The Who's Who of

COLCHESTER UNITED

The Layer Road Years 1937-2008

Jamie Cureton and Chris Iwelumo.

The Who's Who of
COLCHESTER UNITED
The Layer Road Years 1937-2008

Jeff Whitehead & Kevin Drury

First published in Great Britain in 2008 by
The Breedon Books Publishing Company Limited
Breedon House, 3 The Parker Centre,
Derby, DE21 4SZ.

This paperback edition published in Great Britain in 2014 by DB Publishing, an imprint of JMD Media Ltd

A catalogue record for this book is available from the British Library.

ISBN 978-1-78091-433-6

Contents

Acknowledgements

We would like to thank the following people for their help in the production of this work:

Steve Caron of Breedon Books who kindly agreed to produce the book, and to editor Michelle Grainger and graphic designer Matthew Limbert. To Matt Hudson, David Gregory and photographer Rob Sambrook of the Colchester United Media Department for the use of club photographs and advertising. The girls in the club ticket office for leaflet distribution. Jean and Darrell in the club shop. Essex County Libraries Local Studies Centre and the Suffolk Record Office. Francis Ponder of the *Colchester Gazette*. Numerous websites linked to virtually every club, far too many to mention all, but regular visits to since1888.co.uk, Google.co.uk, prideofanglia.com and soccerbase.com. To Michael Middleton, Nick Claydon, Graeson Laitt, Jeff Harris and Alan Dews. Jon Burns and Colchester United Supporters Association. To the many club historians across the country whose own works were used for cross reference and to the former players, and their families, of Colchester United and the private collectors who have loaned the magnificent pictures that really bring this work to life; the late Albert 'Digger' Kettle and the Woolf family, the late Johnny McKim, Peter Wright, Reg Stewart, Russell Blake, Derek Parker, Edgar Rumney, Jamie McLeod (son of Sammy), Shona Willocks (daughter of Sammy McLeod), Bobby Hunt, Terry Price, John Le Mare, Alan Dennis, Mrs J. Webber (widow of Bernie), the late Tony Tasker, Eddie Keegan, Brian Wheeler and Roy McDonough.

Finally to the Board of Colchester United for allowing us to use the club crest and endorsing this book as an official history of the club.

Jeff Whitehead & Kevin Drury
May 2008

Dedications

For my daughter Katie, the fifth generation to support the town's team at Layer Road, and in memory of my Dad who made sure I had the Layer Road bug long before I was old enough for school.

Kevin Drury

For Marilyn, Thomas and Hannah.

Jeff Whitehead

Important notice

The majority of photographs used in this book have come from the club, supporters, families of current and ex-players, scrapbooks, programmes and albums. While the quality of some pictures is not the best, we considered that any reasonably clear photograph was worthy of inclusion in what will be for most players the only time their image will be preserved. We have been unable to establish clear copyright on some of these pictures and, therefore, both the publishers and ourselves would be pleased to hear from anyone whose copyright has been unintentionally infringed.

Note

Colchester United was formed in 1937–38 and played in the Southern League until 1950–51 when they were elected to the Football League. In 1989–90 Colchester were relegated from Division Four and played two seasons, 1990–91 and 1991–92, in the Conference League. In the player statistics the seasons and total lines in italics are the non-League figures.

Foreword

We are positively certain that all U's supporters, young or old, male or female, have, at some time or another, been involved in heated discussion concerning a player, whether from the past or present. When did he join Colchester?...Where did he come from?...How many goals did he score?...What happened to him after leaving Layer Road?

This *Who's Who* will answer most, if not all, of those questions, as well as offering lots more information besides. We are confident that the statistical data regarding appearances and goals, for instance, is the definitive record after assessing a number of irregularities and inaccuracies published previously.

You will find details of every player who has appeared for the U's first team in a competitive match from August 1937 when the club joined the Southern League up to May 2008 when the club vacated Layer Road for their new stadium at Cuckoo Farm. Whether they played 600 games or just six minutes, you will find that every player is featured.

There are details of players who guested for the club in the aftermath of World War Two and of players who made the substitutes bench but did not get on the pitch. There are details, too, of managers and chairmen.

The date and place of birth and death are given if clarified, although occasionally it has only been possible to ascertain limited details, in particular from the war years. Where no information exists the entry has been left blank.

Each player has described, where possible, all of his former and proceeding clubs with appearances, goals, honours and notable feats. His Colchester United career statistics are listed on a seasonal basis. A number of players played both non-League and Football League for United. To differentiate the statistics, all non-League data is printed in italics.

A plus sign (i.e. 100+3) indicates the number of substitute appearances made.

For seasons 1937–38 to 1949–50 'League' appearances refer to the Southern League, 'League Cup' refers to the Southern League Cup while 'Others' contains statistics from the Southern League Midweek Section. Between 1950–51 and 1989–90 'League' applies to the Football League, 'League Cup' to the Football League Cup and 'Others' to the Watney Cup (1971–72) and the Football League Trophy, in its various sponsorship guises, (1982–90). Colchester were relegated to the Conference in 1990, and so between 1990 and 1992 'League' refers to the GM Vauxhall Conference, 'League Cup' refers to the Bob Lord Trophy and 'Others' to the FA Trophy. Returning to the Football League in 1992 the term 'League' reverts back to the Football League, 'League Cup' to the Football League Cup and 'Others' to the Football League Trophy. Appearances and goals in Play-off fixtures are, strangely, not recognised by the Football League. A dash indicates that the particular competition did not run or the club was not eligible to enter, while a zero means that the player was available for selection but did not play.

Much of this information has not been collectively published before, and a reference book is always liable to require updates as new information comes to light. We believe we have researched the information thoroughly over the eight years that this work has taken to compile and cross-check. If you spot any errors and/or omissions, or indeed if you have anything to add, we would be grateful if you could contact the club's Media Department. Furthermore, there is scope for someone to research war records to establish the identities and/or personal details of some of the mystery wartime guests.

A

ABRAHAMS, Paul

Height: 5ft 8in. Weight: 10st 6lb.

Born: 31 October 1973, Colchester.

■ Abrahams developed through United's youth scheme, signing professional in the summer of 1992 having scored 46 goals in 31 youth-team games that season as the young U's were forced out of the South East Counties League and into the local Eastern Junior Alliance because of United's relegation to the Conference. He had already broken into Colchester's successful non-League double-winning side as a playing substitute. He burst onto the scene the following campaign, scoring six goals, the first of which was against Hereford in March 1992 in a 3–1 Layer Road victory. His career was always blighted by injuries, but he showed enough promise to be picked up by Brentford in March 1995 for £30,000. He surprisingly returned to Layer Road on loan in December 1995, playing eight games and scoring twice. He returned to Griffin Park to complete 26(+8) appearances, netting eight times. In October 1996, U's boss Steve Wignall re-signed the player for £20,000, and he will always be remembered for scoring the 'golden goal' winner in the 100th minute of the Auto Windscreens Shield semi-final that sent United to Wembley. Despite those injuries he returned a creditable one-in-three strike rate before turning out in non-League for Kettering, Canvey, Chesham, Wivenhoe, Heybridge and AFC Sudbury. He was finally forced to retire in November 2006 but returned to action with Halstead in 2007–08.

	League		Lge Cup		FA Cup		Other	
	A	G	A	G	A	G	A	G
1991–92	*0+3*	*0*	*0*	*0*	*0+1*	*0*	*1+1*	*0*
1992–93	9+14	6	0+1	0	0	0	1	0
1993–94	1+3	0	0+2	0	0	0	0	0
1994–95	20+8	2	2	0	4	3	2	2
1995–96	8	2	0	0	0	0	1	0
1996–97	27+2	7	0	0	1	0	5+1	2
1997–98	16+9	7	2	0	1+1	0	1	0
1998–99	13+14	2	2	1	0	0	1	0
TOTAL	94+50	26	6+3	1	6+1	3	11+1	4
	0+3	*0*	*0*	*0*	*0+1*	*0*	*1+1*	*0*

ABREY, Brian Anthony

Height: 5ft 11in. Weight: 11st 8lb.

Born: 25 April 1939, Hendon.

■ Ted Drake invited 16-year-old Abrey to join Chelsea's ground staff in 1955. Despite playing in Chelsea's junior teams Abrey never made a first-team appearance at Stamford Bridge in five years. When not required by his club, Abrey worked behind the counter of Drake's betting shop at Butlins in Clacton. After playing for New York in the US International Soccer League in the summer of 1960, Abrey joined United and featured 38 times as Colchester finished runners-up to Millwall in the Fourth Division. His only League goal came in the 2–2 home draw with the Lions, and he weighed in with another in the thrilling 3–3 FA Cup first-round tie against Peterborough. Retiring in April 1963 due to a recurring knee problem, Abrey worked at a school in Hendon and later as a drayman and postman in the same area.

	League		Lge Cup		FA Cup		Other	
	A	G	A	G	A	G	A	G
1961–62	38	1	1	0	3	1	-	-
1962–63	0	0	1	0	0	0	-	-
TOTAL	38	1	2	0	3	1	-	-

ADAMS, Ernest Robert 'Ernie'

Height: 6ft. Weight: 11st 10lb.

Born: 17 January 1948, Hackney.

■ Goalkeeper Adams signed for Arsenal as an apprentice in February 1964, turning professional in January 1965. Despite playing over 160 times for the Gunners' youth and reserve sides, he was unable to break into the first team and was given a free transfer at the end of the 1966–67 season. Missing just two League games in his first season at Layer Road as United were relegated to the Fourth Division, he featured strongly in Colchester's 1967–68 FA Cup run, which culminated in a third-round replay defeat by West Brom at The Hawthorns. Adams succumbed to new manager Dick Graham's clear out and was picked up by Crewe, where he played 112 League games, albeit in a very poor side that conceded 130 goals in two seasons. Joining Darlington for the 1972–73 season, he played 25 times for the

Quakers before turning out for Crook Town. Adams settled in the area and became a prison officer at Frankland Jail, Durham.

	League		Lge Cup		FA Cup		Other	
	A	G	A	G	A	G	A	G
1967–68	44	0	1	0	5	0	-	-
1968–69	4	0	2	0	0	0	-	-
TOTAL	48	0	3	0	5	0	-	-

ADCOCK, Anthony Charles 'Tony'

Height: 5ft 10in. Weight: 10st 8lb.

Born: 27 March 1963, Bethnal Green.

■ Eighteen-year-old Adcock made his League bow in Colchester's last game of their 1980–81 relegation season in a 1–0 win over Carlisle before a then lowest-ever crowd of 1,430. He opened his goalscoring account in only his third League start with a brace against Torquay in September 1981, and he became a prolific scorer for United. He established himself in the side following the tragic death of John Lyons and the departure of contract rebel Kevin Bremner. His 31 goals in total during 1983–84 could not help United to promotion under Cyril Lea, but there was the bonus of hosting Manchester United in the League Cup. The following campaign Adcock was well on course to break the club's seasonal and overall scoring records, having scored 24 League goals in just 27 games up until January. After scoring a hat-trick against Chesterfield, he suffered a knee injury in training that kept him out for the remainder of the season. It was particularly unfortunate for the player as it was rumoured that Liverpool were on the verge of making an offer for him. Returning from injury, Adcock played for Colchester for two more seasons, but the club could not achieve promotion. His last game was in a Fourth Division Play-off semi-final defeat at Wolves in May 1987. In June 1987 Adcock finally got the move to a bigger club that he deserved when he joined Manchester City for a bargain fee of £75,000. He, David White and Paul Stewart all grabbed a hat-trick apiece in City's 10–1 demolition of Huddersfield in November 1987. After just 12(+3) appearances and five League goals, and unsettled by the big-club scene, Adcock moved away from Maine Road in January 1987. Northampton paid a club-record £85,000 and allowed Trevor Morley to go in the opposite direction. He continued his goalscoring prowess with 30 League goals in 72 appearances for the Cobblers, but when they were relegated to Division Four at the end of 1988–89 he secured a £190,000 move to Bradford the following October. The Bantams were relegated to the Third Division, and after scoring six goals in 33(+5) League games Adcock returned to Northampton in a £75,000 deal during January 1991. The Cobblers' dire financial plight proved a blessing for Adcock as after seven goals in 16(+14) games he, along with Bobby Barnes, were off-loaded to Peterborough with Northampton desperate for the £35,000 cash paid. Posh reached the Third Division Play-off Final at Wembley, where they defeated Stockport. Spending the next two seasons in the second tier of English football, Adcock added another 35 League goals to his career total in 107(+4) appearances. When Peterborough dropped out of the First Division, Adcock was sold to Luton in August 1994 for a fee of £20,000. Making just two appearances as a substitute, he was persuaded by Colchester boss Steve Wignall to return to Layer Road. He responded by netting a further 28 League goals as United reached the Third Division Play-off semi-final in his first season back at Layer Road. In 1996–97 he made his second Wembley appearance as Colchester lost on penalties to Carlisle in the Auto Windscreens Shield Final. He was also part of the squad that won the 1997–98 Play-offs at Wembley before scoring his last goal in an infamous 4–1 FA Cup defeat at Bedlington Terriers in November 1998. On leaving Layer Road Adcock turned out briefly for Heybridge. He fell four goals short of equalling Martyn King's all-time club record of 130 goals. His Colchester total included hat-tricks against Crewe (1982–83), Southend (1984–85), Cambridge (1985–86) and Torquay (1995–96). In all Adcock netted 212 League goals, six in the FA Cup, 14 in the League Cup and 17 in Football League Trophy games, for his six clubs.

	League		Lge Cup		FA Cup		Other	
	A	G	A	G	A	G	A	G
1980–81	1	0	0	0	0	0	-	-
1981–82	31+9	5	4+1	0	2+1	1	-	-
1982–83	26+4	17	1	0	0+1	0	2	0
1983–84	41+2	26	5	5	3	0	2	2
1984–85	27+1	24	2	0	3	1	2	3
1985–86	33	15	2	0	1	0	2	1
1986–87	33+2	11	2	0	3	1	5	0
1995–96	41	12	2	1	1	0	3+1	4
1996–97	26+10	11	3+1	1	0+1	0	6	2
1997–98	19+6	5	0+2	0	3+1	0	1	0
1998–99	0+6	0	0+1	0	0+1	1	0	0
TOTAL	278+40	126	21+5	7	16+5	4	23+1	12

AIMSON, Paul Edward

Height: 5ft 11in. Weight: 11st.

Born: 3 August 1943, Macclesfield.

Died: January 2008.

■ Aimson began his career as a junior on the books of Manchester City, signing professional terms in August 1960. After four goals in 16 League starts, he was sold to York for £1,000 in July 1964. He scored 26 times in his first season as York romped

to promotion to the Third Division. After 43 goals in 77 appearances, he transferred to Bury in March 1966 for £10,000, scoring 11 in 30(+1) games, and had spells with Bradford City (£4,000) in 1967–68, scoring 11 times in 23 fixtures, and Huddersfield Town (£20,000), netting 13 goals in 34(+4) starts, before returning to Bootham Crescent in August 1969 for £8,000. He is the fifth-highest scorer in York City's history, with 113 goals from 248 appearances, and was the club's leading scorer in four of his six seasons, achieving five hat-tricks. He scored another 26 goals as the club won promotion again in 1971 and netted in seven consecutive games. Two years later he scored a last-minute header to tie an FA Cup third-round match 3–3 with First Division Southampton. On 18 October 1971 he scored what was believed to be the fastest recorded goal for York City when he slotted home against Torquay United just nine and a half seconds after kick-off. He transferred to Bournemouth in March 1973 for £12,000 to boost the Cherries' flagging promotion drive. Scoring two goals in 7(+2) of the remaining fixtures, Aimson then signed for Jim Smith's Colchester for £8,000 in August 1973. After netting in his second U's League appearance, he suffered cartilage damage. Making his comeback in February 1974, Aimson scored within nine minutes of coming on as a substitute against Hartlepool, but his knee swelled afterwards and he was referred back to a specialist. After undergoing a second operation, Aimson was actually given the last rites as complications set in. He survived and retired from the game to become a sales rep and then a physical recreation officer for Dorset Probation Service. He received a fund-raising match in November 1975 when Bury took on an All-Stars XI containing north-west footballing greats not long after Colchester had also played an end of season promotion celebration friendly against Norwich as a benefit for the player.

	League		Lge Cup		FA Cup		Other	
	A	G	A	G	A	G	A	G
1973–74	3+1	2	1	0	0	0	-	-
TOTAL	3+1	2	1	0	0	0	-	-

AITCHISON, Barrie George

Height: 5ft 9in. Weight: 10st 10lb.

Born: 15 November 1937, Colchester.

■ Aitchison followed in his older brother Peter's footsteps and joined his local club, signing Border League forms in 1953–54. He was considered too slight and was released, spending 10 years with Tottenham's minor sides, during which time they won two Football Combination titles, before a fee of around £750 brought him to Layer Road in 1964. The winger joined a U's side destined for relegation back to the Fourth Division, and it was at Rochdale in September of 1965 that he suffered the injury that would ultimately lead to his retirement from the full-time game. Declining the offer of a part-time contract for 1966–67, he moved to Cambridge City, transferring to Bury Town a season later. He was employed by Alstons of Colchester and endured a cartilage operation, a legacy of his pro career, in 1970.

	League		Lge Cup		FA Cup		Other	
	A	G	A	G	A	G	A	G
1964–65	36	3	2	1	3	0	-	-
1965–66	13+1	3	1	0	0	0	-	-
TOTAL	49+1	6	3	1	3	0	-	-

AITCHISON, Peter Munro

Height: 5ft 9in. Weight: 10st 7lb.

Born: 19 September 1931, Nettleswell.

■ Aitchison, like his brother, was effective on either wing and joined the U's in August 1950 signing pro a year later. He was on National Service when he scored

within 17 minutes of his U's debut against Gillingham on Christmas Day 1951. United won 2–1 with Vic Keeble grabbing the other goal. On leaving Layer Road he turned out for Sittingbourne, Haverhill, Clacton, Stowmarket, Tiptree and Brightlingsea. Aitchison remained in the town and worked for BT until his retirement in September 1991.

	League		Lge Cup		FA Cup		Other	
	A	G	A	G	A	G	A	G
1951–52	9	2	-	-	0	0	-	-
1952–53	3	0	-	-	0	0	-	-
1953–54	0	0	-	-	0	0	-	-
1954–55	6	0	-	-	0	0	-	-
TOTAL	18	2	-	-	0	0	-	-

ALLAN, Cecil

Height: 5ft 10in. Weight: 10st 7lb.

Born: 1 August 1914.

Died: May 2003, Colchester.

■ One of nine brothers and orphaned by the age of seven, Allan's father had been employed during the fit out of the *Titanic* at Harland and Woolf's Belfast yard. Starting his football with Cliftonville, Allan was on the playing staff of Chelsea when he signed for Colchester and was a Northern Irish international, having played as both an amateur and a professional against England and Scotland in 1935. He also featured in Inter League fixtures, representing the Irish League. Chelsea had a hefty £2,000 transfer fee on his head, but he was allowed to join the U's to play non-League football. His spell at Layer Road was mainly confined to reserve-team duties due to the form of Alf Worton and, of course, the interruption of the war. On leaving Layer Road he ran Colchester Casuals from 1949 along with fellow ex-U's player George Leslie. In early 2000 he made a guest appearance at Layer Road as the oldest, at the time, surviving United player.

	League		Lge Cup		FA Cup		Other	
	A	G	A	G	A	G	A	G
1938–39	0	0	0	0	0	0	3	0
1945–46	1	0	0	0	0	0	-	-
TOTAL	1	0	0	0	0	0	3	0

ALLEN, Albert Robert 'Bob'

Height: 5ft 11in. Weight: 10st 12lb.

Born: 11 October 1916, Bromley by Bow. Died: 7 February 1992, Epping Forest.

■ A six-time England Schoolboy International in 1931–32 while on the books of Tottenham, Allen also played tennis at Wimbledon and was a renowned London Schools sprinter. Not making the first team at Spurs he joined Leytonstone and rekindled his League career at Clapton Orient in 1933, making one appearance. He signed a professional contract and made 11 appearances in two years at Fulham before he was tempted north to join Doncaster for a fee of £350, where he made 31 appearances and scored six goals in the 1937–38 season. Moving back to London, Allen signed for Brentford and later Dartford just prior to the war. In wartime he guested for Port Vale and Northampton and joined the Cobblers when football recommenced after the hostilities. Skipper of their reserves, he came to Colchester in May 1947, signing after a handful of trial games in the U's second string. Allen went on to make the left-back spot his own and starred in United's FA Cup run in 1947–48 and was a Southern League Cup winner in 1949–50. He supplied the free-kick from which Bob Curry scored a famous winning goal against First Division Huddersfield. His League career was ended by a serious knee injury sustained at Watford in February 1951, and he went back to the Southern League with Bedford in August 1951. A year later he was lying in hospital with the prospect of at least a year of treatment. Colchester arranged a benefit match at Bedford in September 1952, where a gate of 4,500 helped ease his family's immediate financial needs. Fortunately, Allen recovered and later became a Welfare Officer in the Redbridge area education department.

	League		Lge Cup		FA Cup		Other	
	A	G	A	G	A	G	A	G
1947–48	*31*	*0*	*7*	*0*	*6*	*0*	-	-
1948–49	*23*	*3*	*4*	*0*	*1*	*0*	-	-
1949–50	*16*	*3*	*1*	*0*	*0*	*0*	-	-
1950–51	29	1	-	-	2	0	-	-
TOTAL	29	1	-	-	2	0	-	-
	70	*6*	*12*	*0*	*7*	*0*	-	-

ALLEN, Bradley James

Height: 5ft 8in. Weight: 11st.

Born: 13 September 1971, Harold Wood.

■ Allen came from a famous footballing family. His father was ex-QPR player Les Allen and his brother Clive Allen had also played for, among others, Rangers. He began his career at Loftus Road, signing professionally in September 1998. Scoring 27 times, 20 of which were at Premiership level, in 56(+25) League games, Allen also represented England at Youth level and won eight Under-21 caps, scoring twice. Charlton paid £400,000 for his services in March 1996, and the striker bagged nine goals in 30(+10) First Division starts. Recruited on loan by Mick Wadsworth, Allen made his Colchester debut against Reading in February 1998 at Layer Road and scored his only goal against Oldham two weeks later. He returned to Charlton but was transferred to Grimsby in the summer of 1999. Playing 46(+34) times for the Mariners, Allen continued to plunder goals, netting on 15 occasions. He made a short-lived transfer to Peterborough in August 2002, playing 10(+1) times and scoring three before moving to his final League club Bristol Rovers in November of the same year. Scoring once in 5(+3) games at The Memorial Ground, Allen joined cash-rich non-Leaguers Hornchurch in 2003–04. When the club got into financial difficulty he moved across south Essex to Redbridge and Billericay. He gave up playing to become a PE teacher while running Tottenham's Under-14 side, a position he held in 2007.

	League		Lge Cup		FA Cup		Other	
	A	G	A	G	A	G	A	G
1998–99	4	1	0	0	0	0	0	0
TOTAL	4	1	0	0	0	0	0	0

ALLEN, Leighton Gary

Height: 6ft. Weight: 11st 7lb.

Born: 22 November 1973, Brighton.

■ Released by Premier League Wimbledon, Allen was signed by George

Burley as he sought to build a squad from the aftermath of the Roy McDonough years. Making just two substitute appearances, Allen enjoyed a 100 per cent success rate in a home win over Darlington and an away victory at Hartlepool. He was soon released as Burley built his squad, and he headed back to his south-coast roots to play for Ringmer, Saltdean, Lewes, Crawley, Worthing and Peacehaven.

	League		Lge Cup		FA Cup		Other	
	A	G	A	G	A	G	A	G
1994–95	0+2	0	0	0	0	0	0	0
TOTAL	0+2	0	0	0	0	0	0	0

ALLINSON, Ian James Robert

Height: 5ft 10in. Weight: 11st.

Born: 1 October 1957, Hitchin.

■ Allinson was taken on as an apprentice in the summer of 1974 and made his Colchester debut as a substitute against Bobby Charlton's Preston at Layer Road in April 1975. Picking up United's Young Player of the Year award, he was rewarded with a professional contract October 1975. Playing regularly in U's promotion-winning side of 1976–77, Allinson netted the winning goal in the final game of the season against Bradford at Layer Road that secured a promotion slot. A consistent performer, it was not until the 1981–82 season that Allinson grabbed the attention of the wider football world. United became supreme goalscorers with a strike force of Allinson, Roy McDonough, Kevin Bremner and Tony Adcock. Allinson chipped in with an amazing 43 League goals in just two seasons and was a hot property, valued at £100,000. Unfortunately, someone slipped up when his new contract was being drawn up, and clauses understood to relate to future benefits and bonuses were not as much as his previous contract, entitling him to a free-transfer. Fingers were pointed at outside influences and underhand tactics, with suggestions that Allinson would not have spotted the errors himself. Heads rolled in United's administration, but it was ironic that his intended destination, Malcolm MacDonald's Fulham, were gazumped when Arsenal stepped in with a late bid. In his second season at Highbury, Allinson netted 10 times in just 27 League games and was joint top scorer with Tony Woodcock. The versatile winger also scored in Arsenal's 1986–87 Littlewoods Cup semi-final replay win over Spurs but within three months had been given a free transfer. In June 1987 Allinson signed for Stoke, but within four months and just 6(+3) games he was on the move again to Luton. At Kenilworth Road he played top-flight football again, scoring three goals in 24(+8) appearances. He helped Luton to the FA Cup semi-finals and the Simod Cup Final in 1987–88 before answering a call from Conference-threatened Colchester to help save the club from demotion from the Football League. Signed while under the caretaker control of Steve Foley, Allinson revelled as United clawed their way from the bottom under Jock Wallace and Alan Ball, scoring seven goals including a vital Bank Holiday Monday winner against Halifax. United failed to improve the following season and Allinson was released just before Christmas 1989. He joined Baldock as a player and became manager of Stotfold between 1992 and 1998. He moved to become boss of Barton Rovers in 1998, and he also took charge of Harlow, and was director of football and manager of Borehamwood before returning to Stotfold in December 2006.

	League		Lge Cup		FA Cup		Other	
	A	G	A	G	A	G	A	G
1974–75	0+1	0	0	0	0	0	-	-
1975–76	3+2	0	0	0	0	0	-	-
1976–77	31+9	7	0+2	0	1+1	0	-	-
1977–78	45	6	5	1	4	0	-	-
1978–79	45+1	5	2	0	7	0	-	-
1979–80	37+1	2	4	1	3+1	1	-	-
1980–81	43+3	6	2	0	4	1	-	-
1981–82	41+1	21	5	2	5	3	-	-
1982–83	46	22	4	2	1	0	3	2
1988–89	24+1	7	0	0	3	1	3	1
1989–90	12+1	3	2	0	0	0	0	0
TOTAL	327+20	79	24+2	6	28+2	6	6	3

ALLPRESS, Timothy John 'Tim'

Height: 6ft. Weight: 12st.

Born: 27 March 1971, Hitchin.

■ A youth trainee with his local club Luton, Allpress signed professional forms in July 1989, playing one top flight game that same season. He joined Preston on loan in October 1991 and played 7(+2) games, but when The Hatters were relegated at the end of 1991–92 Allpress was released, spending time with Conference side Boston United (four games) and German Second Division

outfit Bayer Uerdingen. Having been seen playing for Luton's reserves, he was snapped up by Roy McDonough in August 1993 and made his debut as a substitute at Crewe in the second League game of the campaign. He was released by new boss George Burley in the early part of 1994–95, briefly joining home town club Hitchin before moving to St Albans. He had a spell in Hong Kong with the Enterprise club and trained to become a police officer on his return to this country. Allpress featured in a BBC TV documentary about the notorious Blackwater Farm Estate riot in North London, which had become his beat 20 years later and where he worked as a community officer with, among others, Winston Silcott. He also rejoined Hitchin and played in over 300 games for the Canaries.

	League		Lge Cup		FA Cup		Other	
	A	G	A	G	A	G	A	G
1993–94	21+2	0	1+1	0	0	0	2	0
1994–95	3+8	0	2	0	0	0	0	0
TOTAL	24+10	0	3+1	0	0	0	2	0

AMES, Percy Talbot

Height: 5ft 9in. Weight: 11st 3lb.

Born: 13 December 1931, Bedford.
Died: 4 December 1998.

■ Ames was Benny Fenton's first signing, having been recommended by the great Tottenham and England 'keeper Ted Ditchburn. Ditchburn had declared that Ames was far too good for Tottenham's third team. Colchester were already aware of the player as he had undertaken his National Service at the local Garrison in 1954 and had turned out as a trialist in the end-of-season Pearson Charity Cup game in May 1955, being snapped up immediately after. He began his U's

career by saving a Benny Fenton penalty in a Probables versus Possibles pre-season friendly and repeated the feat on his League debut against Exeter. Incredibly Ames missed only three League games in seven seasons, two of them because of a fractured finger, and included a run of 224 consecutive appearances. He starred in United's assault on the Second Division in 1956–57 and in the 1958–59 FA Cup run which finally saw defeat at Arsenal. Ames claimed a Fourth Division runners'-up medal in 1961–62 and was United's first-ever Player of the Year in 1964–65. West Brom made an offer for Ames, but Fenton wanted to hold on to his custodian and did not tell the player of the interest until two years later. On leaving the U's, Ames briefly joined Romford before turning out for his home-town team Bedford.

	League		Lge Cup		FA Cup		Other	
	A	G	A	G	A	G	A	G
1955–56	44	0	-	-	1	0	-	-
1956–57	46	0	-	-	1	0	-	-
1957–58	46	0	-	-	1	0	-	-
1958–59	46	0	-	-	6	0	-	-
1959–60	46	0	-	-	1	0	-	-
1960–61	45	0	2	0	2	0	-	-
1961–62	44	0	1	0	3	0	-	-
1962–63	34	0	2	0	1	0	-	-
1963–64	20	0	0	0	0	0	-	-
1964–65	26	0	2	0	2	0	-	-
TOTAL	397	0	7	0	18	0	-	-

ANDERSON, Terence Keith 'Terry'

Height: 5ft 9in. Weight: 11st 4lb.

Born: 11 March 1944, Woking.
Died: January 1980, Great Yarmouth.

■ Anderson joined the Arsenal ground staff as a 15-year-old and played in their South East Counties League side. Capped by England at Youth level, he was regarded by the then Arsenal manager Cliff Bastin as best left-wing prospect of his generation. Making 25 appearances for the Gunners and scoring six goals, he was in the side that featured in the very first *Match of the Day* televised match. Never quite able to break consistently into the side, he moved to Norwich in February 1965 for £15,000. At Carrow Road he played in 218(+18) League games and bagged 16 goals. He helped City win the Second Division title in 1971–72 and played in the League Cup Final against Spurs in 1972–73. Signed

by Jim Smith on a month's loan in February 1974 after Paul Aimson's comeback failed, Anderson played in four of United's promotion-winning games before returning to Carrow Road. In the summer of 1974 he went to America to play for Baltimore Comets, returning to play for first Scunthorpe (10 games) and then Crewe (four games) at the beginning of the 1974–75 season. He spent his second summer in Baltimore before being signed by Bobby Roberts at the start of the U's manager's first full season in charge. A regular in the early fixtures, Anderson's final game came in a 6–0 drubbing at Brighton in March 1976, and he was released at the end of the season. He took over the licence of a public house in Caister on Sea and also worked in a sports shop. Tragically, he was found drowned after a training run, aged just 35.

	League		Lge Cup		FA Cup		Other	
	A	G	A	G	A	G	A	G
1973–74	4	0	0	0	0	0	-	-
1975–76	13+3	0	0	0	1+1	0	-	-
TOTAL	17+3	0	0	0	1+1	0	-	-

ANDREWS

■ A youthful inside-forward listed as having experience with Yeovil and Cardiff reserves, Andrews made his solitary appearance against Cheltenham in October 1945.

	League		Lge Cup		FA Cup		Other	
	A	G	A	G	A	G	A	G
1945–46	1	0	0	0	0	0	-	-
TOTAL	1	0	0	0	0	0	-	-

ANDREWS, Wayne Michael Hill

Height: 5ft 10in. Weight: 11st 2lb.

Born: 25 November 1977, Paddington.

■ Andrews's career commenced as a YTS scholar with Watford where he made his debut as a substitute in the 1995–96 season, ahead of signing pro forms in the summer of 1996. He scored four goals in 16(+9) appearances in his first full season, but a broken ankle restricted him to just one League substitute appearance in 1997–98. He had 1(+1) games on loan at Cambridge in October 1998 and scored an impressive five goals, four of them against Barnet, in just 8(+2) loan outings for Peterborough the following February. Released by Watford because of his recurring injury problems, Andrew drifted into non-League with St Albans, Aldershot and Chesham United. Chesham were managed by Bob Dowie, and it was through this connection, and 20 goals in 31 games, that Andrews ended up at Oldham where Ian Dowie was the manager. Signing for the Latics in May 2002, Andrews was a losing Play-off semi-finalist when scoring 11 goals in 29(+8) games at Boundary Park. Phil Parkinson tempted Andrews to move back down south when he signed the player for Colchester in the summer of 2003. Andrews was an instant hit, scoring on his debut at Port Vale, and bettered his previous season Oldham goal tally by one as United chased promotion. The lure of the Premiership meant that after just a handful of games in the early part of 2004–05 Andrews re-united with Ian Dowie at Crystal Palace in a deal that saw Gareth Williams move to Layer Road in part exchange. Andrews's fee was believed to be around £100,000. He played just nine Premiership games, all as substitute, as Palace were relegated and a further 5(+19) games during their 2005–06 Championship season. After scoring just once for Palace, Andrews moved on a free transfer to Coventry in July 2006 but was injured in pre-season and did not make his debut until October, scoring once from three substitute appearances. He was loaned to Sheffield Wednesday in the November, netting one goal in 7(+2) games and had a similar spell with Bristol City, bagging two strikes in 3(+4) games before returning to the Ricoh Arena to fight for his Sky Blues place during 2007–08. He joined Leeds in October and Bristol Rovers in the March on loan.

	League		Lge Cup		FA Cup		Other	
	A	G	A	G	A	G	A	G
2003–04	32+9	12	0	0	4+1	0	3+1	2
2004–05	4+1	2	1	0	0	0	0	0
TOTAL	36+10	14	1	0	4+1	0	3+1	2

ANGELL, Darren James

Height: 6ft 2in. Weight: 11st 4lb.

Born: 19 January 1967, Marlborough.

■ Angell, brother of the prolific striker Brett Angell, joined Portsmouth from Newbury Town in June 1985. Without making an appearance at Fratton Park, he was brought to Layer Road during December 1987 in a loan deal by Roger Brown but lasted just 35 minutes of his debut at Tranmere before limping off with knee ligament damage. This proved to be his only appearance in a Colchester shirt. He recovered to play 11(+1) games for Conference side Cheltenham later in the season. Just as he joined Cheltenham, brother Brett was leaving Whaddon Road for Derby. Angell had a brief spell with Lincoln at the beginning of 1988–89 before playing for Barnet in 20 Conference outings. He joined Hungerford Town and also played for Aldershot in 1993–94, retiring due to injury. He then managed Kintbury Rovers in the Hellenic League.

	League		Lge Cup		FA Cup		Other	
	A	G	A	G	A	G	A	G
1987–88	1	0	0	0	0	0	0	0
TOTAL	1	0	0	0	0	0	0	0

ANTUNES, Jose Rodrigues Alves 'Fumaca'

Height: 6ft. Weight: 10st 8lb.

Born: 15 July 1976, Belem, Brazil.

■ Fumaca arrived at Colchester in a blaze of publicity, having had trials with West Ham, Birmingham and Grimsby. He made his debut in only the second-ever TV pay-per-view game when Colchester took on Manchester City in March 1999. Displaying typical Brazilian flair, he lasted just 14 minutes before being stretchered off following a sickening collision with Andy Morrison. He never played for Colchester again, tempted by the lure of more money at Barnsley. He failed to breach the first team at Oakwell and joined Crystal Palace in the summer of 1999, making 2(+1) appearances. Twenty days later he joined Premier League Newcastle, making 1(+4) appearances. He returned to Brazil and rejoined his first club Catuense SA for 2001–02. Later that same season he joined America Rio de Janeiro and Caxias do Sul. Still on his travels, he had a third spell at Catuense SA in 2003–04 before moving to FK Drnovice of Czechoslovakia for 2005–06. In 2006–07 Fumaca was playing with Turkiyemspor of Berlin before joining fellow German side SC Paderborn. He started the 2007–08 season with German regional League side SV Wilhelmshaven.

	League		Lge Cup		FA Cup		Other	
	A	G	A	G	A	G	A	G
1998–99	1	0	0	0	0	0	0	0
TOTAL	1	0	0	0	0	0	0	0

ARNOTT, Andrew John 'Andy'

Height: 6ft. Weight: 13st 7lb.

Born: 18 October 1973, Chatham.

■ Arnott began his career as a trainee with Gillingham and signed full forms in May 1991. After just 20(+12) appearances and eight goals he received the news that he was to be looked at by Premier League champions Manchester United in the form of a loan deal. He did not play for United's first team and returned to Kent to continue his Gills career, ending it with stats of 50(+23) games played and 12 goals scored. In January 1996 Leyton Orient paid £15,000 for his registration, and he played 47(+3) games in a struggling side, scoring six times. He did enough to convince Fulham to pay £23,000 but, with the Al Fayed regime kicking in and the arrival of star players, Arnott managed just one substitute appearance. He was loaned to Rushden & Diamonds before being picked up by Micky Adams at Brighton for £20,000. Completing 27(+1) appearances on the south coast, Arnott was involved in a swap deal that saw Warren Aspinall leave Layer Road in November 1999. Plagued by injuries, Arnott finally had to call it a day after undergoing a hernia operation. He joined Stevenage in 2001 and later played for Dover, Welling and Ashford Town.

	League		Lge Cup		FA Cup		Other	
	A	G	A	G	A	G	A	G
1999–2000	4+8	0	0	0	0	0	0	0
2000–01	1+2	0	0+1	0	0	0	1	0
TOTAL	5+10	0	0+1	0	0	0	1	0

ASABA, Carl Edward

Height: 6ft 1in. Weight: 12st 12lb.

Born: 28 January 1973, Westminster.

■ Spotted playing for Dulwich Hamlet, Asaba was signed by Brentford in August 1994. After impressing in the Bees reserves, he was brought to Layer Road by Steve Wignall on a two-month loan in February 1995. He scored on his debut at Barnet to secure a 1–0 victory and two weeks later repeated the score at home to Darlington in a game where every supporter got in for free, boosting the attendance to 6,055. Having broken the ice on League football, Asaba returned to Brentford and in the 1996–97 season scored 23 League goals as the Bees lost out in the Play-offs. His 23 goals in 49(+5) starts was enough for Reading to pay £800,000 for his services. Unfortunately, Reading were relegated from the First Division, and a year later in August 1998 he was signed by Gillingham for £590,000 as the Gills sought promotion to justify their new-found wealth. His record at Elm Park showed eight goals in 31(+2) starts, but he rediscovered his scoring touch with the Gills to fire 20 goals as the Kent side failed in his first season to get through the Play-offs, with Asaba scoring at Wembley against Manchester City. The Gills made it a year later when defeating Wigan, also at Wembley. Notching 10 goals in the second tier in 2000–01 in just 18 games took his Gills career record to 65(+12) played and 36 scored, so it was no surprise when a bigger club came looking. Sheffield United paid just £92,500, on a contract technicality, on deadline day 2001, and Asaba netted five times in the last 10 games. When the Blades failed to reach the Premiership at the end of 2002–03 Asaba was given a free transfer after scoring 23 in 53(+15) games. He joined Stoke and rose from the bench 30 times as well as making 40 starts, scoring nine times. His final League move was to Millwall in 2005–06 where he played 17(+4) times, recording three League goals.

	League		Lge Cup		FA Cup		Other	
	A	G	A	G	A	G	A	G
1994–95	9+3	2	0	0	0	0	0	0
TOTAL	9+3	2	0	0	0	0	0	0

ASPINALL, Warren

Height: 5ft 9in. Weight: 11st 12lb.

Born: 13 September 1967, Wigan.

■ An apprentice with Wigan, Aspinall gained England Youth honours. Signing professional forms in August 1985, he scored 10 times in just 21(+12) starts at Springfield Park, earning a dream £150,000 move to Howard Kendall's champions-elect Everton squad. He rejoined Wigan on loan at the beginning of 1985–86, playing a further 18 games and scoring 12. Unable to break into the experienced Everton side – he made just seven substitute appearances – Aspinall was sold to Aston Villa in February 1987 for £300,000 and scored 11 of his 14 Villa goals as the club were promoted back to the top flight at the first attempt

in 1987–88. During the close season he moved to the south coast in a £315,000 deal. In six seasons at Portsmouth Aspinall played 97(+35) League games, scoring 21 times but failed to help elevate Pompey into the top Division. In 1993 he had loan spells at Bournemouth and Swansea before signing permanently for the Cherries in December of the same year for £20,000. Scoring eight goals in 26(+1) games, Aspinall headed back north on deadline day 1995 to Carlisle managed by Mick Wadsworth. Carlisle endured successive promotions and relegations and Aspinall was in the side that beat Colchester on penalties to win the 1997 Auto Windscreens Shield at Wembley. He joined Brentford in November 1997 for £30,000, scoring five goals in 41(+2) games, but it was Wadsworth who brought Aspinall to Layer Road in February 1999, initially on a month's loan. An abrasive personality on and off the pitch, he was summed up by one of his teammates as a man you want on your side on the pitch, but you do not even want him in your dressing room at half-time, let alone around the club during the week. Nevertheless, he was probably Wadsworth's best signing for United as his midfield drive saved United from relegation to the Third Division. When Wadsworth left under a cloud at the beginning of 1999–2000 it was not long before Aspinall departed as well, joining Brighton in September 1999. He retired from the game after completing 19(+13) games and scoring three goals for Albion. In all he played 372(+84) League games and netted 91 goals.

	League		Lge Cup		FA Cup		Other	
	A	G	A	G	A	G	A	G
1998–99	15	3	0	0	0	0	0	0
1999–2000	7	2	2	0	0	0	0	0
TOTAL	22	5	2	0	0	0	0	0

ASTILL, Leonard Victor 'Len'

Height: 5ft 11in. Weight: 11st.

Born: 30 December 1916, Wolverhampton.
Died: March 1990, The Wrekin.

■ On the books of Wolves after beginning at local side Heath Town, Astill played for Wolverhampton Schoolboys in the 1931 English Schools Shield. After just two appearances for Wolves, and still only

18, he moved to Blackburn for £3,000 in 1935, having also gained England Junior caps against Scotland and Wales in 1934–35. After one goal in three appearances at Ewood Park he ventured to East Anglia, joining Ipswich's quest for the Southern League title. For Astill to stay at Portman Road his £1,000 price tag would have to be paid. Ipswich refused, despite him being second top scorer with 22 goals in 38 games, and so Astill joined Colchester on 20 May 1938, just one year after arriving at Ipswich. The move proved fruitful as he helped United to clinch the Southern League title with some important goals. Outside of football he became an on-course bookmaker based in Telford, then a newsagent before finally settling as a Walsall market trader for almost 30 years.

	League		Lge Cup		FA Cup		Other	
	A	G	A	G	A	G	A	G
1938–39	27	12	2	3	0	0	12	6
1939–40	3	0	1	2	-	-	-	-
TOTAL	30	12	3	5	0	0	12	6

ATANGANA, Simon-Pierre 'Mvondo'

Height: 5ft 8in. Weight: 12st 11lb.

Born: 10 July 1979, Yaounde, Cameroon.

■ Starting out with Cameroon clubs Fougre and Olympique de Mvolye, Alfath of Saudi Arabia and Tonerre Kalara, Atangana appeared as a substitute in a World Cup qualifier against Somalia in April 2000 and chanced his arm in Britain by joining Dundee United, thus giving up the chance to play for Cameroon in the 2000 Sydney Olympics. Surplus to requirements at Dundee

United after 13 starts, Atangana moved to Port Vale on loan in January 2002 but tore his hamstring in only his second outing. On his recovery he arrived at Layer Road on trial in November, making his debut as a substitute in a shock 1–0 FA Cup defeat to Conference side Chester. He failed to make any real impact and was released, playing for Grays and Halstead. He resumed a nomadic existence, being attached to Turkish Division Two side Antalyaspor in March 2004, Austrian's Sturm Graz, Luch-Energiya Vladivostock, Belarusian's Lokomotiv Minsk and was with Russian First Division side Terek Groznyy of Chechnya in 2006, scoring five times in 31 outings.

	League		Lge Cup		FA Cup		Other	
	A	G	A	G	A	G	A	G
2002–03	1+5	0	0	0	0+1	0	0	0
TOTAL	1+5	0	0	0	0+1	0	0	0

ATKINS, Ian Leslie

Height: 6ft. Weight: 12st 3lb.

Born: 16 January 1957, Birmingham.

■ Atkins began his career at Shrewsbury as an apprentice. Signing professional forms in January 1975, the defender made 273(+5) League appearances for the Shrews, scoring an impressive 58 goals. After winning the Third Division title in 1978–79, Atkins followed his former manager to Sunderland in the summer of 1982 after scoring 17 times in his final season at Gay Meadow. Sunderland struggled in the top flight in his two seasons at Roker Park, and after 76(+1) games and six goals Atkins was signed by Everton in November 1984.

Injuries restricted the player to just 6(+1) League games in which he scored a solitary goal as the Merseysiders won the League title in 1984–85. In September of the following campaign Atkins was sold to Ipswich for a £100,000 fee. Ipswich dropped out of the top flight and then lost to Charlton in the Second Division Play-offs a year later. Accumulating 73(+4) appearances at Portman Road, returning four goals, Atkins signed for his home-city club Birmingham for £30,000 but suffered the ignominy of relegation again as the once Division One giants slipped into the third tier of English football. With six goals scored in 93 starts for Blues he took the plunge into management with newly-relegated Conference club Colchester. Missing just one game in United's inaugural Conference season as player-manager, Atkins was distraught that his side had finished second to Barnet and not claimed their place back in the League. He left Layer Road, having been offered a coaching job under Terry Cooper at St Andrews in the summer of 1991. He appeared 5(+3) times as Birmingham began their climb back up the League tree. Atkins then joined Cambridge as player-manager and played 23(+1) games for the cannon fodder of the second tier. After a non-playing spell at Sunderland, Atkins played his last seven games for Doncaster, having signed non-contract in January 1994. Keeping fit, with spells at Solihull Borough and Redditch, he was appointed manager of Northampton Town in October 1994. At the end of the 1996–97 season Atkins guided Northampton Town to promotion by winning the Division Three promotion Play-offs. They reached the Division Two Play-off Final the following season but lost to Grimsby Town. In 1998–99 Northampton suffered a slump in form, and were relegated to Division Three, with Atkins handing in his resignation soon afterwards. His next post came when he was appointed manager of Division Three strugglers Chester City in January 2000, but he quit six months later having failed to save the club from relegation to the Conference after their 69 years in the Football League. Next up was the Carlisle hot seat where he lasted just the 2000–01 season. Atkins had a spell as assistant manager to Alan Cork at Cardiff City until taking up his next full-time appointment, taking over from Mark Wright as Oxford manager. 2001–02 was Oxford's first season in the bottom division of the football League for over 30 years, and Atkins was unable to prevent them from scoring a record low of 21st place in the final table. An excellent start to 2003–04 saw Oxford leading the Division Three table at Christmas with just one defeat in over 20 fixtures. But Atkins was dismissed in March 2004 for talking to Bristol Rovers about the possibility of taking over as their manager. It was no surprise then when Atkins joined the Gas, but his stay was short-lived as results did not match the club's ambition, and he was sacked in the early part of 2005–06. Answering the desperate plea of Torquay, who were faced with relegation to the Conference, Atkins took over the Devonians for the last few games of the same season and saved them from relegation with four wins and a draw. Appointed full-time manager for 2006–07, Atkins was asked to become Director of Football to allow Torquay to bring in Lubos Kubik as manager, but he refused and left the club. He returned to Sunderland to be their European scout.

** See also Who's Who Managers section*

	League		Lge Cup		FA Cup		Other	
	A	G	A	G	A	G	A	G
1990–91	41	7	1	0	3	1	4	0
TOTAL	41	7	1	0	3	1	4	0

B

BAINES, John Robert

Height: 5ft 11in. Weight: 11st 10lb.

Born: 25 September 1937, Colchester.

■ After the U's scrapped their A team and withdrew from the Border League in 1956, the club set up an arrangement with Colchester Casuals whereby a number of local amateurs held dual registration with the U's for the Eastern Co. League and the Casuals for the Border League. Centre-forward Baines was one such player, splitting his time between the two clubs until called up for National Service and signed as a service pro by the U's in January 1960. He was leading scorer for the reserves in 1960–61 and 1961–62 and made his first-team debut against Halifax in March 1961, replacing the injured Neil Langman for three matches. He was unable to break into the side that gained runners'-up spot in the Fourth Division and only made one more appearance at Bournemouth in 1962, standing in for Martyn King who was engaged in a local table tennis tournament. A former paratrooper, Baines emigrated to Adelaide a couple of months later where he played for South Australia, Port Adelaide, Lion SC and Elizabeth City, who were then coached by former U's player Sammy McLeod.

	League		Lge Cup		FA Cup		Other	
	A	G	A	G	A	G	A	G
1960–61	3	0	0	0	0	0	-	-
1961–62	0	0	0	0	0	0	-	-
1962–63	1	0	0	0	0	0	-	-
TOTAL	4	0	0	0	0	0	-	-

BAKER, James Edward 'Jim'

Height: 5ft 6in. Weight: 12st.

Born: 5 May 1904, Trethomas.
Died: 1979, Solihull.

■ James Baker was a Welshman who began his career playing for Southern League Lovell's Athletic, the football team of a Newport confectionary company. Signed by Wolves in 1926, Baker made 16 League appearances in two seasons at Molineux before being snapped up by Coventry where he was a virtual permanent fixture, notching up 182 League starts with the bonus of 11 goals to boot. While at Highfield Road, Baker made a brief return to Lovell's in 1931. He moved to Bristol City in 1935 but made just 10 first-team League appearances in two seasons. U's boss Ted Davis made Baker one of his first signings in the role of player-coach. A utility player with a preference for a half-back role, he was unfortunate to break his shin bone in a 2–1 Southern League defeat at Swindon reserves in March 1939, a match in which Bob Murray was also carried off unconscious. By then he had already assumed the role of United's reserve-team manager when the club was admitted to the Eastern Counties League in November 1937. Baker helped United to the Southern League Championship and League Cup Finals in 1938–39. The reserves also won the Eastern Counties League title. He returned to Newport in September 1939 with the outbreak of war.

	League		Lge Cup		FA Cup		Other	
	A	G	A	G	A	G	A	G
1937–38	17	1	4	0	-	-	10	1
1938–39	14	1	0	0	2	0	5	0
TOTAL	31	2	4	0	2	0	15	1

BAKER, Terence 'Terry'

Height: 5ft 11in. Weight: 12st 4lb.

Born: 3 November 1965, Rochford.

■ Following his apprenticeship at West Ham, Baker signed forms for the Hammers in November 1983. Failing to make the first team, he was released and went into non-League with Billericay. Cyril Lea resurrected his career when bringing him to Layer Road in November 1985. Baker's chance came when Keith Day suffered a recurring dislocation of the shoulder and the youngster grabbed the opportunity. He made his first start against Torquay in January 1986 and scored the first of his two League goals at Halifax three weeks later. His other goal secured a 2–1 win at Peterborough in the March. Despite playing in United's Fourth Division Play-off semi-final defeat to Wolves, Baker's chances became numbered when

Mike Walker brought in experienced Northern Ireland international Colin Hill, and Baker returned to play for his first club Billericay.

	League		Lge Cup		FA Cup		Other	
	A	G	A	G	A	G	A	G
1985–86	21	3	0	0	0	0	2	1
1986–87	19	0	2	0	0	0	2	0
1987–88	15	0	2	0	2	0	2	0
TOTAL	55	3	4	0	2	0	6	1

BALDWIN, Patrick Michael 'Pat'

Height: 6ft 3in. Weight: 11st 10lb.

Born: 12 November 1982, London.

■ Baldwin began his career as a youth trainee at Chelsea and captained the reserve side. He was released without gaining a professional contract and was signed by Steve Whitton for Colchester in August 2002. He made his debut as a last minute call-up for the League Cup tie at Coventry in the September, and his early mistake gifted the Sky Blues the opener in a 3–0 win. Soon after, Phil Parkinson took over the Layer Road hot seat and Baldwin was sent out on loan to St Albans in December 2003, playing three games, to regain his own self confidence. The treatment had the desired effect, as Baldwin returned to Layer Road stronger and more determined. He scooped all of the available Player of the Year awards in 2004–05 and a season later starred as United finished runners-up in League One to secure their first-ever season in the Championship. He also enjoyed an FA Cup fifth-round tie at former club Chelsea in front of nearly 42,000 fans. Baldwin did not score his first goal for United until November 2006 when U's beat neighbours Southend 3–0. With the departure of Wayne Brown in the summer of 2007, the onus was put on Baldwin to lead United's defence but injuries curtailed his season.

	League		Lge Cup		FA Cup		Other	
	A	G	A	G	A	G	A	G
2002–03	13+6	0	1	0	1	0	0	0
2003–04	1+3	0	1	0	0	0	0+2	0
2004–05	35+3	0	2	0	5	0	1	0
2005–06	20+5	0	1	0	3	0	4+1	0
2006–07	35+3	1	1	0	1	0	-	-
2007–08	23+3	0	1	0	1	0	-	-
TOTAL	127+23	1	7	0	11	0	5+3	0

BALL, Steven James 'Steve'

Height: 6ft. Weight: 12st 1lb.

Born: 2 September 1969, Colchester.

■ An FA Youth Cup winner in 1987–88 with Arsenal, Colchester-schoolboy Ball's Gunners career was effectively ended when being out for nine months with ankle ligament damage. Given a non-contract deal at Colchester, he made his debut against Hartlepool on New Year's Day, scoring his first goal at Maidstone in a Leyland DAF Trophy game – both in January 1990. Ball wrote for a trial at Norwich and warmed the bench in just two League and two Cup ties but kept himself in the picture by scoring 11 goals in 64 Football Combination games. After a further non-contract attachment, this time at Cambridge in August 1992, he signed full-time for Colchester a month later. His career was plagued by injuries, missing the entire 1994–95 season and then breaking his jaw on his comeback, such that eventually he was only engaged on a monthly contract. He left the U's and joined Sudbury where in three seasons he played 77 times, scoring 14 goals. A brief spell with Heybridge saw Ball then become manager of Eastern Counties League Stanway Rovers, taking over from former U's player Phil Bloss. He quit in October 2003 to play for Long Melford. Ball joined a financially resurgent Clacton Town in March 2004, but when the money pot disintegrated Ball left in May 2006.

	League		Lge Cup		FA Cup		Other	
	A	G	A	G	A	G	A	G
1989–90	3+1	0	0	0	0	0	1	1
1992–93	19+5	5	0	0	2	3	1	1
1993–94	27+5	2	2	0	0	0	3+1	0
1994–95	-	-	-	-	-	-	-	-
1995–96	6+2	1	0	0	0	0	1+1	0
TOTAL	55+13	8	2	0	2	3	6+2	2

BALOGH, Bela

Height: 6ft 2in. Weight: 12st 8lb.

Born: 30 December 1984, Hungary.

■ Signed on a season-long loan with an option to buy, Geraint Williams brought the Hungarian international to Layer Road in the summer of 2007 after he impressed in pre-season friendlies, fighting off interest from Cardiff and Hull. Joining MTK Hungaria in 2004 from Bodaijk FC Siofok, Balogh played

79 games for MTK in the Hungarian First Division, scoring nine times. Capped five times at full international level and four times at Under-21, Balogh was invited to travel with the national team for a friendly against Italy in August 2007 despite suffering a broken nose in a pre-season friendly at Bromley and then straining his hamstring. He had made his debut against Canada in November 2006. He finally made his Colchester debut as a substitute in a 2–1 defeat at Stoke in October 2007. Balogh looked a quality footballer but never seemed to adjust to the pace of the English game and the club decided not to take up the contract option.

	League		Lge Cup		FA Cup		Other	
	A	G	A	G	A	G	A	G
2007–08	10+7	0	0	0	0	0	-	-
TOTAL	10+7	0	0	0	0	0	-	-

BAMFORD, Harold Frank Ernest 'Harry'

Born: 8 April 1914, Kingston-On-Thames.

Died: 1949.

■ Bamford started with amateurs Ealing CYC and Hayes before joining Brentford. He scored once for the Bees against Arsenal in a 6–3 win and made two further appearances at Griffin Park. One of six Brentford players borrowed for the Southern League Cup fixture at Guildford on 13 April 1946, Bamford netted a last-minute penalty as 'Colchester' won 5–2. He made eight appearances for Brighton after the war before his early death.

	League		Lge Cup		FA Cup		Other	
	A	G	A	G	A	G	A	G
1945–46	0	0	1	1	0	0	-	-
TOTAL	0	0	1	1	0	0	-	-

BARADA, Taylor

Height: 6ft. Weight: 12st.

Born: 14 August 1972, Charlottesville, US.

■ Barada was in the UK attempting to gain a contract with an English professional club. Having represented the University of Virginia soccer team 'The Cavaliers' alongside future star Claudio Reyna, he had a period on non-contract forms with Notts County when Roy McDonough recruited him as goalkeeper cover on deadline day 1994. He played his one and only game in the penultimate fixture of the season in a 3–1 victory over

Doncaster. Not retained following McDonough's departure, Barada returned to the States to play for Richmond Kickers.

	League		Lge Cup		FA Cup		Other	
	A	G	A	G	A	G	A	G
1993–94	1	0	0	0	0	0	0	0
TOTAL	1	0	0	0	0	0	0	0

BARBER, Frederick 'Fred'

Height: 5ft 10in. Weight: 12st.

Born: 26 August 1963, Ferryhill.

■ When Barber began his career as a Darlington apprentice in August 1981 few would have imagined the shape his future in the game would take. Keeping goal in 135 League fixtures at Feethams, Barber earned a dream £50,000 move to soon-to-be champions Everton in April 1986, but he failed to make the first team and six months later was sold to Walsall for £100,000. Walsall were promoted via the Play-offs but suffered successive relegations, while Barber was loaned to Peterborough in October 1989 for six games. During the 1990–91 season Barber made three further loan spells, playing at Chester in October and March and at Blackpool in November. He also played for the Saddlers that campaign. During the summer of 1991 he joined Peterborough on a permanent basis for a fee of £25,000 and helped Posh to a Wembley Play-off win over Stockport. Peterborough struggled in the second tier, and in February 1993 he spent a non-playing month on loan at Chesterfield. On deadline day 1993 he joined Colchester. United had endured a torrid season with goalkeepers. He played 10 games but will

always be remembered for his ritualistic wearing of a Freddie Krueger face mask upon entering the field for every match. Few Colchester fans would actually be able to put his real face to his name. Despite Peterborough finishing rock bottom, he had caught the notice of Luton for whom he joined for £25,000 in August 1994. Four months later he was back at London Road on loan. He had subsequent further loan spells at Ipswich (November 1995) and Blackpool (December 1995). He left Kenilworth Road without making a start and played his last League game for Birmingham in 1996. Moving into non-League, he kept goal for Conference side Kidderminster on 21 occasions. In all he had 14 different periods of engagement with 10 League clubs. He became Bolton's goalkeeping coach in 1996 and assistant coach to Northern Ireland manager Nigel Worthington in June 2007.

	League		Lge Cup		FA Cup		Other	
	A	G	A	G	A	G	A	G
1992–93	10	0	0	0	0	0	0	0
TOTAL	10	0	0	0	0	0	0	0

BARKER, Christopher Andrew 'Chris'

Height: 6ft. Weight: 11st 8lb.

Born: 2 March 1980, Sheffield.

■ Barker was recruited by Geraint Williams in August 2007, having fallen out of favour at fellow Championship side Cardiff. His career had started on the non-League circuit with Maltby Main and Alfreton Town before being signed by Barnsley in August 1998. He featured 28(+1) times in Barnsley's unsuccessful Play-off campaign and was voted young

Player of the Year for the next two seasons. After Barnsley's relegation and completing 110(+3) League appearances, scoring three goals for the club, Barker joined Cardiff for £600,000 in July 2002 and enjoyed immediate success with a Millennium Stadium Play-off win over Queen's Park Rangers. It took a four-game loan spell at Stoke in August 2004 to revitalise Barker's Cardiff career, and on returning to Ninian Park he went on to win the club's Player of the Year. Despite making 41 appearances in his last season at Cardiff, Barker was informed that he would not be first choice for 2006–07. Signing for Colchester on loan until January 2007, he made his debut at West Brom in the August and added his vast experience to United's first season in the Championship. The loan was later extended until the end of the season. He received red cards against Southend and at Stoke and despite being courted by United in the close season opted to join Queen's Park Rangers on a free transfer in the summer of 2007. Barker's older brother Richard scored prolifically for Macclesfield, Mansfield and Hartlepool during the same period.

	League		Lge Cup		FA Cup		Other	
	A	G	A	G	A	G	A	G
2006–07	38	0	0	0	1	0	-	-
TOTAL	38	0	0	0	1	0	-	-

BARLOW, Herbert 'Bert'

Height: 5ft 7½in. Weight: 10st 5lb.

Born: 22 July 1916, Kilnhurst.
Died: 19 March 2004, Colchester.

■ Barlow began work as a South Yorkshire coal miner before signing for

Barnsley in July 1935. Scoring 12 goals in 58 League appearances and two more in four FA Cup ties, he earned an £8,000 move to Wolves under Major Frank Buckley. Making only three appearances at Molinuex and scoring one goal, he was snapped up by Portsmouth and had the satisfaction of scoring against his old club Wolves in the 1939 FA Cup Final. He also picked up a 1948–49 League Championship medal at Fratton Park before moving to Leicester in December 1949. Bagging nine goals in 42 starts, Barlow headed for Layer Road in the summer of 1952 for a fee of less than £1,000. A knee injury forced his retirement, but he remained prominent in local junior football while running his grocery shop in the town, including coaching Colchester Casuals in the mid-1950s, guiding juniors Barn Hall from the Fifth to the Premier Division of the Colchester and East Essex League, coaching at Long Melford and later, along with brother-in-law and ex-U's reserve Alan Springett, assisting his son Peter (see below) when Peter was manager at Coggeshall.

	League		Lge Cup		FA Cup		Other	
	A	G	A	G	A	G	A	G
1952–53	28	6	-	-	5	1	-	-
1953–54	32	10	-	-	2	0	-	-
TOTAL	60	16	-	-	7	1	-	-

BARLOW, Peter

Height: 5ft 10in. Weight: 10st 10lb.

Born: 9 January 1950, Portsmouth.

■ Barlow, the son of fifties U's player Bert Barlow, became the then youngest-ever United player when he made his debut

against Bournemouth on 27 December 1966 aged 16 years and 342 days. He had been an apprentice since September 1965 but did not become a full pro until he turned 18 in January 1968. Before the end of that year he was on the free transfer list as part of new U's manager Dick Graham's massive clear out, and Barlow moved to Workington in February 1969 where in one and a half seasons he scored 11 goals in 41(+1) League starts. During the summer of 1970 he moved to Hartlepool, playing 8(+3) times before joining Northern Premier League leaders Stafford Rangers. Here he emulated his father, who had played in the 1939 FA Cup Final, by playing at Wembley some 33 years later as Stafford beat Barnet 3–0 in the 1971–72 FA Trophy final. After leaving Stafford, Barlow stayed in the North West with Nantwich and Hednesford Town before returning to Essex with Heybridge and Chelmsford. He took over as player-manager of Coggeshall for 1978–79 and stayed in that role until going to Wivenhoe as a player during 1983–84. After a spell in junior football he was back at Broad Lane past his 41st birthday for a last couple of senior appearances in August 1991 as a number of ex-U's players helped their near neighbours to keep going after the cash tap was turned off and most of the previous senior squad headed off to more lucrative pastures.

	League		Lge Cup		FA Cup		Other	
	A	G	A	G	A	G	A	G
1966–67	3+1	0	0	0	0	0	-	-
1967–68	14+2	4	0	0	2	1	-	-
1968–69	1	0	0	0	0	0	-	-
TOTAL	18+3	4	0	0	2	1	-	-

BARNARD, Charles Henry 'George'

Height: 5ft 7in.

Born: 5 November 1921.
Died: May 1987, Enfield.

■ Barnard created a U's record when he signed for Arsenal for a four-figure fee. West Ham, the club where he began his career, laid claim to his signature even though he was signed as a professional by Colchester. As a compromise United received the fee of £800, with the Hammers collecting the remainder. The 22-year-old was also courted by Tottenham while at Layer Road and played for Spurs against West Bromwich Albion, getting his picture in the national daily newspapers. He trained at White Hart Lane for two days a week but it was Highbury where the bustling centre-forward landed. The young private then duly celebrated his demob from the Army by scoring a hat-trick for the Gunners on his debut. Remarkably, Arsenal trailed Leicester by 4–0 but went on to win the match 5–4. In all Barnard played 10 times for Arsenal before moving to Margate in June 1947 where he scored 26 goals in 43 games in 1947–48. In the summer he moved on to Ashford, following his sacked Margate player-manager Charlie Walker.

	League		Lge Cup		FA Cup		Other	
	A	G	A	G	A	G	A	G
1945–46	3	1	1	0	0	0	-	-
TOTAL	3	1	1	0	0	0	-	-

BARNES, David

Height: 5ft 10in. Weight: 11st 1lb.

Born: 16 November 1961, Paddington.

■ David Barnes was a Barnado's Boy brought up in Felixstowe who as a schoolboy played for the same junior team as Tom English, South Suffolk Old Boys, and was on Ipswich Town's books as a schoolboy. Taken on by Coventry as an apprentice in May 1979 and converted from a striker to a full-back, Barnes won England Youth honours in the victorious 1980 Toulon International Youth tournament. He made nine top flight appearances before being transferred to Ipswich on a free transfer in April 1982. He played 16(+1) times at Portman Road before securing a £35,000 move to Wolves. Unfortunately, the Molineux side were on

free-fall from Division Two to the basement Division. Barnes featured as Wolves overcame Colchester in the 1986–87 Play-off semi-final but was on the losing side against Aldershot in the Final. After 86(+2) games in the Old Gold and four goals, Barnes moved to Aldershot for £25,000 for the 1987–88 season. The Shots survived just two seasons in the Third Division, allowing Sheffield United to pay £50,000 for the full-back who had made 68(+1) appearances at the Recreation Ground. Barnes was not out of place in Division Two and helped the Blades into the top division as runners-up in 1989–90; 58 of his 82 appearances at Bramall Lane were in the top flight as it evolved into the Premier League. In January 1994 he moved back south to Watford, also for £50,000, but struggled with niggling injuries and played just 16 times. Former Aldershot teammate Steve Wignall brought Barnes to Layer Road in August 1996, making his debut in the opening day Layer Road reverse to Hartlepool. Unable to shake off a persistent groin problem, Barnes was forced to call it a day and had his contract cancelled by mutual consent in March 1997.

	League		Lge Cup		FA Cup		Other	
	A	G	A	G	A	G	A	G
1996–97	11	0	1	0	0	0	1	0
TOTAL	11	0	1	0	0	0	1	0

BARNETT, David Kwame 'Dave'

Height: 6ft 1in. Weight: 12st 8lb.

Born: 16 April 1967, Birmingham.

■ Barnett was signed by Roger Brown in the summer of 1988 from non-League Windsor & Eton. His Colchester career went off with a bang when he was sent off on his debut against York on the opening day of the season. Then after serving his suspension he was sent off again in only his seventh League game, at home to Scunthorpe in October. His discipline was such that he earned the tag 'Psycho' from the Colchester fans – not because of his Stuart Pearce approach but for his ability to get in trouble at every opportunity. His indiscipline was not sustainable, and his Layer Road career came to an abrupt end in April 1989 when Jock Wallace saw him commit an off-the-ball indiscretion in a reserve game. He moved to Canada and played for Edmonton Brickmen but returned to England to play for West Bromwich Albion as a non-contract player in October 1989 without appearing for the Baggies. He had 4(+1) games with Walsall in the early part of 1990–91 before drifting back into non-League with Kidderminster, where he played 19 and 20 Conference games in successive seasons, including a game against the U's on the last day of United's first season out of the League. In February of 1992 he was recruited by Barry Fry for his Barnet side at a cost of £17,000 and won promotion the following campaign. The Bees struggled in the higher division, but Barnett himself went on loan to Birmingham in December 1993, playing twice, before returning to Underhill as Barnet were relegated. Having left an impression at St Andrews, Barnett signed for soon-to-be-relegated Blues in February 1994 for £150,000. Birmingham won promotion back to the second tier at

the first attempt, but Barnett only featured six times, taking his City career total to 45(+1) games. He ventured north of the border in 1997–98 and played 21 times for Dunfermline, scoring once before returning to England for a loan spell at Port Vale on deadline day 1998. During the close season he made the move to Vale permanent and went on to make 34(+2) appearances, bagging a single goal. His final move came after impressing in trials at Lincoln in the summer of 1999. He appeared in 25(+2) outings for the Imps and was also sent out on a three-game loan to Conference side Forest Green Rovers. Barnett was set to play international football for the Cayman Islands in 2000, but an FA veto blocked the back-door efforts of such nations in acquiring English players. Notified that he would be given a free-transfer, Barnett actually got injured and announced his retirement. He joined the Birmingham City Academy staff as a part-time coach and turned out for Halesowen Town before taking up his Academy post at St Andrews on a full-time basis.

	League		Lge Cup		FA Cup		Other	
	A	G	A	G	A	G	A	G
1988–89	19+1	0	2	0	3+2	0	3	0
TOTAL	19+1	0	2	0	3+2	0	3	0

BARRACLOUGH, William 'Bill'

Height: 5ft 7in. Weight: 10st 10lb.

Born: 3 January 1909, Hull.

Died: 6 August 1969, Hull.

■ An outside-left, Barraclough began his career with Bridlington Town before joining his home-town club Hull as a 16-year-old. Nine appearances with the Boothferry Park club were enough to convince Wolves to secure his signature. In six years at Molineux, Barraclough made 172 League appearances, scoring 18 goals, as Wanderers won the Second Division Championship in 1932. A clever winger, it was not long before Chelsea took him to Stamford Bridge, where he made his debut on the 3 November 1934. His intricate ball skills were sometimes displayed at the cost of directness; a fact that did not make him popular with the West London faithful, and he became a target for barracking from some parts of the crowd. In two seasons at The Bridge he made 74 League appearances, scoring eight times. He also

notched three goals in seven FA Cup games. With a transfer fee of £2,500 on his head, Barraclough joined the U's at the beginning of their first campaign. He was selected for the Southern League representative team, along with colleagues Alex Wood and Alex Cheyne, that beat the Cheshire League 7–4 at Sealand Road, Chester in October 1937. Barraclough, however, will go down in history as the first-ever United player to be sent off. He received his marching orders at Newport reserves on 25 November 1937 for persistently questioning the referee. Such was the gravity of the offence that the Football Association saw fit to issue a warning as to his future conduct. He was released by Ted Davis and joined Doncaster for a Rovers record fee of £500. That fee went to Chelsea who had retained his League registration. At Doncaster he was involved in a further misdemeanour in a game against Scunthorpe, but the FA took no further action owing to his improvement in character. He later also played for, then non-League, Peterborough. In wartime he turned out once again for Hull in season 1940–41 making 19 appearances, scoring two goals and actually served in Colchester with RADC. He remained in Hull as a clerk in Hull docks and later as a fruit merchant before his death in 1969. Despite releasing the player, Davis said of his sending-off, 'Barraclough suffered a grave injustice in being ordered off for what was a trivial offence'.

	League		Lge Cup		FA Cup		Other	
	A	G	A	G	A	G	A	G
1937–38	19	2	1	0	-	-	6	2
TOTAL	19	2	1	0	-	-	6	2

BARRELL, Leslie Peter 'Les'

Born: 30 August 1932, Colchester.

■ Barrell was an amateur player with local side Lexden Wanderers who first played for the Colchester A in 1952–53. For the next couple of years he flitted between Layer Road and Harwich & Parkeston, finally settling with the U's in summer 1956 and signing part-time pro-forms at the start of December 1956. By that time he had already made three of his four first-team appearances, scoring his only goal on his debut in the opening game of the season against Southend, and was released at the end of the year. On leaving Colchester, he joined Clacton before emigrating to New Zealand in 1963, where he played for North Island side Kamo Whangagarei.

	League		Lge Cup		FA Cup		Other	
	A	G	A	G	A	G	A	G
1956–57	4	1	-	-	0	0	-	-
TOTAL	4	1	-	-	0	0	-	-

BARRETT, Graham

Height: 5ft 10in. Weight: 11st 7lb.

Born: 6 December 1981, Dublin.

■ An Arsenal youngster playing in their FA Youth Cup-winning side of 2000, Barrett made two Premiership substitute appearances in 1999–2000, and his only full appearance for the Gunners was a season later in a League Cup tie with Wolves. He was sent out on loan in December 2000 to Bristol Rovers, making one substitute appearance, and in September 2001 played 2(+1) games

for Crewe. Colchester manager Steve Whitton spent hours watching Premiership reserve matches, trying to unearth talent to bring to Layer Road. In December 2001 Arsenal boss Arsene Wenger agreed that Barrett could spend the remainder of the season at Layer Road. The Republic of Ireland Under-21 international became a hit with the fans after scoring twice in a 3–2 win at Northampton on Boxing Day but suffered an injury at Wycombe in March that curtailed his season. As a mark of appreciation, United fans dressed in green for the last home game of the season to represent Barrett's Irish roots. Whitton wanted to take Barrett for another season, but instead the player joined Brighton in a similar long-term deal. He played 20(+10) games at the Withdean, netting once but began to suffer niggling injuries. After gaining 24 caps at Under-21 level and representing his country at every age group since turning 15, Barrett picked up his first senior cap when scoring in a 3–0 win in Finland during August 2002. He joined Coventry on a permanent deal a year later, having been released from Highbury. Barrett's injuries continued, and in two seasons he completed 32(+23) League games, scoring six times, for the Sky Blues. On deadline day 2005 he moved to Sheffield Wednesday on loan, scoring once in 5(+1) games. Out of the reckoning at Coventry, Barrett went on loan to Scottish Premier League side Livingston in August 2005, playing six games before suffering a season-ending injury. He signed a two-year deal at Falkirk in August 2006, but the luckless Barrett again suffered injury and required an operation on his knee in the October. He returned to action at the beginning of 2007–08, when he scored in a 7–2 reverse at Rangers. In all Barrett gained seven full caps, scoring twice for the Republic of Ireland.

	League		Lge Cup		FA Cup		Other	
	A	G	A	G	A	G	A	G
2001–02	19+1	4	0	0	0	0	0	0
TOTAL	19+1	4	0	0	0	0	0	0

BARRETT, Scott

Height: 6ft. Weight: 12st 1lb

Born: 2 April 1963, Ilkeston.

■ Barrett joined Wolves from Ilkeston Town in September 1984, just as the once-proud Molineux club were plummeting from Division Two to Division Four in successive seasons. Playing 30 games, he was transferred to Stoke for £10,000 in July 1987, playing 51 times for the Second Division outfit. When Mick Mills, formerly manager at Stoke, became U's boss in January 1990 it was Barrett who became his first signing. Barrett played 13 times in a three-month loan spell and steadied a position that had become a big problem for United. With Colchester unable to match his wage demands, he spent the remainder of the season on loan at Stockport, helping them to a Play-off Final defeat to Peterborough. In the close season of 1990 the U's finally got their man, but by this time Mills had left and United had been relegated to the Conference. Barrett became a dependable ever-present in his two non-League seasons with Colchester and will be remembered for scoring the winning goal in a crunch top-of-the-table clash with Wycombe at Adams Park

in September 1991 and for venturing upfield to nod on a late corner for Tony English to grab an FA Trophy first-round equaliser against Kingstonian at Layer Road. Both feats were notable as United won the Conference title, from Wycombe, and topped the season off winning the FA Trophy at Wembley. Returning to the League, Colchester were not able to meet the wage demands of the player, and he joined Gillingham, playing 51 League games in two seasons. In August 1995 he moved to Cambridge, where he added 119 outings to his career total, and his final professional move was to Leyton Orient in January 1999. In his first season he returned to Wembley as the O's lost to Scunthorpe in the Fourth Division Play-off Final, saving two spot-kicks in the semi-final shoot-out at Rotherham. After collecting all six Player of the Year awards in 2001–02, Barrett maintained his registration and became goalkeeping coach at Brisbane Road, being recalled into action in 2002–03 following injury to regular 'keeper Ashley Bayes. He ended his O's career with 99 League starts and turned out for Kingstonian in the Conference on six occasions during that spell. He became assistant manager to Mark Stimson at Grays and enjoyed further FA Trophy success with the South Essex side before following Stimson to Stevenage in the summer of 2006, where he again tasted FA Trophy success in the first ever Cup Final at the new Wembley in May 2007. When Stimson took over at Gillingham in November 2007 it was only natural that Barrett would follow him to Kent.

	League		Lge Cup		FA Cup		Other	
	A	G	A	G	A	G	A	G
1989–90	13	0	0	0	0	0	0	0
1990–91	*42*	*0*	*2*	*0*	*3*	*0*	*4*	*0*
1991–92	*42*	*1*	*2*	*0*	*3*	*0*	*9*	*0*
TOTAL	13	0	0	0	0	0	0	0
	84	*1*	*4*	*0*	*6*	*0*	*13*	*0*

BASHAM, Michael 'Mike'

Height: 6ft 2in. Weight: 12st 8lb.

Born: 27 September 1973, Barking.

■ Representing England at Schoolboy and Youth level, Basham served his YTS with West Ham but did not make the breakthrough after signing professional in July 1992. His first League appearance was with Colchester, although it proved

disastrous for the player. Having been signed on loan by Roy McDonough to help cure U's leaky defence – they had lost 7–3 at Darlington days earlier – Basham made just one appearance in a United shirt at Doncaster on 20 November 1993 before injuring himself. He returned to Upton Park to recuperate and was shipped out to Swansea on deadline day 1994 on a free transfer. At The Vetch he appeared 27(+2) times in the League before joining Peterborough in December 1995. Plagued by injuries he made 17(+2) appearances in a Posh shirt and was released at the end of the following campaign after managing just four starts. Barnet were next to take up his registration, and in four seasons and 74(+1) League games Basham suffered Play-off semi-final heartbreak twice and saw the Bees relegated out of the League. Basham was not at Underhill on the final day of that season as he had moved to York on deadline day March 2001. With lady luck seemingly deserting him, he found City in dire financial straits as they too headed for relegation out of the League. The York City Supporters Trust, who were running the club, had no option but to release some of their highest earners, and Basham was one of four players to be shown the door after 32(+4) games and three goals. He returned to Essex and played with Chelmsford, Grays Athletic and Thurrock.

	League		Lge Cup		FA Cup		Other	
	A	G	A	G	A	G	A	G
1993–94	1	0	0	0	0	0	0	0
TOTAL	1	0	0	0	0	0	0	0

BEACH, Douglas Frederick 'Doug'

Born: 2 February 1920, Watford.

■ A soldier in the 16th Infantry Training Corp and originally on the books of Sheffield Wednesday, Beach played 27 times for Luton in season 1945–46 and a further 23 times in 1946–47 before joining Southend playing 41 games in 1947–48. After guesting for Colchester on four occasions, Beach returned to Layer Road for U's last season as a non-League club in 1949 as a part-time pro, while continuing to work in Watford. On leaving Layer Road he played for Chelmsford and Biggleswade Town, before retiring as a gardener for St Albans Council to Callington, Cornwall in 1985.

	League		Lge Cup		FA Cup		Other	
	A	G	A	G	A	G	A	G
1945–46	3	2	1	0	0	0	-	-
1949–50	30	0	4	0	1	0	-	-
TOTAL	33	2	5	0	1	0	-	-

BEARRYMAN, Henry William 'Harry'

Height: 5ft 9½in. Weight: 11st 2lb.

Born: 26 September 1924, Battersea.
Died: December 1976, Leatherhead.

■ Bearryman joined Chelsea in 1940 as a half-back and, as well as being a regular in their Football Combination side, played first-team wartime football at the age of just 16. He also represented London Schoolboys and during the war served as a Wireless Operator and Gunner in the RAF. In four years he flew 33 missions over Germany. Despite this he still managed a wartime playing record of: 1941–42 Chelsea (13

appearances/1 goal), Watford (1/0); 1942–43 Chelsea (23/0) and 1944–45 Chelsea (1/0). He was demobbed in 1947 with the rank of Warrant Officer and opted to join Colchester in July, despite interest from Hull and Notts County. An ever-present for three League seasons at Layer Road, Bearryman was a rock as United reached the fifth round of the FA Cup in 1948, won the Southern League Cup in 1950 and were elected into the Football League. He quit professional football at the end of 1953–54 to join the Metropolitan Police and served at Tooting, Sutton and Banstead. He also helped the Met Police football team to the 1954–55 Spartan League title.

	League		Lge Cup		FA Cup		Other	
	A	G	A	G	A	G	A	G
1947–48	*32*	*2*	*8*	*3*	*6*	*0*	-	-
1948–49	*41*	*0*	*6*	*0*	*1*	*0*	-	-
1949–50	*46*	*3*	*5*	*1*	*1*	*0*	-	-
1950–51	46	0	-	-	2	0	-	-
1951–52	46	0	-	-	3	0	-	-
1952–53	45	1	-	-	5	0	-	-
1953–54	37	2	-	-	2	0	-	-
TOTAL	174	3	-	-	12	0	-	-
	119	*5*	*19*	*4*	*8*	*0*	-	-

BEATTIE, Thomas Kevin

Height: 5ft 10in. Weight: 12st 2lb.

Born: 18 December 1953, Carlisle.

■ Beattie came through the impressive youth ranks of Ipswich and starred alongside future U's boss Allan Hunter in a side that challenged the elite of English football throughout the 1970s. He became the first-ever winner of the PFA Young Player of the Year Award in 1974. Already recognized at Youth level and nine times at Under-23, Beattie made his England debut against Cyprus in 1975 and went on to win nine caps. Many

expected him to win over 100 caps, but injuries dogged his career. His only goal for England came in the 5–1 thrashing of Scotland at Wembley in the 1976 Home International Championship. He starred as Ipswich won the FA Cup in 1978 but missed their UEFA victory in 1981, having broken his arm just weeks before the Final. In all he played in seven European campaigns. His knees gave him his worst lay-offs, but he also suffered from personal problems. Allan Hunter brought him to Layer Road in the summer of 1982 on a non-contract basis, but Beattie managed just six first-team appearances and suffered a broken nose from a boot in the face. In November of 1982 he tried his luck at Middlesbrough but after just 3(+1) games reluctantly had to call it quits. He had brief spells with local side Ipswich United, Norwegian sides Sandvikens, Konsberg and Nybergsunds and back in England with Clacton. Beattie's autobiography is entitled *The Greatest Footballer England Has Never Had.*

	League		Lge Cup		FA Cup		Other	
	A	G	A	G	A	G	A	G
1982–83	3+1	0	1	0	0	0	2	0
TOTAL	3+1	0	1	0	0	0	2	0

BEDFORD, Kevin Edward

Height: 5ft 9in. Weight: 11st 2lb.

Born: 26 December 1968, Carshalton.

■ Bedford completed his Wimbledon apprenticeship before signing professional in November 1988. He had made his debut in a League Cup tie

against Newcastle a month earlier and enjoyed four Division One games on the bounce after turning out against Tottenham three days later. In February 1988 he was sent out on loan to Aldershot to gain experience, playing 16 times in a side that included Steve Wignall and Ian Phillips, both former U's stars. With the Dons ever-evolving he was never able to force his way back into the side and in the summer of 1988 was signed by Roger Brown, making his debut at Tranmere as a substitute in the second game of the season. He did not get a run in the side until Brown was sacked and Steve Cartwright returned to Tamworth, but he made the left-back slot his own as Steve Foley took over as caretaker manager. Bedford played every game as United reached the fourth round of the FA Cup, but he lost his place when Jock Wallace brought in Clive Stafford.

	League		Lge Cup		FA Cup		Other	
	A	G	A	G	A	G	A	G
1988–89	24+2	0	0+1	0	6	0	3	0
TOTAL	24+2	0	0+1	0	6	0	3	0

BELL, John Russell 'Jackie'

Height: 5ft 6in. Weight: 10st 4lb.

Born: 17 October 1939, Evenwood.
Died: April 1991, Darlington.

■ Starring for Durham Schools, Bell was soon picked up by Newcastle, signing as a junior in October 1956. In all, the wing-half made 111 League appearances for the Geordies, scoring eight goals. In the summer of 1962 he made his way south to Norwich for a fee of £10,000, where he

played 48 times, scoring three goals. Neil Franklin persuaded him to join Colchester rather than non-Leaguers Cambridge United, but after just seven games Bell was diagnosed with diabetes, quit the game and returned north to live in Darlington.

	League		Lge Cup		FA Cup		Other	
	A	G	A	G	A	G	A	G
1965–66	7	0	0	0	0	0	-	-
TOTAL	7	0	0	0	0	0	-	-

BENNETT, Albert

■ A serving soldier in the East Surrey Regiment, 'Drummer' Bennett, who is confusingly noted sometimes with the initial 'C' in local match reports, made just one first-team appearance in a Southern League Midweek League fixture at Norwich in November 1937. A centre-forward for his Regiment, Bennett usually played at outside-right at Layer Road, where most of his appearances were in the handful of games Colchester Town played in 1937–38. The U's offered him pro terms, but he opted to remain in the Army and continued to play the occasional game for the reserves until the end of September 1938.

	League		Lge Cup		FA Cup		Other	
	A	G	A	G	A	G	A	G
1937–38	0	0	0	0	-	-	1	0
TOTAL	0	0	0	0	-	-	1	0

BENNETT, Gary

Height: 5ft 7in. Weight: 9st 13lb.

Born: 13 November 1970, Enfield.

■ Following the sacking of Roger Brown, youth trainee Bennett got an early chance to shine, as caretaker manager Steve Foley opted to use the exuberance of youth to get United away from the Conference trap-door. He made his debut as a substitute in a 2–1 Layer Road defeat to Cambridge in October 1989, scoring his first goal also at Layer Road against Rochdale in March 1990. In United's first Conference season Bennett was second-highest scorer, with his 12 goals only being bettered by Mario Walsh's 18 strikes. The following season he formed a lethal strike-trio with Steve McGavin (26 goals) and Roy McDonough (29), netting 18 goals himself as U's won the Conference title. Bennett was unlucky to only get a substitute's appearance in the Wembley FA Trophy Final of 1992, but he got on the field as United beat Witton 3–1 to complete the non-League double. Much was expected of the youngster as Colchester returned to the League, but in 1993 he was given a free-transfer following the arrival of Steve Brown, a victim of the endemic financial pressures at Layer Road. He joined Conference side Woking, playing three games, scoring once, and in the ensuing two seasons turned out for Dagenham and Redbridge on 12(+5) occasions, netting five times. His non-League career really took off when he joined Braintree and became the club's record scorer with 57 goals in one season. He missed most of 1998–99 with a groin injury and signed for Sudbury in the summer. He continued to find the net regularly in the Eastern Counties League scene and joined Chelmsford in February 2000 for £3,000, scoring 25 goals in 57 games over two seasons. Despite being voted Chelmsford's Player of the Year, he rejoined Sudbury at the start of 2001–02 for £1,500 and completed an unwanted treble by playing and losing in three successive FA Vase Finals. Sudbury lost to Brigg Town at Upton Park in 2003, Winchester City at St Andrews in 2004 and a year later to Didcot Town at White Hart Lane. Bennett left Sudbury in the summer of 2004, having scored a magnificent 172 goals in 243(+10) appearances for the Suffolk side. He joined Witham Town and helped them to promotion to the Ryman Division One North, before becoming assistant manger to Ipswich Wanderers in October 2006.

	League		Lge Cup		FA Cup		Other	
	A	G	A	G	A	G	A	G
1988–89	6+3	1	0	0	0	0	0	0
1989–90	26+10	4	2	1	2	1	2	0
1990–91	*34+2*	*9*	*0*	*0*	*1+2*	*0*	*4*	*3*
1991–92	*31+8*	*16*	*1*	*0*	*3*	*0*	*4+4*	*2*
1992–93	30+8	8	2	0	1+1	2	1+1	0
1993–94	3+1	0	0	0	0	0	0	0
TOTAL	65+22	13	4	1	3+1	3	3+1	0
	65+10	*25*	*1*	*0*	*4+2*	*0*	*8+4*	*5*

BENSTEAD, Graham Mark

Height: 6ft 2in. Weight: 12st 4lb.

Born: 20 August 1963, Aldershot.

■ Benstead began his career as an apprentice with Terry Venables's QPR, where he won England Youth honours, but he failed to make the first team after

joining in the summer of 1981. Signed by Norwich in March 1985, Benstead played just 16 times in three seasons at Carrow Road as understudy to Chris Woods. Soon after he staked his first team claim, Norwich signed Bryan Gunn. Benstead went out on loan to Colchester for the start of the 1987–88 season, making his debut in the opening day fixture at Burnley. Norwich did not want him Cup-tied, which gave Trevor Lake his only outing in United's goal and forced Roger Brown to sign Mark Walton on loan from Luton when Lake got injured. Benstead performed well enough at Colchester to attract a bid from Sheffield United for the Norwich player. He made the move to the steel city in March 1988 and played 47 games for the Blades, winning promotion in his first full season. In July 1990 he signed for Brentford and kept goal on 112 occasions for the Bees, losing the 1990–91 Play-offs to Crewe at Wembley but gaining automatic promotion the next time out. He moved into non-League and played for Kettering, Rushden & Diamonds and Kingstonian, as well as the England semi-professional side, before returning for one non-contract game with Brentford in 1997–98 while serving on the Griffin Park coaching staff. Resuming his non-League travels, he played for Basingstoke, Chertsey, Farnborough and Stevenage, where he became assistant manager between May and October 2004.

	League		Lge Cup		FA Cup		Other	
	A	G	A	G	A	G	A	G
1987–88	18	0	0	0	0	0	1	0
TOTAL	18	0	0	0	0	0	1	0

BETTS, Simon Richard

Height: 5ft 8in. Weight: 10st 7lb.

Born: 3 March 1973, Middlesbrough.

■ Betts signed for Ipswich in February 1991 but failed to make the first team. He had a trial with Wrexham, before signing non-contract forms with Scarborough in November 1992. A month later Roy McDonough brought him to Layer Road, and the full-back made his debut as a substitute in the FA Cup second-round replay defeat to Gillingham. Betts missed just one game in 1995–96 when United lost to

Plymouth in the Play-off semi-finals, and he weighed in with five goals in the process. The following season he was unlucky to injure himself scoring a penalty at Lincoln and struggled thereafter to shrug off knocks and the full-back pairing of Joe Dunne and Scott Stamps. He did, however, regain his place and played at Wembley as Colchester beat Torquay to gain promotion to the third tier. Released from United's new challenge, he joined non-League Scarborough, playing 59 Conference games and scoring nine goals. Fellow Conference side Yeovil paid £10,000 for his services in December 2000, and he appeared 14(+2) times, scoring once. The summer of 2001 brought a return to League football when he signed for Darlington on a free transfer, going on to score one goal in 69 League starts. After two seasons with the Quakers, he joined Whitley Bay before returning to East Anglia, hoping for a trial with Phil Parkinson's U's. Parkinson did not take up Betts's request, and instead he played for Halstead, Needham Market, Mildenhall and Whitton United.

	League		Lge Cup		FA Cup		Other	
	A	G	A	G	A	G	A	G
1992–93	23	0	0	0	0+1	0	1	0
1993–94	31+2	1	1	0	1	0	3	0
1994–95	34+1	2	0	0	4	0	2	0
1995–96	45	5	2	0	1	0	6	2
1996–97	10	1	4	0	0	0	0	0
1997–98	17	0	0	0	2+1	0	3	0
1998–99	22+6	2	2	0	0	0	1	0
TOTAL	182+9	11	9	0	8+2	0	16	2

BEVERIDGE

■ Worcester player Beveridge, along with colleague Hogg, guested for the U's when Shiels, Ferguson and Willmott missed Colchester's train journey to Worcester, arriving five minutes after kick-off. Beveridge left the field injured with 10 minutes remaining as U's lost 6–2. He was a regular in Worcester's Birmingham Combination reserve side.

	League		Lge Cup		FA Cup		Other	
	A	G	A	G	A	G	A	G
1945–46	1	0	0	0	0	0	-	-
TOTAL	1	0	0	0	0	0	-	-

BICKLES, David 'Dave'

Height: 6ft. Weight: 11st 6lb.

Born: 6 April 1944, West Ham.
Died: 1 November 199, Havering.

■ England Youth international Bickles joined West Ham in July 1961, making his debut in the 1963–64 season, and made 24(+1) injury-interrupted appearances before joining Crystal Palace in October 1967. At Upton Park he could count on Bobby Moore and Martin Peters as two of his teammates. Just 11 months later he was recruited in the Dick Graham revolution without breaking into the Palace first team. A regular pick in Graham's U's team, Bickles was released at the end of 1969–70 and joined Romford, becoming player-manager in 1976–77, until their demise the following year. He subsequently became boss of Romford-based Collier Row. He later became a PE teacher at Brampton

Manor School and assisted the West Ham Youth Academy.

	League		Lge Cup		FA Cup		Other	
	A	G	A	G	A	G	A	G
1968–69	34	3	0	0	1	0	-	-
1969–70	33	0	2	0	1	0	-	-
TOTAL	67	3	2	0	2	0	-	-

BICKMORE

■ A soldier from the No. 1 Holding Battalion, Bickmore was attached to Chelmsford but never played in the first team at New Writtle Street. He played just one game for Colchester at Barry Town in December 1945.

	League		Lge Cup		FA Cup		Other	
	A	G	A	G	A	G	A	G
1945–46	1	0	0	0	0	0	-	-
TOTAL	1	0	0	0	0	0	-	-

BICKNELL, Roy

Height: 5ft 10½in. Weight: 11st 10lb.

Born: 19 February 1926, Doncaster.
Died: 31 January 2005, Colchester.

■ Bicknell signed professional for Wolves in September 1943 after first being a junior at Molineux. At Wolves the legendary Stan Cullis restricted his appearances. During wartime he played twice in the Wolves first team and once for Swindon as a guest. He moved to Charlton in 1947, playing seven times as well as representing London in a 1948 fixture in Belgium. The London team included future U's manager Dick Graham of Crystal Palace. Two years later he moved to Bristol City, making 21 appearances before having a spell with Gravesend. Bicknell joined

Colchester in June 1952 and after his first-team career finished captained the reserves for 1954–55 but was forced to retire in September 1955, the cumulative result of a number of knee injuries that had included a cartilage removal in January 1955. He then managed Clacton Town to the 1959–60 Southern League title and had to turn out once or twice in emergencies, including a game at outside-right against Oxford United in February 1962. In October 1963 he obtained a permit to trade as a turf accountant and was obliged by FA rules to sever his ties with Clacton. At the end of the decade he returned to management for a while with Brantham Athletic and for 29 years ran The Hythe Coffee Shop with another ex-U's player, Len Jones, before retiring as an usher at the County Court in May 1987.

	League		Lge Cup		FA Cup		Other	
	A	G	A	G	A	G	A	G
1952–53	6	0	-	-	2	0	-	-
1953–54	19	0	-	-	2	0	-	-
TOTAL	25	0	-	-	4	0	-	-

BIDEWELL, Sidney 'Sid'

Born: 6 June 1918, Watford.

■ An amateur with Wealdstone, Bidewell made a sensational debut for Chelsea on 4 December 1937, scoring two goals against Huddersfield as stand-in following injuries to regular Chelsea forwards Mills and Bambrick. Playing four games at Stamford Bridge, any chance the forceful attacker had of breaking permanently into the team were dashed by the war. Lance Corporal Bidewell served in the Army during the war and played 18 League and Cup games for Chelsea, as well as guesting for Wrexham and Southampton. At Layer Road he met up with former Chelsea teammate Doug Smale, scoring four goals in six Southern League Cup fixtures. Bidewell joined Gravesend and Northfleet after the war and then went to Chelmsford for a three year stint from the 1948–49 season, before becoming manager of Hemel Hempstead.

	League		Lge Cup		FA Cup		Other	
	A	G	A	G	A	G	A	G
1945–46	1	0	6	4	0	0	-	-
TOTAL	1	0	6	4	0	0	-	-

BIGGS, Arthur Gilbert

Height: 5ft 11in. Weight: 11st 5lb.

Born: 26 May 1915, Wooton.

Died: 15 January 1996, Luton.

■ Biggs joined Arsenal as an amateur in October 1933 and became a professional at the turn of the year. Despite hammering in 41 goals in 44 Football Combination games, he had to wait until March 1937 for his Gunners debut. Only two further League games followed, and he was transferred to Hearts in December 1937 for £2,500. Hearts finished runners-up in 1937–38, when he scored eight times in 15 games. He added another four in four games in the early part of 1938–39 before transferring to Aberdeen and was nominally still on their books when he came to Layer Road. With the outbreak of war he returned to Bedfordshire and guested for Luton, playing 19 times in 1939–40, scoring five goals, and he made further guest appearances for Watford, Crystal Palace and Ipswich. Biggs had already played for Bedford during 1946–47 while employed at Vauxhall Motors and joined Colchester for the last four games of the campaign, netting three times. He left the U's in November 1948 and thereafter played for the Vauxhall Motors works team in Colchester Town's old stomping ground, the Spartan League.

	League		Lge Cup		FA Cup		Other	
	A	G	A	G	A	G	A	G
1946–47	4	3	0	0	0	0	-	-
1947–48	8	1	1	1	1	0	-	-
TOTAL	12	4	1	1	1	0	-	-

BINKS, Martin John

Height: 5ft 10in. Weight: 10st 12lb.

Born: 15 September 1953, Romford.

■ A former Leyton Orient apprentice, Binks joined Colchester in the summer of 1972. He made his debut at centre-half in the second game of the 1972–73 season at Hartlepool but was transferred to Cambridge in January 1973 following the arrival of Ray Harford. Binks played just one League game at The Abbey Stadium before moving into the non-League game with Gravesend, Chelmsford and Tilbury. In 1982–83 he was player-manager of Ford United.

	League		Lge Cup		FA Cup		Other	
	A	G	A	G	A	G	A	G
1972–73	10	0	0	0	0	0	-	-
TOTAL	10	0	0	0	0	0	-	-

BIRCH, Clifford 'Cliff'

Height: 5ft 6in. Weight: 10st 8lb.

Born: 1 September 1928, Crumlin, Gwent.

Died: March 1990, Norwich.

■ Birch joined Cardiff as an amateur in 1946 before transferring to Norwich. He signed professional with Norwich in December 1946, making just five League appearances and scoring three goals. He moved to Newport in October 1950 and went on to make 143 League appearances, netting 28 times for his hometown club and gaining representative honours for the Welsh League in 1951. A fee of £1,000 brought him to Layer Road in June 1954, but he was one of a dozen players cleared out at the end of the year by new manager

Benny Fenton, having played 14 matches as U's finished bottom of Division Three South. Although normally a right-winger, he had the novel experience of playing in goal for the reserves at Gorleston in February 1955 when army duties unexpectedly prevented John Wright from travelling. The U's lost that game 3–1. Having married a Norwich girl, he returned to the area and played non-League for Great Yarmouth, where he was leading scorer in 1955–56, Gorleston and Spalding before a twisted knee forced his retirement.

	League		Lge Cup		FA Cup		Other	
	A	G	A	G	A	G	A	G
1954–55	12	3	-	-	2	1	-	-
TOTAL	12	3	-	-	2	1	-	-

BIRCH, Joseph 'Joe'

Height: 5ft 10in. Weight: 12st.

Born: 6 July 1904, Hednesford.
Died: December 1980, Colchester.

■ As an amateur Birch played for Cannock Chase before joining Hednesford Town in August 1920. A coal miner by trade, Birch's stocky build made him a resolute tackler, and he signed for Birmingham in March 1928. Released in May 1929 after just one appearance, Birch moved south to Bournemouth & Boscombe where he added 26 more appearances. His career really took off when he joined Fulham in October 1931 for £600. The Cottagers won the Third Division South title, and Birch went on to make 185 League appearances and a further 10 in the FA Cup in six seasons as regular for

Fulham. He temporarily lost his place in 1935–36 and missed Fulham's run to the FA Cup semi-final. Birch signed for Colchester in June 1938 and was a stalwart defender as United took the Southern League crown. During the war he made a guest appearance for Millwall and later became assistant to Colchester manager Ted Fenton. Birch remained local and was landlord of the Stockwell Arms and the Lexden Crown Inn before retiring in 1976.

	League		Lge Cup		FA Cup		Other	
	A	G	A	G	A	G	A	G
1938–39	44	1	3	0	2	0	13	0
1939–40	3	1	1	1	-	-	-	-
TOTAL	47	2	4	1	2	0	13	0

BIRCHAM, Bernard 'Barney'

Height: 5ft 11½in. Weight: 11st 6lb.

Born: 31 August 1924, Houghton.
Died: 11 October 2007.

■ Goalkeeper Bircham started his career as a Sunderland junior during the war years. He played three games in the Regional League of 1945–46 for the Wearsiders before joining Chesterfield in November of 1946 but failed to break into their first team. He finally made his League debut for Second Division Grimsby in 1949 and went on to to make eight appearances for the Mariners. Brought to Layer Road at a cost of £800 by Jimmy Allen, Bircham had to wait until February 1951 and the home game with Northampton until he could displace regular custodian George Wright, who had suffered a fractured jaw a week earlier at Watford, and in all made seven consecutive appearances before Wright's return. Bircham shared digs in Maldon Road with full-back John Harrison, but he could not displace Wright. He slipped into non-League football before returning to Grimsby where he was employed as a site engineer for a Swedish engineering company.

	League		Lge Cup		FA Cup		Other	
	A	G	A	G	A	G	A	G
1950–51	7	0	-	-	0	0	-	-
TOTAL	7	0	-	-	0	0	-	-

BLACKWOOD, Robert Rankin 'Bobby'

Height: 5ft 7½in. Weight: 11st 2lb.

Born: 20 August 1934, Edinburgh.
Died: 25 June 1997.

■ Blackwood joined Hearts in October 1950 from Kelty Rangers and made his debut two years later. He played a major part in Hearts' most successful period, when between 1953 and 1960 they won the Scottish League twice, were runners-up three times, won the Scottish FA Cup and the League Cup on three occasions. He represented the Scottish League against the English League at Highbury in 1960 and played in the European Cup and Cup-winners' Cup for the Jam Tarts. After 220 games in all competitions and a return of 77 goals, he moved to Alf Ramsey's Ipswich in June 1962 for a fee of £10,000. At Portman Road he scored 11 times in 62 League appearances before receiving a free transfer which took him to Layer Road. Blackwood encountered an amazing case of déjà vu in his second Colchester season. In just the second game of the 1966–67 season he fractured

his jaw in a collision with QPR's Les Allen in a League Cup tie at Loftus Road. Out for 15 games, he had just regained his match fitness when, five games after his return, he fractured his jaw again in a December home League game with QPR in a collision with – yes, Les Allen. This time Blackwood was out for nine games. He refused the part-time terms offered in summer 1968 and returned to Edinburgh, where he was briefly player-manager of Hawick Royal Albert, before returning to Tynecastle for a spell as Hearts reserve's trainer.

	League		Lge Cup		FA Cup		Other	
	A	G	A	G	A	G	A	G
1965–66	41	4	2	0	2	2	-	-
1966–67	20	0	1	0	1	0	-	-
1967–68	43+1	3	1	0	5	0	-	-
TOTAL	104+1	7	4	0	8	2	-	-

BLAKE, Mark Christopher

Height: 6ft. Weight: 12st 4lb.

Born: 19 December 1967, Portsmouth.

■ A Southampton apprentice, Blake's outings for the Hampshire club were restricted to 18 appearances over four seasons with two goals scored. He gained England Under-18 caps in seasons 1984–85 and 1985–86. Jock Wallace brought him to Colchester in September 1989 in a loan deal that saw the player remain undefeated in four starts. Blake also scored the equaliser in a 2–2 draw at Rochdale in the same month. He

returned to The Dell and was loaned to Shrewsbury on deadline day 1990, playing in 10 remaining games. He joined the Gay Meadow club permanently for a £100,000 fee in the summer, scoring three goals in a further 132 starts. A stint in Hong Kong playing for Rangers preceded Blake joining Fulham, where he was voted Player of the Year in 1996 and helped The Cottagers to promotion to Division Two a year later. The Al Fayed and Kevin Keegan revolution spelt the end for his 133(+3) game Fulham career, where he scored an impressive 17 goals. He joined AS Cannes in July 1998 before returning to England with Aldershot in April 2000. He spent time with Andover and Bashley during 2001 before becoming joint player-manager of Winchester in March 2002. He steered the club to FA Vase success against Sudbury in 2004, playing in the Final at St Andrews. However, financial wrangling led the player to join Conference South Eastleigh in January 2005 before setting up his own IT consultancy.

	League		Lge Cup		FA Cup		Other	
	A	G	A	G	A	G	A	G
1989–90	4	1	0	0	0	0	0	0
TOTAL	4	1	0	0	0	0	0	0

BLAKE, Russell Timothy

Height: 6ft. Weight: 11st 6lb.

Born: 24 July 1935, Colchester.

■ Blake was one of the local amateurs who played in the U's A side, first appearing in 1953, and had not yet turned pro when making his debut in a

6–0 thrashing at Leyton Orient in September 1955 as deputy for Peter Wright. A school colleague of U's goalkeeper John Wright, Blake played his early football with Colchester junior side Dedham Old Boys. He got another chance in the first team at the start of April 1956 and played so well at Brighton that the home side made an offer for him, forcing Benny Fenton to offer him professional terms at Layer Road. Blake was in the team that held Arsenal at Layer Road in the 1958–59 FA Cup, which proved to be his most fruitful season. He was leading scorer for the reserves in 1959–60 and on leaving Layer Road spent a year at Chelmsford and also played for Sudbury.

	League		Lge Cup		FA Cup		Other	
	A	G	A	G	A	G	A	G
1955–56	5	0	-	-	0	0	-	-
1956–57	2	0	-	-	0	0	-	-
1957–58	8	2	-	-	0	0	-	-
1958–59	24	5	-	-	5	0	-	-
1959–60	11	1	-	-	0	0	-	-
1960–61	7	0	0	0	0	0	-	-
TOTAL	57	8	0	0	5	0	-	-

BLATSIS, Con

Height: 6ft 3in. Weight: 13st 7lb.

Born: 6 July 1977, Melbourne, Australia.

■ Australian international Blatsis made his SoccerRoos debut against South Korea on 7 October 2000 in Dubai and gained a further cap against Colombia, in Bogotá, the following February. He had already gained international honours at Under-20 level playing in the 1997 World Youth Cup in Malaysia and at Under-23 level in qualifying

matches for the 2000 Olympic Games. He played in the Club World Championship for South Melbourne in Brazil, also in 2000, and marked Romario of Vasco da Gama out of the game in a group that also contained Mexicans Nexcaca and Manchester United. He arrived in England during August 2000, signing for Derby for £150,000. After just two Premiership starts, he was loaned to Sheffield Wednesday in the December, playing six times. Steve Whitton signed the player for Colchester on deadline day 2002 on a non-contract basis after he had spent time with Norwegian side Lillestroem. Making his debut in a 3–1 home win over QPR, Blatsis steadied U's defence. He declined the offer to join United permanently and moved to Turkish side Kocealispor, where he suffered a contractual nightmare. He was forced to take the Turks to FIFA in a long-running arbitration case, which he eventually won. Short of match practice, as a result he signed for Irish side St Patrick's Athletic, managed by former Colchester hero Eamonn Collins, in July 2004. He soon returned to his first club, South Melbourne, after a brief trial with Coventry, where he remained in 2007.

	League		Lge Cup		FA Cup		Other	
	A	G	A	G	A	G	A	G
2001–02	7	0	0	0	0	0	0	0
TOTAL	7	0	0	0	0	0	0	0

BLOSS, Philip Kenneth 'Phil'

Height: 5ft 9in. Weight: 10st 8lb.

Born: 16 January 1953, Colchester.

■ A United apprentice who signed professional in January 1971, midfielder Bloss will be remembered most for scoring the winning penalty-kick in the 1971 Watney Cup Final victory over West Bromwich Albion at The Hawthorns after the U's had earned a 4–4 draw. Bloss also scored on his debut in April 1971 when United beat Barrow 4–1 at Layer Road. The son-in-law of manager Dick Graham had a trial at West Brom in August 1973 after being freed by the U's but never made the first team. Bloss joined Wimbledon, playing 45 League and Cup games in 1973–74 and then moved to Clacton where he picked up an Eastern Counties League Championship medal in 1974–75. In 1977–78 he trod the well-worn path between Clacton and Harwich, the club for which his dad Ken had played centre-half in the 1953 Amateur Cup Final, and later managed local sides Wivenhoe in 1993–94 and Stanway Rovers between 1995 and 2000, while owning an Estate Agency in the town.

	League		Lge Cup		FA Cup		Other	
	A	G	A	G	A	G	A	G
1970–71	1	1	0	0	0	0	-	-
1971–72	19	2	2	0	0	0	1	0
1972–73	12+2	0	0	0	0+2	0	-	-
TOTAL	32+2	3	2	0	0+2	0	1	0

BOND, Leonard Allan 'Len'

Height: 5ft 9in. Weight: 12st.

Born: 12 February 1954, Ilminster.

■ Bond became a Colchester United rarity as he actually played in the U's goal while Mike Walker was still at the club. Beaten 6–0 at Brighton the week previous, Bond arrived on loan from Bristol City, with Colchester being his fifth club in a little over a year. Things did not get any better as U's lost 4–1 at home to Hereford in his first game and lost away games at Rotherham and Chesterfield. Bond had begun his career as a Bristol City apprentice, signing professionally in September 1971. Embarking on a run of loan deals, he joined Exeter in November 1974 (30 appearances), Torquay in October 1975 (three), Scunthorpe in December 1975 (eight) and of course the U's in January 1976. He also completed 30 games at Ashton Gate before being sold to Brentford at the beginning of the 1977–78 season. He established himself at Griffin Park, making 122 League starts, before having a spell in the US with St Louis. On his return in October 1980 he joined Exeter, where he became a teammate of former U's star Roy McDonough and completed a further 138 League games. He moved into the non-League circle and played for Weymouth, Bath, Yeovil and Gloucester before becoming goalkeeper coach at Yeovil.

	League		Lge Cup		FA Cup		Other	
	A	G	A	G	A	G	A	G
1975–76	3	0	0	0	0	0	-	-
TOTAL	3	0	0	0	0	0	-	-

BOOTY, Justin

Height: 5ft 11in. Weight: 13st 12lb.

Born: 2 June 1976, Colchester.

■ A Colchester YTS player and a prolific scorer at schoolboy and youth level where his early physical maturity allowed him to dominate opponents, Booty was given his League debut as a substitute during January 1994 in a 1–0 home win over Hereford. Four days earlier he had made his one and only first-team start against Wycombe in the Autoglass Trophy. Booty remained local for a time, playing for Braintree, Wivenhoe and Brightlingsea following his release from Layer Road before moving to Cumbria where he was content to play Sunday football. His father Keith was a legendary fundraiser for the club's youth department while Justin was coming through the ranks.

	League		Lge Cup		FA Cup		Other	
	A	G	A	G	A	G	A	G
1993–94	0+1	0	0	0	0	0	1	0
TOTAL	0+1	0	0	0	0	0	1	0

BOTT, Wilfred 'Wilf'

Born: 25 April 1907, Featherstone.
Died: July 1992, Hastings.

■ Bott was signed in July 1946 from QPR, having scored 34 goals in 75 League appearances between 1935 and 1938. Previously he had represented Doncaster 1926–30 (111 appearances/32 goals), Huddersfield 1930–34 (110/25) and Newcastle 1934–35 (37/11). He marked his £1,000 transfer to St James' Park with a hat-trick on his debut against Bury. During the war he turned out for Aldershot, Brighton, Chelsea and, predominantly, QPR. He also represented the FA against the RAF in 1941, but he played just twice for Colchester in September 1946. He signed for Guildford City in the October and captained them against the U's the following Easter Saturday. Bott later played for non-League Lancaster.

	League		Lge Cup		FA Cup		Other	
	A	G	A	G	A	G	A	G
1946–47	2	0	0	0	0	0	-	-
TOTAL	2	0	0	0	0	0	-	-

BOURNE, Richard Adrian

Height: 5ft 11in. Weight: 12st.

Born: 9 December 1954, Colchester.

■ Bourne began his football career just down the road from the Layer Road ground at Kingsford Junior School, where in 1965–66 he captained a school team that included one of the authors. He first played for the U's reserves while still at school just before his 16th birthday, but as the U's did not run a youth team between 1970 and 1973 he also played for Tiptree in the Essex Senior League in the early part of 1971–72 as well as the U's reserves in the Midweek League. His Football League debut came as sub at Chester on 3 April 1972, but his first start, seven days later, ended with injury forcing his own substitution. Signing professional forms in 1972–73, Bourne played in the last two games of Colchester's re-election season but was released in Jim Smith's subsequent purge and joined Ramsgate where he was a virtual ever present until they went into liquidation in March 1976. He moved on to Bath, helping them to the Southern League title in 1977–78 and was brought back to the Football League by Torquay in the summer of 1979 at a cost of £10,000. He played in 64(+4) games for the Gulls, scoring seven goals before the arrival of Frank O'Farrell and Bruce Rioch as the new management team at Plainmoor spelt the end of his League career. Ex-U's teammate Stuart Morgan took him to Weymouth, and he made almost 200 appearances to 1987 before joining the Terra's coaching staff. He had a testimonial at Weymouth against Bournemouth in August 1989 and by that time was a newsagent in the town.

	League		Lge Cup		FA Cup		Other	
	A	G	A	G	A	G	A	G
1971–72	1+1	0	0	0	0	0	0	0
1972–73	2	0	0	0	0	0	-	-
TOTAL	3+1	0	0	0	0	0	0	0

BOWDITCH, Benjamin Edward 'Ben'

Height: 5ft 9in. Weight: 11st 7lb.

Born: 19 February 1984, Harlow.

■ Released by Tottenham after serving his youth training at White Hart Lane, Bowditch had already represented England at Youth (as captain) and Under-20 level before Phil Parkinson brought him to Layer Road. He had joined Danish side AB Copenhagen in March 2004 but failed to settle in Denmark. He made his Colchester debut as a substitute in a 2–1 League Cup win over Cheltenham in August 2004 but featured in only a handful of further appearances from the bench as he was unable to displace Neil Danns from

United's midfield. Released at the end of the season, Bowditch joined Barnet on a summer trial but, despite being taken on, managed just 3(+3) appearances and was loaned out to Conference South team Yeading. Released by Barnet, he joined Cambridge City and began the 2007–08 season marshalling their Conference South midfield. Bowditch's younger brother Dean played at the same time on the books of Ipswich.

	League		Lge Cup		FA Cup		Other	
	A	G	A	G	A	G	A	G
2004–05	0+5	0	0+1	0	0+1	0	0	0
TOTAL	0+5	0	0+1	0	0+1	0	0	0

BOWEN, Keith Bryn

Height: 6ft 1in. Weight: 11st 2lb.

Born: 26 February 1958, Northampton.

■ Bowen already had a football pedigree, as his father Dave Bowen had taken Northampton from the Fourth Division to the First Division in the mid-sixties and been manager of the Wales national team between 1964–71. Keith Bowen earned Welsh Schoolboy honours and signed professionally for his home-town club Northampton in the summer of 1976. He scored all of his 24 League goals in a two-season spell between 1979–81. Signing for Brentford in September 1981, Bowen went on to score nine times in 42(+9) games at Griffin Park. On deadline day 1983 U's boss Cyril Lea captured the striker, initially on loan, and he scored on his debut in a 2–1 victory over Bury at Layer Road. Bowen formed a great partnership with Tony Adcock, and his extra-time winner at Reading in the 1983–4 League Cup led ultimately to a home tie with Manchester United. In the same season he also netted a hat-trick in U's 6–0 FA Cup mauling of non-League Wealdstone. His career came to an abrupt end when his car crashed into metal railings just hours after playing against former team Northampton at Layer Road. The broken leg suffered and other injuries spelt the end for Bowen.

	League		Lge Cup		FA Cup		Other	
	A	G	A	G	A	G	A	G
1982–83	13	4	0	0	0	0	0	0
1983–84	46	13	4	1	3	5	2	0
1984–85	41+1	17	2	1	0+1	0	2	0
1985–86	15	4	2	3	0	0	0	0
TOTAL	115+1	38	8	5	3+1	5	4	0

BOWER, Ronald William Charles 'Bill'

Born: 17 November 1911, Wrexham.
Died: December 1998, Colchester.

■ Originally a forward with Merseysiders New Brighton, Bower made 24 League appearances between 1932 and 1934 before joining the prominent non-League side South Liverpool in 1935. Moving to Bolton a year later, he was converted to right-back, which became his career position. After just three games at Burnden Park, Bower moved south to Millwall in 1937, playing in the Lions' Southern League side, but the war curtailed any hopes of a regular League career. He did, however, gain representative honours for the Southern League as a centre-half. During the war he guested for Southend (39 appearances/0 goals), New Brighton (40/1) and Aldershot (44/5) and was selected for the British Army against the Canadian Army at Aldershot. It was while stationed in Colchester that Bower joined United, becoming one of the first post-war professional signings on 28 November 1945 following his demob. Although christened Ronald, U's secretary-manager Syd Fieldus decided that having two Ron's, Hornby and Sales, in the squad was enough and Bower became known by his second name William or rather Bill. During the 1945–46 season, United used 80 players as they battled to field a side following the end of hostilities; incredibly Bower was an ever-present, playing in all 20 Southern League games and 10 League Cup ties. One of only four retained for the following season, he missed just one outing, clocking up a further 30 League, seven League Cup and two FA Cup matches. Moving aside for the up-and-coming Digger Kettle, 36-year-old Bower deputised for Kettle on three occasions in 1947–48 while doubling up as captain and coach of United's Eastern Counties League reserves side. Inspired by this role, he gained an FA coaching badge in 1949–50 and spent the summer months imparting this knowledge to local schools. He also added two last first-team appearances in the early weeks of 1949–50, replacing the injured Kettle against Hereford and finally at Dartford on 1 October. Bower finished his playing days at Sudbury Town, first retiring in September 1956, although he actually turned out for the last time at the ripe old age of 54. Never booked in 25 years of football, Bower retired from his job in the Despatch Department of Woods of Colchester in November 1976.

	League		Lge Cup		FA Cup		Other	
	A	G	A	G	A	G	A	G
1945–46	20	0	10	1	0	0	-	-
1946–47	30	0	7	0	2	0	-	-
1947–48	3	0	1	0	0	0	-	-
1948–49	-	-	-	-	-	-	-	-
1949–50	2	0	0	0	0	0	-	-
TOTAL	55	0	18	1	2	0	-	-

BOWRY, Robert John 'Bobby'

Height: 5ft 9in. Weight: 10st 8lb.

Born: 19 May 1971, Croydon.

■ Beginning his football career as a trainee at QPR, Bowry was unfortunate to be released and joined non-League Carshalton in August 1990. After some sterling displays he was picked up by Crystal Palace in April 1992 and went straight into their relegation-destined

side, making 6(+5) Premiership appearances and scoring the winner against Aston Villa. Palace bounced back the following season as champions and so Bowry enjoyed further top-flight action. Completing 36(+14) games at Selhurst Park, he was sold to Millwall in July 1995 for a fee of £220,000. Unfortunately Millwall were relegated to the third level of English football, but Bowry remained a regular, amassing 125(+15) appearances and scoring five times for the Lions. He played twice for St Kitts & Nevis in April 2000 against St Vincent in World Cup qualifiers. Becoming just a squad player at The New Den, Bowry joined Colchester on a free transfer in the summer of 2001, appearing as a substitute in a stunning 6–3 opening-day win at Chesterfield. He became a valued figure, marshalling the young Colchester midfield. Hip and groin injuries curtailed his Colchester career, and in August 2005, following his release by Phil Parkinson, he joined Conference side Gravesend & Northfleet. He moved to Bromley in November 2006 and helped the club to Play-off promotion to the Ryman Premier League. He remained at Hayes Lane in 2007–08 as player-coach alongside former Colchester players Andy Walker and Gareth Williams.

	League		Lge Cup		FA Cup		Other	
	A	G	A	G	A	G	A	G
2001–02	27+9	1	0+2	0	1	0	2	0
2002–03	33+2	1	1	0	1	0	1	0
2003–04	18+6	0	1	0	1+1	0	2+1	0
2004–05	7+4	0	0+1	0	1+1	0	1	0
TOTAL	85+21	2	2+3	0	4+2	0	6+1	0

BOYCE, Robert Alexander

Height: 5ft 11in. Weight: 11st 12lb.

Born: 7 January 1974, Islington.

■ On the books of Sheffield Wednesday as a schoolboy, Boyce failed to make the grade and dropped into non-League with Stevenage and Enfield before being recruited on trial by Steve Wignall in October 1995. He made his debut as a replacement in a 2–1 win at Cardiff in the same month and made just one further substitute appearance at Doncaster in November of the same season. He was not retained after suffering a shoulder injury and joined Chelmsford. In 1996–97 he played three times for Aylesbury and in 2000 was with Wealdstone.

	League		Lge Cup		FA Cup		Other	
	A	G	A	G	A	G	A	G
1995–96	0+2	0	0	0	0	0	0	0
TOTAL	0+2	0	0	0	0	0	0	0

BRAMBLE, Titus Malachi

Height: 6ft 1in. Weight: 13st.

Born: 21 July 1981, Ipswich.

■ After breaking into the Ipswich team in late 1998 Bramble suffered a series of niggling injuries and arrived at Layer Road as part of his return to fitness, having made just 2(+2) appearances at Portman Road. He made his Colchester debut at Blackpool in January 2000 but injured himself in conceding a penalty to Bristol Rovers' Jamie Cureton in a thrilling 5–4 Colchester win a week later. He returned to Ipswich and won a regular place in 2000–01, scoring against

Torpedo Moscow in the UEFA Cup. In July 2002, after only a further 39(+1) League appearances, Newcastle bid £5 million for the young defender. He took time to settle and scored his first goal for the Magpies also in UEFA Cup action against NAC Breda in 2003–04 and repeated the feat against Basle and Mallorca in subsequent rounds. Despite winning 12 England Under-21 caps between 2000 and 2002, Bramble was often chastised by the Toon Army and the media for basic defensive errors. The arrival of Sam Allardyce at St James' Park in the summer of 2007 signalled the end of Bramble's 96-game Premier League Newcastle career. He moved to fellow top-flight Wigan on a free transfer for the 2007–08 season.

	League		Lge Cup		FA Cup		Other	
	A	G	A	G	A	G	A	G
1999–2000	2	0	0	0	0	0	0	0
TOTAL	2	0	0	0	0	0	0	0

BRAMHALL

■ Centre-half Bramhall, a soldier in the Army Fire Fighting Corps, was said to be attached to Notts County, although he never played for their senior side. His only Colchester appearance came at Yeovil in September 1945.

	League		Lge Cup		FA Cup		Other	
	A	G	A	G	A	G	A	G
1945–46	1	0	0	0	0	0	-	-
TOTAL	1	0	0	0	0	0	-	-

BRANSTON, Guy Peter Bromley

Height: 6ft 1in. Weight: 14st.

Born: 9 January 1974, Leicester.

■ Branston's career began as a youth trainee at Leicester where he signed professional in the summer of 1997. After being let out on loan to Rushden & Diamonds, the centre-half joined Colchester on a similar deal in February 1998, making his debut in a 2–0 win over Mansfield in the same month. He became a solid addition as Steve Wignall's side reached the Third Division Play-off Final. The duration of his loan meant that he could only play in the first leg semi-final at Barnet. He was sent off after 82 minutes along with Bees star Sean Devine, weakening the opposition for the second leg which United won through. He rejoined Colchester at the start of 1998–99 but

made just one substitute appearance because of injury and suspension. On completion of the second loan he joined Plymouth for seven games, scoring once. Attempting to break into the Leicester first team, Branston had another spell with Rushden & Diamonds before joining Lincoln on loan at the beginning of the 1999–2000 season. Just four games convinced Rotherham to pay £50,000 for his services, and the Millers went on to clinch promotion in successive seasons under Ronnie Moore to reach the second tier. Branston scored 13 times in 101(+1) games at Millmoor. He had nine games on loan at Peterborough in September 2003 before making a permanent switch to Sheffield Wednesday in the 2004 close season. He was soon back at London Road, playing a four-game loan spell in December 2004 prior to making a permanent move to Oldham in February 2005. At Boundary Park he featured 44(+1) times, scoring once. His third spell at Peterborough was made permanent in the summer of 2006 with a two-year deal, but, he joined Rochdale on loan at the start of 2007–08 and had similar stints at Northampton in November and Wells County in January 2008.

	League		Lge Cup		FA Cup		Other	
	A	G	A	G	A	G	A	G
1997–98	12	1	0	0	0	0	1	0
1998–99	0+1	0	0	0	0	0	0	0
TOTAL	12+1	1	0	0	0	0	1	0

BREMNER, Kevin Johnston

Height: 5ft 9½in. Weight: 12st 3lb.

Born: 7 October 1957, Banff.

■ Bobby Roberts surprised everyone by signing former Deveronvale striker Bremner from little-known Highland League side Keith in October 1980. Costing £25,000, Bremner was an instant hit with the U's faithful with his tireless running and enthusiasm for the game. His first U's goal came in front of the *Match of the Day* cameras at Plymouth in November 1980, but it was in the following season that he came to the fore, forming a lethal strike partnership with Ian Allinson (21 goals) and Roy McDonough (14). Anxious to improve himself, Bremner rebelled against Colchester and refused a new contract. He touted himself around several loan clubs at the beginning of 1982–83, playing for Birmingham (3(+1) appearances/1 goal), Wrexham (4/1) and Plymouth (5/1). In February 1983 Millwall boss George Graham stumped up the same £25,000 fee that had brought Bremner to Colchester. Millwall were promoted to Division Two at the end of 1984–85, but Bremner signed for Reading for £35,000 despite firing 32 goals in 87(+9) League games for the Lions. He went one better at Elm Park with the Royals, winning the Third Division title in his first season. After a season in the second tier, scoring 14 goals, he moved to Brighton in July 1987 for £65,000 where, incredibly, he won promotion from the Third Division for the third time in succession. Added to his 60(+4) games and 21 goals for Reading, Bremner bagged 36 further strikes in 125(+3) appearances on the south coast despite Brighton struggling to avoid the drop. Peterborough was the next port of call in the summer of 1990 for a fee of £18,000. After scoring three times in 13(+4), games Bremner returned over the border to join Dundee, scoring six in 24 games during the 1991–92 season. Recruited by Shrewsbury on deadline day 1992, Bremner played seven games on loan at Gay Meadow and scored twice before taking up the post of player-manager at Highland Leaguers Brora Rangers and then Deveronvale. Bremner then spent eight years as youth coach at Gillingham before being sacked in a cost-cutting exercise due to the ITV Digital collapse. He took up a similar post at Millwall in 2004.

	League		Lge Cup		FA Cup		Other	
	A	G	A	G	A	G	A	G
1980–81	33+1	8	0	0	4	2	-	-
1981–82	46	21	5	3	5	0	-	-
1982–83	10+5	2	0+2	0	1	0	1	0
TOTAL	89+6	31	5+2	3	10	2	1	0

BRIGHT, Stewart Linden

Height: 5ft 8in. Weight: 10st 10lb.

Born: 13 October 1957, Colchester.

■ Local lad Bright progressed through the Colchester youth ranks to make his debut as a substitute against Shrewsbury at Layer Road in November 1975. An apprentice since summer 1974, he signed pro in January 1976 but was always going to find it difficult to break into the first team with U's stalwart Micky Cook in his position. He had a good run in the team

from the beginning of 1976, but United were a poor side destined for relegation and, while Bright played in a handful of games the following season, manager Roberts had strengthened the side, and as a result Bright was released to Chelmsford where he played over 170 games before moving on to Wivenhoe in early 1981. He gave good service to them as well and was still a regular in 1984–85.

	League		Lge Cup		FA Cup		Other	
	A	G	A	G	A	G	A	G
1975–76	18+2	0	0	0	0	0	-	-
1976–77	5	0	0	0	0	0	-	-
TOTAL	23+2	0	0	0	0	0	-	-

BROOKE, Garry James

Height: 5ft 6in. Weight: 10st 5lb.

Born: 24 November 1960, Bethnal Green.

■ A Tottenham apprentice, Brooke signed professionally at White Hart Lane in October 1978 and completed 49(+24) League appearances, scoring 15 times. During this time Spurs won the FA Cup, the UEFA Cup and the Charity Shield, and Brooke appeared as a substitute in three Cup Finals. He had a spell on loan at Gothenburg in April 1980, but just four months after scoring an October 1982 hat-trick against Coventry he was involved in a near-fatal road crash. On recovering, he joined Norwich in the summer of 1985, scoring twice in 8(+6) games. A £30,000 fee saw him move to FC Groningen in December 1986 before he returned to England in March 1988 to play 5(+7) times for Wimbledon. By March 1990 he had been loaned out to Stoke, adding 6(+2) games to his total before being engaged by Brentford in the summer of 1990. However, after just 8(+3) games and a solitary goal Brooke was on the lookout for a new club. Colchester manager Ian Atkins gave Brooke his only U's appearance as a trialist in a Bob Lord Trophy game at Fisher Athletic in January 1991. He was not retained, and after a spell with Baldock he finished his professional career with 1(+3) games for Reading at the tail end of 1990–91. Moving into non-League, Brooke turned out for Wivenhoe, St Albans, Romford, Worthing and Cornard. Brooke attained his coaching badges and assisted Tottenham in their Football in the Community programme.

	League		Lge Cup		FA Cup		Other	
	A	G	A	G	A	G	A	G
1990–91	0	0	1	0	0	0	0	0
TOTAL	0	0	1	0	0	0	0	0

BROWN, Andrew 'Andy'

Born: 20 February 1915, Coatbridge.
Died: 1973, Colchester.

■ Scotsman Brown began at Cumbernauld Thistle and in 1936–37 joined Cardiff where he made just two League appearances. His next move was to Torquay in 1938 where he made 34 appearances, scoring five times. Signed from Torquay on 17 June 1947, Brown became a regular in United's defence as they embarked on their famous FA Cup run of 1947–48 and scored U's opening goal against Banbury Spencer in the first round. Released in 1949, he spent a couple of years back in the West at Kidderminster before returning to East Anglia to play for Bury Town. After 137 games in three years at Kings Road he returned to Colchester to succeed Bill Light as reserves coach, a position he still held when the club pulled out of the Eastern Counties League in 1959. He also had a spell as player coach at Halstead and worked with Bill Bower in the packing and despatch department of fan manufacturers Woods of Colchester.

	League		Lge Cup		FA Cup		Other	
	A	G	A	G	A	G	A	G
1947–48	28	2	8	0	6	1	-	-
1948–49	29	0	4	0	1	0	-	-
TOTAL	57	2	12	0	7	1	-	-

BROWN, Harold Thomas 'Harry'

Height: 6ft. Weight: 12st.

Born: 9 April 1924, Kingsbury.
Died: 1982.

■ Brown, a goalkeeper, was on the books of QPR during the war and played in each wartime season, notching up 79 appearances. He still found time also to guest for Brentford, Crystal Palace and Spurs during the 1944–45 season. QPR manager Dave Magnall was keen to cash in on Brown's experience, ordering him away from his guest appearances at Layer Road to Notts County in order to put in him in the shop window. Brown had a £3,000 transfer fee on his head, and after 10 games at Meadow Lane he was chosen to guest for Chelsea against Swansea. Unfortunately he was beaten four times and Chelsea never returned their interest; Colchester manager told the local press that it was Chelsea's loss and that one day Brown would play for England. He never quite made that

mantle, but he did guest for Arsenal against the touring Moscow Dynamo side on 11 November 1945. Few of the 54,000 crowd could see the proceedings because of dense fog, but a call came out over the tannoy for a goalkeeper and Wright beat Charlton's Sam Bartram to the Arsenal changing room. Moscow claimed Arsenal were actually the full England side, but although Stan Matthews and Stan Mortensen had guested for them that season they also had two Welshman in Cumner and Cardiff 'keeper Griffiths. The dense fog threatened the game, but Dynamo supplied their own ref and linesmen patrolling the same touchline. Griffiths suffered a head injury and struggled on to half-time. The game ended 4–4 in a spot of Anglo-Russian diplomacy after the Russians had brought on a substitute and not taken anyone off. Unluckily Brown dislocated his knee in a friendly against Ekco Sports at Layer Road in January 1946, but he resurrected his career and went on to play for Notts County (93 League games 1946–48), Derby (37 games 1949–50), returned to QPR (187 games 1951–55), Plymouth (66 games 1956–57) and finally made no appearances on the books of Exeter in 1958–59.

	League		Lge Cup		FA Cup		Other	
	A	G	A	G	A	G	A	G
1945–46	10	0	2	0	0	0	-	-
TOTAL	10	0	2	0	0	0	-	-

BROWN, Ian O'Neill

Height: 5ft 10in. Weight: 11st 5lb.

Born: 11 September 1965, Chelmsford.

■ Starting his career at Birmingham as an apprentice, Brown signed professionally in September 1984, making just a brief substitute appearance in the League Cup the same season. He moved back to East Anglia to play for Felixstowe and proceeded via Stowmarket and Sudbury Town to Harwich from where he signed non-contract terms for the U's in October 1988. It was thought that the manager intended to offer him a full-time deal, but Brown departed after an 8–0 thrashing at Leyton Orient and Ian Brown's first stint at Layer Road, consisted of a friendly at Brightlingsea and a reserve game with Orient. He spent a couple of years at Harwich, then a similar period at

Chelmsford from where he returned to League football in the summer of 1993 when he signed for Bristol City. Scoring once in 5(+7) games, he finally arrived at Layer Road on deadline day 1994 on a month's loan. Despite scoring on his 26 March debut in a 1–1 draw with Preston he returned to Bristol and made just one further League substitute appearance and two more in the League Cup. By December he was with his third club of 1994 when joining Northampton. He played out the remaining 23 games of the season, scoring four times, and later found himself back on the East Anglian non-League circuit where he served a good half-dozen clubs including Braintree, Cambridge City and a second spell with Sudbury .

	League		Lge Cup		FA Cup		Other	
	A	G	A	G	A	G	A	G
1993–94	4	1	0	0	0	0	0	0
TOTAL	4	1	0	0	0	0	0	0

BROWN, Jermaine Anthony Alexander

Height: 5ft 11in. Weight: 11st.

Born: 12 January 1983, Lambeth.

■ Signing full forms for Arsenal in July 2001 after being with them since the age of nine, Brown had a mammoth task ahead of himself in trying to displace the wealth of foreign talent in the Gunners' first team. It was no surprise that he was released at the end of 2002–03. Phil Parkinson brought the player to Layer Road on a short-term deal in October 2003 and Brown made just one substitute appearance in an LDV Trophy tie at Wycombe in the December. It was a notable appearance as the youngster

scored the winner in the eighth minute of injury time, in extra-time, after a serious injury to U's Bobby Bowry. At the end of his contract Brown joined Boston United, playing 3(+2) games before turning out for non-League clubs King's Lynn, Lewes, Aldershot and Margate.

	League		Lge Cup		FA Cup		Other	
	A	G	A	G	A	G	A	G
2003–04	0	0	0	0	0	0	0+1	1
TOTAL	0	0	0	0	0	0	0+1	1

BROWN, John

Height: 5ft 11in. Weight: 10st 12lb.

Born: 6 March 1940, Edinburgh.

■ Brown arrived at Layer Road at the same time as Duncan Forbes in September 1961 but did not have quite the same impact. Originally with Scottish junior side Dunbar United, Brown lodged with U's defender John Harrison and made a solitary League appearance as half-back against Halifax in October 1962. On leaving Layer Road he played for Stenhousemuir before emigrating to Melbourne where he turned out for the Maltese community team George Cross

and then became player-coach of their main rivals Boxhill.

	League		Lge Cup		FA Cup		Other	
	A	G	A	G	A	G	A	G
1962–63	1	0	1	0	1	0	-	-
TOTAL	1	0	1	0	1	0	-	-

BROWN, Michael John 'Micky'

Height: 5ft 7in. Weight: 11st 12lb.

Born: 11 April 1944, Slough.

■ Diminutive winger Brown signed for Fulham in September 1961 and played four times for the Cottagers, making his debut as a 17-year-old at Sheffield Wednesday. Although signed as a professional in April 1962, Brown struggled to break into the First Division side and eventually moved to Millwall where his 10 goals in 28 (+2) appearances helped the Lions to promotion to Division Two in 1965–66. In total he amassed 47 (+5) League appearances for the South London side, scoring 11. Moving to Luton in July 1967, he failed to impress at Kenilworth Road, playing just 9(+5) games and netting twice in the League. Once Dick Graham had assessed the playing staff left to him at the beginning of 1968–69, Brown became one of a number of recruits to Layer Road, with the U's paying a £3,000 fee. He enjoyed a good second season at Layer Road, weighing in with nine goals, but missed much of 1970–71 with injury and departed Layer Road in April 1971 on loan to Romford before leaving permanently in the summer. For 1971–72 he teamed up with fellow ex-U's players Terry Dyson, Eddie Presland and Ray Whittaker at Wealdstone before turning out for Maidstone, Tonbridge and Hillingdon Borough. He later became a newsagent in the Harrow area.

	League		Lge Cup		FA Cup		Other	
	A	G	A	G	A	G	A	G
1968–69	17+3	3	0	0	1+1	0	-	-
1969–70	30+2	9	3	0	1	0	-	-
TOTAL	47+5	12	3	0	2+1	0	-	-

BROWN, R.

■ A young West Ham colt, Brown made his debut against Swindon reserves in February 1946 and went on to play in goal in seven League and Cup games for Colchester.

	League		Lge Cup		FA Cup		Other	
	A	G	A	G	A	G	A	G
1945–46	2	0	5	0	0	0	-	-
TOTAL	2	0	5	0	0	0	-	-

BROWN, Simon James

Height: 6ft 2in. Weight: 15st 1lb.

Born: 3 December 1976, Chelmsford.

■ Beginning his career in the Youth Training Scheme at Tottenham, Brown progressed to the senior ranks in July 1995 but failed to reach the first team. He had one game on loan at Lincoln in December 1997 and a non-playing loan at Fulham at the beginning of the following campaign. Released from White Hart Lane, Brown played non-League with Kingstonian, Gravesend & Northfleet and Aylesbury before being recruited for Colchester in the summer of 1999 by Mick Wadsworth. He made his debut in the opening game of the season in a 1–0 win at Chesterfield but was sent off for handling outside the box in the next game, which was a League Cup tie with Crystal Palace. Brown spent the next two seasons vying with Andy Woodman for the number-one spot. When Woodman departed, Brown made the position his own but refused a new contract and joined Scottish Premier League Hibernian in the summer of 2004. Regarded as a good shot-stopper, Brown often failed to command his area. Ever-present in his first Scottish Premier League campaign, Brown lost his place after a series of blunders and did not feature in the first team again until January 2006. His three-year stint at Easter Road realised 38, seven and then four seasonal appearances, but he did play European football as Hibs entered the Intertoto Cup. In the summer of 2007 he returned to the English League and joined Brentford.

	League		Lge Cup		FA Cup		Other	
	A	G	A	G	A	G	A	G
1999–2000	38	0	1	0	1	0	1	0
2000–01	18	0	4	0	1	0	0	0
2001–02	19	0	0	0	0	0	2	0
2002–03	26+1	0	0	0	1	0	0+1	0
2003–04	40	0	2	0	6	0	5	0
TOTAL	141+1	0	7	0	9	0	8+1	0

BROWN, Stanley 'Stan'

Height: 5ft 7in. Weight: 11st 3lb.

Born: 15 September 1941, Lewes.

■ Brown began as an amateur at Fulham in 1957, signing professional in March 1959. Making 348(+5) League appearances, he appeared in the First Division with the Cottagers and remained as they slipped to the Third Division in the late 1960s. Scoring 16 goals, he was loaned out to Brighton in October 1972 where he made nine appearances. On completion of that loan spell he was signed for Colchester by Jim Smith in December 1972 and was made captain. Playing in all the remaining

fixtures, Brown was unable to help Colchester avoid re-election. On release from Layer Road he moved to Wimbledon and Margate and was player-manager of Hayward's Heath between 1974 and 1977. Staying in Sussex, he took over as manager at Ringmer and Burgess Hill during the 1980s.

	League		Lge Cup		FA Cup		Other	
	A	G	A	G	A	G	A	G
1972–73	23	0	0	0	0	0	-	-
TOTAL	23	0	0	0	0	0	-	-

BROWN, Steven Robert 'Steve'

Height: 5ft 11in. Weight: 11st 10lb.

Born: 6 December 1973, Southend.

■ A YTS player with Southend, Brown signed full forms with the Shrimpers in July 1992. Scoring twice in 10 League starts, he moved to Scunthorpe a year later only to become homesick without kicking a ball. Roy McDonough brought the young forward back to Colchester, and he scored on his first full start against Shrewsbury in August 1993 and proceeded to score five more goals in the next four matches, including a hat-trick against Bury at Layer Road. He was top scorer in that first season, but as George Burley assembled his own side in the following campaign Brown found himself transferred to Gillingham in March 1995 in a swap deal for Robbie Reinelt, where he played 8(+1) times, scoring twice, before moving on once again to Lincoln in October 1995 for £20,000. At Sincil Bank he stayed for three

seasons and was used as a substitute in no fewer than 25 League games as well as making 47 starts. He registered eight goals for the Imps and had a spell with Dover during the 1996–97 season, netting twice in three Conference starts. It would not be his last appearances for the Kent side, but on release from Lincoln he had a short sojourn with Macclesfield, playing 1(+1) League game and equalling that playing record in the League Cup. He returned to Dover and in three seasons between 1998 and 2001 played 57(+13) Conference games, scoring 12. Brown later played in the Ryman League with Kingstonian and Purfleet.

	League		Lge Cup		FA Cup		Other	
	A	G	A	G	A	G	A	G
1993–94	30+4	11	0	0	1	1	3	1
1994–95	26+2	6	2	0	4	2	2	0
TOTAL	56+6	17	2	0	5	3	5	1

BROWN, Wayne Lawrence

Height: 6ft. Weight: 12st 5lb.

Born: 20 August 1977, Barking.

■ Brown originally joined Colchester as a 20-year-old loanee in October 1997. He made his debut as a substitute in a 1–1 draw with Shrewsbury at Layer Road but made just one further appearance from the bench. He did not really establish himself in the Ipswich side until the 1999–2000 season when he played 20 games as Town won through to the Premiership via the Play-offs. Making just four substitute appearances in Ipswich's two seasons in the top flight, Brown had loan spells with QPR in March 2001 playing twice, 17 games and a goal with Wimbledon in September of the same year and with Watford in January of 2003 where he bagged three goals in just 10 starts. He gained UEFA Cup experience in 2002–03 scoring once, against Avenir Beggan, in three European outings. Just before the turn of the year, unable to break into the Ipswich side, he made the move to Watford permanent, playing 24(+1) games over the next two seasons as well as having a loan spell at Gillingham in September 2003 and scoring once in four starts. He rejoined Colchester in the summer of 2004 and steadily matured into a fine defender. He helped Colchester to runners'-up spot in League One in 2005–06, being named Player of the Year. With extensive second tier experience with all his previous clubs,

Brown excelled at Colchester's new level. In the summer of 2007, with a year still left on his contract, Brown acrimoniously left the club for fellow Championship side Hull for a fee of £450,000, winning promotion via the Play-offs in 2008.

	League		Lge Cup		FA Cup		Other	
	A	G	A	G	A	G	A	G
1997–98	0+2	0	0	0	0	0	0	0
2003–04	16	0	0	0	0	0	0+1	0
2004–05	38+2	1	3	0	2+1	0	1	0
2005–06	38	2	1	0	4	1	2	0
2006–07	46	1	1	0	1	0	-	-
TOTAL	138+4	4	5	0	7+1	1	3+1	0

BROWNE, Robert James 'Bobby'

Height: 5ft 7in. Weight: 12st 4lb.

Born: 9 February 1912, Londonderry.
Died: August 1994, Leeds.

■ Irishman Browne was stationed with the Army Air Force Fire Corps at Clacton during the war and was on the books of Leeds. Elland Road manager Billy Hampson had signed Browne from Derry on 1 October 1935, and he went on to make 121 appearances for the Yorkshiremen. It was during his spell at Leeds that Browne won his six Northern Ireland caps. He faced England and Wales in 1936 and 1938 and added games against England and Scotland in 1939 and also had represented the League of Ireland. A left-half, Browne guested extensively during the war, playing for Aldershot (1939–40 three appearances), Leeds (1939–40 six games), single games for Watford and Aldershot in 1941–42, seven games for Luton and three for

Tottenham in 1942–43, once for Swansea in 1944–45 and four games for Leeds in 1945–46. Browne had told the U's that he was a free agent, and Leeds would not renew his contract, but as the U's were about to make him their fifth post-war pro signing Leeds got wind of it and begged to differ. He added 19 more Football League appearances to his Elland Road tally in 1946–47, and his release sparked interest from Bolton and Huddersfield, but he eventually ended up at York in August 1947, making all his five appearances in the first five games. He later had a spell on the coaching staff at Halifax and was briefly in charge at The Shay as caretaker manager.

	League		Lge Cup		FA Cup		Other	
	A	G	A	G	A	G	A	G
1945–46	2	0	0	0	0	0	-	-
TOTAL	2	0	0	0	0	0	-	-

BRUCE, Marcelle Eugene

Height: 5ft 10in. Weight: 11st 7lb.

Born: 18 March 1971, Detroit, USA.

■ Bruce, the son of an American serviceman, had high hopes of being recognised for the USA squad preparing for the 1990 World Cup, but he had to settle for a short career with Colchester where he had signed full-time in the summer of 1989. Jock Wallace gave Bruce his debut against Cambridge in November of the same year and the youngster made the right-back slot his own for the remainder of the season as United were relegated to the Conference. His only goal came against Grimsby in February 1990, a 1–0 win that briefly lifted United off the bottom of the table. Released at the end of the campaign, Bruce joined Baldock Town and later played 291 times for Ryman and Southern League Hemel Hempstead, scoring 21 times.

	League		Lge Cup		FA Cup		Other	
	A	G	A	G	A	G	A	G
1989–90	28+1	1	0	0	2	0	0	0
1990–91	*2+2*	*0*	*2*	*0*	*0+1*	*0*	*0*	*0*
TOTAL	28+1	1	0	0	2	0	0	0
	2+2	*0*	*2*	*0*	*0+1*	*0*	*0*	*0*

BUCK, Alan Michael

Height: 6ft. Weight: 11st.

Born: 25 August 1946, Colchester.

■ Buck was signed by the U's in July 1963 but, with the youth team only playing cup ties and experienced pros Percy Ames and George Ramage to fill the first-team and reserve spots, he had little opportunity for match practice in his first season. That changed for 1964–65 as, until Sandy Kennon arrived on deadline day, he was number two to Ames and the Mercia Youth League had been established. If that was not enough the club had returned to the Border League, and between the A side and the Under-18s there were 64 games to cover, none of which clashed. He got his first-team chance in October 1964 as Ames, nearing the end of his career, was dropped after seven games without a win, but Buck could not take advantage in a struggling side, and after an 11 game run that finished with Southend putting six past him and Bideford three, Ames was back in the first team. Once Kennon arrived he took the number-one spot and the only start Buck got in the next 21 months was scrubbed out of the records when fog forced the game at Doncaster in October 1965 to be called off after 25 minutes. His longest run of games came at the start of 1966–67, but after conceding 12 in three games in the November he was dropped in favour of Kennon and only made three further appearances. On leaving United he played for Southern League Poole and took a job as a lorry driver.

	League		Lge Cup		FA Cup		Other	
	A	G	A	G	A	G	A	G
1964–65	10	0	0	0	1	0	-	-
1965–66	0	0	0	0	0	0	-	-
1966–67	25	0	1	0	0	0	-	-
1967–68	2	0	0	0	0	0	-	-
1968–69	1	0	0	0	0	0	-	-
TOTAL	38	0	1	0	1	0	-	-

BUCK, David Colin

Height: 5ft 8in. Weight: 10st 10lb.

Born: 25 August 1946, Colchester.

Died: 1996.

■ The twin brother of goalkeeper Alan, David Buck appeared as a substitute at Layer Road when he came on for Reg Stratton in the 2–0 win over Hartlepool on 16 October 1965. A knee injury shortly after put him out of action and that was his only outing in a first-team shirt. He continued to play for the reserves as a part-timer until joining

Halstead Town in 1968–69, where he took over as coach in 1972 until going to work in Zambia in 1974.

	League		Lge Cup		FA Cup		Other	
	A	G	A	G	A	G	A	G
1965–66	0+1	0	0	0	0	0	-	-
TOTAL	0+1	0	0	0	0	0	-	-

BUCKLE, Paul John

Height: 5ft 7in. Weight: 11st 3lb.

Born: 16 December 1970, Hatfield.

■ Schooled in Brentford's YTS scheme after being released by Watford, Buckle signed professional forms in the summer of 1989, having already broken in to the side in 1987–88 as a substitute. Making 42(+15) appearances at Griffin Park and scoring a solitary goal, Buckle moved to Torquay in February 1994 and helped them to the Play-off semi-finals. Torquay hit bad times and were destined for the Conference, only to be reprieved on ground-grading issues. Buckle completed 57(+2) games, netting nine times, at Plainmoor before moving across Devon to Exeter in October 1995. Scoring twice in 22 games, Buckle found himself in a football wilderness, having unsuccessful trials at Cambridge, Northampton and Wycombe before finding himself a contract at Colchester. Initially on a week-to-week basis, Buckle made his debut at Mansfield in December 1996. He scored three goals as United progressed to Wembley in the Auto Windscreens Shield including the extra-time 'golden goal' that knocked out Millwall at The New Den and the area semi-final aggregate equaliser against Peterborough. Desperately unlucky, Buckle missed the Final through suspension but appeared at Wembley a year later as Colchester beat his old club Torquay in the Play-offs. He was released by Mick Wadsworth at the end of the 1998–99 season, joining Exeter once again. The Grecians struggled around the lower reaches of the basement division, and after three seasons, 85(+6) appearances and five goals Buckle moved into non-League with first Aldershot, making 29 appearances, scoring five goals, and then Weymouth, netting nine times in 37 games. Exeter, by now, had also been relegated to the Conference, and Buckle returned for a third spell in December 2004, playing 9(+2) games before joining Tiverton for a dozen appearances. The lure of St James's Park was too great, and Buckle returned once again to the cathedral city where he became player-coach in 24(+4) games, scoring three times before being appointed assistant manager to Alex Inglethorpe and later Paul Tisdale. Exeter lost in the 2006–07 Conference Play-off Final at Wembley, at which point Buckle took up the manager's position at Torquay, who themselves had been relegated to the Conference for the 2007–08 season.

	League		Lge Cup		FA Cup		Other	
	A	G	A	G	A	G	A	G
1996–97	24	0	0	0	0	0	5	3
1997–98	33+5	5	2	0	1	0	4	0
1998–99	39+4	2	2	0	1	0	1	0
TOTAL	96+9	7	4	0	2	0	10	3

BUCKLEY

■ A young private in No.1 Holding Battalion, Buckley made one appearance against Bedford in September 1945.

	League		Lge Cup		FA Cup		Other	
	A	G	A	G	A	G	A	G
1945–46	1	0	0	0	0	0	-	-
TOTAL	1	0	0	0	0	0	-	-

BULLOCK, Peter Leonard

Height: 5ft 10in. Weight: 11st 10lb.

Born: 17 November 1941, Stoke-on-Trent.

■ Bullock had won three England Schoolboy caps by the age of 17, was picked for England Youth and played in the same Stoke side as Stanley Matthews. He scored 13 goals in 44 League games in The Potteries,

including being the youngest-ever Stoke player, at the age of 16 years 163 days, before a fee of £15,000 took him to Birmingham where he teamed up with his younger brother Mickey. After three seasons at St Andrews, former U's boss Ted Fenton signed him for Southend in a £5,000 deal in February 1965. Scoring two goals in 12 starts, he found himself one of Neil Franklin's new signings, moving up from the south of the county for a small fee as Colchester won promotion at the first attempt. He scored a hat-trick in the 6–3 win over Bradford Park Avenue in February 1966. With a creditable strike-rate of better than one goal in three games, Bullock suffered injuries during the 1967–68 season and headed west, on a free transfer, to Exeter in the summer. He failed to settle in the area and after just 14 games returned to the Midlands with Walsall, where he played out his last seven League games, and then Stafford Rangers. Bullock spent much of his employment with Michelin and also ran a bookmakers with his brother.

	League		Lge Cup		FA Cup		Other	
	A	G	A	G	A	G	A	G
1965–66	34	11	0	0	2	0	-	-
1966–67	40+1	15	1	0	1	0	-	-
1967–68	20	7	1	0	1+1	0	-	-
TOTAL	94+1	33	2	0	4+1	0	-	-

BUNKELL, Raymond Keith 'Ray'

Height: 5ft 9in. Weight: 11st 3lb.

Born: 18 September 1947, Edmonton.

Died: 15 March 2002.

■ Arriving at Layer Road in the player-plus-£25,000 deal that saw John McLaughlin joining Swindon, Bunkell was unfortunate to break his leg in only his fifth game for Colchester at Crewe on New Year's Day 1974. His earlier career had begun at Tottenham in 1967, and despite winning three England Youth caps he failed to make the grade at White Hart Lane. Transferred to Swindon in the summer of 1971, he made 52(+4) League appearances at the County Ground, scoring three goals. He recovered from his injury and established himself a U's regular, and penalty taker, in 1975–76, which saw United relegated to Division Four. Plagued by injury, Bunkell took charge of United's reserves and filled in for the first team before being forced to retire in 1979. When Bobby Roberts departed in May 1982 Bunkell spent 24 hours as caretaker manager before Allan Hunter arrived, and within a few days he had followed Roberts out of the door to make way for Hunter's chosen coach, Cyril Lea.

	League		Lge Cup		FA Cup		Other	
	A	G	A	G	A	G	A	G
1973–74	5+1	0	0	0	0	0	-	-
1974–75	23+6	1	3	0	1+1	0	-	-
1975–76	40+1	4	2	0	2	0	-	-
1976–77	16+2	2	3	1	3	0	-	-
1977–78	22	1	3	0	1	0	-	-
1978–79	10+2	1	1	0	2	0	-	-
1979–80	1	0	0	0	0	0	-	-
TOTAL	117+12	9	12	1	9+1	0	-	-

BURDITT, Frederick Charles Kendal 'Ken'

Height: 5ft 11in. Weight: 12st.

Born: 12 November 1906, Ibstock.
Died: 27 October 1977, Ibstock.

■ Inside-right Burditt joined Norwich on 1 November 1930 from Gresley Rovers. A double hat-trick for City's reserves culminated in a first-team call-up from which the player never looked back. In five seasons at Carrow Road Burditt scored 61 goals in 173 League and Cup matches. His powerful shot earned him the honour of being the Canaries' top scorer in both 1932–33 and 1934–35. In August 1936 Burditt moved to Millwall where he enjoyed an FA Cup semi-final appearance and 23 goals in 53 games. It was while on the books of Notts County, whom he signed for in January 1938, that Burditt arrived at the reigning Southern League Champions Colchester, signing on 25 May 1939. Twenty League games for Notts had not yielded any goals and so Burditt was available for transfer for £1,000. Unfortunately the war cut short his Colchester career after just three games. In wartime Burditt guested for Leicester on four occasions and once for Norwich. When hostilities ceased Burditt turned out for Ibstock Colliery until 1959. His brother George was also on Norwich's books as an amateur.

	League		Lge Cup		FA Cup		Other	
	A	G	A	G	A	G	A	G
1939–40	2	0	1	0	-	-	-	-
TOTAL	2	0	1	0	-	-	-	-

BURGESS, Eric Robert Charles

Height: 5ft 11½in. Weight: 13st.

Born: 27 October 1944, Edgware.

■ Burgess is recorded as Watford's first-ever apprentice to sign professional in the summer of 1962. Having represented Middlesex Schools at cricket, the full-

back made just three appearances for the Hornets before being transferred to Torquay in July 1965. At Plainmoor he notched up 73(+1) games, won promotion and a subsequent move down the A38 to Plymouth. Playing 14(+1) times for Argyle, he was signed by Dick Graham in December 1970, initially on a two-month trial, after a short spell out of football to help with the family business. Colchester were about to embark on their famous FA Cup run, and so Burgess found it difficult to break into the side until the following campaign when he also picked up a Watney Cup-winners' medal. On leaving Layer Road he played for Weymouth in the 1973–74 Southern League and became player-manager of Bracknell Town.

	League		Lge Cup		FA Cup		Other	
	A	G	A	G	A	G	A	G
1970–71	8+2	1	0	0	0	0	-	-
1971–72	41	8	3	0	0	0	3	0
TOTAL	49+2	9	3	0	0	0	3	0

BURLEY, George Elder

Height: 5ft 10in. Weight: 11st.

Born: 3 June 1956, Cumnock.

■ Burley enjoyed a magnificent playing career in which he represented Scotland at all levels: Schoolboy, Youth, five caps at Under-21, two caps at Under-23 and 11 full caps, which included the 1982 World Cup. He joined Ipswich as an apprentice in 1972 and made his senior debut at Old Trafford a year later, having the unenviable task of marking George Best.

He played a prominent part as Ipswich beat Arsenal to win the 1977–78 FA Cup Final at Wembley and a year later as Town finished runners-up in the old First Division. He missed the UEFA Cup win over AZ Alkmaar through injury but played nine seasons in Europe. He left Ipswich for Sunderland in September 1985 after amassing 394 League appearances, scoring six goals at Portman Road. The second-tier club had designs on promotion, but unfortunately at the end of Burley's second season at Roker Park and 54 appearances later the club were relegated to the Third Division. Burley moved to Gillingham, also in the Third Division, and was ever present as the Gills were relegated to the basement. Disillusioned, Burley returned to Scotland and joined Motherwell in 1990, playing 54 games. He was appointed player-manager of Ayr United in January 1991, appearing 66(+1) times, had a single match at Falkirk in January 1994 then returned to Motherwell in the February from where he was persuaded to revisit East Anglia to take over at Colchester in the close season of 1994. While building the side up he played for United himself but once he had overcome initial hurdles stepped back and let his squad play. Despite being told that they could not talk to him, the manager-less Ipswich board approached Burley to take over the reigns of his old club. He could not refuse, although United later won a court case regarding the illegal approach, which was rumoured to have cost Ipswich £150,000 in compensation and the same again in settling both sides' legal costs. Burley left a stunned United on Christmas Eve 1994, and many fans did not know he had resigned as they took their places for the Boxing Day fixture against Northampton. Burley then moulded an Ipswich team that reached the Play-offs on four consecutive occasions before finally claiming a Premiership spot with a 4–2 win over Barnsley at Wembley in 2000. Ipswich finished fifth in his first season earning a UEFA Cup spot. His second Premiership season resulted in relegation and a humiliating 9–0 defeat at Manchester United. As the slide continued Burley was sacked from his position in October 2002. He was not out of the game long and took over as manager of Derby in March 2003 but walked out on the Rams to manage Hearts in June of 2005 after taking County to the Play-off semi-finals. Despite guiding Hearts to the top of the Scottish Premier League, he again walked out on the Edinburgh side following interference from its Lithuanian owners. In December 2005 he arrived at St Mary's to take on the post at Southampton. He steered the Saints to the 2006–07 Championship Play-off semi-final, and was appointed manager of the Scottish national side in January 2008.

* *See also Who's Who Managers section*

	League		Lge Cup		FA Cup		Other	
	A	G	A	G	A	G	A	G
1994–95	5+2	0	0+1	0	0	0	0+1	0
TOTAL	5+2	0	0+1	0	0	0	0+1	0

BURMAN, Simon John

Height: 5ft 10in. Weight: 11st.

Born: 26 November 1965, Ipswich.

■ Taken on after being released from Ipswich's youth scheme, Burman was given his debut by Cyril Lea at Tranmere in April 1983 and had a run of games when Tony English was converted to left-back for the injured Ian Phillips. Progressing through the reserves, he scored his first goal at Exeter a year later, securing U's a 2–2 draw. His final run of games came as a stand-in for the injured Tony Adcock in 1986–87. The following campaign he joined Weymouth and in two seasons made 84(+10) appearances for the Terras, scoring three times, before moving along the coast to Poole Town. He later came back to Suffolk and played for Bury Town and Brantham Athletic with a short spell at Wivenhoe in between. His younger brother Jason was also on Colchester's books at the same time but did not get beyond the reserves.

	League		Lge Cup		FA Cup		Other	
	A	G	A	G	A	G	A	G
1984–85	8+1	0	0	0	0	0	0	0
1985–86	10+1	1	0	0	0	0	0	0
1986–87	10+2	2	1+1	0	0	0	0	0
TOTAL	28+4	3	1+1	0	0	0	0	0

BURNSIDE, David Gort

Height: 5ft 9in. Weight: 11st 6lb.

Born: 10 December 1937, Bristol.

■ A Bristol lad, Burnside was ignored by both of his home town clubs to join West Brom and had already impressed the crowd at The Hawthorns with his half-time ball juggling skills. He earned £25 a time for his expertise and was reputed to be earning more than Albion's star

international Bobby Robson. Burnside won a *Daily Sketch* competition in 'keepy-uppy' with 495 touches compared to the second-placed entrant who managed 286. Signing for West Brom in February 1957, Burnside amassed 127 League games, scoring 39 goals and won England Youth and two Under-23 caps against Denmark and Turkey in 1961 and 1962 respectively. After refusing to re-sign for the Baggies, it was Southampton who captured the player in September 1962 for £17,000, and he scored twice on his debut against Portsmouth. Before signing for Crystal Palace for a then record £14,000 in December 1964 he completed 61 League games for the Saints, scoring 22 times. At Palace he played out 54(+4) League starts netting eight goals. A £2,500 fee took him next to Molineux in September 1966 where he was part of Wolves' Second Division promotion-winning side of 1966–67. Ironically, he scored against his former employers Palace just 24 hours after completing the deal and was listed in the match programme as a Palace player, so late was the deal. Returning West, Burnside was captured by Plymouth for £7,000 in March 1968, playing 105 times for Argyle and weighing in with 15 League goals. Fed up with commuting from his Bristol home, he joined Bristol City in December 1971, but the move did not work out, and it was at Layer Road under Dick Graham that he ended up in March 1972. His stay lasted until the end of the campaign when he announced his retirement, becoming player-manager of Bath. He also counted touchline positions at Walsall, Bridgwater Town, Taunton Town and Cheltenham. A qualified FA coach, he led the England Youth team and was on the England staff until 1999 when he became Academy Director at Bristol City.

	League		Lge Cup		FA Cup		Other	
	A	G	A	G	A	G	A	G
1971–72	13	0	0	0	0	0	0	0
TOTAL	13	0	0	0	0	0	0	0

BURTON-GODWIN, Osagyefo Lenin Ernesto 'Sagi'

Height: 6ft 2in. Weight: 13st 6lb.

Born: 25 November 1977, Birmingham.

■ A youth trainee on the books of Crystal Palace, Burton made his debut in the Premiership in 1997–98 as Palace were relegated. He staked a claim the following campaign, taking his Palace playing record to one goal scored in 19(+6) appearances. Mick Wadsworth brought him to Layer Road in the summer of 1999 to replace Stephane Pounewatchy, but as quickly as Wadsworth left Layer Road, so too did Burton, as he joined Sheffield United on trial in November 1999 after just nine outings for Colchester including a red card at Bournemouth in only his third League start. Spurned by the Blades, he spent three seasons with Port Vale, notching up 76(+10) appearances and

scoring two goals. He joined neighbours Crewe in early August 2002, but after 21 days and one League game he moved to Peterborough. At London Road he stayed for three and a half seasons, turning out 88(+8) times and scoring eight League goals. During this time he won three caps for St Kitts & Nevis in World Cup 2006 qualifiers. In January 2006 Burton signed for Shrewsbury and completed 41(+3) games, scoring five times. He was released in the summer of 2007 to join Barnet.

	League		Lge Cup		FA Cup		Other	
	A	G	A	G	A	G	A	G
1999–2000	9	0	2	0	0	0	0	0
TOTAL	9	0	2	0	0	0	0	0

C

CADE, Jamie William

Height: 5ft 8in. Weight: 10st 10lb.

Born: 15 January 1984, Durham.

■ Cade represented England Youth while on the books of Middlesbrough and signed professionally for Boro in January 2001. Playing just one League Cup tie as a substitute, he went out on loan to Chesterfield in September 2003, scoring twice in 9(+2) games. Phil Parkinson beat off Chesterfield's attempt to sign Cade following the completion of his loan and signed him on a free transfer. Cade never managed to play in his favoured striking role, being mainly used as a wide player. He was released at the end of the 2004–05 season and joined Conference side Crawley in August 2005, scoring three goals in 15(+4) appearances. A season later he moved to Lewes where he scored 18 goals in 62 appearances up until the start of the 2007–08 season.

	League		Lge Cup		FA Cup		Other	
	A	G	A	G	A	G	A	G
2003–04	6+10	0	0	0	0	0	0	0
2004–05	4+5	0	1	0	0+3	0	0+1	0
TOTAL	10+15	0	1	0	0+3	0	0+1	0

CAESAR, Gus Cassius

Height: 6ft. Weight: 12st 9lb.

Born: 5 March 1966, Tottenham.

■ Caesar joined Arsenal as an apprentice in August 1982, signing professionally two years later. He broke his ankle three times in 30 months but made his debut in a 1–0 win at Manchester United in December 1985. He earned three England Under-21 caps, the first of which was in June 1987, and then embarked on his best run of 22 games deputising for the injured David O'Leary. One crucial error in the 1988 League Cup Final turned Gunners fans against him forever. He slipped and presented Luton with an equaliser, and the Hatters went on to win the trophy. He played just twice more after that error and had a spell on loan at QPR in November 1990, playing five times. Despite this, his Arsenal career of 27(+17) appearances brought that League Cup Finalist medal and a Charity Shield appearance in 1989. He went on trial at Cambridge in July 1991 but signed for Bristol City in the September. After just 9(+1) games he ventured over the border and played for Airdrieonians 57 times, reaching the Scottish Cup Final in 1993–94. George Burley's knowledge of the Scottish game led to Caesar becoming a Colchester player in August 1984. He made his debut in the 3–1 home reverse to Torquay on the opening day of the 1994–95 season and scored his first-ever English League goal in a 5–2 win over Fulham in April 1995. His second season at Layer Road was spent vying with long-term loanee David Greene for the centre-half shirt. Caesar was released at the end of 1995–96 after United's exit to Plymouth in the Play-offs. He played briefly for Dagenham & Redbridge and returned to Scotland with Partick Thistle before emigrating to Hong Kong. He played with Eastern, Sing Tao, Golden and Hong Kong Rangers and was picked to represent Hong Kong following his performances there. His greatest claim to fame is that Arsenal fan Nick Hornby chose to devote a whole chapter in his book, *Fever Pitch*, to Caesar's apparent inability to be a top flight player. As a result Caesar attained cult status as Arsenal's worst-ever player. Caesar remained in Hong Kong, working in the financial sector.

	League		Lge Cup		FA Cup		Other	
	A	G	A	G	A	G	A	G
1994–95	39	1	2	0	4	0	2	0
1995–96	23	2	2	0	1	0	3	0
TOTAL	62	3	4	0	5	0	5	0

CALDWELL, Garrett Evan James

Height: 6ft 1in. Weight: 12st 12lb.

Born: 6 November 1973, Princeton, New Jersey, USA.

■ Although born in the US, Caldwell represented Canada in the Pan-Am Games of 1994, playing alongside future English League star Jason De Vos. He made his debut in an Auto Windscreens Shield tie at Swindon in November 1995. He began the 1996–97 season as first choice but was injured during a League Cup tie at West Brom, a game in which Steve Whitton had to take over in goal for the entire second-half. Caldwell lost his place to Carl Emberson, but when Emberson broke his thumb at the tail end of the season Caldwell was not

available to retake his place as he was away on international duty with Canada. In the summer of 1997 he opted to return to Canada to continue his studies. He joined up with Toronto Supra, playing in the Canadian Professional Soccer League.

	League		Lge Cup		FA Cup		Other	
	A	G	A	G	A	G	A	G
1995–96	0	0	0	0	0	0	1	0
1996–97	6	0	2	0	0	0	0	0
TOTAL	6	0	2	0	0	0	1	0

CAMERON, Daniel 'Danny'

Height: 5ft 7½in. Weight: 11st 7lb.

Born: 9 November 1953, Dundee.

■ Cameron arrived at Colchester in February 1975 as U's boss Jim Smith attempted to overcome a sudden injury crisis. Having lost regular defender Alex Smith, the Sheffield Wednesday full-back arrived at the same time as Ian MacDonald from Liverpool and both played five games during their loan spells. Colchester could not afford Wednesday's asking price, reported to be £10,000, and the player returned to Hillsborough, whom he had joined as an apprentice, to complete 31 appearances, netting a solitary goal. On transfer deadline day 1974 he joined Preston and went on to play 120(+2) times for North End. Moving back across the border, Cameron turned out for his home-town club Dundee 25(+3) times in 1981–82 before carrying out some coaching in South Africa.

	League		Lge Cup		FA Cup		Other	
	A	G	A	G	A	G	A	G
1974–75	5	0	0	0	0	0	-	-
TOTAL	5	0	0	0	0	0	-	-

CAMERON, John S. 'Jock'

Born: Clydebank.

■ A veteran Scottish winger who made just one appearance for Colchester, against Bedford in September 1945, whil serving with the Army Fire Fighting Centre. He is reported to have been on the books of St Johnstone. Dundee and Arsenal, which identifies him as the Cameron who made his Scottish League debut in 1926–27, when his club Motherwell finished runners-up to Rangers in the Scottish Championship, and scored 27 goals in 37 games for St Johnstone in 1930–31. He also had a spell with Dundee before coming South of the border to join Arsenal but never played a first-team game in England.

	League		Lge Cup		FA Cup		Other	
	A	G	A	G	A	G	A	G
1945–46	1	0	0	0	0	0	-	-
TOTAL	1	0	0	0	0	0	-	-

CAMPBELL, Sean Martin

Height: 5ft 11in. Weight: 11st.

Born: 3 December 1974, Bristol.

■ Campbell was a very quick left-footed player who was taken on as an apprentice in 1991 and handed a one year pro contract in summer 1993. Roy McDonough gave him his debut as a substitute at Crewe in the second game of the 1993–94 season and his first full start in an understrength Autoglass Trophy side in the January. He was subbed that night as he was on his only full League start against Chesterfield the following month and released in the summer. He has since played for many of the local non-League clubs including Clacton, Chelmsford, Harwich & Parkeston and Wivenhoe in short spells and more than once for each club. Chelmsford was his first stop after Layer Road and Barry Fry later briefly took him on trial at Peterborough, although he did not play their first team.

	League		Lge Cup		FA Cup		Other	
	A	G	A	G	A	G	A	G
1993–94	1+3	0	0	0	0	0	1	0
TOTAL	1+3	0	0	0	0	0	1	0

CAMPBELL-RYCE, Jamal Julian

Height: 5ft 7in. Weight: 11st 10lb.

Born: 6 April 1983, Lambeth.

■ A schoolboy with Charlton, Campbell-Ryce signed professionally in July 2002 but was restricted to three substitute appearances in the Premiership. In between those games he had a loan spell with Leyton Orient in August 2002, scoring twice in 16(+1) matches. He played 3(+1) First Division games for Wimbledon in February 2004 and had a three-month stint at Chesterfield the following August where he started 14 fixtures. He was chosen for Jamaica in 2003 and went on to earn six caps, including an appearance against England at Old Trafford. At the end of the Chesterfield loan he signed permanently for Rotherham, making 23(+1) appearances for the Millers who remained rock bottom of the Championship all season. Just 4(+3) games into the 2005–06 season he joined Southend on loan, appearing 7(+6) times as the Shrimpers vied with

Colchester for promotion to the Championship. When Southend tried to make the deal permanent Rotherham insisted that a fee of £100,000 had already been agreed so, while the two clubs argued, Colchester manager Phil Parkinson took the player on loan himself. Campbell-Ryce made his debut, coming off the bench at Nottingham Forest, in April 2006, and his only start was in the final game of the season when United secured promotion at Yeovil. It was a double-whammy for Campbell-Ryce as Southend clinched the title on the same day, thus he had two celebrations to attend. In between, and while on United's books, he played for Jamaica against USA on 11 April 2006 in North Carolina. During the close season of 2006 he signed permanently for Southend on a free transfer, scoring twice in 38(+5) games but failing to prevent relegation back to League One. Two games into the 2007–08 campaign Campbell-Ryce returned to the Championship when signing for Barnsley for an undisclosed fee after Southend had earlier rejected a bid of £250,000.

	League		Lge Cup		FA Cup		Other	
	A	G	A	G	A	G	A	G
2005–06	1+3	0	0	0	0	0	0	0
TOTAL	1+3	0	0	0	0	0	0	0

CANHAM, Marc David

Height: 5ft 10in. Weight: 12st 3lb.

Born: 11 September 1982, Wegburg, Germany.

■ Son of a serviceman, Canham caught the eye of the U's youth team hierarchy in Northern Ireland, playing on an adjacent pitch to the boy whose game they had gone to watch. Very conveniently his father was posted back to the UK during his final school year, and he was taken on in 1999 as one of the first batch under the newly introduced three-year scholarship scheme. A midfield playmaker who could do the defensive side of the job as well, he progressed through the youth and reserve teams, captaining both, and made his Colchester League bow as a substitute in a 1–0 home defeat to Cardiff in April 2002. Offered a one year professional contract, he made his first full start at Plymouth a year later but was released at

the end of the term by Phil Parkinson, probably being considered to be half a yard short of the pace needed to bridge the gap to first-team football. He joined Team Bath, the student team representing the University of Bath, and also trialled at Bournemouth after a good first season in the West Country. He played in the World Student Games in 2005 and then continued his career with Team Bath as they won promotion to the Southern Premier League, being named Player of the Year in 2005–06. Canham also represented England at the World Futsal Championship, scoring seven goals in 13 appearances. Team Bath finished runners-up in 2006–07 but lost the Southern League Play-off Final to Maidenhead. Canham remained in the team for the 2007–08 season.

	League		Lge Cup		FA Cup		Other	
	A	G	A	G	A	G	A	G
2001–02	0+1	0	0	0	0	0	0	0
2002–03	2+1	0	0	0	0	0	0	0
TOTAL	2+2	0	0	0	0	0	0	0

CANHAM, Ronald

■ A Colcestrian who had gone to East Ward school and played most of his wartime football in West Africa, Pilot Officer Canham was in the RAF and stationed in Yorkshire when he impressed in the first post-war pre-season trial, scoring a couple of goals. He was one of seven amateurs signed in the first six weeks of 1945–46 but did not play for the club until he was home on Christmas leave when he scored twice in a friendly on Christmas Day and made his only Southern League start at Cheltenham four days later. He signed amateur forms again in February 1947 when home on demob leave but only appears to have played one or two reserve games after his return.

	League		Lge Cup		FA Cup		Other	
	A	G	A	G	A	G	A	G
1945–46	1	0	0	0	0	0	-	-
TOTAL	1	0	0	0	0	0	-	-

CANT, Dennis C.

Born: 1925, Fordham Heath.

■ A 20-year-old Post Office worker who served with the Royal Navy during the war, Cant was signed as an amateur in August 1946 from Crittall Athletic and quickly promoted to the first-team centre-forward spot after scoring twice in half a game in one of the trials and twice in the opening reserve game. He made his debut at Chelmsford on 4 September and scored at Exeter three days later but was displaced after three games when Ted Fenton pulled off his Arthur Turner coup. Cant only got two more first-team starts and could not do much more to advance his cause than the brace he netted each time, including a pair against Norwich Gothic in the fourth qualifying round of the FA Cup as the U's ran out 5–1 winners. He was the reserves' leading scorer with 22 in less than 30 games and briefly rejoined United in 1947–48 before switching to Clacton in October 1947 and on to Harwich in 1948, scoring regularly for both. He played his last game for Harwich before joining the communications department of the police force on 22 December 1951 and was made captain for the day. Cambridge United spoiled his party though, winning 3–1.

	League		Lge Cup		FA Cup		Other	
	A	G	A	G	A	G	A	G
1946–47	5	3	0	0	1	2	-	-
TOTAL	5	3	0	0	1	2	-	-

CAREY, Peter Richard

Height: 6ft. Weight: 12st.

Born: 14 April 1933, Barking.

■ An Essex Schools player, Carey joined Leyton Orient as an amateur in October 1956. He made 34 League appearances at Brisbane Road before joining QPR in May 1960. After just 15 games for Rangers he arrived at Layer Road for a small fee in the November of the same year, making 10 League appearances. Carey, a defender, left Colchester in the summer to join Aldershot where after 47

appearances he moved into non-League, playing for Dover, Ashford, Brentwood and Gravesend. He later managed Walthamstow Avenue.

	League		Lge Cup		FA Cup		Other	
	A	G	A	G	A	G	A	G
1960–61	10	0	0	0	0	0	-	-
TOTAL	10	0	0	0	0	0	-	-

CARTWRIGHT, Stephen Raymond 'Steve'

Height: 6ft 1in. Weight: 13st.

Born: 5 January 1965, Tamworth.

■ Roger Brown returned to his old club Tamworth to sign Cartwright in the summer of 1988 and, despite being ever present at left-back in the first 12 League and Cup games of the season, the left-back was out of his depth and returned to Tamworth in the October following Colchester's appalling 8–0 humiliation at Leyton Orient. Brown also left Layer Road after that defeat. Cartwright then played for Tamworth against Sudbury later that season in FA Vase Final at Wembley which the Midlanders won in a replay at Peterborough. He also later played for Atherstone.

	League		Lge Cup		FA Cup		Other	
	A	G	A	G	A	G	A	G
1988–89	10	0	2	0	0	0	0	0
TOTAL	10	0	2	0	0	0	0	0

CATER, Leonard Arthur 'Len'

Height: 5ft 8in. Weight: 11st.

Born: 8 September 1920, Colchester.
Died: 6 October 2002, Colchester.

■ Cater first played at Layer Road for Colchester Town as a 17-year-old in 1937 and on 13 November 1937 had the rare experience of forming the left-hand side of the Town attack with his 47-year-old father, Arthur Cater, who valiantly agreed to help out as Town struggled to find players in their dying days. Neither completed the game, though, as a torn leg muscle forced Len off during the first half and a similar injury removed his dad in the second period. Town had been forced to find five last-minute substitutes and unsurprisingly lost 9–2. A fortnight later the Town committee, who had completely underestimated the attraction of professional football, threw in the towel and on Christmas Day 1937 Colchester United reserves were born. Len Cater played at inside-left, scoring one of the goals in a 3–1 win over Ipswich Town reserves. He only played once more that year, again finding the net at Bury Town, and did not appear for the U's again until joining permanently after the war. As an amateur he was eligible to represent the Essex FA, and did so on three occasions, and was on the verge of being selected for the England amateur international side. During the war he played his football with Clacton, Rowhedge and Charlton Athletic and represented Northern Command in Army matches in Belgium, Germany and Holland. Following his demob in the summer of 1946 his services were much in demand, with Charlton, Wolves and West Ham all interested. He had also built a reputation as a welterweight boxer during his National Service and lost just four of his 60 bouts. Ted Fenton, United's new manager, persuaded him to sign for United in August 1946, and he would have been an ever-present if he had not missed the train to Merthyr on 19 April 1947. He did not sit idle though and instead went along to Layer Road to play for the reserves. An indication of his keenness to play football came a couple of weeks later when he played in the return game against Merthyr at 3.30pm and, along with Digger Kettle, had a second game for the reserves in their 6.30pm kick off at Chelmsford reserves. As well as providing the ammunition for the prolific 43-goal partnership of Arthur Turner and Bob Curry, he weighed in with a creditable 14 goals himself. The energetic left-winger, at the time still an amateur, was prominent as Fenton's team rocked the football world with their stunning run to the FA Cup fifth round in 1947–48, defeating First Division Huddersfield on the way. Again he helped provide Turner and Curry with many of their 59 goals and scored 12 himself. Ipswich manager A. Scott Duncan sought his services, but Fenton rebuffed him, and Cater finally turned professional in 1948–49 before a knee injury curtailed his career just as United were in the eve of joining the Football League. After leaving Layer Road, Cater spent five years at Clacton and a couple more at Sudbury, also playing for Tunbridge Wells before calling it a day. He retired from his job as a gas fitter in January 1984.

	League		Lge Cup		FA Cup		Other	
	A	G	A	G	A	G	A	G
1946–47	30	9	7	3	2	1	-	-
1947–48	26	6	5	7	6	0	-	-
1948–49	31	5	4	1	1	2	-	-
1949–50	4	0	0	0	0	0	-	-
TOTAL	91	20	16	11	9	3	-	-

CAWLEY, Peter

Height: 6ft 4in. Weight: 13st.

Born: 15 September 1965, Walton-on-Thames.

■ A late starter in the professional game, Cawley was spotted playing for Chertsey Town by Wimbledon in 1986 and signed professionally in January the following year. The top flight club loaned him out the following month to Bristol Rovers in order to gain experience. With Rovers he made 9(+1) starts but did not break into the Wimbledon first team until 1988 when he made his sole appearance. A further loan move to Fulham in December 1988 realised 3(+3) appearances. Unable to break into The Crazy Gang side, Cawley joined Bristol Rovers the following summer but made just 1(+2) appearances. A further year on and he arrived at Southend to make 6(+1) starts before joining Exeter after just four months at Roots Hall. Amassing just seven games for City, he was released and played three games on a non-contract basis for Barnet in November 1991. His career finally started in earnest with his move to Layer Road in October 1992. Missing just four games in the 1995–96, he was a major part of United's journey to the Third Division Play-off semi-finals that ended in defeat to Plymouth and a year later enjoyed a day out at Wembley as Colchester lost on penalties to Carlisle in the Auto Windscreens Shield Final. In an earlier round of the competition against Northampton Cawley had to keep goal for 68 minutes following the dismissal of John Vaughan. During his U's career he formed partnerships with Tony English, Gus Caesar and David Greene. On leaving Layer Road he played for Braintree and Watton United before becoming reserve-team manager and then, assistant manager to Tony Adams, at Wycombe. He was sacked after an FA Cup win over Coalville in November 2004. He had been in temporary charge for that game as Adams had left just prior to the tie.

	League		Lge Cup		FA Cup		Other	
	A	G	A	G	A	G	A	G
1992–93	22+2	3	0	0	2	0	0	0
1993–94	36	1	0	0	1	0	4	0
1994–95	23	2	0	0	4	0	2	0
1995–96	42	1	2	0	1	0	5	1
1996–97	28	1	4	0	1	0	3+1	0
1997–98	27	0	2	0	3	0	1	0
TOTAL	178+2	8	8	0	12	0	15+1	1

CHAMBERLAIN, Alec Francis Roy

Height: 6ft 2in. Weight: 11st

Born: 20 June 1964, March.

■ Chamberlain's career started at Ipswich where he served his apprenticeship, having been spotted playing for Ramsey Town. Signing professional terms in the summer of 1981, he failed to make a start at Portman Road and a year later moved to Colchester as understudy to Mike Walker. Walker had been a difficult player to displace from the United line up but after he suffered a groin strain over Christmas 1982 Chamberlain was given his first start in a 4–1 victory over Hartlepool at Layer Road. At the end of the season Walker took the post of reserves player-coach, and the two 'keepers swapped teams. Chamberlain grabbed the opportunity with both hands and became an immaculate ever-present for four seasons. United huffed and puffed but could not win promotion despite regular top eight finishes. Chamberlain enjoyed a League Cup tie against Manchester United and his last game was as a losing Play-off semi-finalist to Wolves. In the summer of 1987 he made a richly-deserved transfer to Everton for a fee of £80,000. He was unable to displace Neville Southall and was loaned out to neighbours Tranmere in the November, playing 15 League games. Looking for regular football, he moved to Luton the following summer and got his top-flight career up and running. Playing 138 times for the Hatters, he could not help stop relegation in the third of his four seasons at Kenilworth Road and spent a non-playing period on loan at Chelsea in 1992–93. Moving to Sunderland in July 1993, he made 89(+1) appearances for the Wearsiders and had another high profile but brief non-playing loan – this time at Liverpool as the Reds won the League Cup – while winning promotion, with the North East club in 1995–96. Despite promotion, he joined Watford for £40,000 and became first choice when Kevin Miller was sold to Crystal Palace in 1997. He won the Division Two Championship in 1997–98 and helped Watford to the Premiership in 1999 with a penalty shoot-out save in the Play-off semi-final against Birmingham and a clean sheet in the 2–0 Wembley win over Bolton. After Watford's relegation from the Premiership, Chamberlain lost his place to Espen Baardsen but had the character to fight back and become first choice once again. In the autumn of 2004 Chamberlain was made Watford's goalkeeping coach, and when Watford reached the Premiership again in

2006–07 he was retained as a player. At 42 he would have become the oldest player to ever have played in the Premiership. Having played over 700 games in total, Chamberlain received a Testimonial in 2005 when Watford took on Charlton.

	League		Lge Cup		FA Cup		Other	
	A	G	A	G	A	G	A	G
1982–83	4	0	0	0	0	0	0	0
1983–84	46	0	5	0	3	0	2	0
1984–85	46	0	2	0	3	0	3	0
1985–86	46	0	2	0	1	0	2	0
1986–87	46	0	2	0	3	0	5	0
TOTAL	188	0	11	0	10	0	12	0

CHAMBERS, Triston Gregory

Height: 5ft 8in. Weight: 11st 8lb.

Born: 25 December 1982, Enfield.

■ Released at 16 by Tottenham, Chambers was spotted up by the U's youth staff at the Academy exit trials day and taken on a scholar in 1999. He was part of the successful Under-19 side that won the South-East Youth Alliance and got to the final of the Youth Alliance Cup in 2001–02, scoring better than a goal every other game. His only senior appearance came as a half-time substitute in a 1–0 home defeat to Cardiff in April 2002. Given a three month contract for the new season, he failed to make any in-roads to the first team and intermittently played non-League with Harlow, Dagenham & Redbridge, Heybridge, Tilbury and Wivenhoe.

	League		Lge Cup		FA Cup		Other	
	A	G	A	G	A	G	A	G
2001–02	0+1	0	0	0	0	0	0	0
TOTAL	0+1	0	0	0	0	0	0	0

CHATTERTON, Nicholas John 'Nicky'

Height: 5ft 9in. Weight: 11st 4lb.

Born: 18 May 1954, Norwood.

■ A Crystal Palace junior, Chatterton signed professionally at Selhurst Park in March 1972. His father Len had once been Palace's groundsman. Chatterton made his debut on the opening day of the 1973–74 season and went on to complete 142(+9) appearances, scoring 31 goals. He was part of the record-breaking Third Division side that reached the FA Cup semi-final in 1975–76 and won promotion the following season. Palace also won promotion in 1978–79, but Chatterton had already left for Millwall in November for a fee of £100,000 where he played 258(+6) times, scoring 56 League goals and winning promotion to Division Two in 1984–85. Millwall's captain between 1979–83, Mike Walker brought Chatterton, along with Paul Hinshelwood, to Layer Road in September 1986 and the player helped steer United to the Fourth Division Play-off semi-final despite an injury-plagued start when he dislocated his shoulder after just six games. Unfortunately Chatterton then broke his leg while playing for the reserves in January 1988, which effectively ended his playing career. He remained on the U's administration staff for a while and in his career total of 96 League goals 32 of them were from penalties. In 2006 he was running a glazing business in Eastbourne.

	League		Lge Cup		FA Cup		Other	
	A	G	A	G	A	G	A	G
1986–87	20+1	1	0	0	0	0	1	0
1987–88	26	7	2	0	3	2	2	0
1988–89	1+1	0	0	0	0	0	1+1	0
TOTAL	47+2	8	2	0	3	2	4+1	0

CHEESEWRIGHT, John Anthony

Height: 6ft. Weight: 11st 5lb.

Born: 12 January 1973, Romford.

■ Trained at Tottenham as a YTS player, Cheesewright joined Southend on non-contract forms in March 1991 as cover for their promotion run-in. He was not retained and played briefly for Kingsbury Town before signing for Birmingham, also on non-contract forms, in November of the same year. He played one game at St Andrews but did not make the grade and drifted out of professional football with Cobh Ramblers of Ireland, Redbridge Forest and Braintree. Following the departure of Colchester's previous loan 'keeper Jon Sheffield, U's boss Roy McDonough moved quickly to snap up Cheesewright on an 18-month contract from Braintree for £10,000, and he made his debut in an Autoglass Trophy tie against Wycombe in January 1994. He played out the remainder of the season and was first choice the following campaign under new manager George

Burley despite the fact that Carl Emberson had been signed by the board in the summer. When Burley left, his successor Steve Wignall promoted Emberson when Cheesewright began to suffer balance problems due to an ear infection. He was seconded to Wimbledon in the summer of 1995 to assist with their Intertoto Cup qualifying campaign, playing three games in Europe for the Dons. After a spell in Hong Kong, Cheesewright returned to the UK to join Wycombe in March 1996 where he featured in 18 League games. He then embarked on a nomadic non-League career, playing for Wivenhoe, Aldershot, Heybridge, St Albans, Leyton Pennant, both Aldershot and Heybridge again, Eton Manor, Romford and Braintree.

	League		Lge Cup		FA Cup		Other	
	A	G	A	G	A	G	A	G
1993–94	17	0	0	0	0	0	1	0
1994–95	23	0	1	0	3	0	2	0
TOTAL	40	0	1	0	3	0	3	0

CHEETHAM, Michael Martin

Height: 5ft 9in. Weight: 12st 3lb.

Born: 30 June 1967, Amsterdam, Holland.

■ Plucked from the British Army, Cheetham had been playing for Basingstoke before joining Ipswich in October 1988. He made just 1(+3) appearances at Portman Road and signed for Cambridge exactly a year later in a £50,000 deal. The Cambridge side was on their way to rising from Fourth to Second Divisions in consecutive seasons, and it was a Cheetham hat-trick that condemned Colchester to the Conference in the final weeks of the 1989–90 season. Cambridge reached the quarter-finals of the FA Cup twice and narrowly lost to Leicester in the First Division Play-off semi-final, which could have seen them in the Premiership. Unfortunately their fall was as rapid as their rise and, after 123(+9) appearances and 22 League goals, Cheetham moved to Chesterfield in July 1994. Starting just five games, he left Saltergate on deadline day 1995, signing for a Colchester side managed by Steve Wignall. He made his debut as a substitute in a 2–0 home defeat to Scarborough but by the early part of 1996 had been shipped out to Sudbury Town. He later played for Cambridge City and the newly formed amalgam AFC Sudbury. A player, assistant manager and coach, Cheetham played over 200 times for the new Suffolk club and was rewarded with a testimonial pre-season friendly against Colchester in July 2006. In his last three seasons he and joint-manager Gary Harvey had steered the club to three successive League titles but with two successive agonising FA Vase Final defeats.

	League		Lge Cup		FA Cup		Other	
	A	G	A	G	A	G	A	G
1994–95	8+1	1	0	0	0	0	0	0
1995–96	25+3	2	2	1	1	0	3	0
TOTAL	33+4	3	2	1	1	0	3	0

CHEYNE, Alexander George 'Alec'

Height: 5ft 8in. Weight: 11st 4lb.

Born: 28 April 1907, Glasgow.
Died: 5 July 1983, Arbroath.

■ Spotted playing for Shettleston Juniors, Cheyne was signed by Aberdeen as an 18-year-old in December 1925 and, after establishing himself in the first team, was soon attracting the attentions of the Scotland selectors. He made perhaps the most dramatic of debuts for his country on 13 April 1929, scoring direct from a corner kick in the closing minutes of the international against England at Hampden in front of 110,512 spectators. The game went down in folklore as the 'Cheyne International' and it has been said that Cheyne's remarkable 88th-minute winner was the birth of the famous 'Hampden Roar'. The Scot's forward line was Hughie Gallacher (Newcastle), Alex James (PNE), Alan

Morton (Rangers) and Alex Jackson (Huddersfield). England included Dixie Dean. Cheyne had been selected for the team only 48 hours earlier and the Scots played most of the game with only 10 men. The in-swinging corner was obviously a Cheyne speciality, for he is the only player to score two goals direct from a corner in a single game. This was for Aberdeen against Nithsdale Wanderers in the second round of the Scottish Cup at Pittodrie on 1 February 1930. Aberdeen won 5–1. Further caps followed in the 26 May 1929 tour match in Brann Stadium, Bergen, when he cracked a hat-trick in a 7–3 win over Norway, then on 1 June in a 2–0 defeat to Germany at the Grunewaldstadion, Berlin and a 2–0 win over Holland at the Olympic Stadium in Amsterdam on 4 June. He was also selected for the Scottish League XI while at Aberdeen. Cheyne was sold to Chelsea in June 1930 for a £6,000 fee after making 138 appearances at Pittodrie, scoring 55 goals. A versatile forward who played on the wing during the early part of his career, Cheyne was used entirely as an inside-forward for Chelsea. In only his third match he scored a fine hat-trick in a 6–2 win over Manchester United at Stamford Bridge before a 49,000 crowd. He found it difficult to adjust to the speed of the English game and rarely produced his best form south of the border. After 62 League appearances and seven goals, along with seven FA Cup starts and one goal, Cheyne became one of the first British players to play in France in May

1932. Audacious French club Nimes made an advance to four Chelsea players, Hughie Gallacher, Andy Wilson, Tommy Law and Cheyne. Gallacher and Law refused the advances, but the other two, along with a Harry Wilde of Ramsgate FC, took an impromptu 'holiday' to the wine country, 900 miles south of Paris, where they promptly signed up. Somewhat remarkably, those four internationals, along with fellow Scottish cap Alex Jackson, had formed the Chelsea forward line against Sunderland on 13 December 1930. Cheyne returned to Stamford Bridge at the start of 1934–35 where again he failed to do his great ability any real justice. Making only nine further appearances at Stamford Bridge, scoring two goals, he was placed on the transfer list at £3,000, joining Southern League Colchester in preference to Third Lanark. It was at Layer Road that Cheyne re-discovered his shooting boots, scoring a remarkable 59 goals in 97 appearances, as United won the Southern League Cup and Southern League Championship a year later. But for the war, Cheyne, with his fellow prolific United forward Arthur Pritchard, would surely have propelled the U's into the Football League, which was on the verge of expansion or re-organisation. After a brief hiatus, when war was declared, the Southern League restarted in a limited form, but the U's decided not to enter and instead confined themselves to friendlies. These did not prove very attractive, and the U's closed down for the duration at the end of 1939. Cheyne played in most of those games and then guested for Chelmsford for the rest of the 1939–40 season until Chelmsford also ceased operations. Cheyne participated in the D-Day landings, attached to the 1st Canadian Army, and turned out twice for Darlington in 1943–44, scoring once. He intimated a desire to return to Colchester on his demob from the Army in December 1945 but eventually found himself as manager of Arbroath from May 1949 to May 1955, a town where he passed away aged 76 in July 1983.

	League		Lge Cup		FA Cup		Other	
	A	G	A	G	A	G	A	G
1937–38	32	19	6	7	-	-	16	9
1938–39	29	14	3	2	2	0	6	5
1939–40	3	2	-	-	-	-	-	-
TOTAL	64	35	9	9	2	0	21	14

CHILVERS, Liam Christopher

Height: 6ft. Weight: 12st 4lb.

Born: 6 October 1981, Chelmsford.

■ Chilvers became the third young Arsenal player to spend a loan period at Colchester in a little under a year when he signed for Steve Whitton in January 2003. Like Graham Barrett and John Halls before him, he had been a member of their 2000 FA Youth Cup-winning team. He had already had loan deals at Northampton in December 2000, playing seven games, and Notts County in November 2001 where he scored his first League goal in nine starts. Before arriving at Colchester, Chilvers also spent time playing for Belgian side Beveren. The fact that so many Arsenal youngsters were going to Beveren prompted a FIFA investigation into possible financial irregularities, but no charges were brought. Phil Parkinson re-engaged the young defender on loan in August 2003, and the deal was made permanent a year later. After helping Colchester to runners'-up spot in League One during 2005–06, Chilvers rejected the offer of a new contract and joined fellow Championship side Preston. Completing 45 League starts and scoring two goals, Chilvers was still a Preston player during 2007–08.

	League		Lge Cup		FA Cup		Other	
	A	G	A	G	A	G	A	G
2002–03	6	0	0	0	0	0	0	0
2003–04	29+3	0	1	0	7	0	5	0
2004–05	40+1	1	2	0	4+1	0	0	0
2005–06	33+1	2	1	0	2+1	0	2	0
TOTAL	108+5	3	4	0	13+2	0	7	0

CHISWICK, Peter John Henry

Height: 5ft 10in. Weight: 12st.

Born: 19 September 1929, London.
Died: August 1962.

■ Chiswick hailed from Wivenhoe, and his goalkeeping pedigree came from his father who had kept goal for Clacton. Signed as a Colchester amateur on 14 July 1946, Chiswick was also registered as a colt on the books of West Ham. His sterling performances for United during 1946–47 led to West Ham claiming his services permanently and giving him a pro contract in July 1947. The U's asked to borrow him back the next season, but West Ham declined, and he continued his development in their Combination and Eastern Counties League teams before getting his debut in February 1954. He made 19 consecutive appearances before losing his place early the next season. That was the end of his first-team career at Upton Park, and he moved to Gillingham for 1956–57, resulting in 14 further League appearances. Chiswick remained in Kent with Margate, later becoming player-coach at Barking before his tragically early death from a throat infection in August 1962.

	League		Lge Cup		FA Cup		Other	
	A	G	A	G	A	G	A	G
1946–47	11	0	2	0	2	0	-	-
TOTAL	11	0	2	0	2	0	-	-

CHURCH, John 'Johnny'

Height: 5ft 9in. Weight: 10st 8lb.

Born: 17 September 1919, Oulton Broad.
Died: September 2004, Waveney.

■ Prolific local Leagues goalscorer Church signed for Norwich as an

amateur on 27 July 1936 before becoming a full professional in September of the same year. At Norwich he served under five different managers but was robbed of six years of his career by the war years. As a Royal Marines Commando he was awarded the Distinguished Service Medal for his part in a raid on Milos in Greece. He did turn out for Norwich during the war years and scored a stunning three minute hat-trick against Crystal Palace in the Division Three South Cup tie in March 1946, adding a fourth goal later. A fee of £1,000 brought Church to Layer Road, despite the interests of Bristol City, and he made his U's debut in the first-ever League game at Gillingham on 19 August 1950. In October 1953, by now a reserve, Church dropped down to part-time as he had obtained a hotel licence and left at the end of the season to join Crittall's of Braintree, having declined the opportunity to coach in Holland for family reasons. After a year he went back to Norfolk as player-coach of Beccles, and later he joined up with another ex-U's player, Mike Grice, to coach Corton FC while working as a gold and silver sales rep for a London jewelers. His Canaries career spanned 114 League and Cup games in which he scored 16 goals. The war years added a further 13 appearances and seven goals.

	League		Lge Cup		FA Cup		Other	
	A	G	A	G	A	G	A	G
1950–51	40	10	-	-	2	0	-	-
1951–52	38	3	-	-	3	0	-	-
1952–53	34	8	-	-	5	1	-	-
1953–54	6	0	-	-	1	0	-	-
TOTAL	118	21	-	-	11	1	-	-

CLARK, Simon

Height: 6ft. Weight: 12st 11lb.

Born: 12 March 1967, Boston.

■ Clark was a late starter in the professional game, not playing his first game as a non-contract player at Peterborough until the age of 27 in March 1994. His earlier career had seen him turn out for Boston United, Holbeach, King's Lynn, Hendon and Stevenage. He began the following season as a fully-fledged Posh player and went on to make 102(+5) League appearances, scoring four times. In June 1997 Leyton Orient paid Peterborough £25,000 and, after suffering Play-off defeat in 1998–99 at Wembley, Clark missed the latter half of the following season with a viral infection. Signed by Steve Whitton in the summer of 2000, Clark made his debut in an opening day 0–0 draw at Swindon. He formed a good partnership with first Alan White and then Scott Fitzgerald at the heart of United's defence. However, he was involved in a fatal car accident in Colchester in November 2000 and, despite being admonished of any blame, left on compassionate grounds for Singapore, the home of his wife. He played in the S-League for Woodlands Wellington but returned to England in 2004–05, playing for non-League King's Lynn. In August 2005 he became the short-lived manager of Ryman League side Leyton and in 2007–08 was in charge of Peterborough United's youth team.

	League		Lge Cup		FA Cup		Other	
	A	G	A	G	A	G	A	G
2000–01	33+1	0	4	0	0+1	0	0	0
2001–02	19+2	0	2	0	0	0	2	0
TOTAL	52+3	0	6	0	0+1	0	2	0

CLARKE, William Charles 'Billy'

Height: 5ft 8in. Weight: 10st 1lb.

Born: 13 December 1987, Cork, Republic of Ireland.

■ A Republic of Ireland Youth and Under-21 international with 34 appearances and 13 goals at all levels, Clarke was pressing for an Ipswich first team spot after signing professional in January 2005. He was a member of Town's FA Youth Cup-winning squad of 2005, although he missed the Final through injury. Impressing in an earlier round as Town thrashed Colchester's youth team 5–0 at Layer Road, Clarke was recruited by Phil Parkinson to bolster United's run-in to gaining promotion to the Championship at the tail end of 2005–06. He made his debut as a substitute at Scunthorpe in April 2006 but returned to Portman Road to play against United during 2006–07. Clarke scored three times in 11(+18) games during that season and remained on Ipswich's books for 2007–08, being loaned to Falkirk in January 2008.

	League		Lge Cup		FA Cup		Other	
	A	G	A	G	A	G	A	G
2005–06	2+4	0	0	0	0	0	0	0
TOTAL	2+4	0	0	0	0	0	0	0

COLEMAN, David Houston

Height: 5ft 7in. Weight: 10st 8lb.

Born: 8 April 1967, Salisbury.

Died: May 1997, Salisbury.

■ An apprentice with Bournemouth, Coleman made 40(+10) appearances at

Dean Court, scoring twice. During this spell he was loaned out to Poole to gain match experience. Recruited by Roger Brown when having only made three first team appearances, the left-back made his debut against Burnley in February 1988, scoring his only goal in a 2–1 home defeat to Wrexham a month later. Despite being one of Brown's better acquisitions, Coleman returned to Bournemouth prior to deadline day 1988 when United could not raise the necessary transfer fee. Released by the Cherries in 1991, he joined Farnborough and played 39(+3) Conference games over two seasons, scoring three times, and also played non-League for Dorchester, Salisbury, Wimborne, Amesbury and Warminster. Coleman died in 1997 and a Salisbury-based team, Dave Coleman AFC, was born in his memory and competed in the Wessex League.

	League		Lge Cup		FA Cup		Other	
	A	G	A	G	A	G	A	G
1987–88	6	1	0	0	0	0	0	0
TOTAL	6	1	0	0	0	0	0	0

COLEMAN, David John 'Dave'

Height: 5ft 10in. Weight: 11st 6lb.

Born: 27 March 1942, Colchester.

■ By 1958 Coleman was playing in the Border League for Colchester Casuals and first played for the U's in the club's first-ever FA Youth Cup tie, against Aveley on 7 October 1959. Coleman scored twice in the 4–1 win, and that earned the boys a second-round home tie against Chelsea, who were the dominant force in youth football in the southern half of the

country from the mid-1950s through to the early 1960s. Nine of Chelsea's team went on to have significant professional careers including Peter Bonetti, Terry Venables and Bobby Tambling, while Bobby Hunt and Mick Loughton are the only other members of the U's XI who make this book. Incredibly, Bobby Hunt scored the only goal of the first half, but Chelsea hit back with nine after the break and went on to win the Cup. Coleman continued to play for Casuals as well as making nine appearances for the U's reserves in 1960–61. At the start of 1961–62 he joined Harwich & Parkeston and in his three months there scored 21 times in just 15 appearances, including half of the two dozen they scored in reaching the first round of the FA Cup for only the fourth time in their long history. After Harwich's Cup exit Coleman went back to Layer Road as a part-time pro and made his debut at Rochdale almost immediately as stand-in for the injured Martyn King. He became a full-timer in February 1962 but only made one further appearance for Colchester, scoring his only goal in a 4–1 defeat at Wrexham in October 1962. He returned to local football where he maintained his goalscoring exploits for Clacton, Sudbury, where he netted 75 times in two years, Braintree, Brentwood, Halstead, Coggeshall and finally Brightlingsea, where he was player-manager before business commitments brought an end to his playing career in October 1972 .

	League		Lge Cup		FA Cup		Other	
	A	G	A	G	A	G	A	G
1961–62	1	0	0	0	0	0	-	-
1962–63	1	1	1	0	0	0	-	-
TOTAL	2	1	1	0	0	0	-	-

COLEMAN, Philip 'Phil'

Height: 5ft 11in. Weight: 11st 9lb.

Born: 8 September 1960, Woolwich.

■ Millwall apprentice Coleman worked his way into the Lions first team after signing professional terms in August 1978. He scored one of the goals as Millwall Youth sensationally beat Manchester City in the 1979 FA Youth Cup Final. In February 1981, after 23(+13) appearances and a single goal, U's manager Bobby Roberts paid £15,000 for his services. Unfortunately Colchester were relegated, but Coleman virtually made the left-back slot his own, firstly under Allan Hunter and then Cyril Lea. When Lea signed Ian Phillips in September 1983 Coleman was loaned out to Wrexham where he teamed up with former U's boss Bobby Roberts. Scoring twice in 17 games for the Welshmen, Coleman returned to Layer Road but was released to join Chelmsford. In December 1984 he signed non-contract forms with Exeter playing six games for the Grecians. This was enough to convince Aldershot to take a chance on the defender. He joined the Shots in February 1985 and in two seasons appeared 45 times, scoring 5. Released by Aldershot, he drifted back in to non-League with Dulwich Hamlet from where he made a surprise return to Second Division Millwall. From September 1986 he played a further

8(+2) games at The Den before going to Finland to play. With Colchester struggling to avoid relegation to the Conference, caretaker manager Steve Foley brought Coleman back to Layer Road in December 1988 to bolster his defence. Coleman played 6(+4) League games as United, under newly appointed Jock Wallace, succeeded in avoiding the drop. On release Coleman turned out for Wivenhoe, bravely taking over as player-manager in 1991 when the Dragons' finances collapsed and virtually their whole senior squad quit. He became a teacher and is PE Faculty Manager at the Colne Community School in Brightlingsea, a specialist sports college since 2000, where he employs former U's stalwart Micky Cook as head of football. Phil's son Liam came through the U's Centre of Excellence and was an apprentice at the club before playing 14 League games for Torquay in 2005–06.

	League		Lge Cup		FA Cup		Other	
	A	G	A	G	A	G	A	G
1980–81	4	0	0	0	0	0	-	-
1981–82	34+3	4	4+1	0	4+1	0	-	-
1982–83	37	2	4	0	1	0	3	1
1983–84	7+1	0	0	0	0	0	1	0
1988–89	6+4	0	0	0	2	0	2	0
TOTAL	88+8	6	8+1	0	7+1	0	6	1

COLLINS, Eamonn Anthony Stephen

Height: 5ft 6in. Weight: 8st 13lb.

Born: 22 October 1965, Dublin, ROI.

■ Collins became the youngest first-class footballer in British history when he turned out for Blackpool against Kilmarnock, aged just 14 years and 323 days, in the 1980–81 Anglo-Scottish Cup. Collins never actually made another appearance at Bloomfield Road and served his apprenticeship under Alan

Ball at Southampton where the former Blackpool boss had taken over the hot seat. At the Dell, Collins made just 1(+2) appearances before again following Ball to Portsmouth in the summer of 1986. Still only 20 years old, Collins appeared 4(+1) times for Pompey. In November 1987 he was loaned out to Exeter, making 8(+1) appearances and followed the same route to Gillingham a year later without making a start. When Ball joined Jock Wallace as Colchester's assistant manager, Collins followed in May 1989 after his release from Pompey. Making his debut at Chesterfield on the opening day of 1989–90 Collins was unable to prevent United sliding into the Conference. He stayed with Colchester during their two non-League campaigns and was unlucky to drop out of favour as Roy McDonough's side homed in on the title. He faced further heartache when he was only a non-playing substitute in the 1992 FA Trophy Final victory over Witton Albion at Wembley. He magnanimously gave his medal to U's player Jason Cook who had received his marching orders during the match and was therefore not entitled to a winners' medal. Collins left Layer Road in the summer and teamed up with his old friend Ball at Exeter, making 8(+3) appearances for the Second Division outfit. He joined Farnborough Town, playing 11(+2) games in 1992–93, scoring twice, before turning out for Devon junior sides Crediton and Elmore. He returned to his homeland and managed St Patrick's Athletic in 2003, resigning a year later to become assistant manager of Shelbourne where he experienced UEFA Cup football against Lille. His son Joe, on the books of Portsmouth, followed his father into the Republic's Under-17 squad in 2007. Collins himself had won four caps in 1984 at Under-21 level and became a football advisor following the financial collapse of Shelbourne.

	League		Lge Cup		FA Cup		Other	
	A	G	A	G	A	G	A	G
1989–90	39	2	2	1	2	0	2	0
1990–91	*35*	*2*	*0*	*0*	*3*	*0*	*4*	*0*
1991–92	*29+3*	*2*	*1*	*1*	*3*	*0*	*3+2*	*0*
TOTAL	39	2	2	1	2	0	2	0
	64+3	*4*	*1*	*1*	*6*	*0*	*7+2*	*0*

COLLINS, James Frederick Arthur 'Jim'

Height: 5ft 11in. Weight: 12st.

Born: 14 July 1903, Brentford.

Died: May 1977.

■ Jim Collins was the first-ever U's player to be dropped from the starting line-up after featuring in the club's professional debut at Yeovil in August 1937. The brother of the England amateur international Ted Collins, who had played for Colchester Town, Collins started his career with Chelmsford, Clapton and Leyton before joining West Ham in 1923. In 12 years at the Boleyn he made 311 appearances as a half-back, including 160 in a row, scoring three goals. When his first-team career expired he captained the successful Hammers reserve side that pipped Arsenal to the London Combination title. Joining the U's in the twilight of his career, he was one of the few disappointments of United's inaugural season, making only two further appearances, one of which was accidental as he travelled to Bath in October to cheer on his colleagues, only to be roped in to action after Syd Fieldus had missed the train. It was perhaps no surprise when he was released at the end of the 1937–38 season.

	League		Lge Cup		FA Cup		Other	
	A	G	A	G	A	G	A	G
1937–38	3	0	0	0	-	-	0	0
TOTAL	3	0	0	0	-	-	0	0

COLLINS, R.

■ A native of King's Lynn, Corporal Collins served with No.1 Holding Battalion Infantry Training Corps and signed as a U's amateur on 1 May 1946 after playing eight times in 1945–46. He occupied the left-wing spot throughout October and November 1946 but was not seen again after the 5–0 FA Cup defeat at Reading.

	League		Lge Cup		FA Cup		Other	
	A	G	A	G	A	G	A	G
1945–46	2	1	6	1	0	0	-	-
1946–47	7	3	1	2	2	0	-	-
TOTAL	9	4	7	3	2	0	-	-

CONLON, Barry John

Height: 6ft 2in. Weight: 13st 7lb.

Born: 1 October 1978, Drogheda, ROI.

■ Released from his Youth Training Scheme at QPR, Conlon was given a second chance by Manchester City when signing forms at Maine Road in August 1997. Earning seven Republic of Ireland Under-21 caps, he made 1(+6) appearances for City in the First Division and was also loaned to Plymouth for six months in February 1998, scoring twice in 13 games. In September 1998 he moved to Southend for £100,000, scoring seven goals in 28(+6) Third Division matches, and followed up with a transfer to York in the summer of 1999. He bagged 11 goals in 31(+9) games in his first season for the struggling Minstermen but featured only 2(+6) times the following campaign. Steve Whitton signed the big striker on a long-term loan in November 2000, and he made his debut in a surprise 1–0 win at Reading in the same month. He soon became popular with the Layer Road faithful, but cash-strapped United were unable to offer Conlon a deal on the completion of his loan. Instead he joined Third Division Darlington for £60,000 and enjoyed three prolific seasons, scoring 39 goals in 113(+1) appearances. First Division Barnsley signed Conlon in July 2004, but his goals dried up somewhat with just seven strikes in 25(+10) League games. With Barnsley on the verge of promotion he was loaned to Rotherham in October 2005, scoring once in three outings. Re-signed by Darlington in the 2005 close season, he managed a further six goals in 12(+7) appearances. In January 2007 he made a further transfer when joining Mansfield, scoring a creditable six goals in just 16(+1) games for the Stags. In July 2007 he became new manager Stuart McCall's first signing for League Two Bradford.

	League		Lge Cup		FA Cup		Other	
	A	G	A	G	A	G	A	G
2000–01	23+3	8	0	0	1	0	1	0
TOTAL	23+3	8	0	0	1	0	1	0

CONNOLLY, Matthew 'Matt'

Height: 6ft 2in. Weight: 11st 3lb.

Born: 24 September 1987, Barnet.

■ Schooled in the Arsenal Academy and captain of the reserves side, Connolly made his Gunners debut in a League Cup tie against West Brom in October 2006. The following month he was sent on loan to Bournemouth to earn valuable first-team experience and scored one goal in 3(+2) appearances. Having been seen on the Premier Reserve League circuit by Colchester's scouts, Connolly was brought to Layer Road in the summer of 2007 by Geraint Williams to bolster his defence following the departure of Wayne Brown and Chris Barker. In making his debut at Sheffield United on the opening day of the season, he along with fellow debutants Clive Platt, Teddy Sheringham and Luke Guttridge pushed the number of players to represent Colchester United's first team through the 700 barrier. Connolly was unfortunate to receive a contentious red card in the September 2007 match against Charlton at Layer Road when he was adjudged to have fouled former U's favourite Chris Iwelumo. In November 2007 Connolly was called up by England Under-21s and was an unused substitute in the 1–1 draw in Portugal. He returned to Arsenal in order to sign for QPR in the January transfer window for a fee of £850,000.

	League		Lge Cup		FA Cup		Other	
	A	G	A	G	A	G	A	G
2007–08	13+3	1	0	0	0	0	-	-
TOTAL	13+3	1	0	0	0	0	-	-

CONNOLLY, Patrick Joseph 'Pat'

Height: 5ft 11in. Weight: 11st 12lb.

Born: 27 July 1941, Newcastle, Staffordshire.

■ A centre-forward, Connolly began his career at Crewe, scoring three goals in nine League starts, but moved on to local non-Leaguers Macclesfield in April 1963 for a record fee of £1,000. That transfer remained Macclesfield's record transfer until 1990. U's manager Neil Franklin paid £1,200 for his services to replace Martyn King. An impossible act to follow, Connolly netted six League goals before returning homesick to Cheshire. He starred for Altrincham in their 1965–66 FA Cup run that ended in defeat to Wolves in the third round and notched 34 goals that season for the Cheshire League champions. Later he turned out for Northwich, Runcorn and Winsford United.

	League		Lge Cup		FA Cup		Other	
	A	G	A	G	A	G	A	G
1964–65	21	6	1	0	3	1	-	-
TOTAL	21	6	1	0	3	1	-	-

COOK, Anthony 'Tony'

Born: 17 September 1976, Hemel Hempstead.

■ A former YTS player at QPR, Cook was taken on by the Colchester youth set up and given his first-team debut as a substitute in an Autoglass Trophy tie against Wycombe in January 1994. His only full League start came in the penultimate game of the same season against Doncaster at Layer Road when United won by 3–1. He had the misfortune to suffer a cruciate knee ligament injury in March 1995, just as the decisions on the second-year apprentices were being made, and although not offered a contract he remained at the club for his rehabilitation, returning to action just before Christmas. He continued to play for the reserves, but the injury had put paid to any chance he had of a professional career at Colchester and he left at the end of the season. He returned to Hertfordshire briefly to play for Berkhamstead, then joined Roy McDonough's ex-U's colony at Chelmsford, being one of the few to survive when Roy left, and later went back to his Hertfordshire home to play for Hemel Hempstead and Tring Town.

	League		Lge Cup		FA Cup		Other	
	A	G	A	G	A	G	A	G
1993–94	1+1	0	0	0	0	0	0+1	0
TOTAL	1+1	0	0	0	0	0	0+1	0

COOK, Jason Peter

Height: 5ft 7in. Weight: 10st 6lb.

Born: 29 December 1969, Edmonton.

■ Cook failed to make the grade at White Hart Lane after signing as an apprentice in

the summer of 1988. He was released to Southend a year later and played 29 times as Southend won promotion from the old Fourth Division. The Shrimpers achieved the same feat a year later in the Third Division, but Cook did not feature apart from one substitute appearance. It was Roy McDonough who recruited his former teammate in the early stages of the 1991–92 Conference season. Cook bolstered the midfield and scored a thunderbolt at Macclesfield in the FA Trophy semi-final that put United on the road to Wembley. At Wembley it all turned sour as Cook was sent off for striking an opponent. He did not receive a medal as a result, but non-playing substitute Eamonn Collins gave his own medal to Cook. His chances reduced by the arrival of Alan Dickens, Cook was released to Dagenham & Redbridge, appearing 22(+1) times, and later played for Braintree, Chelmsford, Heybridge and Romford.

	League		Lge Cup		FA Cup		Other	
	A	G	A	G	A	G	A	G
1991–92	*28+3*	*2*	*2*	*0*	*2*	*0*	*9*	*1*
1992–93	30+4	1	1	0	2	0	1	1
1993–94	0+1	0	0	0	0	0	0	0
TOTAL	30+5	1	1	0	2	0	1	1
	28+3	*2*	*2*	*0*	*2*	*0*	*9*	*1*

COOK, Michael 'Micky'

Height: 5ft 7in. Weight: 10st 11lb.

Born: 9 April 1951, Enfield.

■ Cook began his long, distinguished career as a schoolboy with Leyton Orient under Dick Graham. When financial pressures led Orient to release Cook in early 1969, Graham, by now the U's boss, brought him to Layer Road on trial and Cook was first seen in a U's shirt for the youth team at Reading on 1 March 1969. His final appearance in the blue-and-white stripes was in a reserves game at home to Clacton on 30 April 1984. Originally an inside-forward, Cook was signed as a pro in July 1969 and at the end of October appeared for the first time at right-back, in a reserve game with Charlton. He had already made his debut by coming on as substitute at Wrexham earlier in the month, and when Duncan Forbes was sold in the first week of November Graham unveiled Cook as his replacement at right-back. Establishing himself in the first team, Cook made the right-back slot his own for the next 12 seasons, missing just 32 League games. He did help further forward as well and weighed in with 21 goals. Cook was unfortunate to be the non-playing substitute on the day that Colchester beat mighty Leeds in 1971 FA Cup fifth round, having played in four of the previous five ties but enjoyed many spats with higher League opposition in both the FA Cup and League Cup in later years and featured prominently against Aston Villa (three times), Manchester United (twice), Southampton (three times), Derby, Leeds

and Newcastle. He suffered re-election pain in 1972–73, promotion under Jim Smith in 1973–74, relegation (1975–76 and 1980–81) and promotion (1976–77) under Bobby Roberts. Cook took several heavy knocks in season 1983–84 and was told by a specialist that his spinal injury would end his professional career. Having become the club's record appearance holder, taking over from Peter Wright, Cook hung up his boots and enjoyed a second testimonial game when a Colchester Past and Present took on their Ipswich counterparts in December 1987. Such was Cook's exemplary long service that he had already had a testimonial in 1979 when Colchester took on West Bromwich Albion. Cook sought a career in Insurance and also took on a coaching role at Wivenhoe Town as the local side rose through the non-Leagues. Cook returned to Layer Road as community officer before becoming youth team manager and being part of the team that set up the Club's centre of excellence in 1998. While Director of Youth, Cook and his team were responsible for producing many players for the first team, most notably Greg Halford, John White, and Dean Gerken. He famously helped unearth the talent of Lomana Tresor Lua Lua who, having been on trial at Layer Road, did not have the mental attitude required. With Cook and his staff's perseverance Lua Lua was moulded into a future Premiership star, earning the Club a £2.25m transfer fee. Cook was unceremoniously sacked from his position as Director of Youth in 2004 and set up his own coaching school at Colne Community College in Brightlingsea with ex-U's player Phil Coleman soon after. He is a true Colchester United legend.

	League		Lge Cup		FA Cup		Other	
	A	G	A	G	A	G	A	G
1969–70	19+1	0	0	0	1	0	-	-
1970–71	34+1	0	1	0	4	0	-	-
1971–72	36+2	1	1	0	1	0	0	0
1972–73	43	0	0	0	2	0	-	-
1973–74	44	4	1	1	1	0	-	-
1974–75	46	4	6	0	2	0	-	-
1975–76	39	1	2	0	2	0	-	-
1976–77	46	3	3	0	6	0	-	-
1977–78	44	1	5	0	4	0	-	-
1978–79	46	1	1	0	7	0	-	-
1979–80	44	0	2	0	4	0	-	-
1980–81	45	0	1	0	4	0	-	-
1981–82	46	4	5	1	5	1	-	-
1982–83	41	1	4	0	0	0	3	0
1983–84	36	2	5	0	2	0	2	0
TOTAL	609+4	22	37	2	45	1	5	0

COOMBE, Mark Andrew

Height: 6ft 1in. Weight: 12st 6lb.

Born: 12 September 1968, Torquay.

■ Coombe started out as a youth trainee at Bournemouth but failed to gain any first-team experience. He joined Bristol City in August 1987 and played in one FA Cup game for the Ashton Gate club. A spell with Carlisle later that same season saw Coombe play in one Sherpa Van Trophy tie for the Cumbrians. Recruited during the caretaker reign of Steve Foley, Coombe made his Colchester debut against Torquay in November 1988, having signed non-contract forms. Conceding eight times in his three League games, he did taste success with a 1–0 FA Cup win at Fulham. Coombe impressed Torquay on his U's debut and they offered him a full contract in December. After playing eight times for them, he drifted in to non-League and played for Salisbury, Dorchester, Elmore and Taunton before spending a brief spell at Exeter as second-choice 'keeper in 1996. Resuming his non-League career, he then turned out for Minehead, Taunton (again) and in 2003 for Bideford.

	League		Lge Cup		FA Cup		Other	
	A	G	A	G	A	G	A	G
1988–89	3	0	0	0	1	0	1	0
TOTAL	3	0	0	0	1	0	1	0

COOMBS, Francis Henry 'Frank'

Height: 5ft 11in. Weight: 11st 3lb.

Born: 24 April 1925, East Ham.
Died: April 1998, Colchester.

■ Goalkeeper Coombs joined Bristol City from Dartford in June 1949 and made 24 appearances for the Ashton Gate club before moving 12 months later to Southend. In a similarly brief spell at Roots Hall he made 20 League appearances before he ended up as second-choice 'keeper at Layer Road, making his debut, ironically, at Bristol City in March 1952. He covered for George Wright on 39 occasions and then headed for Gravesend in the summer of 1954. Coombs had the misfortune to break his leg for Fleet against Headington United just before Christmas. He later worked at Hollington's clothing factory and then Fieldcote and Sons ship brokers until taking early retirement in October 1987.

	League		Lge Cup		FA Cup		Other	
	A	G	A	G	A	G	A	G
1951–52	13	0	-	-	0	0	-	-
1952–53	18	0	-	-	0	0	-	-
1953–54	7	0	-	-	0	0	-	-
TOTAL	38	0	-	-	0	0	-	-

COOTE, Adrian

Height: 6ft 1in. Weight: 11st 11lb.

Born: 30 September 1978, Gt. Yarmouth.

■ Coote arrived at Layer Road with an amazing pedigree. Capped 14 times at Northern Ireland Under-21 level, once at B level and with six full caps, he had been a prolific scorer in the Football Combination for Norwich. Yet the striker had only played 20(+34) League games in the Canaries first team, scoring three times since turning professional in July 1997. He had scored on his international debut against Canada in April 1999. Soon to be out of contract and way down the

pecking order of experienced strikers at Carrow Road, Coote went on loan to Dutch side Roda Kerkrade. This did not work out and, despite an attempt by U's boss Steve Whitton to sign the player on loan, he opted to re-sign for Norwich and fight for a first-team place. Whitton finally got his man in December 2001 and had to pay a club record-equalling fee of £50,000. He made his debut as a substitute in a 3–3 pre-Christmas draw with Huddersfield but did not find the net until February 2002. Coote never settled at Layer Road and was released by Phil Parkinson, having had just two minutes to impress the U's new boss. He spent time on loan at Bristol Rovers in October 2002, scoring once in 4(+1) games. The deal that was struck involved Rovers' Justin Richards making the opposite move. Neither club saw reason to progress the moves. Released by mutual consent and having only just moved into the Colchester area, Coote signed a contract with Wivenhoe in January 2004. Still unsettled, he moved back to Norfolk with Dereham Town in the 2004 close season and subsequently played for Wroxham and Acle (2006–07) while in contract dispute with the former over a move to Gorleston.

	League		Lge Cup		FA Cup		Other	
	A	G	A	G	A	G	A	G
2001–02	5+14	4	0	0	0	0	0	0
2002–03	7+9	0	0	0	0	0	0	0
2003–04	0	0	0+1	0	0	0	0	0
TOTAL	12+23	4	0+1	0	0	0	0	0

COTTON, Russell Andrew

Height: 5ft 10in. Weight: 11st 8lb.

Born: 4 April 1960, Wellington.

■ Cotton developed through United's youth ranks, making his debut as a substitute at Port Vale in April 1978. A regular in U's reserve team, his chances were limited until he finally got a run during Colchester's relegation season of 1980–81. His only senior goal came in a 1–0 victory at Hull in March 1981 – one of only two successes on the road that term. He was released and went to play in Denmark and on his return in December 1982 had half a season with Chelmsford before emigrating to New Zealand where he appeared for Canterbury.

	League		Lge Cup		FA Cup		Other	
	A	G	A	G	A	G	A	G
1977–78	1+1	0	0	0	0	0	-	-
1978–79	1	0	0	0	0	0	-	-
1979–80	4	0	0	0	0	0	-	-
1980–81	18+1	1	1	0	0	0	-	-
1981–82	9+2	0	0	0	0	0	-	-
TOTAL	33+4	1	1	0	0	0	-	-

COULSON, R.

■ One of the 'Brentford Six' seconded to play for Colchester at Guildford in March 1946, Coulson made one appearance for Brentford in 1945–46 and although appearing in the Bees 1946–47 team, he failed to make any further appearances at Griffin Park.

	League		Lge Cup		FA Cup		Other	
	A	G	A	G	A	G	A	G
1945–46	0	0	1	0	0	0	-	-
TOTAL	0	0	1	0	0	0	-	-

COUSINS, Mark

Height: 6ft 1in. Weight: 12st 1lb.

Born: 9 January 1987, Chelmsford.

■ Taken on in his final year of school after being released by Fulham, U's youth-team boss Micky Cook was undecided whether to give him a scholarship and asked him to return for pre season as a trainee. During that pre-season Barnet found themselves desperate for a 'keeper for a friendly and rang the U's asking whether they could borrow Dean Gerken. The U's said no but offered them Cousins and Mark did so well in that game that Micky Cook promptly signed him on. It is a tribute to the way that Mark has continued to develop that when his scholarship finished in 2006 he was given a two-year professional contract despite the club already having two highly rated senior 'keepers in Gerken and Aidan Davison. After keeping the bench warm 30 times as understudy to one or the other, Cousins got a surprise introduction to Championship football when he was called into action following Gerken's red card in the August 2007 home game with Barnsley. Cousins's first taste of League football was to face a Brian Howard penalty which he nearly reached with a full-length dive to his left, and if he had taken the advice of his experienced teammate Teddy Sheringham and gone to the same side he might have reached Howard's second penalty of the game,

given for a second-half handball. Cousins might have been hoping for the start at Preston the week after while Gerken served his suspension but Davison passed himself fit and Geraint Williams preferred to have an old head behind an inexperienced back four.

	League		Lge Cup		FA Cup		Other	
	A	G	A	G	A	G	A	G
2007–08	0+2	0	0	0	0	0	-	-
TOTAL	0+2	0	0	0	0	0	-	-

COYNE, Christopher John 'Chris'

Height: 6ft 2in. Weight: 13st 10lb

Born: 20 December 1978, Brisbane.

■ Despite being born in Brisbane, Coyne grew up in Perth, living in the same street as future U's star Richard Garcia. Garcia, Coyne and his younger brother Jamie were coached by the Coyne's father, John who had played in England for Tranmere, Hartlepool and Wigan. They all joined West Ham, and in Chris Coyne's case the Hammers paid a £150,000 fee to Perth Italia in January 1996. Coyne had come to prominence after being selected for Australia Under-17s for the 1994 World Youth Cup. Also part of the successful West Ham 1999 FA Youth Cup-winning side, which included Garcia, Coyne made just one substitute appearance at Upton Park in 1998–99 against Leeds. He also had 7 games on loan at Brentford in the August of that season, and played a solitary substitute game for Southend the following January. In search of first-team football, Coyne moved to Dundee United in the summer of 1999, making 20 League appearances and playing UEFA Inter-Toto Cup football, over two seasons. Recruited by Luton for £50,000, Coyne became a big hit at Kenilworth Road, being chosen for the PFA League One representative side after Luton won the League One Championship trophy in 2004–05. Appointed club captain, Coyne completed 207(+14) League appearances for the Hatters, scoring 14 goals. Coyne represented his country in 8 warm-up games for the 2000 Sydney Olympics, although he did not make the final 'Olyroos' Under-23 squad, as future Colchester loanee Con Blatsis wore the centre-half shirt and Coyne was on standby. With Luton in administration at the turn of 2008, Coyne joined Colchester for a club-record £350,000 and helped stabilise United's leaky Championship defence. He made his U's debut in a 1–1 draw at Bristol City in January 2008 and his full international debut against Iraq in Dubai during June 2008.

	League		Lge Cup		FA Cup		Other	
	A	G	A	G	A	G	A	G
2007–08	16	1	0	0	0	0	-	-
TOTAL	16	1	0	0	0	0	-	-

CRAM, Robert 'Bobby'

Height: 5ft 11in. Weight: 12st 10lb.

Born: 19 November 1939, Hetton-Le-Hole.

Died: 14 April 2007, Vancouver.

■ Cram joined the West Brom ground staff before turning professional in 1957 and made his debut in October 1960. He became only the second-ever full-back to net a First Division hat-trick in a 5–3 West Brom win over Stoke in September 1964. Two of the goals were penalties, and Cram was Albion's regular from the spot. His last game for the Baggies was in the 1967 League Final defeat by QPR. Amassing 141 League games and scoring 25 goals, Cram also played over 200 games for West Brom reserves. After a spell with Bromsgrove Rovers he moved to Canada where he played for Vancouver Royals. Dick Graham, who had coached at The Hawthorns at the same time as Cram was a player, signed the defender in January 1970. He was made captain and led Colchester to their world famous FA Cup run in 1970–71 when the U's beat First Division Leeds 3–2. Cram also lifted the Watney Cup the following pre-season ironically at The Hawthorns, as once again United upset the form books beating West Brom on penalties after a 4–4 draw. He returned to Canada and played for Royal Canada FC and had a brief spell as player-coach to Bath City during 1973. Cram was also the uncle of Olympic athlete Steve Cram.

	League		Lge Cup		FA Cup		Other	
	A	G	A	G	A	G	A	G
1969–70	21	0	0	0	0	0	-	-
1970–71	43	4	3	0	7	0	-	-
1971–72	35+1	0	2	0	1	0	3	0
TOTAL	99+1	4	5	0	8	0	3	0

CRANFIELD, Harold Richard 'Harry'

Born: 25 December 1917, Chesterton.

Died: December 1990, King's Lynn.

■ A nephew of pre-war international Vic Watson, Cranfield had to wait an incredible nine years for his Fulham debut after joining them from Cambridge Town in December 1937. He

Ray Crawford

did turn out for Fulham in wartime, despite being posted overseas, notching four goals in 11 appearances. 13 goals for Fulham's reserves earned a move to Bristol Rovers in June 1947 and cost them about £3,000. He scored on his debut and played 25 consecutive games before injury and a cartilage operation led to him being released at the end of season. Cranfield played briefly for King's Lynn after leaving Layer Road where he had faced stiff competition from Len Cater for the outside left berth.

	League		Lge Cup		FA Cup		Other	
	A	G	A	G	A	G	A	G
1948–49	6	0	0	0	0	0	-	-
TOTAL	6	0	0	0	0	0	-	-

CRAWFORD, Raymond 'Ray'

Height: 5ft 11in. Weight: 11st.

Born: 13 July 1936, Portsmouth.

■ Crawford installed himself in Colchester folklore by netting twice as United beat the mighty Leeds in the 1970–71 FA Cup fifth round. Starting as a junior at home-town Portsmouth, Crawford signed professional in December 1954. It was not until the 1957–58 season that he made the first team, scoring nine League goals in 19 outings. After completing his National Service in Malaya, he joined Ipswich in September 1958 for £5,000. Crawford scored 143 goals as Ipswich rose to the First Division, culminating in a Championship medal in 1961–62. He was leading scorer in consecutive seasons in two different Divisions. As his goalscoring prowess grew he won two England caps in 1962 against Northern Ireland and Austria as well as representing the Football League. As well as netting hat-tricks in the League, League Cup and FA Cup, Crawford scored five in a 10–0 win over Maltese side Floriana in the European Cup of 1962–63. When Ipswich were relegated Crawford signed for Wolves in a £55,000 deal during September 1963. Scoring 39 times in 57 League games, he moved to WBA for £30,000 in February 1965 where he had an unhappy time, scoring six in 14 League starts. Returning to Portman Road in March 1966, he added a further 61 goals in 123 games and won a Second Division Championship medal in 1967–68. Exactly three years later he found himself at Charlton where he claimed seven goals in the remaining 21 fixtures of the 1968–69 season. Despite having a spell in non-League with Kettering, U's manager Dick Graham snapped up the player for £3,000 at the age of 34 to join his so-called Grandad's Army at Layer Road. Crawford's 24 League goals were not enough to get United promotion, but the double against Leeds assured world acclaim for both himself and Colchester United. He picked up the Player of the Year award, but Crawford's decision to join Johnny Byrne's Durban City at the beginning of 1971–72 turned sour when his wife fell ill and he returned to England. The South Africans refused to release his contract, and he was denied the chance to ever play again in England. He set up home on the South Coast and had spells as youth team coach at Brighton and Portsmouth and a stint at managing Fareham Town and Winchester City. In all Crawford played in 476 League games and scored a magnificent 289 goals.

	League		Lge Cup		FA Cup		Other	
	A	G	A	G	A	G	A	G
1970–71	45	24	3	0	7	7	-	-
1971–72	0	0	0	0	0	0	1	0
TOTAL	45	24	3	0	7	7	1	0

CRISP, George Henry

Height: 5ft 9in.

Born: 30 June 1911, Pontypool.
Died: 27 March 1982, Penrhiwceiber.

■ Crisp was a diminutive winger who was a great favourite with the Layer Road crowd with his dashing play and absolute fearlessness. While scoring a good number of goals himself, it was he more than most that provided the ammunition for United's prolific twin attack of Arthur Pritchard and Alec Cheyne. A member of the Llanelli team that won the Welsh League in 1932–33, he signed for Coventry in November 1933 where he made eight League appearances. Crisp moved to Bristol Rovers the following season notching six goals in 22 starts. At the end of the season he was on his way again – this time to Newport for whom he played 10 games, scoring once. It was from the Welshmen that Ted Davis acquired his services for United's first-ever season. A Southern League Cup and Championship-winner with the U's, he returned a creditable strike rate for a winger of better than a goal in every three games. Signing for Nottingham Forest on 21 July 1939, he failed to make any appearances at the City Ground before the onset of the war. During this time he assisted Notts County for one game in 1940–41 and Welsh side Aberamen Athletic, towards the end of hostilities, declaring an interest in returning to Layer Road but eventually joining Merthyr Tydfil.

	League		Lge Cup		FA Cup		Other	
	A	G	A	G	A	G	A	G
1937–38	19	9	5	1	-	-	15	4
1938–39	20	7	1	0	2	1	8	3
TOTAL	39	16	6	1	2	1	23	7

CROUCH, Nigel John

Height: 5ft 8in. Weight: 10st 7lb.

Born: 24 November 1958, Colchester.

■ Brother-in-law to United's Steve Foley, Crouch had a memorable Colchester debut for all the wrong reasons. He was sent off in the opening fixture of the 1980–81 season, which was a League Cup first round first-leg tie with Gillingham. Gillingham's future Manchester United star Steve Bruce was on the receiving end of retaliation following his own unseen crude tackle on the young full-back. An Ipswich apprentice, Crouch had failed to make the grade at Portman Road, having signed professionally in November 1978. He was loaned out to Lincoln at the start of 1979–80 and made seven League starts and was brought to Layer Road in the summer of 1980 by Bobby Roberts. Chances were limited, and the player filled in at left-back early in the season as United drifted towards relegation.

Released by Colchester, Crouch moved in to non-League where he joined Harwich and had long spells at both the Royal Oak and for Brantham Athletic before finishing with Mistley in the Border League. His son Ross, who was tragically killed in a road accident in May 2008, aged just 23, played for the U's Under-19s as a 14-year-old, and was an apprentice from 2001 to 2004, briefly having a professional contract.

	League		Lge Cup		FA Cup		Other	
	A	G	A	G	A	G	A	G
1980–81	9+1	0	1	0	0	0	-	-
TOTAL	9+1	0	1	0	0	0	-	-

CULLING, Gary

Height: 5ft 9in. Weight: 11st.

Born: 6 April 1972, Braintree.

■ Culling arrived at Layer Road in the early days of the 1994–95 season from Braintree for £5,000. He made just three starts, all of which ended in defeat. When new manager George Burley decided to don his own boots again Culling returned back to Cressing Road. He enjoyed a testimonial in October 1997 when Braintree took on an Ipswich XI.

	League		Lge Cup		FA Cup		Other	
	A	G	A	G	A	G	A	G
1994–95	2	0	1	0	0	0	0	0
TOTAL	2	0	1	0	0	0	0	0

CULLUM, Arthur Richard 'Dick'

Height: 5ft 11in. Weight: 10st 7lb.

Born: 28 January 1931, Colchester.

■ Cullum started at Layer Road in the Colts team that spent 1947–48 in the open-age Suffolk & Ipswich League. Details beyond scores and dates are sketchy, but it is known that he netted a

double hat-trick against Westerfield in November 1947 and four in a friendly against Guildford City, played at Layer Road on Good Friday 1948 as a warm up to and immediately before a Southern League game with the same club. He continued to score regularly the following year when the Colts moved to the Border League and became the A team, shedding their self-imposed age cap, although remaining primarily the youth team of the time. From 1949 to 1955 he was a consistent marksman for both the A team and the reserves but found the competition for first-team places too stiff and only made two senior appearances. His debut came on 26 March 1951 when he got the goal in a 3–1 defeat at Torquay, and it was almost three years before his second and final game as United suffered a 3–0 defeat at Aldershot in January 1954. On leaving Layer Road he signed for Sittingbourne, but by the end of the 1950s he was once again hitting the back of Border League nets for Long Melford and then Halstead. Away from football he became managing director of a Hertfordshire-based printing company.

	League		Lge Cup		FA Cup		Other	
	A	G	A	G	A	G	A	G
1950–51	1	1	-	-	0	0	-	-
1951–52	0	0	-	-	0	0	-	-
1952–53	0	0	-	-	0	0	-	-
1953–54	1	0	-	-	0	0	-	-
TOTAL	2	1	-	-	0	0	-	-

CURETON, Jamie

Height: 5ft 8in. Weight: 10st 7lb.

Born: 5 August 1975, Bristol.

■ Capped by England at Youth level, Cureton scored 126 goals in 180 appearances for Norwich at various levels before making his first-team debut in the Premiership in 1994. Playing 9(+8) games in that first season, he scored against Arsenal, Chelsea, Manchester City and Ipswich. A season later he repeated the feat against Ipswich when he sported green-and-yellow dyed hair. He spent six games on loan at Bournemouth in September 1995 but struggled to get in the Norwich side on return. After 13(+16) League appearances and six goals, Cureton was sold to Bristol Rovers exactly a year later for a fee of £250,000 following an initial loan period. He scored 11 League goals and was voted Young Player of the Year in his first season. He scored three hat-tricks in 1998–99 including four goals at Reading in a 6–0 win, picking up the Second Division's Golden Boot as top scorer. After plundering 72 goals in 165(+9) appearances at The Memorial Stadium it was inevitable that Rovers would have to sell. Cureton joined Reading in August 2000 for £250,000 and scored 26 goals to once again claim the Golden Boot. He also scored the first in Reading's Play-off Final defeat to Walsall at the Millennium Stadium. His goal at Brentford on the last day of the following season helped the Royals to second spot and promotion to Division One. Completing 74(+34) games at The Madejski and scoring 50 League goals, Cureton opted to make a bizarre move to South Korean side Busan Icons in 2002. The move proved ill-fated and Cureton returned to England in February 2003 to join QPR in a £95,000 deal funded

entirely by supporters. He never managed to have an extended run in the Rangers, side and three of his six goals came in one match against Coventry. After only 20(+23) appearances he moved to Swindon in May 2005 on a free transfer. Goals having deserted him, Cureton mustered just 6(+4) appearances at the County Ground before ex-Reading colleague Phil Parkinson brought him to Layer Road in October 2005 on a three-month loan. Cureton scored four League goals in just seven starts and bagged a pair in U's record-equalling 9–1 win over Leamington in the FA Cup a month later. Swindon refused to let Cureton join United on a permanent basis, preferring to take a second look at their discard. Despite netting seven times in 16(+4) appearances, Swindon were relegated and Cureton was able to exercise a clause in his contract that meant he did not have to play League Two football. He re-joined the newly promoted Colchester in June 2006 just days before Parkinson walked out of the club to join Hull. Despondent at first, Cureton completed a hat-trick of Golden Boots by being top scorer in the Championship, forming a lethal partnership with Chris Iwelumo. His goal touch rediscovered, Cureton demanded a move in the summer of 2007, rejoining his first club Norwich for a fee of £850,000.

	League		Lge Cup		FA Cup		Other	
	A	G	A	G	A	G	A	G
2005–06	7+1	4	0	0	2	3	0	0
2006–07	44	23	0+1	0	1	1	-	-
TOTAL	51+1	27	0+1	0	3	4	0	0

CURRY, Robert 'Bob'

Height: 5ft 8in. Weight: 10st 8lb.

Born: 2 November 1918, Gateshead.
Died: 30 June 2001, Halstead.

■ Captain of Ted Fenton's all-conquering FA Cup team of 1947–48, Curry scored the winning goals against Third Division North Wrexham and mighty First Division Huddersfield, as well as two against Second Division Bradford PA, as Southern League United marched on to the fifth round and achieved a place in FA Cup folklore. The run ended at Blackpool where after the game Curry was presented with the match ball in recognition of the club's feat. Starting his career at Gateshead in 1936, Curry failed to break

into the first team there but was plucked from the North East by a Sheffield Wednesday scout for whom he made his debut as a 17-year-old. That became his only appearance at Hillsborough before the war halted the progression of his career. During those war years he guested for: 1939–40 Bradford PA (2 appearances/3 goals); 1940–41 Sheffield Wednesday (7/1); 1941–42 Gateshead (2/0); 1944–45 Sheffield United (14/5) and Mansfield (13/5). He suffered severe wounds at Dunkirk that put him out of football for almost two years. After the war he joined Gainsborough Trinity from whom he was signed by Ted Fenton in June 1946. Curry, a wizard of the dribble, scored within 42 minutes of his U's debut in the 3–2 home defeat by Gloucester in August of that year and notched an impressive 20 goals in 39 appearances. The following season, partnering Arthur Turner, he scored a magnificent 32 goals in 44 matches in all competitions including hat-tricks at Barry and at home to Cheltenham in the League Cup. The headlines earned by the FA Cup run that season prompted a bid from Third Division South Reading, but Fenton turned down the offer. His stubbornness proved wise as he plundered 19 goals in 41 matches as U's sought to obtain Football League status, and this time it was Ipswich who were scorned of his services. When elevation to the elite was achieved at the end of 1949–50, Curry had scored 22 of United's 109 League goals, but they ended with runners'-up spot by just one-fifth of a goal difference to Merthyr. Curry picked up a Southern League Cup-winners' medal in 1949–50 and was losing finalist in both of the previous seasons. Despite having the honour of scoring U's first ever League goal, in the 25th minute of U's second game at Swindon, and finishing the inaugural Football League season as the club's top scorer with 15 goals, Curry left at the end of 1950–51 to become player-manager at Clacton. They did not renew his contract at the end of 1953–54 and, he moved over to Halstead Town as player-coach and was also the licensee of the Nags Head in the town. His grandson Paul Curry became a well-known golf professional.

	League		Lge Cup		FA Cup		Other	
	A	G	A	G	A	G	A	G
1946–47	*30*	*14*	*7*	*4*	*2*	*1*	-	-
1947–48	*31*	*17*	*7*	*6*	*6*	*7*	-	-
1948–49	*40*	*17*	*6*	*2*	*1*	*0*	-	-
1949–50	*37*	*22*	*4*	*2*	*1*	*0*	-	-
1950–51	32	13	-	-	2	2	-	-
TOTAL	32	13	-	-	2	2	-	-
	138	*70*	*24*	*14*	*10*	*8*	-	-

CUSENZA, Calegero 'Leo'

Height: 5ft 8in. Weight: 10st 8lb.

Born: 20 February 1963, Edmonton.

■ Cusenza, whose family originates from Sicily, was a U's apprentice between 1979 and 1981 and got his only first-team start in the opening fixture of the 1980–81 season. U's manager Bobby Roberts faced a defensive dilemma when Steve Wright contracted jaundice, Micky Cook ricked his neck getting out of his car and Steve Dowman had signed for Wrexham, and Cusenza got his chance. It was too soon in a team that was going to struggle all season, for a 17-year-old who was as

much a left-winger as a left-back. The U's lost the first leg League Cup tie to Gillingham by 2–0, and Cusenza returned to the reserves and youth sides before being released at the end of the year when he begun a long association with Harlow Town that lasted the rest of the decade.

	League		Lge Cup		FA Cup		Other	
	A	G	A	G	A	G	A	G
1980–81	0	0	1	0	0	0	-	-
TOTAL	0	0	1	0	0	0	-	-

CUTTING, Noel Frederick Charles 'Fred'

Height: 5ft 8in. Weight: 11st 6lb.

Born: 4 December 1921, North Walsham.
Died: July 1997, Plymouth.

■ On the books of Leicester before the war, Cutting served with the Royal Scots in Burma and Singapore and won the Military Medal. Ted Fenton brought the clever ball-player in to replace Arthur

Biggs, and after a spell with Norwich in 1946–47 Cutting made the inside-left position his own and scored the winning goal against Bradford Park Avenue in Colchester's famous FA Cup run of 1947–48, having made his debut in the first-round tie with Banbury Spencer. Released in 1952, he returned to Norfolk with Great Yarmouth, taking part in another famous Cup run when Yarmouth reached the second-round in 1952–53, their best ever performance. He left them in 1956, having clocked up a half-century of goals and finished his playing days with Boulton & Pauls in the Norfolk & Suffolk League. He became a builder and was Clerk of Works at the Marques Cholmondeley estate at Houghton Hall, King's Lynn and also ran a sub Post Office in the area.

	League		Lge Cup		FA Cup		Other	
	A	G	A	G	A	G	A	G
1947–48	*23*	*12*	*3*	*2*	*5*	*1*	-	-
1948–49	*35*	*14*	*6*	*3*	*1*	*0*	-	-
1949–50	*46*	*19*	*5*	*3*	*1*	*0*	-	-
1950–51	11	3	-	-	1	1	-	-
1951–52	18	9	-	-	2	0	-	-
TOTAL	29	12	-	-	3	1	-	-
	104	*45*	*14*	*8*	*7*	*1*	-	-

Micky Cook.

D

DALE, Robert Jenkins 'Bob'

Height: 5ft 7in. Weight: 10st 7lb.

Born: 5 July 1931, Irlam.

Died: January 2007, Colchester.

■ Dale began as an amateur on the books of Manchester City, but it was from Altrincham that he signed for Bury in September 1951 after being recommended by Bert Head. He made the Bury first team in 1952–53, playing 15 League games at wing-half, and netted two goals. He signed for Colchester on Christmas Eve 1953 for a fee of £1,500, joining a side that was destined for re-election for two successive seasons. He came to the fore under the management of Benny Fenton and played an instrumental part as United surged towards the Second Division in 1956–57. However, in February of 1957 he developed Tuberculosis and never played for Colchester again. His last game was the 0–0 draw with Ipswich which ultimately decided promotion and set the local rivals on opposite courses for the best part of 50 years. Many say that the loss of Dale and fellow player Chic Milligan, through injury, was the main reason United lost out to Ipswich for the coveted Second Division spot. The club continued to pay his wages, and after recuperating in a Manchester hospital Dale returned to the Colchester area to manage local sides Arlesford, Coggeshall, Braintree and Brightlingsea while becoming a Regional Manager for a dairy and then a car salesman.

	League		Lge Cup		FA Cup		Other	
	A	G	A	G	A	G	A	G
1953–54	21	4	-	-	0	0	-	-
1954–55	34	4	-	-	0	0	-	-
1955–56	39	2	-	-	1	0	-	-
1956–57	33	2	-	-	1	0	-	-
TOTAL	127	12	-	-	2	0	-	-

DALLI, Jean

Height: 5ft 9in. Weight: 10st 10lb.

Born: 13 August 1976, Enfield.

■ Dalli was released by Watford as a schoolboy and picked up by the Colchester YTS scheme. At the time the football year did not align with the school year so boys like Dalli with an August birthday could spend three years around the youth team. With United's squad in disarray following the appointment of George Burley, Dalli was pressed into service at left-back in the opening day game of the 1994–95 season when United lost 3–1 at home to Torquay. Unfortunately, he ran up against the flying Barbadian international winger Gregory Goodridge who exposed his limitations, and at half-time a sub was on and Dalli's Football League career was over. Before the end of September he had suffered a groin injury that kept him out of action for five months and, although he was retained on non-contract terms for the first few weeks of 1995–96, he was soon off to try his luck elsewhere, playing a couple of Conference games for each of Dover and Slough and passing through Chelmsford and Baldock without leaving much of an impression.

	League		Lge Cup		FA Cup		Other	
	A	G	A	G	A	G	A	G
1994–95	1	0	0	0	0	0	0	0
TOTAL	1	0	0	0	0	0	0	0

DANIELS, Scott Charles

Height: 6ft 1in. Weight: 11st 9lb.

Born: 12 November 1969, Benfleet.

■ Daniels was promoted from Colchester's youth and reserves to make a substitute debut at Carlisle in April 1988. In doing so he became the 18th debutant of a troubled season. Things did not get any better the following campaign as the U's fought for their Football League lives. The youngster was called upon to do a man's job in a poor side by first Steve Foley as caretaker and then the management duo of Jock Wallace and Alan Ball. Daniels was a rock as United reached the fourth round of the FA Cup and staved off relegation to the Conference. An ever-present the following campaign, United could not keep their heads above water and duly sunk to the Conference. He formed a partnership with Neale Marmon and scored his only goal in a 2–0 win over Telford in September 1990. When United failed to regain League status Daniels moved to Exeter for £50,000 where he teamed up

with Grecians manager Alan Ball who had retained his admiration for the defender. He played 114(+3) times for Exeter, scoring seven goals. In January 1995 he signed for Northampton but made just 5(+3) appearances. Moving in to non-League he played 89(+2) Conference games for Dover between 1995 and 2000 and was club captain for a time before turning out for Ramsgate and Folkestone where he was also club coach.

	League		Lge Cup		FA Cup		Other	
	A	G	A	G	A	G	A	G
1987–88	0+1	0	0	0	0	0	0	0
1988–89	18+8	0	0	0	5	0	2+1	0
1989–90	46	0	2	0	2	0	2	0
1990–91	*40*	*1*	*0*	*0*	*3*	*0*	*4*	*0*
TOTAL	64+9	0	2	0	7	0	4+1	0
	40	*1*	*0*	*0*	*3*	*0*	*4*	*0*

DANNS, Neil Alexander

Height: 5ft 9in. Weight: 11st 12lb.

Born: 23 November 1982, Liverpool.

■ Captain of Blackburn's youth team, Danns had first impressed Colchester in an FA Youth Cup replay at Layer Road in February 2001, a year when Rovers reached the Final only to lose to Arsenal. He made his Blackburn debut against CSKA Sofia in a UEFA Cup tie in September 2002 and his Premiership debut a few days later against Leeds. Loaned to Blackpool in August 2003, he played 12 games at Bloomfield Road, scoring twice, and had a similar spell with Hartlepool in March 2004 where he scored once in 8(+1) games. Phil Parkinson originally signed Danns on a two-month loan in September 2004, and the deal was made permanent at its expiry. He finished the campaign as United's leading scorer in the League and ironically returned to Ewood Park in United's colours for a fourth-round FA Cup tie the following January. He continued to impress as Colchester faced Premiership champions Chelsea a year later, again in the FA Cup, and helped steer the U's to runners'-up spot in League One. The defeat at Chelsea and the arrival of Danns's new baby unsettled both club and player respectively, but a double strike against Hartlepool proved the catalyst for Colchester's promotion revival. Publicly announcing that he desired a move back nearer his Liverpool home, Danns joined Birmingham in the summer of 2006 for a fee of £500,000, rising to £850,000 on appearances, and made his debut against Colchester in their first-ever Championship fixture at St Andrews in August 2006. He featured in most games for Blues although 18 substitute appearances accompanied just 11 starts as they won promotion back to the Premiership. Danns found it difficult to break into a Blues first team awash with foreign imports. After 11(+20) League appearances and three goals he moved to Crystal Palace for £600,000 in January 2008.

	League		Lge Cup		FA Cup		Other	
	A	G	A	G	A	G	A	G
2004–05	32	11	2	1	1	0	1	0
2005–06	38+3	8	1	0	4+1	5	3+1	3
TOTAL	70+3	19	3	1	5+1	5	4+1	3

DARMODY, Aubrey

Born: 17 March 1921, Swansea.

Died: 9 February 2006, Gt Yarmouth.

■ A full-back who began his career at Cardiff Nomads, Darmody joined Norwich as an amateur in September 1946 and signed professional forms just a month later after Army service in Italy and Belgium. He made only two appearances for Norwich after suffering a serious injury. Given a free transfer, he joined United and made just three appearances, deputising for Ted Fenton in March 1948. He spent three years at Gt Yarmouth Town from November 1948 and in 1994 embarked on researching the history of Gt Yarmouth Town, while holding the position of club president.

	League		Lge Cup		FA Cup		Other	
	A	G	A	G	A	G	A	G
1947–48	3	0	0	0	0	0	-	-
TOTAL	3	0	0	0	0	0	-	-

DAVIDSON, Adam Richmond

Height: 5ft 7in. Weight: 10st 6lb.

Born: 28 November 1929, Invergowrie.

Died: 2007, Scotland.

■ Scotsman Davidson spent two of his four years at Sheffield Wednesday away on National Service in the Royal Navy and failed to break into the first team prior to his August 1951 free-transfer move to Layer Road. Initially, Davidson found his chances limited at Colchester as well, due to the form of United's other wingers John Church and Len Jones, but he got his chance when Jones broke his leg in November 1951 and shared the right-wing spot with Peter Aitchison for the rest of the season. Neither made the position their own and neither played more than four games in a row. Davidson scored his only goal directly from a corner kick in an FA Cup tie against Bristol City. Released at the end of the season, he moved to Dundee where he became a painter and decorator and played for Carnoustie in Scottish junior football.

	League		Lge Cup		FA Cup		Other	
	A	G	A	G	A	G	A	G
1951–52	19	0	-	-	2	1	-	-
TOTAL	19	0	-	-	2	1	-	-

DAVIES, Graham Gilding

Born: 3 October 1921, Swansea.

Died: November 2003, Swansea.

■ Capped by Wales at Schoolboy level, Davies joined the ground staff at the Vetch Field. He made over 70 wartime appearances for Swansea while serving in the RAF. In June 1947 he moved to

Watford as second-choice goalkeeper and made nine appearances. Taken on trial by the U's in an emergency at the end of April 1949 when injuries to Ken Whitehead and Harry Wright in successive games led to Vic Keeble keeping goal at Merthyr, Davies played three games for the U's in five days, starting with a clean sheet but conceding nine in the other two, and was not offered terms. After leaving Watford he played at Hereford and then Merthyr Tydfil and spent over 20 years as a licensee in The Mumbles area of Swansea before retiring.

	League		Lge Cup		FA Cup		Other	
	A	G	A	G	A	G	A	G
1948–49	2	0	1	0	0	0	-	-
TOTAL	2	0	1	0	0	0	-	-

DAVIS, Arron Spencer

Height: 5ft 8in. Weight: 11st.

Born: 11 February 1972, Wanstead.

■ A YTS player with Torquay, Davis joined the Gulls in August 1991, going on to make 20(+4) appearances over two seasons before being released to Dorchester. New U's boss George Burley was struggling to get a squad together for the start of the 1994–95 season and gave Davis a trial. The full-back took over from rookie Jean Dalli, after the season opener, starting the next four League games but was not retained as Tony English slotted into the full-back position, and he returned to Dorchester.

	League		Lge Cup		FA Cup		Other	
	A	G	A	G	A	G	A	G
1994–95	4	0	1	0	0	0	0	0
TOTAL	4	0	1	0	0	0	0	0

DAVISON, Aidan John

Height: 6ft 1in. Weight: 13st 2lb.

Born: 11 May 1968, Sedgefield.

■ Davison began his long career on the books of Billingham Synthonia and joined Notts County in March 1988. Playing just one League game, he was sold to Bury in October 1989 for £6,000 but failed to make an appearance, also having non-playing loan spells with Leyton Orient, Chester and Blackpool. In August 1991 Davison moved to Millwall and established himself as 'keeper. Playing 34 times, he was on the move again in the summer of 1993 when Bolton paid £25,000 for his services. He was part of the squad that won promotion to the Premiership via the Play-offs in 1995 but was chiefly understudy to Keith Branagan. He made his top-flight debut during the next season and earned his first cap for Northern Ireland in a 2–1 defeat to Sweden at Windsor Park in April 1996. The following October Davison joined Ipswich on loan as emergency injury cover and a month later played nine games on loan at Hull. On deadline day 1997 he was transferred to Bradford, playing 10 games and earning another international cap in a 0–0 draw in Thailand during the May. In the summer of 1997 he signed for Grimsby and enjoyed his most successful season to date, missing just four games as the Mariners won the Division Two Play-off Final at Wembley, having already collected the Auto Windscreens Shield at the same stadium a couple of months

earlier. Despite gaining his third and final cap in a World Cup qualifier against Germany in August 1997 and another solid season with Grimsby, he was released in the summer of 1999 over a contract dispute. Picked up by Sheffield United in August 1999, Davison played 1(+1) games for the Blades before returning to Premiership Bradford in January 2000. He made 7(+2) appearances and played in the UEFA Intertoto Cup of 2000–01 as City were relegated from the top flight, staying two further seasons and playing a further 42 times. August 2003 saw him return to another of his former clubs when he turned out 32 times for Grimsby. With Colchester manager Phil Parkinson losing both Richard McKinney and Simon Brown in the summer of 2004, it was no surprise that the U's boss opted for the experience of Davison as his first-choice 'keeper. He kept goal for Colchester for the best part of two and a half seasons, highlighted by an FA Cup outing at Chelsea and missing just five games as Colchester finished runners-up in League One in 2006. Intending to retire to the United States, Davison stayed with United to enjoy their first campaign in the Championship while acting as goalkeeping coach to Dean Gerken. Injury saw Gerken take over the goalkeeper's shirt, but Davison returned in September 2007 as a stand-in for the suspended Gerken in a magnificent 3–0 win at Preston before retiring to the US at the end of the campaign.

	League		Lge Cup		FA Cup		Other	
	A	G	A	G	A	G	A	G
2004–05	33	0	2	0	3	0	1	0
2005–06	41	0	0	0	4	0	0	0
2006–07	19	0	0	0	0	0	-	-
2007–08	6	0	0	0	0	0	-	-
TOTAL	99	0	2	0	7	0	1	0

DAWSON, Peter

■ Dawson, who had played in the pre-season trial match, was a late call-up from local side Rowhedge against Bedford in September 1945 when intended goalkeeper QPR pro Harry Brown was pulled out at the last minute by Rangers to play for them. Pre-war 'keeper Bill Light, the nominal deputy, was not fit enough to play and Ray Dring who had played in the previous two games was on leave. Brown began his Layer Road career the following week, and this was Dawson's only game for the U's. He had also played for local works side Paxman's in the Wartime Colchester and District League.

	League		Lge Cup		FA Cup		Other	
	A	G	A	G	A	G	A	G
1945–46	1	0	0	0	0	0	-	-
TOTAL	1	0	0	0	0	0	-	-

DAY, Albert

Born: 7 March 1918, Camberwell.
Died: 1983.

■ Originally on the books of Brighton where he failed to make the first team in the regular season, Corporal Day of the 17th Infantry Training Corps played 13 times for Albion during the war scoring eight goals. He had also guested for Swindon (1939–40 28 appearances/1 goal) and Lincoln (1941–42 1/0) before arriving at Layer Road. Two of his three games for the U's were in friendlies against Ipswich Town, and in the 1–1 draw on 30 August 1945 he scored the U's first goal at Layer Road after the war. He made sufficient impression on Ipswich that they hijacked him and two weeks later he scored a hat-trick for them on his debut. He went on to score 16 times in 22 games and chose to re-join Ipswich for 1946–47 in preparation for his demob from the Army where he hoped to become a professional once again. He scored another debut hat-trick, in the Football League against Norwich in a 5–0 win, and bagged 25 goals in 60 starts. On leaving Ipswich, Day scored one goal in four games for Watford during the 1949–50 season and later played for Folkestone, Ashford and Crawley Town.

	League		Lge Cup		FA Cup		Other	
	A	G	A	G	A	G	A	G
1945–46	1	0	1	0	0	0	-	-
TOTAL	1	0	1	0	0	0	-	-

DAY, Albert James 'Tully'

Height: 5ft 8in. Weight: 10st 6lb.

Born: 10 October 1910.
Died: June 2000, Harwich.

■ Day was a promising youngster with local side Harwich and Parkeston, joining them at the age of 20 from Parkeston Railway. He averaged an astonishing 45 goals a season for six seasons. Indeed, he scored 10 goals for them in an Essex Senior Cup tie against Severalls on 21 January 1936. Courted by Crystal Palace, he declined to turn professional because of work commitments. His employment meant that he could only travel the distances required in midweek. Ted Davis signed him up and he made his debut, appropriately, in the Southern League's Midweek Division at Aldershot's Recreation Ground. A builder, he also resisted United's invitation to turn professional and returned to Harwich and Parkeston before serving in the Merchant Navy during the war aboard SS *Prague*. During service he played against the Norwegian Army at Tain in Scotland and in other services games at Pittodrie Stadium, Aberdeen. Still going strong, he played, aged 42, in the 1952 Essex Junior Cup Final as Harwich Rangers beat Millwall Athletic 3–0. Day scored an impressive 16 goals in 15 appearances for United, including hat-tricks against Folkestone in a 7–1 Southern League win in December 1937 and at Bath in April 1938.

	League		Lge Cup		FA Cup		Other	
	A	G	A	G	A	G	A	G
1937–38	7	9	4	5	-	-	4	2
TOTAL	7	9	4	5	-	-	4	2

DAY, Keith David

Height: 6ft 1in. Weight: 11st.

Born: 29 November 1962, Grays.

■ Day began with Aveley and joined Colchester in the summer of 1984. Recommended by U's physio Bernie Dixon, also linked to the South Essex club, Day made his debut on the opening day of the 1984–85 season in a 3–3 draw against Southend. In the return at Roots Hall the following season Day dislocated his collarbone twice in the opening 20 minutes, an injury he repeated at Swindon on New Year's Day 1986 and two days later at home to Hereford. He had his shoulder pinned as a result. Day's last action in a United shirt was in holding Wolves to a 0–0 draw at Layer Road in the Fourth Division Play-off semi-final of 1986–87. Day missed the second leg which United lost 2–0 and opted to look for a move in the summer. Signing for Leyton Orient in July 1987, Day experienced promotion via the Play-offs in 1988–89, a season in which the O's beat Roger Brown's U's team by 8–0 at Brisbane Road with the defender grabbing one of the goals. Voted Player of the Year in 1991–2, Day's O's career amounted to 184(+8) League appearances with nine goals scored. On leaving East London he turned out for Sittingbourne, Farnborough, Grays, Bishop's Stortford and Romford, as well as having a spell as coach at Chelmsford before taking over as boss of Aveley in late 2005. That was initially on a caretaker basis and just eight weeks after being given the job permanently he resigned, citing difficulties with motivating some of the senior players as a contributory factor. In 2007 he joined the backroom staff at East Thurrock.

	League		Lge Cup		FA Cup		Other	
	A	G	A	G	A	G	A	G
1984–85	45	4	2	0	3	0	2	0
1985–86	30	5	2	0	0	0	0	0
1986–87	38	3	1	0	3	0	4	0
TOTAL	113	12	5	0	6	0	6	0

DENNIS, Alan George

Height: 6ft. Weight: 12st.

Born: 27 December 1951, Colchester.

■ Dennis signed on schoolboy forms in April 1967, along with another Monkwick lad Adrian Webster, and progressed through the U's youth team to a professional contract in August 1970. He made his debut in the third to last game of the 1969–70 season, coming on as a substitute against Lincoln, and with only nine fit professionals he was in the starting 11 for the remaining fixtures at Port Vale and Grimsby. Dennis made two further substitute appearances the following season but could not break into Dick Graham's 'Grandad's Army' of experienced professionals and departed for Dover in January 1972. He returned locally to play for Clacton in 1973 and became part of a large North Essex contingent at Tilbury in 1977–78 who took that club to the third round of the FA Cup for the first and only time in their history. As soon as they were out of the cup the money dried up and within three weeks Dennis was back in North Essex with Harwich, rejoining Clacton in the close season. Later he had a spell as player-manager of Brightlingsea United. In 2007 his son Adam Bailey-Dennis followed in his footsteps as a Layer Road apprentice.

	League		Lge Cup		FA Cup		Other	
	A	G	A	G	A	G	A	G
1969–70	2+1	0	0	0	0	0	-	-
1970–71	0+2	0	0	0	0	0	-	-
TOTAL	2+3	0	0	0	0	0	-	-

DENNIS, John Anthony 'Tony'

Height: 5ft 7in. Weight: 10st 7lb.

Born: 1 December 1963, Eton.

■ Dennis signed professionally for Plymouth in December 1981 after completing his apprenticeship at Home Park and having scored in the League Cup earlier in the same season. Despite this he never stepped up a challenge for a first-team spot and left for neighbours Exeter in August 1983 after just 7(+2) League appearances. With just 3(+1) appearances under his belt at St James' Park Dennis slipped into non-League for Bideford, Taunton and then Slough. He was spotted by Cambridge and joined the club in February 1989 for £15,000 and was with them as they rose from the Fourth Division to the second level of English football in successive seasons. When the 'other' U's were relegated at the end of 1992–93 Dennis joined Chesterfield for £20,000 where he featured 4(+6) times during the season. George Burley brought the player to Layer Road on a free transfer in the summer of 1994 and he also served under Steve Wignall. Dennis played in both legs of the Play-off semi-final defeat to Plymouth and was released in the summer to join Lincoln, scoring twice in 23(+5) games. Those proved to be his last in League football. He remained in Lincolnshire and played for non-League Gainsborough Trinity.

	League		Lge Cup		FA Cup		Other	
	A	G	A	G	A	G	A	G
1994–95	32+1	2	2	0	1+3	0	2	0
1995–96	24+8	3	0	0	0	0	3+1	0
TOTAL	56+9	5	2	0	1+3	0	5+1	0

DESBOROUGH, Michael 'Micky'

Born: 28 November 1969, Newham.

■ Desborough answered Colchester manager Roy McDonough's desperate plea for a goalkeeper when he stepped in at the 11th hour to play at Gillingham on 30 October 1993. With John Keeley and Nathan Munson suspended after both had been dismissed in the same match at Hereford, McDonough only had youth-team 'keeper David Schultz available, and he had not even made his reserve debut. McDonough arranged for his former Southend teammate 41-year-old Mervyn Cawston to step in, but at the last minute it was realised that Cawston had received insurance payments and was therefore ineligible. Desborough, who has kept goal for well over a dozen non-League clubs in and around Essex since first appearing with Clapton, was Cawston's deputy at Chelmsford and in the right place at the right time so got the nod. The U's lost 3–0 at Gillingham, but it was probably lucky for Desborough's self esteem that Keeley was back for the following Tuesday evening trip to Feethams; he had to pick the ball out of the net seven times as Colchester lost 7–3. He returned to Chelmsford soon after and later played for Gravesend & Northfleet, Grays Athletic and Bishop's Stortford and was with Hornchurch in 2004–05.

	League		Lge Cup		FA Cup		Other	
	A	G	A	G	A	G	A	G
1993–94	1	0	0	0	0	0	0	0
TOTAL	1	0	0	0	0	0	0	0

DEVEREUX, Robert 'Robbie'

Height: 5ft 8in. Weight: 10st 9lb.

Born: 31 January 1971, Ipswich.

■ A youth trainee with Ipswich, Devereux joined Colchester in the summer of 1989 in an attempt to resurrect his career. He made his bow as a substitute in a 2–0 defeat to York at Layer Road in October of the same year and started in a 4–0 defeat at Scunthorpe eight days later. A dislocated shoulder in a reserve game at Barnet in November put him out of action until the end of March, and he was released at the end of the season. He went back into the Eastern Counties League with Sudbury and briefly went to live in Dublin before returning to play for Conrad United. Roy McDonough then recalled him to Layer Road in February 1992 on a non-contract basis. He had a spell in Ireland with Shelbourne, where former U's player Eamonn Collins was assistant, before becoming a regular with Sudbury Town and AFC Sudbury, making 68(+9) appearances for the newly-formed club from 2000 before retiring through injury.

	League		Lge Cup		FA Cup		Other	
	A	G	A	G	A	G	A	G
1989–90	1+1	0	0	0	0	0	0	0
1992–93	3+3	0	1	0	0	0	1	0
TOTAL	4+4	0	1	0	0	0	1	0

DICKENS, Alan William

Height: 5ft 11in. Weight: 12st 5lb.

Born: 3 September 1964, Plaistow.

■ Schooled at West Ham, Dickens progressed from his apprenticeship to sign pro forms in August 1982. He won five England Youth caps and appeared once for the Under-21 side. Prominent in seven seasons at Upton Park as a replacement for Trevor Brooking, Dickens missed just two games as the Hammers finished third in the top flight in 1985–86. When West Ham were relegated Dickens moved across London to Chelsea for £650,000. He was used sparingly at Stamford Bridge, largely due to the arrival of Vinnie Jones, completing just 39(+9) games in three seasons while scoring a single goal. Loaned out to West Brom, he played three games in December 1992 and two months later signed permanently for Brentford, playing 13(+2) games as the Bees were relegated from Division One. Roy McDonough brought Dickens to Layer Road in September 1993 and the player made his debut as a substitute at Torquay in the same month. Vying with Steve Ball for the midfield shirt, Dickens was released at the end of the season and later played for Chesham, Collier Row, Billericay and Purfleet. He also studied 'The Knowledge' to become a London taxi driver.

	League		Lge Cup		FA Cup		Other	
	A	G	A	G	A	G	A	G
1993–94	28+4	3	0	0	1	0	3	0
TOTAL	28+4	3	0	0	1	0	3	0

DOBSON, Brian Ashley

Born: 1 March 1934, Colchester.

■ Dobson made his senior debut at Aldershot in March 1956 having been a part-time pro since the January of that year. It was already his fifth season with the club, having started in the Border League team in 1951–52, and he had been leading scorer for the reserves in 1954–55 and 1955–56. He was second-top scorer in 1956–57 with 17 goals despite playing a large chunk of the second half of that season at right-back, and by the time he got back into the first team in 1957–58 he had been converted to centre-half. Injury to Chic Milligan gave him a run of games in the latter part of the season, but it was back to the reserves for 1958–59 again, predominantly at centre-half. Two final League games came his way in autumn 1959, in his original position of centre-forward, before he departed for Clacton in the spring. He was not retained by the Seasiders at the end of the year and joined Sudbury Town. He later became Finance Director of a Colchester company.

	League		Lge Cup		FA Cup		Other	
	A	G	A	G	A	G	A	G
1955–56	6	0	-	-	0	0	-	-
1956–57	0	0	-	-	0	0	-	-
1957–58	16	0	-	-	1	0	-	-
1958–59	0	0	-	-	0	0	-	-
1959–60	2	0	-	-	0	0	-	-
TOTAL	24	0	-	-	1	0	-	-

DOCHERTY, John

Height: 5ft 9in. Weight: 11st 11lb.

Born: 28 February 1935, Glasgow.

■ Having started his career at Albion Rovers in 1955, Docherty was signed by St Johnstone from Stirling Albion for £15,000 in 1958. He won the Scottish Second Division with Stirling in 1957–58 and repeated the feat with St Johnstone in 1959–60. Docherty also played 22 times for Hearts following his move to Tynecastle in March 1961, including three Inter-Cities Fairs Cup games alongside future U's player Bobby Blackwood. A virtual permanent fixture in United's Third Division side, he was released following the club's relegation at

the end of 1964–65 and joined Chelmsford. He moved to Bury Town as player-manager in 1968 and led them to the Metropolitan League Championship in his first season, pipping Spurs A by one point, as well as reaching the first round proper of the FA Cup for the first and only time in their history. He spent four years in the job, playing nearly 200 times in the process, before resigning and returning to his West Lothian roots.

	League		Lge Cup		FA Cup		Other	
	A	G	A	G	A	G	A	G
1963–64	36	1	2	0	2	0	-	-
1964–65	41	1	2	0	3	0	-	-
TOTAL	77	2	4	0	5	0	-	-

DOMINEY, Barry William

Height: 6ft. Weight: 12st.

Born: 21 October 1955, Edmonton.
Died: 22 March 2005.

■ Spotted in local football in the London area and signed a month before his 18th birthday, Dominey made his debut as a substitute in the promotion-clinching

draw at Brentford in April 1974. He gained instant fame when scoring the winning goal in a League Cup replay at Second Division Southampton in November 1974. Colchester eventually bowed out in the quarter finals to Aston Villa. He celebrated getting married at Colchester Register Office on Saturday 11 October 1975 by scoring in United's 2–0 win over Walsall later that same day. A regular in Colchester's relegation side of 1975–76 he was released at the end of the season and joined Yeovil, the club his father had represented. He died, tragically young, in 2005.

	League		Lge Cup		FA Cup		Other	
	A	G	A	G	A	G	A	G
1973–74	1+2	0	0	0	0	0	-	-
1974–75	22+5	2	3	1	2	0	-	-
1975–76	32+6	1	2	0	2	1	-	-
1976–77	1+2	0	0	0	0	0	-	-
TOTAL	56+15	3	5	1	4	1	-	-

DONALD, Warren Ramsey

Height: 5ft 7in. Weight: 10st 1lb.

Born: 7 October 1964, Uxbridge.

■ Beginning his career at Upton Park as a West Ham apprentice, Donald had already gained England Schoolboy honours before signing professional in October 1982. He made just 1(+1) appearances for the Hammers and after completing an 11-game two-goal loan spell at Northampton in March 1985 signed permanently for the Cobblers in the close season of 1985. He established himself in the side and won promotion to Division Three in 1986–87. After completing a further 169(+8) League games, scoring 11 goals, Donald was released following Northampton's relegation at the end of 1989–90. Ian Atkins snapped up the player for Conference side Colchester, and he became a stalwart as United won their way back into the League at the second attempt in 1991–92. Donald collected a Conference Championship medal and a week later won at Wembley as United beat Witton 3–1 in the FA Trophy Final. Notoriously the only member of the regular senior squad who failed to score in 1991–92, he spent the last 20 minutes of the Barrow game at centre-forward as his teammates were more concerned with getting him on the score sheet than adding to the comfortable victory that was securing the club's return to the

Football League. That did not work so in the post season intra-club promotion-celebration exhibition game an early penalty was conjured up for him. However, youth team goalie Paul Gothard (a future England semi-pro international) who had recently been told the club could not afford to offer him a pro contract, had his own point to make to the management and was not about to give a goal away cheaply. He blocked the penalty, but Donald managed to get his goal from the rebound. Donald featured in a handful of United's return to the League fixtures but lost his place to Martin Grainger and joined Kettering, playing a further 80(+2) Conference games for the Rockingham Road club.

	League		Lge Cup		FA Cup		Other	
	A	G	A	G	A	G	A	G
1990–91	*33+5*	*1*	*1*	*0*	*3*	*0*	*4*	*0*
1991–92	*38+3*	*0*	*1*	*0*	*3*	*0*	*8*	*0*
1992–93	8+2	0	2	0	0	0	1+1	0
TOTAL	8+2	0	2	0	0	0	1+1	0
	71+8	*1*	*2*	*0*	*6*	*0*	*12*	*0*

DOWMAN, Stephen John 'Steve'

Height: 5ft 11in. Weight: 12st 4lb.

Born: 14 April 1958, Manor Park.

■ Former apprentice Dowman burst on the scene as an 18-year-old, scoring an incredible 12 League goals in his first professional season. After three substitute appearances, he made his full debut against Torquay in November 1976, scoring in a 4–0 U's win. He formed a formidable central defensive partnership

with Lindsay Smith as United won promotion and took First Division Derby to a replay in the FA Cup. Smith departed, but Dowman teamed up with Mick Packer, and once again Dowman performed on the big stage in a League Cup tie at Leeds. In 1978–79 it was Steve Wignall's turn to become Dowman's defensive partner in a season when U's hosted Manchester United in the FA Cup. With Bobby Roberts's side failing to reach the second tier at the end of 1979–80 Dowman sought new challenges and signed for Wrexham in a £75,000 deal. Scoring two goals in 87 League games, Dowman got the Second Division football he craved. In the summer of 1983 he signed for Second Division Charlton after Wrexham suffered their second successive relegation. He completed 60(+1) games for the Addicks, scoring five times but was sold to Newport in August 1985. After just two months, nine games and a single goal, he joined a Cambridge side that was plummeting from the Second to Fourth Divisions in successive seasons. Scoring three goals in 45 League games, Cambridge incorporated a pre-season friendly with Ipswich in 1987 as a benefit match for the player. A spell in non-League with Heybridge led Dowman to become manager of Essex Senior League side Brightlingsea in 1987, and he led them to the League title in 1989. Dowman went to Ryman League Wivenhoe as a player in early 1992, taking on the management role there a year later, and then had a spell in charge of Jewson League Clacton before returning to Heybridge as boss in the summer of 2001.

	League		Lge Cup		FA Cup		Other	
	A	G	A	G	A	G	A	G
1976–77	33+3	12	0	0	6	0	-	-
1977–78	43	5	5	1	4	1	-	-
1978–79	37+1	2	2	1	7	2	-	-
1979–80	37	2	3+1	0	4	0	-	-
TOTAL	150+4	21	10+1	2	21	3	-	-

DOZZELL, Jason Alvin Winans

Height: 6ft 1in. Weight: 13st 8lb.

Born: 9 December 1967, Ipswich.

■ Dozzell was discovered playing for Langham Lions, towering above youngsters of his own age, and signed as a professional for Ipswich in December 1984. He had already made his First Division debut at the age of 16 years and 56 days against Coventry in 1983–84, scoring in a 3–1 win to become the then youngest-ever player and goalscorer in top flight history. Converted to a striker by John Lyall, Dozzell helped Ipswich to the Second Division title in 1991–92 with 11 goals. On the way he earned England Youth honours and nine caps at Under-21 level. After 312(+20) games for Town he secured a £1.9 million move to Tottenham in the summer of 1993. Things did not go too well at White Hart Lane, and the player made just 68(+16) appearances in five seasons, bagging 13 goals. He returned briefly to George Burley's Ipswich in October 1997, scoring once in eight non-contract games before securing a permanent move to Northampton. The Cobblers

lost in the Second Division Play-off Final of 1997–98, and after completing 18(+3) games and scoring four goals he was persuaded by Colchester boss Steve Whitton to try his luck at Layer Road. He rekindled his career despite a series of brushes with the law but was forced to retire in 2001 because of a niggling toe injury. Dozzell turned out for Canvey Island, becoming player-manager of Ipswich Wanderers in 2003–04. He took over as manager of Eastern Counties League Leiston three seasons later.

	League		Lge Cup		FA Cup		Other	
	A	G	A	G	A	G	A	G
1998–99	23+6	4	0	0	1	0	0+1	0
1999–2000	38+1	5	2	1	1	0	1	0
2000–01	22	0	4	0	1	0	1	0
TOTAL	83+7	9	6	1	3	0	2+1	0

DRING, Raymond 'Ray'

Born: 13 February 1924, Lincoln.
Died: 21 October 2003, Lincoln.

■ Lance Corporal Dring served in the 17th Infantry Training Corps and was on the books of Huddersfield as amateur. He represented England Schoolboys against Ireland in April 1938, but his chances were curtailed by the war. A back injury suffered in an Army game meant he was not available to the U's after October 1945, but he eventually recovered to make his Huddersfield debut against Grimsby in Division One on 10 September 1947. Ten days later he made his fourth and final first-team appearance for the Leeds Road club. After football, he became a PE teacher in the Lincoln area before becoming a storeman at a car showroom.

	League		Lge Cup		FA Cup		Other	
	A	G	A	G	A	G	A	G
1945–46	2	0	0	0	1	0	-	-
TOTAL	2	0	0	0	1	0	-	-

DUBLIN, Keith Barry Lennox

Height: 5ft 11in. Weight: 11st 10lb.

Born: 29 January 1968, High Wycombe.

■ Dublin arrived at Colchester on loan from Southend in November 1998 making his debut in a 3–1 win at Notts County. He only played one further game, citing that he could not bear the extra driving involved in getting to Colchester rather than Southend from his home. Earlier, his career had begun as a Chelsea apprentice, and he made the step up to full forms in January 1984, having been voted

Steve Dowman

Young Player of the Year. All but one of his 50(+1) appearances were in the top flight, but in the summer of 1987 he was sold to Third Division Brighton for £35,000. Albion finished runners-up and Dublin was ever present. Missing only six games over the next two seasons, he earned a £275,000 move to Watford in July 1990. He completed 165(+3) games at Vicarage Road, netting twice, before joining fellow First Division Southend for £100,000 in the 1994 close season. Southend were about to free-fall from the second tier, but Dublin featured 175(+4) times in five seasons at Roots Hall, scoring nine. Following the collapse of his Colchester loan deal, he returned to South Essex but made just two further appearances for the Shrimpers. He moved into non-League and played for Canvey Island, Farnborough and Carshalton.

	League		Lge Cup		FA Cup		Other	
	A	G	A	G	A	G	A	G
1998–99	2	0	0	0	0	0	0	0
TOTAL	2	0	0	0	0	0	0	0

DUDLEY, Frank Ernest

Height: 6ft. Weight: 10st 8lb.

Born: 9 May 1925, Southend.

■ Dudley joined Southend as a 16-year-old and signed professional in October 1945 after serving in the Air Training Corps, scoring a creditable 32 goals in 88 League appearances. This tally included two hat-tricks in March 1947. He scored twice in his only Colchester appearance against Barry in February 1946 as a stand-in for George Barnard who had completed his transfer to Arsenal. Dudley moved to Leeds for the 1949–50 season and went on to score 23 goals in 64 League games at Elland Road. The fee was a Southend record at £10,000 and included Albert Wakefield in exchange. Dudley was top scorer in his first season at Leeds with 16 League and four Cup strikes. After a further 11 goals in 1951–52 he signed for Southampton in February 1952 where he continued his goalscoring with 31 goals in 67 starts for the Saints. In 1953–54 his first three goals all came in different divisions as he scored for Saints in Division Three South, Cardiff (on loan in Division One) and Brentford (Division Two). He retired from League football at Griffin Park in 1958 after 31 goals in 73 games and played non-League for Folkestone. In 1961 he rejoined Southend as coach, having gained FA badges, until 1965 and then worked in local government until his retirement in 1985.

	League		Lge Cup		FA Cup		Other	
	A	G	A	G	A	G	A	G
1945–46	1	2	0	0	0	0	-	-
TOTAL	1	2	0	0	0	0	-	-

DUFFETT, Sean R.

Born: Colchester.

■ The then U's coach Ian Phillips also had coaching connections with Colchester junior side Gas Recreation, and local lad Duffett had caught his eye playing for Gas in 1990–91. Duffett began 1991–92 as a trialist in the reserves at Layer Road and impressed in an Essex Senior Cup tie against Tilbury when he scored both the U's goals. He got his first-team chance in a Bob Lord Trophy tie against Kettering in October 1991, deputising for Roy McDonough in the number-nine shirt and was signed on a non-contract basis. He continued to be a regular member of the reserve squad into the New Year while also playing for Wivenhoe Town whom he had signed for back in September 1991. After cutting his ties with Layer Road, he stayed with Wivenhoe until October 1992 when he switched to Brightlingsea United and subsequently went back to playing locally in the Border and Colchester & East Essex Leagues.

	League		Lge Cup		FA Cup		Other	
	A	G	A	G	A	G	A	G
1991–92	0	0	1	0	0	0	0	0
TOTAL	0	0	1	0	0	0	0	0

DUGUID, Karl Anthony

Height: 5ft 11in. Weight: 11st 9lb.

Born: 21 March 1978, Hitchin.

■ Duguid, a YTS product, epitomises the one-club career that used to be prevalent in English football. A loyal player, whose career was almost ended in 2004, he came back to gloriously captain his club into the Championship two years later. Brave enough to take a penalty at Wembley in the Auto Windscreens Shield Final against Carlisle in 1997, when other more senior players shirked the responsibility, Duguid was endeared for his tears, having missed from 12 yards. Tears turned to joy a year later at the same venue as Duguid once again appeared as a Wembley substitute as United secured promotion from Division Three against Torquay in the Play-off Final. His most prolific scoring season came in 1999–

2000 under Steve Whitton when he finished third-top scorer behind Steve McGavin and Lomana Lua Lua. Duguid enjoyed FA Cup runs in both 2003–04 and 2005–06, the latter when Colchester faced Premiership champions Chelsea at Stamford Bridge live on Sky TV. Having suffered knee ligament damage against Stockport in March 2004 it was fitting that Duguid, after fighting his way back to fitness, be appointed club captain and go on to lead United into the second tier of English football and into a new stadium for 2008–09.

	League		Lge Cup		FA Cup		Other	
	A	G	A	G	A	G	A	G
1995–96	7+9	1	0	0	0	0	0+1	0
1996–97	10+10	3	0+2	0	0+1	0	1+1	0
1997–98	6+15	3	0	0	3+1	0	0+3	0
1998–99	23+10	4	0+1	0	0+1	0	0	0
1999–2000	40+1	12	2	0	1	0	0	0
2000–01	34+7	5	3	0	1	1	1	0
2001–02	36+5	4	1	0	2	1	1	0
2002–03	26+1	3	0	0	0	0	0	0
2003–04	30	2	2	0	6	0	4	0
2004–05	0	0	0	0	0	0	0	0
2005–06	26+9	0	0	0	4+1	0	5	1
2006–07	42+1	5	1	0	0+1	0	-	-
2007–08	37	0	1	0	0+1	0	-	-
TOTAL	317+68	42	10+3	0	17+6	2	12+5	1

DUNN, Ronald Victor 'Ronnie'

Height: 5ft 9½in. Weight: 13st.

Born: 24 November 1908, Southall.
Died: January 1994, Swale.

■ Serving in the 2nd Dorset Regiment, Dunn was a bugler and talented cornet player in the Army and also represented his Regiment at football when 18 years old. In 1929 he played with Wealdstone, and between 1931 and 1936 he kept goal for Crystal Palace on 167 occasions in the Football League. He had originally been spotted in an Armed Services game at Selhurst Park. He was taken on as understudy to Billy Callender, taking up the mantle when his mentor committed suicide. A prominent member of the Crystal Palace Prize Band – when Bath visited for the first-ever professional game at Layer Road on 2 September 1937 in the Midweek section of the Southern League – Dunn used his musical background to welcome the players of both teams onto the pitch. His rendition of the Post Horn Gallop stuck and is still played regularly today as the teams enter the field of play. Dunn was certainly a character, and during one Eastern Counties League game for the reserves against Newmarket Town he was actually seen to light up a cigarette and lean up against a post, unemployed, as his colleagues demolished the Jockeys by 7–1. Due a benefit at Selhurst Park, Palace manager Tom Bromilow instead brought the full Crystal Palace side to Layer Road in recognition of his services. George Williams bagged a pair for United as they ran out 2–1 winners in front of a crowd of 4,614. The game was all the more poignant as Dunn's father had died just two days earlier at his home on the south coast; it was also Cliff Fairchild's last game in a United shirt before he joined Arsenal. Released by United at the end of 1937–38, Dunn was retained to help out United's second string. Called up as a reservist in 1939, Dunn spent five years in West Africa but on his return to Colchester decided not to return to the game.

	League		Lge Cup		FA Cup		Other	
	A	G	A	G	A	G	A	G
1937–38	31	0	5	0	-	-	15	0
1938–39	1	0	0	0	0	0	2	0
TOTAL	32	0	5	0	0	0	17	0

DUNNE, Austin

Born: 31 July 1934, Limerick.
Died: March 2007.

■ Dunne was signed from League of Ireland club Limerick City in October 1953, having played for them from the age of 15 years old. He had won an Irish junior cap against Scotland in 1950 but his solitary first-team appearance for Colchester came at Gillingham in April 1955 as United languished at the bottom of Division Three South. He was released at the end of the season by new manager

Benny Fenton, and he joined non-League Tonbridge.

	League		Lge Cup		FA Cup		Other	
	A	G	A	G	A	G	A	G
1954–55	1	0	-	-	0	0	-	-
TOTAL	1	0	-	-	0	0	-	-

DUNNE, Joseph John 'Joe'

Height: 5ft 8in. Weight: 11st 6lb.

Born: 25 May 1973, Dublin, ROI.

■ Representing the Republic of Ireland at Schoolboy, Youth and once at Under-21 level, Dunne joined Gillingham as a YTS player, signing professionally in August 1990. Scoring once in 108(+7) League games Dunne joined Steve Wignall's U's in March 1996, making his debut as a substitute at Hartlepool in the same month. His first goal for the club was vital as it secured a 19th-minute win at Mansfield in the penultimate game of the season. United qualified for the Play-offs a week later but lost to Plymouth. A year on and Dunne played at Wembley

as United took on Carlisle in the Auto Windscreens Shield Final and again 12 months later as Colchester beat Torquay to secure promotion to the third tier. A steady campaigner, dogged by injury, Dunne was unceremoniously released in the summer of 1999 by new manager Mick Wadsworth who brought in Frenchman Fabrice Richard in his place. Dunne played 11 times for Conference side Dover, and when Wadsworth left new manager Steve Whitton re-engaged Dunne and the defender went on to add to his Colchester career before having to quit following a knee injury against Bury in November 2001. Dunne stayed with the club and became coach of the Under-17 side, replacing Micky Cook as senior youth-team coach in August 2003. He stepped up to reserve-team boss in 2007 and, following the departure of assistant manager Micky Adams, Dunne was appointed first-team coach.

	League		Lge Cup		FA Cup		Other	
	A	G	A	G	A	G	A	G
1995–96	2+3	1	0	0	0	0	0	0
1996–97	23+12	0	3	1	1	0	2+1	0
1997–98	22+3	2	0	0	3+1	0	4	0
1998–99	32+4	0	0+1	0	1	0	1	0
1999–2000	19+1	0	0	0	0	0	0	0
2000–01	31+3	1	3	0	0+1	0	1	0
2001–02	6+2	2	1	0	0+1	0	0	0
TOTAL	135+28	6	7+1	1	5+3	0	8+1	0

DUQUEMIN, Leonard Stanley 'Len'

Height: 5ft 10in. Weight: 12st 9lb.

Born: 17 July 1924, Cobo, Guernsey.
Died: 20 April 2003, Buckhurst Hill.

■ Duquemin was a native of Guernsey during the German occupation. Football continued in Guernsey during this time unless the Germans wanted the fields for military reasons. Food became critically short towards the end of the war, but Duquemin was working in a market garden attached to Vimiera monastery. It was the Brothers of Vimiera, who only spoke French, that let him eat the produce just at the time when his body needed the growing strength that eventually made him a strong centre-forward. Duquemin was recommended by a Spurs fan and attended a trial at White Hart Lane in December 1945. He was immediately signed up and was sent to Chelmsford to gain some experience. He made just one

appearance at Swindon reserves for City and played his one and only game for Colchester at Chelmsford in the Southern League Cup on 3 April 1946. U's lost 2–0. His first game for Tottenham was in March 1946 at Fulham, but it was not until the next season that he was elevated to the first team on a regular basis after Spurs reserves crushed Brighton 13–0. 'Duke', as he would become known, netted the fifth in a 5–1 win over Sheffield Wednesday at White Hart Lane. He then embarked on an incredible career at Tottenham, winning a Division Two Championship medal in 1950 and the First Division equivalent in 1951, becoming Spurs' sixth all-time top scorer behind Jimmy Greaves, Bobby Smith, Martin Chivers, Cliff Jones and G.S. Hunt, with 134 goals in 308 games. His final game was at Newcastle in March 1957. He moved on to Bedford where his 22 goals in 22 games earned Town the Southern League title in 1958–59. The following season he scored 33 times and then had spells at Hastings and Romford. He continued to play for Showbiz XIs and ran a pub before retiring.

	League		Lge Cup		FA Cup		Other	
	A	G	A	G	A	G	A	G
1945–46	0	0	1	0	0	0	-	-
TOTAL	0	0	1	0	0	0	-	-

DYER, Paul David

Height: 5ft 9in. Weight: 12st.

Born: 24 January 1954, Leicester.

■ Dyer was signed by new U's boss Bobby Roberts in the summer of 1975. Initially on trial, the midfielder joined from Notts County for whom he had signed in September 1972 and accrued 1(+6) appearances. His first Colchester

goals came as a pair in a 3–2 reverse at Port Vale. He played regularly in the side that won promotion from Division Four in 1976–77 and in the big Cup ties against Derby, Leeds and Manchester United. On being released from Layer Road he had a spell with Gravesend & Northfleet and managed in the Eastern Counties League. He became chief scout at Layer Road in August 1991 and was still in that role in 2007–08. Dyer has been a publican at various locations over the years and memorably held the licence for The Lamb in Colchester High Street at the time the club were in the Conference. The establishment was much favoured by the players of the time and manager Roy McDonough, a fact commemorated in the title of the contemporary U's fanzine *Always See Him In The Lamb On Saturday Night.*

	League		Lge Cup		FA Cup		Other	
	A	G	A	G	A	G	A	G
1975–76	34+2	2	2	0	2	0	-	-
1976–77	29+5	0	3	0	4+2	0	-	-
1977–78	21+9	0	1	0	0+1	0	-	-
1978–79	37+3	2	2	0	5	0	-	-
1979–80	3+1	0	0	0	0	0	-	-
TOTAL	124+20	4	8	0	11+3	0	-	-

DYSON, John Barry

Height: 5ft 10in. Weight: 11st 7lb.

Born: 6 September 1942, Oldham.
Died: 26 February 1995.

■ Dyson began his career at Bury as an apprentice in September 1960. His career got off to a bang having joined Tranmere in the summer of 1962. Dyson bagged an incredible 100 League goals in just 174 games, twice scoring more than 30 in a season. Sold to Crystal Palace in

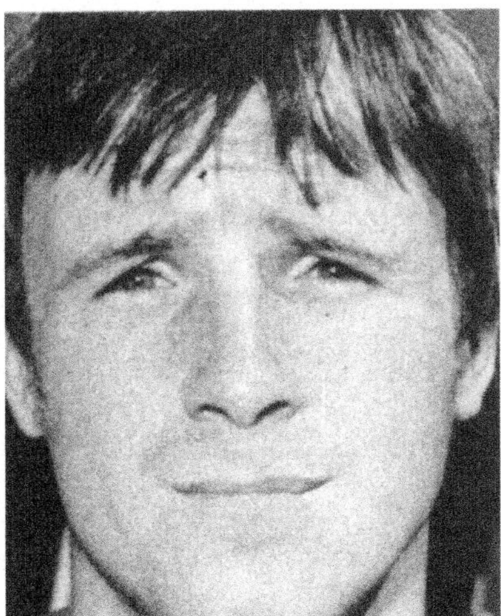

September 1966 for £15,000, he scored a hat-trick in only his second appearance but found the net just six more times in 33(+1) League games for Palace. By January 1968 he had joined Watford for £9,000, scoring 19 in 39 League starts for the Hornets. His stay was short as Leyton Orient paid £8,000 for his services, and he scored 28 times in 154(+6) games for the O's. Converted to a midfielder, he was released at the end of 1972–73 and joined Colchester. Starring in United's promotion to Division Three, he was the regular penalty taker but for 1974–75 was mostly used as the old head in the reserves and A teams. The A team had been resurrected and entered into the Essex Senior League, but well before the end of the season it was decided the cost of running a third team could not be justified and so the venture only lasted the one year. By mid-February 1975 Dyson was on loan at Chelmsford and made the move to New Writtle Street permanent on deadline day. He was manager of Borehamwood in 1984 and ran a Colchester-based haulage firm before suffering a fatal heart attack aged just 52.

	League		Lge Cup		FA Cup		Other	
	A	G	A	G	A	G	A	G
1973–74	36	6	1	0	1	0	-	-
1974–75	5+1	1	0+1	0	0	0	-	-
TOTAL	41+1	7	1+1	0	1	0	-	-

DYSON, Terence Kent 'Terry'

Height: 5ft 4in. Weight: 10st 4lb.

Born: 29 November 1934, Malton.

■ Dyson, the son of a famous jockey – 'Ginger' Dyson, joined Spurs as an amateur in 1954 while on National Service at Woolwich and having been on the books of Scarborough. Turning professional in 1955, he was devastated when Tottenham paid £35,000 to Swansea for Cliff Jones three years later. Dyson thought his Spurs career would be over but resolved to fight on and was rewarded when he was part of the Tottenham side that won the double in 1960–61. One of the shortest players around, Dyson missed only two League games and scored one of the goals that won the FA Cup by 2–0 against Leicester. He also scored twice in the European Cup-Winners' Cup Final of 1963 as Spurs thrashed Atletico Madrid 5–1 in Rotterdam. After a magnificent career at White Hart Lane, he signed for Fulham in June 1965 for £5,000. Playing just 22 games for the Cottagers, scoring three goals, Dyson was brought to Layer Road by Dick Graham on a two-month trial during his restructuring phase and given a contract midway through. After more than a half-century of games for United he joined Guildford in 1970, winning the Southern League Division One South, and had a spell at King's Lynn. Becoming player-coach at Wealdstone in 1972, he again won the Southern League Division One South title in 1973–74, having been joined by Micky Brown, Eddie Presland and Ray Whittaker – all former U's players. His greatest non-League achievement was steering Dagenham to a Wembley FA Trophy win in 1980 after which he managed Borehamwood, Kingsbury Town and Ruislip while teaching at a Hampstead School.

	League		Lge Cup		FA Cup		Other	
	A	G	A	G	A	G	A	G
1968–69	40+1	3	0	0	2	0	-	-
1969–70	13+2	1	0	0	0	0	-	-
TOTAL	53+3	4	0	0	2	0	-	-

E

EAGLES, Alan James

Height: 5ft 10in. Weight: 11st 8lb.

Born: 6 September 1933, Edgware.
Died: 6 November 1995, Pembrokeshire.

■ A right-back by trade, Eagles joined Leyton Orient from Carshalton in May 1957. After 80 League and Cup appearances at Leyton, he signed for United in a £3,000 deal in January 1961. Eagles featured in 16 games at Layer Road as U's were relegated to Division Four. In the summer of 1961 he joined QPR but failed to make a first-team appearance, subsequently joining Aldershot by the November. After just 15 League games for the Shots he drifted into non-League where he played for Yiewsley, Hillingdon, Deal, Gravesend & Northfleet and Pembroke. He became harbour superintendent at Tenby and ran a hotel in Saundersfoot. His only career goal came for United in the 2–1 Essex derby defeat at Southend in February 1961.

	League		Lge Cup		FA Cup		Other	
	A	G	A	G	A	G	A	G
1960–61	16	1	0	0	0	0	-	-
TOTAL	16	1	0	0	0	0	-	-

EDWARDS, Michael 'Mike'

Height: 6ft. Weight: 12st.

Born: 25 April 1980, North Ferriby.

■ A Hull City youth trainee, Edwards made an impressive 165(+13) League appearance for his local club, scoring six times from central defence. Signed by Phil Parkinson on deadline day 2003, Edwards appeared just five times in a United shirt, making his debut at Plymouth in a 0–0 draw. Not retained, he joined Grimsby in the August and scored once in 32(+1) games. Moving to Notts County in August 2004, Edwards sustained a leg injury after just eight games for his new club and missed the rest of the season. He returned to be a virtual permanent fixture over the next two campaigns, missing just one game and scoring 10 at Meadow Lane. Having been voted Player of the Year for 2006–07, Edwards's season was put on hold when breaking his leg in a Notts County friendly in July 2007.

	League		Lge Cup		FA Cup		Other	
	A	G	A	G	A	G	A	G
2002–03	3+2	0	0	0	0	0	0	0
TOTAL	3+2	0	0	0	0	0	0	0

EDWARDS, Stanley Llewelyn 'Stan'

Height: 5ft 11in. Weight: 11st 6lb.

Born: 17 October 1926, Dawdon.
Died: 14 January 1989, Bromley.

■ Edwards's early football was played with Horden Colliery. In 1948 he joined Chelsea and caught the eye in Harry Bearryman's testimonial in April 1952, scoring Chelsea's winning goal. Colchester paid £750 a few weeks later,

and he scored on his debut against Swindon. U's manager Jimmy Allen's resignation prompted a move to Leyton Orient, which resulted in Tommy Harris making the opposite journey – Colchester's first-ever swap deal. At Brisbane Road he was unfortunate to break his leg twice playing for the reserves despite also scoring on his O's debut against Shrewsbury in October 1953. After two seasons and just two League games, he joined Chelmsford but broke his leg again, on 27 December 1955 against Exeter, and had to retire. He took up work as a salesman for a rubber manufacturing company.

	League		Lge Cup		FA Cup		Other	
	A	G	A	G	A	G	A	G
1952–53	16	5	-	-	3	2	-	-
TOTAL	16	5	-	-	3	2	-	-

ELDER, James 'Jimmy'

Height: 5ft 8½in. Weight: 11st 4lb.

Born: 5 August 1928, Perth.

■ Elder became new manager Jimmy Allen's first signing as the League era dawned at Layer Road. Brought in as a left half-back, Elder had broken into the Portsmouth Combination side at the tender age of 17 as a wing-half. He made one full appearance during Pompey's 1949–50 League Championship-winning season and failed by just one game to reach the 200 appearances milestone for the U's. On leaving Colchester, Elder had

three seasons at Yeovil until 1958 before becoming a prison officer in Dover. Arthritis had finally ended his playing career, and he moved to work at a Young Offenders Institution near Olney in Warwickshire.

	League		Lge Cup		FA Cup		Other	
	A	G	A	G	A	G	A	G
1950–51	45	4	-	-	1	0	-	-
1951–52	44	2	-	-	3	1	-	-
1952–53	45	3	-	-	5	0	-	-
1953–54	37	4	-	-	2	0	-	-
1954–55	28	2	-	-	2	1	-	-
TOTAL	199	15	-	-	13	2	-	-

ELITO, Medy

Height: 6ft. Weight: 10st 11lb.

Born: 20 March 1990.

■ Elito made his senior youth-team debut as a 14-year-old substitute in November 2004 and made two further appearances from the bench in FA Youth Cup ties later that month. He had his first run-out with Colchester reserves on 29 August 2006 against the second string of Ipswich. He earned his first England Under-17 cap in February 2007 against Portugal and was part of the England Under-17 World Cup squad in Korea in August and September 2007 playing twice. He was also capped at Under-18 level in both internationals played in that age group during 2007–08 to take his current total to six. Elito finally got his chance for United in unfortunate circumstances. Named as substitute against Plymouth in March 2008 Elito replaced fellow substitute Izale McLeod who had suffered a serious knee injury 11 minutes after entering the field. He scored his first goal at West Brom in March 2008 and started six of the U's last seven games.

	League		Lge Cup		FA Cup		Other	
	A	G	A	G	A	G	A	G
2007-08	7+4	1	0	0	0	0	-	-
TOTAL	7+4	1	0	0	0	0	-	-

ELLIOTT, Shaun

Height: 6ft. Weight: 11st.

Born: 26 January 1957, Haltwhistle.

■ Making his Sunderland debut just two weeks short of his 20th birthday in January 1977, Elliott became a rock in the heart of the Wearsiders defence, turning out in 316(+5) League games and netting 12 times. He missed just one game as Sunderland won promotion back to the top flight in 1979–80 and won three England B caps, including an emotional appearance against Spain at his home ground Roker Park. Set for a testimonial, Elliott was sold to Norwich in the summer of 1986 just a year after being robbed, by suspension, of a Wembley appearance against the Canaries in the League Cup Final. At Carrow Road he made 29(+2) appearances, scoring twice before moving North West to Blackpool in August 1988. When his new club was relegated at the end of 1989–90 Elliott was released after completing 66(+1) outings for the Tangerines. Making his Colchester debut in a shock 3–0 defeat at Merthyr Tydfil in December 1990, Elliott signed full-time after a tribunal-set transfer but was to suffer Wembley

heart-ache once again as U's boss Roy McDonough left the defender out of his side to face Witton in the 1992 FA Trophy Final. In footballing terms the selection of loanee Dave Martin, a seasoned professional with over 400 League games and over six years younger than the 35-year-old Elliott, was a reasonable decision, but it was well known that Martin was also a good mate of McDonough's and Elliott declined the invitation to sit on the subs' bench, leaving Eamon Collins to step into that role. Having collected a Conference Championship medal, Elliott returned to the North East and played for Gateshead 28(+4) times during the 1992–93 Conference season. He also turned out for Whitley Bay and Bishop Auckland before returning to live in Norwich in 2003.

	League		Lge Cup		FA Cup		Other	
	A	G	A	G	A	G	A	G
1990–91	14+5	0	0	0	0	0	3	0
1991–92	32+5	1	0	0	2	0	5	0
TOTAL	46+10	1	8	0	2	0	8	0

ELLIS, Glen Douglas

Height: 5ft 10in. Weight: 12st.

Born: 31 October 1957, Dagenham.

■ England schoolboy international Ellis became one of only two players to interrupt Mike Walker's 451 League game United appearance record. An apprentice with Ipswich, Ellis failed to make a start at Portman Road but was called in as cover by U's boss Bobby Roberts when reserve 'keeper Ian Cranstone was injured (and ruled out for the season) and was on the spot to get a

first-team chance when Walker was injured. Ellis earned a 100 per cent record as U's beat Watford 1–0 on his February 1977 debut at Layer Road and followed up with a 2–1 win at Newport four days later. He left Ipswich in the summer and was initially reported to have signed for the U's, but this was quickly rescinded and he spent some time at Harlow Town during 1977–78.

	League		Lge Cup		FA Cup		Other	
	A	G	A	G	A	G	A	G
1976–77	2	0	0	0	0	0	-	-
TOTAL	2	0	0	0	0	0	-	-

ELOKOBI, George Nganyuo

Height: 6ft 1in. Weight: 13st 2lb.

Born: 31 January 1986, Cameroon.

■ Elokobi was spotted by the Colchester scouting system while playing for non-Leaguers Dulwich Hamlet. Joining United in July 2004, the aim was to mould the player into League standard,

so in January 2005 he was loaned to League Two Chester, managed by Ian Rush, to gain match experience. Playing 4(+1) games, Elokobi also received a red card in a 5–0 defeat at Shrewsbury. He made his U's debut as a substitute in a 2–0 League Cup defeat to Cardiff in August 2006, scoring his first goal exactly a month later in a 1–1 draw with Huddersfield. As a squad member he helped United to runners'-up spot in League One in 2005–06, but chances were limited in U's first season in the Championship by the almost season-long loan of Chris Barker. When Barker opted to join QPR in the summer Elokobi grasped the chance to make the left-back slot his own, despite the attentions of the experienced summer signing of Danny Granville. Vowing not to renew his contract, Elokobi was sold to Wolves in January 2008 for £500,000.

	League		Lge Cup		FA Cup		Other	
	A	G	A	G	A	G	A	G
2005–06	10+2	1	0+1	0	0	0	4	1
2006–07	8+2	0	0	0	0	0	-	-
2007–08	17	1	1	0	1	0	-	-
TOTAL	35+4	2	1+1	0	1	0	4	1

EMBERSON, Carl Wayne

Height: 6ft 1in. Weight: 14st 9lb.

Born: 13 July 1973, Epsom.

■ Emberson began his career at Millwall as a youth trainee, winning the FA Youth Cup in 1990–91. He played just one Anglo-Italian Cup tie for the South Londoners in a qualifying round game against Crystal Palace. Unfortunately Emberson was sent off. Answering Roy McDonough's desperate goalkeeping shortage, he joined Colchester on loan in December 1992, making a winning debut at Gillingham in the same month. Returning to Millwall, he failed to break into the first team and eventually signed permanently for Colchester for a fee of £25,000 in the summer of 1994. Without a manager following McDonough's sacking, Emberson was signed by the board but found himself not in new manager George Burley's plans. Burley preferred to play John Cheesewright. Eventually making the number-one slot his own after Burley's shock exit, Emberson helped United reach the Play-off semi-finals in 1995–96 and enjoyed two Wembley appearances as United faced Carlisle and Torquay in the Auto

Windscreens Shield and Third Division Play-off Finals respectively. Refusing to sign a new contract, he moved to Walsall in the summer of 1999 but played just 6(+2) League games in two seasons. Moving to Luton on a free transfer in July 2001, Emberson re-established himself and featured 51(+2) times for the Hatters, winning promotion in his first season. His final move came in July 2003 when he teamed up with ex-U's manager Steve Wignall at Roots Hall, playing six times in the League for Southend. He then moved into non-League with Conference side Grays Athletic and later Sutton United before becoming part of the 'Keeps' Goalkeeping School. He was assistant manager to former U's player Dave Swindlehurst at Whyteleafe in 2006–07.

	League		Lge Cup		FA Cup		Other	
	A	G	A	G	A	G	A	G
1992–93	13	0	0	0	0	0	0	0
1994–95	19+1	0	1	0	1	0	0	0
1995–96	41	0	2	0	1	0	5	0
1996–97	35	0	2	0	1	0	6	0
1997–98	46	0	2	0	4	0	4	0
1998–99	37	0	2	0	1	0	1	0
TOTAL	191+1	0	9	0	8	0	16	0

ENGLISH, Anthony Karl 'Tony'

Height: 6ft. Weight: 11st.

Born: 10 October 1966, Luton.

■ Capped at England Youth level, English began his apprenticeship with Coventry but was homesick and came back to Colchester just after his 18th birthday. He was quickly snapped up by Cyril Lea and made his bow as a substitute at Wrexham on New Year's Day 1985, a month after

signing pro forms. His first goal came at Blackpool in March 1985. He was joined at Layer Road by his brother Tom who had been engaged initially on a non-contract basis. On 22 April 1986 Tony scored a Layer Road hat-trick in a 5–0 win over Peterborough just four days after Tom had inflicted a similar treble on Preston. Remarkably, the following week both the English brothers and Crewe's Gary Blissett were all sent of after a mêlée at Gresty Road, big brother having run a long way to get involved. English played in Mike Walker's side that lost to Wolves in the 1986–87 Fourth Division Play-off semi-finals and then suffered as United plummeted towards the Conference. He stuck by the U's and was rewarded by captaining Colchester to a glorious Conference and Wembley FA Trophy double in 1991–92 under Roy McDonough. He finally called it a day in 1995–96 as Steve Wignall began to build a new side. A magnificent servant in over 500 games, English moved into local non-League with Sudbury, Heybridge, Harwich & Parkeston before retiring completely from Halstead in March 2005.

	League		Lge Cup		FA Cup		Other	
	A	G	A	G	A	G	A	G
1984–85	20+2	3	0	0	0	0	2+1	0
1985–86	45	10	2	0	1	0	0+1	0
1986–87	32	7	1	0	3	0	4	0
1987–88	43	2	2	0	3	0	3	0
1988–89	36	8	1	0	6	0	2	0
1989–90	44	2	2	0	2	0	1	0
1990–91	*39+1*	*7*	*1*	*0*	*3*	*0*	*3+1*	*0*
1991–92	*37+1*	*6*	*2*	*0*	*3*	*0*	*9*	*2*
1992–93	30+3	1	2	1	3	0	1	0
1993–94	42	4	2	0	1	1	4	0
1994–95	33	2	2	0	4	1	2	0
1995–96	20+1	0	2	0	1	0	3+1	0
TOTAL	345+6	39	16	1	24	2	22+3	0
	76+2	*13*	*3*	*0*	*6*	*0*	*12+1*	*2*

ENGLISH, Thomas Steven 'Tommy'

Height: 5ft 9in. Weight: 11st 6lb.

Born: 18 October 1961, Cirencester.

■ The English family moved to Colchester from Luton when Tommy was 11 years old and younger brother Tony just six, but it was as an apprentice with Coventry that English began his career, signing professional in June 1979 and scoring 17 goals in 62(+4) First Division games. In September 1982 he transferred to Leicester, scoring three goals in 29(+17) appearances. Leicester were promoted to Division One in his first season, but he was released and found himself playing on non-contract forms for, first, Rochdale where he made three appearances, scoring one goal, and Plymouth, completing four substitute appearances with one goal scored. After a spell in Australia with Canberra City, English joined Colchester and rekindled his goalscoring form. He netted a hat-trick against Preston in April 1986 just four days before brother Tony grabbed the match ball himself with a treble against Peterborough. The brothers were both sent off after a retaliatory brawl at Crewe just a week after the family hat-trick double. The following campaign Mike Walker publicly called English's training efforts into question, and the player moved on to Wealdstone and Bishop's Stortford. When United were faced with relegation in 1989 English was re-engaged by Jock Wallace. Despite enjoying cult status as a former Colchester schoolboy, he was largely overlooked when Mick Mills took charge of United's slide into the Conference. He later played for Happy Valley (Hong Kong), Crawley, Wivenhoe, Bishop's Stortford, Harwich & Parkeston and Sudbury. His son Tommy Junior was on the Youth books of Arsenal and Norwich and had a brief trial at Layer Road, playing one reserve game.

	League		Lge Cup		FA Cup		Other	
	A	G	A	G	A	G	A	G
1984–85	0	0	0	0	0	0	0+1	0
1985–86	16+7	11	0	0	0	0	0+1	0
1986–87	18+6	9	1	0	3	3	2	0
1989–90	12+1	3	0	0	2	0	1	0
TOTAL	46+14	23	1	0	5	3	3+2	0

EPHRAIM, Hogan

Height: 5ft 9in. Weight: 11st.

Born: 31 March 1988, Holloway.

■ Signing professionally for West Ham in April 2005, Ephraim made his Hammers debut as a substitute in a League Cup tie with Sheffield Wednesday five months later. He was taken on loan by Geraint Williams in November 2006, making his debut as a substitute in the 5–1 thrashing of Hull at Layer Road in the same month. His loan was extended in January 2007, and he continued to receive England Under-19 caps while at Layer Road scoring his first-ever League goal with a wonderful individual effort at Barnsley in the February. He also represented England at Under-16, 17 and 18 levels and scored four goals against Russia in September 2004. Showing up well in the last few games of the season, it was hoped that Ephraim would renew his loan for the 2007–08 season, however,

following advice from West Ham manager Alan Curbishley, he opted to join Queen's Park Rangers, and his first Rangers goal came at Layer Road in October 2007 in a 4–2 win for United. Ephraim joined QPR on a permanent basis during the 2008 transfer window.

	League		Lge Cup		FA Cup		Other	
	A	G	A	G	A	G	A	G
2006–07	5+16	1	0	0	0	0	-	-
TOTAL	5+16	1	0	0	0	0	-	-

EVANS, Anthony William 'Tony'

Height: 5ft 8in. Weight: 10st 8lb.

Born: 30 August 1958, Colchester.

■ Evans was another United youth product who was blooded at a time when funds for transfers were not generally available. The 19-year-old made his debut as a substitute at Hereford in March 1978 and had a run of games when new signing Eddie Rowles broke his leg against Portsmouth a week later. He had a further run in the side in October 1978 when Steve Foley was injured. Evans responded by scoring his only two senior goals in home games against Swindon and Southend. Along with fellow young U's player Gary Harvey, Evans spent a spell with Norwegian side Kongsvinger in 1980. He was not able to oust the likes of Foley, Rowles, Bobby Gough and Trevor Lee and was released in 1981. He and Harvey were supposed to go back to Norway, but it did not work out, and Evans joined Tiptree, following manager Mick Loughton to Chelmsford when the former U's star took over at New Writtle Street. Evans subsequently returned to Tiptree and later moved to Haverhill, also playing the odd game for Wivenhoe.

	League		Lge Cup		FA Cup		Other	
	A	G	A	G	A	G	A	G
1977–78	5+2	0	0	0	0	0	-	-
1978–79	8+1	2	0	0	0	0	-	-
1979–80	2+4	0	0	0	0	0	-	-
1980–81	6+2	0	0+2	0	0	0	-	-
TOTAL	21+9	2	0+2	0	0	0	-	-

EVANS, John William

Height: 5ft 11in. Weight: 10st 11lb.

Born: 28 August 1929, Tilbury.
Died: August 1999, Brentwood.

■ Starting his career at Tilbury, Evans was soon picked up by Charlton, joining in May 1950. He made his debut after just three reserve games, and in two and a half seasons at The Valley he notched an impressive 38 goals in 90 appearances. On Christmas Day 1953 Evans was 12th man for Charlton as they travelled to Bolton, but he and fellow player Frank Lock signed for Liverpool for £12,000 and on Boxing Day played for the Merseysiders against WBA. Liverpool were relegated that season, and Evans notched 29 goals the following year, including five against Bristol Rovers and four against Bury. A few weeks into the 1956–57 season he lost his place to Jimmy Melia and was snapped up by Benny Fenton for £4,000. Evans had scored 49 goals in 96 appearances for the Anfield outfit. His best goal for Colchester was probably the 82nd-minute equaliser against Arsenal at Layer Road that earned a replay in front of 60,000 at Highbury and a £10,000 gate kitty. On leaving Layer Road in June 1960, he played for Romford for four seasons before becoming a referee in the Grays area.

	League		Lge Cup		FA Cup		Other	
	A	G	A	G	A	G	A	G
1957–58	24	7	-	-	0	0	-	-
1958–59	27	14	-	-	4	2	-	-
1959–60	5	1	-	-	0	0	-	-
TOTAL	56	22	-	-	4	2	-	-

F

FAGAN, Craig Anthony

Height: 5ft 11in. Weight: 11st 8lb.

Born: 11 December 1985, Birmingham.

■ Fagan managed just one League and two League Cup substitute appearances for Premiership Birmingham after serving his YTS at the club. Loaned out to Bristol City in January 2003, he scored his first-ever League goal against Colchester at Ashton Gate in a 2–1 United win a month later. Eyed by Phil Parkinson, Fagan was brought in to Layer Road on the eve of the 2003–04 on a season-long loan and, despite disciplinary problems, netted 10 League and Cup goals, including a hat-trick against Notts County in April 2004. Determined to get back up the ladder and despite two red cards, 11 bookings and a public warning, Parkinson signed Fagan permanently in the summer, although Birmingham insisted on a sell-on clause. Fagan's early season goalscoring prompted ambitious Hull to table a bid for the striker. Having tormented the Tigers' defence, and scoring in United's 2–0 FA Cup third-round win at The KC Stadium in January 2005, Fagan was kept out of Colchester's line up for the League meeting at Hull a little over a month later. Fagan duly signed for the Yorkshire side for an undisclosed six-figure fee and helped them to promotion to the Championship with four goals in 11(+2) appearances until the end of the season. His drive and ambition showed no abatement, and after completing 67(+13) appearances, scoring 15 goals, he was on the move to Premiership-bound Derby in the January 2007 transfer window for £750,000. Scoring once in 12(+5) appearances, Fagan also played in the Wembley Play-off Final win over West Brom. His disciplinary problems did not go away, and he suffered a four-match video evidence ban after stamping on Liverpool's Alvaro Arbeloa in August 2007. Fagan rejoined Hull on loan in March 2008.

	League		Lge Cup		FA Cup		Other	
	A	G	A	G	A	G	A	G
2003–04	30+7	9	2	1	5	0	4	0
2004–05	25+1	8	3	2	5	4	0	0
TOTAL	55+8	17	5	3	10	4	4	0

FAIRCHILD, Clifford C. 'Cliff'

Height: 5ft 11½in. Weight: 11st 5lb.

Born: 23 October 1917, Romford.

Died: 1974, Gt. Yarmouth.

■ Ted Davis signed 19-year-old Fairchild after he impressed in the pre-season Probables versus Possibles trial game. Fairchild had been with Barking but in October 1936 was a professional on the books of Northfleet at the time. Northfleet operated as the nursery side of Tottenham Hotspur. Fairchild was virtually a permanent fixture as United won the Southern League Cup in their first professional season and was impressive enough that Arsenal manager George Allison signed him up. The deal was done in March 1938 but an agreement struck that Fairchild would stay until the end of the season. He moved to Highbury with another Davis prodigy in 18-year-old goalkeeper Ted Platt. The transfer fee was £500 but, significantly, Davis used his powers of persuasion to entice Arsenal to play at Layer Road in the Colchester Challenge Cup as part of the deal. Davis had fixed a similar deal with Wolves for the services of Reg Smith, and the clash of the First Division giants drew a then Layer Road record crowd of 17,854. Fairchild appeared against Colchester in the 1938–39 season for Arsenal Colts in the Southern League and Cup but was released towards the end of that season and joined Southend where he made two Football League appearances before the outbreak of war. He came back to Layer Road with the Southend team to play for the Colchester Challenge Cup on 10 May 1939, a game the U's won 2–1. He played a few war-time friendlies and regional League games for the Shrimpers before being appointed player-coach of Eastern Counties League Great Yarmouth Town in August 1946. In the early 1950s he moved down the coast to finish his playing days at Lowestoft where he was still playing regularly for their reserves in 1955–56 and occasionally deputising in the first team.

	League		Lge Cup		FA Cup		Other	
	A	G	A	G	A	G	A	G
1937–38	30	0	6	0	-	-	16	0
TOTAL	30	0	6	0	0	0	16	0

FARLEY, Craig

Height: 6ft. Weight: 11st.

Born: 17 March 1981, Oxford.

■ Released from Watford's Youth Training Scheme, Farley joined Colchester in the summer of 1999 as a squad player, making his debut as a substitute in a 1–0 home defeat to Scunthorpe in the September. This was the year that the Football League Youth Alliance started with its Under-19 age

limit, and Farley played several times, particularly later in the season, as he dropped out of the first-team squad. His presence in the Under-19s did not go down too well with some of the squad who felt he was not any better than the U's lads of the same age discarded by manager Wadsworth at the end of the previous season. Farley was released at the end of the season and joined Chesham United. In March 2001 he moved on to home-town non-League side Oxford City, and between 2002 and 2005 he turned out for Maidenhead before joining Brackley Town, where he played in the 2007–08 season.

	League		Lge Cup		FA Cup		Other	
	A	G	A	G	A	G	A	G
1999–2000	8+6	0	0	0	1	0	1	0
TOTAL	8+6	0	0	0	1	0	1	0

FARRELL, Andrew James 'Andy'

Height: 5ft 11in. Weight: 11st.

Born: 7 October 1965, Colchester.

■ Spotted playing against the U's for Stanway in the Border League as a 16-year-old, Farrell was brought to Layer Road as an apprentice in 1982 and given his chance in the first team by Cyril Lea at Darlington on the opening day of 1983–84. He filled in at left-back, not his natural spot, until the experienced Ian Phillips arrived a couple of weeks into the season, but Phillips was already League Cup-tied, so Farrell played all five games as the U's got to the third round where they entertained Manchester United at Layer Road. Farrell's dedication and team spirit were shown in early

October when, after returning at 3.30am from playing the full 90 minutes of a League Cup tie at Swansea, he led the youth team in the FA Youth Cup that same evening. He then completed the set of club sides in under five days by playing for the reserves on the Saturday afternoon. His first goal came in a 3–3 draw at Rochdale in April 1986. In the summer of 1987 Farrell made a surprise £5,000 move away from his roots to fellow Fourth Division Burnley. Ironically his debut was against Colchester on the opening day of the 1987–88 season as Mike Walker's side thrashed his new team 3–0 at Turf Moor. A regular in the Clarets side, he made 237(+20) appearances, scoring 20 goals, and played in two Play-off campaigns. The first resulted in defeat, but Farrell appeared as substitute as Burnley beat Stockport in the 1993–84 Division Two Final at Wembley. He also played in a 2–0 defeat to Wolves before 80,000 at Wembley in the Football League Trophy Final. In September 1994 he moved to Wigan for £20,000 and in two seasons for the Division Three side appeared 51(+3) times, scoring once. At the start of 1996–97 he signed for Rochdale and added a further 113(+5) League games to his career total, with six goals scored. Staying in the North West, he appeared in the Conference for Morecambe and Leigh RMI, including a stint as assistant manager to the Bolton-based side, before returning to Turf Moor as Community Officer and having the honour of being inducted into the Clarets Hall of Fame by Burnley fans.

	League		Lge Cup		FA Cup		Other	
	A	G	A	G	A	G	A	G
1983–84	15	0	5	0	1	0	0	0
1984–85	35+3	0	2	0	3	0	3	0
1985–86	24	1	0	0	1	0	0	0
1986–87	24+4	4	2	0	3	0	3	0
TOTAL	98+7	5	9	0	8	0	6	0

FARRELL, Sean Paul

Height: 6ft 1in. Weight: 12st 8lb.

Born: 28 February 1969, Watford.

■ Farrell joined Watford as an apprentice and celebrated turning professional by joining Roger Brown's Colchester on deadline day 1988. He made his first-ever League appearance in a 0–0 draw with Cambridge and scored the winner a week later as United's failing promotion bid

received a brief respite in a 2–1 victory over Halifax. Returning to Kenilworth Road, Farrell had to wait until 1990–91 for his first start for the Hatters. He was loaned to Fourth Division Northampton in September 1991, scoring once in four starts, which was enough for Fulham to sign the young striker for £100,000. Farrell scored a hat-trick in only his fourth game against West Bromwich Albion. Injuries restricted his appearances to 93(+1) but he scored an impressive 31 League goals. When Fulham were relegated to the basement Farrell joined Peterborough in August 1994 for £120,000 and scored 20 times in 49(+17) games. His final League move came in October 1996 when he teamed up with former Fulham teammate Gary Brazil, who was boss of Notts County. For his £80,000 transfer he helped County win the Third Division title in 1997–98, netting 15 times, and completed 58(+30) games, scoring 22 times in all. He joined non-League Burton Albion in September 2001 but retired through injury in the summer of 2003.

	League		Lge Cup		FA Cup		Other	
	A	G	A	G	A	G	A	G
1987–88	4+5	1	0	0	0	0	0	0
TOTAL	4+5	1	0	0	0	0	0	0

FENTON, Benjamin Robert Vincent 'Benny'

Height: 5ft 8½in. Weight: 11st 3lb.

Born: 28 October 1918, West Ham.

Died: 29 July 2000, Dorset.

■ Fenton joined West Ham from school, turning professional on his 17th birthday. While an amateur he followed in older brother Ted's footsteps by playing at Layer Road for Colchester Town, making his debut aged 15 on 1 September 1934 against Hoxton Manor in the Spartan League and played 30 games scoring 9 goals, over the next 12 months. Making 21 League appearances for the Hammers before the war, Fenton scored nine times before joining Millwall on a free transfer in March 1939. Making 20 appearances, scoring seven goals, Fenton's Millwall career was dissected by the war. During this time he guested for several clubs, thus: 1939–40 Millwall 1 appearances/0 goals, Norwich 4/0; 1940–41 Millwall 2/1; 1941–42 Cardiff 5/3; 1942–43 Charlton 1/0, Crystal Palace 1/0, Millwall 19/6, West Ham 1/0; 1943–44 Millwall 4/1; 1944–45 Millwall 11/1, West Ham 1/0, Charlton 10/4; 1945–46 Millwall 17/4. Fenton joined Charlton as a wing-half in January 1947 for £4,000 and went on to make a stalwart 264 League appearances as captain, while weighing in with 22 goals. He missed out on the 1947 FA Cup Final, however, because he had played for Millwall in round three. In February 1955 Fenton became player-manager of Colchester when the ailing Jack Butler was relieved of his duties, but he could not prevent United finishing bottom of the table. Fenton turned the mediocre U's side around, playing 104 games himself, scoring 15, and after finishing 12th in his first full season he almost steered United to Division Two in 1956–57 when they finished third. He was in charge as United held Arsenal 2–2 at Layer Road in 1959 and as they finished runners-up to Millwall in Division Four of 1961–62. He had a penchant for signing Scottish players and frequently scouted junior football north of the border, bringing many fine players to Layer Road. His first signing was goalkeeper Percy Ames. He hung his playing boots up in 1958, having earned a five-year contract at Layer Road but being denied the chance to discuss the possibility of managing struggling Leeds. In October 1963 he became manager of Leyton Orient after nine years at Layer Road and then in 1966 took charge at Millwall. Defensively strong, the Lions almost made Division One in 1971–72 and never finished outside the top 10. After leaving The Den in October 1974 following a poor start to the season, he became secretary at Charlton in 1977 and assistant manager in March 1980.

* *See also Who's Who Managers section*

	League		Lge Cup		FA Cup		Other	
	A	G	A	G	A	G	A	G
1954–55	11	2	-	-	0	0	-	-
1955–56	32	2	-	-	1	0	-	-
1956–57	38	8	-	-	1	0	-	-
1957–58	23	3	-	-	0	0	-	-
TOTAL	104	15	-	-	2	0	-	-

FENTON, Edward Benjamin Ambrose 'Ted'

Born: 7 November 1914, Forest Gate.
Died: 12 July 1992.

■ Ted Fenton signed for West Ham as a 14-year-old and, as was West Ham's practice, spent time out on loan with amateur clubs to aid his development. After a spell with Ilford, Fenton came to Layer Road in September 1931, joining Colchester Town, and made an immediate impact, scoring a hat-trick on his debut in a 9–1 win in a local derby with Ipswich Town at Portman Road. Ipswich were only about three short of their full strength, and 10 of the side that lost to the Oysters represented Town in the FA Cup three days later. Fenton's stint at Layer Road only lasted until February when he turned pro with West Ham, but he made quite an impression, particularly with his heading ability, scoring 26 times at about a goal a game. He got a hat-trick on his Football League debut with West Ham and another in Second Division game with Bury in

1932 and in all played in 166 League games for the Hammers, netting on 19 occasions. As a pro he settled into the right-half position after initially operating at centre-half. In the period immediately before the war he ran a successful painting and decorating business in the East End, employing 25 men. After selling up prior to the outbreak of war, Fenton served as a Physical Training Instructor at Aldershot Barracks until he was posted to Colchester where the professional United had superceded the amateur Town and were re-establishing themselves in the transitional season of 1945–46. Fenton, a Company Sergeant Major, was a Hammers idol and played regularly at Upton Park during the war years, with his career reading as follows: 1939–40 (31 appearances/16 goals); 1940–41 (17/8); 1941–42 (34/5); 1942–43 (21/30); 1943–44 (23/5); 1944–45 (31/3) and 1945–46 (36/3). In addition Fenton also guested for Northampton (2/2) and York (8/2) in season 1943–44. West Ham reached the Football League Cup Final in 1940 beating Blackburn 1–0 in front of 42,399 fans at Wembley, a year Fenton toured South Africa with the FA representative side, for whom he played in three matches. A successful tour led to wartime international caps for England against Wales 1940, Switzerland 1945 and he played for the Army versus the Belgian Army and the Scottish Army. In the summer of 1946 he was appointed player-manager at Layer Road and had the unenviable task of putting together a side to get Colchester into the Football League. His affiliation with Colchester went back to the Spartan League days of the defunct Colchester Town where he travelled from

London on a Saturday while on West Ham's books to play for the Oysters. Fenton took the dishevelled United team and moulded them into a club on the verge of Football League status. His finest hour came during 1947–48, a year after hanging up his playing boots. Southern League United beat Wrexham, Bradford Park Avenue and mighty Huddersfield as they stormed to the fifth round of the FA Cup. The national press had been caught up in the imagination and Fenton had told them that he had a plan to defeat Bradford and the Terriers after having watched them play in the weeks prior to the cup ties. He had his Colchester players practice a routine that he felt sure would expose weaknesses in the Bradford and Huddersfield defences. This became known as The 'F' Plan, and it worked both times. The fifth-round draw paired Colchester with Blackpool and Stanley Matthews. Blackpool were too strong and ran out 5–0 winners, but Fenton had laid the foundations of national recognition. The supporters' club counted on almost 16,000 members, such was the interest in United, and while it was not Fenton who took United into the Football League he had created enough national interest that when it came around for the election to the League in 1949, United, as runners-up to Merthyr, were elected ahead of their Welsh rivals purely on the foundations that Fenton had created.

In the aftermath of United's magnificent Cup run he applied for managerial positions at Blackburn and West Brom, requesting the advice of his former manager Charlie Paynter of West Ham. This alerted the Hammers chairman W. Cearns, and it was announced in late June 1948 that he was to be appointed as assistant to Paynter. He was only on a three-month contract at Layer Road, but in mid-July the U's directors agreed to release him early, and he left at the end of that month. When Paynter retired in 1950 Fenton became manager of an ageing side and struggled to keep them in the Second Division in 1951–52. He was only the third manager to hold the hot seat at the Boleyn and among players in his charge was a host of future managers in Ron Greenwood, Malcolm Allison, John Bond and Frank O'Farrell. Youthful players such as Bobby Moore, Martin Peters and Geoff Hurst were also on the books. He pioneered the use of weights to strengthen thigh and buttock muscles to help prevent injuries, and the 4–2–4 playing formation. After guiding West Ham back to the top flight in 1957–58, with former Colchester players Mike Grice and Vic Keeble in his squad, he went into print, writing a book *At Home With The Hammers* in 1960 but surprisingly quit in March 1961 to become manager at Southend where he remained until 1965. He was succeeded at West Ham by one of his protégées, Ron Greenwood. His son Alan was also on West Ham's books during the 1950s and later ran the family sports shop in Brentwood High Street. Retiring to the Gloucestershire's Forest of Dean, he underwent a hip operation at the age of 71 but was still able to enjoy a round of golf. He died tragically in a head-on road crash on the way to a family reunion in Gloucestershire along with two other passengers. His wife suffered a broken neck in the accident. Probably the ultimate U's legend, it was Fenton's managerial and playing skills that laid the foundations for Colchester to become a Football League club.

* *See also Who's Who Managers section*

	League		Lge Cup		FA Cup		Other	
	A	G	A	G	A	G	A	G
1946–47	27	2	7	0	2	0	-	-
1947–48	20	4	4	1	6	0	-	-
TOTAL	47	6	11	1	8	0	-	-

FERGUSON, Barry

Height: 6ft 3in. Weight: 13st.

Born: 7 September 1979, Dublin, ROI.

■ A product of the same successful Home Farm side that introduced ex-U's star Mark Kinsella to the game, Ferguson won six caps at Under-21 level for the Republic of Ireland and was recruited by Coventry in April 1998. Unable to break into the Sky Blues side, he joined Colchester on loan in March 2000, making his debut against Blackpool in the same month. Ferguson was not pursued by U's boss Steve Whitton and had subsequent loan deals at Hartlepool (4 games) and Northampton (1[+2] games) in the early part of 2000–01. He returned to Ireland and joined Longford Town, captaining their 2003 FAI Cup and 2004 League Cup-winning teams, and later played for Bohemians. In January 2007 he signed for Shamrock Rovers.

	League		Lge Cup		FA Cup		Other	
	A	G	A	G	A	G	A	G
1999–2000	5+1	0	0	0	0	0	0	0
TOTAL	5+1	0	0	0	0	0	0	0

FERGUSON, Jock

■ Lance Corporal Ferguson, an inside-forward with links to Motherwell, although he is not recorded as playing in the Scottish League for them, served in No.1 Holding Battalion and played in wartime football in Colchester. He played four games for Southend in 1945–46 and spent 10 weeks with the U's during the winter of 1945–46, playing nine times in all, always at inside-left, before being demobbed and returning to Scotland. His three U's goals were in the Christmas friendlies against minor opposition.

	League		Lge Cup		FA Cup		Other	
	A	G	A	G	A	G	A	G
1945–46	5	0	1	0	0	0	-	-
TOTAL	5	0	1	0	0	0	-	-

FERGUSON, Michael John 'Mick'

Height: 6ft 1in. Weight: 12st 8lb.

Born: 3 October 1954, Newcastle.

■ Geordie Ferguson started his long career as an apprentice at Coventry, signing as a professional in December 1971. Ferguson formed a strike partnership with Ian Wallace and almost fired Coventry into Europe. After 51 goals in 121(+8) appearances, he moved to Everton for £280,000 in August 1981 and scored four times in 7(+1) games for the Toffees but more often than not was on the physio's couch. He was loaned to Birmingham in November 1982, and his eight goals in 20 starts were enough for City to sign the player permanently in

the summer of 1983. Plagued by injury, he made just two further starts, scoring once before returning back to Coventry in a loan deal in March 1984. Despite three goals in seven games, the Sky Blues were not convinced enough to sign their ex-player. It was Brighton who finally took a chance in September 1984, and the big striker returned six strikes in 17 games. Cyril Lea signed Ferguson on deadline day 1986, as he still sought to replace car-crash victim Keith Bowen. Debuting against Chester, Ferguson scored in each of his next four games, teaming up with another ex-Sky Blue in Tommy English. United missed out on promotion, and in November 1986 Ferguson was 'banished' to U's reserves. Mike Walker signed Simon Lowe, and Ferguson ended up at Wealdstone. Soon after, he quit his Brighton home to return north to Sunderland where he joined the Community Football scheme. From 2000 he was in charge of over 30 coaches in the Leeds United Football in the Community programme.

	League		Lge Cup		FA Cup		Other	
	A	G	A	G	A	G	A	G
1985–86	9+1	7	0	0	0	0	0	0
1986–87	16	4	2	0	1	0	0	0
TOTAL	25+1	11	2	0	1	0	0	0

FERNANDES (AOUF), Tamer Hasan

Height: 6ft 2in. Weight: 13st 8lb.

Born: 7 December 1974, Paddington.

■ England Youth international Fernandes signed for Brentford in the summer of 1993, under his original family name of Aouf, but his chances were restricted to just 10(+1) appearances in four seasons, during which he changed his name. He

had a non-playing loan at Peterborough in October 1997 before being signed by Steve Wignall as a replacement for out-of-sorts Carl Emberson in January 1998. He made his debut in a 2–2 draw with Luton on the second day of the New Year but conceded three in each of his next two games, preceding Wignall's resignation. New boss Mick Wadsworth recalled him for five of the last six games, but he was not retained at the end of the season, joining Hemel Hempstead.

	League		Lge Cup		FA Cup		Other	
	A	G	A	G	A	G	A	G
1998–99	8	0	0	0	0	0	0	0
TOTAL	8	0	0	0	0	0	0	0

FIELDUS MBE, Sidney Albert William 'Syd'

Height: 5ft 11in. Weight: 11st 5lb.

Born: 27 May 1909.

Died: April 1974, Chelmsford.

■ An inside-forward from Brentford, Fieldus signed in June 1937 but never made a great impact on the pitch, making just 24 first-team appearances for Colchester in over 10 years' association with the club. He did, however, play a pivotal role in ensuring that the club re-emerged after the war and was secretary-manager until Ted Fenton arrived in summer 1946. Fieldus started as an amateur with Leytonstone and played at Layer Road in January 1929 as a 19-year-old centre-forward, scoring the only goal of an Essex Senior Cup tie against Colchester Town five minutes from time. He turned pro with Millwall, moving on to Brentford and won London Combination medals with both but never made the Football League. In January 1937 he came to live in Colchester and in the summer was one of the first signings for the newly-formed U's. Once the reserve side started at Christmas he was ever present until early April from when he had a run at right-half in the first team. In the first 12 reserve games he wore seven different shirt numbers, and in 1937 that meant he played in seven different roles. He was rejected from the regular forces but joined the Home Guard where he was commissioned, and in December 1944 the name of Captain Sidney Albert William Fieldus, Estuary Sector, appears in a list of servicemen awarded MBEs for meritous service in the Home Guard. Fieldus was a

commercial traveller by profession and was renowned for being able to get his hands on anything and everything, and along with Claude Orrin, kept the club alive during the war, albeit that it had officially closed down. When football restarted in 1945 it was proposed to run the Southern League in Eastern and Western sections, which would reduce travelling time and costs in the time of shortage immediately after war, but there was not enough teams to make that viable so the Southern League decided on a full single division restart. The U's board did not want to enter but Fieldus persuaded them that they could ill afford not to if they wanted to re-establish Colchester on the football map. In the transitional season of 1945–46, Fieldus had the considerable help of Major Dai Rees, a Welsh rugby international, in ensuring a regular supply of Army personnel turned out for United, many of whom were seasoned Football League professionals. There were no signing-on regulations at the time and so line-ups were sometimes not finalised until kick off. The influx of serving soldiers enabled U's to compete in the 1945–46 Southern League and most of the 80 players used in the 31 Southern League games were military personnel. During the war Fieldus guested for Chelmsford, Clapton Orient (twice) and Southend (15 times). His brother Harry also turned out for the U's reserves.

** See also Who's Who Managers section*

	League		Lge Cup		FA Cup		Other	
	A	G	A	G	A	G	A	G
1937–38	13	3	4	0	-	-	3	0
1938–39	0	0	0	0	0	0	1	0
1939–40	1	0	0	0	-	-	-	-
1945–46	1	0	0	0	0	0	-	-
1946–47	1	0	0	0	0	0	-	-
TOTAL	16	3	4	0	0	0	4	0

FINCH, Jack

Born: 3 February 1909, West Ham.
Died: 15 November 1993, Worthing.

■ Finch joined Colchester in August 1946 on a month's trial after a glowing career at Fulham. Starting with Walthamstow Avenue, Finch was invited for a trial at Aston Villa in 1929 but was signed by Fulham as an amateur in October 1930 and as a professional just a month later. Playing mainly as an outside-forward, Finch played for the Cottagers on 280 occasions, scoring 50 League goals. He also played 15 FA Cup ties, including the 1936 semi-final against Sheffield United, and collected a Division Three South Championship medal in 1931–32. He was chosen to represent London against Diables Rouge of Belgium in February 1937. During the war he continued turning out for Fulham, amassing a further 72 wartime League appearances, as well as guesting for Brentford and Crystal Palace. His Colchester career lasted just two games as new player-manager Ted Fenton began his team building. Finch later became coach to the 1949 Nigerian touring team, who took to the field in bare feet, and coach and manager of Valur of Iceland between 1950 and 1952. He became a freelance reporter in the West Ham area before the offer of a driving job on the coast saw him move to Lowestoft.

	League		Lge Cup		FA Cup		Other	
	A	G	A	G	A	G	A	G
1946–47	3	0	0	0	0	0	-	-
TOTAL	3	0	0	0	0	0	-	-

FISHER, George Sidney

Height: 5ft 10in. Weight: 11st.

Born: 19 June 1925, Bermondsey.

■ During the war Fisher served as a wireless operator and air gunner, seeing service in Italy for nearly two years while playing for the RAF Command. He had been spotted representing London Boys by Millwall boss Bill Voisey and signed professional at The Den in December 1944, having been an amateur for two years. At 18 years of age he played in the 1945 War Cup Final South in front of the king and queen and 90,000 Wembley spectators, in which Millwall lost 2–0 to Chelsea. His father and six brothers were well known at The Den and even had a part of the terracing dubbed 'Fisher Row'. During wartime he played 47 games for Millwall between 1944 and 1946 and totalled 286 League appearances with four goals to his credit before joining Fulham for £10,000 in November 1954. After only eight appearances at Craven Cottage, his final League move came on 1 September 1955 when he joined Colchester for £1,000, making his debut against Bournemouth. Initially a left-back, Fisher moved to the right-back slot following the arrival of John Fowler and represented Division Three South in the annual challenge with Division Three North in April 1957. A regular fixture in Benny Fenton's side, Fisher had hoped to stay on at Layer Road in a coaching capacity but joined Bexleyheath & Welling in the summer of 1960. He added to his impressive tally of six Kent Senior Cup-winning medals from seven Finals with both Bexleyheath & Welling and Millwall, joining Romford in August 1961 and Aveley a year later, where he became manager. In 1965 he was appointed manager of Dagenham but left after three months, disillusioned by the way the club was run, and continued working for Barclays Bank in the city until his retirement in 1990.

	League		Lge Cup		FA Cup		Other	
	A	G	A	G	A	G	A	G
1955–56	42	1	-	-	1	0	-	-
1956–57	45	2	-	-	1	0	-	-
1957–58	45	1	-	-	1	0	-	-
1958–59	28	1	-	-	6	0	-	-
1959–60	3	1	-	-	0	0	-	-
TOTAL	163	6	-	-	9	0	-	-

FITZGERALD, Scott Brian

Height: 5ft 11in. Weight: 12st 8lb.

Born: 13 August 1969, Croydon.

■ Fitzgerald began his career as a youth trainee with Wimbledon. Signing professionally in July 1989 he went on to make 95(+11) appearances for the Dons, 43 of them in the Premiership, scoring once and won Republic of Ireland caps at Under-21 (four) and at B level. He spent loan periods at Sheffield United (six games) and Millwall (7) in November 1995 and October 1996 respectively before signing permanently for Millwall for a fee of £50,000 in the 1997 close season. Completing 79(+3) games for the Lions, scoring once, he was signed by Steve Whitton for Colchester in October

2000 making his debut against Cambridge in a 2–0 Layer Road win. Never managing to find the net but keeping many out of United's, Fitzgerald was sent out on loan to Brentford at the tail end of 2003–04 by Phil Parkinson and helped the Bees stave off relegation. Released by Colchester in the summer, he joined Brentford on a permanent basis and after suffering a series of injuries was forced to call it a day after 21 games at Griffin Park. He became Brentford's youth-team manager for 2005–06, with his side beating Arsenal in the FA Youth Cup, and when first-team manager Leroy Rosenior was sacked in November 2006 Fitzgerald became caretaker manager and was then appointed full-time a month later. Brentford were relegated in April 2007, and days later Fitzgerald was sacked. He took up a position as youth-team coach at Gillingham for the 2007–08 season.

	League		Lge Cup		FA Cup		Other	
	A	G	A	G	A	G	A	G
2000–01	30	0	0	0	1	0	1	0
2001–02	36+1	0	2	0	2	0	1	0
2002–03	26	0	0	0	0	0	0	0
2003–04	22+1	0	1	0	2	0	2	0
TOTAL	114+2	0	3	0	5	0	4	0

FLETCHER, H.

■ A soldier who played just twice for Colchester, making his debut against Swindon reserves in February 1946. He also played once for Tottenham during that season.

	League		Lge Cup		FA Cup		Other	
	A	G	A	G	A	G	A	G
1945–46	1	0	1	0	0	0	-	-
TOTAL	1	0	1	0	0	0	-	-

FLOWERS, Paul Anthony

Height: 5ft 11in. Weight: 12st 6lb.

Born: 7 September 1974, Stepney.

■ Released by Watford, Flowers joined the Colchester youth scheme, making his full debut against League leaders Cardiff at Layer Road in March 1993 following suspensions to Tony English, Peter Cawley and Martin Grainger. Despite a 4–2 defeat in a hostile atmosphere Flowers retained his place for the following game at Carlisle. After a spell at Grays Athletic, he moved to Chesham United for the 1994–95 season and later played for Aveley, Barkingside, Romford and Dagenham & Redbridge.

	League		Lge Cup		FA Cup		Other	
	A	G	A	G	A	G	A	G
1992–93	2+1	0	0	0	0	0	0	0
TOTAL	2+1	0	0	0	0	0	0	0

FOLEY, Stephen Paul 'Steve'

Height: 6ft. Weight: 11st 4lb.

Born: 21 June 1953, Clacton.

■ Foley joined United as a 16-year-old apprentice in July 1969 and was thrust into first-team action by Dick Graham against Exeter at Layer Road in November 1971. He immediately stamped his mark on the game, scoring twice and having another disallowed, as U's won 3–0. Only just signed as a full professional in the September, Foley attracted the attention of First and Second Division clubs, but was dogged by injuries throughout his career. Nicknamed 'Zora', Foley missed out on the promotion run-in of 1973–74 through injury and did not return to action until January 1975. History repeated itself in 1976–77 when Foley had to watch from the sidelines as Colchester regained their place in the Third Division. It was not until the latter part of 1978 that he regained full fitness, and he finally got the break his footballing skills deserved when playing regularly for three consecutive seasons, including an FA Cup tie with Manchester United at Layer Road, and being appointed team captain. Had injuries not been so cruel he could well have challenged Mick Cook's appearance record or graced a higher division. His final game came at Sheffield United in September 1981, and soon after he was advised to retire. The club arranged a testimonial against Ipswich in May 1982 and Foley moved to Wivenhoe, then played in the Border League for Little Oakley, before returning to Layer Road to join the coaching staff in 1986. Initially, he was assistant to youth-team boss Roy Massey, whose job as a teacher made it impossible to supervise the day-to-day training of the growing number of full time apprentices. At the end of the season Foley formally took over as youth-team coach with Roy Massey concentrating on the club's Under-16s. With Roger Brown's appointment, Foley replaced Colin Henson as reserve coach because Brown did not want a part-timer in the job, but within a couple of months he had left to take over as Watford's youth-team coach. Fortunately for the U's, house prices in the Watford area were such that Foley could not move his family there, and it was not long before he was back at Layer Road, even being forced to put his boots on again and play for the reserves at Yarmouth on 19 April 1988 when resources were so stretched that the only substitute was youth-team 'keeper Rhys Jones. Foley had youth-team striker Chris Roll as his front running partner, and it was reckoned that having to do Foley's running as well as his own was the reason Roll failed to wake up when the coach got back to Layer Road and had to be retrieved from the coach company's Tollesbury depot at 2am! Foley had an extremely successful stint as caretaker manager between the sacking of Roger Brown in October 1988 and the appointment of Jock Wallace in January 1989. He took Conference-

bound United and introduced a number of his young protégées. While United did not win any League matches in his charge he instilled a desire within the support to survive and set the team on a remarkable FA Cup run that culminated in a home defeat to Sheffield United in a fourth-round replay. Foley was caretaker twice more but never considered himself to be ready for the job full-time, contrary to many U's fans. After a spell as youth coach at Watford in February 1988, Foley was eventually prised away from Colchester by old teammate Mike Walker and moved to Norwich, where he took responsibility for City's reserves before becoming assistant director of the Norwich Academy. In January 2001 he was appointed first-team coach to Nigel Worthington as City reached the Premiership but was 'relieved of his duties' in the summer of 2006 as the Canaries style of play failed to regain their coveted spot in the elite. At the beginning of 2006–07 he took up a coaching post at Ipswich.

	League		Lge Cup		FA Cup		Other	
	A	G	A	G	A	G	A	G
1971–72	17	4	0	0	0	0	0	0
1972–73	36	8	1	0	3	1	-	-
1973–74	32	8	1	0	1	0	-	-
1974–75	16+2	3	0	0	0	0	-	-
1975–76	26+3	5	0	0	1	0	-	-
1976–77	10	0	0	0	0	0	-	-
1977–78	29+3	7	2	0	1	0	-	-
1978–79	34	6	2	0	6	1	-	-
1979–80	42	8	4	0	4	0	-	-
1980–81	30+1	5	2	0	3	0	-	-
1981–82	1+1	0	0	0	0	0	-	-
TOTAL	273+10	54	12	0	19	2	0	0

FORBES, Duncan Scott

Height: 5ft 11in. Weight: 11st 4lb.

Born: 19 June 1941, Edinburgh.

■ Craggy and muscular, Forbes became another of Benny Fenton's Scottish recruits when he was signed from Musselburgh in September 1961. Fenton had persuaded the 20-year-old brewery wages clerk to make the 10-hour, 400-mile train journey to Colchester. He made his debut in April 1962 at Crewe as United sought to secure promotion to Division Three. Forbes became an almost permanent fixture at the heart of United's defence for the next seven seasons as Colchester yo-yoed between Division Three and Four. He was captain as United won promotion yet again back to Division

Three in 1965–66, a season in which he scored his first goal, against Notts County, in November 1965. Forbes joined Norwich for a criminally low fee of £10,000 in September 1968, having become the then fourth-highest appearance holder for United and being Supporters' Player of the Year in 1967. Forbes's Norwich career was equally impressive as he captained them to two promotions to Division One and two Wembley League Cup Finals and partnered Dave Stringer in the City defence. The Scot was never sent off in his career but was booked on numerous occasions due to his supreme competitiveness. He suffered cut eyes, a broken nose and a punctured lung at various points in his career. Forbes also spent a short time on loan with Torquay in October 1976, and one of his seven appearances for the Devonians was an emotional return to Layer Road. Shortly after, Bobby Roberts was reported as trying to bring him back to Layer Road but nothing came of it. In all he made 565 League appearances and had a spell at Diss Town before returning to Carrow Road as Chief Scout in March 1988, retiring from that position in 2001, having given 33 years of service to Norwich City.

	League		Lge Cup		FA Cup		Other	
	A	G	A	G	A	G	A	G
1961–62	6	0	0	0	0	0	-	-
1962–63	46	0	1	0	1	0	-	-
1963–64	32	0	3	0	1	0	-	-
1964–65	46	0	2	0	3	0	-	-
1965–66	42	1	2	0	2	0	-	-
1966–67	46	0	1	0	2	0	-	-
1967–68	46	1	1	0	5	0	-	-
1968–69	6	0	2	0	0	0	-	-
TOTAL	270	2	12	0	14	0	-	-

FORBES, Steven Dudley 'Steve'

Height: 6ft 1in. Weight: 11st 4lb.

Born: 24 December 1975, Stoke Newington.

■ Millwall plucked Forbes for a Sittingbourne record fee of £45,000 in July 1994. Making just five League and two Cup appearances, all as substitute, Forbes joined Colchester on a free transfer in March 1997, making his debut, and scoring, in a 4–2 win at Barnet on the last day of the season. Forbes was a regular as United reached Wembley in the Third Division Play-offs and played in all three end-of-season games. He lost his place to Jason Dozzell and was loaned to Peterborough in March 1999, playing 1(+2) times. After a couple of substitute appearances at the beginning of the following season he was released to Stevenage and later played for Dagenham & Redbridge, Braintree, Hendon (2002–04), Billericay (2004–05) and Eastleigh.

	League		Lge Cup		FA Cup		Other	
	A	G	A	G	A	G	A	G
1996–97	1	1	0	0	0	0	0	0
1997–98	25+10	1	1+1	0	2	1	3+1	0
1998–99	8+7	2	0+1	0	1	0	1	0
1999–2000	0+2	0	0	0	0	0	0	0
TOTAL	34+19	4	1+2	0	3	1	4+1	0

FORREST, Craig Lorne

Height: 6ft 4in. Weight: 12st 3lb.

Born: 20 September 1967, Vancouver, Canada.

■ Forrest joined Ipswich in 1984, but it was not until Roger Brown took him on loan to Layer Road that he played his first games in England. With Mark Walton still

a rookie and U's struggling to fill the void left by Alec Chamberlain, Forrest was recruited in February 1988 and played 11 times in United's goal before being recalled by Town two games before the end of season. This initial experience paved the way for Forrest to make 263 appearances for Ipswich, including the 1991–92 campaign when they won promotion to the Premiership. In March 1997 he joined Ruud Gullit's Chelsea on loan and played 2(+1) games. Ipswich turned down Chelsea's advances but let the player join West Ham in July of the same year, where he played 26(+4) games in the Premiership. Forrest was first chosen for Canada in 1988 and went on to win 56 caps before retiring from international football in 2002. He was the key to Canada winning the CONCACAF Gold Cup in Los Angeles in 2000, conceding a mere three goals and saving two penalty kicks in his team's five games. He was inducted into Canadian football's Hall of Fame in 2007 as their most capped goalkeeper and represents Canada as a FIFA ambassador while being a football pundit on the TSN network in Canada. He was also appointed Chairperson for the 2007 FIFA World Youth Tournament held in Canada.

	League		Lge Cup		FA Cup		Other	
	A	G	A	G	A	G	A	G
1987–88	11	0	0	0	0	0	0	0
TOTAL	11	0	0	0	0	0	0	0

FOSTER, Michael Sidney 'Mike'

Height: 5ft 8in. Weight: 11st.

Born: 3 February 1939, Leicester.

■ A tricky and thrusting winger, Foster began on the books of Leicester in August 1959. Failing to make the first team, he signed for Benny Fenton's Fourth Division challengers in May 1961 and starred as the club gained promotion at the first attempt, finishing runners-up to Millwall. He netted eight of United's Club record 104 League goals in a season, where Martyn King and Bobby Hunt scored an amazing 79 goals, and had another of his goals knocked off when Accrington Stanley folded. His exploits were spotted by Norwich, and he earned a move to Carrow Road in September 1962 for a fee of £3,000 plus former City favourite Roy McCrohan. He did not impress the City management and was given a free transfer to Millwall for the 1963–64 season. At The Den he scored two League goals in 13 appearances and by April 1967 was back in Norfolk with Great Yarmouth. He later worked for Barclays Bank in Norwich.

	League		Lge Cup		FA Cup		Other	
	A	G	A	G	A	G	A	G
1961–62	36	8	1	0	3	0	-	-
TOTAL	36	8	1	0	3	0	-	-

FOWLER, John

Height: 5ft 9in. Weight: 11st 6lb.

Born: 17 October 1933, Leith.

Died: 28 March 1976, Colchester.

■ Fowler made his United debut against Exeter in August 1955, having been signed along with Sammy McLeod and Bobby Hill from Scottish junior football.

After 10 seasons Fowler was given a free transfer but was re-signed by new manager Neil Franklin as United regained their Third Division status at the end of 1965–66. During his Layer Road career he helped United to their highest League position of third in the Third Division South, played in the FA Cup run to the fourth round in 1958–59 when Colchester eventually lost to Arsenal at Highbury in a replay, and won a Fourth Division runners'-up medal in 1961–62. On departing Layer Road Fowler was appointed player-manager of Heybridge Swifts and a year later moved on to Colchester intermediate side Eastern Gas along with his brother Matt. Fowler tragically died from a heart attack while playing for an ex-U's XI against Layer Fox in a charity game in 1976.

	League		Lge Cup		FA Cup		Other	
	A	G	A	G	A	G	A	G
1955–56	16	2	-	-	0	0	-	-
1956–57	43	1	-	-	1	0	-	-
1957–58	46	0	-	-	0	0	-	-
1958–59	42	0	-	-	6	0	-	-
1959–60	46	0	-	-	1	0	-	-
1960–61	45	2	2	0	2	0	-	-
1961–62	44	0	1	0	3	0	-	-
1962–63	46	0	2	0	1	0	-	-
1963–64	24	0	0	0	1	0	-	-
1964–65	35	0	2	0	3	0	-	-
1965–66	25	0	0	0	2	0	-	-
1967–68	3	0	0	0	0	0	-	-
TOTAL	415	5	7	0	20	0	-	-

FOX, Geoffrey Roy 'Geoff'

Height: 5ft 11in. Weight: 12st 2lb.

Born: 19 January 1925, Bristol.

Died: 1 January 1994, Worcester.

■ Fox, a full-back who joined Ipswich Town from Army football in late 1945, only made one U's appearance, guesting at Chelmsford in a Southern League Cup tie in April 1946 when United's team had been decimated by Army priorities. He played 16 games for Ipswich, as well as cricket for Suffolk, before returning home to Bristol in 1947, signing for Rovers where he played 306 games between 1947 and 1955, winning a Division Three South Championship medal in 1953. On leaving Eastville he headed for Swindon and between 1955 and 1957 played 48 games at the County Ground. During the early 1970s Fox was a director of Bath City, and he died of a heart attack while playing golf on New Year's Day 1994.

	League		Lge Cup		FA Cup		Other	
	A	G	A	G	A	G	A	G
1945–46	0	0	1	0	0	0	-	-
TOTAL	0	0	1	0	0	0	-	-

FOXALL, Joseph Stanley 'Stan'

Height: Weight:

Born: 6 October 1914, Crowle.
Died: 12 August 1991.

■ A prolific scorer for Midland Leaguers Gainsborough Trinity in his native Lincolnshire, Foxall spent nine seasons at Upton Park, scoring 38 goals in 106 League appearances. An RAF Physical Training Instructor during the war, Foxall could play left or right wing and represented West Ham in the 1940 War Cup Final against Blackburn at Wembley in front of 42,339. He played a tremendous amount of football during wartime, appearing over 120 times for the Hammers, scoring over 50 goals, as well as guesting for Charlton, Fulham and Wrexham. He moved to Layer Road in June 1948, but when Colchester gained election to the Football League in 1950 he was unable to play because he had received an insurance pay out from the Football League while at West Ham. He was released by Colchester and had one season at neighbours Chelmsford, finding, along with many of the club's other senior pros, that growing financial problems meant their wages could no longer be afforded.

	League		Lge Cup		FA Cup		Other	
	A	G	A	G	A	G	A	G
1948–49	30	7	4	4	1	0	-	-
1949–50	45	5	5	0	1	0		
TOTAL	75	12	9	4	2	0	-	-

FRENCH, George Noah

Born: 10 October 1926, Colchester.

■ French signed amateur forms for West Ham in August 1948 but by February 1949 had switched allegiance to his home town club and played in the A and reserve teams, usually at left-half or left-back, before making his debut in the latter position against Gillingham in October 1952 as deputy for Phil Rookes. He had joined the Essex Police in October 1950 and rose to the rank of Inspector, winning representative honours with the British Police team several times. A transfer to Laindon brought his U's career to an end in 1957, and he was made captain on his last appearance for the reserves, against Lowestoft on 23 March 1957. In the early 1970s he was a Director of Colchester Sports Council.

	League		Lge Cup		FA Cup		Other	
	A	G	A	G	A	G	A	G
1952–53	1	0	-	-	0	0	-	-
1953–54	2	0	-	-	0	0	-	-
TOTAL	3	0	-	-	0	0	-	-

FROGGATT, John Lawrence

Height: 5ft 11in. Weight: 12st 3lb.

Born: 13 December 1945, Sutton-in-Ashfield.

■ Beginning his football career at East Kirkby Welfare, Froggatt was picked up by Notts County and signed professional in the summer of 1964. After just four appearances, he drifted back to non-League with Buxton. Signed by Boston United for £500, he scored 44 goals in 115 League and Cup appearances before Colchester's former Boston manager Jim Smith paid £6,000 for his services in the summer of 1974. Froggatt teamed up with another former Boston striker in Bobby Svarc and proved the perfect foil for his fellow goal-getter. An ever-present in his first season, Froggatt netted an impressive hat-trick against Grimsby at Layer Road in October 1974 and was equally at home playing alongside Bobby Gough and Colin Garwood after Svarc's transfer to Blackburn. Winning promotion with United in 1976–77, Froggatt moved to

Port Vale for £10,000 in February 1978 following the arrival of Eddie Rowles. He is credited with the quickest-ever goal at Vale Park after scoring just 15 seconds into his debut against Exeter. He scored just twice more in 12(+2) appearances and secured a transfer to Northampton in September of the same year for a £10,000 fee. Plundering 13 goals in 42 League starts for the Cobblers, he returned to Boston in 1980, scoring five goals in 38(+3) starts before being appointed manager at the end of 1980–81 as the Pilgrims became founder members of the Football Alliance (later the Conference).

	League		Lge Cup		FA Cup		Other	
	A	G	A	G	A	G	A	G
1974–75	46	16	6	1	2	1	-	-
1975–76	41	5	2	0	1	0	-	-
1976–77	43	6	3	0	6	2	-	-
1977–78	25	2	5	2	4	0	-	-
TOTAL	155	29	16	3	13	3	-	-

FRY, Christopher David 'Chris'

Height: 5ft 9in. Weight: 9st 6lb.

Born: 23 October 1969, Cardiff.

■ A Welsh Youth international cap, Fry began as a YTS on the books of Cardiff. Making his debut in 1988–99, Fry was with the Bluebirds as they plummeted to the basement division. After 22 starts and a further 33 substitute appearances, he moved to Hereford at the beginning of the 1991–92 campaign. He established himself in the Bulls side and scored 10 goals in 76(+14) League games. Signed by Roy McDonough for a four-figure fee on Christmas Eve 1993, Fry made his debut as a substitute three days later against Mansfield. A firm favourite with the fans, the lightweight winger went on to make 102(+28) appearances for the U's, scoring 16 times. He played in both legs of the Play-off semi-final defeat to Plymouth in 1995–96 and appeared as a substitute at Wembley a year later as United lost on penalties to Carlisle in the Auto Windscreens Shield Final. Leaving Layer Road in July 1997, he joined fellow Third Division side Exeter, ending his League career with 43(+17) appearances in Devon, scoring three times. He returned to his native South

Wales and played for Barry Town, 32 appearances (+2)/9 goals, Haverfordwest 22(+10)/2 and Llanelli 4(+2)/0.

	League		Lge Cup		FA Cup		Other	
	A	G	A	G	A	G	A	G
1993–94	12+5	0	0	0	0	0	0	0
1994–95	24+9	8	1	0	1+1	0	0+1	0
1995–96	35+3	2	0+1	0	1	0	6	0
1996–97	31+11	6	2+2	1	1	0	6+1	1
TOTAL	102+28	16	3+3	1	3+1	0	12+2	1

G

GALLEGO, Jose Augustin 'Joe'

Height: 5ft 8in. Weight: 11st.

Born: 8 April 1923, Renteria, Spain.
Died: 17 September 2006, Cambridge.

■ Gallego moved to England in 1937 at the age of 13 as an evacuee from the Spanish Civil War. Pushed into a refugee boat along with his brother and three sisters by his war-widowed mother, Gallego ended up in Cambridge working on a farm and did not see his mother again until 1947. He first played for Abbey United, the forerunners of Cambridge United, and gained his first League experience at Brentford in 1946, playing six games. Moving to Southampton in 1948, he featured in one game for the Saints, cracking his ankle, before joining Colchester in July 1949. His goalkeeping brother Antonio also managed one game for Norwich. At Layer Road, Gallego was mainly a stand-in player, amassing 12 appearances and joined Cambridge United where he played 142 games in the Eastern Counties League, scoring 37 goals, and then Biggleswade on release from United. He suffered badly from pleurisy, and it was this that forced him to give up the game to become a gas fitter in the Cambridge area. He is recorded as the first Spaniard ever to play in the First Division.

	League		Lge Cup		FA Cup		Other	
	A	G	A	G	A	G	A	G
1949–50	*8*	*1*	*0*	*0*	*0*	*0*	-	-
1950–51	4	0	-	-	0	0	-	-
TOTAL	4	0	-	-	0	0	-	-
	8	*1*	*0*	*0*	-	-	-	-

GAME, Kirk Michael

Height: 6ft 2in. Weight: 12st.

Born: 22 October 1966, Rochford.

■ Released from his Southend apprenticeship, Game joined Cyril Lea's Colchester in August 1985, making his debut against Rochdale in November 1985. The following campaign Mike Walker paired Game with Keith Day at the heart of the U's defence, and the youngster alternated with Terry Baker throughout the season. Released in the summer of 1987, he moved into non-League circles where he had a long career, playing for Maidstone, Chelmsford, Dartford, Braintree, Heybridge, Dagenham & Redbridge and Billericay, as well as spending time coaching in America and playing in Germany.

	League		Lge Cup		FA Cup		Other	
	A	G	A	G	A	G	A	G
1985–86	3+1	0	0	0	1	0	0+1	0
1986–87	25	0	1+1	0	3	0	2	0
TOTAL	28+1	0	1+1	0	4	0	2+1	0

GARCIA, Richard

Height: 5ft 11in. Weight: 12st.

Born: 9 April 1987, Perth, Australia.

■ The then Colchester manager Steve Whitton first wanted to sign Garcia for United in October 2002 after he had watched him playing for West Ham reserves. Serving his traineeship at Upton Park, Garcia scored in every round as the young Hammers won the FA Youth Cup in 1998–99. He was loaned to Leyton Orient in August 2000 and played 18 League games for the O's, scoring four times, before picking up a cruciate injury. On recovery, he made his West Ham debut against Reading in the League Cup and his Premiership bow at Bolton in February 2002. A new injury blow scuppered his chances of establishing himself and also ruined his selection for the 2004 Australian Under-23 Olympic team trial. Colchester finally got their man in September 2004, but Garcia remained plagued by injuries. His cross set up the own goal that gave Colchester a shock, but brief, lead at Chelsea in the 2005–06 FA Cup, and he was part of the squad that finished runners-up in League One that same season. Having appeared to have overcome his injuries nightmare by appearing in 36 of United's Championship matches, and having scored United's first-ever goal at that level at Birmingham on the opening day, Garcia chose to exercise his right of freedom of contract and joined Hull in the summer of 2007, winning promotion to the Premiership via the Play-offs in 2008.

	League		Lge Cup		FA Cup		Other	
	A	G	A	G	A	G	A	G
2004–05	20+4	4	1+1	0	3	1	1	1
2005–06	9+13	5	0	0	3+2	1	4	2
2006–07	33+3	7	1	0	1	0	-	-
TOTAL	62+20	16	2+1	0	7+2	2	5	3

GARVEY, Brian

Height: 6ft. Weight: 11st 8lb.

Born: 3 July 1937, Hull.

■ Garvey, a wing-half, made his debut for his home-town club Hull in season 1957–58 and became a fixture in the

Tigers side, appearing in 232 League games and scoring three goals. Signing for Watford in July 1965, he made a further 179(+1) League starts and notched two goals as Watford won the Third Division Championship in 1968–69 and reached the FA Cup semi-finals in 1969–70. Signed by Dick Graham in June 1970, aged 33, Garvey was prominent in the United side that famously beat Leeds in the FA Cup and won the Watney Cup in 1971–72. He left Layer Road in 1972 to become player-manager of Bedford, returning a year later when appointed U's youth-team coach in July 1973 as the U's resurrected a youth team after a three-year gap. In May 1974 he left in search of a full-time coaching job and had brief spells with Arsenal and Wolves before emigrating to Melbourne, Australia where he coached South Melbourne in 78 games between 1987–89 and was voted National Soccer League coach of the year in 1988.

	League		Lge Cup		FA Cup		Other	
	A	G	A	G	A	G	A	G
1970–71	44+1	0	2+1	0	6	1	-	-
1971–72	31+1	1	3	0	1	0	3	0
TOTAL	75+2	1	5+1	0	7	1	3	0

GARWOOD, Colin Arthur

Height: 5ft 9in. Weight: 10st 13lb.

Born: 29 June 1949, Heacham.

■ Signing professional for Peterborough in July 1967, Garwood scored on his Posh debut against Bournemouth and never looked back, scoring 30 times in just 58(+8) League games including being top scorer in 1970–71 and winning England Youth honours. He was snapped up by Oldham in the summer of 1971 and bagged 35 goals in 84(+9) appearances at Boundary Park. He was used in a swap deal with Huddersfield that saw Les Chapman move to Oldham in December 1974. In 22(+8) games for the Terriers he netted eight times. Colchester manager Bobby Roberts recruited Garwood on loan in February 1976, and the player responded by scoring twice on his home debut against Cardiff. The U's paid £4,000 to keep him as the month's loan came to an end, and over the next two years this proved to be an excellent piece of business. The following campaign his goals were vital as United won promotion at the first attempt. He also scored a memorable equaliser in the seventh minute of injury time against Derby in the FA Cup fourth round, seen by millions on *Match of the Day*. Garwood netted a hat-trick against Millwall in a League Cup two-legged tie in August 1976 but still lost out as United were defeated on penalties for the first time in their history. He also claimed the match ball with a treble against Hartlepool in October 1976. He continued to plunder goals, despite United's elevation to Division Three, and joined Portsmouth in March 1978 for £25,000. Scoring 34 goals in 62(+9) appearances, Garwood was part of the promotion-winning Pompey side in 1979–80 but left in February 1980 for Aldershot in a £54,000 record deal for the Shots. He added a further 25 League goals in 79(+2) games at The Rec. Remarkably, he was top scorer for both Pompey and Aldershot in season 1979–80. He signed for Boston in the summer of 1982, scoring a hat-trick on his Alliance League, debut and later played for King's Lynn while working for an engineering firm in Wisbech.

	League		Lge Cup		FA Cup		Other	
	A	G	A	G	A	G	A	G
1975–76	15	2	0	0	0	0	-	-
1976–77	40+2	16	3	4	6	4	-	-
1977–78	28+2	8	5	2	4	3	-	-
TOTAL	83+4	26	8	6	10	7	-	-

GENTLE, Justin David

Height: 5ft 7in. Weight: 10st 9lb.

Born: 6 June 1974, Enfield.

■ Spotted playing for Borehamwood, Gentle was picked up by Luton in the summer of 1993. He was one of several Luton Under-18s who had caught the eye when easily beating the U's 3–0 in early March 1994 and Gentle and Neal Butler were brought to Layer Road on six-month deals on deadline day when Luton decided they would not offer them contracts. Scott Walters from Watford was recruited at the same time in the same circumstances. Gentle was the only one of the three to make the first team, with substitute appearances in the last two games of the 1993–94 season and all three had gone by mid-September. While they were at Layer Road they were part of the team that set a new ground record score, beating a team playing as St Albans reserves 19–0 on 20 April 1994. Nine of the 12 outfield players used found the net, including Walters(4), Butler(2) and Gentle(1). Gentle later played for Chesham, Enfield, St Albans, Dagenham & Redbridge, Billericay, Harlow and Waltham Abbey.

	League		Lge Cup		FA Cup		Other	
	A	G	A	G	A	G	A	G
1993–94	0+2	0	0	0	0	0	0	0
TOTAL	0+2	0	0	0	0	0	0	0

GEORGE, Norman

■ A 22-year-old recruited from the works team of the Birmingham factory where Jimmy Allen had been Sports & Welfare Officer before his appointment as U's Manager, George made his reserve debut as an amateur on 4 September 1948 and signed pro at the end of the month. Towards the end of the season he played four times on the right-wing as deputy for Dennis Hillman and once at centre-forward for Arthur Turner. His one goal was a 90th-minute equaliser at Tonbridge in April 1949. George was released at the end of the season.

	League		Lge Cup		FA Cup		Other	
	A	G	A	G	A	G	A	G
1948–49	5	1	0	0	0	0	-	-
TOTAL	5	1	0	0	0	0	-	-

GEORGE, Ronald Anthony 'Ron'

Born: 14 August 1922, Bristol.
Died: October 1989, Colchester.

■ George began his working life as an apprentice toolmaker at the Bristol Aeroplane Company. He joined Crystal Palace as an amateur during the war and signed pro in February 1947, got his debut in 1948–49 and was in and out of the team over the next six years, making 122 League appearances in the two full-back positions and scoring twice. A teammate of future U's manager Dick Graham at Selhurst Park, George was signed by Jack Butler in the summer of 1954 but made just eight appearances, never appearing on a winning team, before being released and joining Sudbury as they were finally accepted into the Eastern Counties League. He was

perhaps better known for having a chain of five fashion shops.

	League		Lge Cup		FA Cup		Other	
	A	G	A	G	A	G	A	G
1954–55	6	0	-	-	2	0	-	-
TOTAL	6	0	-	-	2	0	-	-

GERKEN, Dean Jeffery

Height: 6ft 3in. Weight: 13st.

Born: 22 May 1985, Southend.

■ Gerken was with Southend as a schoolboy, starting in midfield, but found his true vocation when pressed into service as an emergency 'keeper. The Southend youth hierarchy thought he was worth a scholarship, but the senior

management of the time did not think it was worth giving a spot to a 'keeper, so Southend's youth department recommended him to Micky Cook at Colchester. Before his U's scholarship ended he was in contention for an England age group cap and was regularly watched by the national selectors, including goalkeeping coach Ray Clemence. Gerken was pressed into first-team action for the first time in a 3–2 defeat at Brentford in April 2004 after sharing the duty of being understudy to Simon Brown with Richard McKinney. When both Brown and McKinney left in the summer of 2004, Phil Parkinson opted to bring in the experienced Aidan Davison as his first choice, but Gerken enjoyed a run of games, including a narrow 3–2 League Cup defeat at Southampton in the October. Gerken remained an important member of the U's squad as they won promotion to the Championship in 2006, and he established himself as first choice in the latter part of the campaign, following injury to Davison. Picking up the Young Player of the Year award, Gerken received an unfortunate red card in the opening home game of the 2007–08 season against Barnsley.

	League		Lge Cup		FA Cup		Other	
	A	G	A	G	A	G	A	G
2003–04	1	0	0	0	0	0	0	0
2004–05	13	0	1	0	2	0	0	0
2005–06	5+2	0	1	0	1	0	5	0
2006–07	27	0	1	0	1	0	-	-
2007–08	40	0	1	0	1	0	-	-
TOTAL	86+2	0	4	0	5	0	5	0

GERMAIN, Steven 'Steve'

Height: 5ft 10in. Weight: 11st.

Born: 22 June 1981, Cannes, France.

■ Germain arrived along with Thomas Pinault from French side AS Cannes with the reputation of having been a high achiever at youth level in France. Signed by Mick Wadsworth, the player initially arrived on loan before signing permanently in the 1999 close season. He made his debut as a substitute against Preston in April 1999 but looked like another example of initial prominence owing much to early physical maturity, and by November 1999, with his champion Wadsworth gone, he found himself in the U's Under-19s. Although he scored three times in his first two

games, his demeanour made it clear he did not think he should be there, and when next time up he was made sub so that a trialist could be looked at, his reaction when introduced at half-time was to claim an Achilles injury inside 10 minutes. The youth team declined to have his assistance again and by Christmas he had been released and returned home to France.

	League		Lge Cup		FA Cup		Other	
	A	G	A	G	A	G	A	G
1998–99	1+5	0	0	0	0	0	0	0
1999–2000	1+2	0	0	0	0	0	0	0
TOTAL	2+7	0	0	0	0	0	0	0

GIBBS, Brian Richard

Height: 5ft 11in. Weight: 12st 6lb.

Born: 6 October 1936, Gillingham, Dorset.

■ Gibbs is regarded as a Gillingham legend after being leading scorer for the Kent club in five successive seasons, following his £4,000 transfer from Bournemouth in October 1962. His career had started at Gosport Borough, and in five years he scored 15 goals in 58 League appearances at Dean Court. He won the Fourth Division title with the Gills in 1963–64 and came close to helping them to Division Two a couple of seasons later. He became the first Gillingham player to notch 100 League goals but became restless as the Kent side's fortunes started to wain. Dick Graham signed him for £8,000 in September 1968, and he repaid the fee with a hatful of goals. During a League Cup tie with Reading in August 1969 he had to play in goal for 66 minutes after regular custodian Ron Willis suffered an eye injury. Gibbs featured strongly in United's famous FA Cup run of 1970–71 when they reached the quarter-finals after beating Leeds in the fifth round. He also won the Watney Cup with the club in the following pre-season. Released at the end of the 1971–72 season, he played for Bletchley while working in the meat industry in Milton Keynes.

	League		Lge Cup		FA Cup		Other	
	A	G	A	G	A	G	A	G
1968–69	37	11	0	0	1	0	-	-
1969–70	41	14	3	0	1	0	-	-
1970–71	45+1	11	3	0	6	0	-	-
1971–72	30+3	4	3	0	1	0	3	1
TOTAL	153+4	40	9	0	9	0	3	1

GIBBS, Paul Derek

Height: 5ft 9in. Weight: 11st 4lb.

Born: 26 October 1972, Gorleston.

■ Gibbs impressed in the 1994 FA Vase Final at Wembley when his Diss Town side beat Taunton 2–1 after extra-time, with his goal being the winner. He had previously been on the books of fellow Eastern Counties League team Gorleston. Steve Wignall brought him to Layer Road in March 1995, and Gibbs made his debut in a 3–1 defeat to Hartlepool. He made a major contribution the following season when in the last game of the season his cross-cum-shot flew into the Doncaster net to secure a Play-off spot for Wignall's men. Unfortunately, Gibbs and United lost to Plymouth, but a year later Gibbs was back at Wembley in the Auto Windscreens Shield Final against Carlisle. He opted to seek pastures new and joined Torquay in the summer of 1997. Gibbs once again had a successful season, scoring seven times in 40(+1) games but again suffered Play-off and Wembley heartache as the Gull's lost to his former employers Colchester in the Third Division Final. Gibbs's spell at Plainmoor will also be noted for his friendship with *Soccer AM* presenter and Torquay fan Helen Chamberlain. Moving across Devon, he joined Plymouth in July 1998 and in over two seasons played 30(+4) times for mid-table Argyle and suffered a broken leg. Gibbs notched up an unenviable hat-trick when moving to Brentford in the summer of 2000 as his new club lost to Stoke in the Millennium Stadium Division Two Play-off. Completing 49(+5) games at Griffin Park, Gibbs made his final League move when joining First Division Barnsley in March 2002. The Tykes were relegated and he appeared 27(+6) times for the Yorkshire club, scoring once. Drifting into non-League, he turned out for Gravesend & Northfleet, Canvey Island, Weymouth and went back to his first club Gorleston in 2006 as a player and coach.

	League		Lge Cup		FA Cup		Other	
	A	G	A	G	A	G	A	G
1994–95	8+1	0	0	0	0	0	0	0
1995–96	13+11	3	0	0	0+1	0	3	0
1996–97	18+2	0	0	0	1	0	5+1	0
TOTAL	39+14	3	0	0	1+1	0	8+1	0

GIBBS, Stanley 'Stan'

■ A schoolboy international, Gibbs joined Charlton in 1938 aged 18. During the war he made seven appearances, scoring three goals at The

Valley. A Flight Sergeant in the RAF, Gibbs joined Colchester on trial in July 1946 and was engaged for the season on a full-time basis in October. He was demobbed from the RAF in January 1947 but was released in the April after just one game. Although we have not been able to identify him for certain, he was probably Stanley Archibald Gibbs, born 13 January 1920 in South London and died September 2004 in Croydon.

	League		Lge Cup		FA Cup		Other	
	A	G	A	G	A	G	A	G
1946–47	1	0	0	0	0	0	-	-
TOTAL	1	0	0	0	0	0	-	-

GILBERT, William Albert 'Billy'

Height: 5ft 11in. Weight: 12st.

Born: 10 November 1959, Lewisham.

■ Gilbert represented England at Schoolboy, Youth and was capped 11 times at Under-21 level while with Crystal Palace, for whom he had served his apprenticeship. Winning the FA Youth Cup in both 1977 and 1978, he missed just one game as Palace stormed back to the top flight in 1978–79, playing alongside future U's players in Nick Chatterton, Dave Swindlehurst and Paul Hinshelwood. Completing 235(+2) League games at Selhurst Park and scoring three goals, the defender moved to Portsmouth in June 1984, where Alan Ball was the manager, after being voted Palace's Player of the Year. Once again Gilbert won promotion to the top division in 1986–87, but Pompey were immediately relegated. Ball was sacked and ended up at Colchester as Jock Wallace's assistant. After 133(+7) appearances at Fratton Park, he teamed up again with Ball at Layer Road in October 1989, making his debut at Scunthorpe in a 4–0 defeat. Initially he was retained at the end of the campaign as United slipped into the Conference but left quickly before the season began, with club sources of the time spreading rumours alleging that he was involved in match-fixing. He signed for Maidstone on a non-contract basis in October 1990 but played just 2(+2) games before moving into non-League with Havant Town, Whyteleafe and Waterlooville where he was manager. When Havant and Waterlooville merged it was Gilbert who became the new club's manager before being responsible for commercial activities.

	League		Lge Cup		FA Cup		Other	
	A	G	A	G	A	G	A	G
1989–90	26+1	0	0	0	2	0	1	0
TOTAL	26+1	0	0	0	2	0	1	0

GILCHRIST, John Skidmore

Height: 5ft 8in. Weight: 11st 10lb.

Born: 5 September 1939, Wishaw.
Died: 1991.

■ A Scottish Schoolboy international, Gilchrist was on the books of Airdrie when he was spotted by Millwall manager Ron Bray playing in an Army match at Aldershot. Millwall duly signed the defender in March 1961, and he helped the Lions rise from the Fourth to the Second Division, including a run of 59 games unbeaten at the Den. Millwall had to pay £70 a time to get him back from Germany where he was carrying out his National Service. In the summer of 1969 after 280 League starts, scoring 10 goals, Gilchrist moved to Fulham in a player-exchange deal that saw Brian Sear and Brendan Mullen move to South London. A year later he was a Colchester player after completing 20(+1) games for the Cottagers. Coming on as a substitute, he inspired United to fight back from 3–1 down at Rochdale in the FA Cup fourth round of 1970–71 to earn a replay that eventually drew Leeds to Layer Road for an historic FA Cup victory. Gilchrist also won a Watney Cup-winners' medal the following season, but as an ageing member of Dick Graham's Grandad's Army he was released to Tonbridge in March 1972 as player-coach. He held a similar post at Tooting & Mitcham before spending the remaining years of

his life on a kidney dialysis machine. Gilchrist enjoyed a testimonial match at Layer Road against his old club Millwall during the 1977–78 season.

	League		Lge Cup		FA Cup		Other	
	A	G	A	G	A	G	A	G
1970–71	28	1	3	0	5+2	1	-	-
1971–72	13	0	2	0	1	0	3	0
TOTAL	41	1	5	0	6+2	1	3	0

GILLESPIE, Ian

Born: 6 May 1913, Plymouth.
Died: 1988.

■ A former Harwich and Parkeston and Suffolk County player and well-known to Colchester football fans from his amateur days playing against the Town, Gillespie was spotted by Crystal Palace and signed pro in February 1937. He played, on trial, for Palace in Ronnie Dunn's benefit match at Layer Road as an inside-forward. He made 21 League appearances for Palace, scoring four goals, but most of his games were during wartime, thus: 1939–40 Charlton (1 appearance/1 goal), Crystal Palace (20/3); 1940–41 Clapton Orient (1/1), Crystal Palace (20/5); 1940–41 Millwall (1/0); 1941–42 Crystal Palace (26/7),

Millwall (2/0); 1942–43 Brighton (1/0), Crystal Palace (16/2), Millwall (2/0); 1943–44 West Ham (1/0); 1944–45 Clapton Orient (14/0), Crystal Palace (2/0); 1945–46 Ipswich (25/4). Having moved to Ipswich as a three-year-old, it was natural that after guesting for Ipswich in 1945–46 he signed for Town in 1946–47. After six appearances and one goal, he moved to Layer Road in the May of that extended season but was almost exclusively a reserve and was released in the summer of 1948. Gillespie later became player-manager of Leiston.

	League		Lge Cup		FA Cup		Other	
	A	G	A	G	A	G	A	G
1946–47	4	1	1	0	0	0	-	-
1947–48	0	0	1	1	0	0	-	-
TOTAL	4	1	2	1	0	0	-	-

GODBOLD, Daryl Martin

Height: 5ft 11in. Weight: 11st.

Born: 5 September 1964, Ipswich.

■ Although a supporter of his home-town club, Godbold joined arch-rivals Norwich as an apprentice and signed professional in September 1982. A member of the Canaries' all-conquering youth side of 1982, Godbold made just two substitute appearances for City against Tottenham and Nottingham Forest. Signed by Cyril Lea in August 1984, he made his debut in the opening day 3–3 Essex derby draw with Southend. Losing his place to Andy Farrell, it was not until November 1984 that he appeared again – twice coming on as substitute and scoring his only goal at Tranmere in a 2–1 defeat. He moved into non-League and played for Wroxham in the Eastern Counties League and assisted Norwich with their Football in the Community Scheme.

	League		Lge Cup		FA Cup		Other	
	A	G	A	G	A	G	A	G
1984–85	4+2	1	2	0	1	0	0	0
TOTAL	4+2	1	2	0	1	0	0	0

GODDARD, Karl Eric

Height: 5ft 6in. Weight: 10st 1lb.

Born: 29 December 1967, Leeds.

■ Goddard's career started as a Manchester United apprentice after winning England Schoolboy honours. He joined Bradford City in the summer of 1986, playing 67(+6) times for the Bantams. He got embroiled in a Sunday

newspaper exposé and was sent out on loan to Exeter in December 1989, making just one substitute League appearance. Mick Mills brought the full-back to Layer Road the following month in a similar deal, and he made the left-back spot his own as United slipped out of the League and into the Conference. Goddard's only goal came in a 1–1 draw at Stockport in March 1990. He tried his luck at Hereford the following season but managed just 8(+1) games, scoring a single goal. He later turned out for Bradford Park Avenue.

	League		Lge Cup		FA Cup		Other	
	A	G	A	G	A	G	A	G
1989–90	16	1	0	0	0	0	0	0
TOTAL	16	1	0	0	0	0	0	0

GODFREY

■ A soldier from the 17th Infantry Training Corps who was reported to have been an amateur with Erith and Belvedere, the 1938 Amateur Cup losing finalists. The importance of local industry meant that the Erith were able to continue through the war and were one of Kent's strongest sides. Godfrey is not recorded as having played for their first team and was only briefly involved at Layer Road, not being seen again after the 8–0 defeat at Yeovil when a last-minute scratch side had to be raised from the Colchester Garrison after a number of U's regulars were refused leave for the day.

	League		Lge Cup		FA Cup		Other	
	A	G	A	G	A	G	A	G
1945–46	3	0	0	0	0	0	-	-
TOTAL	3	0	0	0	0	0	-	-

GOODFELLOW, Marc David

Height: 5ft 10in. Weight: 11st 10lb.

Born: 20 September 1981, Swadlincote.

■ Goodfellow's career began as a Stoke junior where he signed professional forms in January 1999. He made his debut a year later and went on to play 17(+37) games for the Potters, scoring six goals, five of which were in the Play-off winning season of 2001–02. Transferred to Bristol City for £50,000 in January 2004, Goodfellow made just 8(+12) appearances at Ashton Gate in two seasons but had 4(+1) games on loan at Port Vale in October 2004 and scored three times in six loan appearances at Swansea a month later. Phil Parkinson brought Goodfellow to Layer Road on deadline day 2005 in a loan until the end of the season – a deal which saw Joe Keith move in the opposite direction. He made his debut against Sheffield Wednesday at Layer Road and scored his only goal at Peterborough a week later. Despite some interest from United Goodfellow returned to Bristol to negotiate a move to Swansea. After just 5(+6) games, he was unloaded to Grimsby in January 2006, scoring once in 8(+2) appearances. Joining Bury in the summer of 2006, Goodfellow played just 2(+2) League games before being released just three months into his contract because of a back problem. He moved in to non-League in January 2007 and played for Conference side Burton Albion.

	League		Lge Cup		FA Cup		Other	
	A	G	A	G	A	G	A	G
2004–05	4+1	1	0	0	0	0	0	0
TOTAL	4+1	1	0	0	0	0	0	0

GOODWIN, James

Born: 20 July 1974, Colchester.

■ Youth-team skipper Goodwin was brought into the senior squad in the early days of Roy McDonough's tenure as manager as the new boss sought to build a squad with little or no resources. He first appeared as a substitute at Witton Albion in September 1991 and made his first start in a bizarre 6–2 home defeat to Wycombe in the Bob Lord Trophy – a game for which McDonough was fined for fielding a weakened side. His other full appearance came in an FA Cup tie at Exeter. Goodwin was given a short-term pro contract at the end of his apprenticeship, but the club's decision not to run a reserve side for 1992–93 left him with few chances to earn an extension, and he was out of Layer Road in October 1992, trialling briefly at Chelmsford. He later played locally for Earls Colne.

	League		Lge Cup		FA Cup		Other	
	A	G	A	G	A	G	A	G
1991–92	0+3	0	0	0	1	0	1	0
TOTAL	0+3	0	0	0	1	0	1	0

GORMAN, Keith

Height: 5ft 10in. Weight: 10st 10lb.

Born: 13 October 1966, Bishop Auckland.

■ Signed up as a professional in January 1984 after serving his apprenticeship at Portman Road, Gorman joined Colchester on loan in September 1986 and made just one fleeting appearance as a substitute against Wrexham in October 1986. After a Football League Trophy appearance for Northampton in 1986–87 he transferred to Darlington in January 1987 and appeared 4(+3) times for the Quakers, scoring twice. Moving into non-League he represented Brandon United and West Auckland.

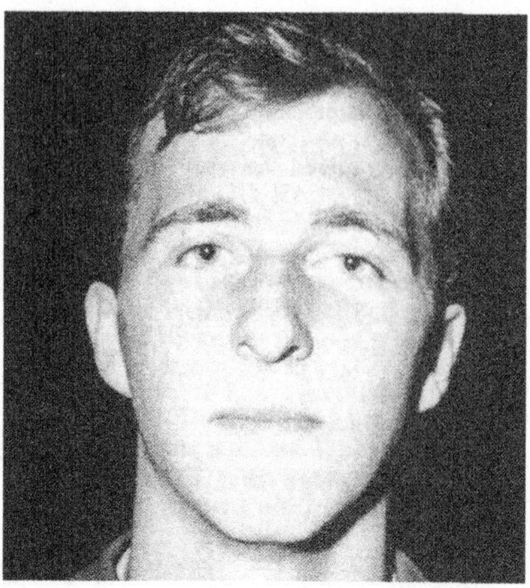

	League		Lge Cup		FA Cup		Other	
	A	G	A	G	A	G	A	G
1986–87	0+1	0	0	0	0	0	0	0
TOTAL	0+1	0	0	0	0	0	0	0

GOTTS, James Atkinson 'Jim'

Height: Weight:

Born: 17 January 1917, Seaton Delaval.
Died: December 1998, Ealing.

■ Gotts was one of the 'Brentford Six' – U's manager Syd Fieldus's old club – who stood in for a depleted United at a League Cup match at Guildford in March 1946 when a number of U's Army regulars were playing in a Regimental Cup Final. Right-winger Gotts started with Ashington and played six times in the League for Brentford in 1945–46, scoring one goal. He also represented Brighton twice during 1946–47.

	League		Lge Cup		FA Cup		Other	
	A	G	A	G	A	G	A	G
1945–46	0	0	1	0	0	0	-	-
TOTAL	0	0	1	0	0	0	-	-

GOUGH, Robert George 'Bobby'

Height: 5ft 7in. Weight: 11st 2lb.

Born: 20 July 1949, Ladywood.

■ Gough started his apprenticeship at nearby Walsall and played just one game after signing professional in July 1967. A year later he transferred to Port Vale, scoring 23 goals in 189(+21) appearances at Vale Park. He won promotion in 1970 and was top scorer in 1971–72. Spending a spell on loan at Stockport in February 1973, he played six times in the League without scoring. In the summer of 1974 he was sold to Southport where he made 61 appearances, netting 16 times. Gough was on Dick Graham's target list in 1968 when he joined Vale and Bobby Roberts finally brought him to Colchester in January 1976 as United fought to maintain their Third Division status. Costing £7,000, Gough made his debut against the star-studded Crystal Palace team. He could not help prevent relegation but more than re-paid his transfer fee with 46 League goals in the next three seasons, including winning promotion back to Division Three. He scored in a 2–0 League Cup win at Villa Park and blasted a hat-trick against Oxford in the FA Cup. Moreover, he formed a lethal strike force with Colin Garwood, ably assisted by John Froggatt. Garwood and Gough became known as 'The G Men'. In 1980–81 Gough suffered broken toes in only the fourth game of the season and never really recovered any form. He joined Hendon in March 1981 and then later played for Chelmsford and Wivenhoe and was licensee of the Layer Fox pub in Layer-de-la-Haye.

	League		Lge Cup		FA Cup		Other	
	A	G	A	G	A	G	A	G
1975–76	22	5	0	0	0	0	-	-
1976–77	43	17	3	1	6	1	-	-
1977–78	42	13	5	3	4	1	-	-
1978–79	42	16	2	0	6	6	-	-
1979–80	31+1	10	4	2	3	0	-	-
1980–81	15	4	1	1	1+1	0	-	-
TOTAL	195+1	65	15	7	20+1	8	-	-

GRACE, John Michael

Height: 6ft 2in. Weight: 12st 7lb.

Born: 16 February 1964, Dublin, ROI.

■ Grace was recruited by Jock Wallace in the summer of 1989 from Irish junior

side Tolka Rovers. Because of his nervy start, Wallace brought in loanee Roger Hansbury, but Grace recovered a little and when Hansbury was re-called by injury-hit Birmingham kept the number-one shirt until Wallace's departure. New manager Mick Mills brought in Scott Barrett on loan, and Grace was released and returned to Ireland where he played for Kilkenny, Limerick and Tolka in the South and Crusaders in the North.

	League		Lge Cup		FA Cup		Other	
	A	G	A	G	A	G	A	G
1989–90	19	0	2	0	2	0	2	0
TOTAL	19	0	2	0	2	0	2	0

GRAINGER, Martin Robert

Height: 5ft 11in. Weight: 11st 13lb.

Born: 23 August 1972, Enfield.

■ A defender from the 'When I tackle them they stay tackled' school, Grainger progressed through United's Youth ranks, representing the FA against The Independent Schools at Bisham Abbey in 1988–89, and was thrown in at the deep end as Colchester battled against relegation to the Conference. He made his debut in Jock Wallace's last game in charge at home to Torquay in a desperately poor 3–0 defeat in December 1989. He scored his first goal on Boxing Day in a surprise 2–0 win at Southend under the caretaker leadership of Steve Foley. He scored again on New Year's Day against Hartlepool as U's threatened to repeat their great escape of the previous season. Unfortunately, United were relegated. Grainger's' appearances were stifled by managers Ian Atkins and Roy McDonough as both banked on experience to get United back into the League. He played more often in 1992–93 and began 1993–94 as a starter before Peter Cawley arrived. Others maybe appreciated his ability more than the U's management at the time, and when Brentford stepped in, offering £60,000 for a player who had been on the bench in four of the last six games, the club thought it was an offer they could not refuse. In his second season Brentford lost in the Play-offs, but his chance to play in Division One soon came when he joined Barry Fry's Birmingham in March 1996 for £400,000 after 100(+1) appearances and 12 goals for the Bees. Suffering three consecutive years of Play-off heartache, Grainger, Player of the Year in 1999–90, and his Birmingham side finally won through to the Premiership against Norwich at the Millennium Stadium in 2002–03. He also played at the same venue against Liverpool in the League Cup Final in the same campaign. The defender made 8(+1) Premiership appearances but suffered a serious injury that kept him out for a long spell. In the course of recovery he spent time on loan at Coventry in February 2004, playing seven times. He returned to St Andrews full of vigour but after 3(+1) games broke down again. Fittingly, Grainger's last game was against Manchester United, and he scored in a 2–1 defeat. His 25 goals in 205(+21) games for the Blues left him as a fans' folk hero, epitomised by playing 43 minutes against West Bromwich Albion without noticing that he had a broken leg. He was rewarded with a testimonial in November 2005, after which he joined

Bishop's Stortford but was thwarted by a thigh injury in 2006. He spent three days in charge of Cheshunt in January 2008 before deciding that management was not for him.

	League		Lge Cup		FA Cup		Other	
	A	G	A	G	A	G	A	G
1989–90	4+3	2	0	0	0	0	1	0
1990–91	3+2	0	1	0	1	0	0+1	0
1991–92	9+2	0	2	0	0+2	0	0+2	0
1992–93	28+3	3	1	0	2	0	1	1
1993–94	5+3	2	2	0	0	0	1	0
TOTAL	37+9	7	3	0	3+2	0	3	1
	12+4	0	3	0	-	-	0+3	0

GRANVILLE, Daniel Patrick 'Danny'

Height: 5ft 11in. Weight: 11st 5lb.

Born: 19 January 1975, Islington.

■ A youth trainee with Cambridge, Granville signed full forms in May 1993 and scored an impressive five goals in just 10(+1) appearances in his first full season. After 89(+10) appearances and seven goals, Granville was snapped up by Chelsea in March 1997 for £300,000. He made his Premiership debut as a substitute against Arsenal and also earned an England Under-21 call up, playing against Georgia at Charlton. Earning two further Under-21 caps, Granville remained understudy to Graham Le Saux, featuring 12(+6) times, but did step in for the full-back, winning a European Cup-winners' Cup medal when Chelsea beat Stuttgart in 1998. Later that summer he joined Leeds for £1.6 million but again was an understudy, this time to Ian Harte. With

just 7(+2) games under his belt and an appearance in the UEFA Cup, Granville moved to Manchester City on a three-month loan, completing a £1 million move in the October and helping City to runners'-up spot in Division One. In October 2000 he spent six games on loan at Norwich. In December 2001 Granville joined Crystal Palace in a £500,000 deal after 56(+14) appearances and three goals for Manchester City. He helped Palace to a Play-off Final victory over West Ham at the Millennium Stadium in 2004 but missed most of the 2005–06 season through injury. Released by Palace in the summer of 2007, Granville was recruited by U's boss Geraint Williams to replace Chris Barker who had opted to join QPR. Granville made his debut in a League Cup tie at Shrewsbury in the August but faced a fight with George Elokobi and then John White for the left-back slot. Granville was released at the end of the season, joining Leyton Orient in June 2008.

	League		Lge Cup		FA Cup		Other	
	A	G	A	G	A	G	A	G
2007–08	14+5	0	1	0	0	0	-	-
TOTAL	14+5	0	1	0	0	0	-	-

GRAY, Simon

Born: 1972, Manchester.

■ Released by Ipswich Town at the end of his apprenticeship, Gray came to Layer Road on trial for the 1992 pre-season and spent the year with the club on non contract terms. He was an unused sub in the first away game, the long trip to Barrow, and made his only start in a 1–1 draw at Cheltenham in September 1991 as stand-in for Steve McGavin. His only other outing was as a substitute in the December of the same year in a Bob Lord Trophy game against Wycombe, and that was the only other time his name appeared in the matchday squad. He started 1992 with the first of several spells at Wivenhoe and has played for many local non-League clubs since including Clacton, Felixstowe, Harwich, Witham and Woodbridge.

	League		Lge Cup		FA Cup		Other	
	A	G	A	G	A	G	A	G
1991–92	1	0	0+1	0	0	0	0	0
TOTAL	1	0	0+1	0	0	0	0	0

GRAY

■ Gray was a Scottish junior player who was serving in the Army Fire Fighting Corps. His only game was in an 8–0 thrashing at Yeovil in September 1945 when the U's found half their regular team unavailable and had to desperately scour the Colchester Garrison for last-minute replacements, most of whom never played for the club again.

	League		Lge Cup		FA Cup		Other	
	A	G	A	G	A	G	A	G
1945–46	1	0	0	0	0	0	-	-
TOTAL	1	0	0	0	0	0	-	-

GREEN, Cecil John

Born : 17 February 1912, Swindon.
Died: January 2000.

■ Cecil Green signed for Swindon Town as an amateur in 1934 but spent most of his playing career in the colours of Cheltenham Town. After hanging up his boots in 1950, he started work as a scout for Swindon Town. In 1959 he joined the board and set up the youth system that produced great players like Don Rogers, John Trollope and Mike Summerbee. Cecil Green took over as chairman of Swindon Town in 1972 – a position he would hold for 11 years. He became president in 1989 and remained a familiar face at the County Ground and at football grounds all over the country. Green was loaned to Colchester by Cheltenham manager Jimmy Brain after Brentford's Sutton, expected to guest for United, did not show up, leaving U's one short for the fixture at Whaddon Road. A second player named Green guested for United in the League fixture at Cheltenham in the same season and, although having a contradictory name initial in the published line up, local press reports indicate that it was the same player in both instances.

	League		Lge Cup		FA Cup		Other	
	A	G	A	G	A	G	A	G
1945–46	1	0	1	0	0	0	-	-
TOTAL	1	0	1	0	0	0	-	-

GREEN, Ronald Rex 'Ron'

Height: 6ft 2in. Weight: 14st.

Born: 3 October 1956, Birmingham.

■ With U's manager Roy McDonough unable to attract a regular goalkeeper following the departure of Scott Barrett in the summer and the ending of Paul Newell's loan spell, he turned his attention to former Walsall colleague Ron Green. The vastly experienced player initially joined the Saddlers from Alvechurch in the summer of 1977 and played 163 times at Fellows Park, winning promotion in 1979–80. Moving to Shrewsbury in the summer of 1984. Green played 19 times before signing for Bristol Rovers eight months later. Completing 56 League games for the Pirates, he was on the move again, this time to Scunthorpe, where he featured 78 times between 1986 and 1988 and was a losing Play-off Finalist. Top flight club Wimbledon signed the 'keeper for £20,000 as back-up to Hans Segers, but his appearances were restricted to just four games. He was loaned to Shrewsbury in September 1988, playing 17 games, and on transfer deadline day of the same season returned to his roots at Walsall to play a further 67 games. Walsall plummeted two divisions and Green was released to Alvechurch. Picked up by Conference side Kidderminster, Green played against Colchester in his 41 starts for the club in 1991–92 and stayed in the Conference for a further three seasons with Bromsgrove Rovers, appearing 59 times after his spell at Layer Road. That spell at Colchester was

something of a disaster. Green conceded 10 goals in just three League games and was blamed for all of them. He had further associations with Cambridge, Shrewsbury, Walsall, Hereford, Redditch, Moor Green, Oldbury United and as Community Officer at Coventry, but his games at Layer Road were his last in League football.

	League		Lge Cup		FA Cup		Other	
	A	G	A	G	A	G	A	G
1992–93	4	0	0	0	3	0	1	0
TOTAL	4	0	0	0	3	0	1	0

GREENE, David Michael

Height: 6ft 4in. Weight: 14st 4lb.

Born: 26 October 1973, Luton.

■ Greene was picked up by Luton from Irish side St Joseph's, signing for the Hatters in September 1991. Capped a then record 14 times at Republic of Ireland Under-21 level, Greene made 18(+1) appearances in the top flight for a struggling Hertfordshire side. He spent time out at Conference side Dagenham & Redbridge and Woking before joining Steve Wignall's Colchester on loan in November 1995. Impressing in 14 games, United could not afford Luton's fee, and the player had a similar spell at Brentford, arriving on deadline day 1996. Greene played out the last 11 games at Griffin Park, but Wignall finally got his man in the close season for £30,000, and he quickly established a partnership with Peter Cawley. He played twice at Wembley for Colchester against Carlisle and Torquay and followed in the footsteps of the likes of Steve Dowman and Wignall, himself in being a goalscoring centre-half. His eight goals in 1998–99 made him second-leading scorer and prompted a move to Cardiff in the summer of 2000. After just 10 starts for the Welshmen, he moved back to East Anglia with Cambridge in March 2001 but made just one appearance.

	League		Lge Cup		FA Cup		Other	
	A	G	A	G	A	G	A	G
1995–96	14	1	0	0	0	0	2	0
1996–97	44	2	4	0	1	0	6	1
1997–98	38	4	2	0	4	0	3	1
1998–99	42	8	2	0	1	0	1	0
1999–2000	29	1	2	0	1	0	0	0
TOTAL	167	16	10	0	7	0	12	2

GREGG, Robert Edmund 'Bob'

Height: 5ft 8in. Weight: 11st 7lb.

Born: 4 February 1904, Ferryhill.
Died: May 1991, Hounslow.

■ Inside-forward Gregg enjoyed a long career. Starting with Ferryhill Athletic, Comford Juniors, Spennymoor United and Chilton Colliery Welfare, Gregg joined Darlington in 1926, scoring 21 goals in 40 matches. Moves to Sheffield Wednesday (1928–30, 37 appearances/7 goals) and Birmingham (1930–33, 66/11) resulted in Gregg signing for Chelsea in September 1933, having already won a Championship medal in 1929. Despite a distinguished career with his previous two clubs, Gregg failed to settle at Stamford Bridge and played the majority of his time in the reserves. He is often remembered as being the scorer of the best disallowed goal in an FA Cup Final, against West Bromwich Albion in 1931. He made his Chelsea debut in September 1933 and briefly played for Boston United in 1938 and Sligo Rovers, and although he signed as a professional for Colchester he was released at the end of 1945–46 after just three games.

	League		Lge Cup		FA Cup		Other	
	A	G	A	G	A	G	A	G
1945–46	2	1	0	0	1	0	-	-
TOTAL	2	1	0	0	1	0	-	-

GREGORY, David Spencer

Height: 5ft 9in. Weight: 12st.

Born: 23 January 1970, Sudbury.

■ Gregory made his debut for Ipswich at Chelsea in December 1988 after signing professionally in March 1987. He scored one goal in the Premiership against Crystal Palace at the end of the 1992–93 season and had netted a hat-trick against Watford in a Full Members' Cup tie in November 1989, but after just 16(+16) appearances in six seasons he sought pastures new. He had two games on loan at Hereford in January 1995 before signing for Peterborough in the summer. With just three substitute appearances at London Road he was brought on trial to Layer Road in December 1995. He established his career at Colchester and will always be remembered for scoring the winning goal from the penalty spot in the 1997–98 Third Division Play-off Final at Wembley. Colchester's win over Torquay began the elevation that would eventually see United in the Championship. Gregory had already scored twice in the semi-final second-leg win over Barnet. He followed that by becoming United's leading scorer in the next campaign before injury curtailed his professional playing career. He was released in the summer of 2002 and joined Canvey, where his brother Neil,

also a former U's player, was playing. In August 2003 he turned out for Wivenhoe before returning to Layer Road to join the successful Media Department, where he continued in to the 2007–08 season as United prepared to move to their new stadium at Cuckoo Farm.

	League		Lge Cup		FA Cup		Other	
	A	G	A	G	A	G	A	G
1995–96	7+3	0	0	0	0	0	0	0
1996–97	32+6	1	1+1	0	1	0	7	0
1997–98	42+2	5	2	0	4	2	4	3
1998–99	43+1	11	2	2	1	0	1	1
1999–2000	45	0	2	0	1	0	1	0
2000–01	27+1	3	1	0	1	0	1	0
2001–02	15+1	0	2	0	0	0	1	0
TOTAL	211+14	20	10+1	2	8	2	15	4

GREGORY, Neil Richard

Height: 6ft. Weight: 12st 6lb.

Born: 7 October 1973, Ndola, Zambia.

■ The younger brother of Colchester's David Gregory started his career on the Youth Training Scheme at Ipswich. Signing professionally in February 1992, Gregory played 18(+29) times for Town, scoring nine League goals. In March 1994 he played 2(+1) games on loan at Chesterfield, scoring once. He had similar spells with Scunthorpe in March 1995, where he scored an impressive seven goals in just 10 starts. During this time Ipswich were in the Premiership and Gregory made 1(+2) appearances in the top flight. November 1996 saw another loan stint, this time at Torquay, where he turned out five times. Almost exactly a year later he had a month at Peterborough, netting once in 2(+1) starts. Gregory also appeared in goal for Ipswich when another former U's man, Craig Forrest, was injured, although he did see four Charlton goals fly past him. Steve Wignall paid a then club-record £50,000 to bring the player down the A12 to Layer Road in March 1998 after an initial three-month loan. Gregory scored twice on his full debut at Darlington in the January and enjoyed a Wembley Play-off outing as United defeated Torquay to win promotion. Never able to live up to the record signing tag, Gregory had a short spell in America with Boston Bulldogs before returning to play regularly for Canvey Island. He carved out a successful time with the South Essex club, winning the FA Trophy and helping the club to promotion to the Conference. He also scored winning goals in the FA Cup as Canvey shocked both Wigan and Northampton. Gregory then joined Wivenhoe, for whom he was still playing in 2007.

	League		Lge Cup		FA Cup		Other	
	A	G	A	G	A	G	A	G
1997–98	12+3	7	0	0	0	0	3	0
1999–99	29+9	4	2	0	0	0	1	0
TOTAL	41+12	11	2	0	0	0	4	0

GRENFELL, Stephen John

Height: 5ft 9in. Weight: 10st 11lb.

Born: 27 October 1966, Enfield.

■ Grenfell's career started as a Tottenham apprentice where he signed forms in August 1984. Unable to make the first team he joined Colchester, initially on loan in October 1986 before completing a £15,000 transfer. He made his first start in a 3–0 Layer Road win over Wolves, scoring his first goal at Scunthorpe in a 5–2 defeat during November. He missed several games through injury but played in the home leg of the Play-off semi-finals at the end of 1986–87. Early into the 1988–89 season Grenfell was placed on the transfer list by Roger Brown and eventually moved into non-League with Bromley, then Dagenham before joining Aylesbury for 1992–93. In 1998 he became Head of Tottenham's Football in the Community scheme.

	League		Lge Cup		FA Cup		Other	
	A	G	A	G	A	G	A	G
1986–87	23	1	0	0	3	1	4	0
1987–88	39+2	0	0+1	0	3	0	4	0
1988–89	5+1	0	2	0	0	0	1	0
TOTAL	67+3	1	2+1	0	6	1	9	0

GRICE, Michael John 'Mike'

Height: 5ft 8in. Weight: 11st 10lb.

Born: 3 November 1931, Woking.

Died: August 2002, Waveney.

■ Lowestoft Town amateur Grice, who had made one of his earliest first-team appearances for the Suffolk club against the U's reserves in August 1948, was taken on the U's post season tour to Holland in May 1952 and signed as a part-time pro with the U's that summer. The 21-year-old made his debut against Bristol Rovers in September 1952 in a 3–0 Layer Road victory and scored his first goal at Walsall at the end of that same month. In the November he started his National Service in the Royal Engineers and after basic training was conveniently stationed in the London area. Just before his demob two years later he played and scored for the British Army against the Belgian Army. For a while after demob he continued his profession as a draughtsman, eventually switching to football full-time in April 1955. Grice soon caught the attention of West Ham, managed by former Colchester boss Ted Fenton, and Ted paid his brother Benny, the Colchester manager, £9,000 for Grice in March 1956. Grice helped the East Londoners into the First Division in 1958, playing 150 League and Cup games, scoring 19 goals, before moving to Coventry in August 1961. This was just as the Jimmy Hill-led Sky Blues were beginning their journey from the Third Division to the top flight, and in his only season at Highfield Road Grice scored six times in 38 League starts. He returned to newly-promoted Colchester for a four-figure sum in 1962–63, becoming the first ex-player to

return for a second spell. When the club were relegated in 1965 Grice stepped down to part-time, resuming work as a draughtsman at Eastern Coachworks, where he stayed until his retirement in 1992, but still played a part of the successful promotion winning-side of 1965–66, particularly in the early part of the season. Grice played under four managers at Layer Road: Jimmy Allen, Jack Butler, Benny Fenton and Neil Franklin, and he was back with Lowestoft in August 1966 after his retirement from the professional game. He missed three-quarters of the 1967–68 season with knee trouble and had a cartilage operation in the summer of 1968 and, although he played in Lowestoft's trial game in August 1968, that injury effectively ended his playing career.

	League		Lge Cup		FA Cup		Other	
	A	G	A	G	A	G	A	G
1952–53	13	1	-	-	0	0	-	-
1953–54	18	2	-	-	0	0	-	-
1954–55	38	6	-	-	2	1	-	-
1955–56	37	6	-	-	1	0	-	-
1962–63	45	8	1	0	1	0	-	-
1963–64	42	4	3	1	2	0	-	-
1964–65	40	1	2	0	3	0	-	-
1965–66	12+1	0	2	0	0	0	-	-
TOTAL	245+1	28	8	1	9	1	-	-

GRIFFITHS, Richard David 'Richie'

Height: 5ft 10½in. Weight: 11st 9lb.

Born: 21 March 1942, Earls Colne.

■ Griffiths was another product of the successful local junior side Colchester Casuals. Signed as a full-back in June 1961, U's manager Benny Fenton saw him as a straight replacement for Tommy Millar who had returned to his native Scotland following the tragic death of his

son. Griffiths played the final 16 games of the 1961–62 season as Colchester won promotion back to Division Three. He continued into the next season, playing 23 consecutive League games, before Keith Rutter arrived to play centre-half and Duncan Forbes switched to right-back. With the experienced Pat Woods around, and able to play either full-back Griffiths did not get a look-in during 1963–64, and although Rutter's departure required Forbes to go back to centre-half for the early part of 1964–65 Mick Loughton's emergence saw Griffiths again lose his spot to Forbes. This time it was for good, and when released at the end of the season he left full-time football to work at Paxman's Diesels and play part-time for Haverhill Rovers, where former U's teammate Peter Wright had just taken over as player-manager. Griffiths moved to Sudbury for 1966–67 and stayed with them until he joined the Police in early 1968, when he stopped playing. He later became a detective, based in Chelmsford.

	League		Lge Cup		FA Cup		Other	
	A	G	A	G	A	G	A	G
1961–62	16	0	0	0	0	0	-	-
1962–63	23	0	2	0	1	0	-	-
1963–64	-	-	-	-	-	-	-	-
1964–65	9	0	2	0	0	0	-	-
TOTAL	48	0	4	0	1	0	-	-

GROVES, Perry

Height: 5ft 11in. Weight: 11st 12lb.

Born: 19 April 1965, Bow.

■ Playing for local youth side Cornard Dynamos, Groves earned a trial at

Wolves before joining Colchester as an apprentice in 1981 and progressed so quickly that he was in the U's first team nine days before his 17th birthday, starting the last nine games of the season. He signed pro forms in June 1982 and was noted for his incredible speed down the wing. He set up countless goals for the strike pair of Keith Bowen and Tony Adcock over two seasons and made a substitute appearance against Manchester United in the League Cup. His greatest U's feat was to score two hat-tricks against Essex rivals Southend in the space of eight weeks. First he hit three in a 4–2 League win at Roots Hall in October 1985 and then repeated the dose in a 4–1 Freight Rover Trophy win the following January. Aspiring to greater things, Groves rejected a new contract and became new Arsenal manager George Graham's first signing when he moved to Highbury for £50,000 in September 1986, following in the footsteps of his Uncle Vic who played around 200 times for the Gunners in the 1950s and early 1960s. Groves played in the Littlewoods League Cup Final in 1987 against Liverpool at Wembley and set up the winning goal for Charlie Nicholas. The following campaign he again reached the final of the same competition but this time lost to Luton. In Arsenal's title-winning campaign of 1988–89 Groves was used mainly from the bench, appearing 15 times as a substitute, along with six starts. Two seasons later he picked up a title medal in similar fashion, coming off the bench 19 times, starting on 13 occasions. In those two Championship-winning seasons he bagged four and six goals respectively. With first-team opportunities becoming increasingly hard to come by he moved to Southampton in August 1992 for a fee of £750,000. He was forced to retire after two Achilles tendon injuries and just 13(+2) appearances for Saints. He attempted to resurrect some football by turning out for Dagenham & Redbridge but lasted just four games. Already a Gunners cult hero, when Groves released his biography entitled *We All Live In a Perry Groves World* in 2006, irate Gunners fans, upset at the manner of Ashley Cole's departure to Chelsea, launched a web campaign to ensure that Groves' book outsold that of Cole. Such was the success of the campaign that the book also outsold the biographies of Rio Ferdinand and Frank Lampard. Groves became a TV pundit on Alpha TV's *Soccer Night*.

	League		Lge Cup		FA Cup		Other	
	A	G	A	G	A	G	A	G
1981–82	9	0	0	0	0	0	-	-
1982–83	8+9	2	2	1	0	0	3	0
1983–84	38+4	2	4+1	0	2	0	1	0
1984–85	44	10	2	0	3	1	3	1
1985–86	42+1	12	1	0	1	0	2	3
1986–87	1	0	0	0	0	0	0	0
TOTAL	142+14	26	9+1	1	6	1	9	4

GUTTRIDGE, Luke Horace

Height: 5ft 5in. Weight: 9st 7lb.

Born: 27 March 1982, Barnstaple.

■ A youth trainee at Torquay, Guttridge played just two minutes for the Devonians, coming on as a substitute against Mansfield in April 2000. Joining Cambridge four months later, he played a couple of LDV Trophy games before scoring on his League debut against Oldham. Unfortunately, he missed the remainder of the season through injury. He became a regular in the Cambridge midfield and turned out 127(+9) times, scoring 17 goals in the League. Charlton looked at the player as a possible £200,000 replacement for Scott Parker, but the deal did not materialise. When it became clear that Cambridge were going to slip into the Conference Guttridge joined Southend on deadline day 2005. He helped Southend to League Two Play-off success and then won

a League One Championship medal in 2005–06 when Southend pipped Colchester to the title. After starting the early games in the 2006–07 Championship season Guttridge fell out with manager Steve Tilson and was loaned to Leyton Orient in November 2006, where he played seven games and scored once. Unable to reconcile the situation back at Roots Hall, Guttridge signed for Leyton Orient in January 2007, playing a further 8(+2) games. Geraint Williams brought the combative midfielder to Layer Road in the summer of 2007 after 59(+4) appearances and six goals for the South Essex side, and he made his debut as a substitute in the opening-day fixture at Sheffield United but was released at the end of the season after making little impact on U's midfield. He signed off in the last-ever fixture at Layer Road, scoring for U's second string against Peterborough reserves.

	League		Lge Cup		FA Cup		Other	
	A	G	A	G	A	G	A	G
2007–08	5+9	0	1	0	1	0	-	-
TOTAL	5+9	0	1	0	1	0	-	-

GUY, Jamie Leslie

Height: 6ft 1in. Weight: 13st.

Born: 1 August 1987, Barking.

■ A West Ham supporter, this Dagenham schoolboy was picked up as an Under-15s player when released by the Hammers, and the powerful Guy progressed through United's youth scheme to make his debut as a substitute

against Blackpool in February 2005. He was leading scorer for the youth team in 2004–05, scoring a memorable goal in the FA Youth Cup win over Chelsea when the Premiership club's international central-defenders just could not handle his pace and power. He was loaned out to Eastern Counties League side Tiptree United to gain experience of adult football during 2004 and, although still eligible for the youth team for 2005–06, it was felt Guy would gain nothing from playing at that level. He continued his development in the reserves and with loan spells at Gravesend, Staines and notably Cambridge United, where he became a big hit with the Conference club's fans, scoring twice in 12 League games 2005. His full U's debut came during 2005–06 in December's LDV Trophy tie at Milton Keynes Dons, and his first Football League start arrived at the impressive surroundings of Sunderland's Stadium of Light in 2006–07. He joined the action from the bench an incredible 31 times in Colchester's first-ever Championship season, scoring goals against West Brom, Coventry and Cardiff. Guy's 2007–08 season was affected by injuries and off-the-field problems.

	League		Lge Cup		FA Cup		Other	
	A	G	A	G	A	G	A	G
2004–05	0+2	0	0	0	0	0	0	0
2005–06	0+2	0	0	0	0	0	1+3	0
2006–07	1+31	3	1	0	0+1	0	-	-
2007–08	0+11	0	0	0	0+1	0	-	-
TOTAL	1+46	3	1	0	0+2	0	1+3	0

H

HADLAND, Phillip John 'Phil'

Height: 5ft 9in. Weight: 11st 5lb.

Born: 20 October 1980, Warrington.

■ A YTS player with Reading, Hadland made just one League Cup appearance for the Royals before being released into non-League with Aldershot. In August 2000 he signed for Rochdale and bagged two goals in 12(+20) games. A year later he signed for Leyton Orient but struggled to break into the first team. Making just five substitute appearances, scoring once, Hadland went on loan to Carlisle in November 2001, scoring once in four outings. On deadline day 2002 he moved to Brighton but appeared just twice as substitute as Albion won the Second Division title. On the move once again, he tried his luck at Darlington playing 4(+2) times for the Quakers before drifting in to non-League with Leek. It was former Reading colleague and U's boss Phil Parkinson that tried to rekindle Hadland's career when bringing him to Layer Road in August 2003. After making his debut as a substitute against Swindon, he was unable to stake a claim for a regular first-team chance and returned to Leek. In July 2004 he moved to neighbours Northwich Victoria and also played for Stalybridge, Bradford Park Avenue, Kidsgrove and was with Hednesford for the 2007–08 season.

	League		Lge Cup		FA Cup		Other	
	A	G	A	G	A	G	A	G
2003–04	0+1	0	0	0	0	0	0+1	0
TOTAL	0+1	0	0	0	0	0	0+1	0

HADLEY, Anthony Paul Frederick 'Tony'

Height: 6ft. Weight: 12st 3lb.

Born: 5 July 1955, Rochford.

■ Hadley signed professional for Southend in July 1974 after joining from Basildon United. He made his debut four months later and twice won promotion with the Shrimpers. Recruited by Cyril Lea in August 1983, Hadley missed just one game in his first season, forming a great defensive partnership with Steve Wignall. He played against Manchester United in the League Cup but failed to turn up at Layer Road for pre-season training the following campaign and then appeared in the Southend defence in the opening day 3–3 draw at Layer Road. Released by Southend at the end of 1984–85, he completed 272(+22) League appearances, scoring 19 goals for the Shrimpers. He moved to Chelmsford and Maldon Town before working as a train driver.

	League		Lge Cup		FA Cup		Other	
	A	G	A	G	A	G	A	G
1983–84	44+1	0	5	0	3	0	2	0
TOTAL	44+1	0	5	0	3	0	2	0

HADRAVA, David Leo

Height: 5ft 10in. Weight: 12st.

Born: 26 February 1983, Enfield.

■ A defender, predominantly at full-back and completely comfortable on either foot, Hadrava established himself in the youth team during the second year of his apprenticeship and progressed so quickly from there that he made his senior debut within about nine months. That debut came in an LDV Trophy match at Reading in October 2001, where he played the last 35 minutes, but this proved to be his only first-team outing. Starting 2002–03 on a short-term pro contract, he was released by Phil Parkinson at the end of September and joined Heybridge, later playing for Thurrock (formerly Purfleet) for four seasons.

	League		Lge Cup		FA Cup		Other	
	A	G	A	G	A	G	A	G
2001–02	0	0	0	0	0	0	0+1	0
TOTAL	0	0	0	0	0	0	0+1	0

HAGAN, James 'Jim'

Height: 5ft 10in. Weight: 10st 9lb.

Born: 10 August 1956, Monkstown, NI.

■ Hagan joined Coventry from Larne Town in November 1977 for £25,000 but made just 12(+1) appearances in the centre of the Sky Blues defence. He was loaned to Torquay in September 1979,

making seven starts for the Fourth Division side. Hagan spent the next two seasons playing in the US with Detroit Express and Washington Diplomats. He also had a stint in Hong Kong with the Seiko club, winning the League title in 1980–81. He was selected for Danny Blanchflower's Northern Ireland 1982 40–man World Cup squad but never made the final 23. Rejoining Coventry in the summer of 1981, he made three further top flight appearances. A year later he was transferred to Birmingham and saw Blues relegated from Division One in 1983–84, only to be part of the squad that won promotion back at the first attempt. Completing 124(+13) games at St Andrews, Hagan moved to Spanish side Celta Vigo in the summer of 1986. He was voted 1987–88 Spanish Overseas Player of the Year, beating off competition from Gary Lineker, while playing 59 times for the Spaniards. Brought to Colchester by Jock Wallace, himself suffering from rapidly declining health, Hagan played in two desperately poor home defeats to Lincoln and Torquay, which culminated in Wallace passing away. In his only other appearance he appeared in a *Match of the Day* main feature against his old club Birmingham in the FA Cup first round. His non-contract deal was not continued and the player spent time in Sweden with IK Oddevold before returning to Northern Ireland, where he became player-manager of Ballymena between 1991 and 1993. He briefly managed Larne in 1993–94 and turned out a handful of times for Carrick Rangers and Crusaders before his final League appearance for Coleraine in 1995 aged almost 40. Hagan was appointed in the Larne hot seat on a permanent basis in the summer of 2006 after previously being assistant manager. After a dismal start to the season, he was sacked in November 2006.

	League		Lge Cup		FA Cup		Other	
	A	G	A	G	A	G	A	G
1989–90	2	0	0	0	1	0	0	0
TOTAL	2	0	0	0	1	0	0	0

HALEY, Ian

■ A soldier with the 14 Field Brigade (from 1939 14 Anti-Tank Regiment) Royal Artillery, a mechanised unit stationed at Reed Hall in Colchester, Haley was a full-back who started playing for Colchester Town in 1935 and when available was a regular first-team starter from early 1936 up until the final game, the Essex Senior Cup tie at Barking in January 1938. He was referred to as the strong man of the Town defence and noted to be a particularly clean kicker of the ball with either foot, appearing many times at both right and left-back as well as having a spell at centre-half for the U's reserves in 1938–39. His first-team appearances for the U's are almost evenly split between right and left-back and he was one of only three to play in both the first U's reserve side at Christmas 1937 and the final game before the war, the delayed 1938–39 Eastern Counties League Cup Final, held over to August 1939. By 1939 he held the rank of Lance Sergeant and played at least twice for Army representative XI's in 1938–39, and for an FA XI against Cambridge University. His regiment were part of the 4th Infantry Division and went to France on 1 October 1939 with the BEF, returning through Dunkirk in June 1940. Later in the war they saw action in North Africa, Italy and Greece. There is no Ian Haley among the published list of World War Two casualties, and it seems likely he was the Yorkshireman born in the West Riding in 1912 who died in Tonbridge in 1960 aged only 48.

	League		Lge Cup		FA Cup		Other	
	A	G	A	G	A	G	A	G
1937–38	5	0	0	0	-	-	4	0
1938–39	0	0	0	0	0	0	1	0
TOTAL	5	0	0	0	0	0	5	0

HALFORD, Gregory 'Greg'

Height: 6ft 3in. Weight: 13st.

Born: 8 December 1984, Chelmsford.

■ A talented all-round sportsman Halford was discovered by the U's at 14, and once he began his apprenticeship and full-time training, developed quickly to get his first-team debut in April 2003. It was not an auspicious start as the U's were thumped 5–0 at home by Luton. He began to establish himself in Phil Parkinson's side the following season with an eye for goal and an enormous long throw-in, an indication of his prowess with the javelin on the athletics field. He gained a taste of the Premiership in successive Colchester FA Cup campaigns when appearing at Blackburn in 2005 and Chelsea in 2006. After being named Young Player of the Year for 2004–05, he won an England call-up and played in the Toulon Under-20 tournament, further impressing the watching scouts. He made his debut against Portugal and scored in a 3–0 success over South Korea. He was also selected for the Football League XI that took on their Italian counterparts at Hull in February and was named in the PFA League One Team of the Year. He missed just one game as Colchester finished runners-up in League One in 2005–06 and, although expected to make a summer move to a top-flight club, remained loyal to the club and played

diligently in United's first-ever season in the Championship. In the transfer window of January 2007 it was Reading who made their move, paying a reported £2.5 million for Halford. The deal was a record for both clubs, and he made his full debut against Tottenham but was unfortunate enough to give away a penalty. Surprisingly, after just 2(+1) appearances Halford made a £3 million move to Sunderland in the 2007 close season. New to the Premiership, Black Cats manager Roy Keane admitted that he had long been an admirer of Halford since a virtuoso display by the player for Colchester at The Stadium of Light in the previous season. But Halford received the wrath of the Wearsiders with two red cards before the end of November. Out-of-favour Halford joined Charlton in January 2006 in a swap with Andy Reid.

	League		Lge Cup		FA Cup		Other	
	A	G	A	G	A	G	A	G
2002–03	1	0	0	0	0	0	0	0
2003–04	15+3	4	0	0	2	0	4	0
2004–05	43+1	4	2+1	1	5	4	1	0
2005–06	45	7	1	0	5	1	3+1	0
2006–07	28	3	1	0	1	0	-	-
TOTAL	132+4	18	4+1	1	13	5	8+1	0

HALL, Brian Samuel

Height: 5ft 9in. Weight: 12st.

Born: 9 March 1939, Burbage
Died: September 2002, Colchester.

■ Hall began his football at Midland League Belper Town before signing professional for Mansfield in April 1959. It was not until he had completed his National Service that Hall struck his best form as he helped Mansfield win promotion in 1962–63. The winger-turned-full-back played 74 times in the League for Mansfield, scoring a creditable 18 goals, and arrived at Layer Road in March 1965. He cemented himself in the club, playing 324(+4) League games in nine seasons, winning promotion in 1965–66, the Watney Cup in 1971, as well as starring in United's famous FA Cup runs of 1968 (losing to West Bromwich Albion) and the world famous victory over Leeds also in 1971. As Colchester headed for re-election in 1972–73 Hall's Layer Road career came to an end, and he joined Chelmsford at Christmas 1972 moving on to link up with manager Dick Graham at

Wimbledon the next season. He returned to play locally for Roy Massey's Eastern Counties League Championship-winning Clacton side in 1974 and had his own first taste of management with Tiptree United in December 1975. He resigned as manager in October 1978, initially agreeing to stay on as a player, but soon moved on to join another ex-teammate Mick Mahon at Rowhedge. Known as 'Henry', Hall was one of the most popular players ever to don a U's shirt and sadly passed away in 2002. In 2007 he was posthumously inducted into United's Hall of Fame.

	League		Lge Cup		FA Cup		Other	
	A	G	A	G	A	G	A	G
1964–65	10	1	0	0	0	0	-	-
1965–66	46	9	2	1	2	1	-	-
1966–67	45	2	1	0	2	1	-	-
1967–68	41	2	0	0	5	0	-	-
1968–69	46	3	2	1	2	2	-	-
1969–70	45	4	3	0	1	0	-	-
1970–71	41+1	4	3	1	7	0	-	-
1971–72	36+2	3	1+1	0	1	1	-	-
1972–73	14+1	0	0	0	3	1	-	-
TOTAL	324+4	28	12+1	3	23	6	-	-

HALLS, John

Height: 6ft. Weight: 11st.

Born: 14 February 1982, Islington.

■ An England Youth and Under-20 international, Halls made three substitute appearances for Arsenal in their 2001–02 League Cup campaign, having been in their 2000 FA Youth Cup-winning side. Signed by Steve

Whitton in January 2002, Halls joined fellow young Gunner Graham Barrett at Layer Road. He made his Layer Road debut against Chesterfield in a 2–1 defeat and struggled a little to adapt to the physicality of the League One game. He returned to Highbury at the end of his loan deal and then spent a similar time at Belgian side Beveren for the whole of the 2003–03 season. His third loan deal came at Stoke where he made eight appearances in October 2003 before securing a permanent £100,000 deal two months later. Completing 59(+2) appearances in The Potteries, scoring three times, Halls moved to ambitious Reading in January 2006 for £250,000, scoring in his only appearance as the Royals stormed to the Championship title. Injury restricted Halls to two League Cup outings in 2006–07, and he remained on Reading's book into the 2007–08 campaign.

	League		Lge Cup		FA Cup		Other	
	A	G	A	G	A	G	A	G
2001–02	6	0	0	0	0	0	0	0
TOTAL	6	0	0	0	0	0	0	0

HAMMOND, Cyril Samuel

Height: 5ft 10in. Weight: 11st 7lb.

Born: 10 October 1927, Woolwich.

■ 'Squib' Hammond joined Charlton from Erith & Belvedere in April 1946. He had to wait until 1950 for his first-team bow but then went on to make 201 League appearances, scoring two goals.

He was an ever-present at wing-half with Benny Fenton in the Charlton side of 1952–53 and joined up with his former teammate at Layer Road in July 1958. A regular in United's side, he was released as U's sunk to Division Four at the end of 1960–61 and retired from full-time football, playing locally for Severalls in the Border League and working in the Building Maintenance department at St Mary's Hospital until his retirement in 1985.

	League		Lge Cup		FA Cup		Other	
	A	G	A	G	A	G	A	G
1958–59	33	0	-	-	4	0	-	-
1959–60	43	1	-	-	1	0	-	-
1960–61	19	4	0	0	0	0	-	-
TOTAL	95	5	0	0	5	0	-	-

HAMMOND, Dean John

Height: 6ft. Weight: 11st 9lb.

Born: 7 March 1983, Hastings.

■ Joining Brighton as a schoolboy, Hammond signed professional forms for Albion in the summer of 2002 after making his debut as a 17-year-old in a

2000–01 LDV Trophy tie against Cardiff. After featuring in four games at the Withdean, Hammond was loaned to Nationwide Conference side Aldershot in September 2003, making seven appearances, and to Leyton Orient a month later, where he played 6(+2) times. Returning to Brighton, he proved himself to manager Mark McGhee and became a regular in the Seagulls midfield. Appointed captain for 2006–07, Hammond completed 122(+14) games, scoring a useful 21 goals and adding a further five strikes in 14(+2) Cup ties. Set to be out of contract at the end of the season, Hammond failed to negotiate a suitable deal for himself, forcing Brighton to cash in on the player or face losing him for free on a Bosman in the summer. A fee of £250,000 brought the player to Layer Road in January 2008 as United sought to stave off relegation from the Championship.

	League		Lge Cup		FA Cup		Other	
	A	G	A	G	A	G	A	G
2007–08	11+2	0	0	0	0	0	-	-
TOTAL	11+2	0	0	0	0	0	-	-

HANNIGAN, Wayne

Born: Republic of Ireland.

■ Combative midfielder Hannigan, nicknamed Spit after the dog puppet in *TisWas*, was one of five Dubliners brought to Layer Road in 1989 by Jock Wallace and the only one apart from Mark Kinsella to make the first team. Hannigan's career path did not quite match his fellow countryman, and he made just two substitute appearances in a Colchester shirt. Both Ian Atkins and Roy McDonough gave the player cameo Bob Lord Trophy appearances against Sutton and Wycombe respectively. Cynics suggested the other four Irish lads were only brought over to keep Kinsella company, but, excluding Martin Grainger three of them, including Hannigan, were probably the next best players, and if the U's finances had been better in 1992 more may have got pro contracts. As it was this was the summer that Chairman Jonathan Crisp departed, and with a second season in the Conference looming future Premiership stars Kinsella and Grainger were the only ones kept. Hannigan spent most of 1991–92 on loan at Wivenhoe, where he

was voted Player of the Year, and the locals were firstly astonished when the U's released him and secondly disappointed when he moved on to Chelmsford. Hannigan's time at Chelmsford was disrupted by injury, and family matters caused him to disappear back to Ireland at short notice on more than one occasion. Eventually he did not come back.

	League		Lge Cup		FA Cup		Other	
	A	G	A	G	A	G	A	G
1990–91	0	0	0+1	0	0	0	0	0
1991–92	0	0	0+1	0	0	0	0	0
TOTAL	0	0	0+2	0	0	0	0	0

HANSBURY, Roger

Height: 5ft 11in. Weight: 12st.

Born: 26 January 1955, Barnsley.

■ Norwich apprentice Hansbury played second fiddle to regular 'keeper Kevin Keelan for the best part of his Norwich career. Signing professional in January 1973, Hansbury played 78 League games for the Canaries but was released in 1981 after first breaking his leg and then contracting jaundice. During his time at City he started 11 times in a November 1977 loan spell at Cambridge. Without a club, he spent time in Hong Kong playing for Eastern. Returning to the UK with Burnley in August 1983, he was a virtual ever-present with 83 games in two seasons. During the close season of 1985 he signed permanently for Fourth Division Cambridge and performed well enough in 37 games to secure a deadline

day move to Birmingham. He was expected to fill the boots of the recently departed David Seaman, but despite making 57 appearances in four seasons he found himself loaned out on three occasions. In October 1987 he had five games with Sheffield United, then three games with Wolves in March 1989 before joining Colchester in August of the same year. The U's seventh 'keeper in less than two years, Hansbury was recruited by Jock Wallace as his new Irish 'keeper John Grace appeared shell-shocked by his introduction to the English game. He played just one more game for Birmingham after his return from Layer Road and was sold to Cardiff in October 1989, going on to complete 99 League starts for the Welshmen before quitting when financial problems prevented wages from being paid by the Welsh club.

	League		Lge Cup		FA Cup		Other	
	A	G	A	G	A	G	A	G
1989–90	4	0	0	0	0	0	0	0
TOTAL	4	0	0	0	0	0	0	0

HARDING, Robert 'Bob'

■ Harding, a Dagenham amateur, signed amateur forms for the U's at the start of 1946–47 and turned pro in November. He had a run in the first team at centre-half early on but was not selected again after the 5–0 FA Cup loss at Reading. Shortly after, player-manager Ted Fenton moved himself into the number-five role. Harding dropped down to the reserves but by the end of the season was carrying an injury that needed a cartilage operation. It was suggested that if the operation was successful he would be back at Layer Road, and in September 1947 the Board were considering whether to re-engage him. They decided not to, and he disappeared from the football map.

	League		Lge Cup		FA Cup		Other	
	A	G	A	G	A	G	A	G
1946–47	8	0	1	0	2	0	-	-
TOTAL	8	0	1	0	2	0	-	-

HARFORD, Raymond Thomas 'Ray'

Height: 6ft 1in. Weight: 12st 2lb.

Born: 1 June 1945, Halifax.
Died: August 2003, Surrey.

■ Jim Smith signed Harford from Port Vale in January 1973 to plug United's defence in a side destined for re-election. He arrived on a month's loan and was signed for a small fee at the end of the month. The following season he formed a rock-like central defensive partnership with Stuart Morgan as the U's won promotion to Division Three. An ever-present in that season, Harford had begun his career as a Charlton junior, playing three games after signing professional in May 1964. Joining Exeter in January 1966, the player scored one goal in 55 League appearances before teaming up with future U's boss Smith at Lincoln. The pair played in the same Imps side, with Harford scoring 10 in 161 starts. He began the 1971–72 season at Mansfield, but after just seven games he moved to Port Vale in December 1971 where he clocked up 20 appearances, scoring one goal. After two cartilage operations at Colchester, Harford was

released at the end of 1974–75 and joined Romford as player-coach. He returned to Layer Road in September 1975 as Bobby Roberts' trainer and youth-team coach, holding an FA coaching badge. A move to Fulham in 1981 was the first stop on a magnificent managerial career. Rising to reserve team manger, Harford then took over the reigns at Craven Cottage in April 1984. He resigned in June 1986 as a reaction to chairman Ernie Clay's selling policy. He became assistant manager to John Moore at Luton, and when Moore quit in June 1987 Harford took over and guided Luton to ninth spot in the top flight and won the club's first-ever major trophy when they beat Arsenal 3–2 in the Littlewoods League Cup Final at Wembley. He took the club to Wembley twice more, losing to Reading in the Simod Cup and then to Nottingham Forest in the League Cup in the same season. By January 1990 Luton were struggling, and Harford was sacked. He moved to Wimbledon and became caretaker manager in the summer of 1990 when Bobby Gould resigned. He took over the manager's role and once again did not suffer fools gladly. When Don's skipper Keith Curle was sold to Manchester City without his knowledge, he gave six months notice of his intention to quit. This was a smart move, as it brought him time to negotiate a move to become Kenny Dalglish's assistant at Blackburn in October 1991. Rovers went on to win promotion to the newly-formed Premiership, winning the title in 1995, and despite his vow never to sit in the hot seat again he took on that mantle when Dalglish retired following the title triumph. He sold Alan Shearer to Newcastle for a then record £15 million, and after that Rovers struggled to emulate their success and Harford resigned in October 1996 with the club bottom of the Premiership. In February 1997 he was appointed manager of West Brom but lasted only until December, when he walked out on the club and joined Queen's Park Rangers. Again his stay was short lived, and by September 1998 he had quit Loftus Road. He was coaxed out of retirement to join Millwall as coach under Keith Stevens and Alan McLeary and remained in the post as

Mark McGhee took the Lions to the 2001 Second Division Championship. A spell as technical advisor at Oxford preceded a battle against cancer, which the much respected coach and manager tragically lost in 2003. As a mark of respect, the England Under-20 team wore black armbands against Croatia, as Harford had also had involvement with the England set up.

	League		Lge Cup		FA Cup		Other	
	A	G	A	G	A	G	A	G
1972–73	21	1	0	0	0	0	-	-
1973–74	46	1	1	0	1	1	-	-
1974–75	40+1	2	6	0	2	0	-	-
TOTAL	107+1	4	7	0	3	1	-	-

HARMAN, Christopher 'Chris'

■ Harman, the spelling used in U's programmes, was a Private in the 15th Infantry Training Corps who was involved in Colchester Garrison football by 1944. His name is also seen spelt Harmon and Harmen in press reports and programmes for Army games, and at least once referred to as Dick Harman in the local press. He was a Bath City player who joined the U's when they restarted in 1945 and played at inside-left at Chelmsford in the first game. Harman was one of four professional players retained at the end of the 1945–46 season, but his work in Glastonbury did not allow him to play on Saturdays so he was released at the start of September without making any further appearances for Colchester.

	League		Lge Cup		FA Cup		Other	
	A	G	A	G	A	G	A	G
1945–46	11	4	3	0	1	0	-	-
TOTAL	11	4	3	0	1	0	-	-

HARRIS, Thomas Alfred 'Tommy'

Born: 8 November 1924, Chelsea.
Died: 11 October 2001.

■ Harris began his career at Fulham in 1947, failing to make the first team. He moved to Leyton Orient in September 1951 and ironically made his mark against Colchester in a 7–0 thrashing when he scored twice. Despite attaining hero status for scoring against Everton and Birmingham in famous Orient FA Cup victories, he lost form and was allowed to join United in June 1953 in an exchange deal for United's Stan Edwards

after 31 League appearances and a respectable 11 goals. He left Layer Road in 1954 and played non-League for Tonbridge, Tunbridge Wells, Yiewsley and Deal Town.

	League		Lge Cup		FA Cup		Other	
	A	G	A	G	A	G	A	G
1953–54	3	0	-	-	0	0	-	-
TOTAL	3	0	-	-	0	0	-	-

HARRIS, Trevor John

Height: 5ft 9in. Weight: 12st 2lb.

Born: 6 February 1936, Colchester.

■ Captain of Essex and London Schoolboys, Harris joined United on leaving East Ward School in July 1951, playing as an amateur in the Border League side until signing as part-time pro in July 1954. As much a centre-half then as his eventual spot of wing-half, he got his first-team chance in April 1955 as deputy for pivot Reg Stewart. One game at right-back and one at left-back came his way in 1955–56 before he did his two

years National Service, and August 1957 saw him in yet another position, left-half, as he made his fourth first-team start. Harris finally broke into the U's first team in the League Cup tie against Newcastle in 1960 and was a virtual permanent fixture, at right-half, for the next two years. His 12 years at Layer Road ended with a free transfer in 1963, and he spent a year in the Southern League with Chelmsford before joining Clacton as they left the Southern League for the Eastern Counties. He later played for Coggeshall, Braintree and Brightlingsea. His son Del became an English International squash player.

	League		Lge Cup		FA Cup		Other	
	A	G	A	G	A	G	A	G
1954–55	1	0	-	-	0	0	-	-
1955–56	2	0	-	-	0	0	-	-
1956–57	0	0	-	-	0	0	-	-
1957–58	7	0	-	-	0	0	-	-
1958–59	1	0	-	-	0	0	-	-
1959–60	0	0	-	-	0	0	-	-
1960–61	27	2	2	0	2	0	-	-
1961–62	43	4	1	0	3	0	-	-
1962–63	18	0	2	0	0	0	-	-
TOTAL	99	6	5	0	5	0	-	-

HARRISON, Derek

Height: 6ft. Weight: 11st 8lb.

Born: 9 February 1950, Leicester.

■ One of ex-manager Jim Smith's summer signings prior to his departure to Blackburn, Harrison began as a Leicester apprentice. Signing professionally in February 1967, he failed to make the first team at Filbert Street and secured a transfer to Torquay in

January 1971. He appeared 124(+3) times in the League for the Devonians, scoring three times. Harrison impressed when scoring in a benefit game for Paul Aimson against Norwich at the end of the 1973–74 season. He suffered injury at Layer Road and never established himself in the side. He was released at the end of the campaign, which saw United relegated to Division Four, and joined Salisbury City.

	League		Lge Cup		FA Cup		Other	
	A	G	A	G	A	G	A	G
1975–76	5+2	0	1	0	0	0	-	-
TOTAL	5+2	0	1	0	0	0	-	-

HARRISON, John Walter

Height: 5ft 10in. Weight: 11st 2lb.

Born: 27 September 1927, Leicester.

■ A tough-tackling full-back, Harrison was signed from Aston Villa for a small fee after making a mark in their Central League side and after completing his National Service in the RAF. His brother Jim played for Leicester in the 1949 FA Cup Final. Harrison's only U's goal was a controversial one. The press of the time gave the goal to Kevin McCurley, but in fact Harrison's shot had taken a massive deflection off a Leyton Orient defender instead. There was no way that the strike was going to be accredited as an own goal in Harrison's eyes and the club officially credited to him in the Manager's Notes of the next week's reserve programme. Eleven months later, in September 1956, Harrison was injured in a collision at Southampton and after an unsuccessful cartilage operation was advised to quit professional football. He took up a position at fan manufacturers Woods of Colchester until his retirement in 1988. During this time he had a couple of spells in charge of Long Melford and managed the very successful Woods football team. He was brother-in-law to United striker Vic Keeble.

	League		Lge Cup		FA Cup		Other	
	A	G	A	G	A	G	A	G
1950–51	31	0	-	-	2	0	-	-
1951–52	41	0	-	-	3	0	-	-
1952–53	46	0	-	-	5	0	-	-
1953–54	41	0	-	-	1	0	-	-
1954–55	35	0	-	-	0	0	-	-
1955–56	40	1	-	-	1	0	-	-
1956–57	3	0	-	-	0	0	-	-
TOTAL	237	1	-	-	12	0	-	-

HARVEY, Gary

Height: 5ft 7in. Weight: 11st 2lb.

Born: 19 November 1961, Colchester.

■ A local lad, Harvey played in the Border League's top division for West End United as a 14-year-old and was taken on as a U's apprentice in March 1978. He got his chance at the tail end of the 1979–80 season as United missed out, by six points, on what would have been their first promotion to the Second Division. He made his debut in a 0–0 stalemate at home to Millwall in the April and three days later grabbed a brace as Colchester won 3–2 at Swindon. Starting a couple of matches in United's relegation season the following campaign, he went to play in Norway with Kongsvinger along with Tony Evans but did not progress as the club had hoped and was released at the end of the season. He and Evans briefly went back to Norway, but the arrangements were not what they expected, and he was soon back and embarked on an extensive local career, representing most of the leading local clubs at some stage.

	League		Lge Cup		FA Cup		Other	
	A	G	A	G	A	G	A	G
1979–80	4	2	0	0	0	0	-	-
1980–81	2	0	0	0	0	0	-	-
TOTAL	6	2	0	0	0	0	-	-

HATHAWAY, Ian Ashley

Height: 5ft 6in. Weight: 10st 6lb.

Born: 22 August 1968, Wordsley.

■ Originally on the books of West Brom, Hathaway was released from The Hawthorns and drifted into non-League with Bedworth United. Spotted by Mansfield, he joined the Stags in February 1989 for £8,000, making 21(+23) appearances in two and a half seasons, scoring twice. He joined Rotherham in March 1991 but made just 5(+8) starts due to injury. Released by the Millers, he signed for Torquay in the summer of 1993 and was part of the club's unsuccessful Play-off campaign. Making 114(+28) appearances for the Devonians, Hathaway netted 14 League goals. Steve Wignall recruited him for Colchester where he joined three other ex-Torquay players in Paul Buckle, Mark Sale and Scott Stamps. His only goal came in a second-leg League Cup draw at Luton in August 1998. Plagued by injury, he was released and joined Aldershot, where he became a cult figure on the Shot's wing over three successful seasons. In 2001 he left Aldershot and joined Andover.

	League		Lge Cup		FA Cup		Other	
	A	G	A	G	A	G	A	G
1997–98	5+7	0	2	1	1+1	0	0	0
TOTAL	5+7	0	2	1	1+1	0	0	0

HAWKSWORTH, Derek Marshall

Height: 5ft 10in. Weight: 11st.

Born: 16 July 1927, Bradford.

■ An amateur with Huddersfield, Hawksworth gained England B honours and a Division Two Championship medal with Sheffield United in 1953. During the war he played 17 times for Bradford Park Avenue, scoring three times. After guesting for Colchester in 1945–46, he played for Bradford in Division Three North, scoring 20 goals in 75 League games between 1948 and 1950. This form alerted Sheffield United for whom he signed in 1950. A Bramall Lane favourite, he notched 88 goals in 255 games. In 1958 he moved to Huddersfield, scoring 14 in 55 matches then appeared for Lincoln in 1959–60 (36/14) and finally Bradford City in 1960–61, where he scored eight goals in 44 fixtures. He then played for non-League Nelson.

	League		Lge Cup		FA Cup		Other	
	A	G	A	G	A	G	A	G
1945–46	4	1	0	0	0	0	-	-
TOTAL	4	1	0	0	0	0	-	-

HAYDON, Nicholas 'Nicky'

Height: 5ft 9in. Weight: 11st 7lb.

Born: 10 August 1978, Barking.

■ A product of Colchester's Youth Training Scheme, Haydon signed professional in August 1995 and made his debut on the last day of the 1996–97 season at Barnet as a substitute. He was booked in his first minute on the field

and scored four minutes from time to secure a 4–2 win. Unlucky to be pressing Joe Dunne, Simon Betts and David Gregory for the full-back berth, Haydon's chances came mainly due to injury. He was loaned to Kettering in March 1999, playing seven Conference games and returned to Rockingham Road the following season on release from Layer Road to play 4(+3) more times. After a failed trial at Norwich, he then joined Heybridge and became almost a permanent fixture in Swifts defence, interspersed with spells at Chelmsford and Braintree and being appointed player-coach at Wivenhoe in the summer of 2003.

	League		Lge Cup		FA Cup		Other	
	A	G	A	G	A	G	A	G
1996–97	0+1	1	0	0	0	0	0	0
1997–98	9+8	0	0	0	1+1	0	1	0
1998–99	7+6	1	2	0	0+1	0	0	0
TOTAL	16+15	2	2	0	1+2	0	1	0

HAZEL (DART), Julian Edward

Born: 25 September 1973, Luton.

■ Known as Dart, his stepfather's name, during his two years as an apprentice at Layer Road, Hazel reverted to his own father's name when he signed a pro contract in the summer of 1992. He made such an impact in his first few weeks that he was given some match time in the first-team pre-season friendly with Southend. He did not immediately fulfill that early promise and only got on to the field three times for the reserves in his first year. At the time he was playing midfield or full-

back, but his true vocation came to light early in 1992 when he was tried up front, 'because he's never going to get a contract as a defender'. Admittedly, the opposition was some way below what was ideal for a professional apprentice, but a double hat-trick in a 14–0 win against Clacton's youth team set him on the way to what would be a prolific career as a goalscorer in non-League football. His full debut came in a League Cup tie at Brighton in August 1992 as he stood in for Steve McGavin who was injured from a holiday prank gone wrong. Unable to make the breakthrough, Hazel moved to Chelmsford and has since had spells at many clubs, including several at Wivenhoe where he was joint manager in 1998 at the age of just 24. Some decent transfer fees have been paid for his services over the years, and some of the U's scouting network still considered him the best prospect on the local circuit at the turn of the Millennium.

	League		Lge Cup		FA Cup		Other	
	A	G	A	G	A	G	A	G
1991–92	*0*	*0*	*0*	*0*	*0*	*0*	*0+2*	*0*
1992–93	2	0	1	0	0	0	1	0
TOTAL	2	0	1	0	0	0	1	0
	0	*0*	*0*	*0*	*0*	*0*	*0+2*	*0*

HEAL, Percival 'Percy'

■ A soldier in No.1 Holding Battalion who had links with Southend and the Irish League, Heal had two months as the U's left-half in October and November 1945, signing pro towards the end of that period. He was then hospitalised with mumps and when demobbed in February 1946 moved to London and was not seen again at Layer Road.

	League		Lge Cup		FA Cup		Other	
	A	G	A	G	A	G	A	G
1945–46	5	0	0	0	1	0	-	-
TOTAL	5	0	0	0	1	0	-	-

HEATH, Matthew Philip 'Matt'

Height: 6ft 4in. Weight: 13st 13lb.

Born: 1 November 1981, Leicester.

■ Heath served his youth traineeship at home-town club Leicester, signing professional in February 2001. Making 42(+9) appearances for the Foxes, including Premier League experience, he scored six League goals and had an eight-game loan spell with Stockport in October 2003. His former Leicester boss, and future Colchester coach, Micky Adams signed Heath for Coventry in 2005, and the defender scored once in 30(+2) League appearances. In November 2006 he was loaned to Leeds and made his debut in a 3–0 win over Colchester at Elland Road. When his loan expired the following January he made the move permanent on a free transfer. After 51(+1) appearances and four League goals, he was sent out on loan to Colchester by new Leeds boss Gary McAllister, having fallen down the defensive pecking order. Heath made his Colchester debut in a 1–1 draw with Cardiff at Layer Road in March 2008, standing in for the injured Chris Coyne

	League		Lge Cup		FA Cup		Other	
	A	G	A	G	A	G	A	G
2007-08	5	0	0	0	0	0	-	-
TOTAL	5	0	0	0	0	0	-	-

HEDMAN, Rudolph Gideon 'Rudi'

Height: 6ft 3in. Weight: 12st.

Born: 16 November 1964, Lambeth.

■ A non-contract player as he came through the U's youth team and reserves until given a pro contract by Cyril Lea in February 1984, Hedman made his debut as a substitute at Bury in April 1984. The following campaign he became a regular after recovering from glandular fever and scored his first U's goal in a 4–1 win over Northampton in February 1985. With Mike Walker in charge, United and Hedman lost out to Wolves in the 1986–87 Fourth Division Play-off semi-finals. Following Walker's sacking, Hedman played through the disastrous spell under manager Roger Brown and was sold to Crystal Palace in December 1988 for a reported £100,000 fee. Steve Foley was in caretaker charge at this time, and Hedman's parting shot was to score in a 2–2 FA Cup draw with Swansea at Layer Road and then repeat the feat as United sensationally beat the Welshmen 3–1 in the Vetch Field replay. In what remained of his first season at Selhurst Park, Hedman found his new club promoted to the top flight via the Play-offs. He played in three of the four Play-off matches in the days before the Final was staged at Wembley. He made 8(+4) appearances in 1989–90 and was loaned out to Leyton Orient in December of that season, where he appeared six times. The following campaign Hedman made just one appearance and returned to Layer Road and Conference football. He could not help United pip Barnet to the coveted place back in the Football League and returned to Palace for 1992–93, where he made just three further appearances as a substitute. He was released to Dulwich Hamlet and had a spell with Sing Tao in Hong Kong and turned out for Witham in 1999. His sister Deta was British Women's Darts Champion in 1994.

	League		Lge Cup		FA Cup		Other	
	A	G	A	G	A	G	A	G
1983–84	3+1	0	0	0	0	0	0	0
1984–85	29+1	2	0	0	1+2	0	3	0
1985–86	38+1	3	2	0	1	0	2	0
1986–87	38+6	4	2	0	2+1	0	4+1	1
1987–88	41+1	0	2	0	3	0	4	0
1988–89	17	1	1	0	3	2	1	0
1990–91	*10*	*0*	*0*	*0*	*0*	*0*	*0*	*0*
TOTAL	166+10	10	7	0	10+3	2	14+1	1
	10	*0*	*0*	*0*	*0*	*0*	*0*	*0*

HETZKE, Stephen Edward Richard 'Steve'

Height: 6ft 2in. Weight: 13st 4lb.

Born: 3 June 1955, Marlborough.

■ Hetzke became the then youngest-ever player to don the hooped shirt of Reading when he made his debut aged 16 years 193 days in December 1971 against Darlington. It was the first of 254(+7) games for the Royals, and he scored nine of his 23 League goals as a converted forward in Reading's 1978–79 Fourth Division Championship side. In the summer of 1976 he also played for Vancouver Whitecaps. Although captain, he was transfer-listed and joined Blackpool for £12,500 in July 1982. In four seasons he scored 18 times in 140 games, winning promotion in 1984–85, and was sold to Sunderland on deadline day 1986. He played 31 times at Roker Park for Lawrie McMenemy's side before finding himself at Chester at the beginning of 1987–88. After completing 14 games, he joined Colchester in March 1988 during the reign of Roger Brown for £10,000, but in only his fifth game he picked up an Achilles injury and missed

the rest of the campaign. Doubling as reserve-team coach for 1938–39, he was injured again in only his second game back and did not return until December. He scored a vital winner against Wrexham in April 1989 as Jock Wallace's side staved off relegation to the Conference and added a goal in a thrilling 3–3 FA Cup fourth-round tie at Sheffield United. On retiring, he worked with the PFA in their youth development programme.

	League		Lge Cup		FA Cup		Other	
	A	G	A	G	A	G	A	G
1987–88	5	0	0	0	0	0	0	0
1988–89	22+2	2	2	0	3	1	3	0
TOTAL	27+2	2	2	0	3	1	3	0

HICKS, Stuart Jason

Height: 6ft 1in. Weight: 12st 6lb.

Born: 30 May 1967, Peterborough.

■ Hicks was released after serving his apprenticeship with Peterborough and spent a year at Rushden Town in the Southern League before moving to Eastern Counties League Wisbech in August 1987. Spotted playing against the U's reserves by manager Roger Brown, Hicks came to Layer Road on trial while serving a two-week suspension in March 1988 and earned a professional contract, making his debut in a 1–0 win over Rochdale the following month. He scored his only goal in a dramatic 3–3 FA Cup fourth-round tie at Sheffield United in January 1989 and epitomised the strength of character that saw U's drag themselves away from relegation to the Conference. When Mick Mills took over as manager in the latter stages of the following campaign Hicks found that his place was taken by Marcelle Bruce. In the summer of 1989 he moved to Scunthorpe and was an ever-present as his new side failed in the Fourth Division promotion Play-offs. In October 1992 he joined neighbours Doncaster, appearing 36 times before securing another move across Yorkshire to Huddersfield a year later. After just 20(+1) games and a single goal, he was picked up by Preston on deadline day 1994 and once again suffered a losing Play-off campaign. Hicks crossed the Pennines again, joining Scarborough in February 1995, playing 81(+4) times for the Seamer Road outfit and being voted Player of the Year in 1995–96. For 1997–98 Hicks signed for Leyton Orient and suffered Play-off heartache for the third time, losing at Wembley to his old club Scunthorpe. Moving to Chester as captain in February 2000, he made 13 starts, but Hicks earned another unwanted record when City were relegated, just like Colchester 10 years earlier, out of the League. He had a short spell at Mansfield in 2000–01, notching up 25 more League appearances before moving in to non-League with Hucknell Town.

	League		Lge Cup		FA Cup		Other	
	A	G	A	G	A	G	A	G
1987–88	7	0	0	0	0	0	0	0
1988–89	34+3	0	0	0	5	1	4	0
1989–90	16+4	0	2	0	0	0	1	0
TOTAL	57+7	0	2	0	5	1	5	0

HILL, Albert 'Bert'

Height: 5ft 8in. Weight: 10st 4lb.

Born: 8 March 1930, West Ham.

■ A former Chelsea junior, Hill signed professionally at Stamford Bridge in May 1950. He joined a struggling United side on a month's trial in August 1952 and was signed for £300 by the end of September. As deputy to Harry Bearryman, he probably thought himself lucky to only have to wait until April for his debut, given that Bearryman had only missed three games in the past five years. He played an important squad role over the next five years but by the end of 1956–57 was transfer listed at his own request because he wanted to find a club nearer his London home. He left Layer Road for Dartford in July 1958, moving to Hastings in June 1959, and later played for Canterbury before knee problems forced him to quit the game. He then had a driving career for Schweppes, worked for a paper bag manufacturer, before becoming a London taxi driver.

	League		Lge Cup		FA Cup		Other	
	A	G	A	G	A	G	A	G
1952–53	1	0	-	-	0	0	-	-
1953–54	16	1	-	-	0	0	-	-
1954–55	19	0	-	-	2	0	-	-
1955–56	22	1	-	-	0	0	-	-
1956–57	15	1	-	-	0	0	-	-
1957–58	31	0	-	-	1	0	-	-
TOTAL	104	3	-	-	3	0	-	-

HILL, Colin Frederick

Height: 5ft 11in. Weight: 12st 2lb.

Born: 12 November 1963, Uxbridge.

■ Hill became an Arsenal apprentice in June 1980, having been with the club on schoolboy forms. He made his debut against Norwich in April 1983 and went on to play 46 times, scoring once. When Arsenal signed Viv Anderson, his first-

team opportunities diminished, and he was given a free transfer in the summer of 1986. He went to Madeira to play for Portuguese League side Maritimo before being signed 15 months later by Mike Walker just days before the U's boss's shock sacking. He made his U's debut as a substitute in a Sherpa Van Trophy tie at Cambridge in November 1987. A polished player in a poor team, it was his display in two FA Cup ties against Sheffield United in January 1989 that persuaded Blades boss Dave Bassett to spend £85,000 on him in the following August. He won promotion in his first season and was picked for Northern Ireland in March 1990. In July 1992, after 77(+5) appearances and a single goal, he was acquired by Leicester for £200,000 and featured in an incredible four Play-off campaigns for the Foxes, playing Premiership football in 1994 and 1996. Completing 140(+5) games for City, he had a spell with Swedish side Trelleborgs in 1997 before joining Northampton in September of the same year. He was involved in yet another Play-off as the Cobblers lost out to Grimsby at Wembley. Hill won 27 caps for Northern Ireland before retiring to run a PR business in Northampton.

	League		Lge Cup		FA Cup		Other	
	A	G	A	G	A	G	A	G
1987–88	22+3	0	0	0	2	1	2+1	0
1988–89	42+2	0	2	0	5	1	1	0
TOTAL	64+5	0	2	0	7	2	3+1	0

HILL, Robert 'Bobby'

Height: 5ft 9in. Weight: 10st 3lb.

Born: 9 June 1938, Edinburgh.

■ Spotted by Benny Fenton when the U's manager went to watch a Scottish junior match between Easthouses Lily and Bonnyrigg Rose, Hill impressed so much that, not only did Fenton capture his signature, but he also signed up Sammy McLeod and John Fowler from the same match. After starring in United's Division Two promotion bid in 1956–57, Hill had to complete his National Service before returning to be a regular in the side and picking up a Fourth Division runners'-up medal in 1961–62. He had become a Jehovah's Witness and in 1965 quit full-time football and worked as a postman until

his retirement. He continued to play semi-pro and after leaving the U's went to Bury Town for just over three years, playing over 150 games, and continued turning out for Wivenhoe Rangers until 1975.

	League		Lge Cup		FA Cup		Other	
	A	G	A	G	A	G	A	G
1955–56	4	1	-	-	0	0	-	-
1956–57	38	7	-	-	1	0	-	-
1957–58	11	0	-	-	0	0	-	-
1958–59	8	1	-	-	0	0	-	-
1959–60	38	4	-	-	1	0	-	-
1960–61	33	1	2	0	2	1	-	-
1961–62	40	3	1	0	3	0	-	-
1962–63	28	4	2	0	1	0	-	-
1963–64	24	0	1	0	0	0	-	-
1964–65	14	0	1	0	0	0	-	-
TOTAL	238	21	7	0	8	1	-	-

HILLMAN, Dennis Victor

Height: 5ft 6in. Weight: 10st 3lb.

Born: 27 November 1918, Southend.
Died: 22 December 1994, Colchester.

■ Previously an amateur with Southend, Hillman served as a Commando in the war and guested for Brighton. He signed for the U's on 21 September 1946 after impressing in a trial for the reserves the previous week. A prominent member of Colchester's 1947–48 FA Cup run, Hillman was also part of the side that gained entry to the Football League in 1949. A very fast winger, Hillman chipped in with some important goals but mainly supplied the ammunition for the likes of Arthur Turner, Bob Curry and Vic Keeble. Hillman joined Gillingham for 1951–52 and made 21 League appearances before turning out for non-League Hastings, Margate and Ramsgate. He helped Hastings to reach the FA Cup third round in two consecutive seasons before being employed at Ford's Dagenham plant and as a Special Constable. Hillman tragically died in a car crash at Birch, near Colchester, after visiting friends from his Wickford home.

	League		Lge Cup		FA Cup		Other	
	A	G	A	G	A	G	A	G
1946–47	*26*	*3*	*7*	*3*	*2*	*1*	-	-
1947–48	*27*	*5*	*6*	*1*	*5*	*0*	-	-
1948–49	*20*	*6*	*3*	*2*	*0*	*0*	-	-
1949–50	*35*	*3*	*5*	*2*	*1*	*0*	-	-
1950–51	4	0	-	-	0	0	-	-
TOTAL	4	0	-	-	0	0	-	-
	108	*17*	*21*	*8*	*8*	*1*	-	-

HILLYARD, Peter

■ Twenty-three-year-old Hillyard, or possibly Hildyard – it is spelt both ways in the local press and there are births registered under both variations in 1925 and 1926 that would fit the age quoted – came in on a week's trial from Leyton Orient but played just one game as a late replacement for centre-half Stamper in United's 4–0 triumph over Hereford on 5 May 1949. Another more successful trialist that day was future goalkeeper George Wright. In July 1951 Chelmsford were reported to have a 6ft 2in centre-half named Peter Hildyard on trial from Hereford United. Nothing came of that trial and it is not known if it is the same gentleman.

	League		Lge Cup		FA Cup		Other	
	A	G	A	G	A	G	A	G
1948–49	1	0	0	0	0	0	-	-
TOTAL	1	0	0	0	0	0	-	-

HINSHELWOOD, Paul Alexander

Height: 6ft. Weight: 12st 6lb.

Born: 14 August 1956, Bristol.

■ Spotted by Crystal Palace playing in a London Schools Cup Final, Hinshelwood was signed up by manager Arthur Rowe to become an apprentice, joining brother Martin who was already on the Eagles books. Originally a striker, Hinshelwood was switched to full-back and won promotion twice as Palace reached the top flight, winning the final promotion in front of a record 51,000 gate at Selhurst Park. Palace fans voted Hinshelwood their Player of the Year in both seasons in the First Division, and he won two England Under-21 caps. After 271(+5) League appearances and 22 goals he moved to Oxford in August 1983, missing just three games as Oxford won the Third Division title. As Oxford pushed and won a second successive promotion, Hinshelwood found himself surplus and joined Millwall in January 1985. Once again he experienced promotion as the Lions moved up to Division Two. Recruited by Mike Walker, Hinshelwood arrived at Layer Road in September 1986 and helped U's reach the Fourth Division Play-offs. After being a virtual ever present, he was discarded by Roger Brown and joined Dartford. Moving into management, Hinshelwood was assistant to Steve Kember at Whyteleafe before taking over the reigns when Kember was appointed boss of Crystal Palace. His sons Adam and Paul are both professionals with Brighton, and his father, Wally, played over 300 League games with Fulham, Chelsea, Reading, Bristol City, Millwall and Newport. Brother Martin played in the League for Crystal Palace and was a very successful youth-team coach at Brighton while nephew Danny, Martin's son, also played a handful of League games for three clubs in the mid-1990s.

	League		Lge Cup		FA Cup		Other	
	A	G	A	G	A	G	A	G
1986–87	41	1	0	0	3	0	5	0
1987–88	40	5	2	0	3	0	4	0
TOTAL	81	6	2	0	6	0	9	0

HODGE, John 'Jack'

Height: 5ft 8in. Weight: 11st.

Born: Plymouth.

■ Hodge was the first U's player to reach 100 first-team appearances. An outside-right, he joined hometown club Plymouth in 1933 but did not make the first team. Moving to Bristol City for the 1934–35 season, he featured in 62 League games, scoring eight goals for the Robins. An £800 bid by Luton saw Hodge moving to Kenilworth Road. Luton were impressed by his speed and good shot, as were Arsenal who offered a big fee to the Hatters in 1935, but it was not enough to entice a sale. Hodge supplied the ammunition for Joe Payne, famous scorer of 10 goals in one match, as Luton won the 1936–37 Third Division title. Further offers followed, as a result, from both Newcastle and Crystal Palace, and when Luton refused those advances as well Hodge refused to re-sign for the next season. Ted Davis infuriated Luton by stepping in and snapping up the forward, thus denying Luton any money at all. Newcastle had finally reached agreement for a deal, but a hitch allowed Davis to sign the player. All that and he had only made 20 appearances for Town, scoring one goal. Despite winning the Southern League Cup in his first season at Colchester and a Championship medal the next, he disliked training and was released at the end of U's second campaign. He moved to Hereford United in July 1939, teaming up with ex-Chelmsford manager Eric Keen. The war cut short his career, although he guested for both Plymouth and Torquay in season 1945–46, making one appearance for each. Retained by Plymouth after hostilities, he made no further League

starts. In 1944, referring to the current activities of ex-U's players, the local press reported that he was playing for the Scottish amateurs Queen's Park with some success. Queen's Park, as is usual with amateur players, just identify the player by Hodge, L J.

	League		Lge Cup		FA Cup		Other	
	A	G	A	G	A	G	A	G
1937–38	30	12	6	4	-	-	15	7
1938–39	42	14	3	1	2	1	13	3
TOTAL	72	26	9	5	2	1	28	10

HODGE, Robert William 'Bobby'

Height: 5ft 9½in. Weight: 11st.

Born: 30 April 1954, Exeter.

■ The Exeter-born winger made his professional debut for his home-town club in 1974 and went on to play in 128

League games in four years, scoring 18 goals. Hodge was part of the Exeter team that accompanied Colchester, Bradford and Cambridge to promotion from Division Four in 1976–77. He joined United in September 1978 for £15,000 and became a fixture on the right side of midfield. He weighed in with a number of valuable goals as Colchester pressed for promotion to Division Two. When United were relegated at the end of 1980–81, Hodge was released and returned westward to join Torquay. He played just 3(+1) games in the 1982–83 season, scoring one goal. He took up a managerial post in Norway but settled in Exeter, where he had a carpentry business.

	League		Lge Cup		FA Cup		Other	
	A	G	A	G	A	G	A	G
1978–79	31	3	0	0	7	1	-	-
1979–80	34+3	5	4	1	3	0	-	-
1980–81	22+2	6	2	0	3	0	-	-
TOTAL	87+5	14	6	1	13	1	-	-

HODGSON, Kenneth 'Ken'

Height: 5ft 11in. Weight: 11st.

Born: 19 January 1942, Newcastle.

Died: 23 October 2007.

■ The Newcastle-born forward joined his home-town club in May 1959 and made six League appearances. Chances were limited, and he moved to Scunthorpe and netted an impressive 30 goals in just 88 starts, including being club's leading scorer in 1963–64. Bournemouth secured his services for £5,000 in June 1964, and he had an equally impressive goal ratio at Dean Court, with 24 goals from 77 League appearances. Neil Franklin paid £4,000 to bring him to Layer Road. In his first season he formed a decent strike force, with his 16 goals being accompanied by 24 from Reg Stratton and 15 from Peter Bullock, but in November of 1967 he suffered a stomach injury, which kept him out until April the following year. In his comeback match against QPR reserves he was unfortunate enough to break his leg. As part of his rehabilitation he went on loan to Chelmsford in early 1969, but he broke down on his U's comeback against Brentford in front of the Anglia TV cameras in February 1969 and was forced to retire from professional football. He joined Poole Town in 1969–70 and later became a sales rep in the Christchurch area. He also ventured to Australia, briefly, playing for Eastern Suburbs.

	League		Lge Cup		FA Cup		Other	
	A	G	A	G	A	G	A	G
1966–67	44	16	1	0	2	0	-	-
1967–68	11+1	3	1	0	0	0	-	-
1968–69	1	0	0	0	0	0	-	-
TOTAL	56+1	19	2	0	2	0	-	-

HODGSON, Robert 'Bob'

■ Hodgson, an amateur from Great Bromley, played for South Shields during wartime. Indeed, on the day war broke out he was due to sign for Huddersfield. Hodgson appeared at Layer Road in February 1946 and signed pro in May. He was also taken on to the ground staff at Layer Road in February 1947 and continued to play for the club, more usually in the reserves, until moving to Brightlingsea United as manager in December 1947. He came back to the U's for 1948–49 to provide an experienced head for the A team in the Border League and then had a couple of years at Sudbury.

	League		Lge Cup		FA Cup		Other	
	A	G	A	G	A	G	A	G
1945–46	3	2	6	3	0	0	-	-
1946–47	7	1	4	2	0	0	-	-
TOTAL	10	3	10	5	0	0	-	-

HOGG

■ Worcester player Hogg, along with colleague Beveridge, guested for the U's when Shiels, Ferguson and Willmott missed the club's train journey to Worcester and did not arrive until five minutes after kick off. Hogg was on trial at Worcester from Stenhousmuir and played a week later for Worcester against an RAF XI and also became a regular in their reserve side.

	League		Lge Cup		FA Cup		Other	
	A	G	A	G	A	G	A	G
1945–46	1	0	0	0	0	0	-	-
TOTAL	1	0	0	0	0	0	-	-

HOINES, Robert 'Bobby'

■ Hoines caught the eye in a 1945 Army Cup Final at Layer Road for No.1 Holding Battalion against the 16th Infantry Training Corps and was noted as among the club's reserve strength by around the turn of the year. The 22-year-old signed professional on 11 January 1946 and made his debut against Hereford the next day, going on to play three of the next five games. By that time Bob Hodgson and Frank Rawcliffe had emerged as the regular inside-forwards and Hoines was not called upon again, being released at the end of 1945–46.

	League		Lge Cup		FA Cup		Other	
	A	G	A	G	A	G	A	G
1945–46	4	0	0	0	0	0	-	-
TOTAL	4	0	0	0	0	0	-	-

HOLMES

■ A soldier serving with the Army Fire Fighting Centre who made a solitary appearance at Yeovil in September 1945 when a decimated United were thrashed 8–0.

	League		Lge Cup		FA Cup		Other	
	A	G	A	G	A	G	A	G
1945–46	1	0	0	0	0	0	-	-
TOTAL	1	0	0	0	0	0	-	-

HONEYWOOD, Brian Roy

Height: 5ft 9in. Weight: 10st.

Born: 8 May 1944, Great Waltham.

■ Honeywood was Dick Graham's first-ever signing for Colchester when he arrived from Ipswich in August 1968 after completing his apprenticeship at Portman Road without breaking into the first team. After a bright start, he struggled to make the first-team defence following the arrival of Brian Wood and was released at the end of the season. He rejoined Chelmsford for 1969–70, having starred in their youth team before being recruited by Ipswich. Honeywood was one of those squeezed out when the cash-strapped City merged with Brentwood in 1970, but he later returned to Chelmsford as Director of Football before being ousted in a boardroom shake up in late 1999. After his football career, he became a market stall holder and in 2007 was involved with Maldon Town.

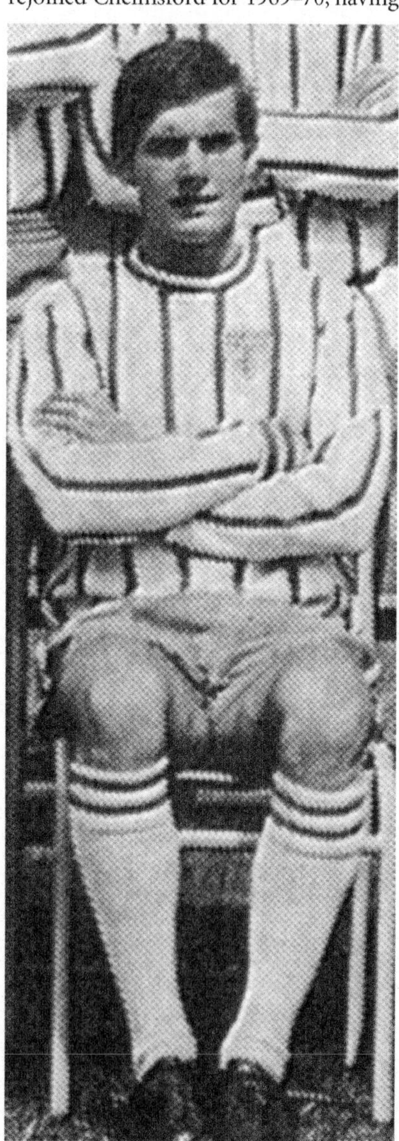

	League		Lge Cup		FA Cup		Other	
	A	G	A	G	A	G	A	G
1968–69	12+6	0	2	0	1	0	-	-
TOTAL	12+6	0	2	0	1	0	-	-

HOPKINS, Robert Arthur

Height: 5ft 7in. Weight: 10st 7lb.

Born: 25 October 1961, Hall Green.

■ Hopkins was an Aston Villa apprentice at the same time as Roy McDonough and signed professionally in the summer of 1979 after captaining their FA Youth Cup-winning team. Scoring one goal in 1(+2) games for Villa, he was used in a swap deal that saw Birmingham's Alan Curbishley arrive at Villa Park in March 1983. He became a regular in Blues midfield, but with a 'bad boy' reputation, and weighed in with 21 goals in 123 League starts. In September 1986 he signed for Manchester City for a fee of £130,000 but played just seven games before being swapped for West Brom's Imre Varadi and £60,000 a month later. He scored on his Baggies debut against Grimsby and bagged a further 10 goals in 81(+2) games at The Hawthorns. On deadline day 1989 he rejoined Birmingham, destined for the third tier of English football, for £25,000. Adding 43(+7) games to his St Andrews total, he netted nine League goals before joining Shrewsbury for the 1991–92 season. After scoring three times in 18(+9) games, he ventured to Hong Kong, where he turned out for the unusually-named Instant Dictionary FC. On returning to the UK he teamed up with McDonough, joining Colchester in February 1993 for a short non-contract spell. He scored on his debut at Shrewsbury but was released at the end of the campaign. Moving into non-League, he spent five seasons as player-coach of Solihull Borough and played for Bromsgrove and Paget Rangers before coaching Pelsall Villa.

	League		Lge Cup		FA Cup		Other	
	A	G	A	G	A	G	A	G
1992–93	13+1	1	0	0	0	0	0	0
TOTAL	13+1	1	0	0	0	0	0	0

HORNBY, Ronald 'Ronnie'

■ A Lance Corporal in the 16th Infantry Training Corps and former Wolves colt, Hornby was virtually ever-present on the left-wing for the first few months of the 1945–46 season and had been one of the first players signed as a pro by the U's. His last game was a friendly against an Arsenal XI on 1 December, watched by over 5,000 and won 2–1 by the U's, and by Christmas he was half a world away in Burma. He had got a bit closer to Colchester by the end of the season, but Palestine was still too far to resume his U's career, and he did not play for the U's again until on demob leave in December 1947. Those were reserve games at Clacton and Chelmsford.

	League		Lge Cup		FA Cup		Other	
	A	G	A	G	A	G	A	G
1945–46	7	3	0	0	1	0	-	-
TOTAL	7	3	0	0	1	0	-	-

HORNSBY, John

Height: 5ft 6in. Weight: 9st 10lb.

Born: 3 August 1945, Ferryhill.

■ Amateur winger Hornsby arrived on trial from the North East in January 1965 and was eventually signed as a professional in the October, his club Northern League Evenwood Town receiving a donation of £25 and five shillings. His chances came mainly when Brain Hall was switched to full-back, and his only goal came in a 3–0 victory over Port Vale at Layer Road in January 1966.

He was released at the end of the season and after spells with South Shields and Ferryhill Athletic took a position as a welder in the Darlington area.

	League		Lge Cup		FA Cup		Other	
	A	G	A	G	A	G	A	G
1965–66	11	1	1	0	0	0	-	-
TOTAL	11	1	1	0	0	0	-	-

HOUSTON, Stewart Mackie

Height: 6ft. Weight: 12st 2lb.

Born: 20 August 1949, Dunoon.

■ Houston was spotted playing for Port Glasgow Rangers by Chelsea and joined the London club in August 1967. His Stamford Bridge career started promisingly but was marred by injuries. After 6(+3) appearances, he joined Brentford on deadline day 1972 and helped the Bees to promotion to Division Three. Establishing himself in the side, Brentford were immediately relegated, but he had done enough to attract the attention of Manchester United. He joined the Old Trafford club in December 1973 and played 20 times as United were

relegated to Division Two. It did not take long for the Red Devils to bounce back and Houston became a permanent fixture at the heart of the Manchester United defence. In total he played 204(+1) times, scoring 13 goals, and played in two Wembley FA Cup Finals winning once. He also played European football on 5(+1) occasions. During this spell he won one Scotland cap to add to his two Under-23 appearances. Moving to Sheffield United in July 1980, he won a Fourth Division Championship medal as his new club vied with Colchester for promotion. Cyril Lea brought Houston to Layer Road at the start of 1983–84, and, ironically, he faced up to his old club Manchester United in a League Cup tie, at Layer Road in the November. Houston's main defensive partners were Keith Day and Steve Wignall. In 1986 he became assistant manager to George Graham at Arsenal. When Graham was sacked in February 1995, Houston took over as caretaker and took the Gunners to the European Cup-winners' Cup Final where they narrowly lost to a spectacular long-range shot from Nayim of Real Zaragoza. Bruce Rioch took over the hot seat and Houston remained as assistant. Just a year later Rioch was sacked, and Houston was once again caretaker manager of Arsenal. Told that he was in charge only while the club waited for Arsene Wenger to work out his contract at Grampus-8, Houston resigned to take over as manager of QPR, with Rioch as his assistant. QPR had just lost their Premiership status, and when they did not regain it Houston was sacked in December 1997. He reunited with George Graham at Tottenham in 1998 but left when the manager was sacked in March 2001. Houston then spent a short time on the staff of Walsall before returning to Highbury as a scout, and in 2007 he could regularly be seen at the Garrison 'B' ground as U's youth team starlet Medy Elito attracted a possee of admirers before signing pro at Layer Road.

	League		Lge Cup		FA Cup		Other	
	A	G	A	G	A	G	A	G
1983–84	42	4	5	0	3	1	1	0
1984–85	28+1	1	2	1	2	1	1+1	0
1985–86	36	0	2	0	1	0	2	0
TOTAL	106+1	5	9	1	6	2	4+1	0

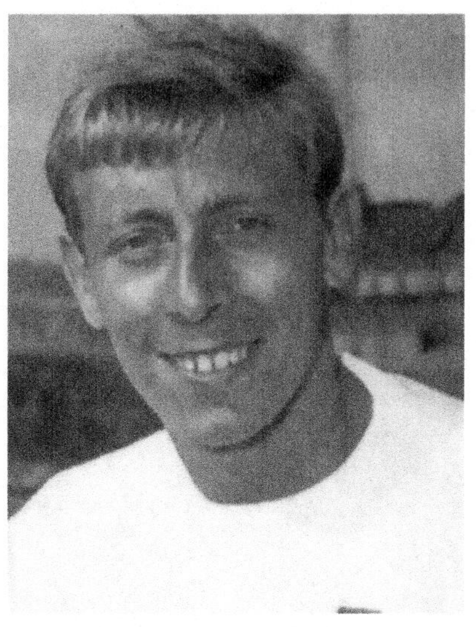

HOWE, Albert Richard Henry 'Bert'

Height: 5ft 8in. Weight: 11st 9lb.

Born: 16 November 1938, Charlton.

■ Howe signed professional with Fourth Division Crystal Palace in December 1958 from Faversham Town as Palace embarked on a steady rise to the Second Division by 1964–65. A steady left-back, Howe followed his former boss Dick Graham to Leyton Orient in January 1967 after 192(+1) appearances at Selhurst Park. When Dick Graham arrived at Layer Road in the summer of 1968, it was not long before Howe joined him for the third time. A close season signing, Howe, without a goal in his professional career, was offered a £5 wager by Dick Graham if he could break his duck. This he duly did against Aldershot in March 1970. At the end of the campaign he was released and joined Romford before becoming a salesman in the London area.

	League		Lge Cup		FA Cup		Other	
	A	G	A	G	A	G	A	G
1969–70	29	1	1	0	0	0	-	-
TOTAL	29	1	1	0	0	0	-	-

HOWE, Anthony Valentine 'Tony'

Height: 5ft 8in. Weight: 11st.

Born: 14 February 1939, Colchester.

■ From 1957 local lad Howe was one of several amateurs who divided their time between the U's and Colchester Casuals until becoming a part-time pro in

March 1960. He made his debut in a thumping 4–0 win over Hull on the opening day of the 1960–61 season and played the next nine games, scoring twice. Unfortunately, the outside-left shirt had been owned by Peter Wright for the past six years, and when Wright recovered from injury Howe was back to the reserves. He did not get another chance at Layer Road and left in summer 1962 joining Haverhill. Southend took him back into the Football League in 1964 for a year and on being freed from Roots Hall he joined Clacton, later playing for Coggeshall and Rowhedge.

	League		Lge Cup		FA Cup		Other	
	A	G	A	G	A	G	A	G
1960–61	10	2	0	0	0	0	-	-
TOTAL	10	2	0	0	0	0	-	-

HOWELL, Dean George

Height: 6ft 1in. Weight: 12st 5lb.

Born: 29 November 1980.

■ Howell began his career as a YTS on the books of Notts County, making one substitute appearance after turning professional in the summer of 1999. He spent a period on loan at Spalding United before joining Dario Gradi at Crewe during the next close season. He found chances equally hard to come by at Gresty Road and again made just one substitute appearance before joining Rochdale on loan in March 2000 to play 2(+1) games. Released by Crewe, he moved to non-League Southport, scoring four times in 50 Conference starts. When Southport

were relegated at the end of 2003–04, Howell joined Morecambe and scored against his home-town club Burton. He failed to live up to his pre-season promise and was released to join fellow Conference side Halifax. At the beginning of 2005–06, with Phil Parkinson keen to bolster squad numbers, Howell joined Colchester. Making just one start, he soon had to make way for the arrival of Mark Yeates. He left Layer Road, returning to play for Halifax and later joined Garry Hill's Weymouth in the 2006 close season playing 11(+6) Conference games before switching to Grays Athletic at the turn of the year when finances turned sour at the Terras. Howell once again teamed up with old boss Hill when signing for Conference side Rushden & Diamonds for the 2007–08 season. He joined League new boys Aldershot in the summer of 2008.

	League		Lge Cup		FA Cup		Other	
	A	G	A	G	A	G	A	G
2005–06	1+3	0	0+1	0	0	0	0	0
TOTAL	1+3	0	0+1	0	0	0	0	0

HOWLETT, Robert Victor 'Bobby'

Height: 5ft 11in. Weight: 12st 1lb.

Born: 12 December 1948, Basildon.

■ Defender Howlett served his apprenticeship at Chelsea before signing professional in December 1965. Failing to make the first team, Howlett moved to Southend in September 1967, playing four League games with a further two substitute appearances. One of Dick Graham's summer 1968 signings, Howlett spent the majority of the season as understudy to Dave Bickles. He did play a few minutes in goal for United in a

League Cup tie at Reading in September 1969 when Ron Willis suffered an eye injury. Brian Gibbs played the majority of the game between the sticks, with Howlett taking over late on. A broken leg after coming on as a substitute at Brentford in April 1970 turned out to be the end of Howlett's Football League career. It was 17 months before he battled back into action, returning in the reserves in September 1971, but before Christmas it was all over for him as the effects of his original injury kicked back in, and he was officially released in the summer. He later played in the Essex Senior League for Bowers United along with former U's colleagues Ken Jones and Mal Slater.

	League		Lge Cup		FA Cup		Other	
	A	G	A	G	A	G	A	G
1969–70	10+6	0	1+1	0	0	0	-	-
TOTAL	10+6	0	1+1	0	0	0	-	-

HUBBARD, C.

■ A West Ham youngster and soldier serving in No.1 Holding Battalion who played just once for Colchester, at outside-left at Bath in February 1946, before suffering a serious leg wound that halted his career.

	League		Lge Cup		FA Cup		Other	
	A	G	A	G	A	G	A	G
1945–46	1	0	0	0	0	0	-	-
TOTAL	1	0	0	0	0	0	-	-

HUBBICK, David 'Dave'

Height: 5ft 7½in. Weight: 10st 10lb.

Born: 16 March 1960, South Shields.

■ 'Rocky' Hubbick began his career as an apprentice at Ipswich, signing in January 1978. He failed to make any first-team appearances and joined Wimbledon in

September 1980. In his first season at Plough Lane he weighed in with four goals as the League's newest team was promoted from Division Four. The Dons were relegated the following season, with Hubbick joining Dagenham. Cyril Lea recruited him on a non-contract basis, and he made his U's bow as a substitute in a 2–2 draw with Northampton in October 1983. His only goal came in the last minute of a 4–1 thrashing of Wrexham at Layer Road in April 1985. Unable to make any in-roads into United's first team, he had spells with Gravesend & Northfleet and then Sudbury, where he scored in the 1989 FA Vase Final draw against Tamworth at Wembley. He also played for Braintree and Cornard among others and later managed and coached Ipswich Wanderers, Woodbridge and Stowmarket, where he was in charge in 2007.

	League		Lge Cup		FA Cup		Other	
	A	G	A	G	A	G	A	G
1983–84	3+7	0	2	0	1+1	0	0	0
1984–85	1+4	1	0	0	0	0	0	0
TOTAL	4+11	1	2	0	1+1	0	0	0

HULL, Jeffrey 'Jeff'

Height: 5ft 6in. Weight: 9st 11lb.

Born: 25 August 1960, Rochford.

■ Rochford-born Hull began his apprenticeship at local side Southend, signing as a full professional in August 1978. Chances were few and far between as Southend were relegated and promoted in successive seasons. At the end of 1980–81, Hull was released and joined Basildon United. Signed by Allan Hunter, Hull made his debut against Stockport in December 1982 as U's ran

out 3–0 winners. In October 1983 Hull suffered knee ligament damage against Crewe after 14 minutes of the match. At the time, many U's fans were still queuing behind the main stand for a ticket for the forthcoming League Cup tie with Manchester United. Hull missed that came but returned later in the season, only to suffer serious pelvic injuries in a 5–0 FA Cup thrashing by Gillingham at Layer Road in November 1984. Despite a brief return, Hull was advised to quit the professional game. He went back to Basildon and also later played for Billericay and Barking.

	League		Lge Cup		FA Cup		Other	
	A	G	A	G	A	G	A	G
1982–83	27	4	0	0	0	0	0	0
1983–84	33	1	4	0	0	0	2	0
1984–85	18	5	2	0	3	0	0+1	1
1985–86	4+1	0	0	0	0	0	0	0
TOTAL	82+1	10	6	0	3	0	2+1	1

HUNT, Robert Rex 'Bobby'

Height: 5ft 10in. Weight: 11st 8lb.

Born: 1 October 1942, Colchester.

■ Hunt was a homegrown player and joined his brothers Ronnie and Billy on the books of Colchester United, marking his Football League debut against York in March 1960 with a goal. A regular in U's side from November 1960 Hunt came to the fore in the 1961–62 Fourth Division Championship battle with eventual winners Millwall. He set the club's current Football League scoring record that season, a record that over the years has been shown in reference books as 37 League goals. However, according to our records, his game-by-game total adds up to 38 without the goal scrubbed out at Accrington when Stanley pulled out during the season. This ties in with the contemporary end-of-year summary in the local press. His haul included a hat-trick against Chester and four-timers against Bradford City and Doncaster. The goals against Bradford helped set a new club record victory 9–1, a record not equalled until the 2005 FA Cup. Hunt's goalscoring attracted the attentions of Northampton who paid £18,000 for him in March 1964 to help continue their high-speed rise from Division Four to Division One. After 40 League appearances and 10 goals, Hunt was on the move to Millwall, where he scored 13 goals in 43 games during the 1966–67 season. November 1967 saw a move back to the region, when he joined Ipswich, as they became Second Division champions in 1967–68. Hunt contributed four goals in 16 full games and appeared as substitute 10 times. He continued his wanderings, joining Charlton in September 1970, scoring 11 goals in 34+2 League games. He suffered from cartilage trouble and was loaned out to Northampton in 1972–73, scoring three goals in five League games. His full career ended at Reading during

the tail end of the 1972–73 season, where he scored three goals in 15 appearances. He briefly turned out for non-Leaguers Maidstone and was player-coach at Bury Town before returning to the U's in 1977 in the dual role of reserve-team manager (and occasional player) and to work for the club's development fund. It was his role as a lottery agent that caused him to quit as reserves manager in April 1980, as he fell out with the Board over his employment status. Hunt was self-employed and wanted to stay that way.

	League		Lge Cup		FA Cup		Other	
	A	G	A	G	A	G	A	G
1959–60	1	1	-	-	0	0	-	-
1960–61	27	4	0	0	2	2	-	-
1961–62	43	38	1	0	3	2	-	-
1962–63	45	19	1	1	1	0	-	-
1963–64	33	20	3	2	2	1	-	-
TOTAL	149	82	5	3	8	5	-	-

HUNT, Ronald Malcolm 'Ronnie'

Height: 5ft 8½in. Weight: 11st.

Born: 26 September 1933, Colchester.
Died: April 1999, Colchester.

■ All five Hunt brothers played for the U's, and Ron was the oldest of the three to make the first team. He spent 15 years at Layer Road, starting as a 16-year-old amateur in 1949, turning pro in October 1951 and making his League debut later that season. Hunt only finally nailed down a regular first-team spot, though, in October 1960, starting with the 4–1 League Cup giant killing of Newcastle, and just a month before his nine year younger brother Bobby broke through. Ron had lost a couple of years in the 1950s to National Service and had his best season immediately on his return in 1954–55. Exceptionally, all his 188 first team games, plus two at Accrington in 1961–62, were in the number-six shirt. Chunky and strong in the tackle, Hunt was a time-served printer, working at the QB company in Colchester for much of his League career. After retiring, he managed local side Mersea from 1967 until 1976 and became a physiotherapist. In later years he suffered from a degenerative disease that brought about his death at 65. His son Andy, who followed him as a physiotherapist, played for the U's youth and reserve teams and was first-team physio for a while.

	League		Lge Cup		FA Cup		Other	
	A	G	A	G	A	G	A	G
1951–52	3	0	-	-	0	0	-	-
1952–53	0	0	-	-	0	0	-	-
1953–54	2	0	-	-	0	0	-	-
1954–55	26	0	-	-	0	0	-	-
1955–56	3	0	-	-	0	0	-	-
1956–57	0	0	-	-	0	0	-	-
1957–58	4	0	-	-	0	0	-	-
1958–59	19	0	-	-	2	0	-	-
1959–60	3	0	-	-	0	0	-	-
1960–61	28	1	2	0	2	0	-	-
1961–62	44	0	1	0	3	0	-	-
1962–63	33	2	1	0	0	0	-	-
1963–64	11	0	1	0	0	0	-	-
TOTAL	176	3	5	0	7	0	-	-

HUNT, Stephen James

Height: 6ft 1in. Weight: 13st.

Born: 11 November 1984, Southampton.

■ Hunt was with Southampton as a schoolboy but failed to make any appearances for the Premiership club. He joined Colchester in July 2004 and had an eventful debut at Chesterfield, being sent off for a rash challenge, 59 seconds after coming on as substitute. His 2005–06 season was disrupted by injury, and he missed the majority of the campaign as his colleagues finished runners-up in League One. Released in the summer of 2006, he joined Notts County and was rewarded with an extended two and a half year contract after scoring once in 24(+8) games at Meadow Lane.

	League		Lge Cup		FA Cup		Other	
	A	G	A	G	A	G	A	G
2004–05	16+4	1	2	0	1+1	0	1	0
2005–06	0+2	0	0	0	3	0	0	0
TOTAL	16+6	1	2	0	4+1	0	1	0

HUNT, William Edmund 'Billy'

Born: 25 November 1934, Colchester.

■ The fourth of the five Hunt brothers, Billy joined the U's as an amateur in 1952, signing pro in August 1953 as he went for his National Service. There seems to have been a clear club policy throughout the 1950s to get their local amateurs onto pro terms as soon as their call-up arrived, and it was presumably a protective move in case they caught another club's eye while they were away from Layer Road. Billy, who played left-back or centre-half, only got one chance in the Colchester team, deputising for skipper Reg Stewart, who had broken his nose in midweek, in a 6–3 Layer Road defeat to Southend in the opening home fixture of the 1955–56 season. Hunt had a difficult opponent in Roy Hollis, who scored over 170 League goals at better than a goal every other game, but handled him well in the first half when the score was just 1–0 to Southend, and McCurley had hit their bar instead of an empty net just before half-time. The second half was a slightly different story, and Hollis ran riot, scoring four times. The match report does not ascribe any particular blame to Hunt, but Stewart was fit for the next game, and by the time he missed an odd game later in the season John Fowler had been converted to a defender and got the nod. Hunt continued to be a regular in the reserves,

generally at left-back before being tried at centre-forward from mid-February. He scored a goal or two, but the writing was on the wall with the positional switch, and he was freed in the summer, joining Sudbury, where he reverted to left-back.

	League		Lge Cup		FA Cup		Other	
	A	G	A	G	A	G	A	G
1955–56	1	0	-	-	0	0	-	-
TOTAL	1	0	-	-	0	0	-	-

HUNTER, Allan

Height: 6ft. Weight: 12st 8lb.

Born: 30 June 1946, Sion Mills, N. Ireland

■ Vastly experienced with 53 full Northern Ireland caps to his name, Hunter joined Colchester in May 1982 as player-manager following the sacking of Bobby Roberts. He made his debut in the last game of the season at Crewe and most notably recruited former central-defensive partner Kevin Beattie to Layer Road in the summer. Just 19 games into the 1982–83 season, Hunter suffered a knee injury that ended his playing career. Distraught also at the tragic suicide of his player John Lyons and the general pressures of management, Hunter resigned in January 1983. He later returned to Layer Road as assistant manager to Mike Walker, departing when Walker was sensationally sacked after leading the club to the top of table. Hunter's playing career had begun at Coleraine. Signing for Oldham in January 1967, Hunter made 83 League appearances at Boundary Park, scoring once. Following Oldham's relegation to Division Four, he joined Blackburn for

£30,000 in the summer of 1969, making 84 appearances and scoring a solitary goal. Spotted by Ipswich's extensive scouting network, Hunter duly signed for Town in an £80,000 deal in September 1971. A permanent fixture in the Suffolk club's defence, Hunter amassed 280 League appearances, scoring eight times. During his Ipswich career he played UEFA Cup football in five seasons and in the Cup-winners' Cup on one occasion. He picked up a FA Cup-winners' medal in 1978 in an Ipswich side that only once finished outside the top six of the First Division. His son Lee was also on the books of Colchester United.

* *See also Who's Who Managers section*

	League		Lge Cup		FA Cup		Other	
	A	G	A	G	A	G	A	G
1981–82	1	0	0	0	0	0	-	-
1982–83	17+1	0	3	0	1	0	1+2	0
TOTAL	18+1	0	3	0	1	0	1+2	0

HUNTER, Lee

Height: 5ft 10in. Weight: 10st 8lb.

Born: 5 October 1969, Oldham.

■ The son of former U's boss, Lee worked his way through United's youth and reserve teams to make his debut in

the last game of the 1987–88 season against Tranmere. It was a fitting reward for having won selection to the Northern Ireland Youth team. Plagued by injuries, the youngster made only a further handful of appearances before being released by Jock Wallace. He got a trial at Wigan for the start of 1989–90 but by September had signed for Wivenhoe. Among his later clubs on the Essex and Eastern Counties League circuit were Braintree, Diss and Clacton.

	League		Lge Cup		FA Cup		Other	
	A	G	A	G	A	G	A	G
1987–88	1	0	0	0	0	0	0	0
1988–89	4+4	0	0	0	0	0	0	0
TOTAL	5+4	0	0	0	0	0	0	0

HUTCHINGS, Robert 'Bob'

Born: Southwark.

■ Hutchings signed professionally for Colchester on 9 February 1946 after

serving with No.1 Holding Battalion. A native of Southwark, he played for junior clubs in the London Area pre-war and was a fixture in the U's side at wing-half from the day he signed until Easter Saturday 1947, only missing the trip to Guildford when most of the team had to be borrowed from Brentford. He also missed just one of the nine friendlies played in that time. One of only four players who had been retained at the end of 1945–46, he lost his place when the ex-Tottenham professional Albert Page arrived, and Hutchings was released at end of 1946–47.

	League		Lge Cup		FA Cup		Other	
	A	G	A	G	A	G	A	G
1945–46	4	0	8	0	0	0	-	-
1946–47	22	0	6	1	2	0	-	-
TOTAL	26	0	14	1	2	0	-	-

HYSLOP, Christian Terence

Height: 5ft 11in. Weight: 11st 7lb.

Born: 14 June 1972, Watford.

■ A YTS player at Southend, Hyslop was recruited by Roy McDonough who himself had been at Southend at the same time. Signed as a professional in April 1990, Hyslop made 16(+3) appearances at Roots Hall. He was loaned out to Northampton in December 1993, making eight League appearances, before arriving at Layer Road in February 1994. Ironically his debut was at Northampton, days after turning down the chance to join the Cobblers, and he was dramatically but correctly dismissed for a blatant body check after just seven minutes. Not retained by Colchester, he moved to Hendon and later Harrow Borough, where he was captain. Hyslop was also briefly with McDonough at Chelmsford in 1996, but when the Board fell out with Roy after just a couple of months Hysslop was one of six of McDomough's

ex-teammates who found themselves following him out of the door within days of his departure.

	League		Lge Cup		FA Cup		Other	
	A	G	A	G	A	G	A	G
1993–94	8	0	0	0	0	0	0	0
TOTAL	8	0	0	0	0	0	0	0

I

IFIL, Philip Nathan 'Phil'

Height: 5ft 9in. Weight: 12st 2lb.

Born: 18 November 1986, Willesden.

■ Ifil joined Tottenham while still at school and progressed through the ranks to make his debut against Liverpool, aged just 17, on the opening day of the 2004–05 season. Although captain of the Spurs youth team and an England Youth international, he was loaned to Millwall in September 2005, making 13 Championship appearances, and he repeated the move in the January 2006 transfer window after recovering from injury, adding three further appearances for the Lions. Returning to White Hart Lane, it was not until April 2007 that he made his next Premiership appearance, against Wigan, although he did take to the field in two Carling Cup ties. In search of first-team football, Ifil joined Southampton in September 2007 on a three-month loan, completing 11(+1) appearances. Despite being a target for the Saints, Ifil joined Colchester in January 2008 for an undisclosed six-figure sum which was said would break the then Colchester United club record transfer fee of £350,000 if certain clauses were satisfied. Ifil made his debut for the U's at Bristol City in the same month, making the right-back spot his own.

	League		Lge Cup		FA Cup		Other	
	A	G	A	G	A	G	A	G
2007–08	20	0	0	0	0	0	-	
TOTAL	20	0	0	0	0	0	-	-

INSKIP

■ There were two players by the name of Inskip who played League football either side of the war, and if the U's guest was either he was surely Frederick Clive, then a 20-year-old on the books of Nottingham Forest. This Inskip, who originated from Cheadle, played all his League football after a move to Crewe in April 1948, and all were at outside-right, the position occupied by the U's Inskip on his one and only appearance. Crewe's Inskip later played for Stafford Rangers and died in Stoke at the turn of the millennium. The other Inskip, Joseph Barton, was a defender for Gateshead.

	League		Lge Cup		FA Cup		Other	
	A	G	A	G	A	G	A	G
1945–46	1	0	0	0	0	0	-	-
TOTAL	1	0	0	0	0	0	-	-

IRVING, Russell

Height: 5ft 8in. Weight: 10st 7lb.

Born: 4 January 1964, Wallsend.

■ Coming from the North-East, Irving was on the books of Ipswich as an apprentice, signing forms in May 1981. He made no appearances for Town's first team and was signed by Cyril Lea in the summer of 1984. He was an able deputy for first Jeff Hull, Keith Bowen and Tony Adcock, who all suffered spells out with injury during the season. Irving only missed playing in five games in his first season and bagged a creditable nine League goals. With Adcock returning to fitness the following season and a new manager in Mike Walker, Irving's chances receded, and he joined Stowmarket and then Sudbury in February 1989. He spent three years coaching in New Zealand before returning to England after suffering a collapsed lung. He later became a lecturer at Suffolk College.

	League		Lge Cup		FA Cup		Other	
	A	G	A	G	A	G	A	G
1984–85	34+7	9	0+1	0	3	1	3	0
1985–86	2+7	0	1	0	0	0	0	0
TOTAL	36+14	9	1+1	0	3	1	3	0

IWELUMO, Christopher Robert 'Chris'

Height: 6ft 3in. Weight: 13st 8lb.

Born: 1 August 1978, Coatbridge.

■ Iwelumo began his career at St Mirren, scoring on his debut, aged 17, in a 5–0 trouncing of Dumbarton in February 1996. Completing 31 appearances, Iwelumo signed for Danish side Aarhus Fremand in 1998. Scoring four times in 27 games, he returned to Britain to sign for Stoke in March 2000. With just three substitute appearances to his name, he was loaned to York in November 2000, scoring twice in 11(+1) games. He spent a further loan spell with Cheltenham in February 2001 scoring once in 2(+2), outings. He established himself in the Stoke side the following season, scoring 10 goals and helping the Potters to a Millennium Stadium Play-off win over Brentford. Reaching the second tier, his appearances were restricted to rising from the bench, but he did score five goals at that level. After 40(+44) appearances and 16 goals Iwelumo moved to Brighton on deadline day 2004, scoring four times in the remaining 10 games and winning a second Millennium Stadium Play-off Final as Albion beat Bristol City 1–0. Despite this, he was released by Stoke and sought his football with German Second Division side Alemania Aachan, joining them in January 2005. Playing just nine times in the League, Iwelumo made UEFA Cup appearances against Sevilla, St

Petersburg, Lille, AEK Athens and AZ Alkmaar. His career was rescued by Colchester manager Phil Parkinson in the summer of 2005. Iwleumo responded by forming a lethal partnership with Jamie Cureton that fired Colchester to runners'-up spot in League One and a first-ever season in the Championship. The strike pairing reformed for the inaugural attempt in the second tier and plundered 41 goals between them. Cureton's 23 League goals earned him the Golden Boot, while Iwelumo's 18 included a club record-equalling four goals against Hull at Layer Road in November 2006, in which the 5–1 victory resulted, ironically, in the sacking of Tigers boss Phil Parkinson. Offered a new contract by new manager Geraint Williams, Iwelumo opted to use the Bosman clause and joined fellow Championship side Charlton in the summer of 2007, who numbered Parkinson as assistant manager and U's legend Mark Kinsella in their coaching staff. His early season goalscoring exploits earned him a call-up to the Scotland B squad, where he played against their Irish counterparts in November 2007.

	League		Lge Cup		FA Cup		Other	
	A	G	A	G	A	G	A	G
2005–06	46	17	1	0	5	2	2+1	0
2006–07	41+5	18	1	0	1	0	-	-
TOTAL	87+5	35	2	0	6	2	2+1	0

IZZET, Kemal 'Kem'

Height: 5ft 6in. Weight: 10st 3lb.

Born: 29 September 1980, Whitechapel.

■ Tenacious midfielder Izzet began his career on the books of Charlton. Released after completing his Youth Training Scheme, he was picked up by U's manager Steve Whitton in March 2001 and made his debut as a substitute in a 3–1 home win over Luton in the same month. He was voted Young Player of the Year in his first full season. He played a key part in United's run to the fifth round of the FA Cup that culminated in a narrow defeat to Sheffield United at Bramall Lane in February 2004. The following campaign proved a disaster for Izzet, as he suffered a groin injury in pre-season and then

ankle problems that required surgery. He missed virtually the whole season, returning as a substitute in the last game against Torquay. He played a supporting midfield role to Kevin Watson and Neil Danns in Colchester's successful 2005–06 promotion-winning side and following the departure of Danns in the close season re-established himself in the engine room of United's first-ever season at Championship level. His older brother Muzzy had a distinguished career at Leicester and Birmingham, while winning nine caps for Turkey.

	League		Lge Cup		FA Cup		Other	
	A	G	A	G	A	G	A	G
2000–01	5+1	1	0	0	0	0	0	0
2001–02	36+4	4	2	1	1	0	2	1
2002–03	43+2	8	1	0	1	0	1	0
2003–04	43+1	3	2	0	6	0	4	1
2004–05	3+1	0	0	0	0	0	0	0
2005–06	19+14	0	1	0	2+1	0	3+1	0
2006–07	45	1	1	0	1	0	-	-
2007–08	35+4	1	0+1	0	0	0	-	-
TOTAL	229+27	18	7+1	1	11+1	0	10+1	2

J

JACKSON, John 'Johnnie'

Height: 6ft 1in. Weight: 12st.

Born: 15 August 1982, Camden.

■ Jackson earned England Youth and Under-20 honours while serving his Youth Training Scheme at Tottenham. He was loaned to Swindon in September 2002 and scored once in 12(+1) games. Phil Parkinson brought the player to Colchester on deadline day 2003, and he made his debut at Brentford. Jackson still had ambitions of Premiership football and returned to White Hart Lane in the summer but had a loan spell at Coventry in November 2003, playing 2(+3), scoring twice. He eventually forced himself into the Spurs side and celebrated with his first and only goal in a 4–2 win over Charlton in February 2004. As Spurs tried to compete financially with the likes of Chelsea and Manchester United, they relied more and more on foreign imports. Jackson was allowed out on loan again in December 2004, playing 14(+1) times for Watford. He then had a further loan at Derby in September 2005, playing 3(+3) times, before being released by Tottenham at the end of 2005–06. U's manager Phil Parkinson moved to sign the midfielder and was also believed to have wanted fellow Spurs players Mark Yeates and Dean Marney. Parkinson resigned and moved to Hull (as did Yeates and Marney), while Jackson buckled down at Layer Road for the club's first-ever season in the Championship. An ankle injury against Sunderland in April 2007 curtailed his season just when United had a glimmer of reaching the Play-offs. An ever present in 2007–08, Jackson scooped the Player of the Year award.

	League		Lge Cup		FA Cup		Other	
	A	G	A	G	A	G	A	G
2002–03	8	0	0	0	0	0	0	0
2006–07	24+8	2	0	0	0+1	0	-	-
2007–08	46	8	1	0	1	0	-	-
TOTAL	78+8	10	1	0	1+1	0	0	0

JAMES, Joseph 'Joe'

Born: 13 January 1911, Battersea.
Died: January 1993, Surrey.

■ Between 1931 and 1939 James made 243 appearances for Brentford, scoring two goals, helping them to promotion to Division One. During wartime he continued to turn out regularly for the Bees thus: 1939–40 32 appearances/1 goal; 1940–41 27/1; 1941–42 38/0; 1942–43 33/1 and 1943–44 23/0. Having broken his wrist playing at Griffin Park, James opted to take compensation and was from then on prevented from playing further in the Football League. His crowning moment was playing in the War Cup Final against Portsmouth on 30 May 1942 in front of a 72,000 crowd. He came to the U's as a professional guest in mid-November 1945, making his debut in a 3–1 defeat at Hereford and only missed the Christmas Day friendly, until an 8–0 defeat at Bath on 2 February 1946. James was one of four of that team who were never seen in a U's shirt again.

	League		Lge Cup		FA Cup		Other	
	A	G	A	G	A	G	A	G
1945–46	8	0	1	0	0	0	-	-
TOTAL	8	0	1	0	0	0	-	-

JARVIS, Ryan Robert

Height: 6ft. Weight: 11st 4lb.

Born: 11 July 1988, Fakenham.

■ With Norwich since his schooldays, Jarvis signed professionally at Carrow Road in August 2003 and represented England at youth level on 22 occasions, scoring eight times. He became Norwich's youngest-ever scorer when netting against Watford in November 2003 and went one better a year later, scoring a sensational Premiership goal against Liverpool as well as being top scorer in the Premier Reserve League. Phil Parkinson took him on loan at Colchester in March 2005 as United sought to bolster their attack. He made his debut at Doncaster in the April and, although appearing in all of the remaining six fixtures, returned to Norwich in the summer. Way down the pecking order at Carrow Road, he was loaned to Leyton Orient in February

2007 and made a big impression, scoring six goals in 14 League starts, including a hat-trick against Millwall. He remained on Norwich's books, alongside his younger brother Rossi, for the 2007–08 season but joined Scottish Premier League side Kilmarnock in August 2007 on a six-month loan deal, scoring once in nine starts. In January 2008 Jarvis fixed up a further loan move to Notts County.

	League		Lge Cup		FA Cup		Other	
	A	G	A	G	A	G	A	G
2004–05	2+4	0	0	0	0	0	0	0
TOTAL	2+4	0	0	0	0	0	0	0

JEFFRIES, Alfred James 'Alf'

Height: 6ft. Weight: 11st.

Born: 9 February 1922, Oxford.
Died: February 1998, Oxford.

■ A soldier serving with the 16th Infantry Training Corps and on the books of Oxford City, Jeffries played just one game for Colchester when he kept goal against Guildford in the Southern League Cup in January 1946. His late call-up was prompted by QPR insisting that their player Harry Brown played for Notts County instead of Colchester. Jeffries signed for Brentford in September 1947, although he had to wait over two years for the first-team shirt and moved on to Torquay in the summer of 1954, playing over 160 games in the Football League for the two clubs.

	League		Lge Cup		FA Cup		Other	
	A	G	A	G	A	G	A	G
1945–46	0	0	1	0	0	0	-	-
TOTAL	0	0	1	0	0	0	-	-

JEFFRIES, William Arthur 'Bill'

Born: 11 March 1921, Acton.
Died: 1981, Hull.

■ Jeffries, a forward, made just one League Cup appearance when he stood in for the Cup-tied Alf Biggs for the semi-final defeat at Gillingham on 7 June 1947. Jeffries had joined Mansfield in March 1946 while stationed in the Army nearby and moved on to Hull, from whom he arrived at Layer Road on a trail at the end of May 1947, playing for the reserves in a game that United's second string lost 6–1. He was reported to have made five first-team appearances for the Tigers that season, but if he did they are recorded under somebody else's name.

	League		Lge Cup		FA Cup		Other	
	A	G	A	G	A	G	A	G
1946–47	0	0	1	0	0	0	-	-
TOTAL	0	0	1	0	0	0	-	-

JELLY, John

■ A local lad, Jelly made two Colchester appearances, keeping goal against Chelmsford in September 1946 when United were forced to field five amateurs, and against Gillingham in the League Cup semi-final of June 1947. He performed very creditably in that semi-final, given that it was his first game since February when a works accident had cost him the tips of his fingers on one hand. He was retained as an amateur for 1947–48 and shared reserve duties with several other local 'keepers until into the New Year, although just before Christmas he switched his main allegiance to Essex & Suffolk Border League side Colchester Casuals.

	League		Lge Cup		FA Cup		Other	
	A	G	A	G	A	G	A	G
1946–47	1	0	1	0	0	0	-	-
TOTAL	1	0	1	0	0	0	-	-

JENKINS, James 'Jimmy'

■ Centre-half Jenkins, a 26-year-old Corporal in the 15th Infantry Training Corps, was one of if not the first player to be signed as a professional by the U's in August 1945, transferring from Bristol City. He had been stationed at Colchester at the Infantry Training Centre for some while and played in one of the handful of games at Layer Road in the depths of the war, the Old Contemptibles Cup Final on Christmas Day 1942. There was a flimsy four-page programme for that game, which lists him as formerly with Bristol City and Bath City, but there is no trace of him playing first-team football for the Bristol club either during or before hostilities. Despite being appointed captain and playing in 19 of the 20 Southern League games during the season, Jenkins was released at the end of 1945–46.

	League		Lge Cup		FA Cup		Other	
	A	G	A	G	A	G	A	G
1945–46	19	0	7	0	1	0	-	-
TOTAL	19	0	7	0	1	0	-	-

JOHNSON, Gavin

Height: 5ft 11in. Weight: 11st 7lb.

Born: 10 October 1970, Eye.

■ Johnson made his Ipswich debut against Barnsley in February 1989, a few days after

signing professional. He established himself in the 1991–92 Second Division Championship-winning side and took his place in the Premiership elite a season later. He unfortunately twisted his foot on a divot in the final League game of the 1992–93 campaign and on recovering, despite 114(+18) appearances and 11 goals, found himself unable to win back his place. He joined Luton for a four-game stint but in December 1995 signed for Third Division Wigan in a £15,000 deal. Johnson helped the Latics to the 1996–97 Third Division Championship but was released in the summer of 1998, after 82(+2) appearances and eight goals, because of a niggling groin injury. Moving north of the border, he signed for Dunfermline, playing 18 times. Signed by Steve Whitton in November 1999, Johnson made his Colchester bow at Oldham in a Sunday fixture and quickly added culture to United's side. He was unfortunate to suffer another groin injury during 2001–02 and on his comeback from injury broke his leg at Port Vale in the early weeks of 2002–03. He spent a year on the sidelines but fought back to regain his place and scored a creditable 10 League and Cup goals in his final season at Layer Road. He joined Boston United in June 2005 but after just 3(+1) games moved to Northampton. He saw out the season at Sixfields, scoring once in 22(+1) games as the Cobblers won promotion. In the 2006 close season he joined Oxford, newly relegated to the Conference and under the guidance of former Colchester manager Jim Smith. After leading the table for most of the campaign, Oxford lost out in the Play-offs and Johnson was released. He teamed up with former U's star Richard

Wilkins, manager at Bury Town, for the 2007–08 season, signing on as a player.

	League		Lge Cup		FA Cup		Other	
	A	G	A	G	A	G	A	G
1999–2000	24+3	0	0	0	0	0	0	0
2000–01	33+4	2	3+1	0	1	0	0	0
2001–02	19+1	1	0	0	2	0	2	0
2002–03	8	0	1	0	0	0	0	0
2003–04	14+4	1	0	0	1	0	1+1	0
2004–05	36+1	9	2	1	4	0	0+1	0
TOTAL	134+13	13	6+1	1	8	0	3+2	0

JOHNSON, Richard Mark

Height: 5ft 10in. Weight: 11st 13lb.

Born: 27 April 1974, Kurri Kurri, Australia.

■ Watford received sterling service from Johnson, who was a product of their Youth Training Scheme. Signing full forms in September 1992, Johnson had already made his Hornets debut in the previous season and won a Second Division Championship medal in 1997–98 and played in Watford's Wembley Play-off victory over Bolton a year later. Scoring three goals in 20(+1) Premiership outings, and earning an Australian cap against the Czech Republic in March 2000 after impressing in two warm-up games against the Brazilian Olympic squad, Johnson's Watford career amounted to 210(+32) League games with 20 goals scored. A knee injury curtailed his Watford career to sporadic comebacks over three seasons, spending a spell on loan at Northampton in February 2003, scoring once in 5(+1) games, and he was released from Vicarage Road the following September by mutual consent. He joined Colchester on trial but made just one substitute appearance, in an LDV Trophy tie at Yeovil in the November. He opted, however, to join Stoke on a three-month contract but figured just 3(+4) times before finishing the season with promotion-winning QPR. Injury restricted his Loftus Road career to just 16(+1) games, and after a two match loan period with MK Dons in October 2004 he had his contract cancelled by QPR and returned to Australia to play for Newcastle Jets in the A-League and later for New Zealand Knights in the same League. Escaping a prison sentence for fleeing the scene of a drink-drive incident in June 2007, Johnson signed for Wellington Phoenix of the A-League.

	League		Lge Cup		FA Cup		Other	
	A	G	A	G	A	G	A	G
2003–04	0	0	0	0	0	0	0+1	0
TOTAL	0	0	0	0	0	0	0+1	0

JOHNSON, Ross Yorke

Height: 6ft. Weight: 13st.

Born: 2 January 1976, Brighton.

■ Johnson joined United from Brighton after a successful loan spell in January 2000. He had served his YTS at Brighton and went on to feature 113(+19) times, scoring twice, for his home-town club. He spent a lot of time on the Layer Road treatment table and as a result was released in April 2002. His only goal was a stunning strike that brought a surprise 3–2 victory over Wigan at the JJB in November 2001. Johnson signed for Dagenham & Redbridge on leaving Layer Road, playing seven Conference games in 2002–03 before joining Canvey Island. During 2003–04 he played 25(+5) games for Worthing.

	League		Lge Cup		FA Cup		Other	
	A	G	A	G	A	G	A	G
1999–2000	17+1	0	0	0	0	0	0	0
2000–01	17+1	0	0	0	0	0	0	0
2001–02	13+3	1	0	0	2	0	1	0
TOTAL	47+5	1	0	0	2	0	1	0

JOHNSTONE, Ian Donaldson

Born: 2 March 1939, Galashiels.
Died: November 1993, Surrey.

■ Johnstone is another player signed on one of Benny Fenton's many scouting trips to Scotland. Signed from Edinburgh side Ormiston Primrose, he made two appearances, with his debut coming against Chesterfield in April 1959. Unable

to break through he then joined Clacton, managed by ex-U's player Roy Bicknell, where he stayed for six years, converting from the inside-forward he had been at Layer Road to a left-half or more usually left-back. After leaving Clacton he had a year with Crittalls (Braintree as is now), then signed for former U's team Peter Wright at Halstead, following Wright when he went to Long Melford.

	League		Lge Cup		FA Cup		Other	
	A	G	A	G	A	G	A	G
1958–59	1	0	-	-	0	0	-	-
1959–60	1	0	-	-	0	0	-	-
TOTAL	2	0	-	-	0	0	-	-

JONES, Charles 'Charlie'

Born: 20 November 1911, Penmaen.

■ Jones began his career with Ebbw Vale but was picked up by Tottenham to play for their nursery side Northfleet United. During season 1934–35 he played for Spurs on 18 occasions. Jones joined the U's Essex rivals Southend in May 1937 and appeared 26 times for them before the war and a further 13 times during 1945–46. Jones guested for the U's over Christmas 1945 and the New Year, managing to fit in two Southern League and four friendly games in that period, mostly at left-back.

	League		Lge Cup		FA Cup		Other	
	A	G	A	G	A	G	A	G
1945–46	1	0	1	0	0	0	-	-
TOTAL	1	0	1	0	0	0	-	-

JONES, Kenneth Brian 'Ken'

Height: 6ft. Weight: 12st 3lb.

Born: 9 February 1941, Keighley.

■ Twice top scorer for Southend, Jones had joined the Shrimpers in October 1960. A healthy 35 League goals in 86

starts earned a move to Millwall in September 1964, where Jones featured in 170(+3) League games for the Lions, scoring 12 times as they rose from the Fourth to the Second Division. Dick Graham paid £5,000 in November 1969 to reinforce the injury stricken Layer Road squad. Jones made his debut against Grimsby in the same month and after settling in for two games scored five goals in the next seven games. He hit a similar vein of form at the end of February, scoring in five consecutive matches (7 goals), and a further four goals in the next five games to finish United's leading scorer. During this spell he succeeded Brian Wood as captain. Much was expected of Jones the following season, and after earning Colchester a 1–1 draw with Birmingham in the League Cup and a 1–0 lead in the St Andrews' replay Jones's title as chief goalscorer was taken over by the signing of Ray Crawford and his own ankle injury. In March 1972 Jones was released, following the signing of David Burnside and joined Margate, scoring the winning goal in an FA Cup giant-killing of Swansea in 1972–73 that eventually led to a third-round tie at home to Tottenham. Unfortunately for Jones, he broke his leg on the Boxing Day prior to the tie and so added the famous Colchester wins over Leeds and West Brom to the list of big games that he was forced to miss. Jones played for Hastings in the Southern League for a season and a half and finished with Bowers United in the Essex Senior League, while running a scaffolding company in Wickford.

	League		Lge Cup		FA Cup		Other	
	A	G	A	G	A	G	A	G
1969–70	28	16	0	0	0	0	-	-
1970–71	31	4	3	4	2	1	-	-
1971–72	13+4	3	1	0	1	0	1+1	0
TOTAL	72+4	23	4	4	3	1	1+1	0

JONES, Leonard 'Len'

Height: 5ft 8in. Weight: 11st 5lb.

Born: 9 June 1913, Barnsley.
Died: March 1998 (aged 84).

■ Yorkshire-born Jones began his career by playing for local side Wombwell before signing for Huddersfield in 1932. After two seasons without breaking into the Leeds Road first team, he joined hometown club Barnsley and between 1934 and 1937 made 57 appearances. An early flirtation with Essex came when he signed briefly for Chelmsford City but he was at Plymouth by the time war came. After arriving at Argyle, Jones made 40 League appearances, scoring two goals between 1939 and 1948, as well as representing them in 30 wartime fixtures. The 1949–50 season heralded a move to Southend, and after 29 appearances Jimmy Allen snapped up Jones for U's League bow to play outside-right. Despite being well into the veteran stage, Jones made the number-seven shirt his own until breaking his leg inside 10 minutes of the FA Cup tie with Port Vale in November 1951. That finished his season, but he was back again the following campaign, primarily to act as

éminence grise to the A team, but also deputising in the first team for three short spells. Released by United in 1953, his professional career was extended following a month's trial with Ipswich Town. He was a regular in their reserves until joining Clacton in March 1954. In 1957, by now 44, he was still active as player-coach at local junior club Great Bentley. He was also well-known around Colchester through his joint ownership, with fellow U's player Roy Bicknell, of the Hythe Hill Coffee House.

	League		Lge Cup		FA Cup		Other	
	A	G	A	G	A	G	A	G
1950–51	41	2	-	-	2	1	-	-
1951–52	17	1	-	-	1	0	-	-
1952–53	13	0	-	-	0	0	-	-
TOTAL	71	3	-	-	3	1	-	-

JONES, Leslie Jenkin 'Les'

Born: 1 July 1911, Aberdare.
Died: 1981.

■ Arsenal player Jones had experience at International level. He won 11 Welsh caps between 1933 and 1939 while playing for Cardiff, Coventry and the Gunners. At Ninian Park Jones scored 31 goals in 140 appearances between 1929 and 1933. His move to Coventry yielded 69 goals in 139 League matches. Such a scoring prowess caught Arsenal's attention, and they signed the player in 1937. The war curtailed any League aspirations, although Jones did notch up 49 Highbury games with a return of three goals. A wartime player, Jones turned out regularly during hostilities, thus: 1939–40 Arsenal 31 appearances/3

goals, Fulham 1/0; 1940–41 Arsenal 7/2, Coventry 1/0; 1941–42 Arsenal 4/0, Lincoln 1/0, West Ham 1/0; 1942–43 Arsenal 2/0, Notts Co 31/11; 1943–44 Notts Co 19/0 and 1945–46 Arsenal 9/2. His efforts did not go unnoticed, as he played for Wales in four wartime internationals against England. His solitary Colchester appearance was as a guest against Yeovil in a 3–3 Layer Road draw during December 1945. After the war he played twice for Swansea, then joined Barry Town, before playing three times for Brighton in 1948–49.

	League		Lge Cup		FA Cup		Other	
	A	G	A	G	A	G	A	G
1945–46	1	0	0	0	0	0	-	-
TOTAL	1	0	0	0	0	0	-	-

JONES Richard Glynn 'Richie'

Height: 6ft. Weight: 11st.

Born: 26 September 1986, Manchester.

■ Jones progressed through the Manchester United Academy to sign full forms in November 2004, having won England youth honours. He made his Red Devils debut in a League Cup tie against Barnet and played in further rounds against Birmingham and West Brom as United went on to lift the trophy. He also played in an FA Cup tie against Burton Albion. He was sent out on loan to United's nursery side Royal Antwerp of Belgium, appearing four times and scoring twice, and returned to play another League Cup tie at Crewe

in October 2006. Geraint Williams brought the player to Layer Road later that month, and Jones made his substitute debut against Southampton. Unable to break into a United side stringing a fine run of results together, Jones returned to Old Trafford before joining Barnsley for 1(+3) games on loan in February 2007. He joined Yeovil in the summer of 2007, on loan, mindful that it was the last year of his contract at Manchester United, but failed to make an impression in nine League games. Jones returned to Old Trafford in January 2008.

	League		Lge Cup		FA Cup		Other	
	A	G	A	G	A	G	A	G
2006–07	0+6	0	0	0	0	0	-	-
TOTAL	0+6	0	0	0	0	0	-	-

JONES, Sidney 'Sid'

Born: 15 February 1921, Rothwell.
Died: 1977, Colchester.

■ Before the war Jones was on the books of Arsenal and turned professional at Highbury in 1937. After playing for Colchester, Brighton and Leeds as a guest, Jones spent three seasons at Arsenal, playing for the Gunners reserve and A teams, after being demobbed with the rank of sergeant. He then moved to Walsall where he spent four years and finally played his first Football League game at the age of 27. He went on to play 151 League and Cup games for the Saddlers scoring once. In the summer of 1952 he moved into Southern League with Weymouth but did not take part in their two FA Cup first-round ties with the U's and ended his football career with a season at Bury Town in the Eastern Counties League while employed as a salesman for Woods of Colchester.

	League		Lge Cup		FA Cup		Other	
	A	G	A	G	A	G	A	G
1945–46	8	1	7	1	0	0	-	-
TOTAL	8	1	7	1	0	0	-	-

JONES, Tecwyn Lloyd

Height: 5ft 9in. Weight: 10st 8lb.

Born: 27 January 1941, Ruabon.

■ Jones arrived at Colchester on 1 October 1964 as make-weight in a deal that saw Martyn King join Wrexham. Jones signed as a junior with Wrexham in May 1959 and made 57 appearances

at wing-half for the Welshmen, scoring two goals. He gained a Welsh Under-23 cap against Scotland in 1953 while at The Racecourse but failed to score in any of his 28 League games for the U's. He was the first U's player to be named as a substitute, filling that role for the first three games of 1965–66, but there were no injuries to require his participation – tactical substitutions were not allowed until the following season. Moving to Crewe in October 1965 for a small fee, Jones played just eight more games before retiring at the age of 30 to take up refereeing. Crewe player Peter Kane was supposed to have swapped places with Jones and join Colchester but turned down the opportunity. Ironically, Jones also played for Portmadoc alongside U's goal hero Martyn King. Jones became a security officer at Brymbo Steelworks until its closure in 1990 when he became an ambulance car driver in the Wrexham area.

	League		Lge Cup		FA Cup		Other	
	A	G	A	G	A	G	A	G
1964–65	25	0	0	0	0	0	-	-
1965–66	3	0	1	0	0	0	-	-
TOTAL	28	0	1	0	0	0	-	-

JOSLYN, Roger Douglas William

Height: 5ft 10in. Weight: 11st 2lb.

Born: 7 May 1950, Colchester.

■ A product of United's youth scheme, Joslyn made his debut against Bristol Rovers in December 1967 and signed professional on 8 May 1968. His first goal

was a 30–yard thunderbolt against Port Vale in September 1968. After becoming a fixture in the side, manager Dick Graham sold him to Aldershot in October 1970 for £8,000, where he won the Player of the Year title in his first season. After 186 appearances for the Shots and 17 goals he was snapped up by the up-and-coming Watford side and their young manager Graham Taylor. His transfer involved a swap with Pat Morrisey, and it was a good move as Watford rose from the Fourth to Second Division. A further 178(+4) appearances and 17 more goals saw his final move to Reading, where he played 67 League games from November 1979 as well as appearing against his home-town club in a third-round FA Cup tie in January 1980. An arthritic hip forced his retirement in 1982, when he set up an interior design company in Hertfordshire.

	League		Lge Cup		FA Cup		Other	
	A	G	A	G	A	G	A	G
1967–68	10+2	0	0	0	0	0	-	-
1968–69	37+1	3	2	0	1	0	-	-
1969–70	38+4	1	2+1	0	0	0	-	-
1970–71	7	0	1	0	0	0	-	-
TOTAL	92+7	4	5+1	0	1	0	-	-

K

KAYE, Arthur

Height: 5ft 4in. Weight: 10st 5lb.

Born: 9 May 1933, Barnsley.
Died: October 2003, Barnsley.

■ Kaye made his debut for his home-town club Barnsley at the age of 17 and earned an England Under-23 cap at 22 years old, as well as representing the Football League against their Irish counterparts. He was also included in full England squads prior to the 1958 World Cup. His party trick was to push the ball past the full-back in the early minutes and then deliberately run into his opponent at the cost of a free-kick, softening up his opponent early on. Scoring 54 goals in 265 League appearances, Kaye earned a £15,000 move to Blackpool in May 1959. Hailed as the replacement for Stanley Matthews, Kaye was unable to displace the maestro from the wing and had to settle for an inside-forward position. Scoring nine goals in 48 League games, he moved to Middlesbrough 18 months later for £9,000 and was unlucky that his silky skills were only on show in the Second Division. Kaye joined Colchester aged 32 for the 1965–66 season and supplied the ammunition for Reg Stratton, Peter Bullock and Ted Phillips as United won promotion back to Division Three. Kaye retired through injury when released in 1967 and became a joiner back in his native Barnsley.

	League		Lge Cup		FA Cup		Other	
	A	G	A	G	A	G	A	G
1965–66	38	2	2	0	2	0	-	-
1966–67	10+1	0	1	0	2	0	-	-
TOTAL	48+1	2	3	0	4	0	-	-

KEANE, Thomas Joseph 'Tommy'

Height: 5ft 6in. Weight: 10st 4lb.

Born: 16 September 1968, Galway, ROI.

■ The young Irishman joined Bournemouth as an apprentice, signing professional in September 1986. His first-team chances were restricted to just 2(+1) games over three seasons, during which time he won Republic of Ireland Youth honours. In December 1987

Roger Brown brought him to Colchester for £10,000, proclaiming him to be the fastest thing on two legs. The expectations proved too great in a poor Colchester side and Keane, after making his debut on New Year's Day 1988 as a substitute in a 3–0 home defeat to Scunthorpe, returned home-sick to Ireland in late summer. He joined Galway United and helped them to the 1991 FAI Cup Final, where they beat Shamrock Rovers and thus qualified for European football. He was leading scorer with eight goals for a side that struggled in the League. However, Keane joined Sligo Rovers and later Finn Harps, missing the opportunity of playing in Europe. In 2007 he was inducted into the Hall of Fame relating to lifetime Sporting Achievement in Galway.

	League		Lge Cup		FA Cup		Other	
	A	G	A	G	A	G	A	G
1987–88	9+7	0	0	0	1	0	2	0
TOTAL	9+7	0	0	0	1	0	2	0

KEARNEY, Noel Michael

Born: 7 October 1942, Ipswich.

■ Kearney received an unexpected visit from U's manager Neil Franklin in September 1964. His United side had a crippling injury list, with Mike Grice, Gareth Salisbury, Billy Stark, Martyn King and Barrie Aitchison all unfit to

play. Having been released by Ipswich three months earlier, Kearney was taken on a one-month trial in mid-September and played in three League games, all of which ended in defeats for Colchester. The Kesgrave-based player later played for both Chelmsford and Haverhill.

	League		Lge Cup		FA Cup		Other	
	A	G	A	G	A	G	A	G
1964–65	3	0	0	0	0	0	-	-
TOTAL	3	0	0	0	0	0	-	-

KEEBLE, Christopher Mark 'Chris'

Height: 5ft 10in. Weight: 10st 7lb.

Born: 17 September 1978, Colchester.

■ A regular in Ipswich's reserve side, Keeble made his debut as substitute at Port Vale in 1997–98 after signing professionally the previous summer. It proved to be his only appearance in a Town shirt, as he was not kept on. He arrived at Colchester on trial and made his debut as a substitute in a 3–0 defeat at Wycombe in April 2000. It was at the same ground just over a year later that he ruptured his Achilles in setting up Scott McGleish's opening goal. The injury meant that he missed the entire 2001–02 season, which effectively ended his League career. He was not retained and joined Heybridge on release in April 2003. His father Vic was a prolific

goalscorer for Colchester in the late 1940s, and the pair join an elite group of fathers and sons to have both played for Colchester.

	League		Lge Cup		FA Cup		Other	
	A	G	A	G	A	G	A	G
1999–2000	2+3	1	0	0	0	0	0	0
2000–01	10+6	1	1+1	0	0	0	1	0
2001–02	0	0	0	0	0	0	0	0
2002–03	0+3	0	0	0	0	0	0	0
TOTAL	12+12	2	1+1	0	0	0	1	0

KEEBLE, Victor Albert William 'Vic'

Height: 6ft. Weight: 11st 6lb.

Born: 25 June 1930, Colchester.

■ Keeble was Colchester United's first local hero. Spotted playing for King George V Boys Club, who received a £10 signing on fee, Keeble actually preferred rugby as a boy and signed as an Arsenal schoolboy in July 1946. He was also proficient at table tennis and cricket. The Gunners allowed him to play more locally with amateur side Colchester Casuals, and he guested for the U's in a friendly on Christmas Day 1946. Arsenal released him shortly before he signed amateur for the U's in late May 1947, and he was still an amateur when he netted a 16-minute hat-trick at Bedford in his first-team debut on the opening day of 1947–48. He marked his first professional game with a hat-trick as well; this was against Norwich A in the Eastern Counties League on 13 September. Keeble scored for Colchester at an incredible rate, which was recognised by selection for the Southern League representative side. His 43 Southern League goals in 1949–50, scored in 45 games, remains a club record that will probably never be beaten. Keeble even played in goal for Colchester on one occasion. Due to fixture congestion and the high costs of travel, United played at Worcester on 21 April 1949, at Merthyr on 22 April in the held-over 1947–48 Southern League Cup Final and again at Merthyr in the Southern League on 23 April. When goalkeeper Ken Whitehead suffered a broken nose at Worcester, Len Cater took over (Keeble was not playing), so Harry Wright, who had already officially retired because of injuries, stepped in for the Cup Final. A leg injury meant he did not finish the game, or play again for the U's, and Keeble, who was one of two changes and known to be a competent 'keeper, completed that game in goal and was between the sticks the next day as United lost 2–0 to the Welshmen in a League match. The next week, in the return game with Worcester, Keeble was initially credited with a hat-trick, but the visitors' late arrival meant the game was reduced to 40 minutes each half, and in the fading light it was Harry Bearryman who had scored one of Keeble's 'goals'. When he carried his goalscoring into the Football League in 1950–51, it was inevitable that bigger clubs would come looking, and Keeble signed for Newcastle on 29 January 1952 in the station buffet of Charing Cross Station. The record transfer fee was a huge £15,000, and there would have been another £1,000 if he had been capped. Keeble was six months into his National Service when the transfer took place, and he was back at Layer Road in February 1952, netting a hat-trick for the Army against Essex. Keeble made 104 League appearances for the Magpies, scoring 56 goals in a side that included the prolific Jackie Milburn and won an FA Cup-winners' medal in 1955. In 1957 Keeble moved south to West Ham and kept up his amazing scoring ratio with 45 goals in 76 League appearances. A back injury contributed to his retirement from the game, but he became Colchester's commercial manager in 1968, carrying out a similar function at Chelmsford in the 1970s. His son Chris played for Colchester at the turn of the millennium.

	League		Lge Cup		FA Cup		Other	
	A	G	A	G	A	G	A	G
1947–48	*12*	*8*	*3*	*1*	*0*	*0*	-	-
1948–49	*12*	*8*	*3*	*1*	*0*	*0*	-	-
1949–50	*45*	*43*	*5*	*4*	*1*	*0*	-	-
1950–51	21	7	-	-	0	0	-	-
1951–52	25	16	-	-	3	1	-	-
TOTAL	46	23	-	-	3	1	-	-
	69	*59*	*11*	*6*	*1*	*0*	-	-

KEELEY, Glenn Matthew

Height: 6ft 2in. Weight: 12st 12lb.

Born: 1 September 1954, Basildon.

■ Keeley, an England Youth international, made his Ipswich debut against Manchester United in February 1972 but made just three further appearances, plus one in the UEFA Cup, before signing for Newcastle in the summer at 1974. He had 43(+1) outings for the Magpies before joining Second Division Blackburn in August 1978. He became a fixture at the heart of the Rovers defence, playing 365(+5) times and adding 23 goals. His Blackburn side vied with Colchester for promotion from Division Three in 1979–80, with Rovers achieving their goal. He also had a spell on loan at Everton in October 1982, making just one start. Remarkably, that was in a Merseyside derby. Keeley was sent off for hauling down Kenny Dalglish, and Everton lost 5–0. He helped Rovers defeat Charlton in the Full Members' Cup at Wembley in 1987. With his career nearing its end he joined Oldham in August 1988, completing 10(+1) games, and it was from Boundary Park that Roger Brown secured the loan services of Keeley in February 1988. A disastrous debut resulted in a 4–1 home defeat by Crewe; however, the U's were intending to keep Keeley at the end of his month-long stay until Steve Hetzke became available, and a choice had to be made. In September 1988 he joined Bolton and started 20 League games. He stayed in the North West and featured in non-League for Chorley and Clitheroe and coached Colne in 2000. Keeley then became Bolton's Community Football officer in 2006.

	League		Lge Cup		FA Cup		Other	
	A	G	A	G	A	G	A	G
1987–88	4	0	0	0	0	0	1	0
TOTAL	4	0	0	0	0	0	1	0

KEELEY, John Henry

Height: 6ft 1in. Weight: 14st 2lb.

Born: 27 July 1961, Plaistow.

■ Keeley was on the books of Southend at the same time as Roy McDonough, and it was no surprise that the U's boss returned to his old club in a bid to cure a goalkeeping crisis. An apprentice with the Shrimpers, Keeley made his debut in the 1979–80 season and went on to make 63 League starts in the Southend goal. After spending a couple of seasons out of the League with Chelmsford, Keeley's career was re-kindled when he joined Brighton in August 1986 for £1,500. He became a regular over the next four seasons, winning promotion to the second tier in 1987–88 while being an ever-present. In August 1990 Keeley moved to Oldham for £240,000 as the Lancashire club won promotion to the top flight. Keeley was second choice at Boundary Park and was loaned out to Oxford in the November and Reading in February 1991, playing six times for each club. He continued to be understudy as the Division evolved into the Premiership and went out on loan again to Chester in August 1991 for four games. He made just two appearances in the top League and signed for Colchester in July 1993, making his debut against Lincoln on the opening day of the season. Sent off at Hereford in October, followed to the early bath by replacement goalkeeper Nathan Munson as well, Keeley was dropped after a series of poor results in which Colchester lost 7–3 at Darlington and were dumped out of the FA Cup at Layer Road by non-League Sutton United. He announced that he was quitting League football and joined Chelmsford, only to sign for Stockport in March 1994, playing the last 10 games of the season and earning a Wembley Play-off appearance in which County lost to Peterborough. After a further 10 games for County the following campaign, Keeley joined Peterborough in January 1995 ending his League career with three starts at London Road. He went into non-League with Worthing, while working as kit man for Brighton from 2001. He was registered as an emergency goalkeeper on non-contract forms in 2002 before becoming goalkeeper coach in 2004. In the summer of 2007 he moved to Portsmouth to take up a similar coaching role.

	League		Lge Cup		FA Cup		Other	
	A	G	A	G	A	G	A	G
1993–94	15	0	2	0	1	0	2	0
TOTAL	15	0	2	0	1	0	2	0

KEENE, Douglas Charles 'Doug'

Height: 5ft 8in. Weight: 11st 2lb.

Born: 30 August 1928, Hendon.

■ Keene began his career at Brentford and in four seasons scored once in 13 Football League outings. A fee of £1,000 took him to Brighton in June 1950, where he returned a tally of 10 goals in 61 appearances. Signed for Colchester by Jack Butler for less than £1,000, Keene made his debut in the opening day fixture of the 1953–54 season at home to Torquay. He never established a regular place in United's side but managed to play 22 games, scoring a solitary goal against Shrewsbury in February 1954. On being freed by the U's in the summer of 1954, he joined Dartford but retired from football because of arthritis.

	League		Lge Cup		FA Cup		Other	
	A	G	A	G	A	G	A	G
1953–54	22	1	-	-	2	0	-	-
TOTAL	22	1	-	-	2	0	-	-

KEITH, Adrian John

Height: 6ft. Weight: 11st.

Born: 16 February 1962, Colchester.

■ Lawford lad Keith, who graduated through the Colchester & District Youth League to be playing for Wivenhoe Town in the Border League at 16, chose Second Division West Ham over the Third Division U's for his apprenticeship, joining West Ham in 1979. In his first year the Hammers won the FA Cup and in his second the Division Two Championship. Keith was made a professional in December 1980 but failed to make the first team at Upton Park and joined Colchester on a non-contract basis in December 1982. He made his debut at Torquay on New Year's Day

1983 and played in three further games as manager Allan Hunter sought to find a replacement for himself at the heart of United's defence. On leaving Layer Road at the end of the season, Keith moved on to Haverhill Rovers.

	League		Lge Cup		FA Cup		Other	
	A	G	A	G	A	G	A	G
1982–83	4	0	0	0	0	0	0	0
TOTAL	4	0	0	0	0	0	0	0

KEITH, Joseph Richard

Height: 5ft 7in. Weight: 10st 6lb.

Born: 1 October 1978, Plaistow.

■ Released by West Ham after serving his youth traineeship, Keith joined Steve Whitton's Colchester in July 1999 and played in every game in his first season,

scoring his first goal in a 3–2 win at Preston – a goal overshadowed by the magnificent Lomana Lua Lua's mazy run and strike that gave United their second in the same match. Keith was Colchester's leading scorer in 2002–03 and featured in big FA Cup ties at Coventry and Blackburn in successive seasons. He was sent out on loan to fellow League One side Bristol City in March 2004, playing three times, but it was Leyton Orient whom he joined in the close season. He missed just four games as the O's won promotion from League Two in 2005–06, as his old teammates at Layer Road also climbed a Division into the Championship. After playing in the first 8(+2) games of the 2006–07 campaign, Keith was loaned to Shrewsbury in the October, making a solitary League start. Returning to Brisbane Road, he found himself out of favour and joined Brentford before the close of the January 2007 transfer window. His two goals in 17(+1) appearances were not enough to lift the Bees off the foot of the table, and they were relegated to the basement Division. In 2007 close season Keith joined the recently re-formed AFC Hornchurch in the Ryman Premier Division.

	League		Lge Cup		FA Cup		Other	
	A	G	A	G	A	G	A	G
1999–2000	45	1	2	1	1	0	1	0
2000–01	21+6	3	1+2	0	0	0	0	0
2001–02	33+8	4	2	1	2	0	1+1	0
2002–03	36	9	1	0	1	0	1	0
2003–04	16+12	2	2	0	4+1	2	5+1	1
2004–05	27+4	4	3	0	4+1	0	1	0
TOTAL	178+30	23	11+2	2	12+2	2	9+2	1

KEITH, Marino

Height: 5ft 10in. Weight: 12st 13lb.

Born: 16 February 1974, Fraserburgh.

■ Keith began his career at Scottish Highland League side Fraserburgh in the 1994–95 season. His goalscoring exploits alerted Dundee United, but the striker played just four times at Tannadice. In 1997 he joined Falkirk and scored 28 goals in 71 appearances over two seasons, winning the Scottish Challenge Cup in 1998. In the summer of 1999 he was signed by Scottish Premier League side Livingston and, after netting seven times in just 21 starts, earned a move to the English League with Plymouth. He became an instant hit, scoring nine times

as Argyle won the Third Division title, and he scored regularly over the next three seasons, picking up another title in 2003–04 as Plymouth won promotion to the Championship. He struggled to win a place and was signed by Phil Parkinson on a free transfer for Colchester in March 2005. He bagged four goals in the 12 remaining games but suffered a summer training injury that kept him out for the entire 2005–06 season. He broke down again on his comeback attempt and was released after two years on the sidelines. Keith returned to Scotland and joined Scottish Third Division side Peterhead for 2007–08 but was struck down again by the injury jinx early in the season.

	League		Lge Cup		FA Cup		Other	
	A	G	A	G	A	G	A	G
2004–05	12	4	0	0	0	0	0	0
2005–06	0	0	0	0	0	0	0	0
2006–07	0	0	0	0	0	0	-	-
TOTAL	12	4	0	0	0	0	0	0

KELLY, Anthony Gerald 'Tony'

Height: 5ft 10in. Weight: 11st 9lb.

Born: 1 October 1964, Prescot.

■ Kelly embarked on a long career when he graduated from his Liverpool apprenticeship in September 1982. Unlikely to break into the star-studded Anfield side, he spent time with Derby before moving into non-League with Prescot Cables. His League career began when he joined Wigan in January 1984, and the following season he tasted Wembley success when the Latics beat Brentford in the Freight Rover Trophy Final at Wembley, with Kelly scoring the second in a 3–1 win. Fifteen goals in 98(+3) appearances earned an £80,000 move to Stoke in April 1986, where he played 33(+3) games, netting four goals. Staying in the Second Division, his next move came soon after when he joined West Bromwich Albion for £60,000 in the 1987 close season. Just one goal in 26 starts saw Kelly loaned out to, first Chester, playing five games in September 1988, and then to Steve Foley-led Colchester a month later. Kelly was a class act in the Colchester midfield, but the club could not agree a permanent deal, despite agreeing a £20,000 fee. Kelly was substituted against York in January 1990 by new signing Les Taylor and was rumoured to have walked straight out the ground, still in his kit, without saying goodbye. Colchester's loss was Shrewsbury's gain as they signed him for £30,000, and he played 100(+1) times, scoring 15 goals in the process. By August 1991 he returned closer to his roots when signing for Bolton in a £100,000 deal. In 103(+3) games he helped Bolton to promotion to the second tier in 1992–93 but was allowed out on loan to Port Vale in September 1994 and appeared 3(+1) times, scoring once before joining Millwall on non-contract terms a month later for a couple of outings. November was spent idle at Wigan, and from December 1994 Kelly made 12(+1) appearances for Peterborough scoring twice. His League journey ended with a barren spell at Wigan in 1995–96. He had a solitary game with Conference side Altrincham and appeared as a substitute for Halifax a season later. In 2006 Kelly embarked on a fund-raising awareness scheme for testicular cancer by visiting all 92 clubs in the 'Keep your eye on the ball' programme.

	League		Lge Cup		FA Cup		Other	
	A	G	A	G	A	G	A	G
1988–89	13	2	0	0	4	0	3	0
TOTAL	13	2	0	0	4	0	3	0

KELLY, Desmond Charles James Jude 'Des'

Height: 6ft. Weight: 11st 6lb.

Born: 1 November 1950, Limerick, ROI.

■ Kelly was brought to Layer Road by Dick Graham as second-string 'keeper in the summer of 1972, having begun his career at Norwich in July 1970. He failed to make the first team at Carrow Road but got his chance at short notice at Layer Road when it was discovered that Barry Smith had been playing with a broken wrist. Kelly made just one League appearance, a 3–0 defeat at Bradford City in November 1972, before Jim Smith brought in John McInally on loan, but Kelly was back in for the 6–0 FA Cup drubbing of Bognor because McInally had not been signed in time. By Christmas, Smith was back in action, and Kelly was unable to get a game for the reserves. In early February 1973 he was released from his contract and departed for Lowestoft.

	League		Lge Cup		FA Cup		Other	
	A	G	A	G	A	G	A	G
1972–73	1	0	0	0	1	0	-	-
TOTAL	1	0	0	0	1	0	-	-

KELLY, Nyrere Anthony Okpara 'Tony'

Height: 5ft 11in. Weight: 11st 8lb.

Born: 14 February 1966, Meriden.

■ Kelly began as a junior at Bristol City, making his debut in September 1982. Making just 2(+4) appearances, he moved to St Albans before reviving his career with a £20,000 move to Stoke in January 1990. He made 33(+25) appearances, scoring five times for the Potters, and had two loan spells with Hull (January 1992) and Cardiff (October 1992) before signing for Bury in September 1993 for £10,000. At Gigg Lane he scored 10 League goals in 53(+4) fixtures. Kelly joined Leyton Orient for £30,000 in July 1995, but an internal bust-up over an unnecessary sending off lead to boss Tommy Taylor terminating his contact. Kelly joined Colchester on trial in October 1996, making his debut against Wigan in a 3–1 Layer Road success. Not retained, he moved back to St Albans for a brief spell before finishing the campaign at Billericay. He moved across Essex to Harlow, scoring 35 in 130 games up until May 2000. He then signed for Arlesey but left after a disagreement over a suspension.

	League		Lge Cup		FA Cup		Other	
	A	G	A	G	A	G	A	G
1996–97	2+1	0	0	0	0	0	0	0
TOTAL	2+1	0	0	0	0	0	0	0

KENNON, Neil Sandilands 'Sandy'

Height: 6ft 1in. Weight: 13st.

Born: 28 November 1933, Johannesburg.

■ Neil Sandilands Kennon, to give him his full name, joined Huddersfield from Queens Park of Bulawayo in 1956, keeping goal for 78 League matches. Previously he had played for South African sides Umbilo and Barea Park. Kennon actually began playing as a centre-half but found he lacked stamina so took up goalkeeping. One of 13 children to a father of Scottish descent, Kennon played left-back for South Africa against Wolves in a special challenge match. When Charlton came asking of his services his father refused to let the 16-year-old travel to England for a trial. After gaining two caps for Rhodesia (now Zimbabwe) against an English FA XI, he joined Huddersfield on £1 per

week. A disagreement with Town manager Bill Shankly resulted in him signing for Norwich in February 1959. He made his debut in an FA Cup quarter-final tie and reached the semi-finals with the Canaries. He missed just one game as Norwich secured promotion to the Second Division in 1959–60 and won the League Cup in 1961–62. After 213 League appearances at Carrow Road he became a Colchester player in March 1965, taking over from Percy Ames. His U's debut came on the same March day as Brian Hall's first game in a home match with Watford. He joined the U's, despite the fact that they were languishing in the relegation zone of the Third Division, and his faith was rewarded as United bounced back at the first attempt as the fourth-placed side in Division Four. Kennon was released at the end of the 1966–67 season and joined Lowestoft Town as a part-timer while setting up Bunny and Kennon bookmakers. Injury brought his Lowestoft career to an end in 1968–69, and he later worked as a sales rep for Highland Distillers.

	League		Lge Cup		FA Cup		Other	
	A	G	A	G	A	G	A	G
1964–65	10	0	0	0	0	0	-	-
1965–66	46	0	2	0	2	0	-	-
1966–67	21	0	0	0	2	0	-	-
TOTAL	77	0	2	0	4	0	-	-

KERNOHAN, Patrick 'Paddy'

■ Kernohan began his career with Derry City and also played for Barry Town. He first appeared for the U's in September 1945, when he played two Southern League games at centre-forward against Yeovil and Bedford, while attached to the Army Fire Fighting Centre. By the time he reappeared on 19 April 1946 the Southern League programme had finished, and he had transferred to the No. 1 Holding Battalion, from where he was demobbed at the end of the month. In the meantime he played four times for the U's in eight days, all friendlies. He also played for Gillingham in April 1946 and was probably stationed away from Colchester over the winter.

	League		Lge Cup		FA Cup		Other	
	A	G	A	G	A	G	A	G
1945–46	2	0	0	0	0	0	-	-
TOTAL	2	0	0	0	0	0	-	-

KETTLE, Albert Henry 'Digger'

Height: 5ft 6in. Weight: 10st 7lb.

Born: 3 June 1922, Colchester.
Died: 1 March 1999, Colchester.

■ Kettle joined as an amateur in September 1946, having previously had a trial with Fulham, and turned professional in December of the same year, prior to joining the RAF. Originally playing for Arclight, a local works side, Kettle was diminutive but never shirked a tackle, and it was sometimes known for his opponents to end up in the boards surrounding the pitch. His attitude was perfectly demonstrated on 3 May 1947 when he played in the Southern League game against Merthyr at Layer Road – a 3.30 kick off – and by 6.30 was down in Chelmsford about to kick off for the

reserves in their League Cup semi-final. He really came to prominence as United embarked on their 1947–48 FA Cup run and was the subject of more than one enquiry from Football League clubs, including Huddersfield, whom United had dumped out in the third round. He chose to continue playing as a part-timer for his local club and combining his football with employment at fan manufacturers Woods of Colchester. Ultimately, it was hip trouble that forced his retirement from the Football League, and when he left Layer Road in summer 1955 he was the last link with the 1947–48 giantkillers. He continued playing for a while with Eastern Counties League Sudbury.

	League		Lge Cup		FA Cup		Other	
	A	G	A	G	A	G	A	G
1946–47	*13*	*0*	*3*	*0*	*0*	*0*	-	-
1947–48	*31*	*0*	*7*	*0*	*6*	*0*	-	-
1948–49	*39*	*0*	*6*	*0*	*1*	*0*	-	-
1949–50	*39*	*0*	*4*	*0*	*1*	*0*	-	-
1950–51	15	0	-	-	0	0	-	-
1951–52	3	0	-	-	0	0	-	-
1952–53	0	0	-	-	0	0	-	-
1953–54	3	0	-	-	1	0	-	-
1954–55	2	0	-	-	0	0	-	-
TOTAL	23	0	-	-	1	0	-	-
	122	*0*	*20*	*0*	*8*	*0*	-	-

KING, Martyn Noel Geoffrey

Height: 5ft 10in. Weight: 11st.
Born: 23 August 1937, Birmingham.

■ King started scoring goals for the U's in the reserves in 1955 and had made his Football League debut before going to Oxford University in autumn 1956. At Oxford he began playing for the famous amateur side Pegasus, as well as assisting the U's during the holidays, and he scored his first League goal at Norwich when home for Christmas 1956. He graduated in 1959 and not long after began his National Service in the RAF, but unlike his time at university it did not get in the way of his football, and he only missed about a dozen games during his stint, and several of those were with a broken cheek bone in early 1961. Bobby Hunt emerged as King's time in uniform was coming to an end, and they formed a formidable striking partnership, scoring close on 200 League and Cup goals between them in under four seasons before Hunt moved on. King's 31 goals in 1961–62 helped United to runners'-up spot behind Millwall in the Fourth Division, and he lost a couple more when

Accrington folded. In all he netted six hat-tricks for Colchester. In 1964–65 he was tempted away from a struggling Colchester side and joined Wrexham in a swap deal for Tecwyn Jones plus £3,000. King made 45 appearances, scoring 15 times for the Welshmen, but his career was ended by knee ligament trouble although he did turn out for non-League Portmadoc before taking up a career in teaching, much of which was spent at the Earls Colne Grammar School near Colchester.

	League		Lge Cup		FA Cup		Other	
	A	G	A	G	A	G	A	G
1956–57	3	1	-	-	0	0	-	-
1957–58	0	0	-	-	0	0	-	-
1958–59	3	0	-	-	0	0	-	-
1959–60	39	30	-	-	1	0	-	-
1960–61	38	23	2	2	1	0	-	-
1961–62	43	31	1	1	2	1	-	-
1962–63	42	26	1	1	1	1	-	-
1963–64	38	18	3	2	2	0	-	-
1964–65	6	2	1	0	0	0	-	-
TOTAL	212	131	8	6	7	2	-	-

KING, Robert James 'Robbie'

Height: 5ft 11in. Weight: 12st 5lb.

Born: 1 October 1986, Chelmsford.

■ King came through the U's Centre of Excellence and by 15 was playing for the Under-19s. Starting as a defender, his future was seen as primarily a defensive midfielder, and he went on to captain the youth and reserve teams and made his first-team debut as a substitute in a live televised game at Bristol City in September 2005. He was sent out on loan

to Staines the following month and in January 2006 was about to embark on work experience (an apprentice's equivalent of a loan) at Cambridge when Conference side Hereford stepped in to sign the youngster until the end of the season. King played 5(+1) times at Edgar Street, scoring on his debut. Like many of the lads coming through the U's youth system in the last two or three years, he had joined the club when its limit seemed to be to survive in Division One, but as he came to try to break through as a professional he found the club's standard had taken a considerable step up. Unable to break into Colchester's Championship side, King spent time on loan at Heybridge in January 2007, and on his release in the summer of 2007 he joined the Ryman League side on a permanent basis.

	League		Lge Cup		FA Cup		Other	
	A	G	A	G	A	G	A	G
2005–06	0+3	0	0	0	0	0	2	0
2006–07	0	0	0	0	0	0	-	-
TOTAL	0+3	0	0	0	0	0	2	0

KINGSTON, Alexander 'Alex'

■ Goalkeeper Kingston was a Private in the 16th Infantry Training Corps and on the books of Southampton. He travelled back from the Colchester Garrison to play his only first-team game for Southampton, against Swansea on 19 January 1946, and three weeks later linked up with the U's for the first time, making his debut against Barry on 9 February 1946. As well as the four Southern League games, Kingston kept goal in four late season friendlies but like many of United's military footballers disappears from sight over the summer.

	League		Lge Cup		FA Cup		Other	
	A	G	A	G	A	G	A	G
1945–46	2	0	2	0	0	0	-	-
TOTAL	2	0	2	0	0	0	-	-

KINSELLA, Mark Anthony

Height: 5ft 9in. Weight: 11st.

Born: 12 September 1972, Dublin, ROI.

■ Kinsella was part of a group of young Irish players brought into Layer Road during the reign of Jock Wallace. Originally with Home Farm, he was the only one to make the grade and was given his debut a few days after his 17th birthday as a substitute against Halifax in a 2–2 Layer Road stalemate during August 1989. Used sparingly over the next two seasons during the U's relegation and first attempt to claw their way out of the Conference, Kinsella was unleashed by Roy McDonough in Colchester's second Conference campaign. His first United goal came at the football outpost of Barrow in August 1991, and he played a prominent part as Colchester won the Conference title and topped the season off by winning the FA Trophy at Wembley. Having gained experience, the

youngster was ready for League football second time round and was a virtual ever present in United's engine room over the next three seasons. He scored a memorable goal in the 1–0 Third Division Play-off semi-final first-leg victory over Plymouth and added the U's other goal in the second leg, where Colchester unfortunately lost 3–1 on the night. He added to his Republic of Ireland Youth caps with eight Under-21 appearances and finally got the move his football deserved. He joined Charlton in September 1996 for a bargain £150,000, the U's negotiating position seriously weakened by the then recently passed Bosman ruling, and captained the Addicks to victory in probably the greatest Wembley Play-off Final ever. Charlton drew 4–4 with Sunderland, winning on penalties, but suffered relegation from the Premiership in their first season. Undeterred, Kinsella led the South London side to the First Division Championship trophy just a year later. He progressed to full international level and partnered Roy Keane and Matt Holland in the Irish midfield. He lost his Charlton place, following a serious knee injury, to Scott Parker and was sold to Aston Villa for £750,000 in August 2002 after completing 200(+8) League appearances at The Valley, scoring 19 goals. At Villa Park he continued to be plagued by his injury and featured just 17(+4) times before moving to West Bromwich Albion in January 2004. Settled in the Midlands, many Colchester fans called for Kinsella to be brought back to Layer Road, but after 15(+3) games for the Baggies, with a single goal, Kinsella opted to join Walsall on a free-transfer as player-coach, with responsibilities for the Bescot club's reserve side in the summer of 2004. He stayed on as a player and turned out 34(+6) times but still suffered from niggling injuries. In April 2006 he took caretaker charge of Walsall for two games but was lured back to Charlton in December 2006, joining Alan Pardew's coaching team as reserve's manager. Pardew's staff also included ex-U's boss Phil Parkinson. Nicknamed 'Sheedy' after the former Irish international Kevin Sheedy, Kinsella represented his country 48 times and the pinnacle of his career was to play in the 2002 World Cup in South Korea/Japan. He scored three international goals and was voted Irish Player of the Year in 2000. He briefly donned his boots again in March 2008 on emergency loan to Blue Square South leaders Lewes.

	League		Lge Cup		FA Cup		Other	
	A	G	A	G	A	G	A	G
1989–90	1+5	0	0+1	0	0	0	1+1	0
1990–91	*6+5*	*0*	*1*	*0*	*0*	*0*	*0*	*0*
1991–92	*37+5*	*3*	*0+1*	*2*	*3*	*1*	*8+1*	*1*
1992–93	37+1	6	2	0	3	0	0+1	0
1993–94	42	8	2	1	1	0	3	1
1994–95	42	6	2	0	4	2	2	1
1995–96	45	5	2	1	1	0	6	3
1996–97	7	2	3	1	0	0	0	0
TOTAL	174+6	27	11+1	3	9	2	12+2	5
	43+8	*3*	*1+1*	*2*	*3*	*1*	*8+1*	*1*

KIRK, James 'Jimmy'

Height: 5ft 11in. Weight: 12st 8lb.

Born: 12 November 1925, Tarbolton.

■ Kirk began his career with St Mirren, signing for them at the age of 16. Demobbed from the Scots Guards at the end of 1947, he played around 100 times for the Buddies before moving south to spend three seasons with Second Division Bury. Arriving at Layer Road in the summer of 1954, he made 32 appearances as United were forced to apply for re-election as wooden-spoonists. New manager Benny Fenton had Percy Ames lined up, and the U's transfer listed Kirk at £1,000, but Kirk appealed to the Football League management committee and won himself a free transfer. Kirk went to Torquay, where he ousted U's wartime guest Alf Jeffries and made 39

appearances before moving again the next summer to Aldershot, where he played his last five League games. He finished his footballing career playing for both Tonbridge and Tunbridge Wells before retiring as a postman in 1990.

	League		Lge Cup		FA Cup		Other	
	A	G	A	G	A	G	A	G
1954–55	32	0	-	-	0	0	-	-
TOTAL	32	0	-	-	0	0	-	-

KNIGHT, Richard

Height: 6ft 1in. Weight: 14st.

Born: 3 August 1979, Burton upon Trent.

■ Recruited by Derby from Burton Albion, Knight won England Youth honours but failed to break into the first team after signing professionally in August 1997. Knight had four loan deals in 1999, playing six times for Carlisle (March), once for Hull (October), no games at Birmingham (August) and three times for Macclesfield (December). At the turn of the year, with chances at Derby remote, he went on a further loan to Oxford with a view to a permanent deal. Impressing in 12 games, Knight signed for Oxford in June 2000, playing a further 36 League games over the next two seasons. The arrival of Andy Woodman at Oxford from Colchester, after his fall out with Steve Whitton, pushed Knight down the pecking order, and so he made the opposite journey to Layer Road but played just once in the penultimate game of the season at Bury, which Colchester won 3–1. Simon Brown had staked his claim for the number-one jersey, and so Knight was not retained and chose to join Oxford City and then turned out for Didcot. He later joined Brackley in October 2004, where he commenced the 2007–08 season.

	League		Lge Cup		FA Cup		Other	
	A	G	A	G	A	G	A	G
2001–02	1	0	0	0	0	0	0	0
TOTAL	1	0	0	0	0	0	0	0

KURILA, John

Height: 5ft 10½in. Weight: 12st 8lb.

Born: 10 April 1941, Glasgow.

■ Kurila began his career as a Celtic Junior and signed for Northampton in August 1962, scoring once in 40 League games. Joining Bristol City a year later, he managed just six games at Ashton Gate before transferring back to

Northampton in November 1963. He added a further 105(+3) appearances to his Cobblers record and netted three times as Northampton made a remarkable rise from Fourth to First Division. In July of 1968 he was sold to Southend, where in two seasons he scored once in 87(+1) League outings. Dick Graham brought Kurila to Layer Road in the summer of 1970, and the player missed just two games in the League as Colchester set the football world alight with their famous victory over Leeds in the FA Cup fifth round at Layer Road. Scoring in his last two League games for United, Kurila was given a free-transfer to Lincoln in December 1971 as financial pressures – the club would soon announce it was carrying a £21,000 accumulated loss – forced Graham to turn to his promising youngsters a little bit earlier than he would have liked. Kurila's League career ended after 23(+1) appearances at Sincil Bank, and he had a spell in Canada, playing for Hamilton Steelers before returning to the Northampton area to become a self-employed carpenter.

	League		Lge Cup		FA Cup		Other	
	A	G	A	G	A	G	A	G
1970–71	44	2	3	0	7	0	-	-
1971–72	9	2	1	0	1	0	0	0
TOTAL	53	4	4	0	8	0	0	0

L

LAIDLAW, John

Height: 5ft 9in. Weight: 11st.

Born: 5 July 1936, Aldershot.

■ Laidlaw was signed in June 1957 from the same Easthouses Lily side that provided Benny Fenton with Sammy McLeod and Bobby Hill. A month later Laidlaw joined the Royal Scots for his National Service and was posted overseas, spending most of next two years in Germany, finally making his U's debut for the reserves at the tail end of 1958–59. Finally able to concentrate on football full time, he made the right-back spot his own in 1959–60, but fate took a hand three days into 1960–61 with a knee injury against Grimsby that necessitated a cartilage operation. He did not recapture his form after his return and could not even force his way into a relegation-bound team. After seeing out the season in the reserves, he was freed and joined Clacton Town, working for Colchester Lathe and as a security officer at the University of Essex. His Wivenhoe home was called 'Ibrox'.

	League		Lge Cup		FA Cup		Other	
	A	G	A	G	A	G	A	G
1959–60	39	1	-	-	1	0	-	-
1960–61	2	0	0	0	0	0	-	-
TOTAL	41	1	0	0	1	0	-	-

LAITT, David John

Height: 5ft 10in. Weight: 11st 2lb.

Born: 1 November 1946, Colchester.

■ Following older brother Colin into the U's youth team, Laitt made his U's debut in 1962, just before his 16th birthday, and was a regular member of the 1964–65 team. This team was the first to play regularly in the newly-established Mercia Youth League. The same team played A fixtures in the Border League, winning 17 Under-18 games in a row from the start of the season, including a perfect 12 out of 12, to clinch the League basis Mercia League Cup. They also had victories in the first three rounds of the FA Youth Cup. A 3–2 defeat at Ipswich Town, whom the U's had already beaten three times, brought the winning run to an end, and Watford put an end to the FA Youth Cup campaign. The young U's grabbed an early lead and held it until midway through the second half, before eventually losing 3–1. Laitt got on the scoresheet, but unfortunately it was at the wrong end. Signing as a part-time pro in 1965–66, he made one substitute appearance in the first team, replacing Reg Stratton in a goalless draw with Southport on 30 October 1965. Released at the end of the season, he joined Crittalls but just over a year later had the misfortune to break his leg in a game against Arsenal A at London Colney, which ended in the unusual score of Arsenal 7 Crittalls 5.

	League		Lge Cup		FA Cup		Other	
	A	G	A	G	A	G	A	G
1965–66	0+1	0	0	0	0	0	-	-
TOTAL	0+1	0	0	0	0	0	-	-

LAKE, Trevor

Height: 5ft 10in. Weight: 10st 12lb.

Born: 2 January 1968, Orpington.

■ Lake, a former West Ham junior, was called up from United's reserve ranks, when Norwich refused to let loanee goalkeeper Graham Benstead become Cup-tied. Lake took his place between the sticks for the League Cup first-round first-leg tie at Fulham in August 1987 and suffered a career-ending knee injury after just 32 minutes, collapsing when launching a kick downfield, just minutes after being caught late by a Fulham forward. He later became manager of local junior side Stanway Rovers at the age of just 21 and after a long spell out of the game resurrected his playing career in 1992 with Wivenhoe Town, playing regularly for the first couple of months of the season before work commitments curtailed his football. He returned to playing for a spell in the mid-1990s at Cheshunt.

	League		Lge Cup		FA Cup		Other	
	A	G	A	G	A	G	A	G
1987–88	0	0	1	0	0	0	0	0
TOTAL	0	0	1	0	0	0	0	0

LAMONT, David 'Dave'

Height: 5ft 9in. Weight: 11st.

Born: 2 April 1949, Glasgow.

■ A combative midfielder, Lamont joined Colchester as an apprentice in July 1965, signing professionally in April 1967 as he turned 18 years old. His only appearance in the U's first team was as a substitute for Tom McKechnie in the 5–3 home defeat to Torquay on 4 November 1967, and before the end of the season the club had dispensed with his services, following an incident away from football that led to a court appearance and custodial sentence. His last appearance

for the club was in mid-February 1968, when he had to come off injured after an hour of a reserve game. He re-emerged in local football with Eastern Gas, coached by former U's stalwart John Fowler, and for much of the 1970s split his time between the Gas in the Border League and Tiptree United in the Essex Senior League. He later had spells at Brightlingsea and Wivenhoe, latterly as assistant manager, before emigrating to Australia in April 1982.

	League		Lge Cup		FA Cup		Other	
	A	G	A	G	A	G	A	G
1967–68	0+1	0	0	0	0	0	-	-
TOTAL	0+1	0	0	0	0	0	-	-

LANGLEY (LONGBOTTOM), Arthur

Height: 5ft 9in. Weight: 11st.

Born: 30 January 1933, Leeds.

■ Langley, then known as Longbottom, joined Queen's Park Rangers from Methley United, following the same route that future Colchester defender Keith Rutter had also taken. In seven

productive seasons at QPR, between 1954 and 1960, Longbottom played 201 League games, netting 63 times. A season and a half at Port Vale, for a fee of £2,000, saw him continue his rich scoring vein as he added 18 goals in 52 starts. He was snapped up by Millwall in January 1962, and, worried by the reaction of The Den faithful over his original surname, he had it changed by deed poll to Langley. One strike in 10 games prompted a move to Oxford for the 1963–64 season, where he scored a useful 14 goals in 34 appearances. In September 1964 Neil Franklin paid a fee of £1,500 for the player, who lasted just one season at Layer Road as United were relegated. Given a free transfer, Langley headed for Nottingham Forest but opted to retire before the season started and turned out for Scarborough, where he set up a guest house.

	League		Lge Cup		FA Cup		Other	
	A	G	A	G	A	G	A	G
1964–65	33	12	0	0	3	1	-	-
TOTAL	33	12	0	0	3	1	-	-

LANGMAN, Hedley Neil

Height: 6ft 1in. Weight: 14st 7lb.

Born: 1 April 1928, Bere Alston.

■ Langman made sure he got his electrical qualifications working for South-West Electricity Board and had to train alone while studying. Before turning professional he served his National Service with RAF Fighter Command. His older brother Peter was already on Argyle's books when he made his debut against Everton. Langman scored two and made two, but remarkably Everton won 8–4. He was leading scorer for Argyle in 1956–57, with 18 goals, and was selected for the Division Three South representative team against their northern counterparts. Langman left for Colchester in November 1957, only a few weeks after having scored against them, having amassed 49 goals in 96 League appearances at Home Park. His transfer fee was then a Colchester club record at £6,750. He scored seven times in the 1958–59 FA Cup run, including four against Yeovil in a 7–1 thrashing and U's first goal in the 2–2 draw with Arsenal in the fourth round at Layer Road. When United were relegated to Division Four in 1960–61 Langman was one of many to fall under Benny Fenton's axe. Despite

requesting a transfer fee of £2,500, Langman was given a free transfer to Bath. Between 1961–63 he was top scorer in both seasons for the West Country side. After short spells with Barnstaple, Falmouth and St Austell, he became caretaker at Tavistock School before retiring after 24 years as Warden at Devon and Cornwall Police HQ in Exeter in December 1997.

	League		Lge Cup		FA Cup		Other	
	A	G	A	G	A	G	A	G
1957–58	23	8	-	-	0	0	-	-
1958–59	44	20	-	-	6	7	-	-
1959–60	27	11	-	-	0	0	-	-
1960–61	34	11	1	0	2	2	-	-
TOTAL	128	50	1	0	8	9	-	-

LAUNDERS, Brian Terence

Height: 5ft 8in. Weight: 11st 10lb.

Born: 8 June 1976, Dublin, ROI.

■ Launders joined Colchester during the Mick Wadsworth era. A promising career began with Irish side Cherry Orchard, where Launders won Republic of Ireland Youth honours. He joined Crystal Palace in September 1993 and made 1(+1) appearances in the Premier League as Palace were relegated. Making just two further substitute appearances, he went on loan to Oldham in 1995–96 but failed to start. In the summer of 1996 he signed for Second Division Crewe but played just 6(+3) times. Moving to Holland, he played with BV Veendam and had a single substitute appearance with Premiership Derby, while on loan, in November 1998. Launders joined Colchester in March

1998, making his debut at Barnsley. He played no further part that season because of injury, and at the beginning of the next season Launders, with nine Republic of Ireland Under-21 caps to his name, was sacked in disgrace by Colchester for an act of gross misconduct. Wadsworth had already resigned and joined Crystal Palace. Launders followed him to Selhurst Park in October 1999 and made 1(+1) appearances. His final English League club was Sheffield United, where he made one substitute appearance in November of the same year. After a spell out of the game Launders resurfaced on trial at Northampton in 2001 and Huddersfield in the summer of 2002, managed by Wadsworth. He had a subsequent trial at St Mirren in 2003 and then disappeared off the football radar.

	League		Lge Cup		FA Cup		Other	
	A	G	A	G	A	G	A	G
1998–99	1	0	0	0	0	0	0	0
1999–2000	6	0	2	0	0	0	0	0
TOTAL	7	0	2	0	0	0	0	0

LAW, Dudley 'George'

Height: 5ft 10in. Weight: 10st 8lb.

Born: 12 May 1912, Wellingborough.
Died: 2 October 1970, Dover.

■ On the books of Northampton since October 1934, Law, as an amateur, was employed in an Earls Barton boot factory scoring a century of goals for Rushden in just 18 months. Law played for Rushden because Northampton had scrapped their A team. Norwich beat Rochdale and Luton to his signature in January 1938. Law netted 16 Southern League goals for Norwich reserves in just three months, including a hat-trick against Torquay reserves in February 1938. This earned him a first-team call-up for the last match

of season against Second Division champions Aston Villa. He never quite established himself in the full side, playing six times and scoring two goals, but notched a further 24 goals for City's reserve side. Law joined Colchester on 18 June 1939 and while at Layer Road had a £100 price on his head, due to the coaching efforts that Norwich had put into him. The war put paid to any aspirations of playing in the Football League, and he became a Lowestoft-based lorry driver afterwards, while turning out for Wellingborough and Lowestoft. Law passed away while on holiday in Kent.

	League		Lge Cup		FA Cup		Other	
	A	G	A	G	A	G	A	G
1939–40	3	1	1	1	-	-	-	-
TOTAL	3	1	1	1	-	-	-	-

LAYTON, William Herbert 'Bill'

Height: 5ft 11½in. Weight: 12st 2lb.

Born: 13 January 1915, Shirley.
Died: February 1984, Ipswich.

■ Layton began as an amateur with Shirley Town before turning professional with Reading, aged 22, in 1937. Either side of the war he made 51 League appearances for Reading, scoring 17 goals, and turned out regularly during the war, thus: 1939–40 Brighton (1 appearance/0 goals), Clapton Orient (1/0), Portsmouth (1/0), Reading (19/8); 1940–41 Reading (30/10); 1941–42 Bournemouth (1/0), Reading (19/0); 1942–43 Reading (16/6); 1943–44 Reading (26/5); 1944–45 Walsall (1/0) and Reading (28/6); 1945–46 Reading (33/3). Layton was chosen for England in 1945 but was an unused player in the game against Wales at Cardiff. He joined Bradford Park Avenue in 1946 for £6,500 and scored five goals in 47 League games. Joining United in August

1949, he took over from Bob Curry as captain in October and was a regular as Colchester gained Football League status in 1950, earning a Southern League Cup-winners' medal. He was not called upon until the end of the 1950–51 season and left Layer Road to become player-manager of Harwich & Parkeston, where he also ran an hotel. Just 12 months after taking the Shrimpers to the FA Amateur Cup Final, a competition his status as a permit player (an ex-pro now playing as an amateur) meant he could not play in, he was told that his contract would not be renewed for 1954–55.

	League		Lge Cup		FA Cup		Other	
	A	G	A	G	A	G	A	G
1949–50	*37*	*7*	*5*	*0*	*1*	*0*	-	-
1950–51	7	0	-	-	1	1	-	-
TOTAL	7	0	-	-	2	1	-	-
	37	*7*	*5*	*0*	*1*	*0*	-	-

LEAH, John Aloysious Peter

Born: 20 July 1924, Liverpool.
Died: July 1999, Sefton.

■ Twenty-three-year-old Leah, an amateur wing-half on South Liverpool's books, was a soldier in No.1 Holding Battalion who still had four years to serve when he signed amateur forms for the U's in July 1946. He only played two games for the first team, the second out of position as a late replacement on the left-wing, and made the odd reserve outing, with his last appearance for the U's being around Christmas 1947. By May 1948 he was out of the Army and on the front page of the local press, rather than the back, as the defendant in a court case. The report of his conviction for stealing an overcoat described him as a former U's reserve footballer who was now a manservant of no fixed abode. The magistrate thought it a particularly sad case and that prison was not the answer to Leah's problem. Instead, he was placed on probation on condition that he took work that the probation service found him and attended the Tavistock Clinic, a specialist trauma institution and presumably an after-effect of some wartime incident.

	League		Lge Cup		FA Cup		Other	
	A	G	A	G	A	G	A	G
1946–47	0	0	1	0	0	0	-	-
1947–48	1	0	0	0	0	0	-	-
TOTAL	1	0	1	0	0	0	-	-

LEE, Trevor Carl

Height: 5ft 11in. Weight: 11st 7lb.

Born: 3 July 1954, Lewisham.

■ Lee began as a Fulham apprentice in 1970 but failed to make the grade and was shown the door in 1972 when he joined non-Leaguers Epsom & Ewell, for whom former Fulham player Brian O'Connell was manager. He played for Epsom & Ewell in their 1975 FA Vase Final defeat to Hoddesdon at Wembley. After scoring prolifically for the Isthmian League side, he and his strike partner Phil Walker were both signed by Second Division Millwall in October 1975. In an age of venomous racism the pair formed a formidable forward line for the Lions. Lee scored 22 times in 99(+9) games at The Den, before U's boss Bobby Roberts paid out £15,000 to bring the striker to Layer Road in November 1978. Lee became the first black player to don the blue-and-white shirt. He made his debut against Plymouth at Layer Road in the November but could not help fire U's to promotion, despite bagging 11 goals. He played against Manchester United in the FA Cup and really came to the fore in 1979–80 when United narrowly missed promotion to the Second Division. The following, season as Colchester struggled at the foot of the table, he joined Gillingham in a then club record £90,000 transfer. Ironically, his last game for United was against the Gills in December, and he scored in a 2–1 win. Over the next season and a half at Priestfield he netted 14 times in 43(+3) League games and was loaned out to Orient in October 1982, failing to score in five starts. Bournemouth paid £5,000 for the player a month later, and he bagged nine goals in 28(+6) appearances. By December 1983 he was on the move again, joining Cardiff for a fee of £2,000. His stay was short-lived as, after just 21

games and five goals, he was transferred to Northampton in the summer of 1984. Failing to score in 24 starts, he returned to Fulham in March 1985, playing just one game. Released by Fulham, he joined Bromley for a spell and then returned to his first club Epsom & Ewell, where he retired in late 1985.

	League		Lge Cup		FA Cup		Other	
	A	G	A	G	A	G	A	G
1978–79	27	11	0	0	5	1	-	-
1979–80	43	17	4	1	4	0	-	-
1980–81	25+1	7	2	0	4	2	-	-
TOTAL	95+1	35	6	1	13	3	-	-

LEIGHTON, William Alexander 'Billy'

Born: 8 December 1914, Walker.
Died: 1981, Southend.

■ Left-half Leighton began at his hometown club Newcastle in 1932, where in five years he made 39 appearances, scoring eight goals. Moving south, he joined Southend and played 16 times up to the outbreak of the war. During wartime, he continued playing for the Essex club, thus: 1939–40 24 appearances/2 goals; 1940–41 23/1; 1945–46 Southend 8/0. In three League

appearances for Colchester he failed to be on the winning side as United lost to Cheltenham, Hereford and Worcester either side of the 1946 New Year, but he was more successful in friendlies, including the Christmas games, where the U's won 7–3, 7–2 and 8–2 in the space of five days against a varying standard of opposition.

	League		Lge Cup		FA Cup		Other	
	A	G	A	G	A	G	A	G
1945–46	3	0	1	0	0	0	-	-
TOTAL	3	0	1	0	0	0	-	-

LE MARE, John Sutton

Height: 6ft 1in.

Born: 15 April 1926, Ipswich.

■ Le Mare, whose name was probably misspelt more often and in more ways than anyone else in this book ('Lamare' was the club programme's usual offering), was a 21-year-old ex-Royal Marines Officer from Ipswich who won representative honours for the Royal Navy while in the services and was playing for Woodbridge when he signed amateur forms for the U's in November 1947. An art student in London at the time, and the London Universities' representative team goalkeeper, he caught the eye of several clubs in the capital, including Second Division Fulham and leading amateur outfits Dulwich Hamlet and Leytonstone, the latter the Amateur Cup holders. They all invited him to trial, but he preferred to play nearer home and was the U's reserve 'keeper during the 1947–48 Cup run. He made his first-team debut at Barry in December 1947 and stood in for Harry Wright on five occasions between the first and fifth rounds, including all the long-distance away trips. One game that

Wright did play – the home game with Cheltenham a week before the Huddersfield third-round tie – saw Wright leave the game with a dislocated finger and Vic Keeble take over in goal. Wright's fitness was in doubt for the Huddersfield game until a few hours before kick-off, and Le Mare actually received the selection card. Ironically, although Wright managed to shrug off the effects of his injury, a broken index finger sustained while playing for the reserves at Harwich on Valentine's Day 1948 brought Le Mare's season to an end, possibly because, unlike Wright, he carried on until the end of the game despite his injury. Le Mare was one of only two of the posse of amateur 'keepers used in 1947–48 to be re-signed the following season, staying until January 1949 when ex-U's boss Ted Fenton asked to take him to his new club West Ham, which was short of reserve 'keepers. By now finished with university and teacher-training, Le Mare signed for his home-town club Ipswich Town for 1949–50, returning to Woodbridge a year later. Teaching posts took him down to the West Country in the mid-1950s, where he first played for Shepton Mallet United in the Somerset Senior League and then stepped up to the Western League with Frome Town, not always between the posts. Both Frome and Woodbridge occasionally used him at centre-forward. He subsequently returned to Suffolk to become a master at the Ipswich School, retiring in 1986 after more than 30 years of teaching, and finished his Territorial Army career as a Lieutenant-Colonel.

	League		Lge Cup		FA Cup		Other	
	A	G	A	G	A	G	A	G
1947–48	4	0	1	0	0	0	-	-
TOTAL	4	0	1	0	0	0	-	-

LEONARD, Patrick Desmond 'Paddy'

Height: 5ft 10in. Weight: 10st 10lb.

Born: 25 July 1929, Dublin.

■ Leonard impressed U's manager Jack Butler when scoring past England international goalkeeper Gil Merrick for Bristol Rovers against Birmingham in a DivisionTwo game. After 14 appearances at Eastville and one further goal, Leonard joined United in July 1954. He was cast

aside by the recently-arrived Benny Fenton at the end of the season and began a brief spell with Tonbridge in July 1955. He later returned to his native Dublin, disillusionedwith the game and reportedly threw his boots away.

	League		Lge Cup		FA Cup		Other	
	A	G	A	G	A	G	A	G
1954–55	34	5	-	-	0	0	-	-
TOTAL	34	5	-	-	0	0	-	-

LESLIE, George William John

Height: 6ft 1in. Weight: 12st.

Born: 9 July 1907, Slough.

Died: November 1986, Colchester.

■ Berkshire-born Leslie started his career as an amateur at Charlton in 1930 but failed to make the first team. A spell in French football was followed by a move to Walsall in 1932. It was at Fellows Park that he played in the famous FA Cup win over might Arsenal. All in all, he made 88 League appearances for Walsall, scoring two goals, but drifted into non-League football with Guildford City. Ted

Davis signed him for United's inaugural season, and he became a stalwart centre-half for the U's. Somewhat ironically, after the damage inflicted by his Walsall colleagues six years earlier, Leslie twice underwent convalescence treatment and fitness training at Highbury. The first was after undergoing a cartilage operation in May 1938, and it is an indication how medical treatment of players has changed for the better that he had to wait six weeks after suffering the injury for that operation. He was back at Highbury in October after another injury at Aldershot earlier that month. On his return to the side, he was appointed first-team captain in 1939, having been voted the best centre-half in the Southern League for the 1937–38 season. Leslie was only just behind John Hodge in notching up 100 appearances for the U's and in 1949 assisted ex-U's full-back Cecil Allan in running the highly successful Colchester Casuals junior side.

	League		Lge Cup		FA Cup		Other	
	A	G	A	G	A	G	A	G
1937–38	24	0	3	0	-	-	15	0
1938–39	40	0	3	0	2	1	13	0
1939–40	1	0	0	0	-	-	-	-
TOTAL	65	0	6	0	2	1	28	0

LESLIE, Steven Robert William 'Steve'

Height: 5ft 10in. Weight: 11st.

Born: 4 September 1952, Brentwood.

■ Leslie signed professionally for Colchester in May 1971 after making his debut at Grimsby on 20 April 1970, in a game that also marked the first appearance of Lindsay Smith. Having just turned 19, he burst onto the scene in his first full season, weighing in with 13 League goals, while gaining three England Amateur Youth caps. A steady fixture on the U's team sheet, Leslie was courted by Spurs and actually turned down the chance to join Norwich. He stayed at Layer Road and won promotion under Jim Smith in 1973–74 and Bobby Roberts in 1976–77. During 1974–75 he scored three important League Cup goals as U's went out in the quarter-finals to Aston Villa after beating Southampton at The Dell, and he was club leading scorer in the relegation season a year later. Voted Player of the Year for 1977–78, he suffered a broken leg at Sheffield Wednesday in only the third game

of the 1978–79 season. Leslie recovered to become an ever present as United almost made the Second Division a season later. Struggling with niggling injuries, Leslie moved into non-League, where he played for Chelmsford and Wivenhoe, later becoming an integral part of the Ipswich Youth Academy.

	League		Lge Cup		FA Cup		Other	
	A	G	A	G	A	G	A	G
1970–71	2	0	0	0	0	0	-	-
1971–72	40+1	13	1+1	0	0+1	0	0+1	0
1972–73	27+3	3	1	0	2	0	-	-
1973–74	21+3	5	0	0	0	0	-	-
1974–75	32+2	3	6	3	2	0	-	-
1975–76	36+3	6	0	0	2	1	-	-
1976–77	40+1	2	3	0	6	1	-	-
1977–78	41	3	4	0	4	0	-	-
1978–79	3	0	1	0	0	0	-	-
1979–80	46	1	4	0	4	0	-	-
1980–81	41+2	0	0	0	4	0	-	-
1981–82	31+3	2	5	0	4+1	1	-	-
1982–83	26+3	1	4	0	1	0	1+1	0
1983–84	25	1	2	0	3	0	1+1	0
TOTAL	411+21	40	31+1	3	32+2	3	2+3	0

LEWIS, Benjamin 'Ben'

Height: 5ft 10in. Weight: 12st 4lb.

Born: 22 June 1977, Chelmsford.

■ A late entrant on the YTS in 1993–94 after been spotted playing for Heybridge Swifts, central-defender Lewis earned a professional contract at the end of his apprenticeship and received a surprise call-up on the morning of United's away match at Scunthorpe in September 1995 when Tony English had to pull out with a severe migraine. Lewis made just one further substitute appearance a month later at Fulham. Released in the summer, he joined neighbours Southend and played 14 times, scoring once. He moved into non-League and had spells with

Rushden & Diamonds, Heybridge, Chelmsford, Grays, Ford United, St Albans (helping them win promotion to the Conference in 2005), Bishop's Stortford, Welling and was with Maidstone United for the 2007–08 season.

	League		Lge Cup		FA Cup		Other	
	A	G	A	G	A	G	A	G
1995–96	1+1	0	0	0	0	0	1	0
TOTAL	1+1	0	0	0	0	0	1	0

LEWIS, Brian

Height: 5ft 9½in. Weight: 10st 7lb.

Born: 26 January 1943, Woking.

Died: 14 December 1998, Dorset.

■ A Crystal Palace junior, Lewis signed professionally in April 1960, going on to score four times in 32 League appearances as Palace finished runners-up in Division Four under Dick Graham. Switching between wing-half and inside

forward, Lewis was unable to retain a regular place and moved to Portsmouth on a free transfer in July 1963. In three and a half years at Fratton Park he notched 23 goals in 134 League appearances, securing a £25,000 transfer to the upwardly mobile Coventry side in January 1967. The Sky Blues won the Second Division title, but Lewis was on the move again, this time to Fourth Division champions Luton in July 1968. A £35,000 fee saw Lewis finishing top scorer for the Hatters with 22 goals, but he was pushed into the shadows by the arrival of Malcolm MacDonald a year later. Oxford was the next stop and a £10,000 transfer saw him score four goals in 14 games, but again he was edged out by other players. With Colchester in something of an injury crisis, Dick Graham paid Oxford £5,000, and the player duly obliged with a goal on his Boxing Day 1970 debut at Lincoln. Lewis was prominent in Colchester's famous win over Leeds in the FA Cup, setting up a couple of goals, and scored three competition goals as United won the Watney Cup at West Brom at the beginning of the 1971–72 season. He returned to Fratton Park in March 1972 for a £8,500 fee and played a further 44(+16) League games, scoring eight goals, until his retirement from the game in 1974. He moved into non-League, where he played for Hastings United.

	League		Lge Cup		FA Cup		Other	
	A	G	A	G	A	G	A	G
1970–71	17	3	0	0	5	2	-	-
1971–72	30	15	3	5	1	0	3	3
TOTAL	47	18	3	5	6	2	3	3

LEWIS, Frederick Arthur 'Fred'

Height: 5ft 9in. Weight: 11st 11lb.

Born: 27 July 1923, Broughton Gifford.

Died: 1975, Aylesbury.

■ Lewis started his career as an amateur with Aylesbury United. Following his demob from the Royal Navy in November 1947, he was signed by Chelsea and made 23 first-team appearances. He captained their reserves in 1952–53, and Jack Butler signed him at the end of that season to partner John Harrison at full-back. Lewis was an ever-present in his first season at Layer Road and, despite only

missing seven games in his second season, was released after Butler himself was sacked, following Colchester's second successive application for re-election to the Football League. A single season at Headington United ensued, and he later became an unofficial scout for Chelsea.

	League		Lge Cup		FA Cup		Other	
	A	G	A	G	A	G	A	G
1953–54	46	0	-	-	2	0	-	-
1954–55	39	0	-	-	2	0	-	-
TOTAL	85	0	-	-	4	0	-	-

LEWORTHY, David John

Height: 5ft 9in. Weight: 12st 7lb.

Born: 22 October 1962, Portsmouth.

■ Portsmouth apprentice Leworthy failed to make the grade at Fratton Park after signing professional in September 1980. He made just one substitute appearance for Pompey before drifting into non-League with Fareham Town. He found his mark, scoring 22 times in the 1983–84 Southern Premier League, and was picked up for £5,000 by Tottenham in August 1984. Scoring three top-flight goals in 8(+3) appearances, Leworthy could not break into Spurs' experienced forward line. He was sold to fellow Division One side Oxford in December 1985 for a then Oxford record £200,000 fee, scoring twice on his Boxing Day debut, but missed their 1986 League Cup triumph through being Cup-tied. Never a regular, Leworthy had a spell on loan at Shrewsbury in October 1987, scoring three times in six appearances. He made a permanent move to Reading in the summer of 1989 and scored seven goals in 23(+21) games for the Royals. During his time at Reading he was recruited by Colchester boss Ian Atkins to bolster the U's attack in the run-in to the Conference title battle with Barnet. Leworthy did his bit, with four goals, but United still finished second to the Bees. Returning to Elm Park, Leworthy turned out three more times in a Reading shirt before becoming the Conference leading scorer in 1992–93 when scoring 32 times for Farnborough and in all netted 45 goals in 61 Conference fixtures. Leworthy earned four England semi-professional caps after joining Dover in the summer of 1993 for a then non-League record £50,000 fee. He made 125(+2) Conference appearances for the Kent club, netting 61 times. He moved to Rushden & Diamonds for the 1996–97 season, bagging eight Conference goals in 18 starts. His next port of call was Kingstonian, who paid £18,000, where he won two FA Trophy Finals under Geoff Chapple, who steered K's to the Conference. Leworthy continued his prolific scoring, netting 22 times in 58(+8) games in 2001–02 and 2002–03. Having spent some time at Havant and Waterlooville as a player and youth and reserves coach, Leworthy became manager between January and November 2004. He then returned to financially-crippled Kingstonian as player-coach in March 2006 until January 2007 and took over as manager of Banstead Athletic a year later.

	League		Lge Cup		FA Cup		Other	
	A	G	A	G	A	G	A	G
1990–91	9	4	0	0	0	0	0	0
TOTAL	9	4	0	0	0	0	0	0

LIGHT, Daniel 'Danny'

Height: 5ft 7in. Weight: 10st 12lb.

Born: 10 July 1948, Chiswick.

■ Light served his apprenticeship at Selhurst Park before signing as a professional in December 1965. He made his debut in 1966–67 and ended the campaign with five goals from 18 (+1) appearances. Dick Graham signed the forward from his old club Crystal Palace in August 1968 for about £4,000, and Light repaid the faith by finishing the campaign as leading scorer – one ahead of Brian Gibbs. On being released by Colchester in 1970, he and teammate Terry Dyson joined Guildford City. Light moved on to Dartford a year later, where he was Player of the Year in 1971–72, and helped the Darts win the Southern League in 1973–74 as they also reached the FA Trophy Final at Wembley. He then moved to Dover, where he featured in the Kent side's 4–1 thrashing of Colchester in an FA Cup replay in 1975–76, following a 3–3 draw at Layer Road. He also represented Wealdstone and Tonbridge as player–coach and took a teaching post in Dulwich.

	League		Lge Cup		FA Cup		Other	
	A	G	A	G	A	G	A	G
1968–69	42+1	12	0	0	2	2	-	-
1969–70	23+1	2	3	0	1	0	-	-
TOTAL	65+2	14	3	0	3	2	-	-

LIGHT, William Henry 'Bill'

Height: 5ft 8in. Weight: 13st 4lb.

Born: 11 June 1913, Woolston.
Died: 15 February 1993, Colchester.

■ Manager Ted Davis secured the services of Light from West Brom, who had him on their transfer list at £1,500 in June 1938. Light's career began at Southampton, where he made 45 appearances between 1933 and 1935. A fee of around £3,500 took him to The Hawthorns, where he made 28 appearances in the ensuing two campaigns. He made his Albion debut against Wolves in March 1936 and was in goal when they suffered their heaviest League defeat, losing 10–3 to Stoke. Light's playing career at Colchester was effectively ended by the war, although he kept goal in the first three post-war games before injury ruled him out. He became player-manager of Clacton Town for a time, before returning to Layer Road in August 1948 to take charge of the third team, which had just switched from the Ipswich & District League to the Border League and metamorphosed from the voluntarily age-restricted Colts to the A team. After two years, during which Light very occasionally kept goal for what was still basically the youth team, he was promoted to look after the reserves and in July 1953 became first-team trainer, a post he held until 1965.

	League		Lge Cup		FA Cup		Other	
	A	G	A	G	A	G	A	G
1938–39	26	0	2	0	2	0	12	0
1939–40	3	0	1	0	-	-	-	-
1945–46	2	0	0	0	0	0	-	-
TOTAL	31	0	3	0	2	0	12	0

LINDSAY, James Young 'Jimmy'

Height: 5ft 7½in. Weight: 10st 2lb.

Born: 12 July 1949, Hamilton.

■ Spotted by the Hammers playing for Possilpark YMCA, Lindsay, a Scottish Youth cap, signed professional terms at Upton Park in August 1968. He made his debut at Sunderland but after eight games was injured and lost his place. The midfielder went on to make 36(+2) appearances, scoring two League goals, before joining Watford in the summer of 1971. In two seasons at Vicarage Road he netted 12 times in 64(+1) League fixtures. Newly promoted Colchester snapped up the Scotsman on a free transfer for the 1974–75 Third Division campaign. Missing just one League and one Cup game, Lindsay helped United to the League Cup quarter-finals, but left during the next pre-season for a £13,000 fee. Moving to Hereford, he helped the Edgar St side to the Third Division Championship in 1975–76 as Colchester were relegated. At Hereford he scored six times in 76 League games, but as the Bull's were relegated from the Second Division he moved to Shrewsbury and repeated his previous feat as they won the Third Division title in 1977–78. In 80(+6) games at Gay Meadow, Lindsay failed to find the back of the net. He remained in the Shropshire area working for the local council.

	League		Lge Cup		FA Cup		Other	
	A	G	A	G	A	G	A	G
1974–75	45	6	5	1	2	0	-	-
TOTAL	45	6	5	1	2	0	-	-

LINFORD, John Russell

Height: 6ft 2in. Weight: 11st 12lb.

Born: 16 February 1957, Norwich.

■ Originally with Gorleston, Linford joined Ipswich in August 1981. Having been a playing substitute against AS Roma in the 1982–83 UEFA Cup, Linford signed for United on New Year's Day 1983, just days before Allan Hunter decided to quit. He filled the centre-forward role, when Roy McDonough was converted to an emergency centre-half, on seven occasions but failed to score and returned to Ipswich when new manager Cyril Lea signed Keith Bowen on deadline day 1983. It was rumoured at the time that the termination of his loan spell and Roy McDonough's end of season free transfer were influenced by something that happened in a boardroom at an away game. Linford did have some scoring joy as he spent a similar loan spell at Southend immediately after his departure from Layer Road. Playing in six games, he found the net three times at Roots Hall. With a lack of opportunities at Portman Road, he moved to Dutch side DS79 and later in November 1984 played 1(+1)

games for Second Division Birmingham during another loan spell. Linford was licensee of a Norwich pub in 2004.

	League		Lge Cup		FA Cup		Other	
	A	G	A	G	A	G	A	G
1982–83	7	0	0	0	0	0	0	0
TOTAL	7	0	0	0	0	0	0	0

LISBIE, Kevin Anthony

Height: 5ft 9in. Weight: 10st 12lb.

Born: 17 October 1978, Hackney.

■ England Youth international Lisbie signed professionally for Charlton in May 1996 and made his debut aged 16, in a League Cup tie at Burnley. Predominantly used from the bench in his early days, Lisbie was sent on loan to Gillingham in March 1999, scoring four goals in just 4(+3) appearances. In November of the same year he played 1(+1) games for Reading, also on loan, but appeared in just one other FA Cup game for Charlton in a frustrating season. He moved across London to Queen's Park Rangers in December 2000 for 1(+1) loan games, and it was only on his return that he began to find the Premiership net. In all, Lisbie scored 14 goals in the top flight, including a hat-trick against Liverpool in 2003. His Charlton career amounted to 62(+93) appearances and 16 League goals. He also had loan deals at Norwich in September 2005, scoring once in 4(+2) games, and at Derby in February 2006 netting once in seven starts. With only one full League appearance for Charlton in his last two seasons at the club, due to a benign tumour, Lisbie was released in the summer of 2007 and after a successful trial at Layer Road was signed by Geraint Williams in the August. He celebrated an early fixture against his former club Charlton by scoring in a 2–2 Layer Road draw and went on to finish the season as leading scorer. Despite representing England at Youth level, Lisbie earned 10 full caps for Jamaica, scoring twice, after making his debut against USA in May 2002.

	League		Lge Cup		FA Cup		Other	
	A	G	A	G	A	G	A	G
2007–08	39+3	17	0	0	1	0	-	-
TOTAL	39+3	17	0	0	1	0	-	-

LOCHERTY, Joseph 'Joe'

Height: 5ft 11½in. Weight: 11st.

Born: 5 September 1925, Dundee.

■ A left half-back, Locherty was reportedly always at loggerheads with manager Jimmy Allen. Allen signed him from Sheffield Wednesday for £1,000 as part of the U's new Football League squad. Locherty had joined Wednesday in September 1947, making his debut the following season and starting 10 Second Division games for the Owls. His Colchester debut came in an Essex Professional Cup tie with West Ham in September 1950 (also John Harrison's debut), and he scored in a 2–1 defeat. Locherty was picked for first team at Northampton two days later and scored, but he was dropped a further week later against Exeter when regular 'Digger' Kettle returned from injury. Released in 1952 to Scarborough, he later returned to his native Dundee. He was given a trial by Dundee United and made his debut for them on 23 January 1954 at Motherwell. Motherwell were on their way to the Championship of Scotland's lower division, while Dundee United would only avoid the bottom spot by goal average. The result, 12–1 in Motherwell's favour, persuaded Locherty to quit football straight after.

	League		Lge Cup		FA Cup		Other	
	A	G	A	G	A	G	A	G
1950–51	10	1	-	-	1	0	-	-
TOTAL	10	1	-	-	1	0	-	-

LOCK, Anthony Charles 'Tony'

Height: 5ft 10in. Weight: 13st.

Born: 3 September 1976, Harlow.

■ Lock looked an outstanding prospect as an apprentice, scoring around a goal a game in a youth team that lost more often than it won, and it was no exaggeration by Mark Kinsella when he said that he looked like he could be as good as anything the club had ever produced. He was introduced to the senior team by Steve Wignall on the 28 January 1995 as a substitute in a 1–0 Layer Road defeat to Wigan and scored his first goal in his third substitute appearance in a 3–1 win over Exeter in March of the same year. Unfortunately, he suffered cruciate and medial ligament injuries in training late that season and was out of the first team picture for almost two years. He spent

time on loan at Chelmsford as part of his recuperation, scoring on his debut, and did the same on his first full start for the U's, at Barnet in a 4–2 win in the final game of 1996–97. Tragically, the injury had robbed him of his exceptional sharpness, and his U's career was mostly spent starting from the sub's bench. He still scored some crucial goals, particularly the six in United's Division Three Play-off success season when he appeared as a substitute in both semi-finals. He also had a run out at Wembley in the 1–0 Play-off Final victory over Torquay in 1998. As Colchester stepped up into the higher division Lock found his chances hard to come by, and his record was not helped when, on one of the odd occasions when he really looked like his original self, he had two goals scrubbed out when the 1998–99 Bournemouth game was abandoned at half-time. During 1999–2000 he had a couple of games on loan at Kettering, and his Layer Road career ended rather ignominiously in November 2000 with two red cards in less than 48 hours as his frustrations got the better of him. The first came for the senior team against Wycombe, not long after coming on as a sub, and sparked a mass brawl, and when he repeated the trick against Norwich reserves it was time for a change. In March 2001 he stepped down two divisions to the Conference to join Dagenham & Redbridge and played 11(+9) games there over two seasons. Later, he played for Grays, signing in February 2002 after a three-month loan spell at The Recreation Ground, and staying there until the end of 2005–06, where initially he partnered Freddy Eastwood.

	League		Lge Cup		FA Cup		Other	
	A	G	A	G	A	G	A	G
1994–95	0+3	1	0	0	0	0	0	0
1995–96	0	0	0	0	0	0	0	0
1996–97	1+5	1	0	0	0	0	0+1	0
1997–98	14+18	6	0+2	0	0+3	0	0+4	0
1998–99	14+9	1	0	0	1	0	0+1	0
1999–2000	12+12	2	0	0	0+1	0	1	0
2000–01	3+11	2	2	0	0+1	0	0	0
TOTAL	44+58	13	2+2	0	1+5	0	1+6	0

LOCKE, Adam Spencer

Height: 5ft 10in. Weight: 12st 2lb.

Born: 20 August 1970, Croydon.

■ A youth trainee with his local side Crystal Palace, Locke was released and

joined Southend in August 1990. He scored four goals in his first season and Southend earned subsequent promotions to reach the second level of English football. Locke first arrived at Layer Road in October 1993 as boss Roy McDonough once again raided his old club for help. He made his debut in a 2–1 home win over Scunthorpe but returned to Roots Hall at the end of his one-month loan spell. George Burley re-signed the midfielder in September 1994, and he appeared twice as substitute against Plymouth in the 1995–96 Play-off semi-final defeat and came off the bench at Wembley against Carlisle a year later in the Auto Windscreens Shield Final. Seeking an improved deal, he was a major part of Bristol City's promotion-winning side of 1997–98, completing 61(+4) League games at Ashton Gate and scoring four times. His final League transfer was to Luton in August 1999, where he played 45(+17) times, scoring five League goals. Moving into non-League, he signed for Hornchurch before the plug was pulled on the non-League club's finances. He returned nearer his roots with Bromley and Tooting & Mitcham, before joining Whyteleafe under former U's player Dave Swindlehurst in 2007.

	League		Lge Cup		FA Cup		Other	
	A	G	A	G	A	G	A	G
1993–94	4	0	0	0	0	0	1	0
1994–95	20+2	1	0	0	4	0	2	0
1995–96	22+3	3	2	0	0	0	2+2	0
1996–97	22+10	4	3+1	0	1	0	4+3	0
TOTAL	68+15	8	5+1	0	5	0	9+5	0

LONGHORN, Dennis

Height: 5ft 11in. Weight: 11st.

Born: 12 September 1950, Hythe, Hants.

■ An apprentice with Bournemouth, Longhorn signed professional terms in the summer of 1968. Playing as a midfielder he made 23(+7) League appearances for the Cherries, scoring once. Transferred to Mansfield in December 1971, he scored five goals in 93(+3) games before securing a dream move to Sunderland. Joining the Roker Park club in February 1974, he was on the club's books when they famously beat Leeds in the 1974 FA Cup Final at Wembley but was Cup-tied, having previously played for Mansfield in earlier rounds. Completing 35(+5) starts, Longhorn scored three goals, but as Sunderland reached the top flight he was sold to Sheffield United in October 1975. At Bramall Lane he turned out 34(+2) times, scoring just once in the League. By February 1978 Longhorn had returned to his Hampshire roots with a move to Aldershot. Narrowly missing promotion twice in his three seasons at The Recreation Ground, the player joined Colchester in May 1980 and suffered relegation in his first season. He failed to find the net for United during his stay and on his release joined Chelmsford then Brantham and later managed Halstead (1988) and was assistant manager at Wivenhoe and Braintree (1993).

	League		Lge Cup		FA Cup		Other	
	A	G	A	G	A	G	A	G
1980–81	21+1	0	1	0	2+1	0	-	-
1981–82	14+7	0	1+1	0	0	0	-	-
1982–83	27+1	0	0	0	1	0	0	0
TOTAL	62+9	0	2+1	0	3+1	0	0	0

LOUGHTON, Michael George 'Mick'

Height: 6ft. Weight: 11st 9lb.

Born: 8 December 1942, Colchester.

■ Taken onto the U's books when he left school in July 1958 Loughton, like most of the U's local amateurs, got his match practice with Colchester Casuals in the Border League. He was first seen by the Layer Road faithful when the U's made their debut in the FA Youth Cup in 1959–60, beating Aveley in the first round and leading the all powerful Chelsea 1–0 at half-time in the second round before being punished for their cheek in the second half. Loughton was an inside-forward at the time, and that was the position he made his reserve debut in during 1960–61. He turned professional, part-time, in August 1961, stepping up to full-time two years later. An established member of the Football Combination side, still at inside-forward, it was not until Neil Franklin, an ex-England centre-half, had the foresight to move Loughton into his old position that Loughton's career took off. Within weeks he had made his first-team debut, even if it was a 6–3 defeat, and he hardly missed a game for the rest of the season or right through the next. That spell encompassed relegation in 1964–65 and promotion a year later at the first attempt, finishing fourth on goal average. Loughton had always had the pull of working the family smallholding and with his father's eyesight fading reverted to part-time status for 1967–68 to give him more time for agricultural work. He still played over half the games as the U's suffered another relegation, scoring five goals in the latter part of the season. In the summer of 1968 he asked for, and was granted, his release so that he could play locally without the nationwide travelling that Division Four demanded. He joined Brentwood Town and in 1970 found himself at Chelmsford when the two clubs combined. He gave outstanding service to Chelmsford, completing 382 appearances for the Clarets between 1970 and 1978, but taking over a player-manager in 1977 led to a parting of the ways the following summer through a dispute over summer wages. Loughton switched to Tiptree as a player under Brian Hall, and a few months later the two ex-U's men switched roles. Loughton went back to Chelmsford in October 1981, now purely as a manager, and stayed until December 1984, again citing budgetary constraints as a factor in his departure. He has subsequently had spells as manager of Wivenhoe Town and then linked up with Colin Hill, enjoying considerable success as Hill's number-two at several clubs, most notably Dagenham & Redbridge.

	League		Lge Cup		FA Cup		Other	
	A	G	A	G	A	G	A	G
1964–65	25	1	0	0	3	0	-	-
1965–66	45	1	2	0	2	0	-	-
1966–67	23	0	1	0	1	0	-	-
1967–68	28+1	5	1	0	1	0	-	-
TOTAL	121+1	7	4	0	7	0	-	-

LOWE, Simon John

Height: 5ft 11in. Weight: 12st 3lb.

Born: 26 December 1962, Westminster.

■ Originally with York as a junior, Barnsley signed the 21-year-old Ossett Town striker in December 1983, but Lowe made just two appearances at Oakwell and was sold to Halifax in the summer of 1984. At The Shay he enjoyed his longest spell of League football, scoring 19 times in 74(+3) appearances. In December 1986 Mike Walker signed Lowe, and he made his debut at Swansea just before Christmas in a 2–1 win. He celebrated his birthday by scoring in the Boxing Day defeat to Cambridge. In March 1987 he bagged a 26-minute Layer Road hat-trick against Stockport in a 5–1 win. He completed his first season ever-present, from arrival, in the number-nine shirt and played in the Play-off semi-finals against Wolves. After Walker was sacked, Lowe became homesick for the north and moved to Scarborough in November 1987. Scoring three goals in 14(+2) games, Lowe entered the non-League scene and played for Frickley Athletic, Goole Town, Glasshoughton Welfare, Pontefract Colliery and both Ossett Albion and Town.

	League		Lge Cup		FA Cup		Other	
	A	G	A	G	A	G	A	G
1986–87	25+1	7	0	0	0	0	2	0
1987–88	7+3	1	2	0	0	0	0	0
TOTAL	32+4	8	2	0	0	0	2	0

LUA LUA, Lomana Tresor

Height: 5ft 8in. Weight: 10st.

Born: 28 December 1980, Kinshasa, DR Congo.

■ Lua Lua, a gymnast rather than a footballer in his schooldays, was spotted playing for Leyton College against Colchester College by U's Recruitment Officer Geoff Harrop in 1997 and played a few games in United's midfield, appearing in the programme as Tresor. His clever footwork caught the eye, but there did not seem to be any particular end product, and with his timekeeping and reliability severely sub-standard the club decided that they did not need to indulge him. Lua Lua reflected on his missed opportunity once he had returned to his part-time job at MacDonald's and begged U's Director of Youth Micky Cook to give him a second chance. 'Lomana Tresor', as he continued to be listed until the end of September, returned for 1998–99 as a non-contract member of the youth squad, initially still playing in midfield. The side struggled for goals, only managing two in the first eight games, so Lua Lua was tried up front, and he blossomed, netting six times in three

games in a week, starting with a game-changing hat-trick against Cambridge United, where he first demonstrated his trademark tumbling goal celebrations. The U's moved quickly to get him on a contract, as opposition youth team bosses realised he was effectively a free agent, and in early January Steve Wignall (not Mick Wadsworth, as is often quoted) gave him his first-team debut at Chesterfield, where he made an immediate impact, scoring four minutes after arriving as a substitute in United's 3–1 defeat. The following season he came to the fore with dazzling speed and ball control and a spectacular somersault goal celebration. It was not long before he caught the attention of the Premiership big boys, and Newcastle's Bobby Robson smashed Colchester's transfer record by paying £2.25 million, with advice from Mick Wadsworth, by now assisting at St James' Park. Scoring twice in Newcastle's 2001–02 Intertoto Cup campaign, Lua Lua started just 14 times, although he came off the bench 45 times to record five Premiership goals. He also played UEFA Champions League football in 2004–05, scoring twice in 5(+4) games. During 2004 he was named captain of the Democratic Republic of Congo's African Nations Cup squad, before moving to Portsmouth in February 2004, initially on loan. At the tournament he was sent off in the group game with Tunisia which led to his country's elimination. He was held to account back in his home country and feared for the safety of his family. Completing his Pompey move for £1.75 million, he played in 64(+24) games at Fratton Park and bagged 19 Premiership goals. Attending the 2005–06 African Nations Cup, Lua Lua fell seriously ill when it transpired that he had failed to take prescribed anti-malaria pills. He had also injured his ankle while celebrating a goal against Arsenal and, worst of all, his baby son Jesus died while he was at the African Nations tournament. The governing body of DR Congo football decided that it was in their own best footballing interests not to inform Lua Lua of the tragedy. In the summer of 2007 he joined Greek side Olympiakos for £2 million on a three-year deal and played UEFA Champions League football.

	League		Lge Cup		FA Cup		Other	
	A	G	A	G	A	G	A	G
1998–99	6+7	1	0	0	0	0	0	0
1999–2000	24+17	12	2	1	1	1	1	0
2000–01	7	2	2	3	0	0	0	0
TOTAL	37+24	15	4	4	1	1	1	0

LUNDSTRUM, Colin Francis

Born: 9 October 1938, Colchester.

■ An amateur at West Ham under Ted Fenton, Lundstrum joined Ipswich in November 1956, scoring one goal in 13 League appearances over five seasons. Signing for United in August 1961 as a part-time professional, Lundstrum made just one appearance, standing in for Mike Foster during a 4–0 defeat at Mansfield in January 1962. He moved to former U's player Roy Bicknell's Clacton Town at the end of the season and then to Sudbury in 1964 and Halstead in 1967 before becoming player-coach of local junior side Donyland Swifts while working at Paxman's Diesels.

	League		Lge Cup		FA Cup		Other	
	A	G	A	G	A	G	A	G
1961–62	1	0	0	0	0	0	-	-
TOTAL	1	0	0	0	0	0	-	-

LYONS, John Patrick

Height: 5ft 10in. Weight: 11st 6lb.

Born: 8 November 1956, Buckley.

Died: 10 November 1982, Colchester.

■ Beginning his career as a Wrexham junior, Lyons had a taste of European Cup-winners' Cup football in 1975–76 as a playing substitute against Djurgården. He repeated the feat in 1978–79, featuring once from the start against Rijeka and as substitute in the return leg. Winning promotion to Division Two in 1977–78, Lyons featured 63(+23) times for the Welshmen, scoring 23 League goals. A £60,000 fee took him to Millwall in the summer of 1979, where he scored 18 goals in his first season. Impressed by his goal touch, Second Division Cambridge paid out £100,000 for the player after he had completed 55 starts and scored 20 goals at The Den. He did not quite find his form at Cambridge, who played a direct, long-ball game. Scoring six in 20(+1) games, he was snapped up by Bobby Roberts in February 1982 and scored within four minutes of his debut in front of the *Match of the Day* cameras, as Colchester walloped promotion rivals Sheffield United 5–2. Tragically, Lyons took his own life less than 24 hours after playing against Chester in November 1982 and four days after scoring both goals in a 2–0 win over Mansfield.

	League		Lge Cup		FA Cup		Other	
	A	G	A	G	A	G	A	G
1981–82	16+2	3	0	0	0	0	-	-
1982–83	15	6	4	1	0	0	3	3
TOTAL	31+2	9	4	1	0	0	3	3

M

McALISTER, Thomas Gerald 'Tom'

Height: 6ft 1in. Weight: 12st 13lb.

Born: 10 December 1952, Clydebank.

■ Scottish-born goalkeeper McAlister began his career as an apprentice with Sheffield United, having been signed from junior side Campsie Black Watch. Signing for the Blades in May 1970, he made four appearances in his first season before becoming the regular 'keeper in 1972–73, completing 63 League starts. He played in the 1972 Watney Cup Final against Bristol Rovers, which United won on penalties. As Sheffield United were facing up to relegation from the top flight in 1975–76, McAlister moved across Yorkshire in the January to Rotherham, playing 159 times and being ever present for four seasons. In the summer of 1979 he signed for Blackpool but after 16 appearances was on the move again in the close season to Swindon. Making just one start at the County Ground, McAlister was loaned out to Bristol Rovers in February 1980. After 13 games and Rovers's relegation to Division Three, McAlister returned to the top flight as second choice West Ham 'keeper in May 1981. Making 85 appearances for the Hammers, he arrived at Layer Road on loan in February 1989, becoming Jock Wallace's first Colchester signing, and adding much needed experience to a key position in the successful relegation battle in preference to rookies Mark Walton and Mark Coombe. He was not retained by West Ham and moved into non-League with Harrow Borough.

	League		Lge Cup		FA Cup		Other	
	A	G	A	G	A	G	A	G
1988–89	20	0	0	0	0	0	1	0
TOTAL	20	0	0	0	0	0	1	0

McCARTHY, Anthony Paul 'Tony'

Height: 6ft 1in. Weight: 12st 3lb.

Born: 9 November 1969, Dublin.

■ Millwall paid £100,000 for McCarthy's services in the summer of 1992. The Irishman was playing for Shelbourne and had already won caps for the Republic of Ireland at Youth level and five caps at Under-21. He had just been named Irish PFA Young Player of the Year for 1991–92. In three seasons with the South Londoners he played 20(+1) games, scoring one League goal. In December 1994 McCarthy was loaned to Crewe, where he played twice. Arriving at Layer Road on a free transfer in March 1995, McCarthy was given his debut by Steve Wignall in a 3–1 Layer Road win over Exeter in the same month. A month later he scored his only goal, also at Layer Road, in a 2–1 defeat to Lincoln. Forming a formidable defensive partnership with Peter Cawley, McCarthy missed just two games as United reached the Third Division Play-offs in 1995–96. A year later he was devastated to miss Colchester's Auto Windscreens Shield Final against Carlisle at Wembley, due to suspension, having been dubiously sent off at Hartlepool, nine days after the U's had qualified for their big day out. He quit English League football to study teaching back home in Ireland and rejoined Shelbourne, where he tasted European Cup-winners' Cup action in 1997, UEFA Cup football in 1998, against a star-studded Glasgow Rangers, 2001, 2002 and 2003 and Inter-Toto Cup preliminaries in 1999 and Champions League qualifiers in 2000 and 2002. He was released by Shelbourne in November 2004.

	League		Lge Cup		FA Cup		Other	
	A	G	A	G	A	G	A	G
1994–95	10	1	0	0	0	0	0	0
1995–96	44	0	2	0	1	0	6	0
1996–97	34+1	0	3	0	0	0	5	0
TOTAL	88+1	1	5	0	1	0	11	0

McCOLL, Thomas Gunn 'Tommy'

Height: 5ft 7in. Weight: 9st 10lb.

Born: 19 September 1945, Glasgow.

■ Signed from Scottish junior side Dennistoun Waverley, McColl scored on his second United start against Walsall in September 1963. The inside-forward was plagued by domestic troubles and made only 11 League appearances before Tommy Docherty took him to Chelsea for a small fee in December 1964. Within weeks he had opted to emigrate to

Australia where, playing for Juventus of Melbourne, he was an automatic selection for the Australian national side from 1967–70. He represented Australia in the 1970 World Cup qualifying rounds, scoring three goals, against Japan (twice) and South Korea, in five games. The Australian team qualified for the 1967 Asian Cup semi-final phase, where they encountered Malaysia in South Vietnam while war rumbled in the background. The match was marred when police and military personnel stormed the ground after a Malaysian player kicked winger McColl as the Australian player was lying on the ground following a tackle. The Malaysian players rushed the Australians and an all-in brawl developed before the police and military personnel restored order.

	League		Lge Cup		FA Cup		Other	
	A	G	A	G	A	G	A	G
1963–64	7	1	0	0	0	0	-	-
1964–65	4	1	2	0	0	0	-	-
TOTAL	11	2	2	0	0	0	-	-

McCOURT, Francis Joseph 'Frank'

Height: 5ft 11in. Weight: 11st 11lb.

Born: 9 December 1925, Portadown.

■ A Northern Irish international with six caps, against England and Wales in 1952 and against England, Scotland, Wales and France in 1953, McCourt began his career with Dundalk, moving on to Shamrock Rovers after serving in the RAF during the war. He also signed for Bristol Rovers but continued to play in Ireland for Shamrock on loan before breaking into the Rovers League team in September 1949. He made 32 League appearances, scoring once, before Manchester City paid the large sum of £2,000 to take him to Maine Road. It was while with City that he gained international recognition, and he played 61 games, scoring four goals, in four years with them. U's manager Jack Butler paid City a small fee in June 1954, but McCourt unluckily broke his leg at Newport in February 1955 and was out of action for a year. He was released in 1956 and joined Poole Town, leaving them in February 1957 to emigrate to British Columbia, where he took charge of recreation at a penitentiary before moving to Concord, California.

	League		Lge Cup		FA Cup		Other	
	A	G	A	G	A	G	A	G
1954–55	12	0	-	-	0	0	-	-
TOTAL	12	0	-	-	0	0	-	-

McCROHAN, Roy

Height: 5ft 11in. Weight: 11st 10lb.

Born: 22 September 1930, Reading.

■ Arriving at Layer Road in a player-plus-cash deal, McCrohan had already notched up almost 400 League appearances. U's winger Mike Foster joined Norwich for £3,000 plus wing-half McCrohan who had started his career at Reading as a junior in January 1949. After just four appearances, he signed for Norwich at the beginning of 1951–52 and went on to make 385 League appearances, scoring 20 goals and missing just 11 games in seven years. During this time he helped Norwich to promotion to Division Two in 1959–60 and starred in their 1958–59 FA Cup run to the semi-finals and League Cup success of 1961–62. He became a regular fixture in the Colchester line-up as U's consolidated their position back in the Third Division. He was released at the end of 1963–64, joining Bristol Rovers, where his career ended with 10 League appearances, his last appearance on a Football League team sheet being as the unused sub on the opening day of 1965–66, the first day that subs could be named. In all he amassed 474 League appearances. At Eastville he turned his attention to coaching and became player-coach of Crawley before teaming up with Bobby Robson at Fulham. When

Fulham were relegated both he and Robson were sacked. In 1968 he became trainer at Aldershot until rejoining Robson as assistant manager at Ipswich a year later. McCrohan took up a similar post at Luton between 1971–75. A qualified FA coach, he moved to the US in 1976 and had spells on the staff of both Detroit Express and Minnesota Kicks.

	League		Lge Cup		FA Cup		Other	
	A	G	A	G	A	G	A	G
1962–63	32	2	0	0	1	0	-	-
1963–64	43	3	3	0	2	0	-	-
TOTAL	75	5	3	0	3	0	-	-

McCURLEY, Kevin

Height: 5ft 10in. Weight: 12st.

Born: 2 April 1926, Consett.

Died: May 2000.

■ McCurley had the difficult task of filling the boots left by Vic Keeble's move to Newcastle. After demob from the Army, McCurley played for Worthing and Wigmore in Sussex before signing for Brighton in 1948. He never held a regular place, playing just 21 times and scoring nine goals, but Liverpool saw his potential and bought him in June 1951. He had not made their first team before a £750 fee brought him to Layer Road in March 1952. His aerial strength was a great attribute, and after playing in the FA Cup against Rotherham the Yorkshire club offered £7,500 for him in February 1953. It was turned down by United so Rotherham upped their bid to £9,250. Manager Allen wanted the cash, and there are conflicting reports as to whether it was the board or McCurley himself who said no. He scored a hat-trick against old club Brighton in

November 1955 on his way to setting a seasonal goal tally that has only been bettered three times in the U's 56-year League history, two of those coming in 1961–62 when the King-Hunt partnership decimated Division Four. He moved to Oldham for a nominal fee in summer 1960 and scored a hat-trick in their trial match, but a couple of minutes before half-time on the opening day of the new season he dislocated his knee cap, and that was the end of his Oldham career. He departed for Tonbridge in March 1961, and then in fairly quick succession had spells with Ramsgate Athletic, Canterbury and Snowden Colliey Welfare. McCurley retired from printing to Broadstairs in 1991.

	League		Lge Cup		FA Cup		Other	
	A	G	A	G	A	G	A	G
1951–52	11	6	-	-	0	0	-	-
1952–53	42	16	-	-	5	3	-	-
1953–54	32	8	-	-	2	1	-	-
1954–55	16	1	-	-	2	0	-	-
1955–56	46	29	-	-	1	0	-	-
1956–57	31	9	-	-	1	1	-	-
1957–58	28	12	-	-	1	0	-	-
1958–59	7	5	-	-	0	0	-	-
1959–60	11	7	-	-	1	1	-	-
TOTAL	224	93	-	-	13	6	-	-

MacDONALD, Charles Les 'Charlie'

Height: 5ft 9in. Weight: 11st 10lb.

Born: 13 February 1981, Southwark.

■ A Charlton trainee, previously on Millwall's books as a schoolboy, MacDonald made three substitute appearances in 1999–2000 as Charlton won the First Division title and

promotion to the Premiership. MacDonald made 1(+4) appearances in the top flight, scoring once, against Newcastle, and was named Young Player of the Year. He was let out on loan to Cheltenham in March 2001, scoring twice in 7(+1) appearances. He played a further five games on loan at Torquay in February 2002 before Steve Whitton, aware of his Football Combination striking prowess, brought him to Layer Road on deadline day 2002. He made his debut as a substitute in a 4–1 Layer Road thrashing by Brighton and scored his only goal, United's second, in a final day 2–2 draw with Wigan. Released by Charlton, he joined Margate and followed up by playing for: Stevenage, three goals in 13(+3) games, Crawley, 10 goals in 30 games, Weymouth and Gravesend & Northfleet. At Gravesend he came to the fore, scoring 39 goals in 60 Conference appearances and was the League's leading scorer in 2006–07. Following the sale of Freddy Eastwood to Wolves in the summer of 2007, MacDonald was recruited by Southend as Eastwood's replacement on a Bosman free transfer.

	League		Lge Cup		FA Cup		Other	
	A	G	A	G	A	G	A	G
2001–02	2+2	1	0	0	0	0	0	0
TOTAL	2+2	1	0	0	0	0	0	0

McDONALD, Ian Clifford

Height: 5ft 7in. Weight: 10st 5lb.

Born: 10 May 1953, Barrow.

■ Suffering from an injury crisis at the turn of 1975, Colchester manager Jim Smith was forced into the loan market. Along with full-back Danny Cameron, from Sheffield Wednesday, Smith signed McDonald from Liverpool. The 22-year-old had begun his career at home-town club Barrow as an apprentice and notched two goals in 31(+5) appearances before being sold for £3,000 to Cumbrian rivals Workington in February 1973. Scoring four goals in 42 League games for the (Workington) Reds, he was surprisingly bought by the Anfield outfit for £35,000 in January 1974. Liverpool wanted to recoup their investment, but, Colchester could not afford the £35,000 asking price after the successful completion of his month's loan. He joined Mansfield in the summer of 1975, for £19,000. He scored just four times in 49(+9) appearances but won a Third Division Championship medal in 1976–77. Transferred to York in November 1977, McDonald netted 29 times in 175 appearances before joining his final professional club Aldershot in November 1981. He became a fixture in the Shots side and scored 50 times in 340 League games as they beat Wolves in the 1987 Division Four Play-off final. He was player-coach at the Recreation Ground and was actually in charge when the club resigned from the Football League in 1992. He then became a coach at Millwall in the same year and later took the same position at Kingstonian under Geoff Chapple. He held the managerial hot seat at Hampton & Richmond, Farnborough in 2003 and also managed Kingstonian in 2005 before retaking charge at crisis-torn Farnborough in 2006.

	League		Lge Cup		FA Cup		Other	
	A	G	A	G	A	G	A	G
1974–75	5	2	0	0	0	0	-	-
TOTAL	5	2	0	0	0	0	-	-

McDONOUGH, Roy

Height: 6ft 1in. Weight: 11st 11lb.

Born: 16 October 1958, Solihull.

■ A Villa fan by birth, McDonough joined his heroes as a schoolboy in 1974 but was shown the door when a change of management brought a restructuring to the club. He signed for local rivals Birmingham and made his debut at Sunderland at the tail end of 1976–77.

He followed that up by scoring against QPR the following week. Those games proved to be his only outings for Blues, and, frustrated, he opted for a move to Walsall in September 1978. Had he waited a week when Birmingham lost both of their first-team strikers, he may well have established himself in the team. At Walsall he suffered relegation in his first season, but the Fellows Park club bounced back in style, finishing runners-up in the Fourth Division. Scoring 15 goals in 76(+6) League games, McDonough asked for an improved contract but was refused. This prompted a move to Second Division Chelsea. Despite scoring regularly for the reserves McDonough never made the first team. In February 1981 U's boss Bobby Roberts, having seen the player on the Football Combination circuit, paid £15,000 for McDonough. He scored on his debut against Burnley and formed a formidable strike partnership in 1981–82 with Ian Allinson and Kevin Bremner who both scored 21 times. McDonough then joined Essex rivals Southend in the summer of 1983, embarking on a run of being relegated with his next three clubs. At Roots Hall he scored four times in 22 League games, before moving west to Exeter in January 1984. Just one goal in 19(+1) appearances saw the Grecians accompany his former club Southend to the drop to Division Four. He joined Cambridge, a club in free-fall, and played 30(+2) games, scoring five times, for a side that set the record of most defeats in an English League season. His career was rescued by Southend, whom he rejoined in August 1985 and duly helped to promotion in 1986–87. When the Shrimpers were relegated two seasons later, McDonough sought pastures new. He teamed up with his former Birmingham teammate Ian Atkins who was in charge of Conference side Colchester. McDonough netted eight Conference goals as United finished runners-up to Barnet and failed to regain League status. When Atkins left in the summer of 1991 McDonough was appointed Colchester player-manager. He gloriously led the re-birth of the club, leading them to the Conference title and a first-ever trip to Wembley where Colchester beat Witton 3–1 in the 1992 FA Trophy Final. Returning Colchester to the League at the age of just 34 was an incredible achievement, but the club's finances did not match McDonough's passion, and the club failed to make any major impact. Big Roy became national news when he became English football's most sent-off player. He collected 13 red cards during his professional career, and disciplinary problems were partly to blame for his eventual sacking in the summer of 1994. He saw service with non-League Dagenham & Redbridge and Canvey Island and had stints as manager of Heybridge and Chelmsford. Moving to Spain in 2004, he became a coach in Charlton's European football academy.

* *See also Who's Who Managers section*

	League		Lge Cup		FA Cup		Other	
	A	G	A	G	A	G	A	G
1980–81	11+1	2	0	0	0	0	-	-
1981–82	40	14	5	2	5	0	-	-
1982–83	38+3	8	4	0	1	0	2+1	0
1990–91	*17+7*	*8*	*0*	*0*	*1*	*0*	*4*	*1*
1991–92	*40*	*26*	*1*	*0*	*3*	*1*	*7*	*2*
1992–93	21+4	9	2	0	3	0	1	0
1993–94	36+2	7	2	1	1	0	3+1	1
TOTAL	146+10	40	13	3	10	0	6+2	1
	57+7	*34*	*1*	*0*	*4*	*1*	*11*	*3*

MACEDO, Eliott 'Tony'

Height: 6ft. Weight: 12st 9lb.

Born: 22 February 1938, Gibraltar.

■ Elliott Macedo, to give him his real name, was evacuated to England as a two-year-old during the war. He was encouraged to take up football by his father who had been on the books of San Sebastian and Barcelona and was a Spanish international in the 1930s.

Representing St Pancras Schoolboys, Macedo was spotted by Fulham and invited to join the ground staff. A very agile 'keeper, Macedo turned professional in 1956 and starred in Fulham's FA Cup runs in 1958 and 1962. During his National Service in Germany, he was considered so vital to Fulham's team that they flew him back for League games. He was the regular goalkeeper as Fulham entered Division One in 1958–59 and was ever-present in 1962–63. A serious injury in August 1963 meant that Macedo lost his place and, although he returned to form, was refused a free transfer in 1967. In all competitions he played 391 times for Fulham and, but for his Gibraltarian roots, he might well have played for England. He did qualify to play for the Under-23s, and he did so on 10 occasions, against Italy and West Germany in 1959, Hungary, France, Holland, East Germany, Poland and Israel in 1960 and Italy and West Germany in 1961. Dick Graham brought him to Colchester, initially on a two-month loan to cover the injury to Ernie Adams, and the inconsistency of Alan Buck. The clubs agreed a fee of £6,000, and it was for the same fee that Macedo was sold to South African side Durban City in August 1969, having played in the first pre-season friendly against QPR. Durban City became national champions in 1970, and Macedo also turned out for Johannesburg side Highland Power while living in

Pinetown, Natal. Macedo was granted a benefit match as part of his Colchester signing-on deal, and 4,500 watched a game against Ipswich in May 1969.

	League		Lge Cup		FA Cup		Other	
	A	G	A	G	A	G	A	G
1968–69	38	0	0	0	2	0	-	-
TOTAL	38	0	0	0	2	0	-	-

McGAVIN, Steven James 'Steve'

Height: 5ft 9in. Weight: 12st 8lb.

Born: 24 January 1969, North Walsham.

■ McGavin, a former Ipswich apprentice, came to the fore with a spell of prolific goalscoring for Eastern Counties League Sudbury Town. Signed for Colchester by Ian Atkins at the tail end of United's first Conference season for a £10,000 fee, McGavin joined Roy McDonough and Gary Bennett in an awesome forward line that propelled Colchester back into the Football League as Conference champions. His season was capped off by scoring one of United's three goals against Witton Albion in the FA Trophy Final at Wembley. Dubbed 'Silky' because of his ability to weave inside and out with the ball, much was expected of McGavin as League football returned to Layer Road. A holiday prank that went wrong meant that he missed the start of the 1992–93 season through injury. In January 1994 he signed for Barry Fry's Birmingham for a reported £150,000. Fry had targeted McGavin while manager at Southend, but the huge first-team squad at St Andrews meant

that McGavin only played 16(+7) League games, scoring twice. In March 1995 he moved to Colchester's former Conference rivals Wycombe. The Chairboys manager, Martin O'Neill, knew all about McGavin from those Conference tussles and splashed out a then club record £140,000 for his services. His spell at Adams Park was not as prolific as expected, with just 14 League goals in 103(+17) appearances in just over three seasons. He was released at his own request in January 1999 and spent time at Southend as a non-contract player, failing to score in 4(+7) games. The summer of 1999 saw him register on the books of Northampton, but without playing a single game he returned to Layer Road in the October. Steve Whitton's signing finished the campaign as top scorer and Player of the Year. His final season at Layer Road was seen mainly from the bench, and he was released at the end of the campaign. Returning to the Conference, he turned out for Dagenham & Redbridge as a midfielder before leaving in September 2002 to take up a brief and disastrous spell as manager of Harwich & Parkeston. Drifting into junior non-League, McGavin played for Cambridgeshire side Tuddenham before teaming up with ex-Colchester player Richard Wilkins at Eastern Counties League Bury. Wilkins had become manager, and McGavin almost earned an historic non-League double of his own when Bury reached the 2005–06 FA Vase semi-finals.

	League		Lge Cup		FA Cup		Other	
	A	G	A	G	A	G	A	G
1990–91	*2+6*	*0*	*0*	*0*	*0*	*0*	*0*	*0*
1991–92	*39*	*20*	*2*	*1*	*3*	*2*	*9*	*4*
1992–93	35+2	9	0	0	3	1	2	0
1993–94	20+1	8	2	0	1	1	3	0
1999–2000	30+4	16	0	0	1	0	1	0
2000–01	19+22	2	3	1	1	0	0+1	0
TOTAL	104+29	35	5	1	6	2	6+1	0
	41+6	*20*	*2*	*1*	*3*	*2*	*9*	*4*

McGEE, Paul

Height: 5ft 6in. Weight: 9st 10lb.

Born: 17 May 1968, Dublin, ROI.

■ McGee joined Jock Wallace's Colchester in February 1989 from Irish side Bohemians in a £35,000 deal. McGee had been voted Irish Young Player of the Year in 1987–88, and a number of English clubs were watching him, but

Wallace had the confidence to step in and had the standing to persuade McGee to join a struggling bottom division team. McGee's immense talent stood out in a consistently underperforming Colchester side, and after just one month and four games he was sold to Bobby Gould's Wimbledon for a £135,000 fee, rising to £150,000. It was a superb piece of business. He scored on his top-flight debut against Arsenal on the last day of the season and went on to win four Irish Under-21 caps. After four campaigns in the top division McGee had amassed 54(+6) appearances, scoring nine times. He was loaned to Peterborough in March the Posh on 5(+1) occasions. He returned across the water but this time to Northern Ireland, where he played for Linfield.

	League		Lge Cup		FA Cup		Other	
	A	G	A	G	A	G	A	G
1988–89	3	0	0	0	0	0	1	0
TOTAL	3	0	0	0	0	0	1	0

McGLEISH, Scott

Height: 5ft 9in. Weight: 11st 4lb.

Born: 10 February 1974, Barnet.

■ McGleish began his career at Edgware Town in August 1993 before being snapped up on a free transfer by Charlton a little short of a year later. Appearing just six times as a substitute, McGleish was sent out on loan to struggling Leyton Orient in March 1995. He left Charlton for Peterborough on a free in the summer of 1995 but made just 3(+10) starts. His career finally kicked off when recruited by Steve Wignall on loan

in February 1996, having scored the winner against United for Posh in an Auto Windscreens Shield tie a month previously. Initially on a month's deal, McGleish had the move extended on deadline day and netted six goals in just 10 starts. He also played in both legs of the Play-off semi-final defeat to Plymouth. Cash-strapped Colchester were unable to prise the player away from London Road, and instead he had a prolific loan spell at Cambridge in the following September, scoring seven goals in 10 outings. New Leyton Orient boss Tommy Taylor, impressed by the player's form, opted to splash out £50,000 on McGleish in November 1996. Scoring seven goals in 36 League games, McGleish was surprisingly sold on to Barnet for £70,000 in October 1997. Completing 106(+28) games at Underhill, he scored 36 times and was suspended by manager John Still in May 1999. Featuring in two Play-off failures for the Bees, he returned to the side but was snapped up by Steve Whitton in January 2001 for £15,000. Back at Colchester, McGleish once again became a fans' favourite, although by now he had dropped his trademark, injury-threatening, somersault goal celebration. Leading scorer in 2001–02, McGleish scored a memorable hat-trick, as a substitute, at Northampton in an LDV Trophy tie in 2003–04, but Colchester lost to local rivals Southend in the Area Final. When he failed to negotiate a new contract at the end of the season, despite again being top scorer, McGleish moved to Sixfields to join Northampton. Maintaining his prolific lower League scoring record, McGleish hit 42 in 106(+5) games as Northampton first failed in the League Two Play-offs before achieving promotion the following campaign in 2005–06. McGleish moved to Wycombe in January 2007 and completed the season, scoring five goals in 11(+3) starts. McGleish passed the 20-goal mark for the season as early as February 2008.

	League		Lge Cup		FA Cup		Other	
	A	G	A	G	A	G	A	G
1995–96	10+5	6	0	0	0	0	2	0
2000–01	11+10	5	0	0	0	0	0	0
2001–02	44+2	14	2	0	2	1	2	0
2002–03	38+5	8	1	0	1	0	1	1
2003–04	25+9	10	1	0	6+1	1	4+2	6
TOTAL	128+31	43	4	0	9+1	2	9+2	7

McINALLY, John Stewart

Height: 5ft 10in. Weight: 11st 6lb.

Born: 29 June 1951, Gatehouse of Fleet.

■ With Barry Smith suffering from a broken wrist and Des Kelly not up to League standard, new U's boss Jim Smith went back to his old club Lincoln for goalkeeper McInally. An ex-Manchester United junior, and with four Scottish Youth international caps, McInally had been at Sincil Bank since August 1970 and played 22 League games. He initially came to Colchester on a month's loan but was signed outright after his first game and played all bar one of the remaining fixtures of the 1972–73, re-election season. The experienced Mike Walker was brought in for 1973–74 and McInally became the first of several deputies to be confined to the reserves. He held the number-two job for two years before quitting full-time football in 1976 and taking over as player-manager of Braintree. He gave up the managerial role in 1977 but continued as a player until going to university in autumn 1978.

	League		Lge Cup		FA Cup		Other	
	A	G	A	G	A	G	A	G
1972–73	27	0	0	0	2	0	-	-
TOTAL	27	0	0	0	2	0	-	-

McKECHNIE, Thomas Sharp 'Tom'

Height: 6ft. Weight: 12st 8lb.

Born: 9 February 1940, Milngavie.

■ McKechnie was spotted by Luton, playing for Scottish junior side Kirkintolloch Rob Roy, and moved south in May 1961 to score 31 League goals in 131 appearances. By 1966 he had moved on to Bournemouth but featured in only 14 League games, scoring twice. Brought to Layer Road by Neil Franklin, McKechnie lasted just one season as United were relegated to Division Four. He started well enough, scoring twice in only his second appearance against his old club Bournemouth, and scored one of the goals in a 2–0 FA Cup victory at Chelmsford that secured a home tie with West Bromwich Albion. He then had a year with Bury Town, where he had more FA Cup glory, being part of the team that took Bury to the first round for the only time in their history. They held his

former club Bournemouth, leaders of the Third Division at the time (the highest placed club in the round), to a goalless draw at Kings Road before losing the replay. He returned to his native Glasgow, where he became a lab assistant.

	League		Lge Cup		FA Cup		Other	
	A	G	A	G	A	G	A	G
1967–68	23+1	5	0	0	4	1	-	-
TOTAL	23+1	5	0	0	4	1	-	-

McKIM, John 'Johnny'

Height: 5ft 8in. Weight: 10st 6lb.

Born: 22 January 1926, Greenock.
Died: June 2000, Colchester.

■ McKim was a clever, ball-playing inside-forward whom Chelsea spotted while playing for Port Glasgow. Despite arriving in June 1947, his first-team chances were limited at Stamford Bridge. A well-spent £1,000 transfer fee brought McKim to Layer Road as Jimmy Allen completed his squad for United's baptism in League football. McKim was second only to Vic Keeble as top scorer in 1951–52, to Kevin McCurley the following campaign and notched an impressive hat-trick as United mauled Walsall by 6–1 in February 1953. In all, McKim returned an impressive goal every three games for United before joining non-League Clacton in August 1955. He holds the less impressive record of being the first U's player sent off in the Football League at Layer Road (Reg Stewart beat him to the overall title), being guilty of a retaliatory kick against Newport in the closing minutes of the game on 28 March 1953. He did not serve his two-game suspension until the early part of the next season, but he found himself in the reserves for the following month, ending an eight-game run in the first team.

	League		Lge Cup		FA Cup		Other	
	A	G	A	G	A	G	A	G
1950–51	24	8	-	-	0	0	-	-
1951–52	26	9	-	-	1	0	-	-
1952–53	28	13	-	-	5	1	-	-
1953–54	19	6	-	-	0	0	-	-
1954–55	32	7	-	-	2	1	-	-
TOTAL	129	43	-	-	8	2	-	-

McKINNEY, Richard

Height: 6ft 1in. Weight: 14st 4lb.

Born: 18 May 1979, Ballymoney, N. Ireland.

■ Irishman McKinney began his career with Ballymena United, being selected for Northern Ireland at Under-18 level, before being signed by Manchester City in August 1999. Failing to make any starts at Maine Road, McKinney joined Swindon in the summer of 2001 but appeared just once in the League. A year later, he was captured by Colchester manager Steve Whitton and made his debut on day one of the 2002–03 season in a 1–0 win over Stockport. Although substituted in only his second game, at Tranmere, he played the first 10 League and Cup games before being dropped following a 4–1 reverse at Northampton. He did not regain his place from Simon Brown until the following March at Oldham, bar an LDV Trophy tie at Cheltenham in which he was sent off for a professional foul. Warming the bench for the majority of 2003–04, McKinney was released at the end of the campaign as a young Dean Gerken began to challenge for the spot of understudy to Brown, who himself left soon after in the same summer, leaving Parkinson with a goalkeeping dilemma. McKinney signed a deal with Walsall in May 2004 but played just three League games for the Saddlers before joining Chelmsford. Signing for Canvey in August 2005, McKinney remained on the Essex non-League scene when returning to Chelmsford in 2006, where he helped the Clarets to the Ryman League Play-off semi-finals. In November 2007 he joined Heybridge Swifts and in February 2008 moved to Wivenhoe.

	League		Lge Cup		FA Cup		Other	
	A	G	A	G	A	G	A	G
2002–03	20+1	0	1	0	0	0	1	0
2003–04	5	0	0	0	1	0	1	0
TOTAL	25+1	0	1	0	1	0	2	0

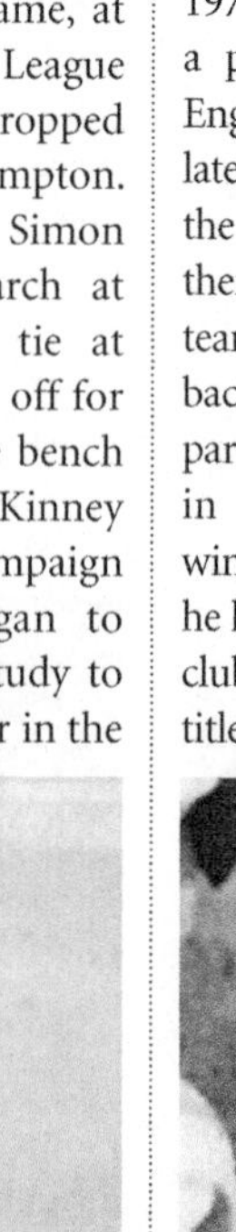

McLAUGHLIN, John

Height: 5ft 10in. Weight: 10st 12lb.

Born: 29 October 1954, Edmonton.

■ McLaughlin was given his League bow by Dick Graham at Hartlepool in March 1972 while still an apprentice and had an eight-game run in the side in April before becoming a full professional. In February 1973 he became the first U's player to win a professional cap when he played for England's Under-18's in Italy. Three days later he dislocated his collarbone early in the game at a fog-shrouded Hereford. By then he had established himself in the first team, switching between right and left-back at will, depending on who he was partnering. Further England caps followed in the successful UEFA Youth Cup-winning team in the summer. Inevitably, he had become a target for higher-division clubs and his contribution to Jim Smith's title chasing team of 1973–74 was ended at

the start of December. Swindon paid £25,000 for him and threw in the skilful midfielder Ray Bunkell. McLaughlin enjoyed 199(+3) starts for Swindon, scoring eight times, before he followed Robins boss Frank Burrows to Portsmouth in a £45,000 transfer. He played 172 League games, as Pompey rose from the Fourth to the Second Division, and netted a solitary goal. On leaving Portsmouth, he had a spell at Bournemouth without making a start and played non-League for Fareham. On retiring from the game, he took up trade as a French polisher in the Portsmouth area.

	League		Lge Cup		FA Cup		Other	
	A	G	A	G	A	G	A	G
1971–72	8+1	0	0	0	0	0	0	0
1972–73	40	2	1	0	3	0	-	-
1973–74	18	0	1	0	1	0	-	-
TOTAL	66+1	2	2	0	4	0	0	0

McLEOD, Izale Michael

Height: 5ft 11in. Weight: 10st 9lb.

Born: 15 October 1984, Perry Barr.

■ McLeod joined Derby on a scholarship, signing professional in February 2003. Debuting as a 17-year-old against Ipswich, he made 24(+15) appearances for the Rams, scoring four goals, and also had a spell on loan at Sheffield United in March 2004, where he appeared 1(+6) times. At the beginning of season 2004–05 McLeod signed for MK Dons for a reported £150,000 fee, netting 16 League goals in his first season at The National Hockey Stadium. After scoring 54 times in 105(+11) League games, including a 43-goal season partnership with future Colchester striker Clive Platt, and being voted League Two Player of the Year, McLeod was bought by Charlton for £1.1 million in a four-year deal that could have seen the fee rise to £1.55 million. In February 2006 McLeod had made his international debut when going on as a 73rd-minute substitute for England Under-21s against Norway at Reading. After just one goal in 2(+16) appearances at The Valley, McLeod rejoined his old strike partner Platt at Layer Road in an initial one-month loan deal in February 2008, making his debut against Wolves within 24 hours. However, three days later McLeod seriously injured his knee at Plymouth, in only his second appearance for United, and was ruled out for up to nine months.

	League		Lge Cup		FA Cup		Other	
	A	G	A	G	A	G	A	G
2007–08	0+2	0	0	0	0	0	-	-
TOTAL	0+2	0	0	0	0	0	-	-

McLEOD, Kevin Andrew

Height: 5ft 11in. Weight: 11st 3lb.

Born: 12 September 1980, Liverpool.

■ McLeod signed professionally for Everton in September 1998 after progressing through their Academy alongside Wayne Rooney, but he did not get a first-team look-in until 2000 when he made five Premiership appearances as substitute. He received his first full outing in a League Cup tie with Crystal Palace the following campaign, and he was voted reserve team Player of the Year in 2000–01. He joined QPR on loan on deadline day 2003, scoring twice in eight games and helping Rangers to a Millennium Stadium Play-off defeat to Cardiff. He signed permanently at Loftus Road in the summer for £250,000 and helped Rangers to runners'-up spot in League One. Used mainly from the bench in the Championship, McLeod concluded his 38(+29) QPR League career, scoring six times, when joining ambitious League Two Swansea in February 2005. The Welshmen won promotion and narrowly missed out on a second elevation when losing in the Play-offs a year later. Lack of professional application, alleged by manager Kenny Jackett, finished McLeod's Swansea career after netting seven goals in 32(+12) games, and he became new Colchester manager Geraint Williams's first signing in August 2006. He made his substitute debut in a 2–1 success at Burnley in the September and scored his first goal in a 2–0 win over Southampton a month later. McLeod scored United's first and last goal of the 2007–08 season at Sheffield United and Scunthorpe respectively, but joined Brighton in the summer of 2008.

	League		Lge Cup		FA Cup		Other	
	A	G	A	G	A	G	A	G
2006–07	13+11	3	0	0	1	0	-	-
2007–08	21+7	4	1	0	1	0	-	-
TOTAL	34+18	7	1	0	2	0	-	-

McLEOD, Samuel Mark 'Sammy'

Height: 5ft 6in. Weight: 10st 4lb.

Born: 4 January 1934, Glasgow.

Died: 29 July 1973, Para Hills, South Australia.

■ Benny Fenton was renowned for his forays north of the border, and it was while watching Scottish junior side Easthouses Lily that Fenton noticed McLeod. Indeed, in the same match he picked up McLeod's teammate Bobby Hill and opponents

Bonnyrigg Rose's John Fowler. Making his debut in same game as Percy Ames and George Fisher, McLeod became the darling of the Layer Road faithful for six seasons. National Service caused him to miss the greater part of 1956–57 and 1957–58 as he was stationed down in the Portsmouth area. Demobbed in August 1958, he enjoyed his best season for goalscoring, including a hat-trick in the 8–2 thrashing of Stockport and two of the seven that put old Southern League rivals Yeovil in their place after an FA Cup draw at Layer Road. He went on the transfer list once or twice and attracted interest from League new boys Oxford in 1962 but opted to stay at Layer Road on that occasion. In the summer he had reverted to part-time status and in December of that year departed for Romford for a fee of about £1,000. In 1968 he and his young family emigrated to Australia, where he played for clubs in Melbourne, Adelaide and latterly Salibury. Tragically he was knocked down and killed as he tried to cross a road to join his wife.

	League		Lge Cup		FA Cup		Other	
	A	G	A	G	A	G	A	G
1955–56	42	2	-	-	1	0	-	-
1956–57	4	2	-	-	0	0	-	-
1957–58	15	2	-	-	1	0	-	-
1958–59	38	7	-	-	6	2	-	-
1959–60	12	3	-	-	0	0	-	-
1960–61	20	3	1	0	1	0	-	-
1961–62	12	3	0	0	1	0	-	-
1962–63	9	0	1	0	0	0	-	-
TOTAL	152	22	2	0	10	2	-	-

McNEIL, Hamish Grant

Height: 5ft 8in. Weight: 10st 8lb.

Born: 16 November 1934, Alva.

■ Reported to be Benny Fenton's most expensive Scottish signing, McNeil joined United in August 1957 from Bonnyrigg Rose for £600. He scored in the fourth minute of his debut against Bournemouth, but despite scoring 23 times in 24 reserve games at Layer Road he made just one other appearance. A small fee took him to Cambridge City on Boxing Day 1958, and he scored on his debut for his new club against Bury Town.

	League		Lge Cup		FA Cup		Other	
	A	G	A	G	A	G	A	G
1957–58	2	1	-	-	0	0	-	-
TOTAL	2	1	-	-	0	0	-	-

MAFFEY, Dennis

Born: 22 February 1922, Sunderland.
Died: August 1995, Ipswich.

■ Maffey started as a centre-forward with amateurs Crook Town and was called for a trial at Sunderland. Unfortunately for Maffey, the war cut short his professional career as he was called up for National Service, and during the war he played for the Army in Palestine alongside Wilf Mannion. In 1948, by now a full-back, he joined Ipswich Town from local club Walton United and scored one goal in five appearances. Arriving at Colchester in May 1948, in time to play in the Pearson Charity Cup game with Chelmsford, he had to wait for his full debut until a Southern League Cup tie against the same team in December 1948. He deputised for Bob Allen for 28 League games thereafter but struggled to displace Bill Bower and Digger Kettle in the following campaign. Freed as the U's entered Division Three South, he joined Yarmouth and had an unhappy return to Layer Road on 9 December 1950 when the U's reserves beat the Bloaters 11–0 in the Eastern Counties League. He later retired to Felixstowe.

	League		Lge Cup		FA Cup		Other	
	A	G	A	G	A	G	A	G
1948–49	28	1	3	0	0	0	-	-
1949–50	5	0	1	0	0	0	-	-
TOTAL	33	1	4	0	0	0	-	-

MAHON, Michael John 'Mick'

Height: 5ft 8in. Weight: 11st 1lb.

Born: 17 September 1944, Manchester.

■ An England Amateur international, Mahon was signed by Port Vale from North Shields in 1966, winning a professional contract in March 1967. Mahon played 91(+1) times for Vale, scoring 22 League goals and was transferred to York in the summer of 1969. A single season at Bootham Crescent returned 10 goals from 27(+2) League starts. Dick Graham brought him to Layer Road in May 1970 and Mahon starred in U's run to the FA Cup quarter-finals in his first season and scored two of the goals in the 1971–72 Watney Cup Final success at West Brom. Personal success followed in August 1972 when, after five years of part-time study, he was awarded his BSc in Geography. Renowned for his corner kicks, Mahon followed Dick Graham to Wimbledon in December 1973 for £3,000 and won back-to-back Southern League titles with the ambitious Southern League side. He also scored the Dons' winning goal at Burnley in the 1974–75 FA Cup run that culminated in a 1–0 replay defeat to Leeds at Selhurst Park in front of 45,000 spectators. In all, Mahon played 122 times for Wimbledon between 1973 and 1976, before becoming player-manager of local Colchester junior side Rowhedge while employed as a PE teacher in the town.

	League		Lge Cup		FA Cup		Other	
	A	G	A	G	A	G	A	G
1970–71	37+1	5	2	0	7	2	-	-
1971–72	41+1	8	3	2	1	0	3	2
1972–73	44	12	1	0	3	0	-	-
1973–74	9+3	0	1	0	1	1	-	-
TOTAL	131+5	25	7	2	12	3	3	2

MAIN, Walter Gay 'Bill'

Height: 5ft 10½in. Weight: 11st 7lb.

Born: 30 November 1915, St Monance.
Died: 1969.

■ Wing-half Main began at his local side St Monance Juniors before joining Raith Rovers. In 1936 he was on the books of Cardiff City and represented the Bluebirds first team on six occasions, playing for their reserves in the Southern League against Colchester in both 1937–38 and 1938–39. Main signed for Colchester on 19 August 1939 making his debut a week later but received what was described in the match report as a crippling injury in a fiery local derby at Chelmsford on 31 August, and the injury kept him out of the last pre-war game. The incident also probably contributed to the sending off of the U's George Wallis shortly after. Main was called up when war broke out and was never seen at Layer Road again.

	League		Lge Cup		FA Cup		Other	
	A	G	A	G	A	G	A	G
1939–40	2	0	1	0	-	-	-	-
TOTAL	2	0	1	0	-	-	-	-

MANSFIELD, John Vincent

Height: 5ft 10½in. Weight: 10st.

Born: 13 September 1946, Colchester.

■ Mansfield was recruited by Benny Fenton at the age of 15 to join United's ground staff. His was signed professional by Neil Franklin in August 1964, making his debut against Brentford in the September. Leading scorer for the reserves in 1964–65 and 1965–66, his first-team chances remained limited, but he was part of the U's squad that won promotion from Division Four in

1965–66 and played in every FA Cup tie in 1967–68 as United bowed out to West Brom in a fourth-round replay at The Hawthorns. He was the unfortunate U's player whose late 'winner' at Layer Road was ruled out for a handball that only the ref seemed to see. Certainly Albion skipper and full-back Graham Williams was reported in a widely-read soccer annual of the time to have thought it was a perfectly good goal. Mansfield was one of several players made available for transfer early in 1968–69 by new boss Dick Graham, and he moved into the Southern League with Brentwood Town. By 1971 he was at Bury Town, managed by ex-U's player John Docherty, and spent five years there before moving to Tiptree United, where he was still playing into the 1980s while working for Hutton Builders in Colchester.

	League		Lge Cup		FA Cup		Other	
	A	G	A	G	A	G	A	G
1964–65	1	0	0	0	0	0	-	-
1965–66	5+2	1	0	0	0	0	-	-
1966–67	7+1	2	0	0	0	0	-	-
1967–68	13+2	0	1	0	5	0	-	-
1968–69	2+1	0	2	0	0	0	-	-
TOTAL	28+6	3	3	0	5	0	-	-

MARDENBOROUGH, Stephen Alexander 'Steve'

Height: 5ft 8in. Weight: 11st 9lb.

Born: 11 September 1964, Selly Oak.

■ An apprentice with Coventry, Mardenborough failed to make the first team at Highfield Road and joined fellow top-flight side Wolves in September 1983. Scoring once, in a famous win at Anfield, in nine starts, he was loaned to Cambridge in February 1984, playing six times. He established himself following a move to Swansea in the close season of

1984, scoring seven times in 32(+4) games. Exactly a year later, he moved to Newport and in a season and a half netted 11 times in 50(+14) games. With Newport destined for relegation to the basement, Mardenborough stayed in the same Division when he transferred on deadline day 1987. A bit-part player the following campaign as Cardiff finished runners-up in the Fourth Division, Mardenborough secured a summer 1988 move to Hereford after scoring just once in 18(+14) games for the Bluebirds. Failing to find the net in 20(+7) games at Edgar Street, Mardenborough drifted in to non-League with Cheltenham, scoring twice in 9(+3) Conference games. He spent time with Sweden's IFK Ostersund before returning to the UK with Darlington as first they took the Conference title and then a season later the 1990–91 Fourth Division Championship. The momentum could not continue, and the North-Easterners were relegated immediately. Mardenborough enjoyed his most prolific season, scoring 11 League goals, in 1992–93, prompting a £10,000 transfer to Lincoln, where he scored two times in 14(+7) games. Released by the Imps, he had a substitute appearance at Scarborough in February 1995 before joining Conference side Stafford, where he scored four times in 22 appearances. In the twilight of his career he was signed by Colchester boss Steve Wignall in August 1995 on a three-month trial scoring on his substitute debut against his former club Lincoln. Not retained, Mardenborough had a single non-contract outing with Swansea in December 1995 before joining Merthyr

Tydfil. He also later played for Gloucester, Cwmbran, Inter-Cable Tel, Aberystwyth, Rhayader, Haverfordwest, Rhayader, Port Talbot, Llanelli, Carmarthen and Barry.

	League		Lge Cup		FA Cup		Other	
	A	G	A	G	A	G	A	G
1995–96	4+8	2	0	0	1	0	1	0
TOTAL	4+8	2	0	0	1	0	1	0

MARMON, Neale Gordon

Height: 6ft 2in. Weight: 14st.

Born: 21 April 1961, Bournemouth.

■ Marmon played four games on a non-contract basis with Torquay in 1979–80 before moving to Germany. He played 129 times for Vfl Osnabruck, scoring 11 goals, before moving to Hannover '96 in 1989–90. After 13 games for the Germans, he was signed by Mick Mills for a small fee. Marmon made his debut against Chesterfield in January 1990 and formed a solid partnership with Scott Daniels, scoring both goals in a 2–0 must-win game against Doncaster. Sadly, that win only prolonged the agony, as United were relegated to the Conference following defeats in the remaining two games of the season. Marmon continued in United's first Conference season and netted the winner as U's beat Third Division Reading in the FA Cup. When Colchester failed to make it back to the League, Marmon opted to return to his wife's German homeland and played 54 times for FC Homburg '08 between 1991 and 1993. He then moved to regional-League FSV Salmrohr and coached Elversburg in the German Division Three South before stepping down in 2001 to become a sports therapist.

	League		Lge Cup		FA Cup		Other	
	A	G	A	G	A	G	A	G
1989–90	22	4	0	0	0	0	0	0
1990–91	*36+1*	*2*	*2*	*1*	*3*	*1*	*2+1*	*1*
TOTAL	22	4	0	0	0	0	0	0
	36+1	*2*	*2*	*1*	*3*	*1*	*2+1*	*1*

MARRIOTT, Andrew 'Andy'

Height: 6ft. Weight: 12st 7lb.

Born: 11 October 1970, Sutton-in-Ashfield.

■ Marriott represented England Schoolboys and graduated from the FA's School of Excellence to become a trainee with Arsenal in the summer of 1987. He won two England Youth caps but already had Alan Miller in front of him waiting for first-team action. He was sold to Nottingham Forest in the 1989 close season for £50,000. From Forest, Marriott set out on a number of loan deals. He played three games for West Bromwich Albion at the start of the 1989–90 campaign and then joined Blackburn for two games in December. Mick Mills signed the youngster for Colchester in March, and he played in the last 10 games of the season as United sank into the Conference. Marriott spent 1991–92 with Burnley, where he appeared 15 times. He finally made his Forest debut later that season and made 15 starts a year later in the inaugural Premiership season, in which Forest were relegated. In October 1993 he was sold to Wrexham for £200,000, having won an England Under-21 cap as well as winning the Zenith Data Systems Cup against Southampton in that last season at The City Ground and playing in the Rumbelows League Cup Final defeat to Manchester United, both of which were at Wembley. He became Wrexham's regular goalkeeper, playing 213 times at The Racecourse, as well as two European Cup-winners' Cup matches in 1995–96. Marriott won his five Welsh international caps during his spell with Wrexham, debuting against Switzerland in April 1996 courtesy of his Welsh grandfather, despite having earlier represented England. In August 1998 he was on his travels again, joining Sunderland for £200,000 as second choice to Thomas Sorensen and as a result only played twice in two seasons. A loan spell at Wigan in January 2001 yielded just two Leyland DAF Trophy games, and it was no surprise when Marriott left The Stadium of Light on deadline day 2001 to join Barnsley as they slipped into Division Two. He gained some stability at Oakwell, playing 53(+1) times and then having another single Premiership game with Birmingham in March 2003. He returned to England halfway through a two-year contract with Portuguese side Beira Mar and linked up with Coventry without making an appearance. Marriott returned to Layer Road in October 2004 and warmed Phil Parkinson's bench as second choice, again without troubling the fourth official. Offered the chance of first-team football rather than staying at Layer Road, he opted to join Bury a month later and completed 19 games for the Shakers. In March 2005 he moved to soon-to-be-relegated Torquay, playing 57 times including being ever present in the 2005–06 season. The summer of 2006 heralded a further move to Boston, where he became the Pilgrims' regular 'keeper. With Boston relegated out of the League, Marriott joined Conference side Exeter for the 2007–08 season.

	League		Lge Cup		FA Cup		Other	
	A	G	A	G	A	G	A	G
1989–90	10	0	0	0	0	0	0	0
2004–05	0	0	0	0	0	0	0	0
TOTAL	10	0	0	0	0	0	0	0

MARSHALL, Alfred George 'Alf'

Height: 6ft. Weight: 11st 4lb.

Born: 21 May 1933, Dagenham.

■ Marshall, an amateur signed from Dagenham, was offered professional terms after a trial for the reserves at Bury in September 1957 and signed on 14 October. Dagenham received a donation

of £25 in appreciation. Marshall shared the right-back shirt with George Fisher during the 1958–59 season but could not dislodge John Laidlaw when the latter returned from National Service the following season. Marshall stayed on the reserve strength at Layer Road until the summer of 1962, when he became one of four ex-U's professionals at Clacton Town. He moved on to Crittalls and then to Coggeshall, taking over as manager at The Crops in 1968. A couple of years later he was managing former club Braintree (the renamed Crittalls) and at the end of 1970s assisted ex-U's reserves teammate Alan Springett at Border League Lexden.

	League		Lge Cup		FA Cup		Other	
	A	G	A	G	A	G	A	G
1958–59	24	0	-	-	0	0	-	-
1959–60	5	0	-	-	0	0	-	-
1960–61	1	0	0	0	0	0	-	-
TOTAL	30	0	0	0	0	0	-	-

MARTIN, David 'Dave'

Height: 6ft 1in. Weight: 11st 8lb.

Born: 25 April 1963, East Ham.

■ A prominent member of Millwall's 1979 FA Youth Cup-winning side,

Martin won England Youth caps and a professional contract at The Den in May 1980. He had already made his debut aged 16 in March of the same year and went on to play 131(+9) times in the League for the Lions, scoring six times. He joined Wimbledon for £35,000 in September 1984, as the Dons reached the top flight. He was not a regular, playing 30(+6) times over two seasons. He moved to Southend in August 1986 and notched 11 goals in 1990–91 as his new club won promotion to Division Two a year after rising from the Fourth Division. He was injured after just five games of the 1991–92 season and once recovered was offered rehabilitation with his old Southend teammate Roy McDonough at Layer Road. He played in just 12 games for United, but his influence helped ensure United carried off the non-League double and returned to the Football League. McDonough hoped to sign the player, but Bristol City were able to offer a more lucrative deal. Martin's stay at Ashton Gate was short-lived as he sought pastures new after 36(+2) games and one goal. He had a spell on loan at Northampton in February 1995, playing seven times before securing a transfer to Gillingham in the summer of the same year. A season-long stay realised 27(+4) appearances and promotion to Division Two, but Martin was on his travels again, joining Leyton Orient for eight games in July 1996. Four months later he was back at Northampton for 10(+2) appearances. His final League club was via a loan deal to Brighton in March 1997. After just one start, he moved to Welling United in the close season.

	League		Lge Cup		FA Cup		Other	
	A	G	A	G	A	G	A	G
1991–92	8+1	0	0	0	0	0	3	0
TOTAL	8+1	0	0	0	0	0	3	0

MARTIN, Dean Edward

Height: 5ft 8in. Weight: 10st 6lb.

Born: 31 August 1972, Islington.

■ Martin joined West Ham in the summer of 1991 from Fisher Athletic for £50,000, after impressing with five goals in 31(+9) Conference appearances. He played 1(+1) game for the Hammers but had also caught the eye of U's boss Roy McDonough who signed the youngster on loan in December 1992. Previous Colchester manager Ian Atkins had also

tried to sign Martin before his move to Upton Park, but United could not afford Fisher's asking price. Making a scoring debut at Walsall on 2 January 1993, Martin celebrated with his trademark aerial somersault. He scored a further goal at Lincoln a month later, but United could still not afford his fee. Unable to break through at West Ham, he joined Conference side Kettering, playing 32(+11) times and netting on six occasions. He joined Dagenham & Redbridge for the 1994–95 season, in a side containing McDonough, and played for Welling United before trying his luck in Iceland with IK Akranes. In October 1995 he returned to League football with Brentford, scoring once in 14(+5) games. Joining Stevenage for 1999–2000, the player completed 48(+5) Conference fixtures, scoring seven times. He returned to Iceland and turned out for KA Akureyri before rejoining IA Akranes in 2005.

	League		Lge Cup		FA Cup		Other	
	A	G	A	G	A	G	A	G
1992–93	8	2	0	0	0	0	0	0
TOTAL	8	2	0	0	0	0	0	0

MARTIN, John

Height: 5ft 9in. Weight: 10st 2lb.

Born: 4 December 1946, Ashington.

■ Martin attended the same Ashington school that counted Bobby Charlton among its former pupils, but it was Aston Villa where he served his apprenticeship, signing professional terms in the summer of 1964. Making just a solitary appearance in the Villa first team, he was signed by Neil Franklin on

a free for his newly promoted Colchester side. Martin was an ever present in his first season, having scored in only his second League appearance against Bournemouth. He was loaned to Chelmsford by Dick Graham at the end of January 1969 and given a free transfer in the summer. Martin moved north and joined Workington, where he added 206(+2) League appearances, scoring 32 goals, and was part of the Workington side that survived a re-election application at the end of 1973–74. He moved to Southport, making a further 54(+9) appearances and adding seven goals over the next two years, again departing as his club survived re-election. He then played non-League for Wigan, Formby and back at Workington and was employed at Heysham Power Station and as a sports administrator on Lancashire County Council.

	League		Lge Cup		FA Cup		Other	
	A	G	A	G	A	G	A	G
1966–67	46	8	1	0	2	0	-	-
1967–68	24	3	1	0	5	0	-	-
1968–69	6+1	0	2	0	0	0	-	-
TOTAL	76+1	11	4	0	7	0	-	-

MASSEY, Roy

Height: 6ft. Weight: 12st.

Born: 10 September 1943, Mexborough.

■ An England Youth international and on amateur forms at Arsenal, Massey refused terms at Highbury, preferring to return north, where he joined Rotherham in the summer of 1964 but continued his studies with a desire to become a school teacher at some time. Scoring six goals in 15(+1) League games, he moved south to Leyton Orient in September 1967 along with Owen Simpson, who would also play for

Colchester. He combined playing football with a teaching post at a junior school in Leyton. Top scorer for Orient in 1967–68, he was plagued by injury the following season and left for Layer Road in July 1969 for a fee of £5,000. At Layer Road he teamed up with his former boss Dick Graham but was destined to be dubbed United's unluckiest-ever player. Getting off to a flyer, he scored 11 goals in his first 13 appearances, including a hat-trick at Reading in a League Cup replay, but broke a bone in his foot and in the next 18 months endured three knee operations. Specialist advice forced him to quit the game, and his retirement was announced in March 1971. He enjoyed a benefit match against Ipswich at the end of 1971–72 and took over as player-manager at Tiptree, while pursuing his teaching career in Colchester. Moving to Clacton in 1973, he led them to the Eastern Counties League title in 1974–75 but as his playing days came to an end returned to Layer Road in 1977–78 as youth-team coach. The youth team at that time only played Cup ties, and the three or four apprentices trained with the small senior squad so the post fitted easily with his teaching. In the mid-1980s the number of apprentices increased substantially with the new Youth Training Scheme, and Steve Foley returned to Layer Road in 1986 to help with the day-to-day training. At the end of the season Foley took over as coach and Massey concentrated on the club's schoolboys, a role he continued in until the financial restrictions imposed by a second year in the Conference saw him depart for a similar role with Norwich. He later moved to Arsenal and is currently head of Under-16 youth development at their Hale End Academy.

	League		Lge Cup		FA Cup		Other	
	A	G	A	G	A	G	A	G
1969–70	18+1	7	3	4	1	0	-	-
1970–71	12+4	4	0+1	0	1	0	-	-
TOTAL	30+5	11	3+1	4	2	0	-	-

MASTERS, Michael 'Mike'

Height: 6ft 3in. Weight: 12st 6lb.

Born: USA.

■ A giant American, Masters had played for Albany Capitals in the American Professional Soccer League. He first featured in a trial match against Ipswich in the autumn of 1990. Also trialling in that game was Roy McDonough as manager Ian Atkins sought to resolve his striking problems. Making his debut as a substitute against Wycombe in October 1990, Masters scored his first U's goal in a 3–1 win at Barnet on New Year's Day. He came to prominence in the tail end of Colchester's second season in the Conference, having had to wait until the January for his international clearance to come through. He netted a hat-trick as United secured the Conference title with a last-day 5–0 win over Barrow and a week later became the first American to score at Wembley as the U's completed the non-League double by defeating Witton Albion 3–1 in the FA Trophy Final. He earned his first international

cap for USA in a New Jersey goalless friendly against Ukraine in June 1992, but this proved insufficient to qualify for a work permit to play in League Football. Playing briefly for Newbury Town in the Ryman League, Masters returned to the States, unable to fulfil his dream of playing in the English League.

	League		Lge Cup		FA Cup		Other	
	A	G	A	G	A	G	A	G
1990–91	2+9	1	2	0	1	1	0+2	0
1991–92	7+8	7	0	0	0	0	2+2	1
TOTAL	9+17	8	2	0	1	1	2+4	1

MATTHEWS, Ernest 'Ernie'

Height: 5ft 10in. Weight: 11st 7lb.

Born: 8 November 1912, Chester-le-Street.

■ Matthews's transfer to Colchester was something of a coup for manager Ted Davis. The centre-forward had a reputation as a professional sprinter, and so Davis took a train journey to York, where he met up with Matthews at an athletics event. Davis signed him at 9pm and arrived back in Colchester at 6am the next morning. Matthews had been a prolific scorer for Bury, notching 46 goals in just 73 appearances between 1935 and 1937. For two seasons he was Bury's leading scorer and third highest in the entire League. Wednesday paid £3,700 for him, and he made his debut on 16 September 1937, scoring a creditable seven goals in 16 appearances. The player joined Colchester with a price tag of £2,500 and scored on his debut against Gillingham but suffered knee ligament damage a fortnight later and was out of action until December. In his absence, Arthur Pritchard had banged in 17 goals at a goal a game, and Matthews's chances receded such that he was freed at

the end of the season and returned to the North East to play for Ashington.

	League		Lge Cup		FA Cup		Other	
	A	G	A	G	A	G	A	G
1938–39	6	3	0	0	0	0	1	1
TOTAL	6	3	0	0	0	0	1	1

MAY, Benjamin Steven 'Ben'

Height: 6ft 1in. Weight: 12st 12lb.

Born: 10 March 1984, Gravesend.

■ A youngster with Millwall, May was spotted by Phil Parkinson on the Football Combination circuit after also scoring once in 4(+6) appearances for the Lions first team. He made his debut against Swindon in April 2003, adding height to United's attack. Brentford, however, stole in and signed the player on a season-long loan during the close season, and he responded with seven goals in 38(+3) games. Parkinson re-signed the player at the beginning of 2004–05, and he scored his first goal at Bournemouth in September and followed it up with a giant-killing winner against Championship side West Brom in a League Cup tie in the same month. When his loan spell ended, Brentford once again took the player to Griffin Park, where he played a further 7(+3) games, netting a solitary goal. Nurtured by his two loan clubs, May was ready to step up to Millwall's Championship side. He finished top scorer in 2005–06 with 10 goals, but his club were relegated. He began to suffer injuries and was restricted to just 7(+6) starts the following season but regained fitness to take his place in Millwall's 2007–08 line-up, having a spell

on loan at Scunthorpe in October 2007, before signing permanently for the Iron in January 2008.

	League		Lge Cup		FA Cup		Other	
	A	G	A	G	A	G	A	G
2002–03	4+2	0	0	0	0	0	0	0
2003–04	-	-	-	-	-	-	-	-
2004–05	5+9	1	0+2	1	0	0	0	0
TOTAL	9+11	1	0+2	1	0	0	0	0

MAYES, Kenneth William 'Ken'

Height: 5ft 6in.

Born: 8 October 1910, Wickford.

Died: 21 February 1975, Havering.

■ Mayes started his footballing career with Brentwood and Warley and played against Colchester Town in the Spartan League. Clever, with dazzling footwork, he moved up the amateur ladder to Barking before signing as an amateur for Southend in October 1930. Scoring one goal in five games for the South Essex club, he had further spells with his two former clubs and won FA XI honours against both the Army and Navy. Fulham persuaded him to turn professional in April 1935 but just two senior appearances at Craven Cottage followed, and he was on their transfer list at £500 when he joined Colchester in June 1937. Mayes left Layer Road for Chelmsford City in January 1939, having refused the U's terms, and was one of three brothers to play for City, including Arnold who played a handful of games in Division One for Chelsea.

	League		Lge Cup		FA Cup		Other	
	A	G	A	G	A	G	A	G
1937–38	19	0	6	0	-	-	12	0
1938–39	2	0	0	0	0	0	1	0
TOTAL	21	0	6	0	0	0	13	0

MERRITT, Harold 'George'

Height: 5ft 7½in. Weight: 11st 7lb.

■ According to the local press reports, when he joined the U's in September 1938 the 20-year-old Merritt had scored 49 goals for Margate, when they did the Southern League and Kent League double in 1935–36. That would make him 17 or 18 at the time. Margate's records, however, only show him in 1936–37, when he scored 11 goals. Margate at the time were a nursery club to Arsenal, and it is possible that Merritt was one of the many players loaned to them by the Gunners. He was at Derby in 1937–38 but refused their terms for the following year because he wanted a move back nearer to London to be closer to his widowed mother. During the summer he had initially been reported to be signing for the newly professional Chelmsford City. He joined the U's in September 1938, making his debut in the reserves' 8–1 win against Yarmouth, and was virtually ever present at inside-left in the second string for the rest of the season. His first-team chances were severely limited though by the presence of Alec Cheyne, and he made just three starts before being released at the end of the season. He reappeared after the war with Bath City, playing for them against the U's in 1946–47 and 1947–48.

	League		Lge Cup		FA Cup		Other	
	A	G	A	G	A	G	A	G
1938–39	3	0	0	0	0	0	1	0
TOTAL	3	0	0	0	0	0	1	0

MILLAR, Thomas Thomson 'Tommy'

Height: 5ft 9in. Weight: 11st.

Born: 3 December 1938, Edinburgh.
Died: 2001.

■ Benny Fenton shrewdly beat a handful of clubs for Millar's signature in July

1959 from Bo'ness United, a prominent Scottish junior club. Signed as a wing-half or inside-forward, the same position his older Scottish international brother Jimmy played in for Glasgow Rangers, Millar played a couple of League games at inside-left soon after his arrival and a couple more at right-half at the end of the season, but Fenton decided full-back was the best way to use his talents and converted him over the summer. He took over the first-team spot in October 1960 and was ever present until suddenly departing to Scotland early in 1961. His wife had failed to settle south of the border, and when she decided to go home Millar had little choice but to follow her. Over the summer Fenton persuaded them to give Colchester another go, and Millar was back at Layer Road for the U's Division Four promotion campaign, netting four times from right-back in the first four weeks of the season and only missing one game until the end of January. Tragedy had struck the family though in October 1961 when their 20-month-old son Scott drowned in the garden of their Colchester home, and shortly after Christmas the club released Millar so he could go back to Scotland. He spent some time on trial at Raith but soon joined Dundee United, where he made over 250 appearances and experienced European glory in 1966 as Dundee United beat Barcelona in the Inter-Cities Fairs Cup. In the latter stages of his time at Tannadice he was joined by brother Jimmy. His Tangerines career was effectively ended by a broken leg in a Scottish Cup-tie against Hearts, but he went on to help Cowdenbeath win promotion in 1969–70 and played a few games for Berwick and Hamilton in 1971–72 before another serious injury, playing for the Accies against Stenhousemuir, finally finished his career. Millar lost two appearances and a League goal from his U's record when Accrington failed to complete the 1961–62 season.

	League		Lge Cup		FA Cup		Other	
	A	G	A	G	A	G	A	G
1959–60	5	0	-	-	0	0	-	-
1960–61	14	0	1	0	2	0	-	-
1961–62	27	4	1	0	3	0	-	-
TOTAL	46	4	2	0	5	0	-	-

MILLER, Alfred George Abraham 'Dusty'

Born: 25 March 1917, Portsmouth.
Died: August 1999, Portsmouth.

■ Miller was a half-back who began his career on the books of Portsmouth in 1935. When he failed to make the first team he drifted in to non-League with Ryde and Margate. In 1936 he was picked up by Bristol Rovers but again failed to make the breakthrough. Eventually he made his debut for Southport in the 1937–38 season, playing 32 games and scoring two goals. His big chance came when he was transferred to Plymouth on the eve of the war, but Plymouth did not compete in wartime football so he guested for the star-studded Aldershot, playing about 25 times from 1942 to 1945. When the League resumed in 1946–47 Miller played in Plymouth's first eight games but was only seen once more before being released at the end of 1947–48 and joined Colchester in the August. Latterly, injuries had not helped his chances in Devon, and his playing days

were clearly coming to an end as he managed just two early season appearances for the U's, at Chelmsford and Barry in September 1948. As it happened, those were the only games lost before mid-January apart from the FA Cup tie against Third Division Reading, although there is no suggestion Miller's presence was anything other than coincidence. In May 1949 he was appointed trainer-coach when Jack Kearton was 'not kept on' after two years in the job and held the post for four years before resigning to go into the grocery business in his native Portsmouth. He had the reputation of being a bit of a martinet, and his attitudes to smoking – no more than one cigarette on the coach journey to an away game and no smoking in the dressing room – were considered rather irksome!

	League		Lge Cup		FA Cup		Other	
	A	G	A	G	A	G	A	G
1948–49	2	0	0	0	0	0	-	-
TOTAL	2	0	0	0	0	0	-	-

MILLER, Anthony William 'Tony'

Height: 5ft 9in. Weight: 10st.

Born: 26 October 1937, Colchester.

■ Miller joined Colchester as an amateur in 1954 and signed part-time pro in May 1958 on his demob from the RAF, but he had to wait until 1 February 1964 to play his one and only Football League game in a 0–0 draw at QPR. At least he got his name in the day's programme. Ten years at Layer Road came to an end in the summer, and he then spent another dozen playing locally before knee problems forced a halt. His first stop was Crittalls (Braintree), soon becoming player-coach and captain. He moved to Coggeshall in 1968 and then Witham in 1970, leading them to the inaugural Essex Senior League title in 1971–72. He managed Maldon from Christmas 1972, going back to Coggeshall in 1975, where he finally called it a day in April 1976, at which time he owned a hairdressing salon in Braintree.

	League		Lge Cup		FA Cup		Other	
	A	G	A	G	A	G	A	G
1963–64	1	0	0	0	0	0	-	-
TOTAL	1	0	0	0	0	0	-	-

MILLIGAN, Charles Campbell 'Chic'

Height: 5ft 10in. Weight: 11st 8lb.

Born: 26 July 1930, Ardrossan.

■ Milligan was another player that manager Benny Fenton picked up on his many forays north of the border. A junior with Ardrossan Winton Rovers, Morton had shown some interest in Milligan, but a fee of just under £1,000 brought him south. A regular in the promotion-chasing side of 1956–57, he was a critical absentee from the last 11 games after breaking his collarbone. The U's dropped 11 of the 22 points available in those games and missed out on promotion to bitter local rivals Ipswich Town by two points, allowing for an inferior goal average, and it would take 49 years to close the gap. Milligan broke his collarbone again in March 1958 but recovered to star in the FA Cup draw with League leaders Arsenal the following January. Milligan's Colchester career ended with the relegation of 1961, and he spent a season at Clacton before moving back to Scotland. He retired in 1994 after having his left leg amputated.

	League		Lge Cup		FA Cup		Other	
	A	G	A	G	A	G	A	G
1956–57	34	1	-	-	1	0	-	-
1957–58	26	0	-	-	1	0	-	-
1958–59	44	1	-	-	6	0	-	-
1959–60	43	1	-	-	1	0	-	-
1960–61	38	0	2	0	2	0	-	-
TOTAL	185	3	2	0	11	0	-	-

MILLS, Matthew Claude

Height: 6ft 3in. Weight: 12st 12lb.

Born: 14 July 1986, Swindon.

■ Mills signed full forms for Southampton in July 2004 after progressing through Saints' Academy. He played four games on loan at Coventry two months later and had a longer spell at Bournemouth in February 2005, where he bagged three goals in just 12 appearances. Returning to St Mary's, he made his debut for Championship Southampton and, after completing just 3(+1) games, was signed by Manchester City for £250,000 in the January 2006 transfer window. Appearing once as a substitute, Mills had to wait until the October to make his full debut against Wigan in a 4–0 defeat. An injury to Pat Baldwin led to Geraint Williams bringing the England Youth international to Layer Road in January 2007. He made his debut against Preston at Layer Road and maintained his place until scoring a disastrous unpressured own goal at Sheffield Wednesday in March that sealed United's 3–0 defeat. During the summer of 2007 he joined Doncaster on a six-month loan, joining up with Sean O'Driscoll who had been boss at Bournemouth during his earlier loan spell, extending the deal to the end of the season in January 2008.

	League		Lge Cup		FA Cup		Other	
	A	G	A	G	A	G	A	G
2006–07	8+1	0	0	0	0	0	-	-
TOTAL	8+1	0	0	0	0	0	-	-

MILLS, Robert Brian 'Robbie'

Height: 5ft 8in. Weight: 11st 2lb.

Born: 16 March 1955, Edmonton.

■ Mills was another product of United's youth scheme. Introduced into the first team by Dick Graham, Mills made his debut at Brentford in March 1972, a few days short of his 17th birthday. He failed to fulfil his early promise, and until deputising for Barry Dyson for a couple of spells in the latter part of Jim Smith's successful 1973–74 promotion campaign he had not played in more than two consecutive games. Although in the team as promotion was secured at Brentford in April 1974, and for the last couple of games, Mills was allowed to join Chelmsford over the summer for a small fee. He played quite regularly for City in a number of positions in 1974–75 but was on the fringes the following campaign and in November 1975 was sacked after not turning up for two games.

	League		Lge Cup		FA Cup		Other	
	A	G	A	G	A	G	A	G
1971–72	3	0	0	0	0	0	0	0
1972–73	3+2	0	0	0	0	0	-	-
1973–74	14+4	0	0	0	0	0	-	-
TOTAL	20+6	0	0	0	0	0	0	0

MILNE, W.

■ A Private in the 16th Infantry Training Corps previously on the books of Hartlepool United, although he only played a couple of times for them, Milne was signed professional by Syd Fieldus in September 1945 and played left-back for the first half-dozen League and friendly games. He missed his first game when he was one of the six prevented from going to Yeovil in September 1945 by their unit, forcing the U's to scratch around the Garrison for last-minute replacements. The more experienced professional Jimmy Southam then appeared and Milne was only called on once more, for the FA Cup tie at Wisbech when guests were not eligible, and a much changed U's side unexpectedly and disappointingly crashed 5–0. Milne returned north shortly after.

	League		Lge Cup		FA Cup		Other	
	A	G	A	G	A	G	A	G
1945–46	3	0	0	0	1	0	-	-
TOTAL	3	0	0	0	1	0	-	-

MOCHAN, Dennis

Height: 5ft 7in. Weight: 11st 2lb.

Born: 12 December 1935, Falkirk.

■ A part-timer with East Fife, Mochan played 53 times for his first club, scoring three goals before moving to Raith Rovers in 1959 where his 85 appearances secured a £12,000 move south to Nottingham Forest in the summer of 1962. Given a free transfer after 108 games, Mochan joined United for their Third Division campaign of 1966–67. Mochan's older brother, Neil, was a Scottish international who had also moved south from Morton to Middlesbrough. Forming a good full-back partnership with Brian Hall at Layer Road, Mochan was released by Dick Graham but invited to stay on as trainer. When Dick Graham resigned as U's manager Mochan stood as caretaker manager before the appointment of Jim Smith in October 1972. Disappointed that his own application to be manager had been overlooked, he too resigned in the November and returned to Scotland and took up a position as a school caretaker in Falkirk.

	League		Lge Cup		FA Cup		Other	
	A	G	A	G	A	G	A	G
1966–67	31+3	0	0	0	1	0	-	-
1967–68	40	2	1	0	5	0	-	-
1968–69	41	0	0	0	2	0	-	-
1969–70	1	0	0	0	0	0	-	-
TOTAL	113+3	2	1	0	8	0	-	-

MONK, Alistair

Born: 8 November 1972, Epsom.

■ A trainee with Everton, Monk was released to Norwich, where he failed to make any appearances. Roy McDonough brought the youngster to Colchester as U's faced a goalkeeping crisis. Monk's only first-team game in a Colchester shirt was in the Associate Members Cup at Barnet four days before Christmas 1992, where the U's interest in the competition could be gauged by the presence of coach Ian Phillips, five years retired as a full professional, in central defence. He had also been between the sticks a couple of months earlier when the U's were obliged to send a side to Wycombe for the GM Vauxhall Conference Shield tie. It was a game the club did not want, and a disinterested scratch side lost 3–0. Not retained, he later played with Brantham Athletic.

	League		Lge Cup		FA Cup		Other	
	A	G	A	G	A	G	A	G
1992–93	0	0	0	0	0	0	1	0
TOTAL	0	0	0	0	0	0	1	0

MOORE, Gary

Height: 6ft 2in. Weight: 12st.

Born: 4 November 1945, Hetton-le-Hole.

■ Moore gained representative honours with both Sunderland and Durham Boys, joining the Roker Park club as a 15-year-old amateur. A year later he played for England Youth, earning a professional contract in November 1962. After 13 appearances in four seasons, scoring twice, he joined Grimsby in February 1967. Scoring 15 goals in 52(+1) starts, he was transferred to Southend in November 1968. Within a month he had scored a hat-trick against King's Lynn in a 9–0 FA Cup victory and went one better in the next round, scoring four as his side defeated Brentwood 10–1. He finished the season on 21 goals but failed to make double figures after that and broke his knee cap during 1970–71. Colchester manager Jim Smith pulled a masterstroke in signing the player on loan on deadline day March 1973, having failed to secure the expected signature of Hereford's Jim Hinch. Moore scored an incredible seven goals in 11 games, including a brace against Brentford that secured promotion on Good Friday 1974. Smith did not pursue Moore, and the striker signed for Chester on a free

transfer in the summer. Scoring just four goals in 29(+14) starts, he moved on two years later to Swansea, adding a further nine goals to his career tally in 30(+4) appearances in the 1976–77 season.

	League		Lge Cup		FA Cup		Other	
	A	G	A	G	A	G	A	G
1973–74	11	7	0	0	0	0	-	-
TOTAL	11	7	0	0	0	0	-	-

MOORE, John William Michael

Height: 5ft 10½in. Weight: 11st 4lb.

Born: 25 September 1923, Chiswick.

■ Moore represented London and Middlesex Schoolboys as a left-half, joining Hayes from school. He became an amateur at Brentford, turning professional there after being demobbed from the Navy. He joined Colchester at the end of 1948–49 after a spell with Gloucester, for whom he played 39 times in 1948–49, scoring their consolation in a 6–1 defeat against the U's in late April. Signed primarily as understudy to Harry

Bearryman, he made his debut at Chingford in September 1949 in place of Bill Layton but could not displace either wing-half as United were on their way to the Football League. By January 1950 he was captaining the reserves, and his two Football League appearances came in a 2–0 win over Swindon and a 7–0 thrashing at Orient. He stayed at Layer Road until the summer of 1952 and in October started a month's trial at Yeovil but cut it short after a fortnight because he wanted a club nearer his London home. He joined Staines Town and later became a car salesman in Garston, Hertfordshire.

	League		Lge Cup		FA Cup		Other	
	A	G	A	G	A	G	A	G
1949–50	*13*	*0*	*0*	*0*	*0*	*0*	-	-
1950–51	0	0	-	-	0	0	-	-
1951–52	2	0	-	-	0	0	-	-
TOTAL	2	0	-	-	0	0	-	-
	13	*0*	*0*	*0*	*0*	*0*	-	-

MORALEE, Jamie David

Height: 5ft 11in. Weight: 11st.

Born: 2 December 1971, Wandsworth.

■ Recruited by Mick Wadsworth in July 1999, Moralee had already had a chequered footballing career and arrived as his name was splashed over the front pages of a Sunday tabloid. A Crystal Palace YTS success, Moralee signed for Palace in the summer of 1990, making his debut a season later. After just 2(+4) games he moved to Millwall in September 1992 on a free transfer. He scored 19 League goals in 59(+11) appearances as the Lions narrowly missed out on reaching the Premiership. He had done enough to convince Watford to pay £425,000 but scored a miserly seven goals in 40(+9) games, resulting in a free transfer to Crewe in August 1996. He managed just 10(+6) games in two seasons without scoring and made his penultimate League move to Brighton in the 1998 close season. With three goals in 22(+9) games, Moralee was released by Albion after just one season from when, as a free agent, he arrived at Layer Road via Wadsworth's contacts. Making his debut at his former club Palace in a televised League Cup tie, Moralee did not score his first goal until January 2000 in a 3–1 win over Bournemouth. It proved to be his only goal, and he was released at the end of

the campaign. He moved to Wales to play at Barry Town, the then giants of Welsh football and managed by former Palace teammate Peter Nicholas. Barry won the title in each of his three seasons there, and as a result Moralee played nine UEFA Champions League qualifiers. When the financial plug was pulled on Barry, Moralee joined Conference side Forest Green Rovers for 2003–04, but he left after just 12 games to join Nicholas, who by then was in charge of Conference South Newport County. He had a few games with Chelmsford in 2005–06 and represented Watford in the London Masters 5-a-side tournaments. On retiring from the game he took up a business dedicated to advising footballers with their property investments.

	League		Lge Cup		FA Cup		Other	
	A	G	A	G	A	G	A	G
1999–2000	20+7	1	0+1	0	0	0	1	1
TOTAL	20+7	1	0+1	0	0	0	1	1

MORGAN, Dean Lance

Height: 6ft. Weight: 12st 1lb.

Born: 3 October 1983, Enfield.

■ Described by a senior member of the U's coaching staff as just about the most complete natural footballer he had seen, Morgan became a major disappointment at Layer Road and ultimately left the club when his alleged attitude towards teammates' property made his continuing presence in the dressing room unacceptable to many of the club's senior pros. Morgan came to the club as a 15-year-old. As an apprentice he was straight into the Under-19s and marked his only appearance for his own Under-17 age group with a spectacular goal,

winning the ball on the edge of his own penalty area and going the length of the field, brushing aside attempted challenges before firing a low shot home across future U's, but then Southend, 'keeper Dean Gerken. Morgan was attracting so much attention that the club gave him a four-year professional contract after just the first of his three year scholarship, but it was too much too young, and he had the fans expecting and demanding another Lomana Lua Lua. Morgan was two years younger than Lua Lua had been when he first came to attention and did not have the same maturity, and unlike Lua Lua, who was a hidden diamond, Morgan's talents were known to the professional scouting network. If football had been the only issue, he would surely have been taken by one of the bigger London clubs and would never have seen Layer Road. He was given his opening first-team outing as a substitute against Northampton in November 2000 and the following season became a regular playing substitute. Morgan's body language gave the impression that he was sullen and lazy, and that did not go down well with fans who did not appreciate that he was an instinctive footballer but some way from knowing how to make best use of his talent. Morgan enjoyed more starts in 2002–03 and hit a stunning 35-yard volley at title favourites Cardiff in April 2003, but a pre-season injury meant new boss Phil Parkinson did not get a proper chance to work on him before he had to leave the club. The fact that Chelsea took him on trial is recommendation enough, but it was Parkinson's old club, Reading, who took the plunge and signed him for the rest of the season, extending the deal in the summer of 2004. He failed to break through in the upwardly mobile Reading team and after 13(+18) appearances and three goals joined Luton in July 2005. Playing 46(+26) games for the club and scoring 10 League goals, Morgan left the Hatters as they went into administration, joining Southend on loan and completing the season on loan at Crewe.

	League		Lge Cup		FA Cup		Other	
	A	G	A	G	A	G	A	G
2000–01	0+4	0	0	0	0	0	0	0
2001–02	1+29	0	0	0	0+2	0	1+1	0
2002–03	22+15	6	1	0	0+1	0	0	0
TOTAL	23+48	6	1	0	0+3	0	1+1	0

MORGAN, Stuart Edward

Height: 5ft 11in. Weight: 12st 7lb.

Born: 23 September 1949, Swansea.

■ A West Ham apprentice, Morgan made his first League starts while on loan at Torquay in February 1969. His 14 League appearances prompted a transfer to Reading in November 1969. At Elm Park he completed 42(+4) games, scoring one goal. Signed by Dick Graham in August 1972, Morgan established his partnership with Ray Harford in the latter part of the season as United headed for re-election. A fixture in the side, Morgan weighed in with eight important goals as Colchester

won promotion at the end of the following campaign. A fiery character, he courted controversy when Steve Leslie was sent off at Bury when it should have been Morgan. That cost him the captaincy, and he received another early bath at Brighton when he refused to give his name for a bookable offence. That proved to be his last game for United, and he moved to fellow Third Division side Bournemouth for £4,000, where he ended his League playing career with five goals in 80(+1) appearances. He became manager of Weymouth in November 1978, finishing runners-up of the Alliance Premier League (the forerunner of the Conference). This prompted an appointment as assistant manger to Harry Redknapp at Bournemouth in November 1983, a position he held for two years before becoming manager of Torquay from September 1985 to May 1987. Torquay had a miserable record in those seasons and narrowly missed dropping out of the League on the last day of the season, when only the bite of a policeman's dog on a Gull's defender set up enough injury time for a Torquay equaliser. Relieved of his job, he returned to Weymouth in the summer of 1987, but the Terras were relegated to the Southern League. He became manager of Dorchester in 1998 for seven seasons and was then chief scout at Portsmouth and Southampton under Harry Redknapp.

	League		Lge Cup		FA Cup		Other	
	A	G	A	G	A	G	A	G
1972–73	30+2	1	1	0	3	1	-	-
1973–74	38	8	1	0	1	0	-	-
1974–75	11	1	2	0	0	0	-	-
TOTAL	79+2	10	4	0	4	1	-	-

MORGAN, Trevor James

Height: 6ft 1in. Weight: 13st 1lb.

Born: 30 September 1956, Forest Gate.

■ Morgan was a late starter in the Football League, joining Bournemouth in September 1980 at the age of 24. He had already played for Walthamstow Avenue, Tonbridge, Dartford and Leytonstone & Ilford. In just over a year at Dean Court the striker bagged 13 goals in 53 starts before joining Mansfield in November 1981. He did not settle at Field Mill, playing just 12 games scoring six times, and returned to the South Coast four months later. Scoring 33 times in 88 League games, he helped

them to promotion to Division Three before securing a £10,000 transfer to Bristol City in March 1984. His five goals in the remaining 15 fixtures helped City to emulate his earlier promotion honour. It was not long before he dropped back down a division to join Exeter in November 1984. Soon after scoring nine goals in 30 appearances, he returned to Bristol. This time it was with Rovers, where he achieved an impressive strike rate of 24 goals in 54(+1) appearances. Blue became red again in January 1987, when he crossed the City back to Ashton Gate, scoring seven in 19 starts. For the third time Morgan won promotion, when in the summer of 1987 he joined Fourth Division Bolton. His 17 goals in 65(+12) caught the attention of Colchester boss Jock Wallace, and the player was recruited in October 1989 for an £8,000 fee. Morgan produced a good goal return in a struggling side, but his goals alone could not help prevent United sliding in to the Conference. His penalty in the last game of the season against Burnley at Layer Road was thought by many at the time to be not just the club's last-ever goal in League football but the last-ever goal of the club's existence. He was released in the summer and went to Hong Kong to play for Happy Valley. When the English season restarted he found himself once again at Exeter, adding another three goals in 14(+3) games for the Grecians. Returning to Hong Kong, he spent the next two seasons with South China and Sun Valley. He had a non-contract substitute appearance with Birmingham in October 1983 and 4(+5) games in his third spell at Exeter in 1994, also on a non-contract basis. He retired in 1994 with 133 League goals to his name.

	League		Lge Cup		FA Cup		Other	
	A	G	A	G	A	G	A	G
1989–90	31+1	12	0	0	2	0	2	0
TOTAL	31+1	12	0	0	2	0	2	0

MORRIS, Robert Arthur John 'Roy'

Height: 5ft 11in. Weight: 10st 9lb.

Born: 11 March 1913, Hatton.

■ Plucked from Brentford's A team, Morris signed for Norwich on 8 May 1933 after also turning out for non-Leaguers Slough, Leyton and Southall. Playing in the half-back position, Norwich's manager Tom Parker continually referred to him as 'Roy' by mistake, and so the name stuck. Morris was a long-throw expert and signed for Colchester exactly three months after scoring against the U's for City reserves in the Southern League. Morris arrived at Layer Road in July 1938 and was a regular member of the Southern League Championship winning side of 1938–39. Morris remained on City's transfer list at £500. Colchester's march on Football League status was cut short by the war, and Morris turned out for Southend in May 1940, as well as: Fulham 1940–41 five appearances/0 goals, Crystal Palace 1942–43 6/0, Reading 1943–44 5/0 and back to Palace for 1945–46 3/0.

	League		Lge Cup		FA Cup		Other	
	A	G	A	G	A	G	A	G
1938–39	44	4	3	0	2	0	16	1
1939–40	3	0	1	0	-	-	-	-
TOTAL	47	4	4	0	2	0	16	1

MORROW, Grant Ralph

Height: 5ft 10in. Weight: 11st 7lb.

Born: 4 October 1970, Glasgow.

■ Spotted playing for junior side Rowntree Mackintosh, Morrow joined Doncaster in July 1989, making 46(+17) appearances at Belle Vue and scoring seven times. Signed by Roy McDonough in August 1993, Morrow suffered cartilage damage in his only appearance as a substitute against Northampton in August 1993 and never played League football again. He did resurrect his career briefly later that season with Boston United, playing 12(+2) games in the Conference, and then joined Gainsborough Trinity.

	League		Lge Cup		FA Cup		Other	
	A	G	A	G	A	G	A	G
1993–94	0+1	0	0	0	0	0	0	0
TOTAL	0+1	0	0	0	0	0	0	0

MOSS, Robert 'Bobby'

Height: 5ft 10in. Weight: 11st 2lb.

Born: 13 February 1952, Chigwell.

■ Moss was a Leyton Orient apprentice and scored five minutes in to his O's debut against Watford in November 1970. He made just two further starts, with three substitute appearances. Signed by Dick Graham in May 1972, he made his debut against League new boys Hereford on the opening day of the 1972–73 season, scoring his first goal at Darlington in September. His services were almost immediately dispensed with by new manager Jim Smith as he endeavoured to save United from re-election, and in November 1972 Moss was on loan to Folkestone. Returning briefly to Layer Road for a couple of sub appearances over the New Year, he joined Dover at the start of February 1973. After spells with Barnet and Wimbledon, he joined Wealdstone in 1974 and netted 71 goals in 265 games, before moving to Chelmsford for 1980–81. In his four-and-a-half years at New Writtle Street he played over 200 times and added another 41 goals to his career tally.

	League		Lge Cup		FA Cup		Other	
	A	G	A	G	A	G	A	G
1972–73	16+2	3	1	0	0	0	-	-
TOTAL	16+2	3	1	0	0	0	-	-

MOUGHTON, Colin

Height: 6ft. Weight: 10st 8lb.

Born: 30 December 1947, Harrow.

■ Moughton began as an apprentice at QPR, signing professional forms in December 1965 and going on to make six appearances at Loftus Road in the same season. The central-defender was brought to Layer Road in July 1968 on a two-month trial and was unfortunate to score an own goal on his debut at Brentford on the opening day of the 1968–69 season. He was not retained and moved to first Bedford and then Cheltenham, where he set up home.

	League		Lge Cup		FA Cup		Other	
	A	G	A	G	A	G	A	G
1968–69	4	0	1	0	0	0	-	-
TOTAL	4	0	1	0	0	0	-	-

MUNRO, Roderick Alexander 'Rod'

Born: 21 February 1920, Inverness.
Died: 1976, Cambridge.

■ A young full-back from Brentford, Munro, with five other Brentford teammates, guested for Colchester at Guildford in March 1946. He played five times for Brentford in the 1945–46 transitional season and then formed a formidable centre-half partnership with Fred Mink at Griffin Park, making 199 League appearances until leaving to manage Cambridge City in the summer of 1953.

	League		Lge Cup		FA Cup		Other	
	A	G	A	G	A	G	A	G
1945–46	0	0	1	0	0	0	-	-
TOTAL	0	0	1	0	0	0	-	-

MUNSON, Nathan Wayne

Height: 6ft. Weight: 11st 4lb.

Born: 10 November 1974, Colchester.

■ Youth trainee Munson was given his League bow by Roy McDonough in the final game of the 1992–93 season at Wrexham. Before a near 10,000 crowd, the Welsh title contenders triumphed 4–3. His next appearance was in somewhat bizarre circumstances. Coming on as substitute at Hereford after regular 'keeper John Keeley had been sent-off in the 43rd minute, Munson himself was dismissed 25 minutes later, leaving player-manager Roy McDonough to go between the posts. Both dismissals were as a result of over zealous interpretation of the professional foul. Munson moved on to Wivenhoe after being released from

Layer Road and later played for Billericay, Woodbridge and Harwich & Parkeston, Stanway Rovers and Needham Market, while joining the Police Force. For 2006 he was on the books of AFC Sudbury.

	League		Lge Cup		FA Cup		Other	
	A	G	A	G	A	G	A	G
1992–93	1	0	0	0	0	0	0	0
1993–94	2+1	0	0	0	0	0	1	0
TOTAL	3+1	0	0	0	0	0	1	0

MURRAY, Robert David 'Bob'

Height: 5ft 11in. Weight: 11st 8lb.

Born: 27 March 1915, Newhaven.

■ An inside-right, Murray played for a trio of Scottish junior sides: Niddrie Strollers, Bo'ness Cadora and Newtongrange Star. He was picked up by Hearts in March 1934 and after 30-odd games for them attracted the interest of Manchester

United, coming south of the border in June 1937. Former Ipswich manager A. Scott Duncan completed the signing. He made his debut against Newcastle on 28 August 1937, but after just four first-team appearances for the Old Trafford outfit he was placed on the transfer list at £800. That only applied to his football League registration though, and while he remained on United's list he joined Colchester's fellow Southern Leaguers Bath for the start of the 1938–39 season. He played for Bath at Layer Road on 10 December, missing a penalty, but it did not make any difference to the result as the U's won 4–0. Murray signed for Colchester on 24 January and was virtually ever present from the middle of February. Concussed in the match against Norwich reserves on 28 August 1939, he actually played against Chelmsford three days later before being admitted to hospital, suffering the after effects of the original injury. Two days later war was declared, and shortly after Murray was reported to have returned home.

	League		Lge Cup		FA Cup		Other	
	A	G	A	G	A	G	A	G
1938–39	21	4	0	0	0	0	8	2
1939–40	2	0	1	0	-	-	-	-
TOTAL	23	4	1	0	0	0	8	2

MUTRIE, Leslie Alan 'Les'

Height: 6ft 2in. Weight: 12st 2lb.

Born: 1 April 1952, Newcastle.

■ Mutrie's early career started at Gateshead, from whom he joined Carlisle in the summer of 1977. The move was not a success, and after just 4(+1) appearances he moved back to the

North East to join Blyth Spartans. A prolific goalscorer, Mutrie was picked for the England semi-professional team and starred as Spartans took Wrexham to an FA Cup fifth-round replay at St James' Park, watched by an incredible 42,000. The following season, with media attention focused on the giantkillers of the previous campaign, Spartans were drawn against Hull. Despite losing, Spartans received a club record £30,000 transfer, as the Boothferry Park club signed up Mutrie straight after the end of the December 1980 second replay. Hull were relegated, but during February and March 1982 Mutrie set a club record, scoring 14 times in nine consecutive games, as they surged to promotion. Scoring 49 goals in 114(+1) appearances, and after falling out with City boss Colin Appleton, he spent December 1983 on loan at Doncaster, scoring once in six starts, before securing a £10,000 move to Colchester in January 1984. He scored just two goals at Layer Road and was clearly unsettled in the South. During the summer he returned to the North East, signing for Hartlepool, where he ended his professional career, scoring four times in 18 appearances. He then turned out for Gateshead and Dudley Welfare before taking over the licence of a pub in Northumberland.

	League		Lge Cup		FA Cup		Other	
	A	G	A	G	A	G	A	G
1983–84	10+4	2	0	0	0	0	1+1	0
TOTAL	10+4	2	0	0	0	0	1+1	0

MUTTITT, Ernest 'Ernie'

Born: 24 July 1908, Middlesbrough.
Died: August 1988, Brentford.

■ Left-sided forward Muttitt was spotted playing for local side South Bank and was signed by Middlesbrough in April 1929. Muttitt enjoyed a memorable debut for Middlesbrough, scoring the winner at Highbury in November 1929. In all, he made 20 appearances at Ayresome Park and scored three goals. Chances were few at Boro due to the form of George Camsell. A £900 fee took him to Brentford, along with fellow Middlesbrough players Billy Scott and Johnny Holliday, where he made 92 League appearances, scoring 25 goals between 1932 and 1933, helping Brentford from Division Three to Division One. Muttitt proved a wartime football nomad, playing for several clubs, thus: 1939–40 Brentford 6/0, Fulham 1/1, Southend 1/0; 1940–41 Brentford 16/2, Clapton Orient 1/0, Fulham 10/0; 1941–42 Brentford 12/1, Crystal Palace 2/0, Fulham 7/1, Charlton 1/0, Chelsea 1/0, Reading 1/0, Millwall 1/0; 1942–43 Aldershot 2/2, Brentford 10/0, Fulham 6/1, Chelsea 2/0, West Ham 1/0; 1943–44 Brentford 11/0, Brighton 2/0, Chelsea 1/0, Clapton Orient 2/0, Crystal Palace 1/0, Fulham 3/0, Reading 2/0, Watford 1/0, West Ham 1/0; 1944–45 Chelsea 1/0, Fulham 3/0, Brentford 18/0 and 1945–46 Brentford 1/0, Luton 1/0. Muttit, therefore, had no qualms about turning out for Colchester and did so on just one occasion against Guildford, along with five other Brentford guests. He later played for both Dartford and Dover.

	League		Lge Cup		FA Cup		Other	
	A	G	A	G	A	G	A	G
1945–46	0	0	1	0	0	0	-	-
TOTAL	0	0	1	0	0	0	-	-

MYERS, Andrew John 'Andy'

Height: 5ft 8in. Weight: 11st.

Born: 3 November 1973, Hounslow.

■ An England Youth and Under-21 cap, Myers included three appearances at the Toulon 95 International Youth tournament on his record. He served his apprenticeship with Chelsea, signing professional in July 1991 and making his debut aged just 17 years old. Completing 74(+10) appearances, scoring twice, Myers was an unused substitute in the 1996–97 FA Cup Final win over Middlesbrough and in the following campaigns European Cup-winners Cup victory over VfB Stuttgart. With experience of 3(+3) games in Europe, Myers was sold to Bradford in the summer of 1999 for £800,000 but lost his place and was loaned to Portsmouth the following March, where he played 4(+4) games. Returning to Bradford, he was immediately involved in the Intertoto Cup as the Bantams sought to

get into Europe via the back door. His Bradford career amounted to 74(+15) appearances and three goals, but at the end of his expensive four-year contract he was released, along with 19 others, with Phil Parkinson picking up the player for Colchester. Myers made his debut at Barnsley on the opening day of the 2003–04 season and was a regular fixture in United's defence until suffering a back injury at QPR in the December. He remained sidelined until the final day of the season and was released in the summer of 2004. Along with fellow defender Scott Fitzgerald, the pair joined Brentford, with Myers making 6(+4) appearances in his one season spell at Griffin Park. The U's wanted him to return for pre-season and prove his fitness before they would consider offering a new contract, so when Brentford stepped in with a firm offer Myers was off to Griffin Park. Unfortunately for his new employers, his injury problems soon reappeared and he did not manage the full 90 minutes of a League game until the very last game of the season. Unsurprisingly, he was not retained.

	League		Lge Cup		FA Cup		Other	
	A	G	A	G	A	G	A	G
2003–04	21	0	1	0	2	0	2	0
TOTAL	21	0	1	0	2	0	2	0

N

NDUMBU-N'SUNGU, Guylian

Height: 6ft 1in. Weight: 12st 8lb.
Born: 26 December 1982, Kinshasa, DR CONGO.

■ Democratic Republic of Congo Under-21 player Ndumbu-N'Sungu arrived at Sheffield Wednesday in September 2003 from French side Amiens for £50,000 after an initial loan spell. Despite scoring nine goals in his first season, he was allowed out on loan in September 2004 to Preston where he played 4(+2) games and to Colchester on a short-term contract in January 2005. He made his Colchester debut against Luton as a substitute and scored his only goal against Bournemouth a month later. Fans dubbed him 'Dave' to counter the difficulty in relaying his name, but he was released in the March after failing to establish himself. He cracked 10 goals in just 11(+10) appearances after signing for Darlington in August 2005, and this earned him a January transfer window move to Cardiff, where he played 4(+7) Championship games before being released in the summer. Joining Gillingham in July 2006, Ndumbu-N'Sungu scored three times in 14(+18) games but was loaned to Bradford in August 2007, scoring 6 in 17(+1) League appearances. In January 2008 he rejoined Darlington on a free transfer.

	League		Lge Cup		FA Cup		Other	
	A	G	A	G	A	G	A	G
2004–05	2+6	1	0	0	0+1	0	0	0
TOTAL	2+6	1	0	0	0+1	0	0	0

NELSON, David 'Dave'

Born: 3 February 1918, Douglas Water.
Died: September 1988, Greenwich, Connecticut, USA.

■ Right-sided Nelson joined Arsenal from Edinburgh-based Scottish League club St Bernards in May 1936 and played 27 times for the Gunners scoring four goals. He played extensively during the war, thus: 1939–40 Arsenal 19/4; 1940–41 Clapton Orient 1/0; 1941–42 Arsenal 24/7; 1942–43 Arsenal 20/2; 1943–44 Arsenal 15/3, Brentford 4/0; 1944–45 Chesterfield 2/2, Arsenal 18/3 and

1945–46 Arsenal 39/2. It was while stationed in Colchester as a sergeant with the 15th Infantry Training Corps that Nelson turned out four times for Colchester between August 1945 and April 1946, all bar once in midweek. After the war he joined Fulham playing 24 times at Craven Cottage, then switched to Brentford, where between 1947 and 1949 he appeared 106 times, scoring five goals. Staying in West London, he played 31 times for Queen's Park Rangers in 1949–50 and ended his League career at Crystal Palace in 1952 after 12 games at Selhurst Park. He became player-manager of Ashford Town before emigrating to the US in 1955.

	League		Lge Cup		FA Cup		Other	
	A	G	A	G	A	G	A	G
1945–46	1	0	2	0	0	0	-	-
TOTAL	1	0	2	0	0	0	-	-

NEVILLE, Percy Herbert 'Bob'

Born: 4 October 1925, Colchester.
Died: March 2000, Colchester.

■ Local lad Neville, a former Bevin Boy, joined the U's as an amateur from Rowhedge in October 1946 and signed pro the following month. He was promoted to the first team after the 5–0 FA Cup defeat to Reading, making his debut in early December in the 3–2 derby win over Chelmsford. He then had a run of seven League and friendly games as first choice outside-left and played a couple more times in February, netting his only goal against Barry, before National Service called. Fortunately, he was only posted to Warley and continued on the reserve strength, latterly usually in the Border League team, until released as the U's were elected to the Football League in 1950. With the likes of Len Cater and Stan Foxall ahead of him, he did not get another first-team chance though, even in minor games and friendlies. On leaving Layer Road, he joined Clacton Town.

	League		Lge Cup		FA Cup		Other	
	A	G	A	G	A	G	A	G
1946–47	5	1	2	1	0	0	-	-
TOTAL	5	1	2	1	0	0	-	-

NEWELL, Paul Clayton

Height: 6ft 1in. Weight: 11st 5lb.
Born: 23 February 1969, Woolwich.

■ Newell served his apprenticeship with Southend, signing professional in the summer of 1987. After 15 League appearances he joined Leyton Orient for a fee of £5,000 in July 1990. Newell broke his ankle soon after but answered former colleague Roy McDonough's cry for help in joining Colchester on loan for the start of the 1992–93 season. He returned to Brisbane Road on completion of his three-month deal and represented the

O's on total on 61 occasions. At the end of the 1993–94 season he was given a free-transfer and joined Barnet, making 16 appearances. A move to Darlington gave the player a Wembley day out as the Quakers lost the 1995–96 Third Division Play-off final to Plymouth in front of 43,000. After 45 starts he joined non-League Sittingbourne in January 1997. He returned briefly to Layer Road in 1997 as a non-contract second-choice 'keeper and then played with St Albans, Dagenham & Redbridge and Grays before becoming player coach at Canvey Island in 2001. He also turned out for Aveley and Ford United.

	League		Lge Cup		FA Cup		Other	
	A	G	A	G	A	G	A	G
1992–93	14	0	2	0	0	0	0	0
TOTAL	14	0	2	0	0	0	0	0

NICHOLLS, Mark

Height: 5ft 10in. Weight: 10st 4lb.

Born: 30 May 1977, Hillingdon.

■ A YTS graduate at Chelsea, Nicholls played 11(+25) games at Stamford Bridge scoring 3 goals after signing full forms in the summer of 1995 including five substitute appearances in the European Cup-winners' Cup and Champions League. Despite being Chelsea's Young Player of the Year in 1994 and top scoring for the reserves with 26 goals and 28 the following campaign, he was loaned to Reading in December 1999, scoring once in 4(+1) appearances, and added two more goals in an Auto Windscreens Shield tie. Chelsea's £800,000 valuation was too much for Reading to make their desired a permanent signing. He had six games on loan at Grimsby in February 2000 before Steve Whitton, using his Football Combination scouting knowledge, brought him to Colchester in October of the same year. He made his debut against Walsall at Layer Road but was clearly not match fit and returned to Stamford Bridge after just three starts. With his career in tatters and, facing imminent release from Chelsea, Nichols was allowed to trial at Aberdeen and Motherwell prior to his May 2001 Stamford Bridge departure. Further trials at Partick, Swindon and Aldershot led to a non-contract spell with Torquay, where he played 4(+5) games in September 2001, scoring once. Next port of call was Hamilton Academical, but he joined Clydebank in November 2001, playing a handful of games for the Glasgow side. In the summer of 2002, after a series of trials with non-League clubs, he joined Maidenhead but by December had left for Uxbridge. In 2003 he turned out for Northwood, joining Hendon in the 2004 close season. In February 2005 he returned to Uxbridge, where he remained at the start of the 2007–08 season.

	League		Lge Cup		FA Cup		Other	
	A	G	A	G	A	G	A	G
2000–01	3+1	0	0	0	0	0	0	0
TOTAL	3+1	0	0	0	0	0	0	0

NICHOLS, Adam Anthony

Height: 6ft 1in. Weight: 12st.

Born: 14 September 1962, Ilford.

■ An Ipswich apprentice, Nichols failed to make a first-team start at Portman Road after signing professional in October 1979. He moved to South Africa where he played for Wits University. Cyril Lea gave him a non-contract opportunity at Layer Road and Nichols made his debut as a substitute at Swindon in October 1983. A week later he stood in for groin-injury victim Steve Wignall for two League games and an impressive League Cup victory over Second Division Swansea that earned a third-round home tie with Manchester United. In his last first-team appearance Nichols scored his only League goal as Colchester demolished Hartlepool 6–0 in December 1983. He played a few reserve games in the early part of 1984 before leaving Layer Road.

	League		Lge Cup		FA Cup		Other	
	A	G	A	G	A	G	A	G
1983–84	4+2	1	1	0	0	0	0	0
TOTAL	4+2	1	1	0	0	0	0	0

NOBLE, Alfred William Thomas 'Alf'

Height: Weight:

Born: 18 September 1924, Hackney.
Died: December 1999, Norwich.

■ Noble, by that time an England Amateur International who played for the South Essex works team Brigg Sports, was registered on amateur forms in September 1955. This was an arrangement whereby he continued to play senior amateur football but was available as cover for the U's. He was only called on once in the Football League, replacing the injured Ken Plant in a 3–1 defeat at Ipswich at Christmas 1955, and also played in an understrength side in a late season Essex Professional Cup tie at Leyton Orient. He re-signed for the U's on the same basis for 1956–57 but did not do any more than take part in the pre-season trial game and continued his career with Briggs while working at the Ford car plant at Chadwell Heath. Earlier in his career he had been a dual FA Amateur Cup winner with Leytonstone in 1947 and 1948 and part of the giant-killing Leytonstone team that beat Watford in the 1948–49 FA Cup.

	League		Lge Cup		FA Cup		Other	
	A	G	A	G	A	G	A	G
1955–56	1	0	-	-	0	0	-	-
TOTAL	1	0	0	0	0	0	-	-

NOBLE, Robert 'Bobby'

Height: 5ft 11in. Weight: 12st.

Born: 25 May 1949, Newcastle.
Died: May 2005, Australia.

■ A Newcastle apprentice, Noble failed to make a start at St James' Park after signing professional forms in April 1967. He was loaned to Barrow in August 1968 and scored 3 goals in 19 League appearances. Sold to Bury in August 1970, Noble made just 8 starts at Gigg Lane before being transferred to Barrow, this time in a permanent deal. Playing a further 72(+1) times for the doomed Cumbrians, he came to Layer Road on trial in July 1972 and was signed for a fee of £1,000 after going on the club's pre-season tour to Cornwall. Ironically, his debut came against Hereford – the club that had replaced Barrow in the Fourth Division. Noble was made captain but his stay at Layer Road was short as Jim Smith sold him to Southport in March 1973 for £2,000. In two seasons at Haig Avenue, Noble scored 6 goals in 61(+2) starts before making his final move nearer to his roots in August 1975. Playing for Darlington, he notched up a further 54 League appearances and netted 3 times. Emigrating to Australia, he played for Sydney side Western Suburbs and was voted New South Wales' Player of the Year in 1981.

	League		Lge Cup		FA Cup		Other	
	A	G	A	G	A	G	A	G
1972–73	25+2	0	1	0	3	0	-	-
TOTAL	25+2	0	1	0	3	0	-	-

NORMAN, Sean

Height: 5ft 6in. Weight: 10st 8lb.

Born: 27 November 1966, Lowestoft.

■ Originally with Lowestoft, Norman played regularly in United's Eastern Counties League reserve side and earned his call-up on the opening day of 1986–87 as a playing substitute at Lincoln. He had to wait until January 1988 to register his only League goal when scoring the equaliser against Tranmere. Chances were limited, especially when Mike Walker was sacked in October 1987. Norman scored his only other goal in a 3–2 Sherpa Van Trophy win over Peterborough at Layer Road in the same month. He joined non-League Wycombe, playing 26 times in 1987–88 and 35(+3) games a year later, scoring 3 and 2 goals respectively. During this spell he won England non-League honours in March 1989. Moving to Wealdstone, he was then transferred to ambitious Chesham United for £25,000, a club record fee equalled only by their sale of Stuart Pearce to Coventry. He played in New Zealand with Papatoetoe, returning to England with Chertsey then to Lowestoft via another spell with Chesham.

	League		Lge Cup		FA Cup		Other	
	A	G	A	G	A	G	A	G
1986–87	12+1	1	1	0	0	0	3	0
1987–88	6+2	0	2	0	0	0	1	1
TOTAL	18+3	1	3	0	0	0	4	1

NUNN, Walter P. 'Wally'

Height: Weight:

Born: 16 January 1920, Deptford.
Died: 1965, Tonbridge.

■ Initially with Bexleyheath & Welling, Nunn was on the books of Charlton during the immediate pre-war period without breaking into the first team. He played 4 games for Swindon in 1947–48 and was signed by Jimmy Allen in June 1948. His 10 appearances came as stand in for Frank Stamper at the heart of Colchester's defence, and he refused the terms offered to re-sign for 1949–50, moving to the U's Southern League rivals Guildford City.

	League		Lge Cup		FA Cup		Other	
	A	G	A	G	A	G	A	G
1948–49	10	0	2	0	0	0	-	-
TOTAL	10	0	2	0	0	0	-	-

O

O'DONNELL, Jonathan David 'Jon'

Height: 5ft 10in. Weight: 11st.

Born: 21 March 1954, Leeds.
Died: April 1997, Yeovil.

■ O'Donnell answered a call from new U's boss Bobby Roberts to help with an early-season injury crisis. He played his one and only game for Colchester in the opening fixture of the 1975–76 season at Preston as United went down 2–1 and by the end of the month was already back at his home club Cambridge United, although his loan still had a couple of weeks left. Cambridge wanted £6,000 for a permanent move but Roberts apparently was not going to be interested even if he were free. O'Donnell begun his career as an apprentice at Leeds and had been signed by Cambridge in the summer of 1973. The full-back scored 8 goals in 79 appearances at The Abbey Stadium, before being transferred to Hartlepool in July 1976. Exactly a year later, and after 30(+1) appearances and a solitary goal, he joined Scunthorpe, where he ended his professional career with 60 more League starts. In 1979 he moved into non-League with Cambridge City and died at the young age of 43 in 1997.

	League		Lge Cup		FA Cup		Other	
	A	G	A	G	A	G	A	G
1975–76	1	0	0	0	0	0	-	-
TOTAL	1	0	0	0	0	0	-	-

ODUNSI, Saheed Adeleke 'Leke'

Height: 5ft 9in. Weight: 11st 7lb.

Born: 5 December 1980, Walworth.

■ Odunsi made his Millwall League debut against Colchester in 2–0 win for the Lions in April 1999. He got his chance as Millwall were visiting Wembley for the Auto Windscreens Shield Final five days later and had made 11 changes from the side that had played three days earlier. He had previously appeared for the Lions in the aforementioned Cup competition. Chances were few and far between at the South London side, and Odunsi made just 6(+12) League appearances in four seasons. He joined Colchester in August 2002 on a season-long loan and made his substitute debut at Peterborough as United won 1–0. Released in December 2002, he decided to quit professional football all together, playing non-League for Kingstonian, Bromley and Carshalton. He made a surprise return to League football in August 2003, playing 12 games for Southend, managed by former Colchester legend Steve Wignall, netting once and succumbing to an ankle injury incurred while scoring at Huddersfield in October 2003 that forced his retirement.

	League		Lge Cup		FA Cup		Other	
	A	G	A	G	A	G	A	G
2002–03	3+3	0	0+1	0	0	0	0+1	0
TOTAL	3+3	0	0+1	0	0	0	0+1	0

OKAFOR, Samuel Amaechi 'Sam'

Height: 5ft 9in. Weight: 12st.

Born: 17 March 1982, Xtiam, Nigeria.

■ Colchester youth teamer Okafor made his only appearance as a substitute at the end of the first year of his three year scholarship in the final game of the 1998–99 season at Blackpool. A midfielder with an excellent engine and work ethic, Okafor went out on work experience, a youth team equivalent of a loan, to Conference club Dover in March 2001 making 3(+1) appearances there. He was very disappointed to be released from Layer Road at the end of the season with the club's senior management considering that he did not have enough quality for Division One. The comment was made that if his athleticism could be combined with midfield partner Marc Canham's creative skills, the club would have had the ideal midfielder. Okafor later played for Enfield, Hampton & Richmond and Bromley, while making a career for himself in the City of London.

	League		Lge Cup		FA Cup		Other	
	A	G	A	G	A	G	A	G
1998–99	0+1	0	0	0	0	0	0	0
TOTAL	0+1	0	0	0	0	0	0	0

OLDFIELD, Craig

Height: 5ft 11in. Weight: 12st.

Born: 24 November 1963, Warley.

■ Oldfield was recruited from Eastern Counties League Stowmarket as an 18-year-old and is actually listed on the programme for both teams when the U's reserves entertained Stowmarket on the opening day of 1982–83. He played for Stowmarket that day and scored their goal in the 1–1 draw but thereafter switched to Layer Road, initially on non-contract terms, and was a regular for the reserves for the next two years. Unfortunately for Oldfield, Colchester had Tony Adcock, Keith Bowen, Perry Groves and, for his first year, Ian Allinson

in the striking positions, and he simply was not as good as them. His first team involvement was limited to the sub's bench, which he occupied 10 times in 1983–84, getting on the field on four occasions, the first in a 2–1 win over Blackpool in September 1983. His last game for the U's is shared with record appearance holder Micky Cook, for the reserves against Clacton on 30 April 1984. He moved to Bury Town and has since had a long career in local non-League football, primarily with Suffolk clubs. During his time at Sudbury he played in the 1989 FA Vase Final at Wembley.

	League		Lge Cup		FA Cup		Other	
	A	G	A	G	A	G	A	G
1983–84	0+3	0	0	0	0	0	0+1	0
TOTAL	0+3	0	0	0	0	0	0+1	0

OLIVER, James Robert 'Jimmy'

Height: 5ft 11in. Weight: 11st 7lb.

Born: 3 December 1941, Falkirk.

■ Oliver joined Falkirk from Scottish junior side Linlithgow Rose in 1958 and in four seasons scored 13 goals in 78 appearances. A Scottish schoolboy international, he was picked up by Norwich, who signed him ahead of enquiries from Arsenal, for a fee of around £12,000 in August 1962. After netting 14 League goals in 40 starts, he joined Brighton, where he picked up a Fourth Division Championship medal in 1964–65, a season in which Brighton averaged crowds of just under 18,000. Oliver joined Colchester in January 1968 for a fee of £2,000 as United were staring

relegation in the face and minus the service of injured forwards Peter Bullock and Ken Hodgson. On leaving Layer Road he played for King's Lynn and became player-coach of Lowestoft in 1971 later moving to Gorleston before setting up a Sports Retailers in Norwich.

	League		Lge Cup		FA Cup		Other	
	A	G	A	G	A	G	A	G
1967–68	14+1	0	0	0	0	0	-	-
1968–69	34+7	9	1	1	1	0	-	-
1969–70	17+2	1	2	0	0+1	0	-	-
TOTAL	65+10	10	3	1	1+1	0	-	-

OPARA, Kelechi Chrysantus 'KK'

Height: 6ft. Weight: 12st 6lb.

Born: 21 December 1981, Owerri Imo, Nigeria.

■ Opara made his debut at Blackpool in the last game of the 1998–99 season coming on as a second-half substitute. While scoring plenty of goals for the U's minor teams, he was never able to cement a place in the first team, and it did not help that he was brought into the senior squad immediately after Lomana Lua Lua departed. Several U's youth teamers suffered over the next two or three years by being compared to the unique Lomana as they tried to make the step up to first team football. KK was released following an alleged act of misconduct at the local college while on the weekly academic day of the scholarship. His brother Lloyd, two years behind him, was also a U's scholar by this time. Leyton Orient took over KK's scholarship, paying the U's a nominal compensation fee, and he was part of their team that won the Youth Alliance Cup at

the Millenium Stadium in 2001. Orient, as was their policy with their scholars, loaned him to local non-League clubs, and when the O's did not offer him a contract at the end of his scholarship he joined one of his former loan clubs, Billericay, on a permanent basis after trialling at Darlington pre-season. He has since played for many clubs in Essex, Hertfordshire and London including Enfield, Dagenham & Redbridge, Purfleet, Redbridge, Heybridge, Erith & Belvedere and Harlow. Opara was involved in an horrific car accident in March 2003 in which five people died but recovered from his serious injuries to resume playing in 2004.

	League		Lge Cup		FA Cup		Other	
	A	G	A	G	A	G	A	G
1998–99	0+1	0	0	0	0	0	0	0
1999–2000	2+14	0	0	0	0	0	0+1	0
2000–01	0+2	0	1	0	0	0	0	0
TOTAL	2+17	0	1	0	0	0	0+1	0

OPARA, Junior 'Lloyd'

Height: 6ft 1in. Weight: 13st.

Born: 6 January 1984, Edmonton.

■ Much was expected of the younger Opara after he progressed through the youth ranks at Layer Road. Considered to have the greater natural talent and athleticism of the Opara brothers, the amiable Lloyd struggled to find the self-discipline to make the full use of his abilities and by autumn 2003 had exasperated the club once too often. Cambridge United grabbed the chance to take over the remainder of his scholarship, but he did not last there either, although he did record his first Football League goal in his 1(+9) appearances. By 2007, he had blown

four chances of a professional career, adding Swindon and Peterborough to the Football League clubs who had tried and discarded him. Steve Whitton gave him his U's debut as a substitute at Blackpool in October 2001, and he nearly made a memorable intervention in a home game with Cheltenham in 2002, picking up the ball near his own penalty area and going the length of the field only to scuff his shot at the business end. In between his stints at professional clubs Opara did a tour of non-League clubs in Essex and Hertfordshire, rarely staying anywhere long enough to make double figures of games played and never reaching 20 until joining Cheshunt in 2005–06. Before being sold to Peterborough for £22,000 he had a brief trial with Chelsea, but that came to nothing and in March 2007 he rejoined Cheshunt from the Posh, where he had scored twice in 8(+11) appearances, on a free transfer. While at Peterborough he featured in the infamous Sky TV documentary *Big Ron*.

	League		Lge Cup		FA Cup		Other	
	A	G	A	G	A	G	A	G
2001–02	0+1	0	0	0	0+1	0	0+1	0
2002–03	0+5	0	0+1	0	0+1	0	0+1	0
TOTAL	0+6	0	0+1	0	0+2	0	0+2	0

ORMESHER, John

■ Ormesher was one of the remnants of the old amateur club, Colchester Town, who briefly co-existed with the U's but found the competition for support from professional football irresistible and ceased operations at the end of 1937. Ormesher, a soldier, first

played for Town in January 1937 in a 6–2 away win at Thetford, the last time the club avoided defeat in an away game, and was virtually ever present at centre-half thereafter. He played three times for the U's first team in October 1937, once at left-half, once at centre-half and once at right-back, and played centre-half in the first five games of the newly-established reserves before leaving for India in mid-January 1938, missing the chance to play in Town's last ever game, an Essex Senior Cup tie at Grays, by a couple of days.

	League		Lge Cup		FA Cup		Other	
	A	G	A	G	A	G	A	G
1937–38	1	0	0	0	-	-	2	0
TOTAL	1	0	0	0	-	-	2	0

O'ROURKE, Kenneth 'Ken'

Height: 5ft 10in. Weight: 11st 4lb.

Born: 8 December 1949, Lambeth.

■ A Leyton Orient apprentice, O'Rourke was signed by Arsenal in February 1967 having shown great promise at Brisbane Road. He failed to get into the Arsenal side but scored 12 times in 42 youth outings at Highbury. Released at the end of the season, he had a two month trial at Ipswich before joining Colchester on a similar basis and for a similar period. His one League appearance came at Swansea in October 1968 when he was also substituted. His also played in the 5–0 FA Cup thrashing of Chesham. He was released at the end of his trial and tried his luck at Bedford before joining the Metropolitan Police and playing for their football club for several years in the Southern League. He also won

representative honours with the British Police team.

	League		Lge Cup		FA Cup		Other	
	A	G	A	G	A	G	A	G
1968–69	1	0	0	0	1	0	-	-
TOTAL	1	0	0	0	1	0	-	-

OSBORNE, Roger Charles

Height: 5ft 9in. Weight: 10st 11lb.

Born: 9 March 1950, Otley.

■ Most famously remembered for scoring Ipswich's winning goal in the 1978 FA Cup Final against Arsenal, and promptly fainting with emotion soon after, Osborne joined Colchester for £25,000 on deadline day 1981 from the Portman Road club and eventually played more games for the U's than he had for Ipswich. Signing on the same day

as Roy McDonough, the pair made their debuts against Burnley in a 2–1 win as manager Bobby Roberts tried to stave off relegation back to Division Four. Osborne originally signed for Ipswich from local junior side Westerfield, a club with which the large Osborne clan had a long association, in March 1971 and scored nine goals from midfield in 109(+15) top-flight appearances. He experienced UEFA Cup football in 1973–74, 1975–76 and 1977–78. At Layer Road he was a regular in a side that just could not quite achieve promotion back to Division Three, with United finishing sixth, sixth, eighth, seventh and sixth in consecutive seasons under Cyril Lea. Osborne later played for Sudbury in the Eastern Counties League and then had spells with Braintree and Felixstowe before returning to Westerfield as manager.

	League		Lge Cup		FA Cup		Other	
	A	G	A	G	A	G	A	G
1980–81	11+1	0	0	0	0	0	-	-
1981–82	39	5	4	0	5	0	-	-
1982–83	45	2	4	0	1	0	3	0
1983–84	34+2	1	4	0	3	0	1	0
1984–85	39+1	2	2	0	2	0	3	0
1985–86	28+6	1	1+1	0	0	0	2	0
TOTAL	196+10	11	15+1	0	11	0	9	0

OSBOURNE, Calbert Gary James 'Gary'

Height: 5ft 7in. Weight: 11st.

Born: 22 October 1969, Wolverhampton.

■ Signing youth trainee forms with Shrewsbury in the summer of 1988, Osbourne made just 3(+4) appearances for the Shropshire club before being released to Telford United. He had moved on to Stourbridge when U's player-manager Ian Atkins recruited him in March 1991 to bolster United's battle with Barnet and Kettering for the 1990–91 Conference title. After some promising performances in the reserves Osbourne made his debut as a substitute at Gateshead in April 1991 but made little impact in the senior side and was released at the end of the season, returning to West Midlands non-League football initially with Cradley Town. He subsequently had spells with Bilston, Redditch, Sutton Coldfield, Tamworth and a second stint at Stourbridge.

	League		Lge Cup		FA Cup		Other	
	A	G	A	G	A	G	A	G
1990–91	5+1	0	0	0	0	0	0	0
TOTAL	5+1	0	0	0	0	0	0	0

O'SULLIVAN

■ A 20-year-old from the RAF, the slightly built O'Sullivan was reputed to have some experience in the Irish League. His only game in Colchester's colours came in October 1945 when he played right-half against Cheltenham where, according to the local press, after a quiet first-half he stood out in the second period with some fine tackling and first-rate positional play.

	League		Lge Cup		FA Cup		Other	
	A	G	A	G	A	G	A	G
1945–46	1	0	0	0	0	0	-	-
TOTAL	1	0	0	0	0	0	-	-

OWEN, Brian Ernest

Height: 5ft 10in. Weight: 12st.

Born: 2 November 1944, Harefield.

■ Owen began his career as a Watford apprentice, signing professional forms in February 1962. He played 148(+5) League games for the Hornets, scoring 17 times as they won the Third Division title in 1968–69 and reached the 1969–70 FA Cup semi-final. He also played for England Under-18's in Switzerland. Signed by Dick Graham along with Brian Garvey in mid-May 1970, Owen had already commenced studying to attain his coaching badges. It was not long before Owen was invited to become part of the England Youth coaching set up. Already suffering from knee problems, he scored twice on his debut against Cambridge in the 1970–71 League Cup, and it was against the 'other' U's that Owen broke his knee cap in an FA Cup tie in December 1970. Owen returned the next season in United colours, but despite picking up a Watney Cup-

winners' medal his knee was not properly recovered. With finances tight, the club had just announced it was carrying a £21,000 loss, his contract was cancelled by mutual consent in January 1972 and he joined Wolves as a coach, now managed by his former Watford boss Bill McGarry. Various injury crises meant he unexpectedly added four more League appearances to his total while at Molineux, and those completed his record of playing in every division during his career. Remaining on the coaching staff as Wolves reached the UEFA and League Cup Finals, he became first-team coach in 1976 as Wolves bounced back to the top flight, winning the Second Division title. A change of management saw Owen move briefly to Peterborough before Bobby Robson took him to Ipswich as youth-team coach. Owen continued his involvement with England Youth, Under-23 and B levels and became reserve coach of Ipswich in 1984. Following a change of management there, Owen took up a post at Crystal Palace under Steve Coppell before returning to Layer Road 1988. After a difficult period, in which Colchester were relegated to the Conference, Owen joined David Pleat at Luton in 1991 but was back for his third stint with United within 18 months. His long association with Colchester was rewarded with a testimonial against Ipswich in August 2005.

	League		Lge Cup		FA Cup		Other	
	A	G	A	G	A	G	A	G
1970–71	4+2	2	2	2	0+1	0	-	-
1971–72	7	0	3	0	0	0	3	0
TOTAL	11+2	2	5	2	0+1	0	3	0

OXBROW, Darren William

Height: 6ft 1in. Weight: 12st 6lb.
Born: 1 September 1969, Ipswich.

■ Signed by Ipswich as a schoolboy, Oxbrow was taken on youth trainee forms but failed to make the first team and was released by new manager John Duncan. He joined Maidstone in the Fourth Division, reaching the Play-off semi-finals in his first season. He played 84(+1) games, netting twice, at Maidstone, who were in financial disarray and sharing Dartford's ground. At the end of 1991–92 they were forced to resign from the League, and Oxbrow found himself on the dole. Signed by Roy McDonough, he made his debut in Colchester's first game back in the League following their sojourn in the Conference. He scored the winner in a 2–1 victory over Lincoln and looked to have established himself at Layer Road with some steady performances. However, there were issues off the pitch that caused problems between him and McDonough, and when Peter Cawley was recruited Oxbrow was the man to give way. After a brief spell on the subs' bench he was released in early December and allowed to join high-flying but financially-troubled Barnet. They loaned him out to Conference club Kettering, and Oxbrow only played one late-season game for Barnet before being released at the end of the year. Disillusioned with lower League football, he applied to join the police force and signed on a permanent basis for Kettering, making 79(+1) appearances and scoring seven goals. Work commitments made Conference football difficult, and he subsequently played at a lower level, including at Chelmsford, Felixstowe, Harwich & Parkeston and Woodbridge.

	League		Lge Cup		FA Cup		Other	
	A	G	A	G	A	G	A	G
1992–93	12+4	4	2	0	0+1	0	1	0
TOTAL	12+4	4	2	0	0+1	0	1	0

P

PACKER, Michael David 'Mick'

Height: 5ft 10in. Weight: 11st.

Born: 20 April 1950, Willesden.

■ Jim Smith signed Packer on a free transfer from Watford in July 1973 as he sought to rebuild the side that had suffered re-election in the previous season. Packer arrived at the same time as goalkeeper Mike Walker. At Watford, Packer had played in the 1970 FA Cup semi-final alongside future U's stars John Williams, Mike Walker and Brian Owen, but after 57(+11) League appearances and 2 goals since signing as a professional in April 1968 he was loaned to Crewe on deadline day 1972. Making 12 appearances at Gresty Road, Packer was released by the Hornets in the summer of 1973. Primarily a left-back, Packer played at the heart of the defence and in midfield, had a no-nonsense attitude and a thunderous shot. He played in United's big Cup ties against Southampton, Derby, Leeds, Manchester United and Newcastle. He also won promotion to Division Three, twice, and played under Jim Smith, Bobby Roberts and Alan Hunter. His long service was rewarded with a testimonial against West Ham in May 1983. On being released from Layer Road, Packer joined Wivenhoe as player-manager. Later, while managing a local leisure centre, he assisted AFC Sudbury and their reserve side.

	League		Lge Cup		FA Cup		Other	
	A	G	A	G	A	G	A	G
1973–74	32+1	0	1	0	1	0	-	-
1974–75	30	1	5	0	2	0	-	-
1975–76	44	2	2	0	2	1	-	-
1976–77	35+4	5	3	0	4+1	2	-	-
1977–78	44	2	5	0	3	0	-	-
1978–79	40+2	1	2	0	5	0	-	-
1979–80	43	4	2	0	4	0	-	-
1980–81	43	3	2	0	4	0	-	-
1981–82	14	1	1	0	0	0	-	-
1982–83	12	0	0	0	0	0	0	0
TOTAL	337+7	19	23	0	25+1	3	0	0

PAGE, Albert Edward

Born: 18 March 1916, Walthamstow.
Died: 10 January 1995.

■ Centre-back Page began his career at Leyton before joining Tottenham in 1936 on a professional contract. He made 56 League appearances at White Hart Lane. During the war he played 29 further games for Tottenham and guested for West Ham and Crystal Palace. Ted Fenton signed him for Colchester, and he made his debut at Cheltenham in March 1947, featuring in every game to the end of the season. He found it hard to displace Fenton and Harry Bearryman in 1947–48 and was released in the summer, joining the newly established and ultimately short-lived Southern League professional club Chingford Town. While with Leyton, who played at a higher standard, he had very occasionally turned out for Colchester Town, a situation possible because the clubs played in different Leagues, and amateur registration forms tended to be specific to a particular League.

	League		Lge Cup		FA Cup		Other	
	A	G	A	G	A	G	A	G
1946–47	11	0	1	0	0	0	-	-
1947–48	6	0	2	0	0	0	-	-
TOTAL	17	0	3	0	0	0	-	-

PAINTER, Trevor Alfred

Height: 5ft 11in. Weight: 11st 6lb.

Born: 2 July 1949, Norwich.

■ Painter first trialled at Ipswich but signed as a Norwich apprentice in May 1966. Captain of both Norwich and Norfolk Boys, it was just over a year later that he signed professional forms but made just two appearances at Carrow Road, accompanied by 103 outings for

City reserves. Signed by Dick Graham at the end of April 1970, Painter made his one first-team appearance for Colchester against Chester at Layer Road in the December. Freed at the end of the year, he spent three years playing for King's Lynn and was reported to have signed for Lowestoft in August 1974 but hardly made a first-team appearance. After full time football he became an insurance worker in Norfolk.

	League		Lge Cup		FA Cup		Other	
	A	G	A	G	A	G	A	G
1970–71	1	0	0	0	0	0	-	-
TOTAL	1	0	0	0	0	0	-	-

PARKER, Derek

Height: 5ft 9in. Weight: 10st 12lb.

Born: 23 June 1926, Colchester.

■ Wivenhoe-born Parker was playing his wartime football for South Essex side Grays Athletic in the Herts & Middlesex League when West Ham signed him up as a professional in October 1944, and he spent 13 seasons at Upton Park, amassing 199 League appearances and scoring nine goals. A single wartime appearance for the Hammers in 1944–45 brought up the 200 mark. Parker was included in the FA tour of Australia in 1951. After Hammers manager Ted Fenton, the ex-U's boss, signed Mike Grice in 1956 it was almost a return of compliment when Ted allowed brother Benny to sign Parker for United in March 1957. Parker was part of

the side that held mighty Arsenal to a draw at Layer Road in 1959. His only goal for United came at Brentford in a 3–3 draw during August 1957. On leaving Layer Road following relegation in 1961 he became player-manager of Eastern Counties League Stowmarket, stopping playing in 1964 but continuing as manager until 1969 when he moved to Coggeshall Town in the same role. In 1973 he swapped to Tiptree United, quitting suddenly at Christmas 1975, citing behind-the-scenes tensions. He worked at the Wakes Hall Centre until he retired in 1991.

	League		Lge Cup		FA Cup		Other	
	A	G	A	G	A	G	A	G
1956–57	6	0	-	-	0	0	-	-
1957–58	29	1	-	-	1	0	-	-
1958–59	38	0	-	-	6	0	-	-
1959–60	43	0	-	-	1	0	-	-
1960–61	14	0	0	0	0	0	-	-
TOTAL	130	1	0	0	8	0	-	-

PARKINSON, Noel David

Height: 5ft 8in. Weight: 10st 7lb.

Born: 16 November 1959, Hull.

■ An England Youth international, Parkinson made just two substitute appearances for Ipswich, for whom he had served his apprenticeship. Both those games were against Skied Oslo in the UEFA Cup of 1979–80. The following month, November, he was loaned to Bristol Rovers, where he scored once in five appearances. Then in February 1980 he spent a further time out on loan at Brentford, where he made 9(+1) appearances. With chances few and far between at Ipswich, he moved to Mansfield in the 1980 close season, establishing himself in midfield and scoring a useful 13 goals in 66(+4) League games. Two summers later, he found himself closer to home when joining Scunthorpe. At The Old Show Ground he added seven goals in 39(+2) appearances and was promoted from the Fourth Division in his first season. Cyril Lea, with his previous Ipswich connections, brought Parkinson to Layer Road in August 1984. Missing the first two games of the campaign, Parkinson played in all 44 remaining fixtures and was a steady influence in U's engine room and weighed in with 13 goals. On leaving Layer Road, he became a sports reporter on local radio in the Humberside area.

	League		Lge Cup		FA Cup		Other	
	A	G	A	G	A	G	A	G
1984–85	44	6	0+1	0	3	0	3	0
1985–86	35	7	1+1	0	1	0	2	0
TOTAL	79	13	1+2	0	4	0	5	0

PARTNER, Andrew Neil 'Andy'

Height: 6ft 1in. Weight: 12st 10lb

Born: 21 October 1974, Colchester.

■ Partner followed his dad Neil through the U's apprentice ranks and inherited his dad's nickname, Twiggy. He got slightly further than his dad by making the first team but his chances of a professional career were shattered, like his knee cap, shortly after coming on as sub at Exeter on 30 August 1994. It was two and a half years years before he played again, in a reserve game with Barnet on 19 March 1997. He took some part in most of the remaining reserve games over the next couple of months before severing his ties with Layer Road in the summer and joining Heybridge. Thereafter, he joined the numerous former U's player on the local circuit with spells at Wivenhoe, Clacton and Harwich. Partner, whose step mother Marie is the club's current Chief Executive, got his first-team debut in manager Roy McDonough's least favourite competition, the Bob Lord Trophy when the senior element in a much weakened side was very content to let promotion rivals Wycombe have the extra fixtures that went with a win. His only other start was in an Autoglass Trophy tie at Barnet in December 1992, another occasion where McDonough picked a distinctly understrength side, and both his Football League appearances were short stints as sub.

	League		Lge Cup		FA Cup		Other	
	A	G	A	G	A	G	A	G
1991–92	*0*	*0*	*1*	*0*	*0*	*0*	*0*	*0*
1992–93	0+1	0	0	0	0	0	1	0
1993–94	0	0	0	0	0	0	0	0
1994–95	0+1	0	0	0	0	0	0	0
TOTAL	0+2	0	0	0	0	0	1	0
	0	*0*	*1*	*0*	*0*	*0*	*0*	*0*

PENDERGAST, William John 'Bill'

Born: 13 April 1915, Pen-Y-Groes.
Died: May 2001, Denbigh.

■ Pendergast was a much-travelled forward who had begun his career at Rhyl Athletic. He became somewhat of a nomad during 1934 and 1935 when he was on the

books of Crewe and Wrexham, both as amateurs, then a pro at Manchester United and Wolves. Remarkably, he did not make a single appearance for any of those teams. He finally made his Football League bow at Bristol Rovers on 10 October 1936 against Southend and scored three goals in seven first-team matches for the Pirates plus an eye-catching 47 times in 45 games for their reserves as they won the Western League. He started 1937–38 in the same vein with 12 goals in 13 reserve games and U's manager Ted Davies had already made one unsuccessful attempt to sign him before Rovers relented, and he came to East Anglia in December. Unfortunately, after scoring six goals in 11 outings, he broke his leg at his old club in March, and the club decided that they could not risk re-signing him because of the injury. Hindsight says that was a slight misjudgement because Pendergast joined Chester and showed not only that he was fully recovered but also that he could transfer his goalscoring prowess to Football League level, including scoring in a record 12 consecutive matches for Chester in Division Three North. In recent times the young Jermaine Defoe came close to equalling that record while on loan from West Ham to Bournemouth. Pendergast also scored in a Cup match in the middle of that run and so is the overall holder, with 16 goals scored in 13 successive League and Cup games. For the record: 10/9 Stockport (h) 4–3 (3 goals), 17/9 Accrington (a) 3–2 (1), 24/9 Barnsley (h) 2–1 (1), 1/10 Oldham (a) 3–1 (2), 8/10 Halifax (h) 5–1 (1), 15/10 Gateshead (h) 2–2 (1), 22/10 Wrexham (a) 2–3 (1), 29/10 York (h) 5–1 (1), 5/11 Rochdale (a) 2–5 (1), 12/11 Rotherham (h) 1–4 (1), 19/11 Doncaster (a) 1–4 (1), 26/11 Doncaster (h) FAC 3–1 (1), 3/12 Crewe (a) 2–0 (1). When war was declared, Pendagast reappeared in Colchester and played in half a dozen of the 15 friendlies played by the U's in autumn 1939. During the war Pendergast continued to bang in the goals for Chester, notching 28 in 42 matches. After the war ended, he joined Third Division North side New Brighton, scoring 26 goals in 69 appearances, and returned to Rhyl Athletic in 1947.

	League		Lge Cup		FA Cup		Other	
	A	G	A	G	A	G	A	G
1937–38	8	5	0	0	-	-	3	1
TOTAL	8	5	0	0	-	-	3	1

PERRYMAN, Gerald 'Gerry'

Height: 5ft 7in. Weight: 10st 12lb.

Born: 3 October 1947, West Haddon.

■ A junior with Northampton, Perryman signed professional in September 1966 but managed just one outing at The County Ground. The full-back joined Colchester in the summer of 1968. He came on as substitute as Dick Graham's team lost 5–1 at Chester on 24 September 1968 and stood in for Dennis Mochan two days later as United were thumped 4–0 by Scunthorpe at Layer Road. Dick Graham took drastic action with the squad he had inherited and

Perryman was one of those to suffer the axe. He moved on to play for Corby and Rushden.

	League		Lge Cup		FA Cup		Other	
	A	G	A	G	A	G	A	G
1968–69	1+1	0	1	0	0	0	-	-
TOTAL	1+1	0	1	0	0	0	-	-

PETTERSON, Andrew Keith 'Andy'

Height: 6ft 2in. Weight: 14st 12lb.

Born: 26 September 1969, Fremantle, Australia.

■ Petterson joined Colchester on loan from Charlton at the tail end of the 1995–96 season when Carl Emberson broke his thumb, and second-choice Garrett Caldwell was away on international duty with Canada. He made his debut in a 1–0 home win over Bury in March 1996 but was recalled by Charlton after five appearances in United's goal. He completed the season as a losing Division One Play-off semi-finalist. Nicknamed 'The Flying Doctor', Petterson played for no less than 13 League clubs, mainly on loan deals, in a 16 year League career. Originally with East Fremantle of Australia, Petterson joined Luton in December 1988, playing 16(+3) games. He had a single-game loan spell at Ipswich in March 1993 before signing for Charlton in the summer of 1994 for £85,000. At The Valley he played 68(+4) times and had loan spells, at Bradford, Ipswich (again), Plymouth, the U's and Portsmouth. Having impressed at Fratton Park, he made the deal permanent in the summer of 1999. After 32 games for Pompey and a

loan stint at Torquay, Petterson signed for West Brom as cover and was also on the books of Brighton and Bournemouth during 2002. Following a spell with Derry City, he had a game with Southend in September 2003 and played three games on trial at Walsall in January 2004, as well as trying his luck at Rushden & Diamonds and Notts County. Joining Farnborough in April 2005, he played 4 times before opting to return Down Under to play for Newcastle United Jets and ECU Joondalup in the Australian State Leagues.

	League		Lge Cup		FA Cup		Other	
	A	G	A	G	A	G	A	G
1995–96	5	0	0	0	0	0	0	0
TOTAL	5	0	0	0	0	0	0	0

PHILLIPS, Edward John 'Ted'

Height: 6ft. Weight: 11st 12lb.

Born: 21 August 1933, Leiston.

■ Phillips was recommended to A. Scott Duncan, the Ipswich manager, by Ian Gillespie, former Ipswich and Colchester player of the war years who was manager of Leiston Town. Within half an hour of his trial he was an Ipswich player and went on to score an incredible 161 League goals in just 269 starts as Ipswich rose from the Third Division South to the First Division. He won Third Division South champions medals in both 1954 and 1957 and became Town's club record scorer with 41 League goals (and five in the FA Cup) in 1956–57 as the Suffolk side pipped Colchester for a place in Division Two. Ipswich duly won the Second Division title in 1960–61 and the First Division Championship in 1961–62 scoring 58 League goals in the process. The following season he played in the European Cup for Ipswich, scoring two in a 10–0 home win over Maltese part-timers Floriana. His main partner was Ray Crawford, who would also eventually turn out in a Colchester shirt. He joined ex-U's boss Benny Fenton at Orient in March 1964 and scored a hat-trick of headers on his debut against Portsmouth. When Fenton was replaced by Dave Sexton at Brisbane Road, he moved to Luton in February 1965, scoring eight goals in 12 games. Neil Franklin brought him to Layer Road as the makeweight in a player-plus-cash deal for Billy Stark, and he repeated his debut feat by scoring a hat-trick against Barnsley at

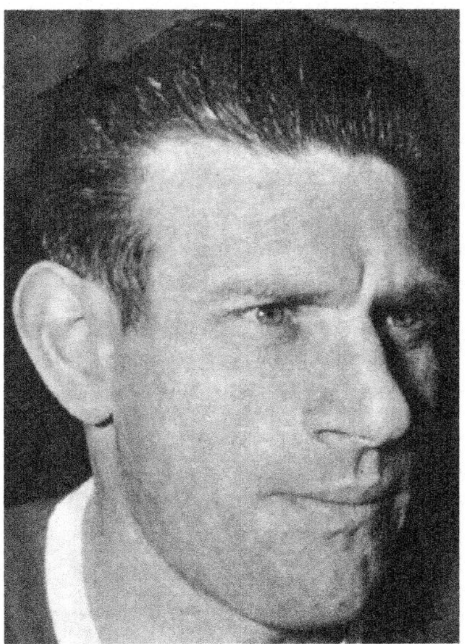

Layer Road, all with his head. He finished second leading scorer in United's promotion campaign, although he only netted once after 12 February. He had fallen out with Franklin by Easter, so spent the promotion run-in in the reserves. He left at the end of the season and went to Malta as player-coach of Floriana but an injured ankle stopped him playing, and he was back at Christmas to sign for Chelmsford. He left New Writtle Street in the summer and accepted a three-year deal to play in Melbourne where he was Player of the Year in 1970–71. He also played locally for Clacton, Lexden, Brantham and Long Melford and was a notable cricketer, playing minor counties for Suffolk as a fast bowler.

	League		Lge Cup		FA Cup		Other	
	A	G	A	G	A	G	A	G
1965–66	32	13	0	0	2	0	-	-
TOTAL	32	13	0	0	2	0	-	-

PHILLIPS, Ian Alexander

Height: 5ft 9in. Weight: 11st 12lb.

Born: 23 April 1959, Kilwinning.

■ Released from his Ipswich apprenticeship, Phillips signed for Mansfield in the summer of 1977 and featured in 18(+5) games for the Stags. In August 1979 he was transferred to Peterborough, where in three full seasons he amassed 97 appearances, scoring three goals. Remaining in Division Four, Phillips moved to Northampton in the summer of 1982, where he scored once in 42 League appearances. Cyril Lea was looking for a left-footed left-back and Phillips had come up against the U's on many occasions. Lea got his man with a £5,000 fee, and the player made his debut at Stockport in September 1983, quickly being appointed captain. His first goals came as a pair in a 6–0 thrashing of Hartlepool in December 1983. A regular in United's defence, Phillips's first stint ended as Colchester lost the 1986–87 Fourth Division Play-off semi-finals to Wolves. He joined Aldershot, the club who beat Wolves in the Final, where he teamed up with ex-U's players Ian McDonald and Steve Wignall, as well as future U's players Paul Roberts, Kevin Bedford and David Barnes. After three seasons and two goals in 106 appearances, Phillips joined then non-League giants Kettering. Ironically, he faced up to Colchester, who had been relegated to the Conference. When Roy McDonough became U's boss for the 1991–92 season, Phillips was recruited as his coach. Colchester gloriously won the Conference and FA Trophy double, with Phillips helping out on a couple of occasions. He was retained on a non-contract basis as United returned to the League, and he made one further appearance in a Football League Trophy tie at Barnet. Phillips also had coaching spells with Halstead and Harwich & Parkeston and helped run the highly successful Colchester junior side Gas Recreation.

	League		Lge Cup		FA Cup		Other	
	A	G	A	G	A	G	A	G
1983–84	43	5	0	0	3	0	2	0
1984–85	37	1	2	0	3	0	3	0
1985–86	37	2	2	0	0	0	2	0
1986–87	33	2	2	0	3	0	3	0
1991–92	*1+2*	*0*	*0*	*0*	*1*	*0*	*0*	*0*
1992–93	0+1	0	0	0	0	0	1	0
TOTAL	150+1	10	6	0	9	0	11	0
	1+2	*0*	*0*	*0*	*1*	*0*	*0*	*0*

PINAULT, Thomas

Height: 5ft 10in. Weight: 11st 1lb.

Born: 4 December 1981, Grasse, France.

■ Pinault arrived from French side AS Cannes in July 1999, along with Steve Germain. He was part of the expected Mick Wadsworth–led revolution and, although originally he spoke very little English, he adapted better than Germain and another Frenchman Fabrice Richard. He made his Colchester debut as a substitute in a 3–0 home defeat to Notts County in August 1999 but was confined mainly to reserve and youth-team football in his first two years, although he did score his first goal in a 3–0 win at Luton in December 2000. He established himself in midfield alongside Kem Izzet but was unable to move up a gear and, despite scoring some spectacular goals, ultimately frustrated the fans with his seeming inability or unwillingness to play forwards rather than across the pitch. He was released at the end of 2003–04, joining Grimsby after rejecting an offer from Northampton and trialling with Dundee United. Scoring 7 goals in 32(+11) games at Blundell Park, Pinault did not play any football at all in 2005–06 after being publicly slated by Mariners boss Russell Slade on local radio and damaging ankle ligaments in pre-season. He was enlisted by Brentford in July 2006 as the Bees sought to capitalise on recent Play-off failures. After completing 24(+3) League games, scoring once, alongside former U's favourite Joe Keith, Pinault was released at the end of the season as the Bees sunk into the basement Division. He kicked off the 2007–08 season on the books of Conference side Crawley.

	League		Lge Cup		FA Cup		Other	
	A	G	A	G	A	G	A	G
1999–2000	1+3	0	0+1	0	0	0	0	0
2000–01	3+2	1	0	0	0	0	0	0
2001–02	37+5	0	2	0	2	0	2	0
2002–03	32+10	4	1	0	1	0	1	0
2003–04	31+9	0	1+1	1	7	0	5	1
TOTAL	104+29	5	4+2	1	10	0	8	1

PITCHER, Geoffrey 'Geoff'

Height: 5ft 7in. Weight: 11st 5lb.

Born: 15 August 1975, Sutton.

■ Pitcher's career started within the YTS ranks at Millwall. Without making the first team he was transferred to Watford in July 1994 as makeweight in the deal that saw Jamie Moralee (later to play for Colchester) move in the opposite direction and made 4(+9) appearances scoring twice. Released by the Hornets he signed for Carshalton and then Kingstonian of the Isthmian League. Given a trial by Steve Wignall at the beginning of the season, Pitcher appeared as a substitute in a 2–1 home win over Mansfield in March 1997 during a second trial period. It proved to be his only appearance for United, and he returned to Kingston and became a fixture in the K's rise to the Conference and subsequent FA Trophy success under Geoff Chapple. He played 109(+2) Conference games between 2001 and 2004, scoring 21 times. His performances earned a spell with Brighton for £25,000 where he made 2(+8) League appearances over two seasons, curtailed by the need for serious bowel surgery. In a much-travelled and much-respected non-League career he also turned out on loan from Brighton for Woking, Dagenham & Redbridge, Farnborough, Stevenage, Barnet, Havant & Waterlooville, Sutton and Haywards Heath before joining Burgess Hill in February 2007. He won eight caps for the England semi-professional side.

	League		Lge Cup		FA Cup		Other	
	A	G	A	G	A	G	A	G
1996–97	0+1	0	0	0	0	0	0	0
TOTAL	0+1	0	0	0	0	0	0	0

PITT, Stephen William 'Steve'

Height: 5ft 8in. Weight: 11st.

Born: 1 August 1948, Willesden.

■ Pitt served his apprenticeship at White Hart Lane and signed professional in August 1965. His only Spurs appearance was against Blackpool, alongside such greats as Jimmy Greaves and Dave MacKay. Signed in the summer of 1969, Pitt made his debut on the opening day of the 1969–70 season at Lincoln, but after a handful of appearances his contract was cancelled by mutual consent at the end of October, and he joined Stevenage, then Corinthian Casuals and more recently has been in management at Heybridge Swifts and Wivenhoe Town.

	League		Lge Cup		FA Cup		Other	
	A	G	A	G	A	G	A	G
1969–70	4+2	0	1	0	0	0	-	-
TOTAL	4+2	0	1	0	0	0	-	-

PLANT, Kenneth George 'Ken'

Height: 5ft 8in. Weight: 10st 8lb.

Born: 15 August 1925, Coventry.

■ Plant had a unsuccessful trial at Coventry in 1947, so spent three years with Nuneaton Borough before Bury gave him his chance in League Football in February 1950. That proved a good decision, and he was Second Division Bury's top scorer in each of his three full seasons there, netting 54 times in 119 games. In January 1954 the U's Supporters Club handed over £3,000 to help manager Jack Butler move into the transfer market, and the local press reported that the U's handed over a 'substantial' fee to Bury for Plant's services. He scored on his debut against Swindon on 6 February, heading the equaliser in the opening minute of the second half as the U's forced a draw from 2–0 down on a hard pitch with a dusting of snow in the shelter of the main stand. Plant was top scorer in 1954–55, 1956–57 and 1957–58 and scored five hat-tricks in his United career. It is a sign of how different football was 50 years ago that in January 1957 the local press should report that Plant had cut smoking down to a minimum and was doing special afternoon training to get that extra edge. He was forced out of full-time football by a knee injury and returned to Nuneaton Borough in July 1959 and then Atherstone. He retired in 1990 after working at British Leyland in Coventry.

	League		Lge Cup		FA Cup		Other	
	A	G	A	G	A	G	A	G
1953–54	17	6	-	-	0	0	-	-
1954–55	40	13	-	-	2	0	-	-
1955–56	36	17	-	-	1	0	-	-
1956–57	46	24	-	-	1	0	-	-
1957–58	44	19	-	-	1	0	-	-
1958–59	7	3	-	-	2	2	-	-
TOTAL	190	82	-	-	7	2	-	-

PLATT, Clive Linton

Height: 6ft 4in. Weight: 13st.

Born: 27 October 1977, Wolverhampton.

■ Platt began his career as a youth trainee at Walsall, signing professional in July 1996, making 18(+14) appearances in the League over four seasons and scoring four times. Two of those strikes came in his first four substitute appearances while still a trainee. He moved to Rochdale in August 1999, initially on loan, for a fee of £100,000 and bagged 30 goals in 151(+18) games. In the summer of 2003 Platt joined Notts County on a monthly contract but only mustered three goals in 19 starts. Discarded by Notts, he joined Peterborough in January 2004, playing 35(+2) League games for Posh, netting six times. Exactly a year later he was on the move again to MK Dons, where he struck a good partnership with Izale McLeod. He helped MK to avoid relegation in that first season but, coinciding with his own barren run, MK slipped to the bottom of League One and were relegated to the basement in 2006. Platt enjoyed his best-ever season in 2006–07, netting 18 League goals in firing MK to the Play-offs, where they lost to Shrewsbury. Despite the lure of playing in MK's new stadium, Platt signed for Colchester in the summer of 2007 for a club record fee of £300,000. Sent off in a pre-season friendly against Bolton, Platt scored the last-minute equaliser on his debut in the opening day fixture at Sheffield United.

	League		Lge Cup		FA Cup		Other	
	A	G	A	G	A	G	A	G
2007–08	34+7	8	1	0	0	0	-	-
TOTAL	34+7	8	1	0	0	0	-	-

POLLARD, Kelly John

Height: 5ft 11in. Weight: 11st 6lb.

Born: 17 November 1971, Chelmsford.

■ Witham youngster Pollard was still in the U's youth team when making his first-team bow in the penultimate game of the 1988–89 season. Colchester needed to beat Exeter to ensure League safety and duly did so with a thumping 4–0 win. Pollard came off the bench to score the third goal in the 83rd minute. He made his only start at Scunthorpe in October 1989, still aged just 18, and was loaned out to Fisher Athletic in March 1991 with Steve Restarick. He played for Bury Town and then Heybridge Swifts, joining St Albans in 1998–99, where in two seasons he played 89(+4) games, scoring nine times. He returned to Heybridge and became the club's record appearance holder, with over 500 starts

for the Ryman League club. Moving to Sudbury in 2005, he completed a further 50 games, scoring four times, before signing for Eastern Counties League Tiptree in January 2007 and following manager Jody Brown to Halstead for 2007–08.

	League		Lge Cup		FA Cup		Other	
	A	G	A	G	A	G	A	G
1988–89	0+2	1	0	0	0	0	0	0
1989–90	1+6	0	0	0	0	0	0+1	0
1990–91	*0*	*0*	*2*	*0*	*0*	*0*	*0*	*0*
TOTAL	1+8	1	0	0	0	0	0+1	0
	0	*0*	*2*	*0*	*0*	*0*	*0*	*0*

POUNEWATCHY, Stephane Zeusnagapa

Height: 6ft. Weight: 15st.

Born: 10 February 1968, Paris.

■ Pounewatchy began his career with French sides Martigues, winning the Second Division Championship in 1993, and Guegnon. He moved to Mick Wadsworth's Carlisle for free in June 1996, despite having a £500,000 price on his head. He inspired the Cumbrians to promotion to the Second Division in his first season but suffered immediate relegation. He played against Colchester in the 1996–97 Auto Windscreens Shield Final at Wembley, which Carlisle won on penalties. After 81 appearances at Brunton Park and a short spell with Dundee, he joined Port Vale in August 1998, making just two League starts. Wadsworth brought him to Layer Road in February 1999, and he made his debut at Gillingham in the same month – a game where fellow defender David Greene was sent off. Although only contracted until the end of the season, Pounewatchy's presence had much to do with the U's staving off an immediate return to the basement Division. His only goal came in his last game and the final game of the season at Blackpool. Wadsworth was keen to keep him the next year but was not prepared to meet his demands and commented that Pounewatchy had a history of pricing himself out of the market. The Frenchman went home until returning to England in January 2000, playing one Auto Windscreens Shield game for Scunthorpe. He was not properly fit though, and no contract was offered. He later became a player's agent, operating out of Bangui, Central African Republic and is still registered with FIFA in 2007.

	League		Lge Cup		FA Cup		Other	
	A	G	A	G	A	G	A	G
1998–99	15	1	0	0	0	0	0	0
TOTAL	15	1	0	0	0	0	0	0

PRESLAND, Edward Robert 'Eddie'

Height: 6ft 1in. Weight: 12st.

Born: 27 March 1943, Waltham Cross.

■ Presland began as a West Ham junior, signing in October 1960. It was not until 1964–65 that he made his Hammers debut, scoring one goal in six League starts. Transferring to Crystal Palace in January 1967, the full-back made 61 appearances for the Eagles and was brought to Layer Road on a three-month loan by Dick Graham to solve his dire injury crisis in October 1969. Presland played just six games in all and, after a spell at Leyton Orient, spent 1970–71 playing for Jewish Guild of Johannesburg. He returned to the UK and joined the ex-U's contingent at Wealdstone, taking over as player-manager when they won promotion from the Southern League Division One South. He subsequently managed Dulwich Hamlet, Hendon and Gravesend, crowning his managerial career by leading Dagenham to the 1980 FA Trophy. Presland also played county cricket for Essex and managed Gravesend and Northfleet between 1985 and 1987. After his professional career Presland became a schoolmaster, teaching PE in East London.

	League		Lge Cup		FA Cup		Other	
	A	G	A	G	A	G	A	G
1969–70	5	0	0	0	1	0	-	-
TOTAL	5	0	0	0	1	0	-	-

PRICE, Raymond 'Ray'

Height: 5ft 10½in. Weight: 11st 7lb.

Born: 18 May 1944, Durham.

Died: 18 November 1990, Grimsby.

■ A former Norwich junior, where he made one League appearance, a very late deputy when tonsillitis incapacitated regular left-back Joe Mullett, Price joined the U's in the summer of 1964. He never established himself at Layer Road, and his most famous contribution to the history of Colchester United is as the first-ever substitute used by the U's. He

came on for Ted Phillips in the 2–0 home win over Rochdale on 18 September 1965. After the game with Doncaster in January 1966 it was found that he had broken his wrist, and his only subsequent first-team involvement was on the subs' bench, being called on just once in March 1967. Released in the summer, he took up badminton and formed a successful club in Norwich before relocating to Lincolnshire, where he was working as an insurance salesman when he suffered a fatal heart attack.

	League		Lge Cup		FA Cup		Other	
	A	G	A	G	A	G	A	G
1964–65	11	0	0	0	0	0	-	-
1965–66	4+1	0	0	0	0	0	-	-
1966–67	0+1	0	0	0	0	0	-	-
TOTAL	15+2	0	0	0	0	0	-	-

PRICE, Terrence Edmund 'Terry'

Height: 5ft 7in. Weight: 10st 10lb.

Born: 11 October 1945, Colchester.

■ Colchester born and bred, Price was snaffled by Leyton Orient, then briefly in the First Division, and progressed through the youth ranks, making his debut before his 19th birthday and scoring against Portsmouth on the opening day of the 1964–65 season. He represented England Youth in a tour to Tenerife. Price also acted as trainer for cash-strapped O's but faded like the team, and when Leyton were relegated in 1966–67 he joined United for a fee of £2,000. He suffered relegation in his first season at Layer Road, but played in the club's FA Cup run, which ended in defeat to West Brom in a replay after the eventual Cup winners had escaped by the skin of their teeth from joining the list of giants slain at Layer Road. Released by Dick Graham, he joined Chelmsford in 1969 and played in their FA Cup run of 1972–73, which ended in defeat to Ipswich. He also turned out for Barnet and Gravesend and had further spells at Chelmsford, latterly moving between New Writtle Street and Tiptree a couple of times. His 389 games for Chelmsford make him their seventh-highest appearance holder, and his 108 goals put him in fifth place in their all-time scoring charts. Renowned for his fitness, Price was still playing Eastern Counties League football in 1985 and still playing

in the local Sunday League many years after that. In 1993–94 he was back at Layer Road for a year as youth-team coach. From a long-established local family of fish and chip shop proprietors, he helped run the family's two shops and in 2007 is still heavily involved in sports and fitness coaching locally.

	League		Lge Cup		FA Cup		Other	
	A	G	A	G	A	G	A	G
1967–68	35	3	0	0	4	0	-	-
1968–69	19+2	2	2	0	1	0	-	-
TOTAL	54+2	5	2	0	5	0	-	-

PRITCHARD, Arthur Brynley

Height: 5ft 9in. Weight: 12st.

Born: 22 October 1917, Newport.
Died: December 2005, Newport.

■ One of three Welshman in U's early line-ups, Pritchard scored eight goals for Yeovil in season 1936–37, joining them midway through the season from Newport County, where he made four Football League appearances. Having started with Oakdale FC, Pritchard was only 24 when Davis signed him. Pritchard formed a deadly partnership with Alec Cheyne, and but for the war their prolific goalscoring would have surely catapulted Colchester into the Football League. A reservist, Pritchard was called to Edinburgh to re-join his regiment, the Royal Scots Greys, as soon as war was

declared, and that was the last heard of him on the football field. The Scots Greys were heavily involved in the fighting during the war, taking part in major campaigns in North Africa, Italy and later North-West Europe, and the local press twice erroneously reported Pritchard killed in action. Pritchard hit seven hat-tricks including two four-timers in two years, feats only bettered by Arthur Turner with eight and three respectively.

	League		Lge Cup		FA Cup		Other	
	A	G	A	G	A	G	A	G
1937–38	22	17	4	4	-	-	11	8
1938–39	40	34	3	3	2	1	14	6
1939–40	1	0	1	1	-	-	-	-
TOTAL	63	51	8	8	2	1	25	14

PUTNEY, Trevor Anthony

Height: 5ft 9in. Weight: 11st 8lb.

Born: 9 April 1960, Harold Hill.

■ Beginning his career with Brentwood & Warley, Putney was snapped up by Ipswich in September 1980 and made 94(+8) appearances, scoring eight goals as well as winning the Player of the Year award in 1983–84. He was transferred to Norwich in the summer of 1986 in a swap deal that saw John Deehan making the reverse move. He had been on the verge of England Under-21 honours but missed out to an ankle injury. At Carrow Road he featured 76(+9) times, netting nine League goals. He also reached the FA Cup semi-final in 1988–89 with the Canaries. A fee of £300,000 realised a move to Middlesbrough, where Putney suffered a broken leg in a game against Aston Villa, which kept him out for eight months. During his spell on the sidelines

he missed the opportunity to play in the Zenith Data Systems Final against Chelsea at Wembley. Completing 45(+3) games for Boro, with a solitary League goal, Putney's next move came in August 1991, when he signed for Watford for £100,000, with Willie Falconer moving to Teesside as well. Two years later, having played 42(+10) games for the Hornets scoring twice, he was on the move again, joining Leyton Orient for £40,000. As a former Ipswich colleague of George Burley, he was tempted to Layer Road, initially on loan, in August 1994. Putney had already made his mind up that he was going to retire from football and work in the financial services sector in London, and this he duly did at the end of his only season at Layer Road. He coached Romford for a spell and worked part-time as a statistician for the Press Association.

	League		**Lge Cup**		**FA Cup**		**Other**	
	A	G	A	G	A	G	A	G
1994–95	28	2	0	0	2	0	0	0
TOTAL	28	2	0	0	2	0	0	0

R

RADFORD, Mark

Height: 6ft 1in. Weight: 11st 8lb.

Born: 20 December 1968, Leicester.

■ Radford progressed through United's youth policy and made his first appearance in a Sherpa Van Trophy tie at Gillingham in January 1987. Radford netted his first goal in a 2–1 home defeat to Darlington in November 1988 that put United bottom of the entire League for the first time since 1972. They battled the season out with the Quakers, and it was Radford's assist that enabled the U's to turn the tables and win 2–1 at Feethams in a crucial game in April 1989 that culminated in Colchester staying up. Despite scoring four times in the following campaign, United were relegated to the Conference, and Radford was a peripheral figure as new manager Ian Atkins attempted to lead the club straight back into the League. Radford was released on deadline day 1991 and, after a time out of football, resumed playing with Wivenhoe and then Bury Town.

	League		Lge Cup		FA Cup		Other	
	A	G	A	G	A	G	A	G
1986–87	0	0	0	0	0	0	0+1	0
1987–88	12+2	0	0	0	0	0	1	0
1988–89	16+14	1	0+1	0	2+2	0	1	0
1989–90	19+1	4	2	0	0	0	1	0
1990–91	*1+3*	*0*	*1+1*	*0*	*0*	*0*	*0*	*0*
TOTAL	47+17	5	2+1	0	2+2	0	3+1	0
	1+3	*0*	*1+1*	*0*	*0*	*0*	*0*	*0*

RAINE, David

Height: 5ft 10in. Weight: 11st 6lb.

Born: 28 March 1937, Darlington.

■ Raine signed as a full-back for Port Vale in May 1957 and appeared 144 times during his spell in Burslem. In the summer of 1962 he transferred to Doncaster, where he completed another 107 starts and scored his first two goals. Neil Franklin signed him for Colchester, and he helped his new side to promotion back to the Third Division in his first season. He continued to be a squad player during the following season and was released at the end of the term. After playing a spell with Burton Albion, he became a joiner, retiring from football with an arthritic hip.

	League		Lge Cup		FA Cup		Other	
	A	G	A	G	A	G	A	G
1965–66	19+3	0	1	0	2	0	-	-
1966–67	25+1	0	0	0	1	0	-	-
TOTAL	44+4	0	1	0	3	0	-	-

RAINFORD, David John

Height: 6ft. Weight: 11st 11lb.

Born: 21 April 1979, Stepney.

■ Midfield playmaker Rainford became a U's apprentice in 1995 and started 75 of the 77 games played by the Under-18s in the two years of his apprenticeship. Rewarded with a one-year professional

contract in July 1997, he was loaned out to Wivenhoe Town to gain experience of men's football. Retained for a second year he made his one and only appearance as a substitute in a 2–1 defeat at York in September 1998. At the turn of the year, he went out on loan to Third Division Scarborough, making two League appearances from the bench, plus a full game in the Auto Windscreens Shield, and by the time he returned to Layer Road, Mick Wadsworth, the man who borrowed him, had already made the same journey. Rainford was one of several players released by Wadsworth to make way for his own men, and so he embarked on a non-League career with Slough, Grays, Heybridge, Bishop's Stortford, where he was Player of the Year in 2004–05, and Dagenham & Redbridge. He was a vital part of Daggers' Conference-winning side in 2006–07 and was in the Essex side's team as they entered the Football League for the first time in 2007–08, still as a part-timer, combining football with teaching duties. Rainford joined Chelmsford in the summer of 2008.

	League		Lge Cup		FA Cup		Other	
	A	G	A	G	A	G	A	G
1998–99	0+1	0	0	0	0	0	0	0
TOTAL	0+1	0	0	0	0	0	0	0

RAMAGE, George McIntosh

Height: 6ft 2in. Weight: 13st 4lb.

Born: 29 January 1937, Newbattle.

■ Ramage can consider himself unlucky to have been understudy to two

consistent goalkeepers during his career. First, he played second fiddle to Third Lanark's Jock Robertson, although he enjoyed a run to the Scottish Cup semi-finals of 1958–59, and then he was in competition with the evergreen Percy Ames. Ramage only cost a nominal fee when he crossed the Border, and the U's could have made a considerable profit when Nottingham Forest offered £4,500 for his signature. U's manager Neil Franklin turned it down but just two months later gave the player a free transfer at the end of 1963–64. Former Colchester boss, Benny Fenton, who signed Ramage originally, grabbed him for Leyton Orient but, after just five League and Cup appearances, a change of manager ended his Brisbane Road career. Dave Sexton showed him the door, and he spent a short time with Luton, notching up seven League appearances, before moving into non-League with Dartford and Dover. He was then on his travels, spending five months playing for Hamilton Steelers in Canada, before emigrating to Australia in July 1967. From his new home Woonona, 50 miles from Sydney, he played for South Coast United, who were crowned New South Wales Champions in 1969. He later played for St George's Bucharest, while plying his trade as an electrician.

	League		Lge Cup		FA Cup		Other	
	A	G	A	G	A	G	A	G
1962–63	12	0	0	0	0	0	-	-
1963–64	26	0	3	0	2	0	-	-
TOTAL	38	0	3	0	2	0	-	-

RANKIN, Isaiah

Height: 5ft 10in. Weight: 11st.

Born: 22 May 1978, Edmonton.

■ Schooled by Arsenal in their YTS scheme, Rankin was given his big break when joining Colchester on a three-month loan in September 1997. He scored in only his third start at Peterborough and signed off with a double in a stunning 4–4 Boxing Day draw against Brighton at Gillingham's Priestfield Stadium. With aspirations of making the big time, Rankin returned to Highbury and made his debut as a substitute in the North London derby with Spurs. First Division Bradford paid £1.3 million for him in August 1998 and the Bantams won promotion to the Premiership in his first season. This limited Rankin's opportunities somewhat, as City's board sought to buy survival with a string of big-money signings. He was loaned out to second-tier clubs Birmingham, in January 2000, scoring four times in 11(+ 2) games, and Bolton in August of the same year, bagging two goals in 9(+7) games. When Bradford were relegated at the end of the campaign, Rankin had already left in the January for Barnsley in a £350,000 deal. Of his 15(+22) appearances at Valley Parade, only 10 substitute appearances were in the top flight. He failed to make any impression at Oakwell as Barnsley were themselves relegated to the Division Two. During three and a half seasons, he made 18(+29) appearances, scoring eight times. In February 2004 he signed for Grimsby, netting four times in the 12 games to the end of the campaign. Moving back to the capital, Rankin joined Brentford in the summer of 2004 and suffered Play-off agony in successive seasons, establishing himself with 64(+18) League appearances and a return of 15 goals. As Brentford re-grouped their squad, Rankin rejoined Grimsby in the 2006 close season to play 16(+5) games, scoring twice, and was loaned to Macclesfield in March 2007 to play 1(+3) times. On 31 January 2008 he joined Conference club Stevenage on a free transfer.

	League		Lge Cup		FA Cup		Other	
	A	G	A	G	A	G	A	G
1997–98	10+1	5	0	0	0	0	1	0
TOTAL	10+1	5	0	0	0	0	1	0

RAPLEY, Kevin John

Height: 5ft 10in. Weight: 12st 2lb.

Born: 21 September 1977, Reading.

■ A youth trainee at Brentford, Rapley signed full forms for Brentford in July 1998. Scoring nine goals in 23(+14) appearances in the 1997–98 season, he could not prevent the Bees from relegation. He became a squad player the following season, as Brentford stormed to the Third Division title, and was loaned out to Southend in November 1998, scoring four times at Roots Hall in nine League starts. He attracted a bid from Notts County and joined the Meadow Lane club for £50,000 in the following February. Finding the net just four times in 21(+31) appearances, he was sent out on loan to Exeter in November 2000 and Scunthorpe on deadline day 2003. He failed to score at either club and was released by Notts on a free transfer in the summer. Steve

Whitton brought the player to Layer Road, and he could not have had a better start scoring on his debut in an astonishing opening day 6–3 win at Chesterfield. Scoring a creditable 10 goals in his first season, Rapley formed an effective partnership with Scott McGleish but was released at the end of 2002–03. He moved to Chester and was in their successful Conference Championship winning squad for 2003–04. Back in the Football League, he scored twice in 12(+9) outings before returning to the non-League scene, on loan, with Conference side Forest Green Rovers. In the summer of 2005 he signed for Droylsden and ended up a Conference North Play-off finalist. For 2007–08 Rapley was on the books of Conference North side Leigh RMI, after his eight goals helped them stave off relegation in the previous campaign. In January 2008 he had a spell with Vauxhall Motors before joining Witton Albion on a permanent deal.

	League		Lge Cup		FA Cup		Other	
	A	G	A	G	A	G	A	G
2001–02	26+9	10	2	0	2	0	1	0
2002–03	14+7	2	0+1	0	1	0	1	0
TOTAL	40+16	12	2+1	0	3	0	2	0

RAWCLIFFE, Frank

Born: 10 December 1921, Blackburn.
Died: December 1986, Blackburn.

■ Rawcliffe represented Chester Schoolboys at the tender age of just 12 and after a spell on Tranmere's books as an amateur turned professional with Wolves in January 1939, being signed to

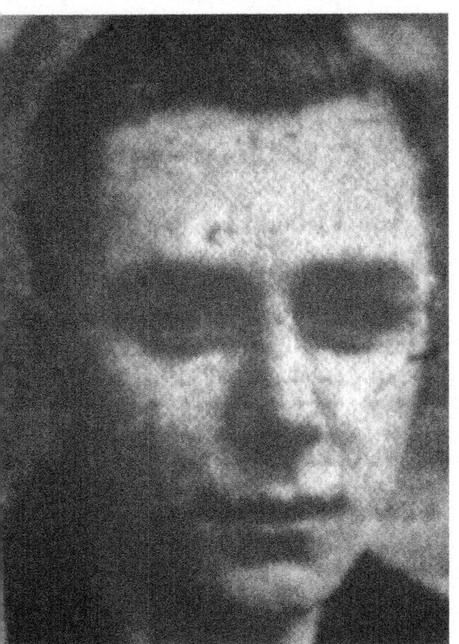

them while guesting for Notts County from February 1943 to February 1944. He later made one guest appearance for his home-town club in 1945–46, and scored, before he appeared at Layer Road in February 1945 and was signed as a professional by the U's in mid-March 1946. Rawcliffe was an ever present until 2 May but refused the terms offered by United for the following season and went looking for a new club, guesting and scoring for Newport County in a late season game. The U's transfer listed him at £500 but took £250 from Newport on 11 May 1946, and in 1946–47 he netted 16 goals in 37 appearances, prompting Swansea to move for him. After his usual one-season stop and 17 goals in 25 games, he was on his travels again, this time to Aldershot, where he spent 1948–49, scoring 14 times in 35 games for the Shots. At the end of the season, he went to Italy for a year, playing for Serie B club Alessandria, where he continued his goalscoring prowess, with 18 in 27 games. His team, however, finished 18th of 22 and were one of five teams relegated to Serie C. Rawcliffe did not stay around to find out how the third tier in Italy compared to the third tier in England and ended his playing career with South Liverpool.

	League		Lge Cup		FA Cup		Other	
	A	G	A	G	A	G	A	G
1945–46	2	0	9	3	0	0	-	-
TOTAL	2	0	9	3	0	0	-	-

RAY, John Walter

Height: 6ft 3in. Weight: 12st 2lb.

Born: 21 November 1968, Newmarket.

■ Centre-half Ray first played for the U's Border League side as a schoolboy and was part of the youth squad as the U's returned to the South East Counties League in 1985, although he was not taken on as a trainee until a couple of months into the season. At the start of 1987–88, with just a couple of months left as an apprentice and just a couple of reserve games to his name, it did not look like Ray would be at Layer Road much longer, but he made considerable progress in those couple of months, as he grew to his strength and impressed manager Roger Brown, himself a centre-half, enough to be given a full contract to the end of the season with a year's option. After sitting on the bench a few times, he

got his one and only League outing in January 1988 as a second-half replacement at Scarborough, where he handled to give them their third goal from the penalty spot as struggling United lost 3–1. He spent time on loan at Wycombe, along with Scott Young, later that season, and new boss Mike Walker did not take up his contract option. Subsequently, Ray had a long career in South Essex non-League circles. Aveley, Barking, Billericay, Ford, Grays, Romford and Tilbury all saw his services, and he was still active 15 years after leaving Layer Road.

	League		Lge Cup		FA Cup		Other	
	A	G	A	G	A	G	A	G
1987–88	0+1	0	0	0	0	0	0	0
TOTAL	0+1	0	0	0	0	0	0	0

REES, Mark

Height: 5ft 10in. Weight: 11st 10lb.

Born: 13 October 1961, Smethwick.

■ An England Schoolboy international, Rees signed apprenticeship forms with Walsall in August 1978. A winger by trade, he made 188(+49) League appearances, scoring 37 goals. While at Fellows Park, Rees was a colleague of Roy McDonough and later helped the Saddlers to promotion via the Play-offs in 1987 and scored the winner as Walsall beat Arsenal at Highbury in the 1984 League Cup. Two successive relegations at the end of the 1980s saw Rees released by Walsall. After a hamstring operation during the summer, he arrived at Layer Road on a weekly basis on 3 September 1990 and played for the reserves a couple of days later. He stayed for a month,

making one substitute appearance in a 3–1 win over Cheltenham. Rees then embarked on a nomadic existence, playing in Luxembourg, in Ireland for Shamrock Rovers, before returning to the UK with Aldershot, Dover, Shrewsbury, Solihull and Stafford.

	League		Lge Cup		FA Cup		Other	
	A	G	A	G	A	G	A	G
1990–91	0+1	0	0	0	0	0	0	0
TOTAL	0+1	0	0	0	0	0	0	0

REEVES, John Charles

Height: 5ft 7in. Weight: 9st 12lb.

Born: 8 July 1963, Hackney.

■ Reeves joined Fulham as an apprentice in July 1979, securing a professional contract two years later. He made his debut for Fulham in January 1982 but broke his arm in 1983–84 and struggled to regain his place. Reeves made 12(+5) League and Cup

appearances for the Cottagers. Signed by Cyril Lea in August 1985, he made his U's debut in the opening day 3–1 win over Stockport but dislocated his shoulder at Crewe in October 1986. Reeves enjoyed three seasons in the Colchester midfield before being released by Roger Brown. He moved onto the non-League circuit, spending 1988–89 in the Conference with Enfield and then joining Diss Town, before heading out to the States with Los Angeles Heat. On his return, he played locally in the Eastern Counties League including spells with Cornard United and Halstead and in 2007–08 was assistant manager at Clacton Town.

	League		Lge Cup		FA Cup		Other	
	A	G	A	G	A	G	A	G
1985–86	24	4	2	0	1	0	0	0
1986–87	16+1	2	2	0	0+1	0	0	0
1987–88	18+2	1	0+2	0	1	0	2	0
TOTAL	58+3	7	4+2	0	2+1	0	2	0

REEVES

■ Reeves was a Private in the 15th Infantry Training Corps and while on the books of Swansea as an amateur had also turned out for Cheltenham and Gloucester. He made a handful of appearances in various positions for the U's in the first few weeks after the war, being seen at centre-forward, outside-right and right-half, and was only called on once after the end of September. His only Colchester goal came in the first League match at Layer Road after the war when he was a late deputy in a 4–3 defeat by Chelmsford on 1 September 1945.

	League		Lge Cup		FA Cup		Other	
	A	G	A	G	A	G	A	G
1945–46	5	1	0	0	0	0	-	-
TOTAL	5	1	0	0	0	0	-	-

REINELT, Robert Squire 'Robbie'

Height: 5ft 10in. Weight: 11st 3lb.

Born: 11 March 1974, Enfield.

■ Reinelt began his career at Aldershot in 1990 as a YTS player. He made his Shots debut later that season and played 3(+2) games before the club was forced to quit the League on financial grounds. The young striker passed under the noses of Colchester when joining local side Wivenhoe Town. He was picked up by Gillingham in March 1993, scoring five times in 34(+18) Third Division games.

U's boss Steve Wignall snapped up the player on a free transfer on deadline day 1995 in a deal that saw U's forward Steve Brown move to Kent. Ironically Reinelt made his debut as a substitute against Gills in a 3–1 win in the same month and also had scored twice for Gills at Layer Road during the season, once against United and the other against Heybridge Swifts in a neutral venue FA Cup tie. He helped Colchester to the Play-offs in the 1995–96 season and was second-leading League scorer behind Tony Adcock. He remained at Layer Road until February 1997, when he joined Brighton for £15,000. He will always be fondly remembered by Albion fans as the scorer of the goal at Hereford on the last day of the 1996–97 season that prevented the club from dropping in to the Conference. Securing cult status in just 32(+12) games, scoring seven goals, Reinelt moved to Leyton Orient in August 1998 on a non-contract basis but made just 2(+5) starts. Not retained, he joined Stevenage in the September, but by January 1999 he was plying his trade with St Albans. In 2000–01 he banged in over 30 goals for Braintree and later played for Aldershot, Grays Athletic, Maldon Town, Ford United (aka Redbridge) and Borehamwood.

	League		Lge Cup		FA Cup		Other	
	A	G	A	G	A	G	A	G
1994–95	2+3	0	0	0	0	0	0	0
1995–96	12+10	7	0+1	0	0	0	3	1
1996–97	8+13	3	4	2	1	0	0	0
TOTAL	22+26	10	4+1	2	1	0	3	1

RESTARICK, Steven Leonard James 'Steve'

Height: 5ft 10in. Weight: 11st.

Born: 28 November 1971, Barking.

■ A former QPR schoolboy and briefly a West Ham trainee, Restarick switched to the U's shortly after the start of his apprenticeship in 1988–89 and in his second year of youth-team football hit a purple patch from October 1989 up to Christmas, when he scored 17 times in 15 games, including a four-timer on his 18th birthday. His one and only Football League appearance came as a substitute at Peterborough in April 1990, as a 1–0 defeat helped push the U's ever closer to relegation, but he was taken on as a pro for the Conference campaign. Briefly loaned to Bury Town in autumn 1990, he scored twice in extra-time, as an experimental United side beat Fisher 3–2 in a January 1991 Bob Lord Trophy tie, before a longer loan at Fisher in March 1991 when he played 11 games and scored once. He was accompanied to the Surrey Docks Stadium by young U's defender John Pollard. Restarick bagged goals in three Cup competitions in United's Conference and FA Trophy double-winning season but found the step up to the first team beyond him and spent a chunk of the year on loan at Wivenhoe, where he finished leading scorer with 11 goals in 17 games. Released as Colchester won back their League status, he joined Chelmsford and scored 23 goals in 1992–93, including a five-timer in an Essex Senior Cup tie with Billericay. His eventual tally was 59 goals in 149 games for the county town before joining Dover (1994–96) for a five-figure fee, where he scored four times in 22(+4) Conference games. Next, he moved to Crawley for the 1996–97 season and was at Dulwich Hamlet in April 1998. After playing for Welling in April 2001, he joined Gravesend & Northfleet a month later. A second spell with Crawley began in the summer of 2001 but by January 2002 Restarick was turning out for Dartford. Loaned to Hastings Town in March 2002, the player decided to try his luck at Folkestone in August 2002 before becoming player-coach of Maidstone three months later. In April 2003 he played for Chatham Town and was back at Maidstone as coach in 2006.

	League		Lge Cup		FA Cup		Other	
	A	G	A	G	A	G	A	G
1989–90	0+1	0	0	0	0	0	0	0
1990–91	*0*	*0*	*0+2*	*2*	*0*	*0*	*0*	*0*
1991–92	*1+6*	*0*	*1*	*1*	*0+2*	*1*	*2*	*1*
TOTAL	0+1	0	0	0	0	0	0	0
	1+6	*0*	*1+2*	*3*	*0+2*	*1*	*2*	*1*

RICHARD, Fabrice

Height: 6ft 1in. Weight: 13st.

Born: 16 August 1973, Saintes, France.

■ Richard was another one of Mick Wadsworth's foreign imports of dubious provenance and from dubious sources. Originally with French side AS Cannes, Richard appeared at Layer Road on 10 March 1999 trialling in a reserve game against Cambridge United. In a game dominated by a Lua Lua hat-trick, and won very comfortably 6–1, he was not properly tested, and at best he was worth another look at because he had not done anything wrong, but he was signed up immediately after the game and made his League debut at Bournemouth in the same month. His arrival spelt the end for Joe Dunne, and he was still continued to be used by Steve Whitton following Wadsworth's departure, despite hardly being able to speak a word of English. The language barrier led to some comical moments, particularly noticeable in reserve games, where the lack of a lingua franca between 'keeper and defender was all too easy for the few present to hear. In March 2000 he was released on trial to Sochaux and later played for Paris-based Red Star until the end of 2001–02.

	League		Lge Cup		FA Cup		Other	
	A	G	A	G	A	G	A	G
1998–99	10	0	0	0	0	0	0	0
1999–2000	13+1	0	0+1	0	1	0	0	0
TOTAL	23+1	0	0+1	0	1	0	0	0

RICHARDS, Garry

Height: 6ft 3in. Weight: 13st.

Born: 11 June 1986, Romford.

■ Richards was thrown into a surprise debut in a live, televised game at Bristol City in September 2005, following injury to Sam Stockley in the warm up. Richards's job was made all the more difficult when fellow defender Wayne Brown was sent off. A strapping lad, Richards had progressed through United's youth ranks and spent a brief loan spell with Gravesend & Northfleet in 2005. His first League goal gave the U's a 1–0 win over Preston in January 2007, but after a difficult time in the local derby at Ipswich, where the lack of regular match practice caused by the erratic fixture list of the Football Combination seemed to catch up with him, he joined ex-U's favourite Scott Fitzgerald's struggling Brentford on loan. A couple of years earlier, Richards had been cleaning Fitzgerald's boots, and now he played a leading role in trying to save his side from relegation. Richards played 10 games, scoring once, before injury sidelined him, but he made a good impression on the locals and many were hoping he would make the move permanent. Richards came back to Colchester, but when he saw the club taking young central-defenders like Matt Connolly and Bela Balogh on season-long loans he asked to be allowed to try for a permanent first-team place elsewhere and League One Southend, whose boss Steve Tilson knew all about

Richards from his days as Southend's youth-team coach, snapped him up for £50,000 on the eve of the 2007–08 season. A regular first-team spot eluded him at Roots Hall as well, and he moved to Gillingham in January 2008.

	League		Lge Cup		FA Cup		Other	
	A	G	A	G	A	G	A	G
2005–06	12+2	0	0	0	1	0	3	0
2006–07	3+2	1	0	0	0	0	-	-
TOTAL	15+4	1	0	0	0	0	3	0

RICHARDS, Justin Donovan

Height: 5ft 10in. Weight: 11st.

Born: 16 October 1980, Sandwell.

■ Richards was brought to Layer Road by Steve Whitton in October 2002 from Bristol Rovers in an exchange loan deal that saw Colchester's record signing, Adrian Coote, go to The Memorial Ground. Earlier, Richards had been an apprentice at West Brom in July 1997, signing professional forms in January 1999. Making just one substitute appearance at The Hawthorns, the England Under-18 international moved to Rovers in January 2001 for a fee of £75,000. Making 3(+13) appearances before arriving at Layer Road, he had already been loaned to non-League Newport, and expectations were that the change would be a new start for both Richards and Coote, both of whom had disappointed. He made little impression at Layer Road and returned to Bristol but was sold to Stevenage in March 2003 for £1,500. In 21(+23) Conference appearances he scored nine goals before moving to Woking in August 2004. He rekindled his League career with 35 goals in 79 Conference games at Woking and signed for Peterborough in July 2006 but after featuring 4(+9) times, scoring once, was loaned to Grays Athletic in the November and relegation-bound League side Boston United for three games in January 2007. Released by Peterborough, he signed for Conference side Kidderminster for the 2007–08 season, before returning to Oxford in January 2008.

	League		Lge Cup		FA Cup		Other	
	A	G	A	G	A	G	A	G
2002–03	0+2	0	0	0	0	0	0+1	0
TOTAL	0+2	0	0	0	0	0	0+1	0

RICHARDSON, John

Born: 28 July 1966, Durham.

■ Richardson signed for Colchester in September 1993 from Chesham United

on non-contract forms and made his debut as a substitute in a 4–1 win over Bury at Layer Road. His only start came against Walsall in November, and soon after he was released and returned to the Ryman League.

	League		Lge Cup		FA Cup		Other	
	A	G	A	G	A	G	A	G
1993–94	1+7	0	0	0	0	0	1+1	0
TOTAL	1+7	0	0	0	0	0	1+1	0

RIGHTON

■ A soldier in the 16th Infantry Training Corps, Righton scored on his Colchester debut in the 5–0 win over Barry Town in February 1946. His only other game was a week later at Swindon reserves. He was attached to non-Leaguers Banbury Spencer but was not part of their team when they came to Layer Road in the FA Cup as part of the 1947–48 Cup run.

	League		Lge Cup		FA Cup		Other	
	A	G	A	G	A	G	A	G
1945–46	2	1	0	0	0	0	-	-
TOTAL	2	1	0	0	0	0	-	-

RIST, Frank Henry

Born: 30 March 1914, Leyton.

Died: 9 September 2001, Highams Park.

■ Rist began playing with Grays Athletic and joined Clapton Orient in 1932. Without making the first team, he was transferred to Charlton in June 1933 and played in 47 League games at The Valley, scoring one goal. His main playing years were interrupted by the war, but he managed to feature during wartime thus: 1939–40 Clapton Orient (31 appearances/0 goals), Norwich (2/0); 1940–41 Bradford (6/0), Clapton Orient (1/0); 1941–42 Bradford (13/0); 1942–43 Southport (17/1), Liverpool (8/0), Walsall (1/0); 1943–44 Walsall (25/0); 1944–45 Walsall (21/0); 1945–46 Charlton (16/0) and Luton (4/0). In his one season at Colchester Rist was reserve centre-half to first Albert Page then Ted Fenton and was restricted to just 13 appearances. His only goal came from the penalty spot in a Southern League Cup tie at Bedford in October 1947. On leaving Layer Road, Rist turned out for non-League Tonbridge and also represented Essex first XI at cricket. In all, he played 65 first-class matches for the County, mainly as wicketkeeper, and averaged 15 runs. He then became coach to the team.

	League		Lge Cup		FA Cup		Other	
	A	G	A	G	A	G	A	G
1947–48	10	0	3	1	0	0	-	-
TOTAL	10	0	3	1	0	0	-	-

RITCHIE, George Thompson

Height: 5ft 10in. Weight: 12st.

Born: 16 January 1904, Maryhill.

Died: 10 September 1978, Leicester.

■ A Scotsman by birth, Ritchie had the unique distinction of being the only U's player who could play the bagpipes. Starting his playing career at Scottish junior side Maryhill, Ritchie moved to Blackburn in 1922, where he made just two appearances. Returning to his native Scotland, he represented Royal Albert and Falkirk before being signed by Leicester City in 1928. In eight seasons at Filbert Street he played in 247 League games, scoring 12 goals, as City won promotion to the First Division and reached the 1934–35 FA Cup semi-finals.

Given a free transfer, and despite overtures from both Derby and Motherwell, he opted to join the newly-formed Colchester United where, with his vast experience, he was appointed club captain. Lifting the Southern League Cup, he won further honours when selected for the Southern League representative side that met the Cheshire League at Sealand Road, Chester in October 1937. In his second season he coached and skippered the U's reserves to the Eastern Counties League Championship and to the ECL Cup Final, which was held over to 1939–40 and was the only reserve game played that season. Ritchie, a certified masseur and having qualified with St John's Ambulance, left Layer Road at the end of 1938–39 to take up the position of assistant coach and trainer to Ipswich's Southern League reserve side. After the war, he was trainer at Leicester City.

	League		Lge Cup		FA Cup		Other	
	A	G	A	G	A	G	A	G
1937–38	20	1	4	0	-	-	8	0
1938–39	0	0	1	0	0	0	0	0
TOTAL	20	1	5	0	0	0	8	0

ROBERTS, Daniel 'Danny'

Height: 5ft 8in. Weight: 10st 8lb.

Born: 12 November 1975, Chelmsford.

■ George Burley was forced into giving youth-team product Roberts his first-team debut due to injuries and suspensions at the very beginning of his spell in the Layer Road hot seat. Predominantly a right-sided wide man, Roberts was also effective at right-back and after sitting on the bench on the first day of the season came on as substitute

in the next game, the 1994–95 first leg League Cup tie with Brentford, replacing winger Chris Fry. He then played the full 90 minutes of the return, a game in which Burley had to put himself and a trialist from Scotland on the bench. The U's lost both legs 2–0, and Roberts failed to feature any further in United's first-team line-up. He moved into non-League and played for Grays, Sudbury, Chelmsford, Clacton, Harwich & Parkeston, Heybridge Swifts and Wivenhoe.

	League		Lge Cup		FA Cup		Other	
	A	G	A	G	A	G	A	G
1994–95	0	0	1+1	0	0	0	0	0
TOTAL	0	0	1+1	0	0	0	0	0

ROBERTS, Paul

Height: 5ft 9in. Weight: 11st 13lb.

Born: 27 April 1962, West Ham.

■ A member of Millwall's 1979 FA Youth Cup-winning side, Roberts signed his apprenticeship four days before his 16th birthday and full terms a year later in April 1979. He made 142(+4) appearances for the Lions and was club captain. The arrival of George Graham as manager forced a squad reshuffle, and Roberts was sold to Brentford for £10,000 in September 1983. At Griffin Park he played 61(+1) times before leaving these shores to play in Finland for Kouvola during the summer of 1985. He returned for the winter and secured a contract at Swindon, where he played 25(+2) times and won a Fourth Division Championship medal. The next season was spent at Southend, where he made 38 starts, this time earning Fourth Division promotion in third place. Despite the Shrimpers' rise, he joined fellow Third Division outfit Aldershot, playing 36(+3) times. A spell outside of League football with Leytonstone & Ilford preceded a December 1988 move to Exeter, where he played just three games. In January 1989 he returned to Roots Hall and added a further 53(+1) games to his record and another third-placed Southend promotion. Released to Fisher Athletic, Roberts was signed by his old teammate Roy McDonough for £750 and was a stalwart as United won the non-League double, capping the season with a Wembley FA Trophy win over Witton Albion. November 1992 was a

momentous month as Roberts scored the only goal of his professional career in a 2–1 win over Carlisle at Layer Road. Determined to keep his ever present record after being written off as a Football League player, Roberts persuaded his mate McDonough to let him play at Crewe at the end of April 1993 while suffering the after-effects of flu. Roberts was way off the pace and Tony Naylor gave him a torrid time, scoring five as the U's lost 7–1. With legs clearly failing, Roberts studied 'The Knowledge' and became a London black cab driver, while playing out his days with Chesham United. He had a brief spell at Chelmsford as player and assistant manager when McDonough was in charge there.

	League		Lge Cup		FA Cup		Other	
	A	G	A	G	A	G	A	G
1991–92	*34*	*1*	*2*	*0*	*0*	*0*	*9*	*0*
1992–93	42	1	2	0	3	0	2	0
1993–94	21	0	2	0	1	0	2	0
TOTAL	63	1	4	0	4	0	4	0
	34	*1*	*2*	*0*	*0*	*0*	*9*	*0*

ROBERTS, Robert 'Bobby'

Height: 5ft 9in. Weight: 11st 4lb.

Born: 2 September 1940, Leicester.

■ Roberts joined Leicester from Motherwell for £40,000 in September 1963, despite interest from Rangers and Ipswich, having gained Scottish Under-23 honours against Wales in 1962 and a Scottish League representative cap against the Irish League. At Leicester he scored in both legs of the 1963–64 League Cup semi-final but was unfortunate to miss the Final itself. He did, however, play in the 1969

FA Cup Final when the Foxes lost to Manchester City. After 25 goals in 225(+6) starts for City, the left-sided midfielder was transferred to Mansfield in September 1970. At Field Mill he made 76(+4) appearances and netted four times before becoming youth-team coach at Coventry. At first he was reluctant to leave Highfield Road but new U's boss Jim Smith finally got his man, and Roberts took up his duties at Layer Road on 1 March 1973. Roberts was registered as a player and had to help out as an emergency substitute on two occasions late in the 1972–73 season. Alongside Smith, the pair engineered United's promotion to Division Three in 1973–74, and when Smith left to join Blackburn, Roberts was the natural choice as his successor in the Layer Road hot seat. His first full season in charge was difficult as United were relegated back to Division Four in 1975–76. He had to field himself in a League Cup tie at Crystal Palace that season, but he turned the situation around, winning promotion at the first attempt. Despite almost leading United to the Second Division in 1979–80, he could not prevent the cash-strapped club from relegation at the end of 1980–81. Asked to resign in April 1982, Roberts refused and was sacked. He immediately found a new job at Wrexham in June 1982 and was even forced to play in goal, aged 43, in a Welsh Cup tie against Worcester. He was in charge when Wrexham famously beat FC Porto in the 1984–85 European Cup-winners' Cup but Wrexham failed to rise out of the Fourth Division, prompting Roberts's departure in March 1985. He coached in Kuwait for two years before returning to the UK to manage Grimsby in July 1987. After a tough season, in which the Mariners continued their fall from Second to Fourth Division, he became coach at Leicester in the summer of 1988. Holding the position for three years, he then took up a scouting position at Newcastle. He teamed up again with Jim Smith, as chief scout, at Derby in the mid-1990s and followed him to Conference side Oxford in 2006.

* *See also Who's Who Managers section*

	League		Lge Cup		FA Cup		Other	
	A	G	A	G	A	G	A	G
1972–73	0+2	0	0	0	0	0	-	-
1973–74	0	0	0	0	0	0	-	-
1974–75	0	0	0	0	0	0	-	-
1975–76	0	0	1	0	0	0	-	-
TOTAL	0+2	0	1	0	0	0	-	-

ROBINSON, John Allan 'Jackie'

Born: 10 June 1917, Shiremoor.
Died: 31 July 1972, Shiremoor.

■ Spotted in a junior game on Tyneside, by Sheffield Wednesday boss Billy Walker, Robinson was signed immediately. He made his Wednesday debut on 22 April 1935 and went on to make 120 League and Cup appearances, scoring 39 goals. Within weeks of making his debut, he was invited to an England trial and earned his first cap against Finland in May 1937, scoring in the 8–0 win. His best League season was 1938–39 when he scored 19 as Wednesday just missed out on promotion to the top flight. It was the wartime seasons that Robinson really made his mark. He scored 90 goals in just over a 100 games. During 1942–43 he bagged 35 in 32 games, including six hat-tricks. It then came to light that he was actually two years older than he had let on when signing. 'Robbo', as he was known, played in the 1942–43 League North War Cup Final, losing to Blackpool by 4–3 on aggregate. The latter stages of the war took its effect on Robinson, and his fondness for a drink meant that on one occasion he was so drunk that Wednesday would not let him play. Robinson spent 12 years at Hillsborough, and but for the intervention of war would have made an even bigger impact than that he did. His other England caps came against Germany and Sweden in 1938 and Wales in 1939. Robinson held the rank of Corporal in the 16th Infantry Training Corps in Colchester and scored in both his competitive games for Colchester, the first home game after the war against Chelmsford on 1 September 1945 and at home to Worcester at the end of November. During that season he also played once for both Ipswich and Southend and scored 11 in 19 games for Wednesday. Robinson returned to the North East on 7 October 1946, joining Sunderland, for whom he scored 32 goals in 82 League games. His League career finished at Lincoln in 1949, where he notched five goals in just eight games before breaking his leg on Christmas Eve.

	League		Lge Cup		FA Cup		Other	
	A	G	A	G	A	G	A	G
1945–46	2	3	0	0	0	0	-	-
TOTAL	2	3	0	0	0	0	-	-

ROBSON

■ An amateur on the books of York City, Robson was a Sergeant Instructor in the 16th Infantry Training Corps. He was another member of the Garrison whose U's career is compressed into the first few weeks after the post-war resumption, and he was not seen again after the 5–0 FA Cup defeat at Wisbech.

	League		Lge Cup		FA Cup		Other	
	A	G	A	G	A	G	A	G
1945–46	2	3	0	0	0	0	-	-
TOTAL	2	3	0	0	0	0	-	-

ROCHFORD, William 'Bill'

Height: 5ft 9½in. Weight: 13st.

Born: 27 May 1913, Newhouse.
Died: March 1984, County Durham.

■ Left-back Rochford joined Portsmouth at 17 from Esh Winning

Juniors, playing in their FA Cup-winning side of 1938–39 with future U's forward Bert Barlow. Between 1932 and the outbreak of war he figured in 140 League games for Pompey, scoring one goal. He was a regular in the War League at Fratton Park, playing 150 games with three goals scored. After the war he joined south-coast rivals Southampton, where he was captain for four seasons in 128 League fixtures. Signed by the U's for £1,000 in August 1950, he became the players' Football League rep. Rochford was injured in training before the season started and made just two appearances for United, deputising for the injured Bob Allen. His debut came against Northampton on 17 February 1951, and a week later in his final League appearance he had the misfortune to score an own-goal as United were trounced 5–0 at Exeter. Rochford moved to the North East, where he took on scouting duties for various clubs. From his Tow Law home he discovered (Sir) Bobby Robson playing for Durham side Langley Park Juniors and later became Southampton's North East Scout.

	League		Lge Cup		FA Cup		Other	
	A	G	A	G	A	G	A	G
1950–51	2	0	-	-	0	0	-	-
TOTAL	2	0	-	-	0	0	-	-

ROE, John

Born: 7 January 1938, Broxburn.
Died: February 1996, Wandsworth.

■ One of Benny Fenton's many Scottish signings, Roe was spotted playing for West Calder and signed as a part-time pro in July 1958. A regular in the Football Combination during his two seasons at Layer Road, Roe got just two first-team chances at the start of October 1959 when he stood in at right-back for John Laidlaw. Both games ended in defeat – the first at Norwich in front of almost 28,000, and the second at Brentford three days later. Roe returned to Scotland and trialled for Stirling Albion before signing for Dundee United and later moving to St Johnstone.

	League		Lge Cup		FA Cup		Other	
	A	G	A	G	A	G	A	G
1959–60	2	0	-	-	0	0	-	-
TOTAL	2	0	-	-	0	0	-	-

ROOKE, Rodney

Height: 5ft 5in. Weight: 10st 3lb.

Born: 7 April 1970, Orsett.

■ Diminutive full-back Rooke came to Layer Road as a trainee in 1986 and at the start of his second year was reported to be training with athletic specialist to try and add some extra pace to his undoubted skill. He did enough that year to be retained as a non-contract pro for 1988–89 and got his debut in a 2–1 Sherpa Van trophy win over Southend in December 1988, but otherwise he was confined to the reserves. The pre-season tour to Scotland in 1989 saw Rooke displace Clive Stafford as first-choice left-back for the first fortnight of 1989–90, but with the defence leaking goals, and 'daft' goals according to manager Jock Wallace, the inexperienced Rooke was the first to go and only got one further chance, when another four goals hit the U's net. Rooke was tried further forward in the reserves, but with Martin Grainger coming through from the youth team he left Layer Road at the turn of the year for near neighbours Wivenhoe. Chelmsford, Dagenham, Grays and Stambridge were among his other Essex non-League stops, as well as a second period at Wivenhoe, and after leaving the U's he was more likely to be seen in midfield than defence.

	League		Lge Cup		FA Cup		Other	
	A	G	A	G	A	G	A	G
1988–89	0	0	0	0	0	0	1	0
1989–90	4	0	2	0	0	0	0	0
TOTAL	4	0	2	0	0	0	1	0

ROOKES, Philip William 'Phil'

Height: 5ft 10in. Weight: 11st.

Born: 23 April 1919, Dulverton.
Died: February 2003.

■ Rookes starred for Portsmouth in the 1930s and 1940s. He played in the 1942 War Cup Final against Brentford at Wembley with future U's players Bert Barlow and Bill Rochford. He also gained two League Championship medals with Pompey. He had originally signed for Bradford City (11 appearances) as an apprentice from Worksop in 1937 after working in a brewery office. Pompey boss Jack Tinn

took him south as an 18-year-old, and he played in the 1939 FA Cup Final before taking Military Service on HMS *Argonaut*. Amassing 114 League appearances and 13 war League games for Pompey, plus one for Oldham, Rookes suffered a serious ankle injury in a 7–0 Cup win over Stockport in 1949 and never fully recovered, playing just six further games before being transferred to Colchester in July 1951. Returning to Hampshire, he managed Chichester City then became publican of the Anerley Arms and then the Dog and Duck in Fratton Road, both Portsmouth. Later, he became a sales rep and then a Norfolk postal worker, retiring in 1997.

	League		Lge Cup		FA Cup		Other	
	A	G	A	G	A	G	A	G
1951–52	25	0	-	-	3	0	-	-
1952–53	43	0	-	-	3	0	-	-
TOTAL	68	0	-	-	6	0	-	-

ROSS, Alan

■ Ross was a right-half who joined Ipswich from Scottish junior football in Dundee and played just one game in September 1945 for Town. Signing for Colchester in July 1946, Ross was considered a bit lightweight and was released in June 1947 after just three first-team games. He picked up an Eastern Counties League Cup-winners' medal with the reserves though and scored one of the goals in the 2–0 replay win over Harwich. After leaving Layer Road, he briefly took up the post of player-coach with Brantham Athletic.

	League		Lge Cup		FA Cup		Other	
	A	G	A	G	A	G	A	G
1946–47	3	0	0	0	0	0	-	-
TOTAL	3	0	0	0	0	0	-	-

ROWAN, Barry

Born: 24 April 1942, Willesden.

■ Winger Rowan, originally a Watford amateur, was signed professional by Brentford in October 1960 but failed to make any appearances. He joined Millwall in the summer of 1964 and scored 13 League goals in 72 appearances before moving into non-League with Dover. He plied his trade in the US during the summer months, playing for Detroit Cougars and Dallas Tornados. Dick Graham brought him to Layer Road in November 1968 on trial, and he signed a full contract at the start

of December but in mid-January after just two games requested his release so he could go to South Africa to play for Durban City. The club agreed and Rowan repaid his signing on fee. He briefly returned to the UK and played one game for Reading before joining Plymouth a month later in September 1969. After one goal in 10 games at Home Park he moved to Devon rivals Exeter and at last enjoyed some stability, turning out 76(+14) times for the Grecians and scoring 14 goals. One of those goals was against Colchester in a 3–3 draw at St James Park in April 1972. After playing non-League for Poole he later became a matchday host at Millwall and a London taxi driver.

	League		Lge Cup		FA Cup		Other	
	A	G	A	G	A	G	A	G
1968–69	2	0	0	0	1	0	-	-
TOTAL	2	0	0	0	1	0	-	-

ROWE, Colwyn Roger

Height: 5ft 7in. Weight: 11st 2lb.

Born: 22 March 1956, Ipswich.

■ Rowe progressed through United's youth ranks, signing pro at the end of October 1973, and made his debut as a substitute in Colchester's second-ever Sunday fixture, at Bury in February 1974. Spending much of the following season on the bench, he made the most of his four senior starts by bagging goals against Halifax and at Gillingham in successive April 1975 fixtures. Freed in 1975, he spent the first month of 1975–76 on trial at Gillingham joining Chelmsford when nothing came of it. By

1976–77 he was at Hadleigh United and spent several seasons there before having a brief second spell at Chelmsford then settling again with Felixstowe. He later managed Ipswich Wanderers (2000), Woodbridge (2004) and was assistant at Heybridge and then Sudbury in 2004–05. In August 2006, after a period spreading the word as an FA coach in Jordan, he became manager of the Botswana national side.

	League		Lge Cup		FA Cup		Other	
	A	G	A	G	A	G	A	G
1973–74	0+1	0	0	0	0	0	-	-
1974–75	4+7	2	0	0	0	0	-	-
TOTAL	4+8	2	0	0	0	0	-	-

ROWLANDS, Trevor Ivor

Height: 5ft 10in. Weight: 11st.

Born: 2 February 1922, Wallston, South Glamorgan.

Died: 22 July 1973, Norwich.

■ A Welsh Schoolboy international centre-half, Rowlands joined Norwich from Cardiff City on 16 August 1946 after just one game for the Bluebirds during the transitional 1945–46 season. A regular in the Carrow Road reserve team – 103 appearances and 11 goals – Rowlands made 10 first-team League appearances, scoring two goals against Crystal Palace in September 1949. He signed for the U's on 20 July 1950. On leaving Layer Road, he returned to Norfolk and signed for Great Yarmouth on 22 August 1953, ironically making his Eastern Counties League debut against Colchester reserves. He was in their 1953–54 FA Cup team that toppled Third Division South giants Crystal Palace, although Palace were a very minor giant at that time and had finished bottom of the League twice in the previous four years. Rowlands amassed 194 games for the Bloaters, scoring three goals. His untimely death came as a result of a tragic construction site accident.

	League		Lge Cup		FA Cup		Other	
	A	G	A	G	A	G	A	G
1950–51	15	1	-	-	0	0	-	-
1951–52	26	1	-	-	0	0	-	-
1952–53	5	2	-	-	0	0	-	-
TOTAL	46	4	-	-	0	0	-	-

ROWLES, Albert Edward James 'Eddie'

Height: 5ft 9in. Weight: 11st 2lb.

Born: 10 March 1951, Gosport.

■ Rowles began as an apprentice at his local club, Bournemouth, scoring his first League goal for the club on 10 February 1968, a month before his 17th birthday. Rewarded with a professional contract a month later, he went on to score 12 League goals in 58(+8) games for the Cherries. Transferring to York in the summer of 1971 he bagged 14 goals in 61(+6) appearances before moving to Torquay in June 1973. At Plainmoor he achieved a similar goal ratio, scoring 13 in 54(+5) outings. Remaining in the Fourth Division, he transferred north to Darlington in August 1975 and in two and a half seasons played 96(+7) League games, scoring 21. Another 1970s Christmas present for the manager from the Board, Bobby Roberts paid £15,000

for his services in a bid to boost U's flagging promotion challenge. In only his ninth game for United he broke his leg, just seven minutes after scoring the second goal of a 4–0 win over Portsmouth. Rowles was continuously plagued by injuries and never got a decent run in the first team and was forced to retire in 1982. He subsequently traded as a painter and decorator in the Colchester area and was one of the U's landlords for their apprentices.

	League		Lge Cup		FA Cup		Other	
	A	G	A	G	A	G	A	G
1977–78	9	3	0	0	0	0	-	-
1978–79	19+2	4	2	1	0	0	-	-
1979–80	26+8	8	2	0	2+1	2	-	-
1980–81	21	2	2	0	3	0	-	-
1981–82	4+2	0	1	0	5	0	-	-
TOTAL	79+12	17	7	1	10+1	2	-	-

RUMNEY, Joseph Edgar

Height: 5ft 11in. Weight: 11st 12lb.

Born: 15 September 1936, Colchester.

■ Rumney signed for United as a 16-year-old amateur in August 1953 and primarily played in the Border League until the U's pulled the A team out in 1956. As with many of the U's amateurs, he then signed Border League forms for Colchester Casuals, while remaining eligible for the U's reserves in the Eastern Counties League but gave up his amateur status on 1 May 1957, ahead of his military service. He made his debut in September 1957, deputising at right-back for George Fisher in a 2–1 win over

QPR, and added four more appearances up to January before being posted overseas. Apart from when he was home on leave, that was Rumney's U's career on hold until he was demobbed in October 1959 and signed full time. It was reserve action only for Rumney until John Laidlaw's knee injury at Grimsby in August 1960 and Rumney then enjoyed a run in the team, up to and including the 4–1 win over First Division Newcastle in the first-ever Football League Cup competition. He played another 33 games over the next four and a half seasons until leaving Layer Road in 1965 to become player-coach of Sudbury Town, a post he also held at Braintree, Coggeshall and Eastern Gas, while working for the family engineering firm.

	League		Lge Cup		FA Cup		Other	
	A	G	A	G	A	G	A	G
1957–58	5	0	-	-	0	0	-	-
1958–59	0	0	-	-	0	0	-	-
1959–60	0	0	-	-	0	0	-	-
1960–61	17	0	1	0	0	0	-	-
1961–62	2	0	0	0	0	0	-	-
1962–63	10	0	1	0	0	0	-	-
1963–64	5	0	0	0	0	0	-	-
1964–65	11	0	0	0	0	0	-	-
TOTAL	50	0	2	0	0	0	-	-

RUTTER, Keith

Height: 6ft. Weight: 12st.

Born: 10 September 1931, Leeds.

■ Benny Fenton signed Rutter when Colchester-born John Bond turned down his agreed £10k move from West

Ham to Layer Road. Rutter cost £4,000 from Queen's Park Rangers, and made his Colchester debut at Coventry in February 1963, wearing basketball boots as he lost his own on the way to the match. An experienced central-defender, Rutter had played 339 times in the League for Rangers between 1954 and 1962. Fenton made him U's skipper, but friction arose with the U's next manager Neil Franklin, and he joined Romford in August 1964. He also played for Ashford and was part of the Hastings side that won promotion to the Southern League Premier in 1967. On leaving football, he ran a Bournemouth hotel and later a restaurant in Bridport.

	League		Lge Cup		FA Cup		Other	
	A	G	A	G	A	G	A	G
1962–63	21	0	0	0	0	0	-	-
1963–64	42	0	3	0	2	0	-	-
TOTAL	63	0	3	0	2	0	-	-

RYAN, Laurence John 'Laurie'

Height: 5ft 9in. Weight: 10st 9lb.

Born: 15 October 1963, Watford.

■ Ryan joined Cambridge United from Dunstable Town in April 1988, having previously played for Chesham United. He made 39(+12) appearances at The Abbey Stadium, scoring 13 times. Under John Beck, Cambridge were on the verge of rising to the second tier of English football. Ryan was loaned to Colchester in September 1990 and scored a hat-trick on his reserve debut, but Cambridge wanted £15,000 for a permanent deal, and so he went back at the end of the month. He was back at Layer Road in December, having now been released by Cambridge, but, despite scoring twice in the last game of the season against Kidderminster at Layer Road and mirroring his debut hat-trick in the last reserve game, he was not retained and joined Cambridge City.

	League		Lge Cup		FA Cup		Other	
	A	G	A	G	A	G	A	G
1990–91	3+10	3	2	0	0	0	1+1	0
TOTAL	3+10	3	2	0	0	0	1+1	0

S

SALE, Mark David

Height: 6ft 3in. Weight: 13st 5lb.

Born: 22 February 1972, Burton upon Trent.

■ A YTS player on the books of Stoke, Sale made just two substitute appearances at Bootham Crescent after signing in July 1990. He transferred to Cambridge in May 1991 but did not make the first team and drifted into non-League with Rocester. Given a second chance, he signed for Birmingham in March 1992 and made 11(+10) appearances for the Blues. Exactly a year later he was on the move again and joined Torquay for £10,000, scoring two goals in the last 10 games of the season. In his first full season he helped Torquay to the Play-offs and impressed Preston boss John Beck enough for the upwardly-mobile Lancashire side to pay £20,000 for his services in the summer of 1994. Preston also failed in the Play-offs, and Sale was on the move within a year to Mansfield for £50,000 after appearing just 10(+3) times for North End, but impressively scoring seven goals. Sale became a target for Steve Wignall and scored against the U's at Field Mill in December 1996. Inadvertently, that goal for Mansfield contributed to United failing to make the Play-offs in his first season. Wignall finally got his man on deadline day three months later for £23,500, and the player made his debut as a substitute in the Auto Windscreens Shield Area Final at Peterborough. Sale played at Wembley in the actual Final a month later and revisited the national stadium again as United beat Torquay in the Third Division Play-off Final of 1998. He was loaned to Plymouth in March 1999 after a dip in form, where he played eight times scoring once. Sale's poor form was eventually diagnosed to the development of Hodgkin's Lymphoma by which time he had joined Rushden & Diamonds for £30,000. After a long spell on the sidelines, he made a triumphant comeback with Doncaster, Tamworth, Alfreton, Hucknall and Northwich. In March 2007 he joined Hednesford, before becoming youth coach at Burton Albion in January 2008.

	League		Lge Cup		FA Cup		Other	
	A	G	A	G	A	G	A	G
1996–97	10	3	0	0	0	0	2+1	0
1997–98	38+1	7	2	0	3	1	4	0
1998–99	21+10	2	2	0	1	0	1	0
TOTAL	69+11	12	4	0	4	1	7+1	0

SALES, Ronald Duncan 'Ron'

Born: 19 September 1920, South Shields.
Died: August 1995, South Shields.

■ Centre-half Sales was plucked from South Shields, a team that included the young Stan Mortensen, while working in the Tyneside factory of Reyrolles, by Newcastle in 1942. He made 42 wartime appearances for the Magpies but moved south to Leyton Orient in 1947 after losing his place while having an appendix operation. At Brisbane Road, Sales made 46 appearances, scoring three goals but suffered injury and on recovery found himself at Colchester. He played just one game for Colchester on a Thursday afternoon in October 1949 at Lovell's Athletic when replacing Reg Stewart. He was a stalwart reserve centre-half and barely missed a game all season, apart from the one in late February when the first team took over the fixture against Chelsea A for match practice and won 6–0. Sales returned to his roots for the 1950–51 season, signing for Hartlepool, but made just three League appearances, having to retire because of a knee injury. In a marvellous gesture, Reyrolles and Newcastle paid for him to visit a top London specialist for treatment.

	League		Lge Cup		FA Cup		Other	
	A	G	A	G	A	G	A	G
1949–50	1	0	0	0	0	0	-	-
TOTAL	1	0	0	0	0	0	-	-

SALISBURY, Gareth

Height: 5ft 9in. Weight: 11st 4lb.

Born: 11 March 1941, Caernarvon.

■ Salisbury gained Welsh Youth International caps with Wrexham, having started as a junior with the Welshmen. After 11 appearances, he joined Norwich but failed to make the grade. Moving to Luton for 1963–64 he scored two goals in 12 League appearances as well as being top scorer

for the Hatters' reserve side. Neil Franklin brought him to Layer Road on a free transfer, but he failed to make much of an impact with two goals from just 14 appearances after dislocating his collar bone 10 days after his 22 August 1964 debut against Carlisle. At the end of the season he moved to Chesterfield for his final taste of League football, scoring nine goals in 34 starts. A brief spell with Kidderminster in July 1966 and then Bangor, saw him emigrate to Australia in 1969, where he turned out for Victoria State side Juventus.

	League		Lge Cup		FA Cup		Other	
	A	G	A	G	A	G	A	G
1964–65	15	2	1	0	1	1	-	-
TOTAL	15	2	1	0	1	1	-	-

SCOTT, Augustus Fisher 'Augie'

Height: 5ft 6in. Weight: 10st 2lb.

Born: 19 February 1921, Sunderland.
Died: 28 November 1998.

■ Before the war, Scott was on the books of Luton, having been spotted playing for Hylton Colliery, but it was not until joining Southampton in July 1947 that his career took off. Scott scored nine goals in 46 games for the Saints. At the time, the £2,000 fee Colchester paid Southampton was a club record, and they had to fight off advances from Cardiff as well. While at Layer Road, Scott was selected for, and scored for, an FA XI against Cambridge University. The inside-forward later became player-coach of Southern League Cheltenham and steered them to the Southern League

Cup win over Gravesend in 1958. Working in the building trade, he retired in the Southampton area in 1986.

	League		Lge Cup		FA Cup		Other	
	A	G	A	G	A	G	A	G
1951–52	45	4	-	-	3	2	-	-
1952–53	38	2	-	-	2	0	-	-
1953–54	37	4	-	-	2	0	-	-
TOTAL	120	10	-	-	7	2	-	-

SCOTT, Keith James

Height: 6ft 3in. Weight: 14st 3lb.

Born: 9 June 1967, Westminster.

■ Scott began his career on the Midlands non-League circuit, playing for Hinckley United, Bedworth and Leicester United. At the age of 22 he was picked up by Lincoln in March 1990, but after scoring just twice in 16 games drifted back into non-League with Wycombe. His goal power fired Wycombe to the 1992–93 Conference title a year after they had vied with Colchester for the same crown. Scoring 44 Conference goals in 79 Conference starts, Scott moved in November 1993 to Premiership Swindon for £300,000, and he went on to make 43(+8) League appearances, scoring 12 goals. In December 1994 he left the struggling Wiltshire club for Stoke, for the same £300,000, playing 22(+3) games and netting three times. In November 1995 he joined Norwich in a swap deal involving Mike Sheron but failed to fill the boots of Dion Dublin. Making just 10(+14) appearances at Carrow Road, scoring five times, Scott was loaned out to Bournemouth in February 1996 (eight games – one goal) and to Watford in February 1997 (six games – two goals). His third loan spell of the campaign was back at his old club Wycombe in March. After netting three goals in nine games, Wycombe manager John Gregory paid £55,000 for the striker in the summer of 1997. Scott rekindled his career in familiar surroundings, grabbing 20 goals in just 60(+16) appearances. This form encouraged Reading to pay an undisclosed fee on transfer deadline day 1999, and Scott scored five times in 20(+15) games at The Madejski Stadium. Following the disappointing form of previous loanee Mark Nicholls, Colchester boss Steve Whitton moved to bring in the big striker in October 2000 in the wake of Lomana Lua Lua's departure to Newcastle. His solitary goal

came on his debut at Port Vale in a 3–1 defeat, but a knee injury cut short his loan. Whitton tried to sign Scott on his recovery in February 2002 but could not agree a fee with Reading. Released by the Royals at the end of the season, Scott joined Dover, scoring 14 Conference goals in 40 appearances. He moved to Scarborough, playing 27(+1) times, before the Seadogs' perilous financial plight forced him to move to Leigh RMI in February 2003. He was later on the books of Dagenham & Redbridge, Tamworth (on loan) and Windsor & Eton. After becoming coach at Northwood, following the acquisition of UEFA A and B coaching badges, Scott became manager of Southern League (Midland) side Leighton Town in October 2006.

	League		Lge Cup		FA Cup		Other	
	A	G	A	G	A	G	A	G
2000–01	8+1	1	0	0	0	0	0	0
TOTAL	8+1	1	0	0	0	0	0	0

SCOTT, Morrys James

Height: 6ft 3in. Weight: 12st 6lb.

Born: 17 December 1970, Swansea.

■ Scott was a schoolboy player with home-town club Swansea but signed as a youth trainee with arch rivals Cardiff in the summer of 1989. He made 1(+8) appearances in the League as the Bluebirds were relegated to the basement division in 1990. Recruited by Ian Atkins for Colchester's inaugural Conference season, the manager soon realised that the Conference was a very physical League, especially with relegation still such a novelty, when the established clubs came up against the ex-Football League clubs, and using the inexperienced Scott as the

target man was like asking a boy to do a man's job. Fortunately, Atkins knew just the man to deal with the Conference's amateur hard men, his old mate and best man U's old boy Roy McDonough. It was a master stroke, and fortunately Southend were willing to swap, and the rest is history. Scott failed to make any appearances at Roots Hall and joined Plymouth in June 1991. After just 3(+3) games for Argyle, he signed for Northampton on a non-contract basis. He scored his only two League goals at The County Ground in 10(+7) League appearances. Moving into non-League, he later turned out for Slough and Merthyr Tydfil.

	League		Lge Cup		FA Cup		Other	
	A	G	A	G	A	G	A	G
1990–91	1+3	0	0	0	0	0	0	0
TOTAL	1+3	0	0	0	0	0	0	0

SCOTT, Robert

Height: 5ft 10in. Weight: 11st 7lb.

Born: 13 January 1964, Broxburn.

■ Jock Wallace returned to his native Scotland to sign Scott from Edinburgh junior side Whitburn Juniors. Originally on the books of Hamilton Academicals before joining Linlithgow Rose until 1988, and already having scored 38 goals for Whitburn with the season only at its mid-point, Scott proved his worth with a hat-trick in a reserve match as a trialist and re-paid Wallace's faith with five vital goals that helped steer Colchester away from the relegation trap door to the Conference. No goal was more precious than his 66th-minute winner at Darlington in April 1989. He struggled to settle so far from home

though, and his appearances the following season became more sporadic, diminishing further when new manager Mick Mills signed Trevor Morgan. He returned to Scotland and played for East Fife between 1990 and 1997, scoring 79 goals in 205 appearances before moving to Ayr United, where in season 1996–97 he scored six goals in 18 games. His next transfer was to Clyde, where in the following season he netted twice in 15 outings, moving mid-term to Forfar, where he failed to score in seven starts. He spent his remaining playing days back at Whitburn Juniors, scoring seven goals to take his club tally to 45 in just 50 appearances.

	League		Lge Cup		FA Cup		Other	
	A	G	A	G	A	G	A	G
1988–89	12	5	0	0	0	0	0	0
1989–90	14+11	3	2	2	0+1	0	1+1	0
TOTAL	26+11	8	2	2	0+1	0	1+1	0

SETCHELL, Ernest Walter 'Ernie'

Height: 5ft 11in. Weight: 11st 5lb.

Born: 9 March 1928, Hammersmith.
Died: August 1999, Colchester.

■ An amateur 'keeper from the Erith area who had previously played for Dartford reserves, Setchell made his debut for the U's reserves in March 1947. He kept a clean sheet on his first-team debut, when he stood in for the not-fully-fit Harry Wright against Yeovil in the last week of the 1947–48 season to save Wright for the League Cup semi-final replay a couple of days later. Setchell

also played in the remaining game of that season and one first team game in 1948–49, although that does not show in the usual statistics because it was a friendly. The opposition were Chelsea reserves, and apart from Setchell it was the U's team that played virtually unchanged for three months.

	League		Lge Cup		FA Cup		Other	
	A	G	A	G	A	G	A	G
1947–48	2	0	0	0	0	0	-	-
TOTAL	2	0	0	0	0	0	-	-

SHARKEY, Patrick George Sharp 'Pat'

Height: 5ft 7in. Weight: 10st 8lb.

Born: 26 August 1953, Omagh, Northern Ireland.

■ Sharkey commenced his career playing for Irish League side Portadown. Spotted by Ipswich's extensive scouting network he moved to Portman Road in September 1973. It was not until 1975 that he made his debut, and he scored

one goal in 17(+1) appearances. He was called up by Northern Ireland for the Home Championship clash at Hampden Park in which Scotland defeated the Ulstermen 2–1. In November 1976 he was loaned out to Millwall, where he played 7 times. Released by Ipswich in the summer of 1977, he spent the following season at Mansfield, appearing 31(+1) times in the League and scoring five goals. Bobby Roberts brought him to Colchester at the start of the 1977–78 campaign, and the player got off to a bad start, missing a crucial penalty in a League Cup tie with Charlton. His apparently lazy attitude did not go down well, and he was sold to Peterborough on deadline day 1979 for £8,000. He played 15 games for Posh but was caught in a scandal when police raided a bar and found several Posh players drinking illegally.

	League		Lge Cup		FA Cup		Other	
	A	G	A	G	A	G	A	G
1978–79	5+1	0	1+1	0	0	0	-	-
TOTAL	5+1	0	1+1	0	0	0	-	-

SHARPE, John

■ Sharpe, 22 years old, had been unintentionally released by Southampton in the summer of 1949 and spent a couple of months on trial at Layer Road. He only got one chance in the first team against Yeovil on 22 October 1949 as deputy for Vic Keeble, who was representing the Southern League against the Cheshire League at Gillingham, and was unable to play on doctor's orders as his extended trial finished. There was a suggestion he might return when fit if the club needed him, but he disappeared from sight.

	League		Lge Cup		FA Cup		Other	
	A	G	A	G	A	G	A	G
1949–50	1	0	0	0	0	0	-	-
TOTAL	1	0	0	0	0	0	-	-

SHEFFIELD, Jonathan 'Jon'

Height: 5ft 11in. Weight: 11st 7lb.

Born: 1 February 1969, Bedworth.

■ Spotted by Norwich taking part in a local soccer camp, Sheffield joined Norwich as an apprentice in August 1985 before turning professional in February 1987. Largely understudy to Bryan Gunn, he was loaned out to Aldershot in September 1989 in a side unbeaten in all 11 of his starts. Sheffield played just one first team game for the Canaries and returned to Aldershot in another loan deal at the start of the 1990–91 season, playing 15 games. Unable to displace Gunn, he joined Cambridge on deadline day 1991, playing 56 times. It was during this period that the goalkeeper arrived, on loan, at Layer Road to replace John Keeley and the inexperienced Nathan Munson. Sheffield became the first U's 'keeper in 31 games to keep two successive clean sheets and was set to sign a further loan deal before Colchester were unexpectedly usurped by the lure of Premiership Swindon. Sheffield played two games for the Robins, including a 5–0 drubbing at Villa Park. At the time, his squad number of 40 was the highest ever in the Premiership. At the beginning of 1994–95 he spent eight games on loan at Hereford before completing a permanent transfer to Peterborough in July 1995 for £150,000. Featuring in 62 League games, Sheffield joined his last League club Plymouth in the summer of 1997 for £100,000, after non-playing loan spells at Oldham and Watford, turning out 155 times for Argyle. A non-contract spell with Yeovil realised just 21 appearances in two seasons, and when the Somerset reached the League in 2003 Sheffield was released, joining Saltash United.

	League		Lge Cup		FA Cup		Other	
	A	G	A	G	A	G	A	G
1993–94	6	0	0	0	0	0	0	0
TOTAL	6	0	0	0	0	0	0	0

SHERINGHAM MBE, Edward Paul 'Teddy'

Height: 5ft 11in. Weight: 12st 5lb.

Born: 2 April 1966, Highams Park.

■ No one could have imagined the wonderful career that Sheringham would have when he set out on his Millwall apprenticeship in the early 1980s. That apprenticeship included playing at Layer Road for Millwall's youth team in October 1982 as a 16-year-old. Signing professionally for the Lions in January 1984, he had a 4(+1) loan spell with Aldershot in February 1985 and a 21-game stint with Swedish side Djurgårdens before going on to complete 205(+15) League games for Millwall, netting 93 goals. A Division Two title winner in 1987–88, Sheringham was top scorer in four consecutive seasons between 1987 and 1991, bagging an amazing 37 goals in that latter campaign as Millwall failed to regain top-flight football, losing in the Play-offs to Brighton. In July 1991 Nottingham Forest paid £2 million for the striker, and he had the honour of scoring the first-ever goal in the newly-sanctioned live coverage of League football. His spell at Forest would later become embroiled in an alleged bung controversy, and a year later, after scoring 14 goals as a 42–game ever present, and being a League Cup finalist and Full Members' Cup winner, he signed for Tottenham for £2.1 million. He top scored in his first two seasons at White Hart Lane, with 22 and 15 goals respectively. At the age of 31, and still to win a major trophy, Sheringham joined Manchester United in July 1997 after scoring 76 League goals in 163(+3) appearances for Spurs. The fee of £3.5 million saw Sheringham labelled as the replacement for Eric Cantona. The arrival of Dwight Yorke pushed Sheringham down the pecking order, but he played enough games in 1998–99 to qualify for a Premiership title medal and scored one of United's goals in their FA

Cup Final victory over Newcastle. Four days later, he ensured his place in United folklore when scoring the late equaliser against Bayern Munich in the Champions League Final moments before setting up Ole Gunnar Solskjaer with the winner to give Sheringham an incredible treble of medals. He picked up another Premiership title the following season and was top scorer in 2001–02, when he received the ultimate accolade of being voted both PFA and the Football Writers' Association Player of the Year. The arrival of Ruud Van Nistelrooy and the offer of just a one-year contract meant that he left United on a free transfer after scoring 31 League goals in 73(+31) games. He returned to Tottenham and was a League Cup Finalist in 2002 under Glenn Hoddle and added 22 goals in 67(+3) games to his Spurs career record. When his contract expired he was not offered a new one but instead the 38-year-old joined Premiership new boys Portsmouth in a season-long deal. Scoring nine goals in 25(+7) appearances at Fratton Park, he joined Championship side West Ham in July 2004 and immediately helped them back to the top flight with a Play-off Final win over Preston, and he top scored with 20 goals. Winning Hammers Player of the Year award, Sheringham signed a new contract and in so doing became the oldest outfield player to appear in the Premiership at 40 years 270 days, culminating in an FA Cup Final penalty shoot out defeat to Liverpool. A free agent, Sheringham opted to continue his football career and duly signed for Colchester in the summer of 2007, shortly after being awarded the MBE for services to football. He scored his first Colchester goal in a 2–2 draw with Barnsley in August. Sheringham also enjoyed an illustrious England career, making his debut at the age of 27 and starring at Euro '96, when both he and Alan Shearer scored two goals in England's 4–1 thrashing of Holland. The emergence of Michael Owen threatened to end Sheringham's England career, but Sven Goran Eriksson continued to use him, and he scored a valuable first goal in a 2–1 win over Greece that saw England qualify for the 2002 World Cup in South Korea and Japan. His final appearance came in that tournament as England lost 2–1 to Brazil in the quarter-finals. His 51 caps were complemented by 11 goals for his country. Announcing his retirement in February 2008 Sheringham bade farewell as a player in the last-ever game at Layer Road against Stoke two months later.

	League		Lge Cup		FA Cup		Other	
	A	G	A	G	A	G	A	G
2007-08	11+8	3	0	0	1	1	-	-
TOTAL	11+8	3	0	0	1	1	-	-

SHERRATT, Brian

Height: 6ft. Weight: 12st 10lb.

Born: 29 March 1944, Stoke-on-Trent.

■ An apprentice with Stoke, Sherratt played just one game for the Potteries side following his promotion to full professional in April 1961. He was snapped up by Oxford for the 1965–66 season as successor to Vic Rouse. Making 44 League appearances, Sherratt was loaned to Nottingham Forest in October 1968, making one appearance before being transferred to Barnsley in the summer of 1969. After 15 appearances at Oakwell, he drifted into non-League

with Gainsborough Trinity, from whom Dick Graham signed him for Colchester in August 1970. At Layer Road he was unable to oust Graham Smith from the green jersey, apart from standing in for injury, and was released to Oxford City in July 1971. He later worked for British Leyland in Oxford.

	League		Lge Cup		FA Cup		Other	
	A	G	A	G	A	G	A	G
1970–71	9	0	0	0	0	0	-	-
TOTAL	9	0	0	0	0	0	-	-

SHIELS, William Francis 'Paddy'

■ Left-back Shiels, a private in the Essex Regiment No.1 Holding Battalion, joined the U's and signed professional shortly after returning from serving in Germany with BAOR. One of only four professionals retained at the end of 1945–46, he briefly returned to Ireland following his demob but was back for the start of the new season and was lodging with teammate Bob Curry at Lexden. He did not stay long though, and by November 1946 he had gone home for good. On Christmas Day 1945 he had been involved in an incident in which a member of the Colchester and District Junior League representative team, a 27-year-old Tollesbury man, had fallen in a tackle during a friendly against the U's at Layer Road and broken his neck. A court hearing absolved Shiels of any blame.

	League		Lge Cup		FA Cup		Other	
	A	G	A	G	A	G	A	G
1945–46	6	0	8	1	1	0	-	-
1946–47	4	0	0	0	0	0	-	-
TOTAL	10	0	8	1	1	0	-	-

SHINNERS, Paul

Height: 6ft 1in. Weight: 12st 7lb.

Born: 8 January 1959, Westminster.

■ Shinners began his career with Southern League Fisher Athletic when he hit over 200 goals and came to prominence as that League's top scorer in 1983–84. Signed by Gillingham in October 1984, he managed just 1(+3) appearances before being taken on loan by Cyril Lea in March 1985. His debut was delayed until mid-April at Torquay because of injury, and his only goal came

at Port Vale in the penultimate game of the season, which helped Colchester to a £2,500 prize from sponsors Canon as the division's top scorers. Leaving Gillingham for Leyton Orient in the summer of 1985, Shinners was top scorer for the O's in his first season, with 19 goals in all competitions. From then on he suffered several injuries, and after completing 73(+4) League games, with a return of 32 goals, he joined Conference side Barnet in January 1989. He later became a well-respected fitness education consultant.

	League		Lge Cup		FA Cup		Other	
	A	G	A	G	A	G	A	G
1984–85	6	1	0	0	0	0	0	0
TOTAL	6	1	0	0	0	0	0	0

SHIRES, Alan Jeffrey

Height: 5ft 8in. Weight: 10st 2lb.

Born: 29 June 1948, Leigh-on-Sea.

■ A young winger who served his apprenticeship with his home-town side Southend, making one substitute appearance in the 1965–66 season, Shires was taken on trial by the U's in the summer and offered terms. His two U's goals both came in the same match at Reading in October 1966, the second of which was a last-minute winner. With few chances to break into the first team, Shires was unfortunate to fracture his collarbone at Gillingham in April 1968 and was released at the end of the season. Like many ex-U's players of the time, he moved down the A12 to Chelmsford and

later spent much of the 1970s with Essex Senior League Basildon United. He was still playing in that competition with Southend Manor in 1986–87.

	League		Lge Cup		FA Cup		Other	
	A	G	A	G	A	G	A	G
1966–67	15	2	0+1	0	1	0	-	-
1967–68	8	1	0	0	0	0	-	-
TOTAL	23	3	0+1	0	1	0	-	-

SILVESTER, Peter Dennis

Height: 5ft 11in. Weight: 11st 8lb.

Born: 19 February 1948, Wokingham.

■ Silvester represented both Reading and Berks & Bucks Schools and joined Reading on leaving school, signing professional in February 1966. He made a scoring debut for the Royals at Exeter in April 1966, and in just over three years he appeared in 76(+3) League games and scored 27 goals for the Elm Park side. Norwich paid £20,000 for his services in September 1969, where he played exactly 100 League games for City, one of which was as a substitute. His 37 goals helped City on their way to the Second Division title in 1971–72, but after suffering a knee injury in January 1972 he underwent three cartilage operations and missed out on playing in the promotion run-in and indeed the League Cup Final of the following season. By the time he returned to action, City boss John Bond had already signed Ted MacDougall and Phil Boyer. Jim Smith brought the player to Layer Road in October 1973, and after four inconspicuous games on loan Silvester decided that he had a better chance of securing a move away from Norwich if he returned there rather than staying at Layer Road. In February 1974 he was sold to Southend and managed 78(+2) League games for the Essex club, netting 32 times. He was loaned back to Reading in March 1975 but played just twice. He then embarked on a transatlantic adventure, playing summer football for Baltimore Comets and San Diego Jaws, followed by Vancouver Whitecaps a year later and Washington Diplomats in 1977. He twice tried to incorporate playing in England in the winter by signing for Blackburn in October 1976 (five games, one goal) and Cambridge in August 1977 (2(+2) games, one goal). Voted Most Valuable Player in the North American Soccer League 1974 season, he also made the All-America Select Eleven. His last port of call was at Maidstone where he played 54 games for the non-League outfit before injury forced him to retire in October 1979. Maidstone entertained Norwich in a benefit game for Silvester in May 1990.

	League		Lge Cup		FA Cup		Other	
	A	G	A	G	A	G	A	G
1973–74	4	0	0	0	0	0	-	-
TOTAL	4	0	0	0	0	0	-	-

SIMMONS, David John 'Dave'

Height: 5ft 11½in. Weight: 12st 13lb.

Born: 24 October 1948, Gosport.
Died: July 2007, Cambridge.

■ Arsenal youngster Simmons failed to make the first team in three seasons at Highbury after signing in November 1965, but scored 70 goals in 94 youth team games and was an FA Youth Cup winner in 1965–66. Spending time on loan at Bournemouth, in November 1968 he made his League debut, scoring three times in seven starts. Being in the shop window paid dividends as he was brought by Aston Villa for £10,000. After netting seven goals in 13(+4) appearances for struggling Second Division Villa, he was sent out on loan to neighbours Walsall in October 1970, scoring twice in five games. This was enough for Dick Graham to put in a bid for the forward, and he was signed in time to make his debut on Boxing Day 1970, when he scored along with fellow debutant Brian Lewis as Colchester won 2–1 at Lincoln. Simmons famously scored the third goal in Colchester's sensational 3–2 win over Leeds in February 1971 and picked up a Watney Cup-winners' medal at the beginning of the 1971–72 campaign. Simmons also suffered a double injury nightmare. While recuperating from a knee injury, he fell down the stairs of his home and crashed through a plate glass door, keeping him out for the remainder of the season. He netted two hat-tricks in 1972–73 against Crewe and Bognor Regis in the FA Cup but moved to Cambridge in March 1973 for £3,000. After a year and three goals in 19(+5) games, he moved to Brentford, where he bagged 17 League goals in 47(+5) appearances. Returning to Cambridge in November 1975, he netted a further five goals in 16(+1) appearances before playing non-League for Bishop's Stortford and Cambridge City. He then took up a position in insurance in the Cambridge area.

	League		Lge Cup		FA Cup		Other	
	A	G	A	G	A	G	A	G
1970–71	10	2	0	0	5	3	-	-
1971–72	20+3	3	2	0	0	0	3	1
1972–73	22+2	6	0+1	0	3	3	-	-
TOTAL	52+5	11	2+1	0	8	6	3	1

SIMNETT, Samuel 'Sam'

■ An RAF player from Felixstowe with Suffolk County honours, Simnett was with Ipswich Town as an amateur and, although predominantly a reserve, played four times for their first team at the end of 1935–36. Ipswich turned

professional that summer, but Simnett stayed with them as an amateur until late January 1938. He first appeared for United's first team in a friendly against Charlton reserves on 22 January 1938, appearing in the programme as 'A. Newman', and was ever present on the reserves right wing for the rest of the season. His only Southern League appearance came in a reserve team in all but name that went to Tunbridge Wells on 23 April 1938 to play the sixth first-team fixture in nine days. He switched to Eastern Counties League side Bury Town for 1938–39 and only missed one game, scoring five times in 34 outings. He played in Bury's first game of 1939–40 before the war intervened.

	League		Lge Cup		FA Cup		Other	
	A	G	A	G	A	G	A	G
1937–38	1	0	0	0	-	-	0	0
TOTAL	1	0	0	0	-	-	0	0

SIMPSON, Owen

Height: 5ft 9in. Weight: 12st.

Born: 18 September 1943, Stockfield.

■ Simpson began at Rotherham, playing six games at left-back between 1964 and his transfer to Leyton Orient in September 1967. He was signed by the then Leyton manager Dick Graham and arrived with fellow Rotherham player Roy Massey, who himself would play for Colchester. Graham converted Simpson into a more forward-thinking player and he scored four goals in 36 League starts at Brisbane Road. When Simpson no longer fitted into new Orient manager Jimmy Bloomfield's plans, he was picked up by the new U's manager Graham for a fee of

£3,500. A consistent player throughout the season, Simpson moved to Southend on 5 August 1969, after playing in the U's pre-season games, for a fee of £4,000. He played 64 times for the Roots Hall club, scoring once. Moving north to Darlington in March 1971, Simpson played 11 games for the Quakers before a change of manager saw him moving on again to Grimsby. Just 6 (+1) more games followed, and so he joined Boston and won the Northern Premier League on two occasions in 1973 and 1974, scoring three in 80 appearances. He settled in Grimsby after turning out for Gainsborough Trinity and Louth United.

	League		Lge Cup		FA Cup		Other	
	A	G	A	G	A	G	A	G
1968–69	41+2	4	1	0	1	0	-	-
TOTAL	41+2	4	1	0	1	0	-	-

SIMS, John

Height: 5ft 11in. Weight: 11st 10lb.

Born: 14 August 1952, Belper.

■ An apprentice at Derby, Sims signed professional for the Rams in August 1970 but made just 2(+1) League appearances. He was a member of the reserves' 1971–72 Central League Championship-winning squad. In November 1973 he was loaned to Luton, for whom he scored once in three League starts. Oxford also took the young striker on loan in September 1974, and he netted once in 6(+1) games at The Manor Ground. Missing Bobby Svarc through injury at the turn of 1975, Jim Smith was forced to delve into the loan market, and Sims, who had come on as a substitute for Derby in a European Cup semi-final

against Juventus, arrived at Layer Road but failed to impress in his two appearances. In December 1975 he was sold to Notts County for £10,000, where he finally established himself, scoring 13 League goals in 48(+13) games. By December 1978 he began a spell that would see him play for all of Devon's senior clubs. First at Exeter (£12,000), he scored 11 goals in 33(+1) fixtures before joining Plymouth for £22,500 in October 1979, following manager Bobby Saxton along the same path. At Home Park he notched 43 goals in 161(+2) games before joining Torquay at the start of the 1983–84 season. He returned to Exeter in February 1984 after playing 30 times for the Plainmoor outfit, scoring eight goals and bagged another six goals in 23(+2) games for the Grecians. His professional career ended with a return to Torquay in November 1984, where he added three goals in 15(+2) outings. In 1985 he was player-manager of Torquay for 33 days but was sacked, and he later played for Saltash United and Waldon Athletic before becoming a licensee in the Devon resort.

	League		Lge Cup		FA Cup		Other	
	A	G	A	G	A	G	A	G
1974–75	2	0	0	0	0	0	-	-
TOTAL	2	0	0	0	0	0	-	-

SKELTON, Aaron Matthew

Height: 6ft. Weight: 12st 6lb.

Born: 22 November 1974, Welwyn Garden City.

■ Skelton's career had already been blighted by injury, having missed the entire 1993–94 season after completing

his YTS at Luton and signing professional forms in December 1992. Battling back to fitness, he played 5(+3) games for the Hatters as they were relegated to Division Two, but he suffered cruciate ligament damage in 1995–96. Picked up by Steve Wignall in the summer of 1997, Skelton carved out a good career at Layer Road, highlighted by a Wembley Play-off win over Torquay. A regular goalscorer, Skelton did so well that his former club tempted him back in the summer of 2001 on a Bosman free transfer, as club captain, and he played 14(+3) games, scoring two goals, over two seasons as Luton climbed out of the basement as champions of the Third Division. Released, he joined Havant & Waterlooville for 2003–04 and three seasons later joined Poole Town, for whom he played in 2007–08.

	League		Lge Cup		FA Cup		Other	
	A	G	A	G	A	G	A	G
1997–98	37+2	7	1	0	3+1	0	3+1	0
1998–99	7+2	0	0	0	0	0	0	0
1999–2000	27+6	4	0	0	1	0	1	0
2000–01	43+1	6	3	0	1	0	1	0
TOTAL	114+11	17	4	0	5+1	0	5+1	0

SLATER, Malcolm Bruce

Height: 5ft 8in. Weight: 9st 12lb.

Born: 22 October 1931, Buckie.

■ Slater began his career at Buckie Thistle and joined Celtic three years later aged 18. Winning three Scottish Amateur caps, he was on the verge of signing

professional at Parkhead when two of his brothers tragically drowned. Slater quit football and joined the Civil Service but was tempted back into the game in 1961 and signed for Montrose, scoring three times in 25 games. He moved south when former U's boss Ted Fenton paid £2,000 to take the forward to Southend in November 1963. After 83 League appearances and six goals, Slater fell out with Fenton and was sold to Leyton Orient in January 1967, only a month after Middlesbrough had bid £15,000 for the player. He moved to Layer Road in October 1969 on a month's loan, making his debut at Aldershot, but after three further starts returned to Brisbane Road as Dick Graham could not raise the £5,000 asking fee. His 111 League games for the O's realised four goals, but in the summer of 1967 he was released and returned to Scotland, where he had spells with Inverness Caledonian and Ross County both in the Highland League. He returned to Essex in the 1970s, playing for and later managing Essex Senior League club Bowers United.

	League		Lge Cup		FA Cup		Other	
	A	G	A	G	A	G	A	G
1969–70	4	0	0	0	0	0	-	-
TOTAL	4	0	0	0	0	0	-	-

SMALE, Douglas Martin 'Doug'

Born: 27 March 1916, London.

■ One of the many players whose professional career was terminated by the war, Smale started with Kingstonian and was on the fringe of the Chelsea first

team at the outbreak of hostilities as deputy for regular left-winger Alf Hanson. He made his Chelsea debut on 29 March 1937 at Charlton and played the last six games of that season and the opening one of 1937–38 but was then only called on twice more before the war. LAC2 Smale served with the RAF in India and during the war made three further appearances for Chelsea and guested for QPR, Norwich, Plymouth and Torquay. He also spent some time with Merthyr Tydfil after the war.

	League		Lge Cup		FA Cup		Other	
	A	G	A	G	A	G	A	G
1945–46	2	2	6	1	0	0	-	-
TOTAL	2	2	6	1	0	0	-	-

SMIRK, Alfred Henry 'Alf'

Born: 14 March 1917, Pershore.

Died: November 1996, Southend.

■ Smirk won an England schoolboy cap in 1931 and by 1935 had signed

professional with Sheffield Wednesday. Despite winning the FA Cup in 1935, the Owls sacked manager Billy Walker, and Smirk no longer fitted in. He ended up playing for Sunderland Bus Company, but Southend manager David Jack took up a recommendation and offered Smirk a contract in 1938–39. He went on to play in many wartime matches for Southend and re-signed professionally with Southend after the war in 1946. An ever present with 12 goals, he joined Gateshead in March 1948, but returned to Essex after just 11 games to play for Chingford Town. He had crossed into Kent by March 1950 when he played for Tonbridge in the Southern League Cup semi-final against the U's at Layer Road. An injury to the 'keeper saw him play in goal for the last 40 minutes, proving an able deputy and handling the ball cleverly and coolly according to the match report. The U's were 2–1 up when he took over and he was only beaten once as the U's won 3–2. Smirk was later player-manager of Loughborough-based Brush Sports and wrote for the *Southend Times* and *Southend Standard* as correspondent for Southend United until his death. There was about a three-month gap between each of his two competitive and one friendly-game appearances for Colchester, which came while serving with the No.1 Holding Battalion.

	League		Lge Cup		FA Cup		Other	
	A	G	A	G	A	G	A	G
1945–46	2	1	0	0	0	0	-	-
TOTAL	2	1	0	0	0	0	-	-

SMITH, Alexander 'Alex'

Height: 5ft 11in. Weight: 11st 9lb.

Born: 11 May 1947, Dewsbury.

■ Yorkshireman Smith began his career playing for non-League Ossett Albion as a 17-year-old. Snapped up by Bradford City in December 1964, he scored two goals in 91(+2) appearances for the Bantams before securing a transfer to Huddersfield in March 1968. After 29 League appearances, he was transferred to Southend in April 1970, where he made the full-back slot his own on 129(+1) occasions in the League, scoring once. With the imminent departure of John McLaughlin, U's manager Jim Smith secured the defender's services on

loan in November 1973. His loan spell ended on 5 January 1974, and with the Colchester Board unwilling to spend £5,000 on him, despite taking in £25,000 for McLaughlin, Smith returned to Roots Hall. Two weeks later though the U's directors changed their minds and agreed to release the cash. Although a vital cog in United's defence as they won promotion to the Third Division at the end of 1973–74, Smith asked to leave over the summer because his wife wanted to return north. He was persuaded to stay for a while, but it was a case of when, not if, and in February 1975 he was sold to Halifax for a small fee and made a further 46(+1) League appearances at The Shay, scoring one goal.

	League		Lge Cup		FA Cup		Other	
	A	G	A	G	A	G	A	G
1973–74	29	1	0	0	0	0	-	-
1974–75	22	0	4	0	0	0	-	-
TOTAL	51	1	4	0	0	0	-	-

SMITH, Barry Anthony

Height: 5ft 11in. Weight: 10st 8lb.

Born: 3 March 1953, Colchester.

■ Home-grown 'keeper Smith signed professional for Colchester in July 1971, and his big goalkeeping chance came when Graham Smith was sold to West Brom in October of the same year. He played in all the remaining games and started the following season as first choice as United struggled. In Jim Smith's first game in charge in October

1972 it was found afterwards that the 'keeper had been playing with a broken wrist, and he was out of action until the New Year. In the meantime, Jim Smith had acquired John McInally and Barry Smith only got one more start, a 4–1 loss at promotion-bound League new boys Hereford United. On being released from Layer Road, he had short spells at Walsall and Sunderland but failed to make any further League appearances. He joined Weymouth in November 1973, starring in their 1974–75 FA Cup run, where they took Peterborough to a second replay, but left shortly after and later played outfield for ex-U's star Roy Massey's Clacton before becoming an insurance agent in Colchester.

	League		Lge Cup		FA Cup		Other	
	A	G	A	G	A	G	A	G
1971–72	31	0	0	0	0	0	0	0
1972–73	18	0	1	0	0	0	-	-
TOTAL	49	0	1	0	0	0	0	0

SMITH, Edmund William Alfred 'Eddie'

Height: 5ft 9in. Weight:

Born: 23 March 1939, London.
Died: April 1993.

■ Originally with non-League Wealdstone, Smith joined Chelsea in May 1950. After two seasons at Stamford Bridge without breaking into the first team, he moved south to Bournemouth for the 1952–53 season. Another season of frustration culminated in a move to

Watford, where in the 1953–54 season he scored 12 goals in 38 League appearances. Following a dispute with one of Watford directors, he signed for Northampton for a fee of £5,000. Smith again fell out with his employers after notching 12 goals in 53 games. Benny Fenton signed Smith in June 1956, and the player weighed in with 13 goals in 36 appearances as United ran Ipswich close for the Third Division South title. Fenton compared Smith to Tommy Lawton, putting him at centre-forward against Crystal Palace. Smith duly notched a hat-trick. He repeated the treble at Reading in January 1957 as United hit the top of the table only to finish third after a poor Easter. He had continued to live in London while playing for the U's and asked for a transfer in June 1957 because he wanted to cut his traveling. The U's received more than they paid for him as he joined Queen's Park Rangers, and the West London club did not get a great return on their investment as he managed just one goal in 17 games and was out for several months with a knee injury. After a season, he moved on to Chelmsford and later played for Wisbech and had an electrical business in the Willesden area.

	League		Lge Cup		FA Cup		Other	
	A	G	A	G	A	G	A	G
1956–57	35	13	-	-	1	0	-	-
TOTAL	35	13	-	-	1	0	-	-

SMITH, Gary Neil

Height: 5ft 10in. Weight: 11st 2lb.

Born: 3 December 1969, Harlow.

■ Smith started as an apprentice at Fulham, making one substitute appearance for the Cottagers at Oldham in May 1986 and turning professional the following September. He was signed by Colchester on a non-contract basis in September 1987 and quickly caught the eye in the reserves as a crunching tackler who could be relied on to mis-time at least one per game. His first-team debut came in a 2–1 win at Halifax in the November in Roger Brown's first match in charge, and not without some pain to his unfortunate direct opponent, who was on a stretcher inside five minutes and was out of action for 16 months. Smith's U's career was over by then, and he moved into the Conference with Enfield in July 1988, playing 40(+5) times before joining the U's then fierce rivals Wycombe, where he played against the U's in his 52(+13) games for the Buckinghamshire side. After a spell with Welling in 1992, he returned to League football with Barnet in September 1993, playing 11(+2) times, before breaking his leg. He later played for Aylesbury United and Gravesend & Northfleet. He became youth coach at Wimbledon, Wycombe and then Watford in 2005, before taking over the reserve team at Vicarage Road.

	League		Lge Cup		FA Cup		Other	
	A	G	A	G	A	G	A	G
1987–88	11	0	0	0	0	0	1	0
TOTAL	11	0	0	0	0	0	1	0

SMITH, George

Height: 5ft 11in. Weight: 12st.

Born: 1910, Connah's Quay.

■ Smith began his career at Bristol City after being spotted at Connah's Quay. He joined the short-lived Thames AFC in 1930 and played 73 times for the Londoners before moving north to Bradford City in 1932. He played just one game in a year at Valley Parade before joining Newport. Four games for the Welshmen saw him move once again to Wolves and then to Bournemouth, where he made 16 appearances. Ted Davis signed the tigerish left-half-back from Bath City, the manager's former club. Smith later played for Clacton after the war with several other U's players.

	League		Lge Cup		FA Cup		Other	
	A	G	A	G	A	G	A	G
1937–38	15	2	0	0	-	-	9	0
1938–39	21	0	2	0	0	0	13	1
TOTAL	36	2	2	0	0	0	22	1

SMITH, Graham William Charles

Height: 5ft 11in. Weight: 12st.

Born: 2 November 1942, Liverpool.

■ Goalkeeper Smith joined Notts County after being spotted playing for Loughborough University in August 1968. His chances were limited at Meadow Lane, but one of his 11 games was at a snowbound Layer Road against the U's in February 1969, where he caught the eye in a 1–1 draw. When County freed him in the summer the U's grabbed him, and Smith missed just three games in his first season at Layer

Road. Best remembered for his acrobatic style, Smith earned rave reviews as he defied a late Leeds onslaught in Colchester's famous FA Cup win in February 1971. In what was described as a world-class save by the watching media Smith prevented Mick Jones from claiming a seemingly odds-on equaliser with just 3 minutes remaining. Smith further enhanced his reputation the following season as he helped Colchester lift the Watney Cup at West Bromwich Albion. The Baggies were impressed enough to sign the stopper as cover for Jim Cumbes, paying £10,000 with another £5,000 in £1,000 instalments payable if appearance targets were met. Smith reached the first one with 10 Division One appearances before moving to Cambridge on a free transfer in January 1973. After 85 League starts at The Abbey Stadium, he was forced to retire with a back injury in 1976. He joined sportswear company Adidas and became general manager of their UK operation before becoming head of marketing at Le Coq Sportif. Between 1985 and 1989 he also served on the board at Chelsea.

	League		Lge Cup		FA Cup		Other	
	A	G	A	G	A	G	A	G
1969–70	43	0	2	0	1	0	-	-
1970–71	37	0	3	0	7	0	-	-
1971–72	15	0	3	0	1	0	3	0
TOTAL	95	0	8	0	9	0	3	0

SMITH, James Michael 'Jim'

Height: 5ft 8in. Weight: 11st 11lb.

Born: 17 October 1940, Sheffield.

■ Smith had joined his home-town club, Sheffield United, in January 1959. Without making an appearance for the Blades he moved on to Aldershot in July 1961, making 74 appearances and netting one goal in three seasons. Returning to Yorkshire in the summer of 1965, he signed for Halifax, scoring seven in 113(+1) outings. Lincoln signed the midfielder in March 1968, where he completed 54 more League games. His big break came with a step backwards. He became player-manager of Northern Premier League Boston United. His team never finished outside the top four and conceded just three home goals in the 1969–70 season. Having gone unbeaten for 40 games (51 eventually following his departure), Smith became manager of Colchester in October 1972. He could not halt the club's slide to re-election but won promotion in his first full season in 1973–74, finishing third behind Peterborough and Gillingham. His ability did not go unnoticed, particularly as Colchester reached the League Cup quarter-finals in 1974–75. He was appointed manager of Second Division Blackburn on 20 June 1975 with United negotiating a £9,000 compensation fee. He was unable to elevate Rovers into the First Division and left to take charge at Birmingham in March 1978. He sold Trevor Francis to Nottingham Forest in British football's first £1 million deal. Relegated at the end of the season, Smith took City back to the top flight in his first full season, but after two mediocre campaigns he was sacked in February 1982. He soon found work at Third Division Oxford and remarkably won the Third and then Second Division titles in successive seasons. Surprisingly, he left Oxford in the summer of 1985 to join

Queen's Park Rangers and took them to a Wembley League Cup Final, where ironically they lost to Oxford. Smith steered Rangers to fifth in the First Division in 1987–88 and then walked into a minefield of trouble at Newcastle in December 1988. Relegated at the end of the season, Newcastle failed to get back to the top flight the following season, losing in the Play-offs. Smith grew tired of the in-fighting and quit to become assistant to Colin Todd at Middlesbrough in March 1991. During the summer of 1991 he was appointed manager of Portsmouth and took them to an FA Cup semi-final in his first season. By 1995 he was in charge at Derby and took them into the Premiership, something he had failed to do at Pompey. In June 2001 he resigned from Pride Park and became assistant to Harry Redknapp at Portsmouth. When Redknapp moved along the coast to Southampton, Smith followed but the former's stay was short-lived. Following relegation from the Premiership, Smith left the Saints and after a spell out of football took charge of Oxford, newly relegated to the Conference, in 2006. He also took on his ex-U's assistant Bobby Roberts as his chief scout. During his career he won Manager of the Month awards with all of his clubs. He stepped down as manager of Oxford in November 2007 to take on a role as Director of Football.

* *See also Who's Who Managers section*

	League		Lge Cup		FA Cup		Other	
	A	G	A	G	A	G	A	G
1972–73	7+1	0	0	0	1	0	-	-
TOTAL	7+1	0	0	0	1	0	-	-

SMITH, John Trevor

Height: 5ft 5in. Weight: 11st.

Born: 8 September 1910, West Stanley.
Died: 23 October 1997, Bracknell.

■ Smith attracted a lot of interest as an amateur with South Moor and Annfield Plain. He attended trials at Portsmouth, Blackpool and Charlton in early 1930. Charlton took the plunge, and Smith scored six goals in 23 games before he joined Fulham in March 1935 for £1,000. At Craven Cottage, Smith scored 19 goals in 93 appearances and helped Fulham to reach the 1936 FA Cup semi-final, scoring against Chelsea and Derby in the fifth and sixth rounds. That prompted a move to Crystal Palace for a fee of £2,500 in February 1938. At Palace 14 goals were scored in 57 games, as well as guest appearances for Fulham, Notts County, Nottingham Forest and Tottenham during the war, before Smith moved to Yeovil in May 1946. U's boss Ted Fenton snatched Smith from the Somerset side and gave him his debut at Yeovil in March 1947. After a run of eight games, Smith was replaced by newcomer Arthur Biggs, but when the U's released him he was taken back into the Football League by Watford and played 10 times for the Hornets in 1947–48, mostly in the first three and a half weeks. Smith went back into the Southern League for 1948–49, captaining Bedford, before becoming manager of Wingate in 1949.

	League		Lge Cup		FA Cup		Other	
	A	G	A	G	A	G	A	G
1946–47	8	2	0	0	0	0	-	-
TOTAL	8	2	0	0	0	0	-	-

SMITH, Lindsay James

Height: 5ft 11in. Weight: 11st 1lb.

Born: 18 September 1954, Enfield.

■ Recommended by his Enfield school teacher, Smith joined United as a 15-year-old and was soon making his mark by becoming United's then youngest-ever debutant. Aged 16 years and 183 days when he came on as a substitute at Grimsby on 20 April 1971, Smith signed pro the following month. Initially a left-sided forward, Smith was converted to left-back and then centre-half, but his early career was as a 'super sub' for United. Winning promotion under Jim Smith in 1973–74, he established himself

in the U's Third Division side for the next two seasons before relegation once again hit the club. During that 1975–76 season he scored in three consecutive games in November, against Millwall, Chesterfield and Shrewsbury, and finished second-leading scorer with six goals. In 1976–77 he missed just one game as Bobby Roberts's United stormed back to the Third Division at the first attempt. Forming a formidable partnership with Steve Dowman at the heart of the Colchester defence, Smith weighed in with six vital goals. Having asked for a transfer, Smith refused a new contract in the summer of 1977 and went on loan to first Charlton (one appearance) and then Millwall (4+1 appearances) before being signed by Cambridge in the October for about £12,000. At the Abbey Stadium 'Wolfie', as he became known, won promotion to the Second Division at the first attempt and went on to play 173(+1) times for the 'other' U's. Desiring regular first-team football after losing his place at Cambridge, he moved to Plymouth in July 1982 and played in an FA Cup semi-final against Watford at Villa Park. After five goals in 76 League games, his family became homesick for Cambridge. He signed for George Graham's Millwall in July 1984 for £17,500 and won promotion to the Second Division in 1984–85, playing 54(+1) times, netting five League goals. His last League club was Cambridge where he played out his days as the club sunk rapidly from Second Division to Fourth, but he still managed to score 16 goals in 102 starts. Moving into non-League, Smith turned out for Bury Town and Ely City from 1989 and enjoyed a testimonial from Cambridge in August 1990.

	League		Lge Cup		FA Cup		Other	
	A	G	A	G	A	G	A	G
1970–71	0+1	0	0	0	0	0	-	-
1971–72	14+4	3	0	0	0	0	0	0
1972–73	26+5	1	1	0	3	0	-	-
1973–74	23+11	1	0	0	0+1	0	-	-
1974–75	38+5	1	2+3	0	1	0	-	-
1975–76	39+2	4	2	1	2	1	-	-
1976–77	45	6	3	1	6	0	-	-
TOTAL	185+28	16	8+3	2	12+1	1	0	0

SMITH, Nicholas Leslie 'Nicky'

Height: 5ft 8in. Weight: 10st 10lb.

Born: 28 January 1969, Berkeley.

■ Signing professional in July 1987, Smith enjoyed four seasons at Southend, winning promotion twice with relegation in between. Released at the end of 1989–90 season, he joined Colchester for their first season in the Conference. He was an ever present the following campaign when United completed the non-League double, winning the Conference title and the FA Trophy at Wembley. Smith notched one of the goals as Colchester beat Witton Albion 3–1. He weighed in with some valuable goals but moreover provided plenty of ammunition for U's rampant strike force of McDonough, McGavin and Bennett. After two seasons back in the League with the U's, Smith was released and joined Wycombe. Despite agreeing a one-year contract, Smith decided the

Buckinghamshire club was not for him and joined Sudbury Town. He briefly rekindled his League career with a spell at Northampton in January 1995, making six appearances and scoring one goal. Taking up a position in the police force, Smith remained a respected player on the local non-League scene, turning out for Braintree, Cambridge City, Maldon Town and Witham. In the summer of 2007 he was appointed assistant manager of AFC Sudbury and retained as a player, becoming manager in the summer of 2008.

	League		Lge Cup		FA Cup		Other	
	A	G	A	G	A	G	A	G
1990–91	*34*	*0*	*1*	*0*	*2*	*0*	*4*	*0*
1991–92	*42*	*8*	*1*	*0*	*3*	*0*	*9*	*3*
1992–93	42	4	2	0	3	0	2	0
1993–94	29+10	0	2	0	1	0	2	0
TOTAL	71+10	4	4	0	4	0	4	0
	76	*8*	*2*	*0*	*5*	*0*	*13*	*3*

SMITH, Reginald George Charles 'Reg'

Height: 5ft 10in. Weight: 11st 5lb.

Born: 1916, Westbury.

■ Smith began his career at hometown club Westbury United and then Trowbridge. He was snapped up by Bristol City for 1935–36 season and scored one goal in seven League starts at Ashton Gate. Smith made an immediate impact in U's first season, scoring 10 goals in 14, and was Colchester's first signing (23 June 1937), first hat-trick hero (against Bath 2 September 1937) and first transfer. Major Frank Buckley, manager of Wolves, spotted Smith's goalscoring ability and promptly signed him for a fee of £500 at the end of October 1937. U's manager Ted Davis also negotiated a clause that meant that Wolves would play at Layer Road in a charity match. Having been sharp enough to ask the same of Arsenal when they signed Cliff Fairchild, Layer Road hosted a crowd of over 17,000 for the clash of the two top-flight sides. While Smith played against Arsenal in that match, he made just two League starts at Molineux before joining Tranmere. After just one appearance for Rovers in 1938–39, he returned west to join Yeovil & Petters. Football was not the only sport that Smith excelled at as he was a good enough tennis player to enter Wimbledon three times.

	League		Lge Cup		FA Cup		Other	
	A	G	A	G	A	G	A	G
1937–38	8	3	1	2	-	-	5	5
TOTAL	8	3	1	2	-	-	5	5

SMITH, Sidney 'Sid'

■ After impressing in a pre-season trial, ex-Dundee United winger Smith was signed on a match basis at the start of 1946–47 and made his only first-team appearance in the first match of the season in a shock 3–2 defeat against Gloucester. After a couple of reserve games in September, including at Gorleston, where he scored his only U's goal in a 1–1 draw, Smith asked for his release and left in mid-November.

	League		Lge Cup		FA Cup		Other	
	A	G	A	G	A	G	A	G
1946–47	1	0	0	0	0	0	-	-
TOTAL	1	0	0	0	0	0	-	-

SODJE, Eftebore 'Efe'

Height: 6ft 1in. Weight: 12st.

Born: 5 October 1972, Greenwich.

■ Sodje was born in London but emigrated to Nigeria aged eight. Having played for Nigerian sides Invincible Leopards and Delta Steel Pioneers, he was tempted to try his luck back in England, having trials with Luton, Millwall and Wimbledon. Unable to obtain international clearance, he joined Conference side Stevenage, playing 99(+7) games between 1994 and 1997 adding nine goals as they won the Conference title but were denied a League place on ground grading rules. He became a prominent player, not least because of his trademark bandana, which he wore in every game. His performances persuaded League new boys Macclesfield to take a £30,000 chance on him, and he helped them to promotion in their first Football League season. Completing 83 appearances scoring three goals, Sodje left the relegated Silkmen in the summer of 1999 to join Luton. He played just 5(+4) games, and it was Steve Whitton that brought him to Layer Road on a three-month loan deal in March 2000. Sodje made his debut against Gillingham in a 2–1 Layer Road win but was called up by Nigeria. While registered with Colchester, he played against Eritrea both home and away in April 2000, becoming the first player ever to win a full international cap while with the club. The game in Eritrea on 11 April was played on a school field as the national stadium was under repair. The Nigerians won the return fixture 4–0 in Lagos three weeks later. Whitton was not happy with the defensive interruptions to United's run in to the season, and Sodje managed just two other games for United. In the 2000 close season he joined Crewe, playing 86(+12) games scoring three as Crewe were promoted back to League One at the first attempt after being relegated at the end of 2001–02. Sodje had fallen out of favour with his

country's management, having been an unused member of the 2000 African Nations Cup squad, but was called up for, and impressed in, World Cup warm-up friendlies against Scotland, Paraguay and Kenya, while scoring the winner in a 2–1 victory against Ireland in Dublin. He was included in the Nigerian World Cup squad for 2002 and made appearances against Argentina and England in the group stages. Surprisingly, Sodje was released from Crewe by Dario Gradi and joined Huddersfield in the 2003 summer break. He kept up his promotion-winning streak as the Terriers beat Mansfield in the Millennium Stadium Play-off Final, despite being stretchered off himself. A run of poor discipline saw him stripped of Town's captaincy and, completing 61(+6) appearances at The McAlpine, he moved again to Yeovil in March 2005 and once again enjoyed promotion. Steadying himself at League Two level, with 23(+3) games under his belt, he was enticed to join Southend as they vied with Colchester for the title and elevation to the Championship. Both Essex sides secured promotion in 2005–06 with Sodje picking up a League winners medal. When Southend were relegated, Sodje started the 2007–08 campaign on the books of Gillingham, moving to Bury on loan in February 2008. In all he earned 10 full international caps for Nigeria.

	League		Lge Cup		FA Cup		Other	
	A	G	A	G	A	G	A	G
1999–2000	3	0	0	0	0	0	0	0
TOTAL	3	0	0	0	0	0	0	0

SORRELL, Anthony Charles 'Tony'

Height: 5ft 11in. Weight: 12st 4lb.

Born: 17 October 1966, Hornchurch.

■ Starting out at Barking and then Bishop's Stortford, Sorrell joined League new boys Maidstone in August 1988 and featured as the Stones narrowly lost to Cambridge in the Fourth Division Play-off semi-final. Released after 46(+9) games at the end of 1990–91, having scored eight League goals, Sorrell joined Conference side Boston United, playing just a single game. A player whose lifestyle and reputed associates away from football made him a challenging proposition to manage, he spent a short

time at Peterborough before arriving at Colchester in November 1992, making his debut in a 3–1 defeat at Cardiff. Sent off in the FA Cup first-round tie at Gillingham a week later, he allegedly became embroiled in a training ground incident and was sacked by the club. He played eight games for Barnet from February 1993, scoring twice but drifted into non-League with Wycombe and Dagenham & Redbridge, where he played 29(+1) times in the following two seasons. He later turned out for Romford, where he was sent off four times between April 1996 and April 1997.

	League		Lge Cup		FA Cup		Other	
	A	G	A	G	A	G	A	G
1992–93	4+1	1	0	0	3	1	0	0
TOTAL	4+1	1	0	0	3	1	0	0

SOUTH, John Alan

Height: 6ft. Weight: 11st 4lb.

Born: 30 November 1952, Bow.

■ Yet another Leyton Orient youngster whom Dick Graham recruited to Layer

Road in an attempt to shake off the 'Grandad's Army' tag and save wages, South was taken on a three-month trial. He played just four games, all of which ended in defeat, during which time Graham resigned. South's days were numbered, and he was released by new manager Jim Smith at the end of his trial, initially being reported to have returned to Orient before disappearing into non-League football.

	League		Lge Cup		FA Cup		Other	
	A	G	A	G	A	G	A	G
1972–73	4	0	0	0	0	0	-	-
TOTAL	4	0	0	0	0	0	-	-

SOUTHAM, James Henry 'Jimmy'

Height: 5ft 7in. Weight: 11st 2lb.

Born: 19 August 1917, Willenhall.

Died: October 1996, Walsall.

■ A full-back on the books of West Bromwich Albion, Southam was a private in the 15th Infantry Training Corps. Although not making any official League appearances for Albion, he played 34 times during the war years and also guested for Arsenal, Aberaman and Newport. A regular in the Colchester side in 1945–46 until just after Christmas, Southam got fed up with continually being asked to play in different positions – he had worn six different shirt numbers and the position went with the number in those days – so he defected to Ipswich Town and played 10 times at Portman Road in 1945–46 as he prepared himself for a professional career after demob. He guested a couple more times for the U's in April 1946, adding the centre-half spot to the list of positions previously played. Having played three times in wartime for Newport, he joined the Welshmen for the 1946–47 season for £300, playing eight times, and a year later moved to Birmingham, playing a solitary League game at St Andrews. The core of his League career, however, came at Northampton where he played 144 games between 1949 and 1954. His career ended on the books of Walsall in 1955, but he remained as trainer at Fellows Park into the early 1960s.

	League		Lge Cup		FA Cup		Other	
	A	G	A	G	A	G	A	G
1945–46	11	1	2	0	0	0	-	-
TOTAL	11	1	2	0	0	0	-	-

STAFFORD, Clive Andrew

Height: 6ft 1in. Weight: 12st 2lb.

Born: 4 April 1963, Ipswich.

■ Originally with Diss Town, Stafford joined Colchester in February 1989, making his debut in a 3–1 defeat at Cambridge the following month. He replaced Kevin Bedford at left-back and played in all of Jock Wallace's side's remaining games, bar one, as Colchester saved themselves from relegation to the Conference. When Mick Mills took over, Stafford played second fiddle to Karl Goddard at left-back and as a result went to Exeter on loan in February 1990, playing two games for the eventual Fourth Division champions. Stafford had been given a three-year contract to persuade him to give up his lucrative job to become a full-time footballer, but he played just one further first-team game for the U's on his return from Devon. He was made available for a free transfer by Ian Atkins and in October 1990 went on loan to Bury Town, signing permanently for the Suffolk club at the start of December. He later also played for the other leading non-League club in the county, Sudbury.

	League		Lge Cup		FA Cup		Other	
	A	G	A	G	A	G	A	G
1988–89	16	0	0	0	0	0	0	0
1989–90	15+2	0	0	0	1	0	1	0
TOTAL	31+2	0	0	0	1	0	1	0

STAMPER, Frank Fielden Thorpe

Height: 5ft 11in. Weight: 11st.

Born: 22 February 1926, West Hartlepool.
Died: July 1999, Hartlepool.

■ Stamper was a Hartlepool amateur who had played for Hesledene Colliery before joining the Army and was stationed with the Army Fire Fighting Centre at the Cherry Tree Camp. He signed pro forms with the U's on 3 March 1947 and played a couple of late-season games at left-half as deputy for Ted Fenton. All his 10 or so reserve games were at inside-right, and he continued with the reserves through 1947–48 playing in either wing-half spot, and appeared in half a dozen late-season first-team games again at wing-half. He was demobbed in July 1948 and, with full-time training and a switch to centre-half, made his breakthrough in the spot vacated by Ted Fenton's departure to West Ham. At the end of 1948–49 Stamper refused the U's terms in favour of a move back to his native North East and joined Hartlepool, going on to play 301 League games for his home town scoring 25 goals. He also scored against the famous Busby Babes of Manchester United in the FA Cup third round of 1956–57. After football, Stamper became a builder, before retiring in 1991.

	League		Lge Cup		FA Cup		Other	
	A	G	A	G	A	G	A	G
1946–47	2	0	0	0	0	0	-	-
1947–48	4	0	2	0	0	0	-	-
1948–49	37	0	5	0	1	0	-	-
TOTAL	43	0	7	0	1	0	-	-

STAMPS, Scott

Height: 5ft 10in. Weight: 11st.

Born: 20 March 1975, Edgbaston.

■ Stamps served his Youth Training Scheme at Torquay, signing professionally in July 1993, having already made his debut for the Third Division side. Completing 80(+6) games at full-back, Stamps scored five times. Steve Wignall signed the player in March 1997 for £15,000, and he made his debut at Hartlepool in the same month, replacing Paul Gibbs. His only goal came in a stunning 4–4 draw with homeless Brighton at Gillingham's Priestfield Stadium on Boxing Day 1997. Released by Mick Wadsworth, Stamps joined Conference side Kidderminster, appearing 34(+1) times, as they won the title and promotion to the League. He played a further 123(+6) times for Harriers in the Football League. Released by Kiddy, he joined Tamworth in August 2004 and played 60 more games in the Conference. Stamps had a spell with Bromsgrove in 2006–07 and then joined Boldmere St Michaels in the Midland Alliance.

	League		Lge Cup		FA Cup		Other	
	A	G	A	G	A	G	A	G
1996–97	7+1	0	0	0	0	0	0	0
1997–98	26	1	2	0	2+1	0	1	0
1998–99	19+2	0	2	0	1	0	0+1	0
TOTAL	52+3	1	4	0	3+1	0	1+1	0

STANYON

■ Stanyon was a soldier with the Army Fire Fighting Service and was one of four members of his unit recruited at the last minute, whose only connection with the U's is the scratch team sent to Yeovil and hammered 8–0 in September 1945, when the Army refused six regular Colchester players leave. The provenance of the club connections claimed for this quartet seem dubious, given that none can be verified and none of the four were invited to play again. That is not to say that Stanyon, for example, had no connection with the club quoted, in his case Barnsley, but it is certain he never played for their first team.

	League		Lge Cup		FA Cup		Other	
	A	G	A	G	A	G	A	G
1945–46	1	0	0	0	0	0	-	-
TOTAL	1	0	0	0	0	0	-	-

STARK, William Reid 'Billy'

Height: 5ft 8in. Weight: 11st 8lb.

Born: 27 May 1937, Glasgow.

■ Stark came from an elite band of players who had been on the books of both Glasgow giants. Having joined Celtic in 1956, he moved to Ibrox two years later on a free transfer but did not make a first-team appearance for either. His first English club was Crewe for whom he signed at the start of 1960–61 scoring 13 League goals in 38 League appearances. He also featured in Crewe's FA Cup run, which included a 2–1 victory over Chelsea, in which he scored. Carlisle grabbed his signature for the 1961–62 season, and the Cumbrians were promoted, helped by his 17 goals in 35 League starts. Colchester signed him in November 1962 for about £3,500, and he played a part as United consolidated their Third Division status. He became a prolific scorer but could not stop United suffering relegation back to Division Four at the end of 1964–65. After three games of the following season, he was transferred to Luton in a deal that saw Ted Phillips and £1,000 arrive at Layer Road. An arthritic knee restricted his Luton career to just 8 games, although he kept up his impressive goal ratio with four goals. He drifted in to non-League with Corby but was signed by Chesterfield for the 1966–67 season, where he was the Spireites' leading scorer with 15 goals. Not one to rest on his laurels, Stark was on his way again at the end of that season, joining Newport, where his League career ended with two goals in 11 League appearances. He finished his playing career with Matlock Town and Boston United. Initially employed in Sheffield, he then took up a position as an open cast coal field production manager in the Chesterfield area.

	League		Lge Cup		FA Cup		Other	
	A	G	A	G	A	G	A	G
1962–63	21	3	0	0	0	0	-	-
1963–64	43	16	2	2	2	0	-	-
1964–65	28	13	0	0	2	1	-	-
1965–66	3	1	0	0	0	0	-	-
TOTAL	95	33	2	2	4	1	-	-

STEELE, Daniel 'Danny'

Height: 6ft 2in. Weight: 13st 6lb.

Born: 11 October 1982, London.

■ A junior with Millwall, Steele failed to make the grade at The New Den, having signed professional forms in February 2000. A regular in the reserves, he was released and snapped up by Steve Whitton in the summer of 2002, making his debut as a substitute against Brentford in August but unfortunately giving away a penalty moments after arriving on the pitch. The successful spot-kick gave the Bees a 1–0 win. Looking unlikely to displace regular centre-backs Alan White and Scott Fitzgerald, and with the club under caution from the League following a punch-up with Oldham in which the club video showed Steele to be a very active participant, he departed by mutual consent in the December. He later played for Fisher Athletic, the South London non-League side.

	League		Lge Cup		FA Cup		Other	
	A	G	A	G	A	G	A	G
2002–03	6+2	0	0	0	0	0	1	0
TOTAL	6+2	0	0	0	0	0	1	0

STEELE, Ernest 'Ernie'

Height: 5ft 11in. Weight: 11st.

Born: 18 June 1908, Middleton.
Died: 1972.

■ A former Millwall colleague of Bill Bower, Steele was recommended to guest for United at Bath in February 1946 by Bower from his Army station at nearby Yeovil. Unfortunately, United were thrashed 8–0 for the second time during the season. His career began before the war at Rochdale in 1931, where he scored three goals in 19 games. Moving to Oldham he scored once in 14 starts for the Latics. Next it was Torquay for the 1933–34 season, then Notts County, where in two seasons he notched up 54 League appearances, scoring nine goals. A brief spell at Bath City came before a

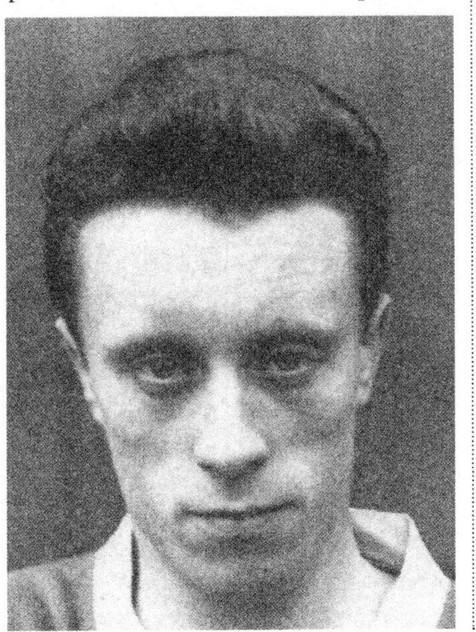

move to Millwall (1936–37 37 appearances/9 goals) and Crystal Palace (1938–39 33/9). He joined Rochdale for the 1939–40 season, but his League career was then interrupted by the war, and he later played for Barry, Northwich and Ossett.

	League		Lge Cup		FA Cup		Other	
	A	G	A	G	A	G	A	G
1945–46	1	0	0	0	0	0	-	-
TOTAL	1	0	0	0	0	0	-	-

STEWART, Alexander 'Alex'

Height: 5ft 9in. Weight: 12st 7lb.

Born: Perth.

■ Stewart joined Colchester on a month's trial on 28 July 1946 but was only seen three times at Layer Road before being released, netting twice in a trial game and again against Gloucester on the opening day of the 1946–47 season. Dropped after that game, he played once for the reserves before departing. It is possible that he was somewhat older than the 30 reported at the time as an authorative modern reference source for Scottish players traces him back to having made his Scottish League debut for Queen's Park in October 1928. His, though, is quite a common name in Scottish football; at least four Alexander Stewarts played in the Scottish League between the wars, and two contemporary sources suggest that the modern one may have combined the records of two individuals. We are confident that our Alex Stewart had a spell in Sheffield with the Wednesday in or around 1935–36, without playing in the Football League, and then returned to Scotland with Motherwell and hit the most prolific form of his career, being leading scorer in 1936–37 and 1937–38 with 28 and 18 goals respectively, including six against Celtic in 1937. He played for the Scottish League against the English League in 1937 and moved on to Falkirk, his club before arriving at Layer Road, during 1938–39. The Alexander Stewart who started with Queen's Park in 1928 moved to St Mirren, where he scored at well over a goal a game in 1929–30 as they finished fifth in the League before trying his luck in Wales and England in 1931 with Rhyl then Sheffield United. He did not break into the first team at Bramall Lane and in early 1933 returned to Scotland with St Johnstone, the club of our Stewart's home town Perth, playing over 70 times to the end of 1934–35 and scoring 16 times in 28 games in that season. The unresolved question is whether he then goes back to Sheffield but this time with the Wednesday.

	League		Lge Cup		FA Cup		Other	
	A	G	A	G	A	G	A	G
1946–47	1	1	0	0	0	0	-	-
TOTAL	1	1	0	0	0	0	-	-

STEWART, Ian Edwin

Height: 5ft 7in. Weight: 11st 9lb.

Born: 10 September 1961, Belfast, NI.

■ A QPR junior, Stewart signed forms at Loftus Road in May 1980. He began to establish himself in Rangers's side in 1982–83, helped by a loan spell with Millwall, where he scored three goals in 10(+1) starts following his transfer deadline move. Returning back to his club, he found Rangers promoted to the top flight, and he enjoyed 30 starts in that First Division season. A Northern Ireland international, Stewart scored the goal on his home debut that defeated the might of West Germany at Windsor Park in November 1982. He also played in the World Cup in 1986 and in all gained 31 full caps. Completing 55(+12) games for the R's, Stewart moved to Newcastle at the start of 1985–86, scoring three times in 34(+8) games. A move to Portsmouth in the summer of 1987 yielded just one substitute appearance, and he had a loan spell at Brentford in February 1988. A year later, Stewart signed for Aldershot, appearing 94(+6) times at the Recreation Ground, before the Hampshire club were forced to close mid-season on financial grounds. U's boss Roy McDonough stepped in and recruited Stewart for the run-in to the Conference title. His presence certainly helped, but he fell foul of McDonough when he refused to go on a three-day bonding trip to games at Boston and Macclesfield. Stewart spent some time with Harrow Borough before becoming a respected member of the Irish Football Association with a UEFA 'A' coaching badge and with responsibilities for youth development and as manager of the national ladies Under-19 side.

	League		Lge Cup		FA Cup		Other	
	A	G	A	G	A	G	A	G
1991–92	6+4	2	0	0	0	0	3+1	3
TOTAL	6+4	2	0	0	0	0	3+1	3

STEWART, Reginald 'Reg'

Height: 6ft 2½in. Weight: 12st 10lb.

Born: 3 October 1925, Sheffield.

■ Tough, no-nonsense centre-half Stewart began on the books of Sheffield Wednesday. He made six full appearances for the Owls and moved to Colchester in 1949 in preference to York and Accrington Stanley. Stewart, whose uncle Ernie Blenkinsop played for England in the late 1920s and early 1930s, missed just one game as Colchester got their most welcome Football League status in 1950. He also picked up a Southern League Cup-winners' medal on the way. The U's had to pay Wednesday £1,000 for his League registration but it was money well spent, and he remained a fixture in Colchester's defence for the ensuing seven seasons amassing 269 League appearances. His two goals came against

Southend in April 1955 (2–0) and a 1–1 draw with Gillingham in September of the same year. A broken arm forced him to miss the start of 1956–57, and that allowed Chic Milligan to establish himself until ruled out for the last couple of months by a broken collar bone. Stewart was made captain for the final game of 1956–57, so it was probably already decided that he was leaving, and he joined Hastings in July 1957. A year later he returned to the local area to play for Clacton and continued with them into the 1960s. He ran the successful Paxman's Social Club and was guest of honour at Layer Road on his 80th birthday in 2005. One U's landmark he would probably prefer not to hold is that of being the first player sent off for the club in the Football League. It happened at Millwall on 8 December 1951, and the ref's report said it was for a deliberate kick. Stewart was fined £5, severely censured and warned as to his future conduct by the disciplinary hearing and missed two games over the New Year.

	League		Lge Cup		FA Cup		Other	
	A	G	A	G	A	G	A	G
1949–50	*45*	*0*	*5*	*0*	*1*	*0*	-	-
1950–51	46	0	-	-	2	0	-	-
1951–52	44	0	-	-	3	0	-	-
1952–53	40	0	-	-	5	0	-	-
1953–54	27	0	-	-	0	0	-	-
1954–55	45	1	-	-	2	0	-	-
1955–56	13	1	-	-	0	0	-	-
1956–57	41	0	-	-	1	0	-	-
1957–58	13	0	-	-	0	0	-	-
TOTAL	256	2	-	-	13	0	-	-
	45	*0*	*5*	*0*	*1*	*0*	-	-

STOCKLEY-PHILLIPS, Samuel Joshua 'Sam'

Height: 6ft. Weight: 12st 11lb.

Born: 5 September 1977, Tiverton.

■ Stockley commenced his career on the books of Southampton but, after serving his youth traineeship, failed to make the first team. He was transferred to Barnet in December 1996 five months after signing his professional contract with the Saints. He was used as the makeweight in the deal that saw Barnet goalkeeper Maik Taylor journey in the opposite direction for a fee of £500,000. Stockley became a regular fixture at Underhill and twice was a losing Play-off semi-finalist – the first of which was against Colchester in 1998. When Barnet were relegated out of the League just a season after the second Play-off defeat Stockley was snapped up by former Colchester manager Ian Atkins at Oxford for £150,000. He had already racked up 177(+5) appearances, scoring twice, and played a further 39(+2) games for Oxford in the 2001–02 season. Steve Whitton brought Stockley to Layer Road in August 2002, initially on loan, and he became an instant hit with fans. He featured in memorable FA Cup runs in successive seasons, only tasting defeat to big guns Sheffield United and Blackburn. Colchester enjoyed an amazing unbeaten run in their 2005–06 season when they won promotion to the Championship for the first time. Stockley was blamed by manager Phil Parkinson for the goal that

ended the run at Swindon on Boxing Day 2005 and for the goal scored by Nottingham Forest at Layer Road a week later. After that he only appeared in LDV Trophy ties and was loaned to Blackpool on deadline day 2006, along with teammate Gareth Williams, in a deal that saw Tangerines' Scott Vernon arrive at Layer Road. Stockley played 3(+4) games for Blackpool but joined Wycombe on a two-year deal in the summer after a trial at Luton. He made 33(+1) appearances in 2006–07, scoring one League goal, and remained at Wycombe in 2007–08 before joining Port Vale in the summer of 2008.

	League		Lge Cup		FA Cup		Other	
	A	G	A	G	A	G	A	G
2002–03	31+2	1	0	0	1	0	1	0
2003–04	44	0	2	0	6	0	5+1	0
2004–05	33+4	1	2	0	5	0	0	0
2005–06	21+6	1	1	0	2+1	0	4	0
TOTAL	129+12	3	5	0	14+1	0	10+1	0

STOCKWELL, Michael Thomas 'Micky'

Height: 5ft 9in. Weight: 11st 4lb.

Born: 14 February 1965, Chelmsford.

■ Stockwell served his apprenticeship at Ipswich but after signing on full forms in December 1982 had to wait exactly three years for his debut at Coventry. An ever-present in Ipswich's 1991–92 Second Division Championship-winning side, Stockwell was named Player of the Year in the following Premiership campaign. Part of three successive Play-off failures, he missed the entire 1994–95 season

through injury. When Ipswich finally did return to the Premiership, Stockwell was released and teamed up with his old Portman Road colleague Steve Whitton at Layer Road in the summer of 2000. A model of consistency, Stockwell was ever present in his first season and scooped the Colchester Player of the Year award and was top scorer. He retired at the end of the 2002–03 season, aged 38, to become player-coach at Heybridge and also figured at nearby Maldon. In 2004 he became manager of Eastern Counties League Woodbridge Town. In all, he played 464(+42) League games for Town, scoring 35 times in a career spanning over 700 first-team games for Ipswich and Colchester. In November 2007 Stockwell stepped down from his post at Woodbridge.

	League		Lge Cup		FA Cup		Other	
	A	G	A	G	A	G	A	G
2000–01	46	11	4	0	1	0	1	0
2001–02	45+1	8	2	1	2	0	1+1	1
2002–03	30+10	2	1	0	1	0	1	0
TOTAL	121+11	21	7	1	4	0	3+1	1

STONEMAN, Paul

Height: 6ft 1in. Weight: 13st 6lb.

Born: 26 February 1973, Whitley Bay.

■ Stoneman first appeared for Blackpool in their Fourth Division Play-off-winning campaign of 1991–92. In four seasons at Bloomfield Road he made 38(+5) appearances after progressing through the YTS ranks. George Burley signed the centre-half as emergency loan cover for Gus Caesar, just days before the U's boss was to walk out on the club. Stoneman made his debut in a surprise 2–1 win at Fulham on 27 December 1994 and four days later scored at Layer Road as United drew 2–2 with Hereford. Stoneman joined Halifax on a free transfer and spent 10 seasons at The Shay in both the Conference and the League. Playing 118(+3) games in the Conference, he added another 137(+2) games back in the League, scoring 10 and 11 goals respectively. He was voted Halifax Player of the Year in 1998–99, and when released in April 2005 he joined Harrogate Town and later played for Wakefield and Bridlington Town, where he became player-manager at Christmas 2006.

	League		Lge Cup		FA Cup		Other	
	A	G	A	G	A	G	A	G
1994–95	3	1	0	0	0	0	0	0
TOTAL	3	1	0	0	0	0	0	0

STRATTON, Reginald Malcolm 'Reg'

Height: 5ft 10in. Weight: 10st 12lb.

Born: 10 July 1939, Farnborough.

■ An England Amateur and Youth international, Stratton joined Fulham from Woking in May 1959 after netting for Woking in a 3–0 1956 FA Amateur Cup Final win over Ilford in front of 71,000 at Wembley. He won Amateur caps against Germany, Ireland and Switzerland in 1957. Surprisingly, after scoring 64 goals in 123 games for Woking, he found the net just once at Craven Cottage, against Liverpool in March 1964, from 21 League appearances. He also added a couple of FA Cup goals for the Cottagers. He regained his scoring touch at Layer Road, being leading scorer in three consecutive seasons, notching 17, 24 and nine goals respectively as United won promotion in his first season 1965–66. He scored the goal that put United into a 1–0 lead against West Brom in the FA Cup third round of 1967–68. Refusing new terms, Stratton spent time on United's transfer list and in the summer of 1968 was due to go to Canada to play for Vancouver Royals alongside future Colchester captain Bobby Cram, but the deal fell through, and instead he joined Brentwood Town, later playing for Basingstoke and Dover.

	League		Lge Cup		FA Cup		Other	
	A	G	A	G	A	G	A	G
1965–66	37	17	2	3	0	0	-	-
1966–67	46	24	1	0	2	0	-	-
1967–68	29	9	1	0	3	2	-	-
TOTAL	112	50	4	3	5	2	-	-

SUTTON, John B.

■ Sutton was an amateur centre-forward with Brentford who played just one game for that club in 1945–46 and was in the squad for 1946–47 but failed to play first-team football at Griffin Park. He had guested for Bristol City in March 1946 and was one of the 'Brentford Six' who completed the U's team at Guildford on 13 April 1946 for a Southern League Cup. The U's won 5–2, and Sutton scored a hat-trick.

	League		Lge Cup		FA Cup		Other	
	A	G	A	G	A	G	A	G
1945–46	0	0	1	3	0	0	-	-
TOTAL	0	0	1	3	0	0	-	-

SVARC, Robert Louis 'Bobby'

Height: 5ft 7in. Weight: 11st 2lb.

Born: 8 February 1946, Leicester.

■ Midlands born Svarc, of Czech descent, followed in manager Jim Smith's footsteps when he joined Colchester from Boston United in

December 1972. His earlier career had started at Leicester in March 1963, for whom he scored twice in 13 appearances. Transferred to Lincoln in September 1970, he netted 16 League goals for the Imps in 40(+5) appearances. After a loan spell at Barrow in September 1970, in which he scored four times in 15 appearances, and a return to Sincil Bank he drifted into non-League, where he joined Boston for £2,000 in 1972. Netting 17 times in 23 appearances was enough to convince the U's board to give manager Jim Smith a Christmas present and pay out £6,000 to bring him to Colchester. His eight goals in the half season that followed were not enough to save United from re-election, but he found his feet in the next two seasons and formed a lethal partnership with fellow Boston recruit John Froggatt in the Third Division campaign of 1974–75. Scoring 25 League goals as United won promotion in 1973–74, Svarc also became the first U's player to score four goals in a match since Bobby Hunt and Martyn King had done so in the club's record 9–1 win over Bradford in December 1961. Svarc's quartet came at Chester in November 1973, although the national press originally only credited him with two of the goals in the 4–0 win. U's manager Jim Smith had moved to Blackburn, and it was no surprise when he came in with a £25,000 bid to take Svarc to Ewood Park in October 1975. Despite scoring 16 goals in 42(+1) games, he was dogged by serious injury. He joined former Lincoln colleague Graham Taylor at Watford in October 1977 on loan, but his single appearance saw him suffer the injury that finished his career. He was forced to retire from the game and set up a security installation company in the Blackburn area. In May 1996 he received a testimonial from Colchester, although it was somewhat overshadowed by the club's preparations for the Third Division Play-off semi-finals against Plymouth. Jim Smith, then manager of Derby, brought his promotion-winning side to Layer Road, and the small crowd that turned up failed to do justice to one of Colchester's sharpest-ever strikers.

	League		Lge Cup		FA Cup		Other	
	A	G	A	G	A	G	A	G
1972–73	20	8	0	0	0	0	-	-
1973–74	46	25	1	1	1	0	-	-
1974–75	42	24	6	1	2	0	-	-
1975–76	8	3	2	2	0	0	-	-
TOTAL	116	60	9	4	3	0	-	-

SWIFT, Don

■ A local man who worked at Severalls Hospital and played in the Border League for their works team, Severalls Athletic, Swift signed amateur forms for the U's in October 1946 and re-signed at the start of the 1947–48 and 1948–49 seasons, although he usually played for Severalls. All his first-team appearances came in December 1946 when he was tried at centre-half in preference to Bob Harding before Ted Fenton decided to move himself over from right-half to make space for Digger Kettle.

	League		Lge Cup		FA Cup		Other	
	A	G	A	G	A	G	A	G
1946–47	2	0	1	0	0	0	-	-
TOTAL	2	0	1	0	0	0	-	-

SWINDLEHURST, David 'Dave'

Height: 6ft 2in. Weight: 13st 23lb.

Born: 6 January 1956, Edgware.

■ England Youth international Swindlehurst served his apprenticeship with Crystal Palace, signing professional in January 1973. In a prolific goalscoring career he bagged 73 goals in 221(+16) appearances. He was leading scorer for Palace in four seasons as they clawed their way back from the Third Division. He scored the goal that won Palace promotion in 1976–77 and repeated the feat two seasons later as the Eagles beat Burnley in front of 51,000 at Selhurst to return to the top flight. He also played in the 1975–76 FA Cup semi-final when Palace were still a Third Division side. Earning one England Under-21 cap, he moved to Derby in February 1980 scoring 29 in 110 starts, but the Rams were relegated to Division Two in his first season. On deadline day 1983 he moved back to the capital with West Ham for £200,000 and once more was back in the top flight. Eighteen goals in 52(+9) starts followed before Swindlehurst moved to Second Division Sunderland in the 1985 close season. Despite 11 goals in 59 games in the North East, Sunderland were dramatically relegated to the Third Division, and Swindlehurst was the victim of a mass clear-out. He played briefly in Cyprus with Anorthosis before playing a couple of games for Wimbledon in March 1988. Roger Brown brought the player to Colchester in the summer of 1988. When Brown was sacked following an 8–0 humiliation at Leyton Orient, his assembled team was broken up, and Swindlehurst was loaned to Peterborough in December 1988. After one goal in four games, Swindlehurst hung up his professional boots and joined non-League Bromley. He subsequently had spells as reserves coach back at Palace, before being sacked in September 2002, was assistant manager at Crawley until September 2005, where he won an unfair dismissal case before becoming manager of, firstly, Chipstead and in November 2006 Whyteleafe, where he included ex-U's 'keeper Carl Emberson in his side.

	League		Lge Cup		FA Cup		Other	
	A	G	A	G	A	G	A	G
1988–89	12	5	2	0	2	0	2	1
TOTAL	12	5	2	0	2	0	2	1

T

TANNER, Adam David

Height: 6ft. Weight: 13st.

Born: 25 October 1973, Maldon.

■ Tanner's career began brightly after completing his Ipswich apprenticeship. In 1994, two years after signing professional, he made his debut in the Premiership, going on to play 9(+1) games and scoring twice, one of which was a glorious winner at Liverpool. He remained a squad player with Ipswich but was found guilty of taking cocaine as a result of a random drugs test and banned for three months in January 1997. Ipswich stood by him, and he resumed his place in the squad on completion of the ban. After making 49(+24) appearances, scoring seven goals, Tanner was released from Portman Road after being arrested for drink-driving following a car crash, to join Peterborough in March 2000. He failed to appear for Posh and in the summer was given the opportunity to rekindle his career at Colchester by former teammate Steve Whitton. He made his debut as a substitute at Bury in September 2000 but failed to make any impact. He was released and signed for Canvey Island.

	League		Lge Cup		FA Cup		Other	
	A	G	A	G	A	G	A	G
2000–01	1+3	0	1+1	0	0	0	0	0
TOTAL	1+3	0	1+1	0	0	0	0	0

TAYLOR, John Patrick

Height: 6ft 2in. Weight: 11st 12lb.

Born: 24 November 1964, Norwich.

■ John Taylor came through the U's junior ranks in the early 1980s, starting in the Border League side at 16. He was considered a utility player and wore virtually every shirt number in the reserves between 1981 and 1984 appearing most often at right-back. His slender frame was thought not to have the strength for full-time training, and with the club running on a shoestring budget there was not scope to carry a 20-year-old who was not ready for first-team action so Taylor was released at Christmas 1984 having made just one substitute appearance, in a League Cup tie at Reading in August 1983. He joined Sudbury Town, where he matured physically, winning two Eastern Counties League titles and reaching the FA Vase semi-finals, before John Beck decided Taylor would be suitable for his particular brand of football and took him to Cambridge in August 1988. Taylor enjoyed three fantastic seasons as the Abbey Stadium side rose from the basement to Division Two in successive seasons before failing to Leicester in the 1991–92 Play-offs, which could have brought Premiership football to Cambridgeshire. He played at Wembley as Cambridge won the 1989–90 Play-offs against Chesterfield and also scored five goals in successive FA Cup campaigns as

Cambridge lost narrowly to Crystal Palace in 1988–89 and to Arsenal at Highbury a year later in quarter-final ties. During the Second Division Play-off campaign he moved to Bristol Rovers on deadline day 1992 in a swap deal with Devon White, and scored 44 goals in 91(+4) appearances to add to the 46 goals he had scored in 139(+21) games at The Abbey. Rovers were relegated in Taylor's second season, and in the summer of 1994 he moved to Bradford in a £300,000 deal. His 11 goals in 35(+1) games for the Bantams were enough to persuade Luton to spend £200,000 on the player in March 1995. His goalscoring dried up a little as Luton were relegated. His three goals in 27(+10) resulted in two loans spells. First he joined Lincoln in September 1996 scoring twice in five games. In November of the same year Taylor returned to Layer Road under Steve Wignall. He scored both goals in a 2–1 win at Chester – his first senior goals for the club coming 13 years after his debut. He repeated the feat a week later with two penalties in a 7–1 thrashing of Lincoln and added his final goal against his old club Cambridge in the last game before Christmas 1996. Wignall wanted to sign the player, but Cambridge could offer a coaching role as a bonus. He added a further 40 League goals to his Cambridge statistics in 103 appearances, plus an incredible 72 further cameos as substitute. In 1998, Cambridge fans voted Taylor their all-time most influential player. Taylor celebrated by surpassing Alan Biley's club record goalscoring total in April 1999. In January 2002, after a six-week spell as caretaker manager, he was appointed player-boss of Cambridge following the sacking of John Beck. Although he led his side to a 4–1 defeat to Blackpool in the LDV Final at the Millennium Stadium, he was unable to prevent Cambridge from sliding into the basement division. In March 2004, after two seasons of financial re-management following the ITV Digital collapse, he was relieved of his duties as the side headed for the Conference. A brief non-contract spell at Northampton yielded one goal in the remaining 3(+5) games of the 2003–04 season. He returned to local football, coaching Mildenhall before turning out as player-manager for Long Melford in the Eastern Counties League. He was sacked as manager of Newmarket in August 2007.

	League		Lge Cup		FA Cup		Other	
	A	G	A	G	A	G	A	G
1983–84	0	0	0+1	0	0	0	0	0
1996–97	8	5	0	0	0	0	1	0
TOTAL	8	5	0+1	0	0	0	1	0

TAYLOR, Leslie 'Les'

Height: 5ft 8in. Weight: 11st 7lb.

Born: 4 December 1956, North Shields.

■ Spotted playing for the famous Wallsend Boys Club, Taylor had three trials with Leeds before joining Oxford. He was captain of Oxford's youth side in 1974–75 and earned his debut in March 1975. He was voted Third Division Player of the Year in 1977–78 and became the youngest-ever Oxford captain at the age of 21. He completed 219 games at The Manor Ground, scoring 15 goals, before being involved in a then club record £100,000, plus striker Keith Cassells, transfer to Watford in November 1980. Watford were promoted to the top flight in his second season and finished second in Division One in the next. The pinnacle of his career was leading Watford to the 1984 FA Cup Final, where they lost to Everton. Completing 167(+5) games, scoring 13 times, he lost his place to new arrival Brian Talbot and moved to Reading in October 1986. He once again played at Wembley as the Royals won the Simod Cup in 1988. U's caretaker manager Steve Foley was in charge when Taylor arrived

at Layer Road in January 1989 for a £20,000 fee, after playing 69(+6) times at Elm Park. A steadying influence in Colchester's midfield, Taylor's only goal came in a 4–1 win over Maidstone in September 1989. Sadly, United were relegated to the Conference at the end of the campaign, and despite having two years left on his contract Taylor was clearly not in Ian Atkins's plans for the return journey, being transfer-listed early in the season and leaving by mutual consent by April 1991. He was head of youth development at Oxford in 2005 after having a spell as assistant manager to the first team in 1999.

	League		Lge Cup		FA Cup		Other	
	A	G	A	G	A	G	A	G
1988–89	14+2	0	0	0	0	0	0	0
1989–90	30+6	1	0+2	0	0+2	0	1	0
1990–91	*0*	*0*	*1*	*0*	*0*	*0*	*0*	*0*
TOTAL	44+8	1	0+2	0	0+2	0	1	0
	0	*0*	*1*	*0*	*0*	*0*	*0*	*0*

TAYLOR, Paul Anthony

Height: 5ft 11in. Weight: 11st 8lb.

Born: 3 December 1949, Sheffield.

■ Taylor made his debut for home-town club Sheffield Wednesday against QPR in August 1971 and made a further 4(+1) appearances for the Owls before transferring to York in the summer of 1973. After just four games for the Bootham Crescent side he was loaned to Hereford in January 1974 and appeared just once as a substitute. As Colchester pressed for promotion to Division Three, manager Jim Smith bolstered his squad with Taylor's signature on deadline day March 1974. Taylor appeared in all but two of United's remaining games as they secured the third promotion spot behind Gillingham and Peterborough. Released at the end of the season, Taylor signed for Southport and eventually carved out a sustained career, scoring 16 times in 95 games. Taylor switched to the US and played for Tampa Bay Rowdies. In 1982 he became assistant manager to Keith Peacock at Gillingham as the Gills almost made it to the second tier, losing a Play-off Final replay to Swindon. When Peacock was sacked, Taylor took over the reigns in December 1987 and suffered a torturous time, being sacked himself in October 1988. In early 1989 he became assistant to John Barnwell at Walsall and had a spell as caretaker manager between

March and May 1990. In 1994–95 he became general manager of Walsall and is currently director of football at The Bescot.

	League		Lge Cup		FA Cup		Other	
	A	G	A	G	A	G	A	G
1973–74	6+3	0	0	0	0	0	-	-
TOTAL	6+3	0	0	0	0	0	-	-

TELFORD, William Albert 'Billy'

Height: 5ft 11in. Weight: 11st 3lb.

Born: 5 March 1956, Carlisle.

■ Telford began his career as a Tranmere apprentice without making an appearance at Prenton Park. He joined Manchester City in August 1975 and made one substitute appearance against Coventry before being transferred to Peterborough just a month later. Despite scoring two goals in 3(+1) appearances during September, he failed to establish

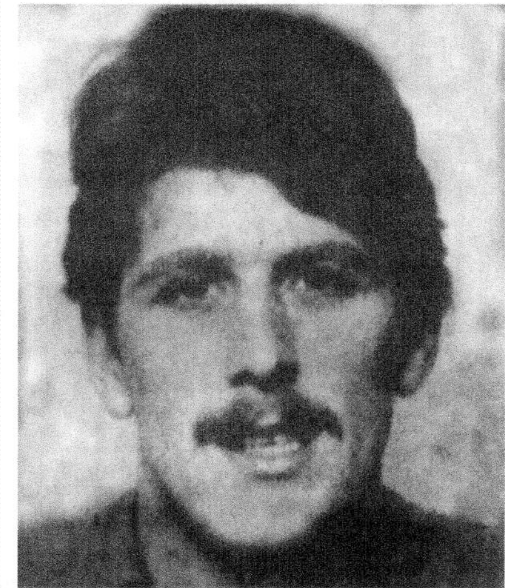

himself in the team and joined struggling Colchester in January 1976. U's were in the midst of a seven-game losing run, having been thrashed 6–0 at Brighton a week earlier. Telford scored within three minutes of his Layer Road debut against Hereford, but United were already a goal down and went on to lose 4–1. On returning to London Road, he was loaned out again to Crewe but failed to make an appearance at Gresty Road. He later played non-League for Runcorn, Bangor, Worcester and Oswestry Town.

	League		Lge Cup		FA Cup		Other	
	A	G	A	G	A	G	A	G
1975–76	1+1	1	0	0	0	0	-	-
TOTAL	1+1	1	0	0	0	0	-	-

TEMPEST, Dale Michael

Height: 5ft 11in. Weight: 12st 4lb.

Born: 30 December 1963, Leeds.

■ Signing professional in December 1981 after serving his apprenticeship with Fulham, Tempest made 25(+6) appearances for the Cottagers. He joined Huddersfield on loan in August 1984, making the deal permanent for a £15,000 fee two months later. At Leeds Road he played 63(+2) League games, returning 27 goals. Fifteen of those goals came in his first season for the Second Division club, but in March 1986 he was loaned out to Gillingham, scoring four in nine games. Tempest moved to Belgian side Lokeren and helped them to reach the UEFA Cup before he was snapped up by Mike Walker in a then Colchester record £40,000 purchase. He scored in only his second game, at home to Scarborough in August 1987, and returned a reasonable strike rate in a rapidly declining team. He

was placed on the transfer list during the caretaker managership of Steve Foley in January 1989 and featured infrequently as Jock Wallace's side escaped the drop to the Conference. On leaving Layer Road, he went to Hong Kong and played for Eastern and South China. He was top scorer in the Hong Kong First Division in five out of six seasons between 1989–90 and 1994–95. Playing in a friendly for South China against Brazilians São Paulo, Tempest earned national acclaim when scoring a hat-trick in a 4–2 win. He began his TV career giving betting tips and commentary on the Hong Kong League before returning to the UK on the commercial staff at Huddersfield, ahead of becoming Chief Betting Correspondent for Sky TV.

	League		Lge Cup		FA Cup		Other	
	A	G	A	G	A	G	A	G
1987–88	44	11	0	0	3	1	4	2
1988–89	25+8	7	2	0	3+1	0	2	1
TOTAL	69+8	18	2	0	6+1	1	6	3

THACKER, Ivan

Height: 5ft 10½in. Weight: 11st 3lb.

Born: 1 October 1913, Lowestoft.
Died: 1976, Waveney.

■ A native of Lowestoft who had represented Lowestoft schools, Thacker started his senior career with neighbouring Kirkley in the Norfolk & Suffolk League, scoring 19 goals in as many games before the Town team signed him. He went on to be a phenomenal goalscorer in the Eastern Counties League, hitting the 100 mark in just over 70 games for Lowestoft and the U's between 1935 and 1946, and his three seasons at Crown Meadow saw an incredible 156 goals in all competitions. Lowestoft fans dubbed him 'Ivan the Terrible', and he set an Eastern Counties League record with nine in Lowestoft's 16–0 win over Bury on 28 December 1935. He also netted seven in a 19–0 demolition of Thetford during the same season. During 1936–37 he was an amateur on West Ham's books but did not get a full contract from the Hammers and declined an offer from Portsmouth, so continued playing for his works side Hoffmans Athletic of Chelmsford. On 28 June 1937 he scored seven as Suffolk beat Norfolk 8–1 at Portman Road, and his debut for Colchester was equally spectacular as he notched all five U's reserves goals in a 5–5 draw with Clacton

on 26 February 1938. He repeated the feat twice the following season against Gt Yarmouth and Newmarket and was leading scorer in the League but could not break into the U's first team, where Arthur Pritchard's goalscoring was not much less spectacular and the other main striking position was occupied by the peerless Alec Cheyne. Thacker served in the Royal Navy during the war and was one of the very few to play for the U's both sides of the conflict. He only played four times after the war though, the last of them in November 1945, before rejoining Lowestoft, where he stayed just long enough for the ECL to re-start and scored six goals in his five games to reach his League century.

	League		Lge Cup		FA Cup		Other	
	A	G	A	G	A	G	A	G
1937–38	2	0	0	0	-	-	2	1
1938–39	0	0	0	0	0	0	1	1
1945–46	3	0	0	0	0	0	-	-
TOTAL	5	0	0	0	0	0	3	2

THOMAS, Philip Leslie 'Phil'

Height: 5ft 10in. Weight: 10st 8lb.

Born: 14 December 1952, Sherbourne.
Died: August 1998, Poole.

■ Thomas began his career at Bournemouth, serving his apprenticeship and signing professional terms in July 1971. He failed to get into the Cherries side and was recruited by Dick Graham on a free transfer in the summer of 1972, making his debut in a League Cup tie at Gillingham in the first month of the season. His speedy wing play featured strongly as Jim Smith's side won promotion to the Third Division in 1973–74. He was forced to quit the

professional game in January 1976 because of a recurring knee injury. He took over as Landlord of Public Houses in Norwich and then Ipswich before returning to his Dorset roots to become a Locksmith in the Poole area. Granted a testimonial by United against Ipswich in May 1977, Thomas died at the young age of 46 in 1998.

	League		Lge Cup		FA Cup		Other	
	A	G	A	G	A	G	A	G
1972–73	32+1	2	1	0	1	0	-	-
1973–74	38+2	4	0+1	0	1	0	-	-
1974–75	26+1	2	6	0	2	0	-	-
1975–76	7+1	0	2	0	0	0	-	-
TOTAL	103+5	8	9+1	0	4	0	-	-

THOMPSON, Niall Joseph

Height: 5ft 11in. Weight: 11st.

Born: 16 April 1974, Birmingham.

■ Thompson's family emigrated to Canada when he was just two years old. He began playing his football with Edmonton Brickmen and Winnipeg Fury. Trying his luck in the UK Thompson had signed for Crystal Palace in the summer of 1992. Failing to make the breakthrough, he had a spell in Hong Kong before joining Colchester on trial in November 1994. Already a youth and full Canadian cap, he made his debut as a substitute in the 7–1 mauling of Yeading in the FA Cup. He soon made an impact as his brace of goals completed an incredible comeback at Scunthorpe three months later. United trailed 3–0 at one stage but fought back to win 4–3, with Thompson's 82nd and 85th minute strikes. Despite being offered an 18-month contract, Thompson moved to Seattle Sounders and then played in his adopted Canada for Montreal Impact. He also had a spell with Sweden's Oesters before playing for Belgian Second Division side FC Zulte V.V. during 1996–97. In February 1998 he briefly returned to the UK and played 6(+2) games for Brentford before returning to Canada to score 18 goals in 24 games for Vancouver 86ers. Having won nine full caps, including a CONCACAF Gold Cup game against Brazil in 1996, Thompson turned out for Airdrieonians, scoring five goals in 25 appearances, during the 1999–90 season and returned stateside with San Francisco side Bay Area Seals. He joined Wycombe in October 2000, appearing 6(+2) times and scoring his only goal in an LDV Trophy tie. He rejoined Vancouver and scored 12 in 22 games in the 2002–03 season.

	League		Lge Cup		FA Cup		Other	
	A	G	A	G	A	G	A	G
1994–95	5+8	5	0	0	0+1	0	0	0
TOTAL	5+8	5	0	0	0+1	0	0	0

THOMPSON

■ A soldier serving in No.1 Holding Battalion, Thompson played one game for Colchester at inside-right in a 4–1 home defeat to Bedford in September 1945 and was reported as being on the books of St Mirren. As with several of the one-game wonders from the Garrison in 1945–46, all we can say for certain is that no one of his name played first-team football for the club they were linked to.

	League		Lge Cup		FA Cup		Other	
	A	G	A	G	A	G	A	G
1945–46	1	0	0	0	0	0	-	-
TOTAL	1	0	0	0	0	0	-	-

THORPE, Anthony Lee 'Tony'

Height: 5ft 9in. Weight: 12st 6lb.

Born: 10 April 1974, Leicester.

■ Thorpe was a youth trainee at home-town club Leicester but failed to make the first team. Released by the Foxes, he joined Luton in August 1992. Scoring 28 League goals in 1996–97, Thorpe won the Golden Boot as Second Division leading scorer and was named Luton's Player of the Year as well as being selected in the PFA representative team. Completing 93(+27) games at Kenilworth Road, Thorpe's 50 League goals persuaded ambitious Fulham to pay £800,000 in February 1998. He did not settle at Craven Cottage as the Al Fayad revolution took hold, and he joined Bristol City for £1 million just four months later. Again finding it difficult to slot in, Thorpe was loaned to Reading for six games in February 1999, scoring once, and returned to Luton in a similar deal on deadline day, netting four goals in 7(+1) starts. Thorpe joined Luton on loan again in November 1999, scoring once in 3(+1) games. It was a change of manager at Ashton Gate that re-ignited his career, and he ended the season top scorer with 16 goals. In 2000–01 he scored 19 League goals and 16 the season after. In the summer of 2002 he rejoined Luton, at the end of his contract, on a free transfer after amassing 102(+26) League games for Bristol City and for the second time scoring 50 goals for one club. In his

fourth spell with Luton he bagged another 15 goals in 30(+2) appearances before joining QPR for £50,000 in August 2003, when hard-up Luton needed a cash injection. Although scoring 10 times in 26(+15) games at Loftus Road, Thorpe's goal touch deserted him, and after a five-game spell at Rotherham on loan in March 2005 he was released in the close season and joined Swindon, where he was expected to form a formidable strike partnership with fellow ex-Ranger Jamie Cureton. When Cureton was called back from his own loan deal at Colchester, Thorpe made the journey to Layer Road, signing for Phil Parkinson in January 2006. He made his debut as a substitute in the same month against his former club Bristol City but in 14 outings in a Colchester shirt failed to find the net. Released, he joined Conference club Stevenage. After just three games he was taken on loan by Grimsby in September 2006, playing five times, and again in the November, playing once. Not retained, he signed for Conference North side Tamworth in the summer of 2007 and also registered to play for Leicestershire Sunday League side Hockley Rangers.

	League		Lge Cup		FA Cup		Other	
	A	G	A	G	A	G	A	G
2005–06	5+9	0	0	0	0	0	0	0
TOTAL	5+9	0	0	0	0	0	0	0

TIERNEY, Paul Thomas

Height: 5ft 10in. Weight: 12st 5lb.

Born: 15 September 1982, Salford.

■ Tierney arrived at Colchester with an impressive pedigree, having been schooled at Manchester United and collecting seven caps at Under-21 level for the Republic of Ireland. Signing professionally in August 2000, Tierney made just one appearance for the Red Devils in a League Cup match against West Brom in December 2003, having previously had a 14(+3) game loan spell at Crewe in November 2002, where he scored his first-ever League goal. Phil Parkinson introduced the player to Layer Road in January 2003, but the full-back had a nightmare time as Colchester were knocked out of the FA Cup fifth Round at Sheffield United and Auto Windscreens Shield Area Final to Southend in the space of a few days. He returned to Old Trafford and 11 months later had 14(+2) games on loan at Bradford. Released by Sir Alex Ferguson, he joined Scottish Premier League Livingston in August 2005, playing 25(+6) times. In the summer of 2006 he joined Blackpool but found games hard to come by, completing just 8(+2) matches. At the beginning of 2007–08 he was sent to Stockport on loan in a deal lasting until January 2008.

	League		Lge Cup		FA Cup		Other	
	A	G	A	G	A	G	A	G
2003–04	2	0	0	0	1	0	1	0
TOTAL	2	0	0	0	1	0	1	0

TITCOMBE, Stanley 'Stan'

■ Titcombe, a Corporal in the 15th Infantry Training Corps, was an amateur on the books of Swindon and acknowledged as a fine sprinter. He scored the U's first post-war goal in the 2–1 win at Chelmsford on 25 August 1945 but did not hit the target again until his last appearance in the blue-and-white stripes in a friendly on 5 January. Finding himself second choice for his favoured right-wing position, and with the U's only running one team, he went to Suffolk to play for Ipswich reserves in March 1946.

	League		Lge Cup		FA Cup		Other	
	A	G	A	G	A	G	A	G
1945–46	5	1	0	0	1	0	-	-
TOTAL	5	1	0	0	1	0	-	-

TOBIN

■ A Glaswegian amateur who first played for the U's in a Southern League Cup tie against Bedford in April 1946. He added one more senior appearance, plus a handful of reserve outings, up to January 1947 before moving on to Clacton Town and was still at Old Road in December 1948 when he played for Clacton reserves against the U's A team.

	League		Lge Cup		FA Cup		Other	
	A	G	A	G	A	G	A	G
1945–46	0	0	1	0	0	0	-	-
1946–47	1	0	0	0	0	0	-	-
TOTAL	1	0	1	0	0	0	-	-

TOWNROW, Raymond Frank 'Ray'

Height: 5ft 11in. Weight: 11st 5lb.

Born: 20 December 1925, West Ham.

Died: December 1990, Chelmsford.

■ Townrow, the son of an ex-professional and nephew of an English international, joined the U's from Wolves in January 1948 and made his Colchester debut in a Southern League Cup tie against Bedford on 17 January 1948 in between the third and fourth rounds of the U's famous FA Cup run, in order to give United's forward Bob Curry a rest. His second appearance between the fourth and fifth rounds was for the same reason, and he never played more than two games in a row in his 18 months with Colchester. He refused the U's terms at the end of 1948–49 and joined Clacton Town, moving to Bury Town in 1950, where he was leading scorer for the next two seasons. His father Francis Albert, known as Frank, played for Arsenal and both Bristol clubs, while Frank's brother Jack was at Orient, Chelsea and Bristol Rovers, being capped against Scotland and Wales while at Stamford Bridge.

	League		Lge Cup		FA Cup		Other	
	A	G	A	G	A	G	A	G
1947–48	8	3	3	2	0	0	-	-
1948–49	1	0	0	0	0	0	-	-
TOTAL	9	3	3	2	0	0	-	-

TOWNSEND, Leonard Francis 'Len'

Born: 31 August 1917, Brentford.

Died: August 1997, Lewes.

■ A centre-forward who played for Hayes before the war, Townsend was a busy player during the war years, playing thus: 1939–40 Brentford (8 appearances/5 goals); 1940–41 Brentford (10/8), Leeds (12/14); 1941–42 Brentford (13/9), Chelsea (5/6); 1942–43 Brentford (20/19); 1943–44 Brentford (15/15); 1944–45 Swansea (2/2, West Ham (1/1), Brentford (28/30), Brighton (1/1); 1945–46

Brentford (18/15). A serving soldier in the 16th Infantry Training Corps, Townsend scored a hat-trick in his only Colchester appearance against Guildford in the January 1946 League Cup tie. Remarkably, Townsend was due to guest for Tottenham that day but missed his train at Colchester's North Station and so turned out for United instead. His full League career amounted to 12 goals in 33 games for Brentford either side of the war years, 45 goals in 74 games for Bristol City during 1947 and 1948, before ending his football at Millwall in 1949. He later played non-League for Guildford, Hayes, Slough and Maidenhead.

	League		Lge Cup		FA Cup		Other	
	A	G	A	G	A	G	A	G
1945–46	0	0	1	3	0	0	-	-
TOTAL	0	0	1	3	0	0	-	-

TREVIS, Derek Alan

Height: 5ft 11in. Weight: 11st 2lb.

Born: 9 September 1942, Birmingham.
Died: 2000, Sacramento, California.

■ A combative midfielder, Trevis joined

Colchester in March 1964 from Aston Villa, where he had been since 1962 and was new manager Neil Franklin's first signing. He missed only five League games in his four full seasons at Layer Road and captained the club to promotion in 1965–66 and was Supporters' Player of the Year for 1967–68. He also starred in United's FA Cup run that season when they eventually bowed out to West Bromwich Albion after a replay. Moving to Walsall in September 1968, Trevis appeared 65 times for the Saddlers in League games, having cost the Midland club £10,000. In the summer of 1970 he signed for Lincoln making a further 100 (+8) starts. His English League career ended with 33 games for Stockport in 1973–74. Trevis emigrated to the US as the North American Soccer League was getting off the ground and featured for Philadelphia Atoms, NASL champions of 1973, San Diego Jaws, Las Vegas Quicksilver and Philadelphia Fury.

	League		Lge Cup		FA Cup		Other	
	A	G	A	G	A	G	A	G
1963–64	9	0	0	0	0	0	-	-
1964–65	46	6	2	0	3	1	-	-
1965–66	43	4	2	0	2	0	-	-
1966–67	45	0	1	0	2	0	-	-
1967–68	45	2	1	0	5	2	-	-
1968–69	8	1	2	0	0	0	-	-
TOTAL	196	13	8	0	12	3	-	-

TURNER, Arthur Alexander

Height: 5ft 10in. Weight: 11st 3lb.

Born: 22 January 1922, London.

■ Turner was the only survivor of an RAF bomber shot down during the war

Arthur Turner

and played as an amateur with Charlton during this time. His wartime record was thus: 1943–44 Charlton (3 appearances/ 2 goals); 1944–45 Charlton (20/17); 1945–46 Charlton (33/34), and obviously Charlton were keen for his signature. He was the only amateur on the pitch when Charlton lost 4–1 to Derby in the 1946 FA Cup Final at Wembley. He refused Charlton's approaches, as he had a successful timber merchant business with his brother, and joined Colchester as an amateur in mid-September 1946, being persuaded to sign a professional contract a couple of months later, much to Charlton's displeasure. His Colchester record was impeccable, with 74 goals in 94 Southern League starts, and in all he claimed eight hat-tricks for the U's, including three four-timers. His career was interrupted by a cartilage operation at the beginning of the 1949–50 season, which allowed Vic Keeble to blossom, but he returned to fitness and the army made sure that he got the number-nine shirt for much of Colchester's first-ever Football League season. During and after the 1947–48 FA Cup run, he attracted interest from Brentford and Southend, but Ted Fenton put a massive £9,000 transfer fee on his head to ward off any deals. By 1951–52 he was mainly a reserve, and in mid-March, shortly after the last of his nine appearances, he broke his wrist at work and had not resumed playing when he was released at the end of the season. On leaving Colchester, he moved to Headington United for 1952–53, scoring 16 goals in 21 League and Cup games for the club who would become Oxford United. Incidentally, he is not the Arthur Turner who led Oxford into the Football League in 1962.

	League		Lge Cup		FA Cup		Other	
	A	G	A	G	A	G	A	G
1946–47	*25*	*21*	*6*	*3*	*1*	*0*	-	-
1947–48	*30*	*25*	*7*	*1*	*6*	*1*	-	-
1948–49	*31*	*29*	*4*	*3*	*1*	*0*	-	-
1949–50	*5*	*0*	*1*	*0*	*0*	*0*	-	-
1950–51	36	12	-	-	2	2	-	-
1951–52	9	2	-	-	0	0	-	-
TOTAL	45	14	-	-	2	2	-	-
	91	*75*	*18*	*7*	*8*	*1*	-	-

TURNER, Robin David

Height: 5ft 9in. Weight: 10st 8lb.

Born: 10 September 1955, Carlisle.

■ Representing England Youth as an Ipswich apprentice, Turner signed for the Portman Road club in April 1973, making his debut in 1975 and playing his last game in 1985. Turner played European football for Town and scored against Skeid Oslo in the 1979–80 UEFA

Cup competition. In all his 10 years at Ipswich he played just 22(+25) times, scoring twice, and spent time out on loan at Beerschot and M.V.V. Maastricht. He transferred to Swansea on deadline day 1985, scoring 8 times in 20 starts. Cyril Lea recruited the player, initially on loan, in November 1985, but he failed to make any impact and was released after just 12 appearances for Colchester. Turner played non-League for Bury Town and made a cameo appearance in the film *Escape To Victory*, playing the part of a football-playing German soldier, before moving to County Mayo in Ireland to work in a school.

	League		Lge Cup		FA Cup		Other	
	A	G	A	G	A	G	A	G
1985–86	6+5	0	0	0	1	0	2	0
TOTAL	6+5	0	0	0	1	0	2	0

VAUGHAN, John

Height: 5ft 10in. Weight: 13st 1lb.
Born: 26 June 1964, Isleworth.

■ Vaughan joined West Ham as an apprentice in September 1980, signing professionally two years later. It was not until he went on loan to Charlton (six appearances) in March 1995 that he made his League bow. The following season he went out on loan to Bristol Rovers (six games), Wrexham (four) and Bristol City (two) before signing for Fulham for £12,500 in August 1986. He was in goal when Fulham lost 10–0 at Anfield in a League Cup tie in 1987. Losing his place to Jim Stannard after 44 games, he returned to Bristol City on loan in January 1988, making three more starts. His days at Craven Cottage were numbered, and he left on a free transfer to Cambridge in June 1988. Cambridge climbed from the Fourth to the Second Division in consecutive seasons and reached the FA Cup quarter-finals, with Vaughan playing in 178 League games and the Wembley Play-off win over Chesterfield. He moved to Charlton in August 1993, playing just 5(+1) times, before rejoining his old Cambridge boss John Beck at Preston in July 1994. Appearing 65(+1) times for North End and winning a Third Division Championship medal, Vaughan followed Beck to Lincoln in August 1996. It was

from Lincoln that Vaughan twice had loan spells at Layer Road. Firstly, Steve Wignall brought him in during February 1997 to cover for the injured Carl Emberson and Garrett Caldwell. Vaughan was sent off in the 22nd minute of the Auto Windscreens Shield tie, with Northampton forcing Peter Cawley to take over in goal. United won through the tie and eventually reached the Wembley Final. Vaughan's second U's loan was in November 1999 when Steve Whitton drafted him to stand in for Simon Brown. Vaughan made one more loan move to Chesterfield in January 2000 before ending his League career in May 2000, with 66 appearances accumulated at Lincoln, marked by a promotion in 1997–98. He had brief spells with western non-League sides Torrington and Barnstaple before offering coaching services to York, Macclesfield and Grimsby. In August 2006 he was appointed goalkeeping coach at Huddersfield.

	League		Lge Cup		FA Cup		Other	
	A	G	A	G	A	G	A	G
1996–97	5	0	0	0	0	0	1	0
1999–2000	6	0	0	0	0	0	0	0
TOTAL	11	0	0	0	0	0	1	0

VERNON, Scott Malcolm

Height: 5ft 1in. Weight: 11st 6lb.
Born: 13 December 1983, Manchester.

■ Vernon began his career as a schoolboy on the books of Oldham. He signed professional in July 2002 and came to prominence in his second season when scoring 12 League goals for the Latics. Unfortunately, he fractured his eye socket, which restricted his appearances in 2004–05 to just 11(+9) games; however, he did spend September on loan at Blackpool, bagging three goals in just four games. Vernon will be best remembered by Oldham fans for his winning goal against Manchester City in an FA Cup third round shock in January 2005. Out of contract in the summer, he had impressed enough for Blackpool to sign him permanently. He could not repeat his loan-spell form and was out of the side for most of the term. On deadline day 2006 Colchester manager

Phil Parkinson, having already loaned Sam Stockley to Blackpool, agreed a swap deal that saw Vernon arrive at Layer Road and U's striker Gareth Williams travel in the opposite direction. The deal was designed to boost both players' careers. Vernon responded with the winning goal at Bournemouth in April, which proved crucial in United's elevation to the Championship. He returned to Bloomfield Road in the summer revitalised and scored 11 goals in 21(+17) games, helping Blackpool to Wembley Play-off success against Yeovil. In all, Vernon scored 20 League goals in 43(+32) games at Boundary Park and had appeared 35(+24) times for Blackpool, scoring 15 times to the end of 2006–07. After spending the first half of 2007–08 on the fringes of the starting XI, Vernon made a return to Colchester in the January 2008 window and scored a fine double as United beat neighbours Ipswich at Layer Road in April. He also scored the last ever League goal at Layer Road against Coventry on 19 April 2008.

	League		Lge Cup		FA Cup		Other	
	A	G	A	G	A	G	A	G
2005–06	4+4	1	0	0	0	0	0	0
2007–08	8+9	5	0	0	0	0	-	-
TOTAL	12+13	6	0	0	0	0	0	0

VINE, Rowan Lewis

Height: 6ft 1in. Weight: 11st 12lb.
Born: 21 September 1982, Basingstoke.

■ Portsmouth trainee Vine's career was rescued by two season-long loans. Signing professionally with Pompey in

April 2001, Vine made 3(+10) appearances at Fratton Park before joining Brentford on loan in August 2002. He had a prolific season, scoring 10 times in 37(+5) League games, and Colchester manager Phil Parkinson pulled off a coup when engaging the striker on a similar deal in the 2003 close season. Vine continued where he had left off, bagging important goals, and capped his Colchester career with a hat-trick in a thrilling 3–1 FA Cup fourth-round replay victory over Championship side Coventry in February 2004. The attention from the national media following the feat turned Vine's head, and he stumbled through the remaining weeks of the season while dreaming of bigger things, falling foul of United fans as a result. He signed for Luton in the summer of 2004 for £250,000 and won a League One Championship medal in his first season. Completing 90(+4) appearances and scoring 31 goals, Vine earned a move to Premiership-bound Birmingham in the January 2007 transfer window for a fee of £2.5 million. He scored once in 10(+7) appearances as City achieved their goal as runners-up to Sunderland. In October 2007 he joined QPR on loan and scored on his debut in a 4–2 defeat against Colchester at Layer Road before making a permanent £1 million move to Loftus Road in January 2008.

	League		Lge Cup		FA Cup		Other	
	A	G	A	G	A	G	A	G
2003–04	30+5	6	1	0	5+2	4	4+2	2
TOTAL	30+5	6	1	0	5+2	4	4+2	2

VIRGO, Adam John

Height: 6ft 2in. Weight: 13st 7lb.

Born: 25 January 1983, Brighton.

■ Virgo signed for home-town club Brighton in July 2000 after progressing through their youth ranks, making his debut in an LDV Trophy tie with Brentford. With Brighton winning successive promotions, Virgo's chances were limited due to the strength of their squad. He moved to Exeter on loan in November 2002 and played 8(+1) times for the Grecians. Establishing himself in Albion's side, he scored a last gasp equaliser against Swindon in extra-time of the 2003–04 Play-off semi-final, and scored in the ensuing penalty shoot-out, earning the Seagulls a Millennium Stadium tie against Bristol City, which they won 1–0. They also included future U's star Chris Iwelumo in their side. Converted to a striker during Albion's Championship campaign, Virgo smashed in nine goals in 36 games, winning the Player of the Year vote and earning a call up to the Scotland B international side for a game against Germany. In the summer of 2005 he joined Celtic in a £1.6 million deal but played just 3(+7) games due to injury. He returned south to Coventry, managed by his former Brighton manager Micky Adams in August 2006 on a season long loan, but suffered further injury nightmare in completing just 10(+5) games, scoring once. When Adams became assistant manager at Colchester in the summer of 2007, he recommended that Virgo was rescued from his Celtic nightmare, and the player duly signed a six-month loan deal. He made his debut as a substitute against Barnsley in August 2007 and scored his first goal in the following month against Burnley. Employed as centre-half for the majority of the season, Virgo and his defence suffered a torrid time as United were relegated from the Championship.

	League		Lge Cup		FA Cup		Other	
	A	G	A	G	A	G	A	G
2007-08	30+7	1	0	0	1	0	-	-
TOTAL	30+7	1	0	0	1	0	-	-

WALKER, Albert

Born: 4 February 1910, Little Lever.
Died: April 1993, Barking & Dagenham.

■ Left-sided Walker started at Little Lever United before signing for Southport in 1928. In the same year, he moved to Bolton but did not make any first-team appearances for either club. He finally made his debut for Barrow in 1929 and went on to score 11 goals in 72 appearances. By 1932 he had joined West Ham and played for them in the FA Cup semi-final of 1938 against Everton. Walker was well known to U's boss Ted Fenton as he made 162 appearances for the Hammers during Fenton's time at Upton Park. In 1938–39 he was released to Doncaster and played 40 times before the outbreak of war. Ted Fenton brought him in when United had lost the first three games of 1946–47, and Walker missed only two of the remaining Southern League fixtures. He then spent two years as one half of a veteran reserve full-back pairing alongside Bill Bower, with the two frequently demonstrating the old adage that there is no substitute for experience. By the time they played their last game together, before Walker was released at the end of 1948–49, their combined age was considerably nearer 80 than 70.

	League		Lge Cup		FA Cup		Other	
	A	G	A	G	A	G	A	G
1946–47	27	0	7	0	2	0	-	-
1947–48	2	0	1	0	0	0	-	-
TOTAL	29	0	8	0	2	0	-	-

WALKER, Andrew William 'Andy'

Height: 6ft. Weight: 11st 10lb.

Born: 30 September 1981, Bexleyheath.

■ Playing with Charlton as a schoolboy, Walker was taken on by the U's when the Addicks decided not to offer him a scholarship, and for a while it looked like Walker would be the most successful 'keeper the club had produced for over 20 years. He was given his debut as a 17-year-old in the final game of the 1998–99 season at Blackpool and taken on as pro after just one year of his scholarship. A sending off for Simon Brown in the League Cup first-round first-leg tie against Crystal Palace at Layer Road brought Walker off the bench and made him the starter in the return leg, a match shown live on Sky TV. A couple of League starts came his way after Christmas, but he did not really seem to be progressing, and when another experienced 'keeper arrived in November 2000, and with another promising 'keeper in Glenn Williamson following him through the youth team, there were too many 'keepers at the club, and Walker was the one to go. He joined St Albans and then signed non-contract forms for Exeter in August 2001, playing one League game. Failing to earn a contract, he returned to his home in Kent and Tonbridge Angels. Ex-U's boss Steve Wignall took him up to Doncaster where

he was managing the then Conference side Doncaster but Wignall was soon to leave and his replacement did not keep Walker. After a spell with Wingate & Finchley, Walker joined Bromley and has established himself there, where he plays alongside fellow ex-Colchester players Bobby Bowry and Gareth Williams. Bromley secured the Ryman League Play-offs in 2006–07, and Walker remained the regular custodian in the ensuing Conference South campaign.

	League		Lge Cup		FA Cup		Other	
	A	G	A	G	A	G	A	G
1998–99	1	0	0	0	0	0	0	0
1999–2000	2	0	1+1	0	0	0	0	0
TOTAL	3	0	1+1	0	0	0	0	0

WALKER, Michael Stewart Gordon 'Mike'

Height: 6ft 1in. Weight: 13st 2lb.

Born: 28 November 1945, Colwyn Bay.

■ Goalkeeper Walker qualified for Wales after being born in Colwyn Bay while his father was completing army service in North Wales. Based in Reading, Walker represented Berkshire, Buckinghamshire and Oxon Boys and joined home-town club Reading as a junior in January 1963. Failing to make a start, he moved to Shrewsbury in the 1964 close season and made seven appearances. Still only 21, he signed for York in the summer of 1966 and established himself at Bootham Crescent, making 60 League appearances in just over two seasons. Spotted by Watford, he joined the Hertfordshire outfit in September 1968, making 137 League appearances, winning the Third Division title in 1969 and appearing in the 1970 FA Cup semi-final. Capped four times at Under-23 level, Walker was also reserve 'keeper on two occasions for the full Welsh squad. Acquired by Jim Smith for £4,000, Walker was the model of consistency, playing 451 League games, including 310 consecutive games between February 1977 and January 1983, for Colchester. In that time he saw off five deputies, preventing any of Lee Smelt, Ian Cranstone, Bobby Hamilton and Jeff Wood from making a first-team appearance at Layer Road and thwarting any ambitions John McInally might have

of adding to the appearances he made before Walker's arrival. Walker kept goal in big Cup ties against Manchester United, Aston Villa, Derby and Southampton and twice won promotion to the Third Division. Missing just nine League games in 10 seasons at Layer Road, he became reserve-team manager, and when Cyril Lea was sacked in April 1986 he saw out the season as caretaker boss. Appointed full-time U's boss for 1986–87, he steered United to fifth place in Division Four before narrowly losing a two-legged Play-off semi-final to a resurgent Wolves. Walker had Colchester nearing the top of the Fourth Division table the following campaign when the chairman incredibly sacked the U's boss over an alleged personal matter. Walker was named Manager of the Month for October 1987 AFTER his sacking. He was soon picked up by Norwich, where he became reserve-team coach, and when Dave Stringer was sacked by the Canaries, Walker was promoted to first-team manager in June 1992. Norwich were early pacesetters in the Premier League, eventually finishing third and earning a UEFA Cup place. It was in Europe that he steered Norwich to their greatest triumph, a UEFA Cup win over Bayern Munich in Germany, but in January 1994 he resigned as Norwich boss to sign a three and a half year contract with Everton, who only escaped relegation by beating Wimbledon on the final day of the 1993–94 season. After poor start to the 1994–95 campaign, he was sacked by the Toffees in November. In June 1996 he was appointed Norwich boss again, two and a half years after quitting Carrow Road, following the departure of chairman Robert Chase and manager Gary Megson. His second spell ended by mutual consent in April 1998 with the club safe from relegation in 16th place in Division One, but in poor form. Following the resignation of Colchester boss Steve Wignall in January 1999, Walker became the fans favourite to retake the Layer Road hot seat. However, nothing transpired and it was Cyprus where Walker took up his next appointment. In November 2000 he took over as coach of Apoel Nicosia, but lasted until just two games into the 2001–02 season. His son Ian, after playing youth football in the Colchester area, became a full England international and carved out a top-flight career, most notably at Tottenham. Ian actually made his debut in senior football for the U's while his dad was club manager. Injuries left the club without a 'keeper for the reserves' first game of 1986–87, and the 15-year-old Ian stepped in to keep a clean sheet in an Eastern Counties League fixture at Ely in August 1986.

* *See also Who's Who Managers section*

	League		Lge Cup		FA Cup		Other	
	A	G	A	G	A	G	A	G
1973–74	46	0	1	0	1	0	-	-
1974–75	46	0	6	0	2	0	-	-
1975–76	43	0	2	0	2	0	-	-
1976–77	44	0	3	0	6	0	-	-
1977–78	46	0	5	0	4	0	-	-
1978–79	46	0	2	0	7	0	-	-
1979–80	46	0	4	0	4	0	-	-
1980–81	46	0	2	0	4	0	-	-
1981–82	46	0	5	0	5	0	-	-
1982–83	42	0	4	0	1	0	3	0
TOTAL	451	0	34	0	36	0	3	0

WALKER, Robert 'Bob'

Height: 5ft 11in. Weight: 11st 8lb.

Born: 23 July 1942, Wallsend.

■ Walker joined Brighton from Gateshead in May 1962. A central-defender, he made just 12 appearances at The Goldstone before drifting into non-

League with Ashford Town and Margate. He joined a Football League club in August 1965 when he signed for Bournemouth. Just 10 League starts at Dean Court saw him signed by Neil Franklin for Colchester on a free transfer. Walker was mainly used at the expense of Mick Loughton, who was not seeing eye to eye with Franklin as United's leaky defence propelled the team towards relegation. Walker was among those shown the door by Franklin before he resigned at the end of the campaign, and he trialled at Bedford during 1968–69 and had a short spell at Dover in 1969–70 before later playing for Salisbury.

	League		Lge Cup		FA Cup		Other	
	A	G	A	G	A	G	A	G
1967–68	13+4	0	0	0	0+2	0	-	-
TOTAL	13+4	0	0	0	0+2	0	-	-

WALLIS, George H.

Height: 5ft 11in. Weight: 12st.

Born: 1910, Sawley.

■ Wallis served 18 months with Birmingham, having been signed from Sandiacre Excelsior. A thrusting inside-left, Wallis moved to Bristol City without getting into the first team at St Andrews. Three seasons at Bristol City realised 14 goals in 42 appearances. When Bath City, his next club, were forced to reduce their wage bill it was Ted Davis who stepped in to sign the player on 28 February 1938. Wallis had scored both Bath's goals the previous weekend, and his fierce shot proved a potent weapon in his first full

season at Layer Road, where United went on to lift the Southern League Championship. In an era of few sendings off, Wallis received his marching orders in the penultimate game before the war for what the press reports described as 'an inexcusable foul', although the fact that it followed very shortly after an incident that put the U's Bill Main out of the game 'with a crippingly injury' may have had something to do with it. Things also overheated off the field as well, with a minor riot, in which U's fans clashed with Chelmsford City fans, players and staff.

	League		Lge Cup		FA Cup		Other	
	A	G	A	G	A	G	A	G
1937–38	10	5	0	0	-	-	6	2
1938–39	43	15	3	1	2	1	15	6
1939–40	3	0	1	0	-	-	-	-
TOTAL	56	20	4	1	2	1	21	8

WALSH, Mario Markus

Height: 6ft 1in. Weight: 11st 12lb.

Born: 19 January 1966, Paddington.

■ Walsh served his apprenticeship with Portsmouth, signing professional in January 1984. Exactly a year later, he was sold to Torquay and suffered three seasons of struggle as the Devon side had to apply for re-election in his first two seasons and only went one better in his last as they staved off relegation to the Conference. Signed by Mike Walker in the summer of 1987 for £15,000, Walsh scored on his debut at Burnley on the opening day of the season but suffered with injury. A creditable goal return in his next season was supplemented as United went on an FA Cup run to the fourth round, with Walsh starting the Cup journey with a goal in the first-round win over Fulham and adding further goals against Swansea and Shrewsbury. Perhaps his most important goal was the equaliser in U's crunch bottom-of-the-table clash at Darlington in April 1989. Colchester went on to win 2–1 and condemned the Quakers to the Conference. He moved to Southend in the close season for £25,000 but scored just twice in 10(+1) games as the Shrimpers were promoted to the Third Division, while United finally did sink to the Conference. New U's boss Ian Atkins paid out the same £25,000 fee for Walsh to return to Layer Road in their inaugural Conference season. The striker scored twice in his first game as United beat Northwich 4–0. He missed the vital run-in to the title race with Barnet after suffering a nasty clash of heads against Kettering in April 1990 but still finished club's leading scorer as United were pipped by the Bees. When Atkins left, new player-manager Roy McDonough claimed the number-nine shirt for himself and Walsh, after a loan spell with Kettering, moved to Redbridge Forest, scoring the Boxing Day winner against the U's in one of only four defeats for eventual champions Colchester. He stayed with Dagenham & Redbridge in their various guises for three seasons, completing 34(+11) games.

	League		Lge Cup		FA Cup		Other	
	A	G	A	G	A	G	A	G
1987–88	4+7	2	2	0	0+2	0	0	0
1988–89	25+2	8	0	0	6	3	3	2
1990–91	*31+1*	*17*	*0*	*0*	*3*	*0*	*3*	*1*
1991–92	*0+1*	*0*	*0*	*0*	*0*	*0*	*0*	*0*
TOTAL	29+9	10	2	0	6+2	3	3	2
	31+2	*17*	*0*	*0*	*3*	*0*	*3*	*1*

WALTON, Mark Andrew

Height: 6ft 2in. Weight: 13st 13lb.

Born: 1 August 1969, Merthyr Tydfil.

■ Walton began his career at Fourth Division Swansea, where his father Ron was the youth-team coach, before being taken on by top-flight Luton in February 1987. He answered United's desperate goalkeeping plight the following August when first Norwich refused to allow Graham Benstead to become Cup-tied and Benstead's replacement Trevor Lake suffered a severe injury against Fulham in the League Cup. When Benstead returned to Carrow Road in November, Walton made his loan deal permanent for £17,500 and saw out the season, vying with Craig Forrest in United's goal. He played in United's run to the FA Cup fourth round in 1988–89 but was replaced by the experienced Tom McAlister between the sticks as U's boss Jock Wallace recognised the youngster's frailties. However, in the summer of 1989 a transfer tribunal set a fee of £75,000, doubling to £150,000 after 50 appearances, on his head as he moved to Norwich, making 22 top flight appearances as understudy to Bryan Gunn. Walton played in the 1991–92 FA Cup semi-final defeat to Sunderland and also won his only Welsh Under-21 cap against Poland during 1991. Retained only on a monthly contract, in August 1993 he joined Wrexham on loan and played six times before crossing another border to play for Dundee. He then had three games for Second Division Bolton in March 1994 as understudy to Aidan Davison before dipping into non-League with Fakenham Town, Wroxham, Barry and Merthyr Tydfil. His career was resurrected by Fulham in August 1996, where he played 40 times and was loaned out to Gillingham for a single game in February 1998. He was re-employed by his old boss Mike Walker at Norwich as standby for Andy Marshall on deadline day 1998 and in the summer secured a £20,000 move to the south coast when he signed for Brighton, playing 58 times before ending his career at Cardiff with 40 games in their Third Division promotion campaign. Walton moved to Australia in 2004 and played for Bentleigh Greens.

	League		Lge Cup		FA Cup		Other	
	A	G	A	G	A	G	A	G
1987–88	17	0	1	0	3	0	3	0
1988–89	23	0	2	0	5	0	2	0
TOTAL	40	0	3	0	8	0	5	0

WARD, Wayne Walter

Height: 5ft 10in. Weight: 10st 8lb.

Born: 28 April 1964, Colchester

■ Ward was in the U's FA Youth Cup team from the age of 15 and was still an apprentice when drafted into United's side by Bobby Roberts just prior to the U's boss's sacking. The full-back made his debut against Darlington in April 1982 on the left side of the defence, and, although the clean sheet helped secure the first win for six games, it was not enough to rescue the promotion bid that had floundered so badly since February. His first call-up of 1982–83 was the U's second-leg League Cup defeat at Southampton in October 1982 against the likes of Mark Wright and Peter Shilton, and injuries to Phil Coleman then Allan Hunter gave him a 13-game mid-season run in the side. Coach Cyril Lea took over when player-manager Hunter resigned, and the two young defenders in the side, Ward and Adrian Keith, were very soon discarded. Released at the end of the season, Ward moved onto the local non-League circuit with Wivenhoe, Tiptree and Haverhill.

	League		Lge Cup		FA Cup		Other	
	A	G	A	G	A	G	A	G
1981–82	3+2	0	0	0	0	0	-	-
1982–83	14	0	1	0	1	0	0	0
TOTAL	17+2	0	1	0	1	0	0	0

WARNER, John

Height: 5ft 10in. Weight: 12st 3lb.

Born: 20 November 1961, Paddington.

■ On a Sunday in November 1987 the U's sent a reserve team to mid-Essex non-League side Burnham Ramblers for the official opening of their new ground. The game was drawn 3–3, and the following summer Burnham found themselves invited to be on the first team's pre-season agenda. Not for the first time in the 1980s, it was not long before suspicion arose that their new-found friends Colchester were looking for more than match practice, as it was the pace and awareness of Burnham's prolific striker Warner that had caught the eye. A security guard at Ford's Dagenham plant, Warner trialled for the U's reserves at Cambridge and three days later came off the first-team bench to score the winning goal at Scunthorpe. That was the first win in 19 games and started the revival of fortunes under Jock Wallace. Warner further enhanced his reputation when scoring a vital equaliser against Halifax on Easter Monday, just two days after Colchester had beaten their main relegation rivals Darlington 2–1 at Feethams. When Ian Allinson netted the winner five minutes later United's safety was virtually assured. The U's wanted Warner to sign full-time but could not offer the security, or even compete financially, with the

combination of Fords and a semi-professional wage packet, and he returned to the non-League circuit for 1989–90, initially with Heybridge. When Steve Foley took over as caretaker boss just before Christmas, he persuaded Warner to come back and, although not scoring this time, Warner again came off the bench in an away game to contribute to the first League win in a long time – 13 games. A scoring appearance in the reserves and a start against Stockport followed in the next 10 days, but when Mick Mills took over the hot seat Warner was allowed to go and joined Dagenham. Mills, meanwhile, led the U's out of the League. Warner later played for Collier Row before becoming player-manager of Bowers & Pitsea United.

	League		Lge Cup		FA Cup		Other	
	A	G	A	G	A	G	A	G
1988–89	7+8	3	0	0	0	0	0	0
1989–90	1+1	0	0	0	0	0	0	0
TOTAL	8+9	3	0	0	0	0	0	0

WARREN, Mark Wayne

Height: 5ft 11in. Weight: 13st 2lb.

Born: 12 November 1974, Hackney.

■ A YTS player on the books of Leyton Orient, Warren represented Essex Schools and signed professionally at Brisbane Road in July 1992. An England Youth international, he made his debut as a substitute in 1991–92 season and soon created an impression, such that he was taken on trial by Nottingham Forest and also had a spell on loan at West Ham before establishing himself in the O's first team. His first goals came in the shape of

a hat-trick at Peterborough in February 1995. Winning Player of the Year in both 1996–97 and 1997–98, Warren spent four games on loan at First Division Oxford in December 1998 but joined Notts County a month later after refusing a new deal at Leyton. Spending four seasons at Meadow Lane, Warren clocked up 76(+8) appearances, scoring once before Steve Whitton secured the player's services on a free transfer in the summer of 2002. After making his debut against Stockport on the opening day of the season, he was involved in a mid-pitch fracas against Oldham at Layer Road, which resulted in a red card and a fine for the club for failing to control their players, this only four games after having been red-carded for two bookings at Peterborough. His last game for Colchester was in January 2003 against Blackpool, which was also Steve Whitton's last game in charge of United. Warren strained his groin and missed the rest of the campaign. He joined neighbours Southend in November 2003, playing 27(+5) games and bagging two goals, and featured in their 2–0 defeat to Blackpool in the Millennium Stadium LDV Trophy Final. He joined Fisher Athletic and later captained King's Lynn helping them to promotion in the 2005–06 season and appearing 40 times in the next. He was with the Southern League side for the 2007–08 season.

	League		Lge Cup		FA Cup		Other	
	A	G	A	G	A	G	A	G
2002–03	20	0	0	0	1	0	0	0
TOTAL	20	0	0	0	1	0	0	0

WATSON, Kevin Edward

Height: 6ft. Weight: 12st 6lb.

Born: 3 January 1974, Hackney.

■ Watson served his apprenticeship at Tottenham, breaking into the side shortly before signing professional in May 1992. Playing 4(+1) Premiership games, he was loaned out to Brentford in March 1994, playing 1(+1) in the League, Bristol City the following December, appearing 2(+1) times, and Barnet in February 1995, starting 13 League fixtures. Released by Spurs in the close season of 1995, despite playing in four UEFA Intertoto Cup matches through the summer, he signed for Swindon and in three seasons played 39(+24) times, scoring once. Dropping down two divisions, he enjoyed the most productive seasons of his career thus far as his new side Rotherham, for whom he was made captain, took the Third Division title in 1999–2000 and followed that up with the Second Division title a year later. Spending November 2001 on a six-game loan deal at Reading, Watson joined the Royals in March of 2002 for £150,000 as they too gained promotion to the second tier. Watson played a further 40(+20) games for Reading, scoring twice, before joining his former playing colleague Phil Parkinson at Colchester in the 2004 close season. He had made his debut on the opening day 3–0 win at Sheffield Wednesday in 2004–05 and scored his first goal three days later against Stockport. He missed just 10 games over the next three seasons at Colchester, finished runners up in League

One in 2005–06 and had memorable FA Cup runs, playing against Sheffield United, Blackburn and Chelsea. Watson's 2007–08 season was curtailed by recurring injuries and he was released at the end of an excellent Layer Road career.

	League		Lge Cup		FA Cup		Other	
	A	G	A	G	A	G	A	G
2004–05	44	2	3	0	5	0	1	0
2005–06	43+1	0	1	0	4	1	2+1	0
2006–07	38+2	1	1	0	1	0	-	-
2007–08	7	0	0	0	0	0	-	-
TOTAL	132+3	3	5	0	10	1	2+2	0

WATTS, Grant Steven

Height: 6ft. Weight: 11st 2lb.

Born: 5 November 1973, Croydon.

■ Another of Roy McDonough's signings, Watts began as a YTS player at Crystal Palace before signing professionally in June 1992. He made 2(+2) appearances for Palace in the Premiership and arrived at Layer Road on loan in January 1994. He made his Colchester debut against Wycombe in an Autoglass Trophy tie and scored his first goal against Gillingham before the month was out. His only other goal came at Rochdale, and he was returned to Selhurst Park at the end of his loan to make way for the arrival of Steve Whitton. After spending non-contract time with Sheffield United, Watts signed for Gillingham in September 1994, where he made 2(+1) appearances. He joined Sutton United, Welling, Bromley and Dartford on the non-League circuit.

	League		Lge Cup		FA Cup		Other	
	A	G	A	G	A	G	A	G
1993–94	8+4	2	0	0	0	0	0+1	0
TOTAL	8+4	2	0	0	0	0	0+1	0

WEBB, Thomas 'Tom'

Height: 5ft 11in. Weight: 10st 5lb.

Born: 17 April 1989, Chelmsford.

■ Webb has been at Layer Road and scoring goals since he was an Under-11. He played 13 times for the senior youth side, which then had an Under-19 age limit, before his 16th birthday and was leading scorer for both years of his apprenticeship, and his willingness and ability to use touch and finesse stood out in an arena where pace and power are often the surest way to catch the eye. He was rewarded with a professional contract and earned his first outing for the senior side during an injury and

suspension crisis at the start of the 2007–08 season. He appeared as a substitute at Shrewsbury in the first competitive match at their brand new stadium as United were surprisingly beaten by the League Two side after extra-time. Webb was loaned to Ryman League Folkestone Invicta in March 2008, and despite finishing as the U's reserves leading scorer he was released at the end of the campaign.

	League		Lge Cup		FA Cup		Other	
	A	G	A	G	A	G	A	G
2007–08	0	0	0+1	0	0	0	-	-
TOTAL	0	0	0+1	0	0	0	-	-

WEST, Ronald 'Ron'

■ West, a corporal in the No. 1 Holding Battalion, was among the amateurs listed before the 1945–46 season as a 'possible' for the U's squad. In the event was only seen once in a Colchester shirt, playing right-half at Barry Town in December 1945 while most U's regulars had an Army Cup Final at Layer Road.

	League		Lge Cup		FA Cup		Other	
	A	G	A	G	A	G	A	G
1945–46	1	0	0	0	0	0	-	-
TOTAL	1	0	0	0	0	0	-	-

WESTLAKE, Brian

Height: 5ft 11in. Weight: 12st 4lb.

Born: 19 September 1943, Newcastle, Staffordshire.

■ A centre-forward, Westlake signed for his local side Stoke in September 1961 but failed to make the first team. Doncaster signed him in the summer of 1963, and he scored once in five appearances before joining Halifax at the

turn of 1964. At The Shay he notched 28 goals in exactly 100 League starts. Moving again, he signed for Tranmere for the start of 1966–67, but after three goals in 14 appearances he was recruited by Neil Franklin in mid-February for a small fee and notched a creditable five goals in his 15 League appearances for United. A bustling and feisty character, quickly given the tag 'Jungle Boy' by the Layer Road End (copied from Ipswich Town star Ray Crawford, who earned it from his National Service in Malaysia), Westlake once waved a corner flag at a Layer Road linesman after a decision went against him. Only he knows if he was play-acting. His stay at Layer Road was short as he moved to Belgian side Royal Daring for a fee of £5,000 in July 1967.

	League		Lge Cup		FA Cup		Other	
	A	G	A	G	A	G	A	G
1966–67	14+1	5	0	0	0	0	-	-
TOTAL	14+1	5	0	0	0	0	-	-

WESTWOOD, John 'Johnny'

Born: Edmonton.

■ Westwood represented Edmonton Schoolboys and signed amateur forms with Tottenham in 1945. He built his reputation in army representative games during his National Service with the 15th Infantry Training Corps and Athenian League football with Finchley. He turned professional with Tottenham in 1948 but failed to make the first team. Westwood scored in his only appearance at Layer Road, against Swindon reserves in February 1946.

	League		Lge Cup		FA Cup		Other	
	A	G	A	G	A	G	A	G
1945–46	1	1	0	0	0	0	-	-
TOTAL	1	1	0	0	0	0	-	-

WHITE, Alan

Height: 6ft 1in. Weight: 13st 7lb.

Born: 22 March 1976, Darlington.

■ White served his Youth Training Scheme at Middlesbrough, signing professionally in July 1994. He made his only appearance for Boro in an Anglo-Italian Cup tie against Ancona. He joined Luton for £40,000 in September 1997 and went on to make 60(+20) appearances at Kenilworth Road, scoring three goals. Steve Whitton brought White to Colchester in November 1999 on a month's loan during that Luton career, but White was sent off at Gillingham in the last of his four-game spell. Released on a free transfer in the summer, White returned to Layer Road and became a virtual permanent fixture at the heart of United's defence. He starred as United reached the fifth round of the 2003–04 FA Cup competition, losing narrowly to Sheffield United at Bramall Lane, and scooped all the Player of the Year awards at the end of that season. Offered just a single-year contract extension, White joined Leyton Orient, playing 26 times at Brisbane Road, before signing for Boston United in March 2005. He played 48 League games for Boston, scoring four goals and was Player of the Year in 2005–06. He moved on to Notts County in the summer of 2006 but ended the campaign playing seven games on loan at Peterborough. Despite being captain of Notts, as he had been at Colchester, and making 32(+3) appearances, White opted to join home-town club Darlington for the 2007–08 season in preference to a bid from Peterborough.

	League		Lge Cup		FA Cup		Other	
	A	G	A	G	A	G	A	G
1999–2000	4	0	0	0	0	0	1	0
2000–01	29+3	0	4	0	1	0	0	0
2001–02	28+5	3	0+1	0	0+1	0	0	0
2002–03	41	0	1	0	0	0	1	0
2003–04	30+2	1	2	0	5+1	0	5	0
TOTAL	132+10	4	7+1	0	6+2	0	7	0

WHITE, Eric Winston

Height: 5ft 10in. Weight: 10st 12lb.

Born: 26 October 1958, Leicester.

■ White made his debut for home-town club Leicester after completing his apprenticeship with the Filbert Street club. Although that first game came as a 17-year-old in 1976, he never established himself in the side and moved to Hereford in March 1979. He became a regular on the right wing and completed 169(+6) League appearances, scoring 21 goals, but the club had to be re-elected three times. Incredibly, he played for four different clubs in 1983–84, and all involved transfers. In September he made a substitute appearance for Chesterfield and repeated the feat for Port Vale in October. In November he played four times for Stockport before joining Bury in December. Finally planting some roots, White made 125 starts and scored 12 goals at Gigg Lane, winning promotion in 1984–85, before being loaned to Rochdale in October 1986. Mike Walker signed him for Colchester on a free transfer in February 1987, hoping that the winger would fill the hole left by the departure of Perry Groves to Arsenal. White helped United to the Fourth Division Play-off semi-finals and then played through the Mike Walker sacking fiasco. After just 10 games of Roger Brown's first season in charge, White saw the writing on the wall and moved back north to Burnley in October 1988 following the debacle of an 8–0 defeat at Leyton Orient. Ironically, White's first goals for Burnley came in a 2–2 draw at Layer Road in February 1989. White scored 14 goals for the Clarets in 93(+11) appearances before joining West Bromwich Albion on deadline day 1991. Turning out 13(+1) times for the Baggies and scoring a single goal, he was on his travels again in October 1991, when he returned to Bury to play 1(+1) game. In January 1992 he joined Doncaster, scoring twice in four games and in February 1992 played six times for Carlisle. His last club was Wigan in March 1992, for whom he played 10 games adding two goals. He was only loaned out once and so had an incredible 11 transfers during his career.

	League		Lge Cup		FA Cup		Other	
	A	G	A	G	A	G	A	G
1986–87	14	1	0	0	0	0	2	0
1987–88	40+1	7	2	1	3	0	4	3
1988–89	10	0	2	0	0	0	0	0
TOTAL	64+1	8	4	1	3	0	6	3

WHITE, John Alan

Height: 6ft. Weight: 11st 1lb.

Born: 25 July 1986, Maldon.

■ Local lad White, who joined the U's youth system at 12 years old, is a shining example of the virtues of hard work and making the most of your opportunities and not assuming that a professional contract is guaranteed the day you sign your apprenticeship. White made notable physical progress over the summer of 2004 and, instead of returning to a final year with the youth squad, earned himself a permanent promotion to the senior set up, making his debut as a substitute against Cheltenham in a League Cup tie in August 2004. First and foremost a

defender, White operated at full-back, centre-back and in a man-marking midfield role and came to the fore in Colchester's successful 2005–06 campaign, when they finished runners-up in League One and gained promotion to the Championship as well as enjoying an FA Cup outing at Premiership champions Chelsea. White became a squad player in United's inaugural season in the second tier, unable to displace Greg Halford and then Karl Duguid from the right-back spot. In November 2007 he went on loan to Conference club Stevenage to get some more competitive match practice. On his return he established himself in the left-back spot, allowing the club to cash in on Wolves' interest in George Elokobi.

	League		Lge Cup		FA Cup		Other	
	A	G	A	G	A	G	A	G
2004–05	16+4	0	0+1	0	3	0	0	0
2005–06	32+3	0	0	0	4	0	1+1	0
2006–07	8+9	0	1	0	0	0	-	-
2007-08	21	0	1	0	1	0	-	-
TOTAL	77+16	0	2+1	0	8	0	1+1	0

WHITEHEAD, Kenneth 'Ken'

■ Whitehead signed pro for the U's from Clacton Town in May 1948 and had earlier been on Ipswich Town's books as an amateur. After a couple of games in the reserves, injury to the veteran Harry Wright gave him the first-team job a fortnight into the season, and he was ever present until breaking his nose during the game at Worcester in April 1949. Harry Wright tried to make a comeback but did not last 90 minutes and for the second time in two days the U's had to put an outfield player in goal. Graham Davies was brought in on trial and, although impressive on his debut, he was less so in his next couple of outings and was allowed to depart. Unfortunately for Whitehead, the next man through the door was George Wright, and the U's were well into their first Football League season by the time he gave anyone else a chance of a first-team outing. Whitehead was his deputy throughout 1949–50 but was not retained for the Football League adventure and joined Ipswich based Border League club Whitton United.

	League		Lge Cup		FA Cup		Other	
	A	G	A	G	A	G	A	G
1948–49	34	0	3	0	1	0	-	-
TOTAL	34	0	3	0	1	0	-	-

WHITTAKER, Raymond Henry 'Ray'

Height: 5ft 8in. Weight: 12st 9lb.

Born: 15 January 1946, Bow.

■ An England Schools and Youth international, Whittaker gained six caps, including a 1963 Little World Cup-winners' medal, while on the books of Arsenal, for whom he had signed in May 1962. Despite 35 goals in 149 reserve and youth-team games at Highbury, Whittaker failed to make the first team and joined Luton in March 1964 for £3,000. Winning promotion with the Hatters in 1967–68, he made 169(+1) appearances at Kenilwotth Road, scoring 40 goals, and was the regular penalty taker. Signed for Colchester by Dick Graham, Whittaker scored seven goals from the left wing but failed to make his mark the following season and was released to Wealdstone, where he joined three other ex-U's players, while running a confectioner's in Forest Gate. From Wealdstone he later played for Dartford and Dunstable.

	League		Lge Cup		FA Cup		Other	
	A	G	A	G	A	G	A	G
1969–70	36+1	7	3	0	1	0	-	-
1970–71	5+3	0	0	0	1	0	-	-
TOTAL	41+4	7	3	0	2	0	-	-

WHITTON, Stephen Paul 'Steve'

Height: 6ft 1in. Weight: 13st 6lb.

Born: 4 December 1960, East Ham.

■ Whitton began his long career as a Coventry apprentice, signing professionally in September 1978 and establishing himself in the Sky Blues top flight side in the early 1980s. After 64(+10) games and 21 goals West Ham were persuaded to spend £175,000 in the summer of 1983. Not quite living up to expectations, Whitton managed just six goals in 35(+4) games for the Hammers. He moved across the division to struggling Birmingham, on loan, and did enough with his three goals in eight starts to convince Blues to sign him on for £60,000 in the summer of 1986.

Birmingham had been relegated in the meantime, and the expected return to the top division did not materialise even though Whitton returned a creditable 28 League goals in 94(+1) starts. On transfer deadline day 1989 he returned to the First Division with Sheffield Wednesday for £275,000, but the Owls were also relegated in his first full season. Scoring four times in 22(+10) games at Hillsborough, he left Wednesday on a £150,000 transfer to Ipswich in January 1991. Whitton weighed in with nine goals in 1991–92 as Town took the Second Division title to earn a place in the Premier League. It took a charm offensive from Roy McDonough to persuade Whitton to drop four divisions to join Colchester but a £10,000 fee saw the player arrive at Layer Road on deadline day 1994. He scored his first U's goals when bagging a pair in the penultimate game of the season against Doncaster after missing penalties in his first two starts. A scything challenge from Darlington's Sean Gregan put paid to most of his 1995–96 campaign, and then a pulled calf muscle following his return meant that he was only a playing substitute in United's Play-off semi-final with Plymouth. A year later, however, he played at Wembley as United faced Carlisle in the Auto Windscreens Shield Final. Whitton also played 45 second half minutes in goal in a shock Colchester League Cup win at West Brom in 1996–97. Engaged as player-coach, Whitton had a one-game spell as caretaker manager of United, between Steve Wignall's resignation and the appointment of Mick Wadsworth, before finally taking the reigns in 1999, following the departure of Wadsworth.

** See also Who's Who Managers section*

	League		Lge Cup		FA Cup		Other	
	A	G	A	G	A	G	A	G
1993–94	8	2	0	0	0	0	0	0
1994–95	36	10	2	0	4	3	2	0
1995–96	10+2	2	2	0	0	0	0+2	0
1996–97	36+3	6	2+1	0	0	0	5	1
1997–98	15+6	1	0	0	2	0	0	0
TOTAL	105+11	21	6+1	0	6	3	7+2	1

WHYMARK, Trevor John

Height: 5ft 11in. Weight: 11st 2lb.

Born: 4 May 1950, Burton.

■ Whymark joined Ipswich from Diss Town in May 1969 and made his Town debut in February 1970 at Manchester City. Forming a formidable partnership with David Johnson, Whymark regularly returned a double-figure seasonal goal total as Ipswich challenged at the top of Division One, and he won seven England Under-23 caps, scoring three times, as well as one full England cap in a World Cup Qualifier against Luxembourg. He had an impressive European record, scoring 13 times in 23(+1) UEFA and Cup-winners' Cup appearances, including all the goals in a 4–0 win over Lazio and another four against Landskrona Bois. In the early part of 1979 he moved to Sparta Rotterdam but played just six times without scoring. He returned to England, where he played a couple of games on loan at struggling Derby, before completing a £150,000 move to Vancouver Whitecaps. He resurrected his career by returning to Grimsby in December 1980, scoring 16 in 83(+10) games for the Mariners. Moving to Southend in January 1984, he was not able to help prevent the Shrimpers from being relegated to Division Four, despite scoring six goals in 37(+2) appearances. Peterborough was the next port of call at the start of 1985–86, but after just three goalless appearances he returned to his first club Diss. Cyril Lea brought the player to Colchester on a non-contract basis, and Whymark played just two away fixtures

for Colchester at Preston and Hartlepool in November and December 1985. Whymark took up youth coaching at Norwich in 1999 before becoming part of the Ipswich Academy set up.

	League		Lge Cup		FA Cup		Other	
	A	G	A	G	A	G	A	G
1985–86	2	0	0	0	0	0	0	0
TOTAL	2	0	0	0	0	0	0	0

WIGNALL, Jack David

Height: 6ft 1lb. Weight: 11st 7lb.

Born: 26 September 1981, Colchester.

■ The son of former U's legend Steve Wignall, the young central-defender came through the Centre of Excellence to start his apprenticeship in 1998 at a time when the club played a three centre-back system. Along with Greg Heighway and Nicky Gyory, he formed a powerful barrier in the youth team's 2000 FA Youth Cup run that saw them draw with

the Leeds at Elland Road and only lose the replay on penalties in front of 2,199 at Layer Road. Wignall had already made both his first-team appearances the previous month, his debut coming as a sub at Swansea in an Auto Windscreens Shield fixture and his League bow also from the bench at Bristol Rovers a few days later. He was unable to get into United's first team the following year and was released to Dagenham & Redbridge in March 2001, playing 2(+3) Conference games. With good habits engrained by his dad and youth-team boss Micky Cook, Wignall apparently found some of his new teammates' attitude to training and match preparation a bit of a culture shock, and he soon moved on to Cambridge City before settling at Wivenhoe, where his father became assistant manager. Joining AFC Sudbury in February 2007, he became an instant hit and commanded a transfer fee when joining Heybridge for the 2007–08 season.

	League		Lge Cup		FA Cup		Other	
	A	G	A	G	A	G	A	G
1999–2000	0+1	0	0	0	0	0	0+1	0
TOTAL	0+1	0	0	0	0	0	0+1	0

WIGNALL, Steven Leslie 'Steve'

Height: 5ft 11in. Weight: 11st 12lb.

Born: 17 September 1954, Liverpool.

■ Wignall proved a bargain buy when Bobby Roberts paid Doncaster £5,000 for the defender in September 1977. Originally on the books of Liverpool as a schoolboy, Wignall moved to Belle Vue in March 1972 and amassed 127(+3) League games for Rovers, scoring one goal. He made his full U's debut at Carlisle in October 1977 and made the left-back slot his own. A consistent performer for six more seasons, Wignall almost helped U's into the second tier in 1979–80 and played in Colchester's big Cup ties against Aston Villa, Manchester United and Newcastle. By this time Wignall was back in his original central-defensive position, where his main partners included Steve Dowman, Mick Packer, Steve Wright and Stewart Houston. With wage cuts hitting the U's hard Wignall took the opportunity to move on and signed for Brentford in August 1984. Completing 67 League games, scoring two goals, the defender enjoyed an outing at Wembley as Brentford lost 3–1 to Wigan in the 1985 Freight Rover Trophy Final. In September 1986 he moved to Aldershot and became a stalwart in the Shots defence on 158(+3) occasions scoring four goals. Aldershot won through in the Play-offs in his first season but crumbled financially over the ensuing years and folded in April 1992. Wignall was appointed manager of the reborn Aldershot and guided them to the Diadora League Division Three

Steve Wignall and Trevor Lee

Championship in his first season. Shots were promoted the next season and reached the quarter-finals of the FA Vase. Wignall's leadership did not go unnoticed, and he was employed by Colchester in January 1995 following the acrimonious departure of George Burley. In 1996 he led the U's to a Third Division Play-off semi-final defeat against Plymouth Argyle, but made it to Wembley the following season in the Auto Windscreens Shield. There was more heartbreak for Wignall, however, as his men missed out on the hallowed turf as Carlisle United pulled off a penalty shoot-out triumph. It all came right in front of the Twin Towers in the end though, as Wignall won Colchester promotion in 1998 thanks to a Play-off Final victory over Torquay United. U's fared well among the big boys in the third tier of English football. Such names as Fulham, Manchester City and Stoke squared up to Wignall's side. By January 1999 Wignall became increasingly frustrated at his attempts to bolster his squad and resigned, saying that he had taken his present squad as far as he could. He continued scouting and was appointed manager of Conference side Stevenage in April 2000. After just six weeks in charge, he was tempted to take over the reins at another of his former clubs Doncaster Rovers, but failure to lift Rovers out of the Conference led to his sacking in December 2001. In April 2003 he was appointed manager of Southend, but with just six wins in 23 games was sacked in November 2003 with the Shrimpers second from bottom of the entire League. In the summer of 2005 he accepted an invite to become assistant manager to former U's player Steve Pitt at Wivenhoe Town, where his son Jack, also a former Colchester player, was on the books. His brother David also played for Doncaster.

** See also Who's Who Managers section*

	League		Lge Cup		FA Cup		Other	
	A	G	A	G	A	G	A	G
1977–78	32+2	2	0	0	4	0	-	-
1978–79	42	4	2	0	7	0	-	-
1979–80	40	3	4	0	2	0	-	-
1980–81	42	1	2	0	4	1	-	-
1981–82	43	0	5	0	5	1	-	-
1982–83	44	4	4	1	1	0	3	0
1983–84	36	8	4	2	3	0	2	0
TOTAL	279+2	22	21	3	26	2	5	0

WILES, Ian Robert

Height: 6ft. Weight: 11st 13lb.

Born: 28 April 1980, Woodford.

■ Defender Wiles was almost the ugly duckling who turned into a swan starting as a marginal member of the youth-team squad who, even for the latter part of his first year, was unlikely to be more than a sub. He blossomed during his second year to claim a professional contract for 1998–99 and joined the exclusive club of people who can say 'I played in the Football League'. Wiles only made one first-team appearance, as a substitute in the second game of the 1998–99 season at Wrexham. He sat on the bench again a couple times, but when Mick Wadsworth arrived he suffered the fate of most of the home-grown talent on the fringes of the squad and was discarded in favour of other club Academy cast-offs. Wiles joined Heybridge, earning a good reputation with his classy displays and enjoying success in their 2000–01 Ryman League Cup-winning season. He spent two years with Chelmsford and after a spell with Welling returned to Heybridge and was Player of the Year at Scraley Road in 2006–07.

	League		Lge Cup		FA Cup		Other	
	A	G	A	G	A	G	A	G
1998–99	0+1	0	0	0	0	0	0	0
TOTAL	0+1	0	0	0	0	0	0	0

WILKIE, William 'Bill'

■ A Lance Corporal in the No.1 Holding Battalion, Witham-based Wilkie kept goal for Crittalls and signed amateur forms for the U's. He was only called on for one competitive game, a 3–1 defeat at Hereford in November 1945, and three friendlies in five days over the Christmas holiday. He later played three games for Chelmsford in February 1948 when they had an injury crisis but otherwise played his football locally at a lower level. In the late 1960s he was reserve manager at Sudbury Town and when he stepped up to the senior job in 1971 was their first non player-manager. That only lasted for a year, when he moved on to manage Needham Market, then in the Suffolk & Ipswich League.

	League		Lge Cup		FA Cup		Other	
	A	G	A	G	A	G	A	G
1945–46	1	0	0	0	0	0	-	-
TOTAL	1	0	0	0	0	0	-	-

WILKINS, Richard John

Height: 6ft. Weight: 12st.

Born: 28 May 1965, Lambeth.

■ Wilkins joined Colchester on trial after impressing for Haverhill Rovers against U's reserves and scored twice on his debut in a 4–2 Freight Rover Trophy defeat at Aldershot in November 1986. He was promptly signed up by Mike Walker and became a stalwart in midfield. He helped United get to the Fourth Division Play-off semi-finals in 1987 when U's lost 2–0 on aggregate to Wolves. When Colchester were relegated to the Conference in 1990, Wilkins moved on to Cambridge for a fee of £65,000. Under John Beck, Cambridge almost made it to the Premiership, losing to Leicester in the Play-offs, but by then Wilkins had already broken his thigh bone. During his Cambridge career, he

amassed 79(+2) appearances and bagged seven goals. Once recovered, Wilkins moved to Hereford on a free transfer in the summer of 1994 and played 76(+1) games, scoring five times and failing with a Play-off bid in 1995–96. Steve Wignall paid £18,000 for his services in the summer of 1996, and Wilkins repaid every penny by helping United to a Wembley Auto Windscreens Final against Carlisle and missing out on the Play-offs by a single point. The following season was equally successful as Wilkins hoisted the Third Division Play-off trophy aloft at Wembley when U's beat Torquay 1–0. Troubled by neck injuries in his last seasons, Wilkins was rewarded by a testimonial match against a strong Tottenham side in July 2002. He joined Bury Town in 2000 as manager and led them to runners'-up spot in the Eastern Counties League and to an FA Vase semi-final.

	League		Lge Cup		FA Cup		Other	
	A	G	A	G	A	G	A	G
1986–87	22+1	2	0	0	0+2	0	4+1	2
1987–88	46	9	2	0	3	2	3	0
1988–89	39+1	9	2	0	2+1	2	1+1	1
1989–90	43	5	2	0	2	0	1+1	0
1996–97	40	2	3	0	1	1	6	0
1997–98	37	5	2	0	2	0	2	0
1998–99	25+1	2	0	0	0	0	0	0
1999–2000	23+1	2	2	0	0	0	0	0
TOTAL	275+4	36	13	0	10+3	5	17+3	3

WILKINSON, Harry Sanderson

Height: 5ft 9in. Weight: 11st 3lb.

Born: 20 March 1926, Sunderland.

■ Wilkinson started his wing-half career at Chelsea in 1945 but did not break into

the Stamford Bridge first team. He moved to Exeter for the 1950–51 season, where he made his full professional debut. Despite moving to Layer Road in 1951, it was not until 14 March 1953 that he made his solitary United appearance against Watford. After leaving Layer Road, he later played for Folkestone and Ramsgate but quit after three seasons with varicose veins. He continued to work for North Thames Gas, and his son David was also a Chelsea trainee.

	League		Lge Cup		FA Cup		Other	
	A	G	A	G	A	G	A	G
1952–53	1	0	-	-	0	0	-	-
TOTAL	1	0	-	-	0	0	-	-

WILLIAMS, David Geraint

Height: 5ft 8in. Weight: 13st.

Born: 5 January 1962, Treorchy.

■ Williams began his career as an apprentice with Bristol Rovers, joining the professional ranks in January 1980. Capped at Youth level for Wales, Williams made 138(+3) appearances for Rovers scoring eight times. In March 1984 he secured a £40,000 transfer to Third Division Derby, winning two successive promotions including a Second Division title in 1986–87. Williams added to his international honours with two caps at Under-21 level and 13 full appearances. He played in the first international ever staged at the Millennium Stadium when Wales hosted Germany. After four seasons in the top flight, Derby were relegated in 1990–91 and when they lost the Play-offs the following season Williams was on the move to Premier League Ipswich via a £600,000 fee. Of his 217 appearances for Town, 109 were in the Premier League, but after relegation in 1994–95 Ipswich suffered successive Play-off failures. Having been captain in 1996–97, Williams moved south down the A12 to Colchester in July 1998. He retired at the end of his first season at Layer Road to join the coaching staff under first Steve Whitton, then Phil Parkinson, before being asked to take over the manager's chair for United's first campaign at Championship level in 2006–07, following Parkinson's defection to Hull. Williams defied the doubters and steered Colchester to 10th place, just six points off the Play-offs and a possible place in

the Premiership. A remarkable achievement for a club on such a small budget in a sea of wealth. After losing star strikers Jamie Cureton and Chris Iwelumo, as well as defender Wayne Brown, Williams was set the task of ensuring that Colchester entered their new stadium as a Championship club in 2008–09.

* *See also Who's Who Managers section*

	League		Lge Cup		FA Cup		Other	
	A	G	A	G	A	G	A	G
1998–99	38+1	0	2	0	1	0	1	0
TOTAL	38+1	0	2	0	1	0	1	0

WILLIAMS, Gareth Ashley

Height: 5ft 10in. Weight: 11st 13lb.

Born: 15 August 1982, Germiston.

■ Williams's career started at Crystal Palace, where he made his debut in the

2002–03 season, appearing as substitute on three occasions in the League as well as having a full outing in a League Cup tie with Oldham, where he had to be sacrificed when future U's player Danny Granville was sent off. A Welsh Youth and five-cap Under-21 international, Williams was noted as a prolific scorer on the Football Combination circuit by Steve Whitton, and he arrived at Layer Road in January 2003 and scored an impressive six goals in just 6(+2) starts. Unfortunately, Whitton lost his job as U's manager following the 2–0 defeat to Blackpool that marked Williams's debut. The striker responded in tremendous fashion by grabbing a hat-trick in a 4–1 win over Port Vale a game which was the first under new manager Phil Parkinson. After such a promising spell, Palace wanted to take a second look at Williams, but he featured in just two more substitute appearances. In October 2003 he joined Cambridge on loan, scoring once in four games, and had one substitute appearance at Bournemouth in an injury-curtailed loan during February 2004. Parkinson brought Williams back to Layer Road in March 2004, and the striker again showed his striking prowess. He joined Colchester on a permanent deal in the September 2004 in a swap that saw Wayne Andrews join Palace. Despite scoring the winner in a shock FA Cup win at Sheffield United in January 2006, Williams never revived his early Colchester promise. He was sent out on loan to Blackpool, along with Sam Stockley, scoring three times in 6(+3) games in a deal that saw Scott Vernon move to Layer Road. Released by Colchester in the summer, Williams had an unsuccessful trial with Yeovil and then joined Weymouth, playing twice as a substitute. In November 2006 he joined former U's favourite Bobby Bowry at Bromley, and his goals helped fire the club to Ryman League Play-off success and a place in the Conference South for 2007–08, joining Braintree in the summer of 2008.

	League		Lge Cup		FA Cup		Other	
	A	G	A	G	A	G	A	G
2002–03	6+1	6	0	0	0	0	0	0
2003–04	5+2	2	0	0	0	0	0	0
2004–05	12+17	3	1	0	2+1	2	1	0
2005–06	6+12	1	0+1	0	0+4	1	4+1	0
TOTAL	29+32	12	1+1	0	2+5	3	5+1	0

WILLIAMS, George

Height: 5ft 11in. Weight: 12st.

■ Formerly with Northern League South Bank and Middlesbrough as an amateur, Williams scored 37 times for Ipswich reserves in 1936–37. He signed amateur forms with the newly formed United at the start of 1937–38, scoring a hat-trick in the pre-season trial, but spent the first part of the season playing for the dying Colchester Town. He was their top scorer with five of their 20 goals when they collapsed in late November, although H. Martin caught him up when Town fulfilled their Essex Senior Cup fixture a couple of months later. Williams stayed at Layer Road right through to the war, but only made four first-team starts, all in 1937–38. He did not score in those games but did get both in the otherwise first-team line up that beat Crystal Palace 2–1 in Ronnie Dunn's benefit match. At the time of his marriage in early 1941 – when he is described as an ex-U's footballer – his home address was in Ipswich, and he was serving as an anti-aircraft gunner. He may be the otherwise unidentified G. Williams who played one post-war game for Ipswich Town at outside-left in the 1945 FA Cup, a competition where guest players were not allowed, causing clubs considerable disruption and difficulties in completing teams.

	League		Lge Cup		FA Cup		Other	
	A	G	A	G	A	G	A	G
1937–38	3	0	0	0	-	-	1	0
TOTAL	3	0	0	0	-	-	1	0

WILLIAMS, J. 'Taffy'

■ Winger Williams successfully concealed his first name at both Layer Road and his previous club, Northampton, and identifying him is not helped by a commercially produced but officially sanctioned 1949–50 Southern League handbook that gives Chingford Town's new signings as J. Williams from Cardiff and L. Williams from Colchester. That is the wrong way round. Invariably referred to as 'Taffy', he had a spell at Leicester before joining Northampton in 1946–47 but was only a reserve at either club, and that did not change a great deal at Layer Road, where all his half-dozen senior starts came in odd games. Naturally right footed, he could play on either wing and was a competent deputy but lacked the electric bursts of pace of first choice outside-right Dennis Hillman. Chingford, who had only been formed in 1947 and turned professional in 1948, were always beset by limited finances and a mudpatch of a ground that had not long since had the River Ching flowing across the centre of the site. They lost 72 of the 104 Southern League games they played and gave up the struggle in November 1950.

	League		Lge Cup		FA Cup		Other	
	A	G	A	G	A	G	A	G
1947–48	4	0	1	0	1	0	-	-
TOTAL	4	0	1	0	1	0	-	-

WILLIAMS, John Robert

Height: 5ft 10in. Weight: 11st 10lb.

Born: 26 March 1947, Tottenham.

■ Williams started out as an apprentice at Watford before becoming full-time in

October 1964. A left-back, he completed 371(+3) League games at Vicarage Road and weighed in with two goals. During that time, he played in the same 1970 FA Cup semi-final side as future U's stars Mike Walker, Mick Packer and Brian Owen. Although the Hornets lost 5–1 to Chelsea, Williams had already picked up a Third Division Championship medal in the previous campaign. Signed in mid-June 1975, Williams was Jim Smith's last recruit to the club before departing for Blackburn, and he proved a dependable left-back until being the man to lose his place when Steve Wignall arrived in autumn 1977. He had just scored his first and only U's goal and later filled in on the left side of midfield before departing at the end of the season. He joined Southern League Margate for a year and stayed in Kent to be a regular in Gravesend's 1979–80 Conference side before moving to Chelmsford in 1980–81.

	League		Lge Cup		FA Cup		Other	
	A	G	A	G	A	G	A	G
1975–76	36	0	1	0	2	0	-	-
1976–77	43	0	3	0	6	0	-	-
1977–78	28+1	1	5	0	3	0	-	-
TOTAL	107+1	1	9	0	11	0	-	-

WILLIAMS, Keith David

Height: 5ft 9in. Weight: 11st 10lb.

Born: 12 April 1957, Burntwood.

■ An apprentice with Aston Villa, Williams signed pro in April 1975 but failed to make the first team. He joined Northampton in February 1977, scoring six goals in 128(+3) games before moving to Bournemouth in August 1981. He won promotion in his first season at Dean Court, where he teamed up with Roger Brown, and it was that friendship which enabled Brown to take Williams to Layer Road in December 1987 as his player-coach. Williams had seemingly finished his League career by joining Bath City after 99(+3) appearances for the Cherries, where he had not been a regular since 1982. It was soon clear that his mobility had gone, and he was playing on memory, but he struck lucky, initially coming into a side that had only lost once in 15 games and was still riding the crest of the Mike Walker-inspired wave. The run came to an end on New Year's Day, and the change in fortunes could hardly have

been more stark with one win in 16 to the end of March. Williams was quickly out of the team and left the club at the end of the season. After Colchester, he returned to the south coast, where he had coaching and managerial associations with non-Leaguers Swanage, Salisbury, Poole, Bournemouth Poppies and Ringwood.

	League		Lge Cup		FA Cup		Other	
	A	G	A	G	A	G	A	G
1987–88	9+1	0	0	0	0	0	0	0
TOTAL	9+1	0	0	0	0	0	0	0

WILLIAMS, Martin Keith

Height: 5ft 9in. Weight: 11st 12lb.

Born: 12 July 1973, Luton.

■ Released by Leicester from their Youth Training Scheme, Williams was given a

second chance by Luton in September 1991. He made his top-flight debut in the last season before it became known as the Premier League and went on to score two goals in 12(+28) appearances in the second tier following Luton's relegation. Spotted on the Football Combination reserve-team circuit, Williams was recruited on a month's loan on deadline day 1995 and made his debut at Hartlepool in a rain-sodden 3–1 defeat. He was not quite ready for basement level football but none-the-less earned a move to Reading in the summer of 1995. At Elm Park he played 99(+29) times and scored an impressive 26 goals from the wing. He moved to Swindon in August 2000, bagging two goals in 17(+2) starts, and his final move was on loan to Peterborough in January 2001 where he also scored two in 13(+2) League appearances. Dropping into non-League, Williams played for Stevenage, appearing 41(+7) times and scoring five Conference goals, Woking, St Albans and was with Maidenhead in 2007.

	League		Lge Cup		FA Cup		Other	
	A	G	A	G	A	G	A	G
1994–95	3	0	0	0	0	0	0	0
TOTAL	3	0	0	0	0	0	0	0

WILLIAMS, Thomas John 'Tommy'

Height: 5ft 8in. Weight: 10st 7lb.

Born: 10 February 1935, London.

Died: 25 August 1967.

■ Benny Fenton signed Williams from amateurs Carshalton Athletic, with whom he had also been playing for Leyton Orient's reserves, in September 1956, and the Londoner became a regular at Layer Road over five seasons. Following relegation to Division Four in

1961, Williams signed for Watford and after just 12 games and a creditable six goals developed knee problems that forced him to quit the professional game. In two seasons at Southern League Gravesend, Williams was part of their 1962–63 FA Cup run to the fourth round beating Exeter, Wycombe and Carlisle before losing 5–2 to Sunderland in a replay. After a brief spell with Margate in 1963–64, Williams became a heating engineer in the Lambeth area.

	League		Lge Cup		FA Cup		Other	
	A	G	A	G	A	G	A	G
1956–57	23	3	-	-	0	0	-	-
1957–58	28	5	-	-	1	0	-	-
1958–59	29	6	-	-	1	1	-	-
1959–60	35	9	-	-	1	0	-	-
1960–61	36	8	2	1	2	1	-	-
TOTAL	151	31	2	1	5	2	-	-

WILLIAMS

■ A 19-year-old on the books of West Ham, Williams was with the No.1 Holding Battalion when twice leading the U's line in eight days in October 1945. He was seen once more, in a friendly at the start of January, but from the limited information available about him all that can be said is that he did not ever play for West Ham's first team.

	League		Lge Cup		FA Cup		Other	
	A	G	A	G	A	G	A	G
1945–46	2	0	0	0	0	0	-	-
TOTAL	2	0	0	0	0	0	-	-

WILLIS, Ronald Ian 'Ron'

Height: 5ft 10in. Weight: 11st 7lb.

Born: 27 December 1947, Romford.

■ A trialist with both Coventry and Spurs, Willis was signed for Leyton Orient in January 1966 by Dick Graham. Gaining England Youth caps, Willis made 45 appearances in the O's goal, standing in when regular 'keeper Vic Rouse was sidelined for the entire 1966–67 season. Graham sold him to Charlton in October 1967 for £5,000, but with just a solitary appearance under his belt he was loaned out to Brentford at the beginning of 1968–69 and became a Colchester player a month later in October. Graham signed the player for a second time and for a fee of £1,500, with the deal being completed in the station buffet at Liverpool Street. Willis covered for Tony Macedo in three games in his first season and was unfortunate to suffer a serious eye injury in a League Cup tie at Reading the

following campaign. Freed in summer 1970, he briefly moved to Natal, South Africa in 1971 to play for Arcadia Shepherds but had to return to the UK at short notice, for business reasons. Arcadia refused to terminate his contract, and he was left in limbo, unable to join another club.

	League		Lge Cup		FA Cup		Other	
	A	G	A	G	A	G	A	G
1968–69	3	0	0	0	0	0	-	-
1969–70	3	0	1	0	0	0	-	-
TOTAL	6	0	1	0	0	0	-	-

WILMOTT

■ A youthful ex-Barnet amateur who first played for the U's at the start of October 1945 and signed professional in late November, Wilmott played 13 out of 17 games, including friendlies, until his unit posted him to Leicester in February 1946. Unable to get weekend leave, that was the end of his connection with Layer Road. Wilmott played for No.1 Holding Battalion in the December 1945 Old Contemptible's Cup Final. Barnet had a reserve player named Joe Wilmott around this time, and it is possible he is the same person but Wilmott definitely did not play for Barnet's first team.

	League		Lge Cup		FA Cup		Other	
	A	G	A	G	A	G	A	G
1945–46	6	1	1	0	1	0	-	-
TOTAL	6	1	1	0	1	0	-	-

WINGATE, Tony

Height: 5ft 10in. Weight: 11st 2lb.

Born: 21 March 1955, Islington.

■ Signed as an apprentice in 1970, Wingate had the shortest U's first-team career on record, coming on as an 88th-

minute substitute at a fog-shrouded Hartlepool on 18 March 1972, three days before his 17th birthday. He broke his leg in a reserve game at Southend in March 1973 and suffered a second break in the same place training in August that year. In the meantime, he had been given his professional contract and was back in action by January 1974, playing right-back in the predominantly first-team squads that contested end-of-season games with Southend (Essex Professional Cup) and Norwich (a promotion celebration friendly). Wingate was released that summer and was reported to be trialling at Enfield.

	League		Lge Cup		FA Cup		Other	
	A	G	A	G	A	G	A	G
1971–72	0+1	0	0	0	0	0	0	0
TOTAL	0+1	0	0	0	0	0	0	0

WOOD, Alexander Lochlan 'Sandy'

Height: 5ft 9in. Weight: 11st 7lb.

Born: 12 June 1907, Lochgelly.

Died: July 1987, Gary, Indiana, USA.

■ Wood, aged 14, emigrated with his family to the US in 1921 and became a naturalised American. During his time in the States, he played for Chicago Bricklayers, Holley Carburettors, Detroit and Brooklyn Wanderers. Chosen as a USA international, he played in the inaugural 1930 World Cup in Uruguay, including the semi-final. Many British professionals had emigrated to the US, particularly Scots, and had become the backbone of the USA side. Wood, James Gallacher, Andrew Auld, James Brown,

Bart McGhee and George Moorhouse were all Brits, but some had seen better days and appeared rather large and unfit. They were quickly dubbed the 'shot putters' by the French national side. Surprisingly they beat Belgium by 3–0, then Paraguay by the same score to reach the semi-finals, where they faced Argentina. Three of the USA players were crippled before half-time by the rough tactics of the Argentinians, such that at the final whistle the USA trainer ran on the pitch and threw his medical box at the Belgian referee. Not surprisingly, the Americans were hammered 6–1 in front of 80,000 spectators. On the way home, the squad stopped off in Brazil for a friendly and lost 4–3. Wood played all of those international matches. In 1932 he found his way back to England, joining Leicester City, where he played 52 League games in three seasons. Wood played his part as Leicester reached the 1933–34 FA Cup semi-final, where they lost to Portsmouth. At the beginning of the 1936–37 season Nottingham Forest paid £750 for his services, and he played in 21 League games before joining Colchester on 16 July 1937. A polished full-back, he earned Southern League Representative honours when he played against the Cheshire League at Sealand Road Chester with U's colleagues Bill Barraclough and George Ritchie in October 1937. At Newport, on 6 November 1937, he became the first U's outfield player to play in goal when he deputised for 30 minutes for Ronnie Dunn who had become concussed. A fearless defender, Wood refused terms at the end of U's first season and moved to the new professional club at Chelmsford, a signing that earned Nottingham Forest £800. At New Writtle Street he featured in Chelmsford's giant-killing FA Cup run in 1938–39. Released at the end of that season, he was re-engaged as a part-timer prior to the onset of war and played his last game for Chelmsford before returning to America on 21 October 1939, being made captain for the day. He worked in US Steel Industry until his death in July 1987.

	League		Lge Cup		FA Cup		Other	
	A	G	A	G	A	G	A	G
1937–38	32	1	6	0	-	-	16	0
TOTAL	32	1	6	0	-	-	16	0

WOOD, Brian Thomas

Height: 5ft 11in. Weight: 12st 11lb.

Born: 8 December 1940, Hamworthy.

■ Dick Graham, a former West Brom trainer, signed Wood on a free transfer for Crystal Palace after the central-defender had been on the ground staff at Albion since January 1958. He became a fixture in the Palace defence, playing 142(+1) times in the League, scoring a single goal. He won promotion with Palace in 1963–64 but lost his place after breaking his leg twice. Moving to Leyton Orient to rejoin Graham in December 1966, he made 58 League appearances scoring three goals and was club captain. With the U's defence leaking goals at the start of 1968–69, Graham once again turned to Wood, bringing him to Layer Road on loan at the start of September and paying £3,500 for him within a couple of weeks. Freed after two seasons at Colchester, he opted to move north to Workington with the ambition of pursuing his FA coaching badge. He made over 200 League appearances at Borough Park and was appointed player-coach in the dark days at the end of Workington's League career. The club were not re-elected in 1977 and were replaced by Wimbledon. Wood maintained his friendship with Graham when the two worked at the Willis Faber Dumas sports centre in Ipswich up until 1996, when he then became licensee of the Doberman Public House in Framsden, Suffolk.

	League		Lge Cup		FA Cup		Other	
	A	G	A	G	A	G	A	G
1968–69	28	1	0	0	2	0	-	-
1969–70	43	1	3	0	1	0	-	-
TOTAL	71	2	3	0	3	0	-	

WOODMAN, Andrew John 'Andy'

Height: 6ft 3in. Weight: 13st 7lb.

Born: 11 August 1971, Camberwell.

■ A youth trainee with Crystal Palace, Woodman failed to make the first team at Selhurst Park and joined Exeter in July 1994. Playing just six League games for the Grecians, he was released after receiving two red cards in close succession – one of which was against Colchester in a second round

FA Cup tie in December 1994, when he handled outside the area. Signing for Northampton, he established his career, missing just three games in three full seasons. He played at Wembley in two successive Play-off Finals, beating Swansea in 1997 and losing to Grimsby a year later. In January 1999 he moved on to Brentford after amassing 163 League games at Sixfields. He immediately helped Brentford to the Third Division Championship in the remainder of the season. On deadline day 2000 he moved to Peterborough on loan, playing five games, but was recalled by Brentford because of injuries in their squad. That summer proved to be the end of Woodman's 61-game career at Griffin Park, as he moved to Southend on loan, starting the first 17 games of the 2000–01 season. When his loan expired it was Steve Whitton who brought the experienced 'keeper to Colchester to compete with Simon Brown. Over the remainder of the season the pair tussled for the number-one jersey, sharing the responsibility, but Woodman became first choice in his second campaign at Layer Road. Disappointed to be dropped for a visit to Tranmere in January 2001, he asked for a transfer and moved to Oxford, initially on loan, playing 101 League games. He moved into non-League, playing Conference football for Stevenage in 2004 while doubling up as goalkeeper coach. He also turned out for Redbridge and then Thurrock in April 2005 after a brief spell as second choice 'keeper on a short-term basis at Torquay. He was appointed goalkeeping coach at Rushden & Diamonds in the summer of 2005 and rekindled his League career with three games for the League new boys before ankle ligament damage ended his playing career. Woodman joined Charlton in a coaching role in the 2007 close season. He also co-wrote a book with Gareth Southgate, detailing the differing paths the two one-time Palace trainees' career path led. The book was called *Woody and Nord*.

	League		Lge Cup		FA Cup		Other	
	A	G	A	G	A	G	A	G
2000–01	28	0	0	0	0	0	1	0
2001–02	26	0	2	0	2	0	0	0
TOTAL	54	0	2	0	2	0	1	0

WOODS, Charles Morgan Parkinson 'Charlie'

Height: 5ft 8in. Weight: 10st 10lb.

Born: 18 March 1941, Whitehaven.

■ Woods began playing for Whitehaven while still at school and was signed up by Cleator Moor Celtic. It was while at Cleator Moor that he earned a trial at Aston Villa but was not signed on by the Midlanders. Undaunted, he was invited for a trial at Newcastle and impressed sufficiently in helping to win an international youth tournament in Holland to be signed by the Magpies in May 1959. He made his debut the following season and scored seven times in 26 League appearances, but Newcastle were relegated and had a change of management. Transferred to Bournemouth in November 1962, he bagged 26 goals in two seasons at Dean Court from 70 League starts. Exactly two years later he signed for Crystal Palace, scoring five in 49 games under Dick Graham, and played in nine different numerical shirts. Next he joined Ipswich in the summer of 1966 featuring 65(+17) times while bagging five goals, including one on his debut against Brentford. He won a Second Division Championship medal in 1967–68, but Ipswich sold him to Watford, and during the 1970–71 season he appeared 40(+2) times, netting on three occasions. Dick Graham brought him to Layer road on loan in November 1971 but after three games cash-struck United could not afford Watford's £1,500 asking fee. He joined the coaching staff of Blackburn and returned to Portman Road to be reserve manager, first-team coach, assistant manager and finally chief scout. He followed Bobby Robson to Newcastle, where he became chief scout of his first professional club.

	League		Lge Cup		FA Cup		Other	
	A	G	A	G	A	G	A	G
1971–72	3	0	0	0	0	0	0	0
TOTAL	3	0	0	0	0	0	0	0

WOODS, Patrick James 'Pat'

Height: 5ft 7in. Weight: 11st.

Born: 29 April 1933, Islington.

■ Woods formed a formidable partnership with Tony Ingham at the heart of the QPR defence and made 304 League appearances at Loftus Road before emigrating to Australia in 1960 to play for Queensland side Hellenic, and Sydney area clubs South Coast United, Melita Eagles and Western Suburbs. He returned to England and signed for Colchester in August 1963 and was ever present until the end of February, by which time it had been agreed that he would be released to return to his family in Australia in time for the new Australian season. He was recalled for one last game at Bristol City on Easter Saturday before flying to Australia a few days later, where he re-joined South Coast United. Woods settled at Nambucca Heads and eventually gained full Australian 'Socceroo' status.

	League		Lge Cup		FA Cup		Other	
	A	G	A	G	A	G	A	G
1963–64	36	0	3	0	2	0	-	-
TOTAL	36	0	3	0	2	0	-	-

WOOLDRIDGE, Stephen Joseph 'Steve'

Height: 5ft 8½in. Weight: 12st 6lb.

Born: 18 July 1950, Chiswick.

■ Crystal Palace apprentice Wooldridge signed professional at Selhurst Park in July 1967 but failed to progress to the first team. He moved to Plymouth on loan at the start of the 1970–71 season and featured 20 times for the Devon side. Dick Graham brought him to Layer Road in the summer of 1972, but after making his debut against Hereford on the opening day of the new season he made just two further League appearances, once at right-back for Micky Cook and once at left-back for John McLaughlin. Before the end of November his U's career was over, and he was on a month's loan to Folkestone, signing permanently for them just before Christmas.

	League		Lge Cup		FA Cup		Other	
	A	G	A	G	A	G	A	G
1972–73	3	0	1	0	0	0	-	-
TOTAL	3	0	1	0	0	0	-	-

WORDSWORTH, Anthony

Height: 6ft 2in. Weight: 12st 4lb.

Born: 3 January 1989, London.

■ Wordsworth joined the U's as an Under-16 when released by Charlton and was taken on as a full professional in 2007 after completing his apprenticeship. He answered an early season call to cover for injury and suspensions to come off the bench in Colchester's extra-time League Cup

defeat in the inaugural match at Shrewsbury's New Meadow stadium in August 2007. An accomplished penalty taker for the youth team and confident in his own ability, the youngster wanted to take what would have been an equalising penalty kick but was out ranked by Johnnie Jackson who promptly missed from 12 yards. Wordsworth continued his footballing education, being a regular in United's reserve side. He made his full debut against Hull in March 2008 in the last League game under the Layer Road lights.

	League		Lge Cup		FA Cup		Other	
	A	G	A	G	A	G	A	G
2007–08	1+2	0	0+1	0	0	0	-	-
TOTAL	1+2	0	0+1	0	0	0	-	-

WORTON, Alfred James 'Alf'

Height: 5ft 10in. Weight: 11st.

Born: 4 April 1914, Wolverhampton.

Died: December 2000, Stourbridge.

■ Left-back Worton began playing with local Midlands sides Ettingshall Westley and Bilston Borough. He joined Walsall in 1933 and, despite playing over 60 times for their reserves, failed to break into the first team. He signed for Norwich on 9 June 1934 for a City side that had just won promotion to Division Two. Nicknamed 'Ginger' due his flame red hair, Worton represented Norwich on 23 occasions before arriving at Layer Road in July 1938 on a free transfer. He picked up a Southern League Championship-winning medal in his first season at Layer Road and made the left-back position his own. He returned to his Midlands home at the outbreak of war and retired from his post as a manager in a Wolverhampton Boilermakers in 1977.

	League		Lge Cup		FA Cup		Other	
	A	G	A	G	A	G	A	G
1938–39	44	0	3	0	2	0	15	0
1939–40	3	0	1	0	-	-	-	-
TOTAL	47	0	4	0	2	0	15	6

WRIGHT, George William

Height: 6ft 2½in. Weight: 12st 10lb.

Born: 10 October 1919, Plymouth.

■ The tall fair-haired Wright joined Plymouth in 1937 and was in goal for their reserves when they beat the U's 5–4 in the Southern League in October 1937. He made his League debut aged just 17 and a half in 1938 and went on to make 11 appearances for the Pilgrims, plus another seven in 1945–46. He asked to leave Plymouth when football resumed after the war after not getting the assurance of a first-team place at Home Park, due to the presence of Welsh international Bill Short. Taken on trial by the U's for the last two games of the 1948–49, after regular 'keeper Ken Whitehead broke his nose and the first trialist replacement flattered to deceive, Wright did not look back and secured a £1,000 transfer in May 1949. Generally the regular U's 'keeper for five years, his career straddled the election to the Football League, and he won a Southern League Cup-winners' medal in 1949–50. He reduced to part-time terms for 1954–55 and, although originally released at the end of the season, was re-engaged as a stand by for another season. He was hardly needed though, with

Percy Ames and John Wright (no relation) ahead of him and youngster Bill Dalziel the regular A team custodian. Wright left Layer Road in 1956 and spent a year at Sudbury before retiring from football. Away from football he became a taxi driver and a carpenter until his retirement in 1984.

	League		Lge Cup		FA Cup		Other	
	A	G	A	G	A	G	A	G
1948–49	*2*	*0*	*0*	*0*	*0*	*0*	-	-
1949–50	*46*	*0*	*5*	*0*	*1*	*0*	-	-
1950–51	39	0	-	-	2	0	-	-
1951–52	33	0	-	-	3	0	-	-
1952–53	28	0	-	-	5	0	-	-
1953–54	39	0	-	-	2	0	-	-
1954–55	12	0	-	-	2	0	-	-
TOTAL	151	0	-	-	14	0	-	-
	48	*0*	*5*	*0*	*1*	*0*	-	-

WRIGHT, Harold Edward 'Harry'

Born: 3 June 1909, Tottenham.
Died: April 1994, King's Lynn.

■ Initially with Harwich and Parkeston, playing against the old Colchester Town, Wright was at Charlton between 1932 and 1935 as they rose from Division Three to Division One as understudy to Sam Bartram. Despite this, he managed 38 League appearances. In 1936–37 Wright played 28 times for Aldershot before a £2,500 fee took him to Derby, where he played 25 times the next year. Wright played in an 'extra' international for England against Scotland for the King's Jubilee Cup in 1935. He played with Fenton for Eastern Command at Layer Road during the war and signed for United on 11 July 1946. At the end of the season he was not on the retained list to start with, but the club changed their mind a month later, which was fortunate for Wright, who otherwise would have missed out on the U's march to the fifth round of the 1947–48 FA Cup. Injury within the first couple of weeks of 1948–49 lost him his place, and he only attempted a comeback at Merthyr in April because Ken Whitehead had been injured the day before. Wright did not last 90 minutes and in the summer, now aged 40, was appointed trainer-coach at Guildford. A fully-qualified FA coach and physiotherapist, he held coaching posts at Walsall and Luton before becoming head coach of Everton in September 1956. Wright spent 1961–63 coaching in India, preparing the Indian youth team for the 1963 Asia Youth tournament in Malaya. He retired to King's Lynn in Norfolk.

	League		Lge Cup		FA Cup		Other	
	A	G	A	G	A	G	A	G
1946–47	19	0	4	0	0	0	-	-
1947–48	28	0	7	0	6	0	-	-
1948–49	3	0	2	0	0	0	-	-
TOTAL	50	0	13	0	6	0	-	-

WRIGHT, John Francis Dominic

Height: 5ft 11in. Weight: 10st 11lb.

Born: 13 August 1933, Aldershot.

■ Wright signed amateur forms for the U's in May 1952 and, like many of the local amateurs, became a part-time professional as he began his National Service. He was a serviceman when he got his first-team debut in the last two games of 1954–55, and in fact four of his five appearances came before he was demobbed from the RAOC in November 1956. That was due to the presence and

consistency of Percy Ames, and Wright epitomised patience as Ames clocked up four ever-present seasons. Wright finally got another chance at Coventry in January 1961 and marked the occasion by saving a penalty from the usually reliable Bill Myerscough, although it did not save the points. That was it, though, as Ames made a quick recovery from injury, and Wright quit at the end of the season to join the police. He left the force in summer 1963, going to work for the Electricity Board and joining Clacton, the town where he lived.

	League		Lge Cup		FA Cup		Other	
	A	G	A	G	A	G	A	G
1954–55	2	0	-	-	0	0	-	-
1955–56	2	0	-	-	0	0	-	-
1956–57	0	0	-	-	0	0	-	-
1957–58	0	0	-	-	0	0	-	-
1958–59	0	0	-	-	0	0	-	-
1959–60	0	0	-	-	0	0	-	-
1960–61	1	0	0	0	0	0	-	-
TOTAL	5	0	0	0	0	0	-	-

WRIGHT, Peter Brooke

Height: 5ft 11in. Weight: 12st.

Born: 26 January 1934, Colchester.

■ An outside-left, Wright signed as a part-time professional in November 1951 and held the club record appearance record until it was taken by Micky Cook in the 1980s. His incredibly consistent and almost injury-free first-team career started against Northampton on 22 March 1952 and ended on 20 April 1964 against Shrewsbury, and the U's probably at least in part have the

Peter Wright.

maximum wage rule to thank for the fact that he resisted all the periodic attempts to tempt him away. Birmingham offered £15,000 for Wright in October 1957, and there was also interest from Fulham and Bolton, but Wright was content to stay part-time and combine his football with employment as a draughtsman at Paxman's Diesels in Colchester. Despite playing in contact lenses and having a couple of goals scrubbed off in 1961–62 when Accrington resigned mid-season, he notched an impressive goal tally from the wing, as well as providing ammunition for Colchester's forward line. That was still his second best season for goals – he had hit 16 in 1957–58 – and he also saw his first hat-trick in the 6–1 win against Workington in September 1961. Another hat-trick followed in the 1963–64 League Cup against Northampton to mark his final year at Layer Road, after which he had a year at Romford then took over as player-coach of Haverhill Rovers. 1967–68 saw him move on to Halstead Town in the same role, staying there for three years before going to Long Melford for a couple of years. His oldest son Steve played over 140 first-team games for the U's in the 1970s and 1980s, younger son Clayton briefly played for the reserves in 1977 while grandson Jamie, Steve's son, is in the second year of his apprenticeship in 2007–08.

	League		Lge Cup		FA Cup		Other	
	A	G	A	G	A	G	A	G
1951–52	9	0	-	-	0	0	-	-
1952–53	12	2	-	-	0	0	-	-
1953–54	22	2	-	-	1	0	-	-
1954–55	23	9	-	-	0	0	-	-
1955–56	45	9	-	-	1	0	-	-
1956–57	44	8	-	-	1	0	-	-
1957–58	45	16	-	-	1	0	-	-
1958–59	43	5	-	-	6	0	-	-
1959–60	46	11	-	-	1	1	-	-
1960–61	21	3	2	1	0	0	-	-
1961–62	44	12	1	0	3	1	-	-
1962–63	38	6	2	0	1	0	-	-
1963–64	34	7	3	3	2	0	-	-
TOTAL	426	90	8	4	17	2	-	-

WRIGHT, Stephen Peter 'Steve'

Height: 6ft. Weight: 10st 11lb.

Born: 16 June 1959, Clacton.

■ Wright, the son of former U's winger Peter, joined the club from local junior club Woods Athletic in 1976 and spent a year as a non-contract player in the reserve and youth teams before landing a professional contract on his 18th birthday. He made his debut at Swindon in April 1978 and, although more naturally a central-defender, established himself at left-back the following campaign, playing in that position in the side that took on Manchester United in the fifth round of the FA Cup at Layer Road. Wright netted his first goal a year after his debut by scoring the equaliser in a 2–2 draw at Bury. During the summer of 1980 he contracted hepatitis and was out of action until December. Returning to the team with the turn of the year, he formed the central-defensive partnership with Steve Wignall, but they could not prevent the U's from being relegated to Division Four, just a year after they had been in the promotion race for much of the season. Wright left Layer Road for Finnish side HJK Helsinki when Allan Hunter succeeded Bobby Roberts as manager, and the following year he found himself playing in the European Cup against, among others, Liverpool. The Finns, with Wright at centre-half and ex-Us reserve 'keeper Jeff Wood in goal, pulled off a spectacular shock, winning the first leg 1–0, but succumbed at Anfield. Returning to the UK, Wright joined Wrexham, managed by former Colchester boss Bobby Roberts, in September 1983 and completed 76 games for the Welshmen. Wrexham won the Welsh Cup, and Wright was part of the team that defeated FC Porto and narrowly lost to AS Roma in the European Cup-Winners' Cup. Then followed a move to Torquay in the summer of 1985, where he played 33 times. His final professional move was to Crewe in July 1986, where in two seasons he turned out 67(+5) times and netted three goals. He then played non-League in the North West for Chorley and Rhyl before returning to Essex and, like many ex-U's players, did the rounds of the North Essex non-League circuit, playing for most of the senior clubs in the area and being involved in the management at Brightlingsea, Clacton and Harwich. He was still playing the odd game in an emergency and on one such occasion scored for Harwich in 2005–06. His son Jamie has followed him into the U's youth and reserve teams and Wright himself has been involved in the club's youth set up, managing the Under-17s before Joe Dunne's appointment and latterly as part of the scouting network.

	League		Lge Cup		FA Cup		Other	
	A	G	A	G	A	G	A	G
1977–78	1	0	0	0	0	0	-	-
1978–79	33+2	1	0	0	6+1	0	-	-
1979–80	23+3	1	3	0	3+1	0	-	-
1980–81	17	0	0	0	0	0	-	-
1981–82	38	0	5	0	5	0	-	-
TOTAL	112+5	2	8	0	14+2	0	-	-

Y

YATES, Mark Jason

Height: 5ft 11in. Weight: 11st 9lb.

Born: 24 January 1970, Birmingham.

■ Youth trainee Yates signed for Birmingham in the summer of 1988 after breaking into the first team a season earlier. Birmingham were on a downward spiral and suffered relegation to the Third Division. U's player-manager Ian Atkins used his contacts at his former club to bring the youngster in on loan, and Yates made a useful contribution to United's effort to get back to the League at the first attempt. By the time he returned to Birmingham they were on their way back up, and so his appearances at St Andrews were limited to 38(+16) in the League, with six goals scored, and an outing in the Wembley Leyland DAF Final in 1991. Moving to Burnley for £40,000 in August 1991, he made just 9(+9) appearances, with a solitary goal. He was loaned to Lincoln in February 1993 and made 10(+4) starts for the Imps. Unable to get into the Clarets side, he joined Doncaster in the summer of 1993, scoring four goals in 33(+1) League games. Slipping out of the League, he joined Kidderminster, playing 185(+2) Conference games and scoring 32 times, while picking up two caps for the England Semi-Professional side. Yates signed for neighbours Cheltenham for £25,000 as they reached the Football League under Steve Cotterill. At Whaddon Road he enjoyed the most consistent spell of his career, playing 190(+4) times and netting 19 times as the Robins remarkably climbed into the third tier, winning a Millennium Stadium Play-off final against Rushden & Diamonds. His former club Kidderminster also by now had made it to the League, and he returned for 14(+2) games in February 2004. The summer of 2004 saw Yates returning to Burnley, managed by Cotterill, as player-coach. Eighteen months later he was tempted into his first management job when he took over the reigns at Conference side Kidderminster. He steered his side to the 2007 FA Trophy Final, losing to Stevenage, in what was the first competitive game at the new Wembley.

	League		Lge Cup		FA Cup		Other	
	A	G	A	G	A	G	A	G
1990–91	22+3	6	1	0	3	0	0+1	0
TOTAL	22+3	6	1	0	3	0	0+1	0

YEATES, Mark Stephen Anthony

Height: 5ft 9in. Weight: 10st 7lb.

Born: 11 January 1985, Dublin.

■ A schoolboy on the books of Tottenham, Yeates signed professional in July 2002, having represented the Republic of Ireland at Youth and four times at Under-21 level. His first appearances, however, came during a loan spell at Brighton in November 2003, where he made 11 starts. He was rewarded with his Premiership debut in the final game of the 2003–04 season, when his pass set up Robbie Keane for Spurs' second in a 2–0 win over Wolves. Furthering his football education, Yeates spent August 2004 on loan at Swindon, playing 3(+1) games, as well as featuring in two further substitute appearances for Spurs. In the second week of the 2005–06 season Colchester manager Phil Parkinson brought Yeates to Layer Road on a season-long loan. Yeates featured prominently as United finished runners-up in League One and enjoyed an FA Cup run that culminated in a visit to Premiership champions Chelsea. Yeates

struck the post with the score at 0–0 in the live televised game, which United eventually lost 3–1. It was hoped that Parkinson would capture Yeates for the following campaign, which indeed he did, only the U's boss had walked out on the club to join Hull. The move proved disastrous for both as Hull struggled and Yeates played just 2(+3) times. A change of manager saw Yeates return to White Hart Lane to negotiate a further loan to Leicester. Joining the Foxes in January 2007, Yeates again was frustrated by lack of games. Scoring once, he registered just 5(+4) appearances at the Walkers Stadium. Colchester manager Geraint Williams broke the club transfer record when bringing Yeates back to Layer Road in July 2007 for a fee in the region of £150,000. The record did not last long as Clive Platt was signed later in the day for £300,000, but Yeates repaid the faith with some stunning goals direct from free-kicks, culminating in being selected for the Republic of Ireland B team that faced their Scottish counterparts at Airdrie in

November 2007. Yeates missed the latter part of the season with a dislocated shoulder.

	League		Lge Cup		FA Cup		Other	
	A	G	A	G	A	G	A	G
2005–06	42+2	5	1	0	5	1	1+1	0
2007–08	29	8	1	0	1	0	-	-
TOTAL	71+2	13	2	0	6	1	1+1	0

YOUNG, Scott

Height: 5ft 6in. Weight: 10st 5lb.

Born: 22 July 1969, Shoreham.

■ Young was a regular in United's youth and reserves sides but made the first team on just one occasion when

coming on as a substitute in a Sherpa Van Trophy tie at Aldershot in December 1986. He spent time on loan at Wycombe in 1987–88, before signing permanently for the Choirboys for a fee of £5,000. He made 12(+13) appearances, before departing in October 1988 for Bishop's Stortford. After a spell at Witham Town, he joined Wivenhoe in September 1991 and also had spells with Brightlingsea and Bury that season and joined Cornard and Halstead in 1992–93.

	League		Lge Cup		FA Cup		Other	
	A	G	A	G	A	G	A	G
1986–87	0	0	0	0	0	0	0+1	0
TOTAL	0	0	0	0	0	0	0+1	0

YOUNGMAN, Stuart Trevor

Height: 5ft 10in. Weight: 10st 7lb.

Born: 15 October 1965, Beccles.

■ Given a trial in a couple of late season youth-team games in 1983, Youngman was taken onto the second year of the U's youth scheme in August 1984. A year later Cyril Lea gave him a year's professional contract, and after a season disrupted by injury he got his only first-team outing when he appeared as a substitute at Aldershot in April 1985. He later played for Wroxham, Lowestoft and was captain of Gorleston in the Eastern Counties League as well as his home town team Beccles and was assistant manager at the latter before stepping down due to family commitments in January 2007.

	League		Lge Cup		FA Cup		Other	
	A	G	A	G	A	G	A	G
1984–85	0+1	0	0	0	0	0	0	0
TOTAL	0+1	0	0	0	0	0	0	0

YOUNGS, Donald 'Don'

■ With the U's forming a Reserve XI at Christmas 1937, they found themselves in need of an additional 'keeper, and Youngs, from RAF Martlesham and with Suffolk County honours, was brought to the club in mid-January. When Ronnie Dunn left the club at the end of February, Youngs got the nod over young professional Ted Platt, who would subsequently be transferred to Arsenal and would play the last of his century of League games nearly 20 years later. Youngs twice represented the RAF in March 1938 and continued to be an integral part of the U's squad throughout 1938–39, taking over as first choice from March 1939 when Light was injured. He was expected back for 1939–40 but in July 1939 came the news that he had been posted to Lincolnshire and would no longer be available.

	League		Lge Cup		FA Cup		Other	
	A	G	A	G	A	G	A	G
1937–38	3	0	1	0	-	-	3	0
1938–39	17	0	1	0	0	0	2	0
TOTAL	20	0	2	0	0	0	5	0

The Subs' Bench

Substitutes were introduced to English football in the summer of 1965, and Ray Price has the distinction of being the first U's sub to take the field when he replaced Ted Phillips at home to Rochdale on 18 September 1965.

By the end of 2007–08, 2,580 sub appearances had been made, with current club skipper Karl Duguid's 82 the largest single contribution. Conversely, there were 21 who had got as far as the team sheet and got to warm up on the touchline during the game but never got the boss's nod to join the action.

Local lad Dennis Barrett, an inside-forward, was the U's first ever apprentice professional when he was taken on in the summer of 1964, and from autumn 1965 he was the first member of the bench club. Plenty of bodies passed through, but it was not until the end of March 1982 that the second permanent member appeared in another apprentice Andy Gooding.

The introduction of the Associate Members' Cup in 1983 considerably increased the chances of the club's youth teamers to be involved with the senior side and over the years that competition has added five to the list – Robin Reid 1984–85, Scott Ridges 1992–93, Daryl Craft 1995–96, and Craig Hughes and Matt Paine both 2005–06.

Another innovation – the introduction of substitute goalkeepers in 1993 – provides the pair who topped the individual count by some way. Mark Cousins had clocked up 28 bench appearances at the end of 2006–07 and taken his tally to 30 before Dean Gerken's red card against Barnsley gave him his first-team break in the opening home League game of 2007–08. That means the record is jointly held by David Schultz, son of a former U's director, who sat on the bench 18 times in 1993–94, and Glenn Williamson, cruelly robbed of a chance to take up the professional contract offered to him at the end of his apprenticeship by a serious medical problem that ended his football career at 19. His 18 were spread over the three seasons of his scholarship 1999–2000 to 2001–02.

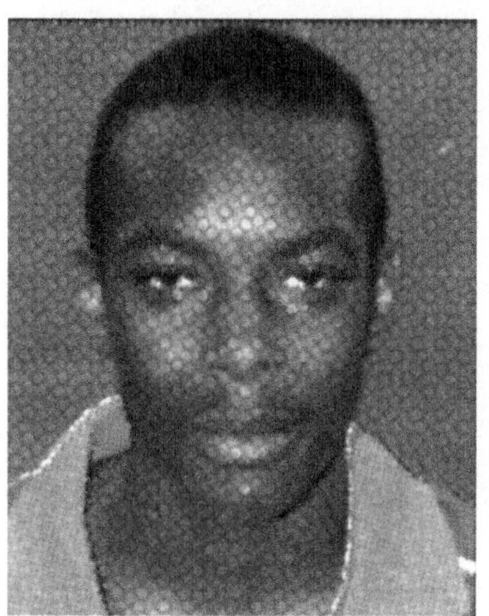

Tristian Toney

Daryl Craft

Craig Johnston

Patrice Tano

Sean Hillier

Ollie Blackwell

Andy Gooding

Dennis Barrett

Ben Cranfield

Glen Williamson

Anthony Allman

Matt Paine

Matt Hearn

Craig Hughes

Lawrie Wilson

Scott Ridges

David Schultz

Robin Reid

Ademole Bankole

James Hammond

All those mentioned so far are our own youth-team products, and another eight share that status. Central-defender Ollie Blackwell, with five in 2001–02, is the one of only two outfield players to have more than the two recorded by Matt Hearn, Sean Hillier, Craig Johnston and Triston Toney. Ben Cranfield's prolific goalscoring for the youth team earned him a call-up for Peterborough's visit in 2001–02, and 2007–08 youth-team skipper James Hammond completes the home-grown list, being called on to the bench for the final Championship game at Scunthorpe in May 2008 when Chris Coyne broke down in the pre-match warm up.

Two short-term trialists, Barry Scott, who spent a week on trial from manager George Burley's old club Ayr United in August 1994, and the Ivory Coast born French-based Patrice Tano, who stayed for the month of February 2002 and who next moved on to Falkirk, have since played in the Scottish League, but none of United's own protégés were taken on by other Football League clubs.

Two full-backs released by Charlton at the end of their apprenticeships were given one-year contracts at Layer Road. Lawrie Wilson was at Layer Road in 2006–07 and was sub for the unsuccessful League Cup tie at MK Dons, while seven times Anthony Allman got no further than the bench in the first half of 2001–02, which makes him unluckiest of the outfield players. Finally much-travelled Nigerian goalkeeper Ademole Bankole, on the coaching staff at Layer Road, stepped in as unused cover for appendicitis-suffering Mark Cousins for seven matches in March 2008.

DAVIS, Edwin 'Ted'

Born: January 1891, Bedminster.
Died: 6 March 1954, Bath.

June 1937 to September 1939

Davis, a goalkeeper, began his footballing career with Bristol City in 1911. He failed to make any first-team appearances and joined Southern League Brentford. In December 1912 he signed for Clapton and played four games, covering injuries, for the East London Division Two side. He played one game for Portsmouth's Southern Alliance team in 1913–14 before signing for Huddersfield in February 1914. He played 16 Second Division games before the onset of World War One and returned to Leeds Road at its conclusion. In the first season after the war, Town were runners-up in the League and reached the FA Cup Final. Davis contributed six League appearances. He established himself in Huddersfield's second season in the top flight, playing 27 times and played in seven FA Cup ties up to and including the fourth round, in which the Terriers went on to beat Preston 1–0 in the Final. Following Town's FA Cup success, he moved to Blackburn in the close season of 1922 after totalling 50 appearances at Huddersfield. Completing 24 games over two seasons, Davis returned to his roots in 1925 and signed for Third Division South Bristol City, playing in four League games. On leaving League football he joined Bath City, where he later became manager. It was from Bath that he became the first-ever manager of the newly-formed Colchester United on 21 June 1937. He set about assembling a side to compete in the Southern League on a limited budget. He steered United to the 1938–39 Southern League title and, but for World War Two, might well have got Colchester in to the Football League sooner than they actually did. Davis did not go back to Colchester after the war, returning to his Bath home.

FIELDUS MBE, Sydney 'Syd'

Height: 5ft 11in. Weight: 11st 5lb.

Born: 27 May 1909, Romford.
Died: April 1974, Chelmsford.

June 1945 to April 1946

Fieldus must be credited with ensuring that football took place in Colchester following the cessation of World War Two. He, along with secretary Claude Orrin, helped sway the minds of the divided U's Board of Directors into entering the abridged Southern League for 1945–46. Awarded the OBE for his services to the Home Guard during the war, Fieldus used his military contacts, in particular Major Dai Rees, to ensure that United could always field a side. Colchester often made up their XI from military personnel stationed in the town. Some happened to be experienced professionals while others might well have claimed to be on the books of one club or another just to get leave from the barracks on a Saturday afternoon. As a result, United used 81 players in just 31 games. With Fieldus needing to concentrate on his real job as a commercial traveller, he informed the Board that they should look for a new manager for the following season. This they did, appointing Ted Fenton, although Fieldus stayed on as his assistant and as secretary until 1949.

* *See also Who's Who Players section.*

FENTON, Edward Benjamin Ambrose 'Ted'

Born: 7 November 1914, Forest Gate.
Died: 12 July 1992, Glouestershire.

April 1946 to June 1948

Fenton was no stranger to Layer Road, having played several games for Colchester Town in 1930–31 while an amateur on the books of West Ham. He played extensively during the war years for West Ham, winning the Football League War Cup Final at Wembley in 1940 and representing England twice in wartime internationals. Appointed on 15 April 1946, he took over a club with a small budget but used his contacts in the game to bring in seasoned professionals, which culminated in a magnificent FA Cup run in 1947–48 that saw his Southern League side defeat League sides Wrexham, Bradford and Huddersfield before finally succumbing to the might of Stanley Matthews's Blackpool in the fifth round. That FA Cup run endeared the club to the nation and led to Colchester being elected to the League in 1950. Fenton, meanwhile, had moved on back to his beloved West Ham, first as assistant manager to Charlie Paynter before becoming manager at Upton Park in 1950. He returned the Hammers to the top flight in 1957–58 but quit in March 1961 to take over at Southend. Fenton was tragically killed in a car crash in 1992, but he will always be remembered as the inspired leader of United's FA Cup glories that ultimately led to League status.

* *See also Who's Who Players section.*

ALLEN, James Phillips 'Jimmy'

Height: 6ft 1in. Weight: 11st 12lb.

Born: 16 October 1909, Poole.
Died: February 1995, Portsmouth.

July 1948 to May 1953

Allen began his career with Poole Town in 1927, joining Portsmouth in February 1930. He played in the 1934 FA Cup Final defeat to Manchester City and totalled 132 League games for Pompey, scoring once. Having played for England against Northern Ireland and Wales in 1934, and also the Football League Representative side, he created what was thought to be a British transfer record when Aston Villa paid £10,775 for his services in the June of the same year. In fact it later became public that David Jack's transfer fee from Bolton to Arsenal in 1928 had been £11,500, not the lower figure reported at the time. Portsmouth actually used the proceeds to build their North Stand at Fratton Park. Although relegated in his second season at Villa Park, Allen's club won the Second Division title in 1937–38 and also reached the FA Cup semi-final, with himself as captain. Having scored twice in 146 League appearances Allen's League career was brought to an end by the onset of war. He officially retired in 1944 after turning out as a wartime guest for Fulham, Portsmouth and Birmingham. Taking up a position as Sports and Welfare Officer in a Birmingham company, Allen was offered the Colchester job, which he took on 22 June 1948. After a bedding-in season, Allen steered United to runners-up spot in the Southern League in 1949–50 behind Merthyr Tydfil, but it was Colchester that got the nod to join the Football League when it was expanded from 88 clubs to 92. After the initial furore, and crowds of over 10,000, interest in a struggling United side dwindled and when the club was forced to apply for re-election at the end of 1952–53, Allen was given a vote of no

confidence by the Supporters Club. He tended his resignation on 2 May 1953 and returned to Southsea, where he later ran a public house.

MEADES, Ron

1 June 1953 to 15 June 1953

While Secretary Claude Orrin and trainer Alf 'Dusty' Miller took over team responsibilities following the departure of Jimmy Allen in May 1953, the Colchester Board set about finding a successor. Les Henley (Reading), George Hepplewhite (Preston), Harry Medhurst (Chelsea) and Ron Meades (Cardiff) were all interviewed on I June 1953. Ten days later it was announced that Meades was the successful applicant. He claimed to have

been on the books of Cardiff and that at the time was managing West Country side Wadebridge Town. A local journalist contacted both Cardiff and Wadebridge for some background information on Meades for an article to be published. It soon transpired that Meades had no associations with either club, and his contract was hastily terminated just four days later on 15 June 1953.

BUTLER, John Dennis 'Jack'

Height: 5ft 11in. Weight: 11st 5lb.

Born: 14 August 1894, Colombo Ceylon.
Died: 5 January 1961, South East London.

16 June 1953 to 14 January 1955

Butler stepped into the Colchester manager's hot seat very much at the 11th hour, following the fiasco of the appointment of Ron Meades. Recommended by Arsenal secretary-manager Tom Whittaker, Butler himself had a distinguished career at Highbury. He began his football with the junior side Fulham Thursdays before joining Dartford in 1913, moving to Arsenal as a centre-forward in March 1914. With his career immediately curtailed by war, Butler rejoined the Gunners in 1919 but as a centre-back. He went on to play 267 League games, scoring seven goals, and played for England against Belgium at West Bromwich in December 1924. Butler is credited with being the first stopper/centre-half in English football. In a then novel experiment, Arsenal's innovative Charles Buchan persuaded manager Herbert Chapman to use Butler as a third centre-half so as to combat the new offside law introduced by FIFA in 1925–56. The plan worked like a dream. Butler also lined up against Cardiff in the 1927 FA Cup Final, which Arsenal lost, and remains the only time the famous old trophy was won by a non-English club. In May 1930 he joined Torquay in a £1,000 deal, playing 50 times for the Third Division South club. He retired in 1932 to become coach of Belgian club Daring for seven years before once again war interrupted football. Just before hostilities commenced Butler had been rewarded for his efforts at Daring by being appointed manager of the Belgium national side for the 1938 World Cup Finals. When football restarted he was

appointed manager of Torquay in June 1946, leaving a year later to take over the reins at Crystal Palace, where he remained until May 1949. Returning to Belgium, he once again became manager of Daring until 16 June 1953, when he was put in charge of Colchester. His first season was chaotic, and for the second season in succession United had to apply for re-election. Colchester were not even close to being voted out of the League, but alarm bells rang the following season when United won only three of their first 13 home games. As 1954 turned into 1955, Butler was given leave and sent on holiday at the club's expense. It emerged that he had had a nervous breakdown, and the club gave him indefinite leave until the end of the season. Butler, in fact, handed in his resignation on 14 January 1955.

FENTON, Benjamin Robert Vincent 'Benny'

Height: 5ft 8½in. Weight: 11st 3lb.

Born: 28 October 1918, West Ham.
Died: 29 July 2000, Dorset.

March 1955 to September 1963

Despite Colchester's recent poor League positions and inability to appoint a long term manager, there were 42 applicants for the post vacated by Jack Butler. Fenton, then with Charlton, was offered the post and for the second time followed in his older brother Ted's footsteps at Layer Road, now as player-manager where previously it had been as a player for Colchester Town. Picking up the pieces of Butler's squad, where trainer 'Dusty' Miller and Secretary Claude Orrin had been in charge of team selection between December and March, Fenton only managed 8 points from a possible 30, losing seven of the last eight games. For the third season running Colchester had to apply for re-election, but this time they had finished rock bottom of Division Three South. He slowly turned United around, with regular forays in to Scotland to recruit players, and in 1956–57 he steered United to their then highest-ever League finish when finishing third behind Ipswich and Torquay in Division Three South. United had led the table virtually all season until an Easter collapse saw them slip back and lose out to their Suffolk neighbours for the only available promotion spot. It would be nearly 50 years before the same opportunity would arise again. United were never able to regain that push again and after being founder members of Division Three in 1958. Fenton, retired from playing, picked a side that held Arsenal to a 2–2 draw at Layer Road in the FA Cup fourth round in January 1959. Season 1960–61 proved a disaster as Colchester were relegated to Division Four, but they bounced back a year later as runners-up to Millwall, scoring a club record 104 League goals. Fenton left United in September 1963 to take over at Leyton Orient but was sacked a little over

a year later with the O's demanding instant success. He stayed out of the game until the summer of 1966, when he became manager of Second Division Millwall. He went agonisingly close to getting the Lions into the top flight in 1971–72, being pipped by Birmingham, but resigned after a poor start to the 1974–75 season. He ended his footballing career in the administration department at Charlton.

* *See also Who's Who Players section.*

FRANKLIN, Cornelius 'Neil'

Height: 5ft 11in. Weight: 11st 4lb.

Born: 24 January 1922, Stoke.
Died: 9 February 1996, Stoke.

December 1963 to May 1968

Franklin arrived at Layer Road on 5 December 1963 following Benny Fenton's decision to join Orient. Franklin came with a distinguished, if not latterly tarnished, career. Joining Stoke as an amateur in 1936, he signed professionally three years later, but his career was put on hold by the war, although he did play a number of games for both Stoke and Gainsborough Trinity in wartime football. He also earned three caps for England in wartime internationals, and when football resumed he established himself as one of the finest centre-halves in English football history. He had an unbroken run of 27 full caps for his country after winning two caps at B level and representing the Football League on five occasions. After 142 League games for Stoke, he was tempted by the lure of big money to play in Colombia. On a fixed wage of £20 per week at Stoke, Franklin and his fellow mercenaries moved to Bogotá to play for Independiente Santa Fe on a salary of £3,500 per year and win bonuses of £35, funded by the cattle barons of Colombia in a League not recognised by FIFA. The fact that he had broken his contract angered the FA and he never played for England again. He was also banned on his return when goings on in Colombia turned sour within just four weeks. He missed out on playing at the 1950 World Cup, and it was not until February 1951 that he was allowed to play English football again,

joining Hull, who paid Stoke £22,500, which was a world record at the time for a defender. Hull were only a Second Division club, testament to the fact that the top-flight clubs would not touch him with a barge pole. After 95 games at Boothferry Park, he joined Crewe for £1,250 in February 1956, scoring four goals in 66 matches and ending his League career with a move for the same fee to Stockport in October 1957, completing 20 League starts. Joining non-League Macclesfield whetted his appetite to take up coaching. Shropshire side Wellington (later Telford United) were his first experience of training a side. Franklin retired from football in April 1962 but was tempted back by the chance to coach Cypriot side Apoel, which he did between February and November 1963. Applying for the vacant Colchester job, Franklin's first disappointment was the break up of Colchester's star striking partnership of Martyn King and Bobby Hunt. Eventually, Franklin earned success in guiding United back to Division Three in 1965–66 with a fourth place on the slimmest of goal averages. A good start to the following season was not maintained, and following relegation at the end of 1967–68 Franklin was sacked on 13 May 1968.

GRAHAM, Douglas Richard 'Dick'

Born: 6 May 1922, Corby.

June 1968 to September 1972

A goalkeeper by trade, Graham began his career at Corby and joined Northampton just before World War Two. During hostilities, he guested for Southport, Crewe and Crystal Palace while in the RAF, joining Leicester in 1944. It was with Crystal Palace, however, that he made his debut in a January 1946 FA Cup tie against Queen's Park Rangers. Going on to make 155 appearances in Division Three South, Graham was forced to retire in November 1950 due to a persistent back injury. He took over a Surrey pub and assisted the Surrey FA with coaching before becoming assistant trainer at West Brom in November 1956. Exactly four years later, he became assistant manager at Selhurst Park before taking over the managerial reins in November 1962. He took Palace to promotion to the Second Division in 1963–64 and the FA Cup quarter-final a year later, but unrest among fans led to the cancellation of his contract in January 1966. He assisted Charlton for the remainder of the season before being appointed manager of Leyton Orient in June 1966, lasting only until February 1968 when he resigned because of the clubs refusal to invest in new players. He was not out of a job long, taking over at Walsall in March 1968 but stepping down to assistant-manager in the summer when a full-time appointment was made. On 31 May 1968 Graham emerged from a short list of three to take charge of Colchester. He brought in lots of new players to Layer Road, after giving some of the existing squad just a couple of games to prove themselves. His greatest moment came in February 1971 when he masterminded Colchester's sensational 3–2 win over First Division top guns Leeds United in the FA Cup fifth round. Despite losing to Everton at Goodison Park in the quarter-finals 'Grandad's Army', as his team of 30-something journeyman professionals became known, had created world news. In August 1971 he also guided United to the Watney Cup, defeating West Brom on penalties at The Hawthorns after a thrilling 4–4 draw. He began to introduce youth to his side with the likes of Steve Foley, Steve Leslie and Micky Cook, but following a stormy shareholders meeting on 7 September 1972 he walked out on the club. A shareholder with only minimal shares won, incidentally in a raffle, had exercised his right to question the club. When the shareholder dared to question Graham's team selections and training methods it proved too much for the U's manager. He scouted briefly for Cambridge before becoming manager of non-League Wimbledon in September 1973, a position he held until March 1974 when he took a position outside of football as manager of a sports centre in Ipswich. Graham returned to Layer Road as guest of honour many times over the ensuing years when health allowed, and the club's bar was re-named The Dick Graham Lounge.

SMITH, James Michael 'Jim'

Height: 5ft 8in. Weight: 11st 11lb.

Born: 17 October 1940, Sheffield.

October 1972 to June 1975

Smith had played all of his football in Division Four after being discarded by Sheffield United in July 1961. He numbered Aldershot, Halifax and Lincoln among his clubs, leaving the latter in the summer of 1968 to become player-manager of Northern Premier League Boston United. Following Dick Graham's shock departure in September 1972, Smith was approached to become United's new manager, a position he took up on 25 October 1972. He could not prevent Colchester having to seek re-election at the end of that campaign but rebuilt the side and won promotion to

Division Three in his first full season. League Cup giant-killings of First Division Carlisle and Second Division Southampton brought Smith's efforts to the attentions of bigger clubs, and after just two successful seasons at Layer Road he was appointed manager of Blackburn in June 1975. He was unable to give Blackburn the First Division football the club desired and moved on to Birmingham in March 1978, suffering relegation and instant promotion. Sacked after lack of top-flight success, he finally got some silverware at Oxford when his side won the Third Division Championship in 1983–84 and the Second Division title a year later. Enticed to Queen's Park Rangers, Smith saw his new club lose to his old club Oxford in the League Cup Final at Wembley, but his Rangers side could finish no higher than fifth in the top division. He had subsequent managerial stints at Newcastle, Portsmouth, Derby and Oxford, where he remained in charge as his team tried to regain their place in the Football League after failing in the Conference Play-offs in 2006–07.

* *See also Who's Who Players section.*

ROBERTS, Robert 'Bobby'

Height: 5ft 9in. Weight: 11st 4lb.

Born: 2 September 1940, Leicester.

June 1975 to May 1982

When Jim Smith joined Blackburn in the summer of 1975 Roberts became the ideal choice to take over at Layer Road and he was handed the role on 20 June 1975. Recruited by Smith himself, Roberts knew exactly what made the team tick, having been assistant manager-coach in Colchester's 1973–74 promotion season and in their giant-killing surge to the League Cup quarter-finals just a season later. He took time to adjust to the role, especially when Smith came back to Layer Road to sign star striker Bobby Svarc. Unfortunately relegated in his first season, Roberts bounced back a year later, earning promotion from the Fourth Division. He made shrewd signings in Colin Garwood, Bobby Gough and Steve Wignall and also brought in a handsome profit when selling Trevor Lee to Gillingham for £90,000. Desperately close to achieving the club's goal of reaching the second tier of English football when finishing just six points short in 1979–80, Roberts's side suffered the ignominy of relegation a year later. Despite employing a free-scoring side, United were unable to bounce back and Roberts was invited by the Colchester board to resign. He refused and was sacked acrimoniously on 3 May 1982. Roberts took up managerial roles at Wrexham and Grimsby, later returning to his original vocation of being number two at Leicester and Oxford. He also had a spell coaching in Kuwait as well as scouting duties at Newcastle and Derby.

* *See also Who's Who Players section.*

HUNTER, Allan

Height: 6ft 0in. Weight: 12st 8lb.

Born: 30 June 1946, Sion Mills, N. Ireland.

May 1982 to January 1983

Hunter had enjoyed a distinguished career, partnering Kevin Beattie at the heart of the successful Ipswich side of the 1970s. Winning the FA Cup in 1978, Hunter also won the UEFA Cup a year later. He had represented Northern Ireland in 53 full internationals and in all turned out in 466 League games for Oldham, Blackburn, Ipswich and Colchester, scoring 10 goals. Appointed player-manager following the departure of Bobby Roberts, Hunter took charge for the final-day fixture at Crewe on 15 May 1982 that resulted in a 3–1 success. It became clear that Hunter enjoyed purely being a tracksuit manager. Matters came to a head when striker John Lyons took his own life in November 1982, and Hunter tendered his resignation in January 1983. He returned to the club in a coaching capacity when Mike Walker took charge in 1986.

* *See also Who's Who Players section.*

LEA, Cyril

Height: 5ft 9in. Weight: 11st 2lb.

Born: 5 August 1934, Wrexham.

January 1983 to April 1986

Lea joined Orient from Welsh amateurs Bradley Rangers in May 1957. An ever present in 1961–62, Lea helped the O's into the First Division. Completing 205 appearances, Lea was transferred to Ipswich in November 1964 for £20,000. At Portman Road he played 103(+4) League games, netting twice, and was briefly caretaker manager in 1968 prior to the appointment of Bobby Robson, before retiring from playing in May 1969. Capped twice by Wales in 1964–65 against Northern Ireland and Italy, he joined the Ipswich coaching staff and was coach to the Welsh national side. He left Portman Road in August 1979 to become assistant manager to Alan Durban at Stoke, before joining Hull as joint manager with Mike Smith in 1980. Arriving at Colchester, initially as assistant to Allan Hunter, Lea took over as caretaker manager until the end of the 1982–83 season. Rumours flew around that United wanted Arsenal's John Hollins as manager but were waiting for the player to finalise his own personal dream of playing in the FA Cup Final. Lea's record was so impressive in the remainder of the season when United narrowly missed out on promotion that he was offered the job full-time in the summer of 1983. He introduced former Manchester United player Stewart Houston as his number two. After missing out on promotion in three successive seasons finishing sixth, seventh and eighth and on the verge of finishing sixth, both Lea and Houston were sacked on 10 April 1986 by Colchester's new owner Jonathan Crisp, with three weeks of the 1985–86 season remaining. Working on a miniscule budget with a fine array of talent including

Tony Adcock and Perry Groves, Lea could consider himself unlucky that Crisp's money had not been forthcoming in each of the previous campaigns when a transfer boost around Easter time might well have turned those near-misses into promotion. Lea became responsible for youth development at Leicester between May 1987 and May 1989 and then youth coach at West Brom in July 1989. He later worked in the youth set-up at Rushden & Diamonds, managed by former Town colleague Brian Talbot. He had a second spell at Rushden assisting Barry Hunter before leaving in February 2006.

WALKER, Michael Stewart Gordon 'Mike'

Height: 6ft 1in. Weight: 13st. 2lb.

Born: 26 November 1945, Colwyn Bay.

April 1986 to November 1987

After a distinguished career as a goalkeeper for Reading, Shrewsbury, York, Watford, Charlton and Colchester, Walker cut his teeth in management as manager of United's Eastern Counties League reserve side in 1985–86, while doubling up as assistant to Cyril Lea. Having made 451 League appearances for Colchester's goalkeeper, he knew the club inside out, having been at Layer Road since the summer of 1973. When Lea was sacked in April 1986, Walker took over the reins in a caretaker capacity for United's remaining nine games of the season, in which United remained unbeaten, rejoining the race for promotion and narrowly missing out by just nine points. Appointed full-time U's boss for 1986–87, he steered United to fifth place in Division Four before losing a two-legged Play-off semi-final to a resurgent Wolves. Despite the then chairman Jonathan Crisp introducing a total ban on away fans at all home League games, and paltry attendances, Walker had Colchester nearing the top of the Fourth Division table the following campaign when Crisp incredibly sacked the U's boss on 1 November 1987 over an alleged personal matter. Walker was named Manager of the Month for October 1987 after his sacking. He was soon picked up by Norwich, where he became reserve-team coach and when Dave Stringer was sacked by the Canaries

Walker was promoted to first-team manager in June 1992. Norwich were early pacesetters in the Premier League, eventually finishing third and earning a UEFA Cup place. It was in Europe that he steered Norwich to their greatest triumph, a UEFA Cup win over Bayern Munich in Germany, but in January 1994 he resigned as Norwich boss to sign a three-and-a-half-year contract with Everton, who only escaped relegation by beating Wimbledon on the final day of the 1993–94 season. After a poor start to the 1994–95 campaign, he was sacked by the Toffees in the November. In June 1996 he was appointed Norwich boss again, following the departure of Chairman Robert Chase and manager Gary Megson, two and a half years after quitting Carrow Road. His second spell ended by mutual consent in April 1998, with the club safe from relegation in 16th place in Division One but in poor form. Following the resignation of Colchester boss Steve Wignall in January 1999, Walker became U's fans' favourite to re-take the Layer Road hot seat. Nothing transpired, however, and it was Cyprus where Walker took up his next appointment. In November 2000 he became coach of Apoel Nicosia, but lasted until just two games into the 2001–02 season. His son Ian, after playing youth football in the Colchester area, became a full England international and carved out a top-flight career, most notably at Tottenham.

* *See also Who's Who Players section.*

BROWN, Roger William

Height: 6ft 1in. Weight: 11st 10lb.

Born: 12 December 1952, Tamworth.

November 1987 to October 1988

Brown began his career as an apprentice with Walsall in 1970 but failed to earn a professional contract. He joined non-League Paget Rangers in 1973 and was with AP Leamington a year later, staying with them as they became founder members of the Alliance Premier League (now the Conference). Signed by Bournemouth in February 1978 for £5,000, Brown scored three goals in 63 League appearances. His performances persuaded Norwich to pay out £85,000 in the summer of 1979, but after just 16 games he moved to Fulham the following March for £100,000. Injured on his first game, against Chelsea, Brown missed the rest of the season as Fulham were relegated. He played in every game during the next campaign as the Cottagers bounced back to the Second Division. Indeed, Brown created a club record by scoring 12 goals from defence. Despite making 141 League appearances at Craven Cottage and scoring 18 goals, Brown fell out with manager Malcolm MacDonald and returned to the south coast with Bournemouth in December 1983 for £35,000. Finishing his professional career with 83(+1) games at Dean Court, Brown netted 5 times. He then had spells as player-coach of Weymouth and as player-manager of Poole Town. Appointed Colchester manager by Jonathan Crisp on 4 November 1987, Brown was cited as having managerial experience from his day job in an engineering environment. The *Colchester Evening Gazette* headlined his arrival with 'Roger Who?' Still riding on a crest of a wave from the team that Mike Walker built, Brown won Manager

of the Month for December but then won just five of the remaining fixtures. Brown was sacked on 16 October 1988 following a club-record 8–0 defeat at Leyton Orient. The day before he had told the local press 'sooner or later one of our opponents is going to get a hiding. Let's hope its Orient tomorrow'. Brown became an insurance salesman and later worked for the East Anglian Probation Service.

WALLACE, John Martin Bokas 'Jock'

Height: 5ft 11in. Weight: 12st 5lb.

Born: 6 September 1935, Wallyford.
Died: 24 July 1996, Spain.

January 1989 to December 1989

Wallace followed in his fathers footsteps by becoming a goalkeeper. While Jock senior had played for Raith Rovers, Blackpool and Derby, Jock junior began his own career as an amateur with Blackpool. Released, he joined Workington in September 1952, playing eight games. Completing his National Service, Wallace joined Berwick Rangers in 1955 as the club nearest his army base, moving to Airdrieonians a year later. In October 1959 he returned to the English game, joining West Brom for £10,000, where he featured 89 times, before joining non-League Bedford in the summer of 1962. Wallace set a record when he played in the 1966–67 English, Scottish and Welsh Cups in the same season while turning out for non-League Hereford and Berwick, where he had become player-manager. His rise to prominence came when minnows Berwick beat Glasgow Rangers in the Scottish Cup of 1967. A year later, he joined Hearts in a coaching capacity, a similar position to that he took at Ibrox in 1970. His partnership with Willie Waddell helped Rangers to the European Cup-Winners' Cup in 1972. When Waddell stepped down as manager it was Wallace who was the ideal choice to step into his shoes. He won the Scottish Cup in his first season and in 1974–75 broke Celtic's nine-year dominance in the Scottish game. Rangers won the Scottish treble in 1975–76 and 1977–78. He sensationally resigned in 1978 over transfer budgets and took over at Leicester. He took City back to the top flight and to an FA Cup semi-final with

Gary Lineker as his main striker. In 1982 he returned north of the border to Motherwell but within a year was back at his spiritual home of Ibrox, winning the Scottish League Cup twice. Dundee United and Aberdeen were the new kids on the block, and Rangers could not break through their title challenge. Wallace was sacked by Rangers in 1986 and took over at Spanish side Sevilla for 1986–87. Remaining in Spain, Wallace was enticed out of his retirement to take over at Layer Road on 10 January 1989. His arrival doubled gates to 4,000 in a team that had not won in the League since early October 1988 and were rock bottom of Division Four with just three wins all season. Under Wallace, United won nine and drew eight of their remaining matches, crucially beating main rivals Darlington at Feethams in April 1989. The addition of England World Cup hero Alan Ball as his assistant was another major coup for United, but when Ball left in October 1989, and with Wallace's health deteriorating fast (unknown to all but those inside the club), United plunged once again into a battle against relegation to the Conference, which they would ultimately lose. Wallace was moved upstairs to become a director on 20 December 1989, with Steve Foley again taking caretaker charge. Wallace returned to Spain, suffering a vicious mugging, before passing away from motor neurone disease in 1996.

MILLS MBE, Michael Denis 'Mick'

Height: 5ft 8in. Weight: 11st 10lb.

Born: 4 January 1949, Godalming.

January 1990 to May 1990

Mills began his career as a Portsmouth apprentice but joined Ipswich when Pompey abandoned their youth policy in 1966. He made his first senior start as a 17-year-old, becoming the first player in the club's history to make 100 appearances before reaching the age of 21. He was made captain in 1970, earning his first England call-up three years later. He captained his country for the first time against Wales in 1978. In all, he earned 42 full caps, playing in the 1980 European Championships and the 1982 World Cup, to add to five Under-23 outings and Youth and Football League honours. At Portman Road he was ever present for four seasons in the mid-1970s and led Town to the FA Cup in 1978 when future Colchester star Roger Osborne scored the winner against Arsenal. The following season he lifted the UEFA Cup when Ipswich defeated AZ Alkmaar over two legs. In all, Mills played 741 first-team games for Town, leaving to join Southampton in November 1982 for £50,000. Earning an MBE for services to football, he added a further 121 games to his incredible career total before moving to Stoke as player-manager in the summer of 1985. Ironically, after a series of dismal seasons in the Potteries, he was sacked and effectively swapped places with Colchester's outgoing assistant manager Alan Ball who had taken over at the Victoria Ground. Mills was appointed manager at Layer Road on 3 January 1990. The U's were already on the slide, suffering from the loss of Ball and the publicly unknown serious illness affecting previous manager Jock Wallace.

Mills brought in ex-Wolves coach Sammy Chung as his assistant but could not prevent the slide into the Conference. Quitting Layer Road on 9 May 1990, he spent time as chief scout at Sheffield Wednesday and then coached Birmingham, where he stood in as caretaker manager for one fixture. He helped set up Galaxy Sports Management, where he remains a technical director.

ATKINS, Ian Leslie

Height: 5ft 6in. Weight: 10st 1lb.

Born: 16 January 1957, Birmingham.

June 1990 to June 1991

Atkins began his career as an apprentice with Shrewsbury in 1975 and amassed a total of 534 League appearances with the Shrews, Sunderland, Everton, Ipswich, Birmingham, Cambridge and Doncaster. He took charge of Colchester in the summer of 1991 as the club embarked on their first season in the Conference. Remaining full-time, Colchester soon rekindled their self-belief after a disastrous season under the seriously ill Jock Wallace and his predecessor Mick Mills. Colchester had lost their hard-won League status after just 39 years. Atkins's remit was to get United back in the League at the first attempt. Remaining as a player himself, Atkins marshalled the defence and was the regular penalty taker. He brought in old pal, and former U's hero, Roy McDonough to lead his attack, but with a penchant for defensive safety United lost out to Barry Fry's Barnet after letting a number of narrow leads slip into draws. Atkins refused to accept the runners'-up trophy and left after just a year for a coaching job at Birmingham. He subsequently managed Cambridge, Northampton, Chester, Carlisle, Oxford, Bristol Rovers and Torquay.

* See also Who's Who Players section.

McDONOUGH, Roy

Height: 6ft 1in. Weight: 11st 11lb.

Born: 16 October 1958, Solihull.

July 1991 to May 1994

Having assisted Ian Atkins in Colchester's inaugural season in the

Conference, Roy McDonough was the surprise choice to take over the hot seat as United desperately sought to fight their way back into the League. McDonough had enjoyed a colourful career since starting as a Birmingham apprentice, picking up no fewer than 13 red cards. Soon after making his debut for Blues, he opted to join Walsall, winning promotion honours in his second season. Frustrated with the deal he was offered, McDonough joined Chelsea, but the move did not work out, and it was from Stamford Bridge that he joined Colchester for £15,000. Finding his goal touch, McDonough had spells with Southend, Exeter, Cambridge and a return to Southend before being contacted by Atkins to boost United's Conference strike force. Unlike Atkins's defensive tactics, McDonough adopted a gung-ho approach and spearheaded a forward line with Steve McGavin and Gary Bennett that just could not stop scoring. McDonough, aged just 34, steered Colchester to the 1992 Conference title and, as icing on the cake, the FA Trophy in Colchester's first-ever trip to Wembley stadium. Backed by a paltry budget, McDonough was unable to make any in-roads into the Division Three promotion race and was relieved of his duties on 15 May 1994 following the last game of the 1993-94 season, which incidentally was his 500th League appearance. McDonough had spells as manager at Heybridge and Chelmsford before moving to Spain to coach in Charlton's European Academy.

* See also Who's Who Players section.

BURLEY, George Elder

Height: 5ft 10in. Weight: 11st.

Born: 3 June 1956, Cumnock.

June 1994 to December 1994

Scottish international Burley, who played at every level for his country, earning 11 full caps, began his football career as an Ipswich apprentice. At a time when Ipswich were threatening the dominant forces in English football, he picked up an FA Cup-winners' medal in 1978 and a UEFA Cup-winners' medal a year later. Burley also played for Sunderland and Gillingham, amassing 494 Football League appearances. He returned to his native Scotland, turning out for Motherwell, Ayr and Falkirk. He began to learn the managerial trade while retaining a playing contract at Ayr. He took over at Colchester in the summer of 1994 and struggled at first as the players he had at his disposal were thumped in a series of friendlies against local non-League opposition. He gradually formulated a winning team and by Christmas Eve had United sitting handily in fifth place, ready for an assault on promotion from Division Three. Unfortunately for Colchester, his emerging talents had not gone unnoticed

by his former club Ipswich, and in an illegal approach they enticed Burley to quit Layer Road on 24 December 1994 and take up the manager's position at Portman Road. Despite leading Town to the Premiership, a series of annual Play-off defeats, relegation and a dip in form spelt the end for him at Ipswich. He subsequently managed Derby, Hearts and Southampton and was never far from controversy when dealing with his own boards of directors. Burley was appointed Scotland manager in January 2008.

* *See also Who's Who Players section.*

WIGNALL, Steven Leslie 'Steve'

Height: 5ft 11in. Weight: 11st 12lb.

Born: 17 September 1954, Liverpool.

January 1995 to January 1999

Following the acrimonious departure of George Burley after just six months in charge, the Colchester Board were once again on the look out for an up-and-coming manager. On 12 January 1995 they turned to former Colchester defensive stalwart Steve Wignall, who had performed miracles with the re-born Aldershot in their rise through the non-League pyramid from the depths of the Isthmian League. Wignall had played in 281 League games for United and also counted Doncaster, Brentford and the previous version of Aldershot as his clubs, in which he made a total of 639 League appearances. In his first full season he led United to the Third Division Play-off semi-finals, where they narrowly lost to cash-rich club Plymouth. Undeterred, Wignall earned Colchester fans a second-ever Wembley outing a year later in April 1997 when his side lost to Carlisle on penalties after a 0–0 stalemate in the Auto Windscreens Shield Final. United finally climbed out of the basement division 12 months later, again at Wembley, when David Gregory's penalty beat Torquay in the Division Three Play-off Final. Probably the most successful manager in Colchester's history, Wignall stepped down on 21 January 1999, citing that he had taken the club as far as he could with the players available and needed to spend money to press on. He had subsequent managerial spells with Stevenage, Doncaster and Southend and assisted at Ryman League Wivenhoe.

* *See also Who's Who Players section.*

WADSWORTH, Michael 'Mick'

Born: 3 November 1950, Barnsley.

January 1999 to August 1999

Wadsworth began his footballing career with non-League Gainsborough Trinity and was signed by Scunthorpe in the summer of 1976. He played just 19(+9) games at The Old Show Ground, scoring three times in the League. Released at the end of the campaign, he joined Frickley Athletic, playing 76 games in the Alliance Premier League (the forerunner of the Conference), scoring 21 goals, including being the clubs top scorer in 1980-81 as player-coach. He became FA Regional coach for the North West area before his appointment as a technical co-ordinator with the FA's Excellence Programme. Wadsworth was also involved for two years as coach of the England non-League side before taking similar roles with the Youth and Under-21 squads. During his time with the England set-ups he was also an official match observer for both Bobby Robson and Graham Taylor, with the former utilising his coaching skills during the World Cup Italia '90 campaign. After the tournament Robson stepped down as England boss and took over at PSV Eindhoven. Wadsworth had been invited over to join him as coach but was not allowed to take up the offer because he was not qualified to coach in the Netherlands. His first managerial job came in August 1993 when he took over at Carlisle United, a position he held for

three years, leading the club to the Third Division title in 1995 and to Wembley for the Auto Windscreens Shield Final, where they lost to Birmingham. His achievements that season were rewarded with the Manager of the Year award for Division Three. He left Brunton Park, following their relegation after only one season in Division Two, taking up a position as assistant to the inexperienced Gary Megson at Norwich in January 1996 and then spent two and a half years as manager of Scarborough. Wadsworth left the Seadogs to join Colchester on 28 January 1999, with the North Yorkshire side dropping out of the League less than four months later, thanks in no small part to goalkeeper Jimmy Glass who ran the length of the field to score deep in injury time for Wadsworth's old club Carlisle to maintain their own League status. Wadsworth, breaking the chain of previous U's managers either being a former player or having connections with Ipswich, kept on Steve Whitton as his assistant, and the introduction of key players Warren Aspinall and Stephane Pounewatchy, both ex-Carlisle, helped United avoid the drop back to the basement. A summer of controversy followed, when Wadsworth released nine players, including stalwart Joe Dunne, and brought in a host of foreign mercenaries and has-been British professionals, allegedly all via the same player's agent, while spending a brief period coaching the St Kitts and Nevis international squad. Just three League games into the season, and following a League Cup defeat at Crystal Palace, Wadsworth resigned on 25 August 1999, citing that he found the travelling from his Yorkshire base too much. Within days he had joined Palace, a club much further south than Colchester, as assistant to Steve Coppell. Wadsworth's reign left a sour taste in the boardroom at Colchester, which resulted in the instigation of a club policy of never dealing with players' agents. He was not at Selhurst Park very long before Bobby Robson returned to English shores to take up the job at Newcastle and Wadsworth was invited over to St James' Park, an offer he could not refuse. He remained at Newcastle until the summer of 2001 and was in part responsible for recommending the talents of Colchester's £2.25 million starlet Lomana Lua Lua to The Toon, before making another move, this time to Southampton, as Stuart Gray's number two, but after only three months in the job the entire management team was dismissed, leaving Wadsworth to find yet another club. It did not take him long, and in November 2001 he replaced Andy Ritchie as manager of Oldham after his shock dismissal. His time at Boundary Park seemed to go well, with the club challenging for a place in the Play-offs. He had appointed Iain Dowie as his assistant, and ironically it was Dowie that replaced him when he was also given the boot, despite losing only nine of his 35 games while in charge. Next, he took charge of Huddersfield in the summer of 2002, and although sacked in January 2003 he remained as manager until the March while his pay-off was arranged. In November 2003 he was appointed coach of the Democratic Republic of Congo national side who included Lua Lua in their ranks. DR Congo failed miserably at the African Nations Cup in January 2004, losing all their games, and Wadsworth was sacked again. In June 2004 he was appointed manager of Portuguese side Beira Mar but resigned in the September, complaining of Boardroom interference. He then joined Shrewsbury as assistant manager in January 2005 before leaving a little over a year later. Appointed

Director of Club Development, Wadsworth at last tasted success as his new club Gretna was promoted to the Scottish Premier League at the end of 2006–07. Wadsworth was appointed assistant manager in the summer of 2007 as Gretna struggled to come to terms with life in the top flight of Scottish football. He then became caretaker manager in February 2008 to the end of the season.

WHITTON, Stephen Paul 'Steve'

Height: 6ft 1in. Weight: 13st 6lb.

Born: 4 December 1960, East Ham.

August 1999 to January 2003

After being U's player-coach and then assistant manager to both Steve Wignall and Mick Wadsworth, it was decided that Whitton would succeed Wadsworth as manager when the position became vacant on 25 August 1999. Whitton had also been caretaker manager along with Micky Cook for one game at Stoke in January 1999. His football had begun as a Coventry apprentice, and in a 16-year career Whitton played in 452 League games, scoring 98 goals. In addition to the Sky Blues, he numbered West Ham, Birmingham, Sheffield Wednesday, Ipswich and of course Colchester as his League clubs. His club-to-club transfers amounted to almost £700,000. Brought to Layer Road by Roy McDonough in March 1994, Whitton played at Wembley in 1997–98 as United lost to Carlisle in the Auto Windscreens Shield Final. Despite victory in his first game in charge, Whitton's team failed to win the next 11 games and found themselves rock bottom of the Second Division. United eventually pulled away to finish 18th. In his first full season Colchester finished one place better in 17th but were limited by a miniscule playing budget ,despite the sale of Lomana Lua Lua to Newcastle for a then club-record £2.25 million. Publicly stating that his goal was to finish one place better than the previous season, harking to the budgetary restraints, Whitton left by mutual consent after a seven-game winless streak on 29 January 2003.

* *See also Who's Who Players section.*

PARKINSON, Philip John 'Phil'

Height: 6ft. Weight: 12st 9lb.

Born: 1 December 1967, Chorley.

February 2003 to June 2006

Parkinson left his home town of Chorley to embark on an apprenticeship with Southampton. Unable to break into the first team, he returned to the North West in the summer of 1988, joining Bury for a fee of £13,000. In four seasons at Gigg Lane he completed 133(+12) League games, scoring five times, but when Bury were relegated he joined Reading for a fee of £35,000 in July 1992. Parkinson quickly became a firm favourite with the Elm Park faithful with his combative midfield style and was rewarded with a Division Two Championship medal in 1993–94 as club captain. He also managed one of the Reading Academy sides and continued his studies with The Open University, achieving a BSc in Sociology. Parkinson gained his UEFA A coaching badge in 2000–01 while still on the books at Reading, now at their new Madejski Stadium. Completing 322(+30) League games, Parkinson netted 20 times for the Royals. He was a surprise, even unheard of, choice to take over from Steve Whitton, but his attributes were clear to see. He took Colchester from being a backwater, behind-the-times club to one with a bold new professional outlook. He, along with his staff, introduced new training methods, improved fitness, introduced diet regimes and was able to entice young Premiership hopefuls to put themselves in the shop window with

extended loan deals. He reinstated Colchester's historical Cup fighting spirit, earning big ties against Sheffield United, Blackburn, Southampton and Chelsea in what, in hindsight, was preparation for United's next momentous move. Colchester finished runners-up in League One in 2005–06 and for the first time in their history reached the Football League Championship. What should have seen Parkinson lead United into the their highest level of football, and with a new stadium on the horizon, turned sour in the summer of 2006 when Parkinson failed to get the level of transfer funding he desired. He accepted what was allegedly an illegal approach from Hull and moved to the Yorkshire club after resigning on 14 June 2006. Colchester Chairman Peter Heard fought tooth and nail, winning compensation from the Tigers. Parkinson never lived up to the expectations of fans at The KC Stadium as City struggled at the foot of the table. The curtain fell on his Hull career, ironically at Layer Road, in November 2006 when four-goal Chris Iwelumo spurred Colchester to a 5–1 thumping of Parkinson's side. Parkinson teamed up with Alan Pardew at Charlton in the latter part of the 2006–07 season as the Addicks were relegated to the Championship. He remained on the backroom staff in 2007–08 alongside another former Colchester favourite Mark Kinsella but continued to be linked with a number of high-profile managerial jobs that came to light.

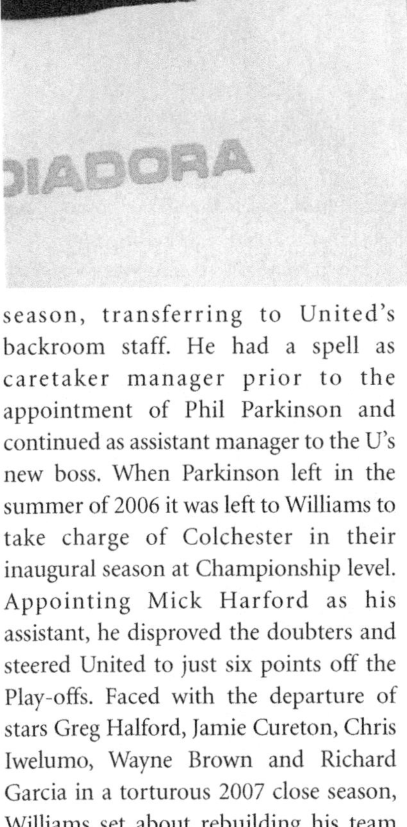

WILLIAMS, David Geraint

Height: 5ft 8in. Weight: 13st.

Born: 5 January 1962, Treorchy.

June 2006 to publication date

A 13-cap Welsh international, Williams had enjoyed a long League career after starting as a Bristol Rovers apprentice in 1980. Spanning 18 years, Williams also played for Derby, Ipswich and Colchester. Completing 674 League games, he scored 20 goals and was capped twice at Welsh Under-21 level and earned 13 full caps. Williams's only season at Layer Road saw him play 38(+1) games during the 1998–99 season. He hung up his boots in the close season, transferring to United's backroom staff. He had a spell as caretaker manager prior to the appointment of Phil Parkinson and continued as assistant manager to the U's new boss. When Parkinson left in the summer of 2006 it was left to Williams to take charge of Colchester in their inaugural season at Championship level. Appointing Mick Harford as his assistant, he disproved the doubters and steered United to just six points off the Play-offs. Faced with the departure of stars Greg Halford, Jamie Cureton, Chris Iwelumo, Wayne Brown and Richard Garcia in a torturous 2007 close season, Williams set about rebuilding his team with the goal of staying in the Championship, in readiness for the opening of Colchester's new community stadium in August 2008, with Micky Adams as his assistant.

* *See also Who's Who Players section.*

Caretaker Managers

1954–55	'Dusty' Miller/Claude Orrin
1972–73	Denis Mochan
1987–88	Steve Foley
1988–89	Steve Foley
1989–90	Steve Foley
1994–95	Dale Roberts
1998–99	Steve Whitton/Micky Cook
2003–04	Geraint Williams

The Chairmen

Maurice Pye,
Summer 1937 to August 1939.

Walter Clark,
August 1939 to World War Two.

William 'Bill' Allen,
Summer 1945 to January 1967.

Harold Moore,
January 1967 to January 1968.

Arthur Neville,
January 1968 to summer 1969.

Bill Graver,
Summer 1969 to March 1971.

Roy Chapman,
March 1971 to summer 1973.

Robert Jackson,
Summer 1973 to November 1974.

Jack Rippingale,
November 1974 to summer 1981.

Maurice Cadman, Summer 1981 to May 1985.

Jonathan Crisp, May 1985 to summer 1991.

Robert Bowdidge, Summer 1991 to summer 1992.

Gordon Parker, Summer 1992 to summer 1998.

Peter Heard, Summer 1998 to summer 2006.

Robbie Cowling, Summer 2006 to publication date.

Roll of Honour

Maisie Adams – 26.12.1996
Graham Duthie
Michael Duthie
Paul Watsham
Phyllis Aitken (nee Brock)
Kevin Cain
Raymond Castle
Peter Chisnall
Gary Bird
Barbara Wortham
Gary Bloor
Peter Osborne
David Jenkinson
Duncan Wyatt
Jane Butler
Richard Fisher
Robin Fisher
Terry Lawrence
Derek Salmon
Bob Miller
Michael Middleton
Terry Poulter
Maurice P. Turner
Russell P. A. Turner
Gerald Robinson
Tim Perry
Stuart Jon Oxford
Mark Dobson
Mark Joyce
Terance Horsfall
Ronald Kirkham
Rosemary Moles
David Grubb
John Elliott
Judith Musgrove
Jonathon Johnson
Bob Semple
Phil Gladwin
Marius Nieuwenhuis
Steve Peacock
Jerry Everett
Kerstin Fletcher
David Amoss
James Nason
Wayne Reece
Andy Diaper
Brian Francis
Gordon Howard Ambridge
Graham G. H. Ambridge
Bryan Gordon Ambridge
Derek James
Ron Flicka Aitken
Craig Aitken
Rob Aitken
Edward and Steve Storey
Aron Storey
Graham Storey
George Peter Chris Ball
Chris Rout (Club Shop 27yrs)
Christian Abbott
Des Abbott
Matthew Abbott
Michael Allen
George Allen
Danny Boreham
David Chadwick
Steve Chamberlain
Peter Clarke
Mark Cutting
Peter Bower
Michael Barrenger
Terry Langohr
Chris Carr
Martin Bloomfield

Tony Adcock.

Ray Chisnall
The Everitts
Julyon Everitt
Julian Lamb
Colin Frost
Chris Fincham
Matthew Everson
Julian Ewers
Colin Hutson
Wayne Perkins
Kevin Harrington
Aaron Wilkinson
Karl Groome
Tanya Groome
Clifford Hogg-Wyatt
Andrew Weston
Alan Weston
Gadbury Family
Adam Wilkin
Fraser Eadie
Peter Meacock
Janet Meacock
Derek King
Tony Boddy
Dr John Graham Rankin
Tabitha Gault
Duncan Stonehouse
John Stonehouse
Steve Wood
Steve Forrester
The Blaxall Family
Simon Warr
Harvey Monk
Leo Reid
Alastair Riley
Mr Eric Meadows
Mr Peter Kelly
Richard Rose
Raymond Harvey Youngs
Kenneth Wightman
Norah Miller
Sue Miller
John Richardson
Peter Leatherdale
Jason John Harris
Dartmoor Wickendens
Nicola Dines
David Dresch
Jenny Amos
Stephen Cook
Stephen Jackson (Mad Milkman)
David, Nicola and Jenny Braid
Bill Chatten (1936-2007 R.I.P.)
Cliff Shepherd
Ray Clark
Dorothy J. Davies (R.I.P. G.M.D.)
Deb Clitheroe
Steve Bracey
Loren Murphy
Tom Bush
Daniel Battersby
Brian Burscough
Joe Budgen
Liam David Bloomfield
Trevor Bailey
The Dunn Family
Matt Mills
Bruce McLellan
Stephen White
David J. Fordham
Andy Hoy
Michaela Edgar
Harry Gladwin
John Tweed
Matthew Smith
Ian Humberstone
Martin James Green
Elijah and Ottillie
Peter Haynes
Ken Mahoney

Duncan Forbes.

Mr Reginald (Tony) Self
Sarah Johnson
Nick Johnson
Matty Elliott
Darrell Weaver
Andy Totham
Roger Matthews
Kieron Matthews
Gair Matthews
Ben Landon (Northern Exile)
Eric Lee
Lee Harris
Terry Lawrence
Susie Owers
David Parr
Charlie Howlett
Oliver Howlett
Lewis Howlett
Ken Houghton
Steve Wright
Robert Simmons
John W. Simmons
Janice Simmons
Colin Whybrew
Elaine Soame
Ed Henshall
Glyn Jenkins
Jim Landon
Matt Hudson (Media Manager)
Geoffrey Fairweather
Andrew Cock-Starkey

Mark Kinsella.